THE
HISTORICAL HANDBOOK
TO
SCOTLAND

DUNCAN MACPHAIL

QUICKREF
PUBLICATIONS

Published in Great Britain 2003 by Quickref Publications, Suite 230, 12 South Bridge Edinburgh.
Copyright held by Clifford Tindale. Typeset by Patrick Armstrong of Book Production Services London. Printed
by Antony Rowe Ltd, Chippenham, Wiltshire, England. All Rights Reserved. With the exception of book reviews
written or broadcast, no part of this work may be photocopied, stored in a retrieval system, published,
broadcast, adapted, transmitted, recorded or reproduced in any form or by any means, without the express
written permission of the copyright owner.
©Quickref Publications 2003
Email : Info@quickref̓org www.quickref.org

ISBN 0 9542805 0 4

CONTENTS

INTRODUCTION

The Historical Handbook To Scotland is a comprehensive alphabetical reference work composed of the facts and figures relating to the main areas of Scottish life down through the ages, that have come to form a rich tapestry of places and events in which the Scottish character was shaped. Since early settlers in Scotland curbed their practices as inveterate hunters to tame the land in settled communities which in Scotland were later to become farmtouns, villages towns and cities provided the bedrock which, to varying degrees, ensured the continuity from which the political and religious structures, traditions and customs developed.

Among the country's more populus centres today, and obvious examples of this are Aberdeen, Edinburgh and Glasgow, each of which had at different times their own ascendant cultural components that reflected their historical ties and geographical location in the north, south and west of the country respectively.

The castles, cathedrals, palaces, abbeys and churches which, although often the outposts of these rural, provincial, and urban centres, often served as the nucleus around which the communities survived and grew. Most notable among these were Aberdeen, Dryburgh, Dumbarton, Dunkeld, Edinburgh, Glasgow, Kelso, Paisley and Saint Andrews. Within the walls of their defensive structures and places of worship were played out some of the more far-reaching acts of allegiance, devotion, greed and profanity in the struggle for military conquest, religious domination, economic control and personal aggrandisement.

The more pleasurable endeavours in past times helped to make golf clubs and whisky distilleries the living parts of Scotland's history that frequently provided an alternative to the more pressing issues of the day, while also becoming two of Scotland's most popular exports. The game of golf, which began in Scotland, is now one of the world's foremost recreational pursuits. Whisky distillation, which has a history stretching back centuries and takes its name from the Gaelic 'uisg beatha' meaning 'water of life' was largely made in crude stills up until the 19th century and since then has built up a reputation as one of the world's premier spirits. While fire and water play a central part in the process, the main ingredient in this is of course the water which over the years filters down through Scotland's mountains and hills and is released at the numerous springs around which the various distilleries were built.

The main motivating forces that served as the catalyst for Scotland's historical milestones while also affecting the overall development of all the other subjects are to be found in the country's military history. The most notable milestones in this are the battle of Mons Grapius in 84 AD when the Romans defeated the Caledonians and the Viking invasions between the 8th and 11th centuries when the more Nordic traditions became rooted in the north west of the country. In addition to these were the battle of

Carham in 1018 when Anglo Saxon laws and customs were preserved in parts of southern Scotland; the Scots victory at Bannockburn in 1314 which marked the re-assertion of the Scottish identity, in contrast with the defeat at Flodden in 1513 when the lifeblood of the nobility and male population was considerably depleted. The 18th century was to be marred by the Jacobite defeat at the battle of Culloden in 1746 when the clan system was broken and thousands of Scots were forced to emigrate. In the 19th century the Radical War of 1820 flared up in the midst of the country's industrialisation when a force of disgruntled workers sought to effect change in pay and living conditions, thus contributing to the development of the Scottish socialist tradition, which was to shape the political landscape of Britain in the 20th century. Although these periods engendered much death and carnage, they paved the way for the fusion of races, values and traditions that make up the people now known as the Scots.

ACKNOWLEDGEMENTS

The author would like to show his thanks and give recognition to the following individuals, publishers, organisations and institutions for their assistance in providing information for this book, without which it would not have the same diverse level of content:

THE SCOTTISH ACADEMIC PRESS; THE ROYAL COMMISSION ON ANCIENT AND HISTORICAL MONUMENTS; THE NATIONAL ARCHIVES OF SCOTLAND; EDINBURGH CENTRAL LIBRARY; THE NATIONAL LIBRARY OF SCOTLAND; MICHAEL RIDINGS, THE UNIVERSITY OF EDINBURGH; THE EDINBURGH MAP LIBRARY; THE GAELIC COLLEGE, ISLE OF SKYE SABHAL MOR OSTAIG (THE OLD STEADING); R.E.ESSON & COWAN, MEDIEVAL RELIGIOUS HOUSES OF SCOTLAND, 1967, ADDISON WESLEY LONGMAN PUBLISHER; LANGSYNE PUBLISHERS; GEORGE PRYDE, THE BURGHS OF SCOTLAND, 1965, AND HENRY HAMILTONS, THE INDUSTRIAL REVOLUTION IN SCOTLAND, 1932, "BY PERMISSION OF OXFORD UNIVERSITY PRESS"; STUART REID, THE CAMPAIGNS OF MONTROSE, 1990, THE MERCET PRESS, EDINBURGH; UNITED DISTILLERS; ALLIED DISTILLERS; THE BRUNTSFIELD LINKS GOLFING SOCIETY; DAVID CLARKE OF GOLF WORLD MAGAZINE; THE CHIVAS GLENLIVIT GROUP; PRESTWICK ST NICHOLAS GOLF CLUB; THE SCOTTISH TOURIST BOARD; TOMATIN DISTILLERY; MERCAT TOURS, EDINBURGH; ROYAL & ANCIENT GOLF CLUB OF ST ANDREWS; PHIPPS PUBLIC RELATIONS; WHYTE & MACKAY GROUP PLC AND DAVID CLERK, BATTLEFIELD WALKS, SUTTON PUBLISHING.

QUICKREF
PUBLICATIONS

Numbered Areas

1. City of Edinburgh
2. West Lothian
3. East Renfrewshire
4. City of Glasgow
5. Renfrewshire
6. Inverclyde

SHETLAND ISLANDS

SUMBURGH

ORKNEY ISLANDS

KIRKWALL

THURSO

WICK

LEWIS

STORNOWAY

WESTERN ISLES

DORNOCH

DINGWALL

FRASERBURGH

MORAY

PORTREE

HIGHLAND

INVERNESS

ABERDEENSHIRE

SKYE

ABERDEEN CITY

EIGG

FORT WILLIAM

ANGUS

PERTH AND KINROSS

MONTROSE

MULL

OBAN

DUNDEE CITY

STIRLING

CLACKMANNAN

FIFE

ST ANDREWS

ARGYLL AND BUTE

WEST DUNBARTONSHIRE

EAST DUNBARTONSHIRE

FALKIRK

DUNBAR

ISLAY

6

5

4

2

EDINBURGH

EAST LOTHIAN

3

MIDLOTHIAN

NORTH AYRSHIRE

SOUTH LANARKSHIRE

SCOTTISH BORDERS

ARRAN

EAST AYRSHIRE

AYR

SOUTH AYRSHIRE

DUMFRIES AND GALLOWAY

DUMFRIES

PORT PATRICK

ISLE OF WHITHORN

XVII

XX

The publishers would like to point out that some of the information in the text pertaining to the distilleries, golf clubs and museums are subject to fluctuations and alterations with the passage of time. In addition to this the figures for the mileage of some of the more isolated locations in the book are approximate calculations.

A

ABBEY ST BATHANS NUNNERY
SCOTTISH BORDERS

It stands on the Whiteadder River 7 miles NW of Duns. The site of an early religious settlement, as it was built on the site of the original 6th century church of St Baithene, the cousin of St Columba and his successor at Iona. Of the Cistercian Nunnery founded here in the late 12th century by Ada the Countess of Dunbar/March and daughter of William I, the east wall and lower portions of the north wall are all that remain. In a recess of the former is a late 16th century recumbent effigy probably of a nun of this or another nunnery. At the Reformation and after the death of Elizabeth Lamb (the last Prioress) it became the property of Elizabeth Hume, 1566, and by 1622 it was erected into a Temporal Lordship for David Lindsay. In the 18th century the remains of the church were incorporated into the Parish Church, north west of which on Shannabank hill are traces of a Pictish Hill Fort.

ABBOTSFORD
SCOTTISH BORDERS

Mansion house situated about 2 miles W of Melrose. Originally called Cartley Hole Farm, it was purchased in 1811 by Sir Walter Scott, who had the Baronial pile of today built between 1817-24. Scott changed its name to Abbotsford because it was near the site where the Abbots of Melrose crossed the River Tweed with their cattle. Built with a diversity of style to satisfy his antiquarian tastes, including a gateway from Linlithgow Palace, a portal from Edinburgh's Old Tolbooth, a roof from Roslin Chapel, oak from Holyrood Palace and a mantelpiece from Melrose Abbey. The rare book collection, which once amounted to 20,000, was accumulated by Scott, along with other historical relics, when he stayed here from 1812 until his death in 1832, when the mansion passed to J. Hope, who married his granddaughter.

ABERCORN CHURCH
CITY OF EDINBURGH

Situated in the village to which it gives its name, on the south shore of the River Forth near Queensferry stands an ancient church. Once the site of a monastery founded by the Northumbrian Bishop Trumwin which became the first Scottish Bishopric 681-685. After the victory of the Picts at Dunnichen in 685 Trumwin fled to Whitby, but the legacy of his work is this fine Medieval building. The land was held by the Grahams in the 12th century but by 1329 had passed through marriage to Reginald Mure Chamberlain of Scotland, while its castle, which stood on a green mound fronting the church, was captured from the 9th and last Earl of Douglas by James II (1437-1460). Although retaining significant traces of the Norman structure, particularly the Norman doorway in the south wall alot of the structure was refitted in 1579 and thoroughly repaired in the 19th century. From the early 17th century onwards it was held by the Hamiltons, Mures, Lindsays of the Byres and Setons, but in 1678 was sold by Walter Seton to John Hope from whom the Earls of Hopetoun are descended. Although containing richly embellished stone and panels and heraldic reminders of the families connected to its history (this is also apparent in the layout with the Hopetoun aisle of 1704, Duddingston aisle, 1605 and Binns aisle, 1618) it is the richly embellished ancient hogback and cross shaft stones that are a testament to Abercorn's antiquity.

ABERDEEN
CITY OF ABERDEEN

City situated at the mouth of the River Dee and River Don on Scotland's NE coast. Once the site of an ancient settlement, its name is derived from the Brythonic 'aber' meaning 'mouth of the water' the water being not the Dee or the Don but the Denburn. Old Aberdeen with its age-old Cathedral and University stood at the mouth of the Don, while New Aberdeen grew out of a trading settlement at the mouth of the Dee. As the seat of a bishopric and site of a castle, its Royal Burgh status under David I (1124-53) was confirmed in 1179 by William I who founded a mint here before the town was destroyed by fire in 1224. Aberdeen figured in the Wars of Independence when the construction of a castle by Edward I in 1296 led to the burning of the English supply ships by William Wallace, 1297; the burghers giving refuge to Robert the Bruce in 1306 resulting in the ejection of the English forces and the war cry 'Bon Accord' becoming the city's motto. The town was destroyed by Edward III in 1336 but was rebuilt on four hills by David II who re-established a Royal Mint and made it a Parliamentary Burgh. The city was firmly established as a seat of learning by the building of St Machar's Cathedral in the 14th century which paved the way for King's College, 1495, and Marischal College in 1593, all of which provided the bed'rock on which the city embraced and sustained the Reformation in 1560. Occupied by Montrose in 1639 after rejecting the Covenant and by Cromwell in 1651 for supporting the Restoration of Charles II, Aberdeen displayed lukewarm support for the Jacobites in 1715, it was the point of departure for Sir John Cope's forces in 1745 prior to his defeat at the battle of Prestonpans: and was later visited by the Hanoverians before their victory at Culloden in 1746. From a small trade in knitted stockings before 1745 its linen manufacture grew to employ 4,000 people by 1840 making sailcloth, osnaburgs, brown linen and sacking mainly for export to Hamburg. Similarly its harbour which started as a single pier in 1610 with a shipbuilding dock by 1661 was greatly extended between 1810 and 1886 with contributions by Telford that facilitated its main exports flax, cotton, wool, granite and livestock. Additional prosperity from whaling which started in 1753 came to be seen as the first oil boom after record amounts of whale oil extracted in one season in 1823 totalled 1,841 tons, but fortunately the trade had ceased by the 1860s due to the change over to gas for street lighting. Suffering the same fate though less fortuitous was its once proud fleet of herring trawlers which numbered 200 in 1900. The Act of Parliament in 1800 authorising the building of Union Street, King Street followed by St Andrew's Cathedral in 1817 gave rise to the Granite City of today for which much of the credit goes to Archibald Simpson, John Smith (Tudor Johny) and James Gibb. All of whom have successfully blended classical forms with personal style while preserving the town's appeal to both architect and antiquary. With continued growth during later decades it became established as the main city on Scotland's north-eastern seaboard. Lost before the Town & Country Planning Act of 1947, after the clearances of 1930 and the air raids of 1942 a lot of the Medieval burgh was swept away and during the latter the barracks of the city's regiment, the Gordon Highlanders was hit. Its function as a supply base for the oil and gas fields of the North Sea in the 1970s brought much inward investment that has revitalised the area with a renewed sense of optimism and pride that is reflected in the city's most interesting domestic buildings. Provost Skene's House, a typical 16th century house, now serves as a museum, Provost Ross's House was once owned by a 16th century merchant but now houses the Maritime Museum, and James Dun's House, a Georgian building of 1769, now holds historical exhibitions. See St Andrews, St Machars & St Marys Cathedral

ABERDOUR
FIFE

A coastal village situated in SW Fife. Name derived from the Brythonic 'aber' and the Gaelic 'dobhar' meaning 'mouth of the water', which frequently functioned as the royal landing place for Dunfermline. The possible site of a monastery in the 12th century, and the site of a Franciscan Nunnery founded in the 15th century by James Earl of Morton, whose family seat was Aberdour Castle. St Fillan's Church built in the 12th century is the burial place of Robert Blair (Chaplain to Charles I) and served as the Parish Church until the late 19th century. Strongly linked to the church, Aberdour was made a Burgh of Barony for the Abbot of Inchcolm in 1500. Although traditionally a fishing village, after its subsequent decline as a coal port for the area after 1918, it became popular with pleasure boats from Granton en route to Burntisland, which in turn gave rise to its development as a holiday location and residentail town, which it still is today. See Castle

ABERDOUR CASTLE
FIFE

Standing near the village overlooking the harbour are the substantial ruins of the Douglas' 14th century keep, with the main additions made up to the 17th century. The land was granted to William Douglas of Liddesdale in 1341 but was transferred to James Douglas of Dalkeith in 1351. Three storeys high, the keep had a range with adjoining stair added by the Regent Morton, who was beheaded in 1581 for his involvement along with other nobles in the murder of Lord Darnley. Later surrounded by domestic buildings including the brew house, an office to the SW and the hall kitchen and store room to the SE which has a 17th century extension probably built by William the sixth Earl (Lord High Treasurer of Scotland) who became Lord Aberdour in 1638. It was partly destroyed by a fire in 1715 and around 1750 was vacated by the Mortons, later having its decline hastened by the collapse of the keep's west wall in 1844. The castle is now held in trust for the nation.

ABERFELDY
PERTH & KINROSS

Town situated 32 miles SW of Perth. Name derived from the Brythonic 'aber' meaning 'mouth of the river' and possibly 'Peallaidh' (an old water spirit). Commanding a view down the Tay is the Aberfeldy five-arched bridge, started in 1733 by Robert Adam for General Wade and still regarded as one of his finest despite being described by Dorothy Wordsworth in 1803 as being 'of ambitious and ugly architecture'. At the south end stands the Black Watch monument erected to mark the regiment's enrolment by the General in 1739 during his attempts to quell unrest and in particular cattle raiding in the Highlands; but the name comes from the regiment's dark green tartan, not any nocturnal activity. Benefiting from an abundant supply of water, the town is predominantly 19th century, as is the Aberfeldy Water Mill and the Aberfeldy Distillery. Since the 1950s much advantage has been gained from the Forestry Commission projects (notably its forest walks) while the Scottish Hydro Electric's scheme in the Tummel Valley, though started in 1945, was first promoted by the Highland Water Power Bill in 1899. See Distillery

ABERFELDY DISTILLERY
PERTH & KINROSS

Located near the town. To ensure supplies of malt for their own brands the distillery was founded in 1896 by Perth's leading wine and spirit merchant John Dewar & Sons, who took out a lease from the Marquis of Breadalbane near the crucial Pitillie burn that had been the site of an earlier distillery and the scene of illicit distilling for centuries. Born two miles away, the founding father John Dewar, who started business in 1846, became a pioneer of whisky blending, with his products in demand from Edinburgh to Inverness, before his death in 1880. Under his son Thomas Dewar the demand for Dewar products and for Aberfeldy Malt exploded, with a London office opened in 1887 and thirty-two agents in twenty-six countries, bringing a new headquarters to Perth with a door-to-door rail link that operated for decades. A part of the Malt Distillers Ltd in 1930. The distillery's hand-fired stills were replaced in 1960 with mechanical coal-fired stills and in 1973 its stillhouse and tunroom were rebuilt using the original stonework. In the same year it converted its malt kiln to a pot ale syrup plant producing animal feed from distillery by-products. The attention paid to the natural ambience, including a nature trail contrasts well with its railway links as symbolised by one of the old puggies once used to pull the whisky wagons.

OWNERS
John Dewar & Sons Ltd ?

REGION
Highland

PRODUCT
Aberfeldy 15 year old single malt 43% vol

NOTES
Slightly peaty nose with a soft round taste.

ABERGELDIE CASTLE
ABERDEENSHIRE

A former Gordon stronghold situated on the south bank of the River Dee 6 miles below Ballater. In 1482 the lands were acquired by Sir Alexander Gordon, the 2nd son of the Ist Earl of Huntly, whose son Alexander built this 16th century Manor Tower House. Its walls bore witness to future centuries of strife, for in 1594 it was damaged by James IV and during the Covenanting Wars its garrison was besieged by Highlanders until General Hugh Mackay relieved them in 1689, destroying the surrounding countryside in the process. In 1715 it was garrisoned again but by 1848 Prince Albert had purchased the lease for 40 years.

ABERLOUR DISTILLERY
MORAY

The distillery takes its name from the town and its water from the underground springs in nearby Ben Rinnes. The former was where St Drostan or Dunstan, a disciple of the Columbian Church, used its pure waters to baptise the Pictish Clan Chiefs in the sixth century. The spot is now clearly marked in the distillery grounds. The site of some kind of distillery from 1780 but officially producing whisky since 1826, the present distillery was built after the fire during the winter's night in 1879 when the villagers leapt from their beds to save the maturing casks of whisky. From the top of the brae can be seen Aberlour village surrounded by a handful of distilleries which produce the classic Speyside Malt, along with over forty other distilleries in the heartland of the world's whisky producing region. The size and shape of Aberlours stills are exceptionally broad and fashioned like rising swans which traps the concentrated vapours within the dome so that only the purest, most rarefied vapours ascend to the elegant neck to become whisky. The spirit is then matured in a mixture of cherry and bourbon oak casks with cork bungs to allow the harsher vapours to evaporate, producing a delicate balance between richness and lightness on the palate. In 1974 Aberlour was taken over by Pernod Ricard, whose later success at promoting it in Europe and particularly France owed much to Aberlours, ranking as the first single malt to ever win the Gold Medal and Pot Still Trophy at the International Wine and Spirit Competition in 1986, and the only whisky to win the award twice in 1990, which further helped to elevate it to the world's sixth best selling malt by 1992.

OWNERS
Chivas Brothers Ltd ?

REGION
Speyside

PRODUCT
Aberlour 10 & 12 year old single malt 40% & 43% vol

NOTES
A malty aroma with a dry spicy flavour and silky malt finish.

ABERNETHY
PERTH & KINROSS

Village situated 6 miles SE of Perth. Name derived from the Brythonic 'Aber', therefore 'mouth of the River Nethy'. This was once the ancient Capital of Pictavia and the site of a religious foundation erected by Pictish Kings and dedicated to St Bridget in the 6th century. Although the village was a royal and Episcopal Capital in the 9th century it was replaced by Saint Andrews in the 10th century, and the Celtic Church where Malcolm III paid homage to William the Conqueror in 1072 (Treaty of Abernethy) was supplanted by an Au-

gustinian Priory in the 13th century. Its Irish round tower nearby was built in the 11th century to protect the clergy from marauding Norsemen. Constituted a Burgh of Barony for the Earl of Angus, 1495. The community has long served as a supply point for farmers, fishermen and foresters while Glenmore Forest Park, a legacy of its former status as a royal hunting ground, has continued to make Abernethy a popular stopping place for hunters, hill walkers and hikers.

ABERUCHILL CASTLE
PERTH & KINROSS

Positioned at the base of mountains 2 miles SW of Comrie. The granting of the Charter of Aberuchill by the Crown to Colin Campbell of Lawers was followed by the erection of this L plan mansion in 1602. So long contested between the Campbells and the Macgregors, the district was the scene of much conflict in times past. In the 19th century the tower was incorporated into the house.

ABOYNE
ABERDEENSHIRE

Town situated on the bank of the Dee 32 miles SW of Aberdeen. Name derived from the Gaelic 'ath bo fhionn' meaning 'ford of the white cows'. The site of a settlement in the 10th century, its 17th century castle was once a motte and bailey which belonged to the Bissets from the 12th century. The town was once called Charlestown of Aboyne after Charles Gordon Ist Earl of Aboyne in 1660, today's town, built around the village green to designs by Sir William Brook, is a typical Victorian Market Town that prospered with the coming of the Aboyne & Braemar Railway in 1865 and the Aboyne Highland Games in 1867. The gathering continues to reaffirm its status in the area. Standing out from the rest of its architecture is the Victory Hall, built in 1921 by Lord Glentanner, the railway station built by the square in 1863 and St Thomas Episcopal Church which was consecrated in 1909.

ACHADUN CASTLE
HIGHLAND

Situated on the Island of Lismore in Loch Linnhe are the substantial ruins of a 13th-century courtyard structure built by the Bishops of Argyll when the see of the bishopric was transferred to Lismore. The Cathedral later became the Parish Church.

ACHALLADER CASTLE
ARGYLL & BUTE

By Loch Tulla in Glenorchy is the ruined baronial fortalice of the Campbells of Glenorchy which was built by Black Duncan Campbell in the 17th century, when it was the scene of a clan battle. The Treaty of Achallader, 1691 signed here by several Highland Chiefs sought to bring stability to the Highlands.

ACKERGILL TOWER
HIGHLAND

Perched on the coast 3 miles N of Wick is a late 15th century tower house built by the Keiths of Inverugie, on land originally belonging to the Cheynes, a powerful family in the north during the 13th century. Passing through marriage to the Keiths, in 1538 the castle and lands were granted by James V to William Keith, Earl Marischall and Lady Margaret. Surrounded by a moat on three sides and the sea on the other, in 1547 the castle was occupied by the Earl of Caithness, who detained Sir Alexander Keith here, but in 1549 Queen Mary bestowed it on Lord Oliphant. Despite being surrendered by George Earl of Caithness to the forces of Sir Robert Gordon in 1623 and being garrisoned by Cromwell's forces in 1651, the success of its restoration by William Dun-

bar moved Bishop Forbes to describe it as 'pretty elegant' during a visit in 1762. In the 19th century extensions were made by David Bryce, including cape house, reinforced wall turrets and enlarged windows.

AFFLECK CASTLE
ANGUS

Located 15 miles NE of Dundee. This 15th century oblong keep was built by the Auchinlecks, whose son-in-law was given further grants of land by James IV in 1504. Containing five floors with a battlement and two watchtowers which served as a landmark for sailors, despite its built-in obsolescence, due to the advent of gunpowder it continued to be occupied until 1760 and still stands as a fine example of its period.

AIRDRIE
NORTH LANARKSHIRE

Town situated 11 miles E of Glasgow. Name derived from the Gaelic 'aird' and 'ruidh' meaning 'high slope' (hill pasture). As part of the Barony of Monkland the land was held by the Hamiltons. Mentioned in 1670 as a farm with three other houses, a typical Scottish 'ferm-toun', it was developed by Robert Hamilton who through an Act of Parliament had it constituted a Market Town by 1695, with four fairs and a weekly market. Its rapid expansion in manufacturing was due to its iron and coal deposits and its position between Edinburgh and Glasgow which also made it a stopping place for the stage coach between 1797 and 1842. A Burgh of Barony for Aitchieson of Rochsolloch in 1821 and a Parliamentary Burgh by 1833, the influx of Irish workers and the subsequent growth of its cotton manufacture furthered its infrastructure to make it the first town in Scotland to adopt the Free Libraries Act in 1866. After continuing well into the 20th century, its textile trade has since made way for lighter industries.

AIRDRIE HOUSE
FIFE

Situated on rising ground 3 miles W of Crail. Consisting of a 15th century tower and a 17th century mansion built on the site of an old seat of the Dundemons, who occupied the land in the 14th century. It passed to James Lumsdaine in 1566 and after his death in 1598 it became the property of Sir John Preston, Lord President of the Court of Session. Greatly enlarged in the 17th century by General Anstruther who brought workmen from Italy. It was purchased in 1793 by Methven Erskine, later Earl of Kellie, who died here in 1830 and whose heir David Erskine made some alterations.

AIRDS MOSS, BATTLE OF, 1680
EAST AYRSHIRE

On a morass near the village of Cumnock was the scene of a battle between around 63 Covenanters, some of them armed and led by their illustrious leader and fugitive Richard Cameron who encountered a party of dragoons. The dissenters were defeated by superior numbers and their leader killed, but for a time his name became synonymous with those who held unusual unorthodox opinions (Cameronians).

AIRLIE CASTLE
ANGUS

On a rocky promontory by the River Isla 5´ miles SW of Kirriemuir is the former seat of the Earls of Airlie which was built by Sir Walter Ogilvie of Lintrathen in 1432. Although deemed impregnable, its ten foot thick walls which were once surrounded by a deep ditch failed to prevent the castle's destruction by 4,000 clansmen led by the Earl of Argyll with a writ of fire and sword issued in 1640 by the Committee of Estates. The reminders of this episode include a large east wall of enceinte and the lofty north tower which form the last vestiges of the Bonnie House of Airlie, which was replaced by an 18th century mansion.

AIRTH
FALKIRK

Coastal town situated 8 miles SE of Stirling. The name is probably derived from the Gaelic 'ard' meaning 'a hill'. Once a village of promise, Airth was created a Royal Burgh by William I (1195-1203) but was eclipsed by the development of Alloa. Long associated with the river, at the Pool of Airth in 1511, James IV built a naval dockyard which also thrived as a trading port until 1746 when it was severely damaged during a skirmish between the Jacobite and Hanoverian forces. Despite this sloops were being built here up until 1820. A Burgh of Barony for Bruce of Airth in 1597, its Earldom was conferred on William Graham Esq in 1633 but was in abeyance by 1694. Modern Airth's raison d'etre was as part of Scotland's industrial supply line which the areas coal mines and quarries supplied up until the early 19th century when much of the present town was built. The main object of interest is the Mercat Cross, adorned with the arms of the Bruce and Elphinstone families; it was once the site of public trials and executions and up until 1935 public obituaries were read from its steps. See Castle

AIRTH TOWER
FALKIRK

On top of a hill near the River Forth 2 miles NW of Kincardine is a late 15th-century keep with extensive 16th and 19th century additions. The first tower, occupied by an English force and taken by William Wallace during the Wars of

Independence, was replaced by a castle built by the Bruces of Airth, which was itself supplanted by the present structure when it was burnt following the battle of Sauchieburn in 1488. The extensions to the east were followed by a north wing added by Sir Alexander Bruce, which is inscribed 'LAT THAIM 1581' and gave the keep the shape of an L plan structure. During the 17th and 18th centuries, the estate was acquired through marriage by the Elphinstones and the Dundas families, before being bought in 1717 by the Judge James Graham. Development plans drawn up by William Adam were not acted upon and the building remained unchanged until 1807, when David Hamilton added an impressive facade with gate tower and portico entrance flanked by curtain walls and round angle towers.

ALDIE CASTLE
PERTH & KINROSS

Built on a steep bank 4 miles SW of Kinross. It was acquired by the Mercers in the mid 14th century and was thought to have been named after Aldia Murray, daughter of William Murray of Tullibardine. Essentially a 16th century oblong keep, it rises four storeys high with vaulted ground floor and turrets above. Its 17th century additions, which made it into an L plan courtyard structure with improved domestic facilities, were in keeping with the more relaxed mood of the times and the house remained occupied until the 19th century, when the property passed to Baroness Nairn.

ALFORD
ABERDEENSHIRE

A small town situated 27 miles W of Aberdeen. Name derived from the Gaelic 'ath' and 'aird' or 'ord' meaning 'high ford'. Virtually guaranteed some prosperity owing to its position in the agri-cultural supply line to Aberdeen. Its most notable family were the Forbese's who occupied the nearby Balfluig and Forbes castles. In 1645 Montrose defeated the Covenanters near here. Once comprising a church shop and smithy, the completion of the rail link with Aberdeen in 1859 boosted the town's grain and cattle market economy that was helped along by the revolution in farming techniques. Although Alford was the birthplace of Charles Murray (1864-1941) whose poems aptly describe the area's rich rural culture, today the town is better known for its Transport Museum and the nearby Haughton Country Park. See Battle

ALFORD, BATTLE OF, 1645
ABERDEENSHIRE

Taking its name from the place, this was one of the six victories gained by the Marquis of Montrose in 12 months when his Royalist force defeated the Covenanters under General Baillie. Through Montrose's military genius as a tactician, Baillie was lured across the River Don and a bog, convinced the enemy was in retreat, only to be surprised by Montrose's strong defensive position, leading to the Covenanters being routed and suffering heavy losses. The victory gave more momentum to Montrose's campaign and military carreer which was finally ended by his defeat at Carbisdale and his execution at Edinburgh Cross, 1650.

ALLOA
CLACKMANNAN

Town situated on the River Forth W of Stirling. Name derived from the Gaelic 'ailbheach' meaning 'a rock in the plain'. Its value as a Supply Port, which often made it a strategic prize for invading armies, undoubtedly encouraged the rich trading tradition that ultimately gave rise to its regional status which began in 1360 when David II bestowed the lands on Sir

Robert Erskine, Chamberlain of Scotland, and builder of Alloa Tower. For his descendant Lord Erskine it became a Burgh of Regality in 1479. A supplier of coal, iron, and whisky, wool and glass production was started in 1750 by Lady Francis Erskine followed by brewing in 1774. In the 18th century Defoe wrote that 'a merchant at Alloa may trade to all ports of the world as well as Glasgow and Leith', and it was on the back of its trade with Baltic, French, German and Dutch ports that it was able to maintain its commercial status up until the 20th century. Today its traditional glass and brewing industry contrast successfully with the new service industries. See Tower

ALLOA TOWER
CLACKMANNAN

Close to the town are the substantial remains of a late 14th century tower house built by Robert Erskine (Chamberlain of Scotland), whose descendant became the Earl of Mar. Thought to stand on the site of a 13th century castle, the 10 foot thick walls of the tower which climb four storeys high are crowned with bartizan battlements, but unfortunately the overall structure was greatly altered when additions, made at later dates to accommodate Mary I, James VI and Prince Henry during their childhood sojourns, were destroyed in the great fire of 1800. It was at that time that one of the last paintings of Queen Mary, bequeathed to her attendant before her execution, was lost. In 1706 the 11th Earl of Mar (Bobbing John, turncoat) introduced the French style of gardening here but in 1716 he returned to France while under forfeiture for supporting the Jacobites.

ALLOWAY KIRK
SOUTH AYRSHIRE

Located about 3 miles S of Ayr on the bank of the River Doon below the Brig of Doon. In contrast to the more modern church are the ruins of the older kirk. In the 16th century James VI annexed the church to the Chapel Royal of Stirling, but by 1690 the Parish of Alloway was annexed to that of Ayr which marked the beginning of the church's fall into ruin through neglect. Although the walls are from an early period, the exact date of the kirk remains uncertain; for a long time this served as a resting place for travellers owing to its proximity to the bridge, which also adds weight to its antiquity. It is, however, the events of the 18th century and its associations with Robert Burns who was born in the village, that have guaranteed its place in Scotland's history for it was here that the bard chose as the setting for his poem 'Tam O Shanter', who from its windows saw the warlocks and witches. The kirk was stripped of its woodwork for the making of snuffboxes which no doubt hastened its decline, but its two most distinctive features are its two light windows in the east gable wall, probably dating from the same time before the 17th century and the belfry above which is post Reformation. In the churchyard is the grave of the poet's father William Burness. In 1820 a cenotaph was erected to the poet to the east of the Old Kirk. The modern church was built in 1858 by Campbell Douglas and contains a number of memorial windows to distinguished individuals like Robert Burns and D.F.McIntyre, the pilot who flew the first solo flight over Mount Everest in 1933.

ALNWICK, BATTLE OF, 1093

After failing to negotiate with William Duffus who had subdued Cumbria and expelled Malcolm III's administrator, the King invaded Northumberland with his army but was surprised by its Earl and defeated near the River Alne and castle of Alnwick. This resulted in the death of the

King and the dispersal of his army by brute force and the winter floods.

ALYTH
PERTH & KINROSS

Town situated 20 miles NE of Perth. Whilst the exact derivation of its name is obscure it would seem to mean 'mound' or 'bank' which was where its ancient church once stood. Although the land was connected with the Ramsays, Lindsays and Crawfords from the 13th to the 17th centuries, Alyth appears in a charter from James II in 1488 as a Burgh of Barony for the Earl of Airlie, whose descendant erected the Mercat Cross at the Causeway in 1670. During Cromwell's invasion when General Monck was attacking Dundee town in 1651 the Committee of Estates was held here. Its original early handloom weaving and later woollen and linen factory flourished up until 1914 when manpower were diverted for the war effort. Built in 1839 in a Norman style, the Parish Church incorporates a much earlier church dedicated to the 12th century Saint Moluag, while in the vestibule of the High Kirk is a 7th century Celtic stone with carved Latin Cross. NE of the town are the remnants of an ancient fort of the Britons which local tradition claims was the prison of King Arthur's Guinevere.

AMISFIELD TOWER
DUMFRIES & GALLOWAY

On a steep bank 5 miles N of Dumfries stands a lofty tower that was once the seat of the Anglo-Norman Charteris family who came to Scotland in the 12th century. In 1280 Sir Thomas Charteris became Lord High Chancellor and a descendant, Alex Charteris, was beheaded at Edinburgh Cross in 1650 for his Royalist sympathies. Above the entrance to the second floor are the family arms with the initials I . C . and the date 1600, when the tower was erected, probably by the same builder who previously designed the nearby Elshieshields, albeit in a less imaginative way. Three storeys high, the first floor comprised a hall and kitchen, the second floor the proprietor's living room with guard-robes, and almonries within the walls with access stairs to the tower and courtyard, while the third floor includes the family bedroom with access to three of the corbelled turrets with their shotholes. Above these is a small attic room overhung by two storeys which lead to the watch tower. In 1636 the barony passed to John Dalziel of Newton and in 1720, Janet, daughter of Francis of Amisfield, married James, 4th Earl of Wemyss. Close by is a later house built in the reign of Charles I which is now absorbed into a more recent mansion.

ANCRUM
SCOTTISH BORDERS

Village situated 6 miles NW of Jedburgh. The original name of Alnecrumb, meaning 'crook of the Alne', is derived from the River Alne now called the Ale. Its proximity to the river and the northern extremity of the Cheviot Hills made the area ideal for early hill fort settlements to which the remains of an Iron Age hill fort at Castlehill testify. The Malton Walls, which stood near the village, and where the Knights of St John had a settlement, were later followed by a bishop's mansion. For a time it was renamed Nether Ancrum to distinguish it from adjoining Over Ancrum, both of which were burnt by Sir Ralph Evers, 1544 and the Earl of Hertford in 1545 when the latter was the site of a Kerr seat which was itself destroyed by fire in the 19th century. See Battle

ANCRUM MOOR, BATTLE OF, 1545
SCOTTISH BORDERS

The site is located to the NW of Jedburgh. In response to incursions by Sir Ralph Evers and Brian Latoun the Earl of Angus urged the Regent Arran into a defensive stance, and on Ancrum Moor the Scottish force led by Angus decisively defeated the army of Henry VIII on their return from their raid of Melrose Abbey. The honours of the field were awarded to the Earl. The battle was part of what came to be known as the Rough Wooing of Mary Queen of Scots by Henry VIII, and with its outcome came decades of strife between the two nations.

ANDERSTON
CITY OF GLASGOW

A suburb of Glasgow, its name derived from a Mr John Anderston of Stobcross who designed the original weaver's village in 1725 on building lots from his most unproductive farmland. For a long time separated from Glasgow by a wide rural tract, in 1824 it was constituted a Burgh of Barony by a Crown Charter but had been annexed to the Municipal City of Glasgow by the 1850s. Its factories, foundries and shipbuilding yards shared in the city's industrial growth throughout the 19th century and in its subsequent post-war decline in the 20th century.

ANNAN
DUMFRIES & GALLOWAY

Town situated at the mouth of the River Annan. The possible site of a Roman Station and of a Royal Mint, like its neighbouring towns it experienced the vicissitudes of border life which had as much to do with its status as a Bruce burgh and family stronghold from the 13th century as its location. Burnt by the English in 1296, after his coronation at Scone in 1332, Edward Balliol summoned his nobles here to pay him homage. After recovering enough to be granted a charter by James V, (1538), Annan was again

burnt in 1547 by Lord Wharton while the stone from its castle (destroyed by the Earl of Sussex, 1570) was eventually used to build a church in 1609. With commercial links throughout the British Isles, by 1840 a brisk trade was done through its cattle and sheep auction and its pork flesh and fish markets. But with the founding of John Nicholson & Co in 1818, shipbuilding became the main industry by 1827, producing schooners, brigs, clippers, (the largest being 'The Elizabeth' weighing 904 tons and launched 1863), and until 1939 fishing boats were being built here. Among its native sons were Hugh Clapperton (1788-1827) the African explorer, Edward Irving (1792-1834), preacher and Thomas Blacklock (the blind Thomas .Blacklock) an associate of Robert Burns, while the writer Thomas Carlyle (1795-1881) studied as a pupil and later taught at Annan Academy. See Battle

ANNAN, BATTLE OF, 1332
DUMFRIES & GALLOWAY

The battlefield is located near the town of the same name. Owing to the disquiet of the Scottish nobles after the crowning of Edward Balliol, the vassal of Edward of England, to consolidate his hold the former summoned the nobility to pay him homage, but the event was marred when Sir Archibald Douglas appeared with 1000 horse; then surprised and defeated Balliol, who fled half naked to Carlisle. Through restoring Balliol to the throne Edward III secured his hold in the north for a time until David II invaded England in 1346.

ANSTRUTHER
FIFE

Seaport town situated in SE Fife. Name derived from the Gaelic 'an sruthan' meaning 'the stream', denoting marshy ground. A fishing village from an early period, it now consists of Anstruther Easter (AE) and Anstruther Wester (AW) both of which were created Royal Burghs in the 1580s. The nearby church of Kilrenny served as a Parish Church from the 13th century, while the later church at AW was the destination for the rascal multitudes led by John Knox in 1559, culminating in a sermon and a riot. Visited by two straggling ships of the Spanish Armada,1588, and plundered by the English in 1651, the town later settled into expanding its trade and trawling activities when a port and Customs House was built in 1710 at AE. Although a centre for herring fishing by the 19th century, the drift of the herring shoals from the Forth, and the young from the trade of their fathers by the 1940s sounded the death knell for the industry; this was cushioned by the building of the Life Boat Station, (1933), summer trade and the Rosyth Naval Dockyard. Among its sons are Dr Thomas Chalmers (1780-1847), the religious reformer who was a leading light in the Disruption Debate of 1843 and William Tennant (1784-1848) author of 'Anstruther Fair'. The Scottish Fisheries Museum, housed in a 16th century building by the shore, skilfully recreates the area's rich fishing tradition.

ARBROATH
ANGUS

Ancient coastal town situated 17 miles NE of Dundee. Originally called 'Aberbrothock' meaning 'at the mouth of the River Brothock'. Up until the Reformation much of the town's history revolved around its Abbey, which was founded in 1178. A signal bell erected on a nearby island in the 14th century, when the Abbots Harbour was built, and which successfully guided shipping in the way that its Abbey guided pilgrims, was aptly described in Southey's poem:

No stir on the air no swell on the sea,
The ship was still as she might be,
The sails from heaven received no motion
The keel was steady in the ocean,
With neither sign nor sound of shock,
The waves flowed over the Inchcape Rock;
So little they rose so little they fell,
They did not move the Inchcape bell

In 1446 Arbroath was the scene of a conflict between the Lindsays and the Ogilvies over the erection of a Bailie of Regality. The town was created a Burgh of Barony by 1488 and Parliamentary Burgh in 1579. Despite being elevated to a Royal Burgh by James VI in 1599, the decline of its Abbey after 1560 marked the end of the town's influence in matters of state and it thereafter resigned itself to a more provincial role. A long-standing fishing community, the Bell Rock Lighthouse off its coast was built by Robert Stevenson to replace an earlier wooden beacon, and ranks, along with its harbour built in 1846, as a sound example of 19th century engineering. With the revenue from the profusion of mills and factories along with a 154 boat fishing fleet, by 1882 it was host to the Vice-consulships of Germany, Sweden, Norway and Belgium. Sadly its textile trade was later eclipsed by engineering. In the Arbroath Signal Tower Museum once used to service the Bell Rock Lighthouse, are housed exhibits which provide an insight into the town's seafaring past. See Abbey & Battle

ARBROATH ABBEY
ANGUS

The ruins of the Abbey which stand in the town's High Street and near the Parish Church were founded by William the Lion in 1178 (who was buried here in 1214) in honour of Thomas a Becket. Completed in 1233 in a blend of late Norman and early Gothic styles, its plan was of the usual cruciform church bordering the south side of the cloister garth with the domestic buildings on either side. The dexterity of its Benedictine monks who were of the Tironesian Order from Kelso and the large endowments from royalty made it one of the richest abbeys in Scotland by the 13th century, and the heartbeat of the area which provided the impetus for growth of the east coast towns from Montrose to Dundee. The monks were also custodians of the Brecbennach, the consecrated banner of St Columba which he had acquired from Pope Benedict and which was carried by the Scots at Bannockburn. From 1288 under Abbot Henry and Henry de Linton it became the hub of nationalist activity culminating in the Scottish nobility signing the Declaration of Arbroath here in 1320, which was a reaffirmation of Scotland's sovereignty that was dispatched to Rome. Frequently attacked by English ships in the late 14th century when its church was also struck by lightning. The blend of piety and warlike countenance of its many abbots was indicative of their noble birth. Amongst them were Abbot Hepburn who died at Flodden, 1513, while its Commendators included three successive members of the Beaton family, the last of whom was James Beaton, before the Abbey was burnt by the Reformers. Later it passed to a number of owners who included Lord Claud Hamilton and the Earl of Dysart. The last before its final decline was Patrick Maul of Panmure, the minister of James VI, after which it was continually pillaged for its red sandstone until it received protection from the Government in 1815. Shortly after the tomb of William I was discovered before the high altar. The last chapter in the Abbey's history came in 1951 when it was thrust into the limelight by a group of Scottish students reasserting Scotland's claim to the Stone of Destiny, thought to have been Jacob's pillow at Bethel which had served as the Westminster Coronation Stone since its seizure by Edward I from Scone in 1296. After a nation-wide police hunt it was found in the Abbey and returned to Westminster Abbey, where it was used for the coronation of Elizabeth II in 1953, but it was returned to Scotland in 1996 and is now housed in Edinburgh Castle. Today's substantial ruins, mainly of the church, are of the entrance doorway, many of the support pillars of the nave with its south wall, transept, sacristy and the east gable. The Chapter House and domestic buildings are to the south and the Abbot's House and gatehouse to the west. In its graveyard are a number of interesting gravestones.

ARBROATH, BATTLE OF, 1446
ANGUS

Fought near the town when the removal by the monks of Alexander Lindsay as Justiciary of Arbroath Abbey (owing to his excesses) for Alexander Ogilvy led to a feud between the two families. With the support of the powerful Sir Alexander Seton (Earl of Huntly 1449), the Ogilvie Clan met the Lindsays at the gates of the town prior to their defeat by the Lindsays which brought about the mass destruction of their estates and murder of their kinsfolk.

ARDBLAIR CASTLE
PERTH & KINROSS

By Loch Ard, 1 mile W of Blairgowrie. In the 14th century the land was held by Thomas Blair of Balthayock, whose original castle, once defended by the loch was replaced by today's 16th century oblong mansion house with vaulted cellars and L plan tower, which bore witness to many of the local feuds the Blairs were involved in. On the family's fall from grace the castle passed to the Oliphants of Gask, who were staunch Jacobites and were frequently visited by Lady Nairn

(1766-1845), who wrote 'Charlie is my darling' and ' Will ye no come back again' ?

ARDMILLAN CASTLE
SOUTH AYRSHIRE

About 3 miles SW of Girvan is a former seat of the Kennedys of Ardstinchar. The present L plan courtyard keep was built in the late 16th century by Thomas Kennedy, known as the 'Gudeman of Ardmellan', who bore the honours of his house at the 7th Laird's funeral after he was killed in a feud with Kennedy, Earl of Cassillis. In 1642 Hugh Kennedy supplicated the Presbytery of Ayr that his 'twenty pund land of Ardmillan might be annexed to the Parish of Colmonell'. After passing to the Crawfords in the late 17th century, it was described by a visitor as 'so much improven of late, that it looks like a palace, built round courtwayes; surrounded with a deep, broad ditch and strengthened with a moveable bridge at entry; able to secure the owner from the suddain commotions and assaults of the wild people of this corner set upon robbery and depredation'. Added to at later dates, in the 20th century it suffered a fire.

ARDROSS CASTLE
FIFE

By the coast 1 mile ENE of Elie are the scant remains of the Dischington's 14th century baronial fortalice built by William Dischington, who held important positions in the court of David II. It passed to William Scott at the beginning of the 17th century and then to William Anstruther at the close of the century.

ARDROSSAN
NORTH AYRSHIRE

Town situated NW of Irvine near the entrance to the Firth of Clyde. Name derived from the Gaelic 'ard' and 'ross' meaning 'headland' or 'height of the little cape'. Possibly one of the earliest sites of human habitation in Scotland, the place played a comparatively unimportant role in Scottish history and owes its existence to its harbour. This saw major construction work which was started in 1806 by the 12th Earl of Eglinton and Baron of Ardrossan, who envisaged a western supply port for Glasgow, but it was the 13th Earl who completed the project in 1844, at considerable cost. Through its export trade in coal and iron from Glasgow and the import of timber from America, corn and cattle from Ireland and manufactured goods from England, the town rose from a Sub Port of Irvine to become a Head Port in 1858, with 120 vessels on its register by 1880. While its failure to boost trade for its shipwrights through its 19th century infrastructuring was compensated for by its popularity as a holiday resort, its shipbuilding revived in later decades with the Ardrossan Harbour Co, Ardrossan Dockyard Ltd and the Shell Marketing Co, making Ardrossan a dual economy that lasted up until the 1970s. See Castle

ARDROSSAN CASTLE
NORTH AYRSHIRE

Positioned on land overlooking the town NW of Irvine, and on the site of an earlier castle are the fragmentary ruins of a 13th-century courtyard keep acquired by the Montgomeries around 1376 through marriage to the Eglinton family. According to Timothy Pont (geographer) this was the scene of Wallace's larder, when after luring the English garrison from the building to put out a fire, he took up positions with his patriots and slew them on their return, putting their bodies in the dungeon which became known as Wallace's larder. Demolished by Cromwell in 1650 before he used its stone to begin a fort at Ayr. In 1806 the harbour was built by the 12th Earl of Eglinton.

ARDSTINCHAR TOWER
SOUTH AYRSHIRE

Erected close to the village of Ballantrae near the River Stinchar. This ruined 15th-century tower commanded the entrance into Carrick from the south since it was built on the land bought by Hugh Kennedy after he distinguished himself at the battle of Beauge (1421), while in the service of Charles VII of France. Established as the seat of the Kennedy Lairds of Barganny, in 1601 the family's feud with the Kennedy Earls of Cassillis resulted in the murder of young Kennedy at the Brig o' Doon. Sold in 1650 to Sir John Hamilton of Lasterick, in 1796 it passed to Hugh Dalrymple.

ARDVRECK CASTLE
HIGHLAND

The ruins of a keep built by Macleod of Assynt in 1591 stand at the E end of Loch Assynt. Scene of the imprisonment of the Marquis of Montrose in 1650, before his transportation to Edinburgh and subsequent execution, 21st May 1650. The nearby Calder House was built by Kenneth Mackenzie, 3rd Earl of Seaforth, in 1660, but was destroyed by fire in the 18th century which also saw the forfeited Seaforth estate being purchased by the Earl of Sutherland, 1758.

ARKINHOLM, BATTLE OF, 1455
DUMFRIES & GALLOWAY

Fought during the Douglas Rebellion when after a series of engagements the three brothers of the 9th Earl of Douglas, who had denounced King James II as a traitor for the assassination of their brother William, were forced into submission. On their defeat by the Crown the Earl fled to England and was forfeited in 1455. The battle was significant in that it precipitated the fall of the Douglases from their long-standing position at the side of the Stewart Kings.

ARNAGE CASTLE
ABERDEENSHIRE

Situated 4 miles NW of Ellon. Formerly the seat of the Anglo Norman de Cheyne family who held large possessions in Aberdeenshire and who owned the land until 1630. The present Z plan structure, probably built around 1650 by the Rosses of Auchlossan incorporates vaulted cellars, and rises three storeys high, with a hall on the first floor, and sleeping quarters above which adjoin the towers and apex roof. In 1702 it was purchased by John Ross, later Provost of Aberdeen, whose descendants still held it in the 20th century.

ARNISTON HOUSE
MIDLOTHIAN

About 10 miles S of Edinburgh by the River Esk is a massive Palladian edifice that stands amidst finely wooded gardens which combine to provide a pastoral setting with a strong Dutch influence. From the 16th century the land was held by the Dundas family who distinguished themselves as politicians and lawyers by holding the offices of Lord President of the Court of Session, Lord Advocate, and Solicitor General. Built in 1726 to designs by William Adam, the building, which incorporates the older house, conforms to the traditional plan of a central block containing the principal apartments flanked by two Palladian style wings which mark some of Adam's other works. Its impressive exterior is second only to its richly embellished interior which displays finely carved woodwork and elaborate plasterwork, with immense variety although all kept subordinate to a leading idea, which was executed by a Dutchman named Enzer. In 1755 the house was completed by the brothers John and Robert Adam following their father's death.

ARNOT TOWER
FIFE

It stands on the Lomond Hills 3 miles W of Leslie. The ruins of the Arnots' 15th-century tower, probably built on the site of an earlier castle, once conformed to an oblong plan with courtyard to the south and tower with 6ft walls and vaulted ground floor, before their destruction during some onslaught. In 1296 a David de Arnot of Fife appeared on the Ragman Roll (register of those who swore allegiance to Edward I) and in 1334 a Michael de Arnot was at the siege of Leven Castle in support of John Balliol, Edward's vassal. In 1507 the lands and tower were incorporated into a Free Barony for Walter Arnot .

AROS CASTLE
ARGYLL & BUTE

Located on the south shore of the Sound of Mull is a pre-13th-century ruin originally erected for the Lords of the Isles who built its keep with a moat and drawbridge to protect the landward side. In 1608 Lord Ochiltree invited the dissenting island chiefs to dinner on his ship moored in the bay and in the course of the meal the guests were told they were prisoners of His Majesty James VI and were subsequently deposited in Dumbarton, Blackness and Stirling castles.

ASHINTULLY CASTLE
PERTH & KINROSS

Conforming to an L plan, the castle was built 15 miles NW of Blairgowrie by Andro Spalding in 1583 for his wife, a member of the Wemyss family. Besieged in 1585 by a lawless band who imprisoned and maltreated its owner. In 1677, another Andrew Spalding (probably a great grandson), received a charter under the Great Seal, erecting the lands into a Barony and Free Forest of Ashintully and Kirktown, with yearly fairs and weekly markets and Ashintully as burgh. By 1750 the castle was acquired by the Rutherfords.

ATHELSTANEFORD CHURCH
EAST LOTHIAN

Occupying land in the village of the same name about 4 miles NE of Haddington, the location of the church is itself steeped in history and takes its name from Athelstane, who was commander of the Saxon Northumbrians, and was defeated by the Picts in the 8th century. The original church was founded in the 12th century by the Countess of Northumberland and was granted to the Cistercian Nunnery of Haddington. A daughter-in-law of David I, like the King, by the time of her death she had left a number of reminders of her pious inclinations which in this case stood as the only church here until 1780 when a second church was built, but it in turn gave way to the present church built in 1868. The Parish's literary past revolves around Robert Blair who was Minister here from 1731, but is better known for his book 'The Grave' and was succeeded by Mr John Hume, author of 'Tragedy of Douglas' from 1749. See Battle

ATHELSTANEFORD, BATTLE OF, 735?
EAST LOTHIAN

Although located near Haddington, it gives its name to the place which was the scene of a victory by Hungus (or Angus) King of the Picts, 731-61, over Athelstane, a Danish Chief who had received land from the King of Northumbria. According to legend, the vision of St Andrews saltire promising him success the following day was the reason the Pictish King founded the Culdee Church in Saint Andrews, which contributed to the rise of Saint Andrews as the ecclesiastical capital and the adoption of the saltire as Scotland's flag.

AUCHENTOSHAN DISTILLERY
WEST DUMBARTONSHIRE

Located to the east of Dumbarton and NW of Glasgow. Founded in the early part of the 19th century, its name in Gaelic means 'corner of the field'. Since 1823 its producers have defined it as a Lowland Malt despite its closeness to the Highland Line and its water supply coming from the Kilpatrick Hills. Unlike other single malts Auchentoshan is distilled not twice but three times to give it the light flavour that appeals to younger whisky drinkers. Having all the advantages of its location with road rail and sea links to four points of the compass, it was also used for blending with other Lowland Malts and was sold in the markets of the south that now include the exclusive stores of London, Paris, Berlin and Tokyo.

OWNERS
Morrison Bowmore Distillers Ltd ?

REGION
Lowland

PRODUCT
Auchentoshan 10 & 21 year old single malt 40% & 43% vol

NOTES
A sweet fruity aroma and a hint of oilyness that are harmonised in the taste
An elegant taste with undertones of quince and caramel and a melting finesse.

AUCHINDOUN TOWER
MORAY

About 2 miles SE of Dufftown on the site of an earlier hillfortress are the remains of a three storey L plan tower dating from the 12th century. In the 15th century it was rebuilt into a court yard structure with enclosure by the Mason Robert Cochran, James III's favourite who was hanged over Lauder Bridge by jealous nobles. It later passed from the Ogilvies of Deskford and then the Gordons in 1535 who added a courtyard with round tower to the NW and extensive ranges along the east and south walls with a main arched entrance. Burnt in 1592 by William Mackintosh Chief of Clan Chattan. Queen Mary rode by here in 1562 and Queen Victoria picnicked nearby with the Duke of Richmond and Gordon in 1867. By the late 17th century it was uninhabited.

AUCHTERARDER
PERTH & KINROSS

Town and Castle (now a fragmentary ruin) situated 25 miles SW of Perth. Name derived from the Gaelic 'uachdar ard dobhair' meaning 'upland of the small stream'. A one time hunting seat of Malcolm Canmore (1058-1093), in 1227 Alexander II granted the teinds (taxes) of the land to Inchaffray Abbey. Represented in Parliament as the Head Burgh of Strathearn, it was elevated to Royal Burgh status by 1246 but had its land granted by Robert I to Sir William Montifix in 1328 and later passed through marriage to Sir William Drummond (Earl of Perth). Although important in Medieval Scotland, Auchterarder had declined by the 16th century when it figured in the Reformation and was burnt by the Earl of Mar in 1716 after the battle of Sheriffmuir, losing the Jacobites some support. Taking centre stage in the events leading up to the Disruption Debate in 1843 and the forming of the Free Church of Scotland, the Auchterarder case involved the rejection of a lay preacher for advancing the belief that predestination exempted certain people from renouncing sin. Today's textile trade was started around 1860 by the local weavers selling their wares in Glasgow and gave rise to a single mill at nearby Ruthvenvale by 1892 and an export market to China, India, Australia and New Zealand.

AUCHTERGAVEN
PERTH & KINROSS

Village situated in Strathtay, NW of Dunkeld. Name derived from the Gaelic 'uachdar-gamhainn' meaning 'upland of the yearling cattle'. The property of Thomas Nairn of Mukkersy in 1605 and created a Burgh of Barony for his grandson Lord Nairn in 1681, it was however the actions of John, the 3rd Lord, that first put the place on the map when he welcomed Prince Charles Edward here in 1745. The nearby Cairn-leith Moss, once a robbers' fastness was where retribution was exacted on highland caterans. Styled as Scotland's second Burns, in 1814 this was the birthplace of Robert Nicholl who is commemorated by the Nicholl monument, a prominent landmark built by the townsfolk of whom he wrote:

Happy happy be their dwellins'
By the burn and in the Glen
Cheerie lasses, cantie callans
Are the a' in Ochtergaen'

The area later became known for its cattle fairs and its slate and sandstone quarries.

AUCHTERMUCHTY
FIFE

Town situated 12 miles NE of Strathmiglo. Name derived from the Gaelic 'uchtar' and 'muc' meaning 'upland of the swine' (pig). The lands originally belonged to the Earls of Fife and later passed through marriage to the Duke of Albany before reverting to the Crown in 1425. Through the enterprise of its weavers it earned itself a Royal Burgh Charter in 1517, which although inactive and confirmed in 1595 failed to halt its steady decline and by 1707, the year of the Treaty of Union with England, it failed to return a member to parliament. The burgh became bankrupt in 1816 and was sequestrated for its corporation property except the Town House, Jail, Steeple bell and Customs. Reaching its heyday in 1851 the last echo of its weaving trade sounded in 1912 when the last shuttle clicked in the last Auchtermuchty handloom, which was later replaced by the more diverse distilleries, sawmills and linen factories. These in turn gave way to its oldest industry, metal beam and scale making, revived by John White & Son.

AULDEARN
HIGHLAND

Village situated 4 miles SE of Nairn. Name derived from the Gaelic 'Allt' meaning 'stream' or 'brook' while 'ern' was once the name of the nearby River Findhorn. The age old seat of the Deans of Moray Auldearn was constituted a Royal Burgh, 1179-82 and created a Burgh of Barony for Dunbar of Cumnock in 1511. The scene of a battle in 1645 when Montrose's forces defeated the Covenanters under General Hurry. The earlier village was also the site of a royal castle which is now marked by a 17th century Boath Doocot, but in 1650 parts of the town were annexed to Nairn, Cowder and Ardlach with Nairn providing the burghers with a market for their produce. See Battle

AULDEARN, BATTLE OF, 1645
HIGHLAND

One of the many victories gained by the Marquis of Montrose and the Highlanders owing to his consummate skills as a tactician. After beguiling Montrose into hostile country in the hope of surprising him, General Hurry (or Urray) with his superior force of Covenanters en route north to raid the Gordons' land, suffered a total defeat, compelling Hurry to join the Royalists. Like other victories, Auldearn contributed to the excessive confidence of the Royalists that was dashed by their eventual defeat at Carbisdale, after which the General was executed.

AULTMORE DISTILLERY
MORAY

About 10 miles SE of Buckie on the B9016 is one of Speyside's traditional 19th century distilleries. When Alexander Edward, a second generation whisky distiller and pioneer expanded his father's legacy, which included Benrinnes Distillery, he founded Aultmore in 1895. A favoured spot for illicit distilling since 1800 thanks to the abundance of springs, the peat on Foggie Moss and its proximity to Keith, Fochabers, and Port Gordon, production began here in 1897, followed by extensive improvements bringing the capacity to 100,000 gallons a year by 1898. With electricity replacing its paraffin lamps and the Abernethy 10 horsepower steam engine (now preserved) replacing the water wheel, Aultmore was equipped to produce large quantities of whisky in the 20th century. Further endeavours by Mr Edwards like the purchase of the Oban Distillery and the forming of the Oban Aultmore Glenlivit Distilleries Ltd, with a share capital of £160,000, were stifled by the collapse of the investors, blenders Pattison Ltd of Leith, 1899, and a shrinking market due to over production by 1900. The misfortune was compounded by a shortage of barley during World War I later followed by a recession in Britain and prohibition in the USA, forcing the sale of Aultmore to John Dewar & Son Ltd of Perth in 1923. Later to become part of Scottish Malt Distillers, later part of United Distillers, Aultmore closed between 1943-45 but its fortunes revived in the 1950s when it pioneered new techniques for recycling distillery effluence and new dried high protein animal feed. Improvements in 1967 such as the conversion of the stills to steam heating forced the steam engine

into retirement, paving the way for two additional stills and the boiler's conversion from coal burning to oil firing.

OWNERS
John Dewar & Sons Ltd ?

REGION
Speyside

PRODUCT
Aultmore 12 year old single malt 43% vol

NOTES
A slightly sweet nose with a well balanced mellow flavour.

AVONDALE TOWER
SOUTH LANARKSHIRE

Overlooking Strathaven town, 7 miles S of Hamilton, are the remains of a mid-15th century tower built by the 2nd Duke of Albany's grandson, Andrew Stewart, who obtained the barony in 1456, becoming Lord Avondale in 1457. The family exchanged it for the Barony of Ochiltree with Sir James Hamilton in 1543, after which further additions were made which remained intact until 1717, when following the death of the Duchess of Hamilton it was allowed to fall into ruin.

AYR
SOUTH AYRSHIRE

Coastal town situated 33 miles SW of Glasgow. Name derived from the river which is either from the Old Norse 'egri' meaning 'tongue of land'/ 'gravely bank' or from the Gaelic 'ar' meaning 'clear water'. With traces of a Roman presence, Ayr was probably used as a port to service the army's supply line which has contributed to its status as one of Scotland's longest standing burghs, something firmly established by the building of Ayr Castle by William I around 1190. Holding a Royal Burgh Charter by 1205, the town's oldest institution is Ayr Academy, which grew from a school located here in 1233. Constantly seen as a strategic prize for friend and foe alike, in 1263 Ayr was taken by the Norsemen under King Haakon prior to their defeat at Largs; to prevent its use by the English its castle was burnt by Bruce in 1298 but was repaired years later in 1314 by the King's brother Edward before his expedition to Ireland, when it disappeared from record. In 1242 a Dominican Monastery was founded here by Alexander II. Another Scottish warrior who left his mark in the town's historical annals was William Wallace when in 1297 he led a force of compatriots who burnt the timber dwellings of Edward I's invasion force, killing 500 men, an act which later became known as the Barns of Ayr. Subsequent to this was the meeting held in the 13th century church of St John when Bruce and his nobles decided on Edward Bruce as the King's successor before granting a Charter of Constitution to Newton upon Ayr. In 1513 the Scottish fleet anchored in Ayr harbour. The nearby Loudon Hall, Town House of the Sheriff of Ayrshire, was built in 1534, while to the east of the old castle, the fort built during Cromwell's occupation in 1652 incorporated St Johns Church for use as an armoury, resulting in its destruction and the building, up river, of the present church (Auld Kirk) 1653-55. The renaming of the Citadel Land to Montgomerystown and its erection into a Burgh of Regality for the Earl of Eglinton in 1633 further stimulated its trade in coal, leather and wool with Ireland, the Isle of Man, England and France. Though in 1686 the Chevalier Andrew Ramsay, tutor to the Young Pretender, was born here, the burghers supported the Government in the 1715 and 1745 rebellions, raising funds to maintain a company of foot during the latter, and escaped any contact with the rebels. Born at Alloway in 1759, Robert Burns received much of his inspiration from the characters and

daily life of 18th century Ayr. The 'Twa Brigs' from Burn's poem are positioned 150 yards apart. The Auld Brig dates from the 15th century, while the New Bridge built in 1788 by Robert Adam was damaged in the floods of 1877 and rebuilt in 1879. Its former status as the chief west coast port in the Middle Ages, was in evidence in the 18th century when the revenue from tobacco, sugar and rum from America and the West Indies helped to found the Ayr Bank, thus providing the catalyst for the town's 19th century export trade in wool, cotton muslin and shoes with Europe and America. Despite this acts passed in 1792 and 1817 failed to develop its harbour and prevent its eclipse by the newer Clyde ports, resulting in coal exports to Ireland being the staple trade here by 1880. Its more recreational pursuits such as the Ayr Races, Scotland's premier horse racing event which dates from around 1700, were along with its railway link to Glasgow (started 1840) and the rising popularity of golf instrumental in making Ayr a popular West Coast holiday retreat and sporting venue which it still is today, albeit on a much more limited scale. In the town centre are concentrated its oldest buildings, the Loudoun Hall, a 16th century merchant's Town House that belonged to the Sheriffs of Ayr, Wallace's Tower, built in 1834 on the site of an older edifice, The Tam O'Shanter Museum, a former 18th century tavern belonging to Douglas Graham of Shanter, and the not so old Town Hall of 1882.

B

BALBLAIR DISTILLERY
HIGHLAND

Six miles NW of Tain on the shore of Dornoch Firth is one of the Highland's oldest distilleries. Probably the site of an illicit still decades before 1750, when Balblair emerged as a farm steading with a still on the Ross family estate. It wasn't until 1790 that it firmly comes on record, when it was built by John Ross in the grounds of Balblair Farm near a small hill with nearby water supply. But following Ross's bankruptcy in 1817, production ceased until 1824. After his death in 1836 his son Andrew Ross ran it with his partner William Matheson (maltsman), with both partners' involvement in other distilleries helping to build its reputation as a recognised producer of quality Highland Malt. After being run by several family members, on the death of the founder's grandson Andrew Ross, in 1872 his son James took over. It was rebuilt in 1896 by the then leaseholder Alexander Cowan, on whose sequestration in 1911 it returned along with the land, to Lord and Lady Ross of the Balnagowan Estate. In 1933 the distillery's warehouses were empty, and from 1939 it was used by the British Army as a workshop and dormitory, eventually returning to production in 1949 after Bertie Cummings had bought the liquidated Balnagowan Estate. Sold by 1969 to Hiram & Walker & Sons of Canada, in the late 1980s it became part of Allied Distillers, later part of Allied Domecq. In 1996 it was purchased by Inver House Distillers Ltd and later by Blairmhor Ltd.

OWNERS
Blairmhor Ltd ?

REGION
Highland

PRODUCT
Balblair, 10 and 16 year old single malt 40% vol

NOTES
A fresh fruity nose and a balanced slightly bittersweet taste.

BALCOMIE CASTLE
FIFE

North of Crail village stands a large late 16th century tower and 17th century gatehouse attached to an 18th century farm steading with mansion. The lands which were held by John de Balcomie in 1375, were granted in feu-ferm by James V to James Learmouth of Clatto in 1526, whose successor Sir James Learmouth of Dairsie entertained Mary of Guise here in 1538 after her arrival at Crail prior to her marriage to the King. In the 18th century, although reduced in size by the Earl of Kellie, it continued to serve as a landmark to mariners.

BALGONIE CASTLE
FIFE

Built on the edge of a slope 1 mile SE of Markinch. To this 15th century keep started by John Sibbald of Balgonie with wall and gatehouse to the SW, a north range was added by Sir Robert Lundie after his marriage to Elizabeth Sibbald in 1419. And it was further extended in the 16th and 17th centuries with a west range and south wall forming a courtyard plan. Held by Sir Andrew Lundy of Balgonie (Sheriff of Fife) in a charter of 1511. Between 1632 and 1635 it was bought by the Covenanting General Leslie, who was created Baron Balgony, Earl of Leven in 1641 twenty years before dying here, 1661. A favourite residence of successive earls, and garrisoned by the Hanoverians in 1716 when it was besieged and taken by Rob Roy. In the 19th century it was bought by James Balfour.

BALLANTRAE
SOUTH AYRSHIRE

Coastal village situated 12 miles SW of Girvan. Name derived from the Gaelic 'Baile an traigh' meaning 'village or town on the shore'. The ancient seat of the Kennedy lairds, it was created a Burgh of Barony in 1541 for Kennedy of Barganny who from the family seat at Ardstinchar Castle ruled the Baronies of Ballantrae and Ardstinchar until the late 17th century. A noted smuggler's haunt, the village was sold in 1816 to the Earl of Stair who introduced many improvements. See Ardstinchar Castle

BALLATER
ABERDEENSHIRE

Village situated 40 miles SW of Aberdeen. Name derived from the Gaelic 'bealaidh tir' meaning 'broom land'. Although the outlying area has some objects of interest, Ballater village dates from the 18th century. Encouraged by its fresh air, picturesque scenery and natural spring water, the village was built by William Farquharson of Monaltrie to accommodate visitors to the Pananich Mineral Wells, while its proximity to the royal retreat at Balmoral further improved its appeal by giving it the semblance of royal approval. The present five arched bridge was built in 1885 to replace earlier bridges that were swept away in the Great Floods of 1799 and 1820.

BALLENCRIEFF HOUSE
EAST LOTHIAN

Standing 2 miles SE of Aberlady village are the ruins of a 17th century mansion house. Lands were granted to John Murray of Blackbarony in 1511, for whose descendent Sir Gideon Murray, an eminent lawer and acting Lord High Treasurer of Scotland, they were erected into the Barony of Ballencrieff in 1617, prior to the building of the house by his son Patrick

in 1625. After the death of his father in prison for corruption, he was raised to the peerage in 1643 as Ist Lord Elibank. In the 18th century the east wings were added and a north front done in a Renaissance style, but by the 19th century the house was reduced to a burnt-out shell.

BALLINDALLOCH CASTLE
MORAY

Positioned at the junction of the rivers Avon and Spey 12 miles SW of Craigellachie. As a Z plan castle and seat of the Grants from 1546, it was built near the site of a previous castle and was greatly altered and enlarged, with its cape house erected by Patrick Grant in 1602. Further enlargements in 1845, making it a castellated mansion, were carried out by the father of Sir George Macpherson Grant, who succeeded him in 1850 and later became MP for Elgin.

BALLINSHOE TOWER
ANGUS

A small tower situated 2 miles SE of Kirriemuir. The land was originally held by the Scrymgeours of Dudhope, who were succeeded by the Ogilvies in the 16th century, but after a dispute over title John Lindsay took possession of it. However, it was probably a succeeding Lindsay Laird who built the tower, to no specific plan, in the late 16th or early 17th century, before it passed to the Fletchers.

BALLOCH CASTLE
PERTH & KINROSS

About 5 miles SW of Aberfeldy at the mouth of Loch Tay, its name denoting opening or pass in Gaelic, is the former seat of the Breadalbane family. Before leaving Kilchurn castle this Z plan structure was built by Sir Colin Campbell, 6th Laird of Glenorchy, who died here in 1583. Partly demolished in 1801, it was incorporated into the renamed Taymouth castle, the new family seat.

BALMANNO CASTLE
PERTH & KINROSS

Occupying land at the entrance to Glen Farg 10 miles SE of Perth. A good example of a Scottish Baronial Mansion, it was built between 1570 and 1580 by George Auchinleck, in whose family it remained until becoming a possession of the Murrays of Glendoick in the 17th century. Passing through marriage to the Belshes of Invermay in 1752 and later held by the Forbeses of Pitsligo, it was saved from ruin when it was used as a farmhouse and restored by Robert Lorimer between 1916 and 1921.

BALMERINO ABBEY
FIFE

Standing on rising ground overlooking the Firth of Tay 5 miles W of Newport is the ruined Cistercian Abbey founded in 1227 by Ermengarde (widow of King William I) and her son Alexander II. Dedicated to the Virgin Mary and St Edward (the Confessor) it was a stately 2nd pointed edifice with work from four subsequent periods. Its patchy remains include part of the church entrance, the north wall of the nave with parts of the transepts; the adjoining sacristy and the Abbey's finest ruin, the Chapter House. Outside this are the domestic buildings and the ruined Abbot's House. As with most of the senior clergy, its abbots were more like statesmen with seats in parliament while often acting as arbiters in civil disputes. Abbot John de Hayles, 1408-35, negotiated with the English for the ransom of James I and also served in France and Italy. Despite its repairs after being burnt by Somerset's invasion force in 1547 and being visited by a special Commission for reform, 1533, to arrest the Abbey's spiritual decline, the monks' continued acts of depravity resulted in the Abbey's destruction by the Lords of the Congregation at the Reformation and its present decay. Created a Temporal Lordship for Sir James Elphinstone Lord Balmerino in 1603 and partly demolished by the 2nd Lord for its stone. Though stone pillaging continued in subsequent periods it is now in a state of preservation.

BALMORAL CASTLE
ABERDEENSHIRE

Situated on the banks of the River Dee 50 miles SW of Aberdeen. Originally consisting of a 16th century tower belonging to the Gordons. The property was later held by several owners before Queen Victoria purchased the estate in 1848. Prince Albert initiated the building of the present granite structure in a Scottish Baronial style, overseen by Sir Robert Gordon to designs by William Smith. It comprises two blocks connected by wings with a large eastern tower. The Queen and Prince Albert first occupied the building on Sept 7 1855 and it quickly became the Royal couple's favourite summer retreat while in Scotland, an allure it has held for the Royal Family up to the present day.

BALMUTO HOUSE
FIFE

Located 3 miles NW of Burntisland. The land, which belonged to the Glen family from the 13th century, passed to Sir John Boswell through marriage to Lady Mariote Glen, whose son Andrew Boswell probably built the original tower in 1477, when Balmuto and their other lands were united into the Barony of Glassmount. This was confirmed in a charter of 1587 for Sir John Boswell, a favourite in the court of James VI and builder of its southern section in 1594. It was further altered by a David Boswell in 1680 before being sold to the Boswells of Auchinleck in 1722, who added a mansion house in the 19th century.

BALVAIRD TOWER
PERTH & KINROSS

Perched on a hill at the head of Glenfarg is a late 15th century L plan keep with 16th century additions. Between 1487 and 1513 Sir Andrew Murray, the youngest son of William Murray of Tullibardine, built this tower after he was married (around 1486) to Lady Margaret Barclay the Balvaird heiress. Considerable additions were made by Andre Murray (grandson) in 1567, who developed the keep into an L plan courtyard castle that was still held by the family in 1618 when the barony was conferred on Andrew Murray (Minister of Abdie). The new owner was made Lord Balvaird by Charles I in 1641, before succeeding to the Lordship of Stormont in 1642.

BALVENIE CASTLE
MORAY

On the left bank of the River Fiddich just north of Dufftown. Probably built on the site of a more primitive fortress, with its well-preserved 13th century shell, its oldest part is called a Pictish tower but its style is Scottish Baronial. Successively the property of the Comyns, the Douglases, the Stewarts and of the Inneses by 1615. In the 15th century, John Stewart of Balveny, the son of the Black Knight of Lorn, was granted the land by his half brother James II on his marriage to Margaret, widow of the Earl of Douglas. Made Earl of Atholl in 1457, his daughter married a John Forbes, who added stair turrets and the SE angle tower.

BALVENIE DISTILLERY
MORAY

Founded outside Dufftown at the mains of Balvenie Farm by William Grant in 1892. The sale secured for Grant the rights of the Robbie Dhu spring which Balvenie shares with its sister distillery the Glenfiddich. Flowing from the stills in 1893, Balvenie's reputation as an old-fashioned backwoods distillery in the shadow of Glenfiddich is proudly upheld by the local farmers, maltmen, cooper and coppersmiths and is in keeping with the Grant family's policy. Grown locally, the barley is steeped and malted on the traditional floor maltings; the germinating barley is then turned by hand before being dried in peat kilns. While the process has remained the same, the range of products has changed and in 1993 to mark the centenary the 12 year old Double Wood 40% vol was added to the long established 10 year old Founders Reserve 40% vol.

OWNERS
William Grant & Sons Ltd ?

REGION
Speyside

PRODUCT
The Balvenie 10 year old Founders Reserve 40% vol

NOTES
A slightly sweet and fruity aroma, that carries through to the palate and blends with a hint of sherry.

BANFF
ABERDEENSHIRE

Coastal town situated 46 miles NNW of Aberdeen. The name may derive from the Gaelic 'banby' meaning 'land unplowed for a year' or possibly from the Irish 'banbh' meaning 'little Ireland'. Though the ancient capital of Banffshire it retains few relics of antiquity as the House of Airlie and the Ogilvies, stately palace are no longer. Standing near the Earl of Findlater's 18th century building are the ruins of Banff Castle which still retains its outer wall and moat which frequently provided security for 11th and

12th century kings, the most notable being Malcolm Canmore (1058-1093). Although the town's development had more to do with the east coast's defensive network than with trade it nevertheless received a Royal Burgh Charter from William I in 1165 that was confirmed by Robert I, 1324, Robert II in 1372 and James VI in 1581. Its old Kirk was once the burial place of the Ogilvies. A Carmelite Friary bestowed by Robert I in 1321 had its property granted to King's College Aberdeen by James VI in 1574. Unable to avoid the historical instability like some of its neighbours, in 1644 it was pillaged by Montrose and during the Jacobite Rebellion of 1745 the Hanoverian forces en route to Inverness bivouacked here. During a visit by Robert Burns in 1780, the bard composed the poem 'Macpherson's Farewell' to the memory of James Macpherson, a Highland free-booter who played the fiddle while being escorted to the gallows:

Sae rantinly, sae wontonly, sae dauntinly, gaed he;
He played a spring and danced it round below the gallows tree.

Its harbour, built by John Smeaton in 1775 and extended by John Telford in 1816, was used by craft carrying wool, whisky, rope, sailcloth and iron to Sweden, Russia, Germany and Holland. Built in 1740 by William Adam for a Mr Duff, later Lord Braco and Earl of Fife, Duff House by the golf course ranks as one of the finest examples of Georgian Baroque architecture in Britain. It was used for various purposes from a sanatorium to a hotel and POW camp but now houses Burgh art exhibitions. The original Parish Church of St Mary's, built by the Adam brothers in 1790 in a Renaissance style, greatly benefited from the renovations of 1927, while at the Plawstones stands the 16th century Mercat Cross and one-time Exchange.

BANNOCKBURN, BATTLE OF, 1314
STIRLING

One of the classic victories of Medieval warfare fought between the Scots under Robert the Bruce and the English under Edward II. Following the siege of Stirling Castle, the key to the Highlands, Edward led around 100,000 men to its relief. With around 30,000 men Bruce chose his ground carefully near the Bannockburn, which along with its marsh and the Scottish pike men proved fatal to the English horse, before the appearance of a Scottish reserve force caused panic broken ranks and eventual defeat. This stratagem was recalled in Sir Walter Scott's 'Marmion':

The landscape like a furnace glowed,
And far as eer the eye was borne,
The lances waved like autum corn.
In battle four beneath their eye,
The forces of King Robert lie
And one below the hill was laid,
Reserved for rescue and for aid.

The victory forced the abandonment of the invasion and paved the way for the Declaration of Arbroath six years later.

BARCALDINE CASTLE
ARGYLL & BUTE

Positioned on rising ground on the south side of the Creran Water 12 miles NE of Oban. According to the 'Black Book of Taymouth' this L plan structure was built in the late 16th century by Sir Duncan Campbell, 7th Laird of Glenorchy, who, as a man of distinction, did much to improve the area before his death in 1631. Garrisoned against Montrose during the Covenanting Wars, 1645. It was enlarged and embellished by Sir Colin Campbell, 8th Laird of Glenorchy, in 1690 and though it fell into decay in the 18th century when the family left for Barcaldine House, it has since been restored.

BARHOLM TOWER
DUMFRIES & GALLOWAY

Located between Gatehouse of Fleet and Creetown inland from Wigtown Bay. Although the property of the M'culloch family from the early 16th century, the present ruined L plan keep was built in the early 17th century. Figuring in the Covenanting Wars, Major M'culloch of Barholm accommodated government troops here prior to fighting in the Pentland Rising, and was subsequently executed in 1666 when his estates were forfeited. The adjacent farmhouse is dated 1797.

BARJARG TOWER
DUMFRIES & GALLOWAY

Standing in a wood 4 miles SE of Penpont. The land originally belonged to Holyrood Abbey, but was later given by the Earl of Morton in 1587 to Thomas Grierson, a prominent landowner who probably started this L plan tower house along with the surrounding woodland. Occupied in 1603 by Robert Maxwell , whose shield is inscribed on the west wing, further additions were made in 1680 by a John Grierson, who lived here with his wife Grizzel Kirkpatrick. After a number of owners including a judge and a professor, in the 19th century a central dwelling house was built.

BARNBOUGLE CASTLE
CITY OF EDINBURGH

Now part of a 19th century structure situated on the shore of the Firth of Forth 3 miles E of Queensferry. In the 12th century the land belonged to the Moberys, who probably built the first fort. It was sold in 1615 to Sir Thomas Hamilton, later Earl of Haddington, but was resold in 1662 to Sir Archibald Primrose Bart from whom it descended to the Earls of Rosebery. In 1880 its shell was restored and incorporated into the building we see today.

BARNS HOUSE
SCOTTISH BORDERS

This well preserved pele house which forms a rectangular keep was built on high ground on the south bank of the Tweed 4 miles SW of Peebles inorder that it served as a signal tower. It was built either around 1591 for Lady Margaret Stewart of Traquair or by her husband William Burnet, who inherited the estate in 1574 and whose family, the Burnets of Burnetland, lived here from the 14th century. A charismatic and chivalrous figure, he was nicknamed the Howlet due to his midnight expeditions, and lived until until he was 107 years old. Vacated by the family in the 18th century for nearby Barns House, the tower now stands empty.

BARR CASTLE
RENFREWSHIRE

Occupying land 1 mile W of Lochwinnoch village. This ruined courtyard keep, crowned with battlements and corner turrets, was started by the Glen family in the 15th century on land received from Paisley Abbey when castle design was changing from slits for arrows to port holes for guns. A James Glen of Barr fought with Queen Mary at Langside in 1568. In the late 16th century it became the property of the Hamiltons of Ferguslie who added to it and held it until the 18th century.

BARRA CASTLE
WESTERN ISLES

On the SW of the island stands an ancient stronghold of the Macneils of Barra. The island and other domains were restored to Ranald son of Malan when pardoned along with the Lord of the Isles by David II in 1334 in order to secure their involvement in the wars with England. Consisting of a tower erected in 1427 with an additional curtain wall built when Roderick

Macmurchan Macneil was granted a charter of the island by the Lord of the Isles. Additional internal structures were added in the 17th and 18th centuries.

BARRA CASTLE
ABERDEENSHIRE

About 2 miles S of Old Meldrum, near the site of Bruce's victory over Comyn Earl of Buchan at Barra Hill, stands a 17th century turreted courtyard structure with buildings around three sides. The castle displays a modern style with the old ideas blending to form a picturesque effect. Alas, the building's total lack of history leaves one focusing on its architectural merits.

BARRA HILL, BATTLE OF, 1307
ABERDEENSHIRE

About 2 miles S of Old Meldrum around the one time prehistoric fort, the recently crowned and ailing King Robert the Bruce with 700 men engaged John Comyn, Earl of Buchan's army of around 1,000 men advancing from Old Meldrum. Comyn's force was soon routed which led to the decimation of his family's land and forced him to retire to England. This was the last battle fought between Bruce and one of the Comyn faction, who was the cousin of Bruce's arch rival and competitor for the Crown who Bruce had killed at Dumfries one year before.

BARSCOBE HOUSE
DUMFRIES & GALLOWAY

Located 3 miles NE of New Galloway is a typical L plan country house built for a 17th century laird. Developing from an old pele tower, it was built in 1648 by William Maclellan of Bombie (from a notable Galloway family) for his wife Mary Gordon, and in 1664 passed to their son Robert, who was a prominent Covenanter, but by 1880 the property had passed out of the Maclellans' possession.

BATHGATE
WEST LOTHIAN

Town situated 18 miles W of Edinburgh. While the exact etymology is uncertain the name would seem to mean either 'house in wood' or 'boarwood'. Under Saxon rule up until the 10th century, its church was granted by Malcolm IV to Holyrood Abbey, 1315. Along with its castle (now gone) the land later formed part of the dowry for Marjory Bruce (daughter of Robert I) on her marriage to Walter Stewart, who died here in 1326. This one-time Sheriffdom was created a Burgh of Barony for Hamilton of Bathgate in 1663 which, despite holding an annual fair from 1600, remained a hamlet until the 18th century, when the area's mineral wealth provided the impetus for growth along with its industrial twin Armadale. In 1811 Sir James Young Simpson, an early promoter of chloroform, was born here, the son of a baker. Created an Independent Burgh in 1824, as a significant source of coal, slate, silver, paraffin and limestone in later decades the area acquired the scars of heavy industrial mining, owing to its position between Glasgow and Edinburgh's industrial belt. This was transformed in the 1970s with the cultivation of the Bathgate Town Wood and Bathgate Park of Peace by the Scottish Development Agencies.

BAVELAW CASTLE
CITY OF EDINBURGH

It stands on high ground overlooking Thriepmuir Reservoir 10 miles W of the city centre. The land was thought to have been a Royal Hunting Seat but the main L plan structure was probably started by Walter Dundas in the 17th century before Charles I granted the land of Easter and Wester Bavelaw with manor and tower to Scott of Harperrig (Advocate) in 1628. In the 19th century the tower was restored.

BEDLAY HOUSE
NORTH LANARKSHIRE

Located 7 miles NE of Glasgow. The land and manor was granted to the Church of Glasgow in the 12th century by David I. Acquired by James Boyd in 1580, whose kinsman Robert, 4th Lord Boyd, built its late 16th century tower in the NE section. In 1642 it was bought by James Robertson, advocate and later Lord Bedlay, whose family purchased its superiority in 1740 and added its western section with turrets before its sale in 1786.

BEMERSYDE
SCOTTISH BORDERS

Positioned on the E bank of the Tweed 2´ miles NE of St Boswells. From the 12th century this was the seat of the Haig or de Hagus family of Norman origin, whose ownership down through the centuries vindicated Thomas the Rymer's prophecy 'Tide, tide, whatee'er betide, Theres aye be Haigs in Bemersyde'. The oldest section consists of a rectangular keep built in 1535 with walls six to ten feet thick in accordance with the Act of Parliament drafted to reinforce the Borders region, probably in response to the Scots' devastating defeat at Flodden a generation before. Additions were made in 1691. It stands on the crest of a public road, commanding a view over the Tweed Valley. During his many jaunts throughout the Borders, Sir Walter Scott often reined up his horse here, and in 1832 his horse and his hearse was seen to come to a standstill here during his funeral procession.

BENHOLM TOWER
ANGUS

A 15th century keep built into a mansion on high ground 2 miles N of Montrose. As the seat of the Keiths, Earls Marischal, it was once a place of considerable strength owing to its position on a penin-sula formed by a stream on the east and south sides and by a deep moat on the west. In 1623 this was the scene of the theft of a large amount of money and jewels by the 5th Earl's widowed Countess.

BEN NEVIS DISTILLERY
HIGHLAND

Unmistakably identified by its name and location at the foot of Ben Nevis, Scotland's highest mountain. Its founding in 1825 by John Macdonald, who was born in Lochaber into a branch of the Keppoch Macdonalds, made him one of the earliest legal distillers in Scotland, in an area awash with illicit stills. The distillery takes its water from the Allt a' Mhuilinn (The Mill burn) which flows from two small lochans in Coirs Leis and Coire na Ciste which are located 3,000 feet up Ben Nevis, arguably one of the most attractive spots for a distillery. Although its closeness to Fort William, the gateway to the Highlands, brought it recognition, the more enduring legacy of this story is the name of its founder who was known throughout the Highlands as Long John. In 1848 it merited a mention in 'The Illustrated London News' following a visit from Queen Victoria who was given a cask of whisky from Macdonald. Known as the Dew of Ben Nevis, the area's bounty of water, barley, yeast and peat assured the production of a quality whisky long before and long after the death of its founder in 1865. In 1885 it reached an annual output of 152,798 gallons of pure Highland Malt. With increased production came more rebuilding facilitating a pier where the whisky was transported by the steamers that plied Loch Linnhe. The distillery was run by the founder's grandsons John and Archibald Macdonald from 1891, under whose stewardship an amicable deal was struck with the North British Railway, bringing a siding and turntable facilities that complemented the fine harbour pier and fleet of steamers for decades afterwards. In 1941 the distillery passed out of the family's hands to a Mr Joseph Hobbs whose coffey stills helped make Ben Nevis by 1955 one of the first distilleries in Scotland that could produce both malt and grain whiskies under one roof. Purchased and used for storage purposes by Long John International in 1978, it was reopened in 1984 and extensively modernised prior to being acquired by the Nikka Whisky Distilling Co of Japan in 1989. Latterly the distillery has changed hands again.

OWNERS
Ben Nevis Distillery Co Ltd ?

REGION
Highland

PRODUCT
Dew of Ben Nevis 12 year old 40% vol & 26 year old 58% vol

NOTES
A floral aroma with a hint of mint, a malty taste with a peaty element and a rounded finish
A flowery, sweet, herb-like aroma with a trace of rum toffee leading to a smooth, rich, liqueurish-sweet taste.

BENRIACH DISTILLERY
MORAY

Easily identified by the pagoda-style roof of its kiln on the main Elgin to Rothes road. Since it was established in 1898 by John Duff, owner of the nearby Longmorn distillery, it has taken its water from the Burnside Springs. Its other enduring qualities have been its kiln and one of the few remaining original floor maltings in Scotland, which continued to produce malt for the industry following Benriach's closure in 1900. Here the malt is regularly plough turned by hand to keep it aerated, and dried over a peat fire. The malt is then dressed and milled before mashing in a traditional cast iron mash tun, during which time the starch turns to sugar. The spirit is produced in small, steam heated stills which preserve its unique flavour. Also popular with blenders, Benriach is the main malt that goes into the distillery's '100 Pipers' brand. Notwithstanding renovations in 1965 by the then owners The Longmorn Distillery Co Ltd, and in 1978 when it was acquired by Seagram Distillers Plc, and later by Chivas Brothers Ltd, the kiln buildings remain as part of the working legacy of the original Benriach.

OWNERS
Chivas Brothers Ltd ?

REGION
Speyside

PRODUCT
Benriach 10 year old single malt 40% vol

NOTES
A soft sweet flowery scented aroma with a balanced fruity slightly sweet flavour and a dry finish.

BENRIG, BATTLE OF, 1382
Alarmed at the many border incursions by the Scots, Richard II appointed Baron Greystokes as Keeper of Roxburgh Castle, a border stronghold. But during his journey to take up the post the Baron and his party were attacked by a force under the Earl of Douglas. Imbued with confidence, in 1388 the Earl led another raid into England which culminated in victory at Otterburn.

BENRINNES DISTILLERY
MORAY

Just south of Aberlour is the granite massif of Ben Rinnes (2755ft high / 840m) which is estimated to be 480 million years old. Through the fissures in the rock, the rainwater is filtered to the Scurran and Rowantree burns that provide the natural spring water for the distillery below.

The first distillery recorded here in 1826, near Whitehouse Farm, was swept away in the great flood of 1829, but was replaced in 1835 by an adapted farmsteading at Lower Lyne of Ruthrie, and licensed to a Peter Mackenzie. Following the bankruptcy of its third owner, William Smith, in 1864, the lease was acquired by David Edward, a farmer whose son Alexander, owner of other distilleries, promoted the Benrines Glenlivet Co Ltd, acquiring the lands, buildings, water rights, plant and vessels following the fire of 1896. Owing to the purity of its supplies of peat barley and especially water, it achieved a high standard of excellence and reputation in the industry that continued until the collapse of its sole agent in 1899. This was compounded by the industry's recession between 1900-03. Failing to revive its flagging fortunes, in 1922 it was taken over by John Dewar & Sons Ltd and later became part of Scottish Malt Distillers in 1930. Discouraged by restrictions during World War II, production ceased between 1943-45. The post-war period saw its transformation when it was connected to the national grid in 1951; and electricity replaced the petrol engine generator, water wheel and the Rushton-Hornsby steam engine. The major reconstruction of the century-old farm-steading by 1956 spared visitors the ritual encounter with cows emerging from the byres. With the doubling of its stills to six in 1966 came increased production, the building of a bonded warehouse in 1978 and improved mashing methods in 1991, whilst preserving its traditional production method, a form of triple distillation which is a distinctive feature of Benrinnes.

OWNERS
Diageo plc ?

REGION
Speyside

PRODUCT
Benrinnes 15 year old single malt 43% vol

NOTES
A medium sweet nose with a round honeyed flavour.

BIGGAR
SOUTH LANARKSHIRE

Town situated 13 miles NE of Abington. Name either derived from the Gaelic 'bigthir' meaning 'soft land' or from the Old Norse 'bygg garthr' meaning 'barley enclosure'. In a charter from David I the land belonged to a Baldwin of Biggar for whose descendants, the Fleming family, overlords and occupants of Boghall Castle (fragmentary ruin), it was made a Burgh of Barony in 1451. The 'Cadger's Bridge' was so named after William Wallace spied out the English position while dressed as a cadger before defeating them at the battle of Biggar in 1297. Once well known for its communication links, an old Roman road passed through here, and the Moat Hill to the north of the High Street was once part of a chain of beacon towers that stretched from the Vales of the Clyde and Tweed. Biggar's religious history concerns the Collegiate Parish Church of St Mary which, regarded as one of Scotlands last pre-Reformation churches, was founded in 1545 by Malcolm, 3rd Lord Fleming, while its involvement in the Covenanting Wars of the 17th century is recalled in the Covenanters Museum. The town also has an industrial history including a gas works and car plant that are remembered in the Gas Works Museum. See Battle

BIGGAR, BATTLE OF, 1297
SOUTH LANARKSHIRE

Fought on Biggar Moss during the campaign launched by Edward I to subdue the unruly Scots under their leader William Wallace. Though said to be superior in numbers, Edward's force was completely defeated and many of them slain owing to the thoroughness of Wallace's horsemen. As one of the many victories achieved under Wallace's leadership, Bigger gave heart to the Scottish cause that reached its height at the battle of Stirling Bridge.

BINNS, HOUSE OF
WEST LOTHIAN

Located 4 miles E of Linlithgow is a castellated structure. Started around 1621 by Thomas Dalyell, a merchant and burgess of Edinburgh who acquired the property in 1612. This was the seat of the Dalyells of the Binns for more than three centuries and birthplace of Sir Thomas Dalyell (1599-1685) who routed the Covenanters at Rullion Green in 1666. In his old age Sir Thomas cultivated the estate with fine gardens where in 1681 he embodied the Scots Greys Regiment in support of Charles II. Enlarged in 1820, its original interior is richly embellished with fine plaster ceilings.

BIRSE TOWER
ABERDEENSHIRE

Situated in what was once Birse Forest 6 miles S of Aboyne. The land and forest were granted by Alexander II in 1240 to Bishop Gordon of Aberdeen, whose descendants, the Gordons of Clunie, built this late 16th century L plan keep with round tower which was extended in the 20th century.

BISHOP'S PALACE
ORKNEY

Within 35 yards of Kirkwall Cathedral are the substantial 15th and the 16th century ruins of a palace built on the site of a 12th century building where King Haakon of Norway died after returning from his defeat at the battle of Largs in 1263. The main oblong block, built of local rubble around 1500, is two storeys high with gardrobe in west wall. The additions made by Bishop Reid, 1541-58, including reinforced walls raised three storeys with garret on top and a large five-storey round tower transformed the structure. In the 17th century buttresses were added to the walls and the vaults, and the ground floor removed when the building was joined to the Earl's Palace at a time when the palace and town were becoming more remote. See Earl's Palace

BLACKHALL HOUSE
CITY OF GLASGOW

Occupying land 1 mile from Paisley town. In 1396 Robert III conferred the land on Sir John Stewart, whose ancestors, the Stewarts of Blackhall and Ardgowan, built this two-storied mansion for use as a family home; it became a farmhouse in 1710.

BLACKNESS CASTLE
WEST LOTHIAN

It stands on a rocky promontory 3´ miles E of Boness. Developing from a 15th century tower, thought to mark the eastern extremity of the Antonine Wall and one of the most important castles in Southern Scotland. It was burnt in 1443 during the conflict between the Douglases, Livingstones, Crichtons and Forresters. During later decades the castle had a colourful history for it was burnt by the English Navy in 1481, witnessed a meeting of James III and his rebellious nobles in 1488, was garrisoned by a French force in 1548 and held for Queen Mary by Lord Hamilton between 1571 and 1573. An enclosing wall was built in the 16th century and it was acquired by the Crown in 1667, when more work was done, before being used as a prison for distinguished Covenanters in 1670. Between 1870-1874 it functioned as a barracks and central ammunitions depot for Scotland, when parts were reinforced and alterations made.

BLAIR HOUSE
NORTH AYRSHIRE

Mansion House located 2 miles SE of Dalry village. Developing from a 15th-century keep, built on land that was held by the Blair family from the 13th century when a Bryce Blair was slain by the English after being invited to Ayr under pretence of holding a Justiciar Court with some other Ayrshire Barons. In 1617, a Bryce Blair extended it for his wife Annabel Wallace and it was further enlarged in 1668 by William Blair who married Lady Margaret Hamilton. As Commissioner of the Peace he tried numerous Covenanters in Ayrshire, many of whom hid on his land, before he became a member of the Convention of Estates (name given to parliament when not summoned by the King) in 1689.

BLAIR ATHOLL CASTLE
PERTH & KINROSS

About 9 miles NW of Pitlochry is the age old seat of the Dukes of Atholl. A four-storey Scottish Baronial Mansion with tower and battlements, it was probably started as a 13th century tower by John Comyn of Strathbogie, 9th Earl of Atholl, in 1296, and was added to in 1457 when the Earldom passed to Sir John Stewart of Balveny, the half brother of James II (1437-1460). Visited by James V in 1529 while hunting in Glen Tilt Forest, and also by Queen Mary in 1564. The castle often served as an important military post for its distinguished occupants; before his victory at Tippermuir Montrose raised 3,000 Highlanders here and after its destruction by Cromwell's forces it was rebuilt in 1689 and served as the headquarters of John Graham of Claverhouse, who was buried in the family vault after his death at Killiecrankie. In 1745 Prince Charles Edward stayed here, followed in 1746 by the Hanoverians, who were reduced to eating horse flesh when it was besieged by Lord George Murray. Following the removal of its two upper storeys, in 1844 it was described by Queen Victoria during her twenty-day stay with Prince Albert as 'a large white building' which by the late 19th century had been fashioned by David Bryce in the Scottish Baronial style we see today.

BLAIR ATHOL DISTILLERY
PERTH & KINROSS

Long famous for its 'Uisge beatha', meaning 'water of life'. It stands to the SE of Pitlochry and Blair Atholl town. The failure of the first distillery founded here in 1798, and named 'Aldour' after the Ault Dour, the 'burn of the otter', didn't discourage John Robertson from reviving Blair Athol in 1826 after the absurdly high excise duties were reduced in 1823 to prevent illicit distilling. Its water from Ben Vrackie flows directly into the distillery grounds. In 1827 it was run by Alexander Connacher, an alleged descendant of the chivalrous young Connacher who figured in Sir Walter Scott's 'Fair Maid of Perth', but was taken over and improved by Peter Mackenzie & Co around 1850, later producing over 1500 gallons (6,800 litres) per week. Made part of Arthure Bell & Sons in 1933, the distillery closed during the Depression and during World War II but in 1949 was extensively rebuilt and, in continuing to share in the traditions of the Vale of Athol, has stayed in production ever since.

OWNERS
Diageo plc ?

REGION
Highland

PRODUCT
Blair Athol 12 year old single malt 43% vol

NOTES
A fresh medium sweet nose with a full, slightly spicy taste.

BLAIRFINDY TOWER
ABERDEENSHIRE

Positioned on high ground above the River Livet 7 miles S of Ballindalloch is a ruined L plan structure. Built by the Gordons to defend the passes from Banffshire to Aberdeenshire and as a hunting seat for the Earls of Huntly close to the ruined castle of Drumill, a former Gordon seat. In 1594, nearby Glenlivet was the scene of a battle in which the Earl of Huntly defeated the Duke of Argyll's forces.

BLAIRGOWRIE
PERTH & KINROSS

Town situated 18 miles NW of Dundee. Name derived from the Gaelic 'blar' meaning 'plain of cleared land' while Gowrie was the old district name, is thought to come from Gabran, an Irish warrior. Historically this is one of the conjectured sites of the battle of Mons Graupius, 84 AD, when the Romans defeated the Caledonians. The nearby Hurcheon or Urchin Hill was where the Earls of Gowrie held their courts in more remote times before dispatching the accused to Gallowbank. During Charles I's visit to Scotland in 1634 it was made a Burgh of Barony but remained an obscure village until its prosperity from the flax and jute mills funded the building of the present town on the slope which still bears the name Wellmeadow, owing to the many springs at its base that provided the domestic water supply. Today Blairgowrie is a typical rural burgh and popular stopping place for tourists and hill walkers attracted to the area's many historical sites. See Newton Castle

BLAIRLOGIE TOWER
STIRLING

Situated 3 miles NE of Stirling. By 1513 the lands were granted by James IV to James Spittal a Stirling merchant, but it was an Alexander Spittal who in 1543 built the tower which had an east wing added by Adam Spittal in 1582. Other than its function as a rest home before being bought by Lieutenant Colonel Hare in 1891 (who made further extensions and alterations), the place has had an uneventful history.

BLANTYRE
SOUTH LANARKSHIRE

Village situated 9 miles SE of Glasgow. Name derived from the Brythonic 'blaentir' meaning 'projecting land' or 'foreland'. Belonging to the Dunbars of Enteckin from a very early period, the lands and its 13th century Augustinian Priory were granted by James VI at the Reformation to Walter Stewart, who became Commendator of the Priory by 1580 and Lord Blantyre in 1606. This was once the site of a mineral spring which was frequented by Glasgow families suffering from tuberculosis. Started by the philanthropist David Dale and by Henry Monteith, 1785, the areas cotton manufacture, which employed 1,000 people working 69 hours a week by 1813, included David Livingstone 1813-73 (explorer) among its more notable employees. As a son of Blantyre, he educated himself while working at the local factory and his personal effects are now in the local museum. The cotton trade was gradually replaced by the coal mining industry which in 1877 and 1878 suffered two tragic explosions, in which 220 and 26 people died respectively. This in turn suffered a marked decline when most of the mining community was transferred to Fife.

BLERVIE CASTLE
MORAY

It stands on a hill 4 miles SE of Forres near Burgie Castle. The site of an early royal fortress which the Earl of Buchan fortified and used to repel King Haakon's invasion forces in the 13th century. The present Z plan structure, built by the Dunbars in the late 16th century, was purchased by Alexander Mackintosh between 1713 and 1724 and was later sold to the Earls of Fife. Afterwards its stone was used to build Blervie House.

BOGHALL CASTLE
SOUTH LANARKSHIRE

To the S of Biggar are the fragmentary remains of the powerful family seat, of the Flemings who held prominent positions in 15th and 16th century Scotland, such as Lord High Chamberlain. Originally a 16th century courtyard keep with large enceinte walls protected by round towers, in 1670 a mansion house was added. After falling into ruin it became a favourite haunt of stone pillagers.

BO'NESS
FALKIRK

A seaport situated 5 miles NE of Grangemouth. Formerly called 'Borrowstounness' and before that 'Burwardstoun' which may derive from the Old English 'burgess tun' therefore 'burgh town'. Its coastal position and its proximity to the Antonine Wall made it important during the Roman occupation, but much of its later history is tied up with trade. Described by Defoe in the 18th century as having 'one straggling street extended along the shore' , when constituted a Head Port in 1707 it did a brisk trade in salt, iron, fish and whisky with France and Holland. Notwithstanding its Burgh of Barony status in 1748, it suffered a comparative decline owing to the opening of the Forth and Clyde Canal in 1770 and the development of Grangemouth in 1810. The deepening of the harbour in 1881, which had cleared over 2,200 vessels in 1880, offered only temporary respite until its port and harbour facilities were revived in the 20th century. It was then used as a base for destroyers during World War I and for landing craft during World War II. Since the decline in its importance after 1945 Boness today appears more like a dormitory town, albeit somewhat residential.

BONNYMUIR, BATTLE OF, 1820
FALKIRK

About 2 miles W of Falkirk was the scene of a skirmish during what became known as the Radical Rebellion. Encouraged by the revolutions in France, a group of thirty weavers armed with pikes and seeking political reform was attacked and subdued by a detachment of Hussars and Yeomanry from Glasgow. The defeat terminated a period of political excitement in the west of Scotland and helped discourage unrest throughout the industrial belt in future decades.

BONSHAW TOWER
DUMFRIES & GALLOWAY

Picturesquely situated above the River Kirtle SE of old Kirtle Bridge Station is a courtyard tower built by the Irvings in the 16th century. Despite being burnt by Wharton, Warden of the West Marches in 1544, it was considered one of the strongest houses in the Borders in 1585 when it repelled two attacks by Lord Maxwell, resulting in his capture and confinement here in 1586.

BORTHWICK CASTLE
MIDLOTHIAN

On the former site of the Old Moat of Lochorwart (an old name for Borthwick) 2 miles NE of Gorebridge stands the castle of Lord William Borthwick, who erected it after being granted a licence by James I. Surrounded by curtain walls with outer ditch this is the noblest of Scotland's pele towers and of astonishing strength, with walls rising six storeys high and up to fourteen feet thick near the bottom. The castle accommodated Queen Mary and Bothwell after their marriage in 1567 and was briefly encircled by the rebel Lords Morton, Mar, Hume and Lindsay, provoking Mary's flight to Dunbar Castle two days later. In 1650 it witnessed the brief resistance of the 10th Lord Bothwell to the forces of Cromwell before his honourable surrender.

BOTHWELL CASTLE
SOUTH LANARKSHIRE

Positioned on the summit of a sloping green bank by the River Clyde 6 miles NW of Hamilton. Developing from a 13th century tower and fortalice built by the Morays or De Moravia family who acquired the land through marriage in 1242. It figured in the Wars of Independence when it was besieged and taken by Edward Ist after a month-long siege and was then garrisoned by the Earl of Pembroke, who as Governor of Scotland from 1309 provided sanctuary for English nobles after Bannockburn (1314), when it was destroyed by Bruce. It was repaired and occupied by Edward III for 25 days in 1336 but was stormed by the Scots under Sir Andrew Murray, who dismantled it in 1337. After passing to the Black Douglases in 1361 under Earl Archibald the Grim, who built its chapel and courtyard buildings, Bothwell was largely restored by 1400 making its most distinctive feature the 13th century donjon tower with walls 90ft high and 15ft thick. After the Douglas's forfeiture (1455), it was held successively by John Ramsay and Patrick Earl of Bothwell, (1488) before being acquired by the Red Douglases in 1492. It was with that period as a backdrop that the castle figured in Sir Walter Scott's poem 'Marmion', when the Lord Marmion realised he had been betrayed by the Earl of Douglas:

Lord Angus, thou hast lied !

On the Earl's cheek the flush of rage
O'ercame the ashen hue of age :
Fierce he broke forth, and darest thou then
To beard the lion in his den
The Douglas in his hall ?
And hopest then hence unscathed to go
No by St Bride of Bothwell, no !
Up drawbidge, grooms what warder, ho !
Let the portcullis fall

Visited by James IV in 1503 and 1504, it was occupied by Dame Margaret Maxwell, Countess of Angus, in 1594 when after holding mass she was forced to surrender it to the Crown and by 1669 it was the property of the Earl of Forfar, who used its stone for his mansion. By the 19th century it was held by the Earls of Home.

BOTHWELL CHURCH
SOUTH LANARKSHIRE

Standing in the village of Bothwell is a fine example of Gothic architecture that was built on the site of an earlier church from the 6th century. Founded by Archibald Douglas (The Grim) Lord of Galloway in 1398, it became one of the most important Collegiate churches in Lanarkshire. Dedicated to St Bride by its founder, whose family seat Bothwell Castle was in the vicinity. It was founded with a provost and eight prebendaries and it was at its altar that David Duke of Rothesay married the founder's daughter Marjory in 1400. St Brides functioned as a Parish Church until 1828, and by 1833 it was incorporated into the present Gothic structure. With its 1150 sittings, its large square tower rises 120ft high, to the east of which is the Medieval (2nd Pointed style) choir of the old church. Restored in 1933 by David Hamilton, the building's more distinguishing features are the monuments to the Douglases, Earls of Forfar, along with its stained glass windows.

BOTHWELL BRIDGE, BATTLE OF, 1679
SOUTH LANARKSHIRE

North of Hamilton. In a bid to crush the Covenanters the Duke of Monmouth (son of Charles II) led a force in the West Country where he engaged the rebel army of around 4,000 men. While attempting to hold the defensive position on Bothwell Bridge over the Clyde, the rebels were forced to retreat after a fierce bombardment. But it was their shortage of ammunition and their blind faith in divine providence that brought about a full scale retreat, the capture of 1200 men and the gradual collapse of the rebellion.

BOWMORE DISTILLERY
ARGYLL & BUTE

Situated in the village by the shore of Loch Indall is the Island of Islay's oldest official distillery, started in 1779 by the Simpson family, whose farm provided a ready supply of barley. Standing near the harbour by the village, with its own jetty and its whitewashed buildings and their pyramid-shape roofs, Bowmore blends with the nearby houses, combining to form the perfect setting for Bowmore's distinctive label with its three seagulls. Its water is taken from the Laggan River after percolating through the surrounding rocks for centuries, gathering the flavours of rich Islay peat that survive the maturation process in Spanish Sherry or American oak casks, in the moist cellars below sea level. Later sold to James Mutter, it changed hands throughout the 20th century and was used as a base for coastal command during World War II. The buildings of today owe much to the modernisation of the 1960s by the then owners Stanley P Morrison Ltd.

OWNERS
Morrison & Bowmore Distillers Ltd ?

REGION
Islay

PRODUCT
Bowmore 10 (40%) 12 and 25 year old single malt 43% vol

NOTES
A peaty nose that is consistent with the balance of sweetness and peaty smoky flavour.

BOYNE CASTLE
ABERDEENSHIRE

A large picturesque ruin situated 2 miles E of Portsoy. The Thanedom of Boyne was granted by David II to Sir John Edmonstone in 1368 but passed through marriage to Sir John Ogilvie in 1486. The land was acquired by Sir George Ogilvie of Dunglass in 1575, who built this 16th century parallelogram courtyard castle shortly after. In 1731 it was purchased by the Earl of Findlater.

BRACKIE HOUSE
ANGUS

In a field about 4 miles W of Inverkeilor Railway Station stands a 16th-century Manor House. Conforming to the L plan, Brackie stands three floors high and includes the familiar crow stepped gables with pepperbox turrets with shot holes. Above the main entrance is a shield surmounted with the letters T.F and C.K with the date 1581 and the arms of the Fraser family impaled with those of the Kinnaird family, along with the motto "soli deo confido". Thomas Fraser was the son of Alexander, 5th Lord Lovat. After the Restoration of Charles II the lands were granted to the Earl of Southesk, 1663, as part of the Barony of Carnegie but were later held by a number of owners after the family's forfeiture in 1716, before being reacquired by the family in 1764.

BRAEMAR CASTLE
ABERDEENSHIRE

Located just N of the town. The original castle, once the 11th century hunting seat of King Malcolm Canmore, and later the feudal stronghold of the Erskine Earls of Mar, was replaced around 1620 by the new L plan castle built by the 7th Earl of Mar, which was burnt by the Jacobites in 1689. In the surrounding countryside the 11th Earl of Mar (Bobbing John) raised the Jacobite standard in 1715, which culminated in his forfeiture and the estate later being sold to Farquharson of Invercauld in 1730. Leased to the Government for 90 years to house a garrison in 1748, it was later repossessed by the family and has since been restored.

BRALL TOWER
HIGHLAND

Situated 6 miles S of Thurso. It is said that the area was once occupied by a palace belonging to the Bishops of Caithness. The present structure is a 14th century keep built by the Sinclairs, who later started a house nearby which much later became a hotel.

BRANXHOLM CASTLE
SCOTTISH BORDERS

Positioned 2 miles above Hawick town. In 1420 the lands were acquired by the Scotts, who built the first fort, which became the centre of the barony created in 1463 for Sir Walter Scott of Buccleuch, whose son David enlarged the structure in 1472. Burnt by the Earl of Northumberland in 1532 and dismantled by the Scotts before a raid by the Earl of Sussex in 1570, it was fully restored by Sir Walter Scott by 1576 into the Z plan courtyard structure of today. As a long-standing part of the Borders defensive network, Branxholm was immortalised in Sir Walter Scott's 'Lay of the Last Minstrel' in 1805:

To see St George's red cross streaming,
They watch against southern force an guile,
Lest Scroop, or Howard, or Percy's power,
Threaten Branxholm's lordly towers.
From Workworth, or Naworth, or Merry
Carlisle.

The residence of the Dukes of Buccleuch in the 18th century, it was again altered in the 19th century when in 1803 Dorothy Wordsworth described it as 'a large strong house old but not ancient'.

BRECHIN
ANGUS

Town situated 9 miles W of Montrose. The name is either derived from a mans name Brechan / Brychan or from the Brythonic 'Brychan' meaning 'the brae' as the town seems to have been built on a slope. One of the oldest towns and ecclesiastical centres in Scotland, according to Hector Boece it was a capital for the Picts. Between 791 and 795 Kenneth II helped found a church here which by 1150 had had like some other foundations become a Cathedral with a Culdee College, and in 1264 a hospital with Maison Dieu was founded by William Brechin. Owing to the constant threat from Scandinavian sea rovers Brechin quickly became a fortified town with its castle, now a 17th / 18th century structure with 16th century foundations, witnessing a siege by Edward I in 1303 and the battle of Brechin in 1452. Receiving a Royal Burgh Charter from Charles I in 1641, it was plundered by Montrose in 1645 and in 1715 James VII was proclaimed King here. The Cathedral was small by comparison with others around Scotland with the distinctive 10th century round tower adjoining it. Damaged at the Reformation, the building now functions as the Parish Church. The Guildry Incorporation of Merchants and Millmen founded in 1629 and incorporated in 1666 has no official status today but once played a pivotal role in Brechin's coarse linen trade from which the East Mill Co derived much benefit up to and during the First World War. Closing down in 1920 it later became adapted for the Engineering Division of the Coventry Gauge & Tool Co in 1939. See Battle

BRECHIN, BATTLE OF, 1452
ANGUS

Fought near the town between the forces of the King led by the Earl of Huntly, who as Lieutenant General of the North defeated the rebel army headed by the Earl of Crawford for the Douglas faction. The victory curbed the Douglas's influence in the north but caused the death of the Earl's brothers and of his many supporters, while hastening the decline of the Douglases.

BRIDGE OF ALLAN
STIRLING

Village situated 5 miles NW of Stirling which takes its name from its 19th century bridge. Once consisting of two villages, Pathfoot and Inverallan, it became a fashionable Victorian spa town created out of Airthrey springs with water noted for its saline content. Its appeal as a rural retreat was greatly enhanced when Burns romanticised the area in his 'By Allan Stream' in 1793:

By Allan Stream I chanced to rove,
While Phoebus sank beyond Benledi;
The winds were whispering through the
grove, The yellow corn was waving ready

Like many of Scotland's rural communities Bridge of Allan was opened up by the railways in the 19th century, and developed like a residential suburb of Stirling, with a growing emphasis on tourism which on an increasingly larger scale continues to the present day. Its

Gothic church was built in 1859 and the village was constituted a Police Burgh in 1870. The Stirling University complex of the 1960s engulfed the nearby Airthrey Castle Estate and further enhanced the village's suburban qualities.

BRIG O DEE, BATTLE OF, 1639
ABERDEENSHIRE

Just outside Aberdeen. The capture of Aberdeen by Viscount Aboyne, a member of the dissenting Gordon family, who the Marquis of Montrose had defeated at the Trott of Turriff, led to Montrose and his Covenanters launching an attack on the enemy. The stratagem employed by Montrose to draw the defenders away from their position brought about the bridge's capture and the retaking of Aberdeen. The victory itself engendered a more pragmatic approach by Charles I to the Covenanters.

BRODICK CASTLE
NORTH AYRSHIRE

Positioned overlooking Arran Bay and Brodick village on the Isle of Arran. For a long time the site was a strategic prize that was occupied by a Norse fort and then an age-old fortalice of the Lords of the Isles. The later structure was fought over by Robert the Bruce and John Balliol after the battle of Methven (1306), when the Douglases tried to take it, but was eventually destroyed by the Earl of Ross in 1455 for James II. Essentially an oblong keep built around 1500, Brodick was damaged by the Earl of Lennox in 1544 for Henry VIII but was rebuilt and fortified by the Marquis of Hamilton in 1638-9 for Charles I. Occupied in 1652 by Cromwell's forces, who added a battery before being massacred by the islanders', it eventually became a Hamilton seat. It was further developed in the 19th century and is now owned by the National Trust.

BROUGHTY CASTLE
DUNDEE CITY

Standing on the Firth of Tay 4 miles E of Dundee is a fortalice of 1514 built by Andrew, 3rd Lord Grey, who was granted a charter by James IV in 1490. Comprising a five storey keep with battlemented top and round towers, it was occupied by the English after the battle of Pinkie in 1547, but after two failed sieges by the Earls Arran and Argyll it was stormed and taken by a Franco-Scottish force in 1550. Held by the forces of the Lords of the Congregation in 1556, it became ruinous after the Union of the Crowns in 1603 and was eventually purchased by the government for £1500 and used as an artillery battery.

BRUICHLADDICH DISTILLERY
ARGYLL & BUTE

Scotland's most westerly distillery is located on the Isle of Islay and takes its name from a Gaelic derivation meaning 'brae of the shore'. The island is thought by many to be the cradle of the Scotch Whisky industry; it was started by the island's Christian monks but was latterly mentioned in the 'Oban Times' of 1881, when the brothers Robert, William and John Harvey declared their intention to build on the site later described by Alfred Bernard as ' the most finest and healthy spot on Islay'. Its water source comes from the hill of Gartacharra meaning ' the field of the stone' in Gaelic. As members of the Harveys of Yoker and Dundas Hill, a family whose experience in distilling stretched back into the 1780s, the brothers took its output to 94,000 gallons and in 1886 rebuilt it and formed the Bruichladdich Distillery Co Ltd. Much of the building's exterior survives from this period. After ceasing production in 1929, increased demand in the USA post-prohibition brought American investors to Scotland, and in 1937 a group led by Joseph

Hobbs and backed by National Distillers of America acquired Bruichladdich, quickly transferring it to Associated Scottish Distillers Ltd. In 1952 it was bought by the whisky brokers Ross & Coulter, but it was its sale to A.B Grant in 1960 that coincided with the freeing of Scottish Whisky exports from post war rationing, bringing expansion and nearly doubling capacity by 1962. Later owned by Invergordon Distillers from 1969, two stills were added much later, and with an enlarged tun room took its potential capacity up to 800,000 proof gallons by 1976, five years before its centenary in 1981.

OWNERS
Bruichladdich Distillery Co Ltd ?

REGION
Islay

PRODUCT
Bruichladdich 10 and 15 year old single malt 40% and 43% vol

NOTES
A seaweedy aroma with a peaty sweet taste and a satisfying finish
A malty seaweed nose with a palate that is slightly salty and slightly sweet and malty to produce a varied finish.

BRUNTSFIELD LINKS GOLF CLUB
CITY OF EDINBURGH

When its was founded in 1761 as 'The Bruntsfield Links Golf Society', the membership mainly consisted of old Edinburgh merchants whose practice was to shut up shop, particularly in the afternoon, to play golf. It was at this time that the passionate golfer Alexander Mckellar 'The Cock' O the Green' who haunted the Links all day and most of the night, gained immortality through the caricaturist John Kay (1724-1826) whose portraits included over 900 prominent figures of Edinburgh society. On removing to Musselburgh in 1870 (then regarded by some as the home of golf before the rise of St Andrews), owing to an increasingly hostile Town Council and general congestion, the members, then numbering 120, used a former Episcopal church as a clubhouse and had to share with three other clubs the use of the Links, where it wasn't uncommon to see the local fishwives play on the course. In 1873, at the Spring meeting the Ladies' Cup was presented to the club. The clubhouse served its function for generations until 1898, when due to congestion the members, encouraged by the efforts of The Burgess Club, secured a new green of 97 acres on the Barnton Estate to the east of the Burgess Golfing Society land. Also acquiring an acre for the clubhouse, the members then changed its name to the Bruntsfield Links Golfing Society Limited which led to an 18 hole course being laid out under the watchful eye of Willie Park. During World War One, the club forged ties with the Royal Navy officers serving at Rosyth, a reminder of which is the Grand Fleet Cup presented in 1919, five years before the Prince of Wales became an Honorary Member. In the run up to World War II, 1939-45 fixtures were held for the officers of the Royal Navy's Grand Fleet, Atlantic Fleet and the Home Fleet but during the war the members were to spend more time engaged in the typical worthy charitable initiatives. In later years the club witnessed a steady increase in activity which culminated in the 200th anniversary celebration in 1961. In the late 1990s plans were initiated for a permanent clubhouse, the society was turned into a limited company; and the membership stood at 450. The club has since operated a spirit of openness and encouraged a junior membership since 1981 while infrastructuring the amenities to accommodate a wider clientele.

BUNNAHABHAIN DISTILLERY
ARGYLL & BUTE

In the most northerly point of the windswept Island of Islay is the legacy of the Greenlees Brothers who built Bunnahabhain with houses for its workforce, and a nearby pier on desolate moorland between 1881-83. Attracted by its position on the shore of the Sound of Islay, (its name in Gaelic means ' mouth of the river') and its fresh peaty water from Loch Staoinsha, the brothers' considerable investment included the land buildings and the latest labour-saving devices, giving it an annual capacity for 200,000 gallons. The demand for blended whisky after sherry and brandy had been tainted with the phylloxera disease which had ravished Europe's vineyards, coincided with the board's plan in 1883 to produce whisky principally for blending, leading to an enlarged workforce and a distillery school for the community's children. As the Islay Distillery Co Ltd in 1887 it amalgamated with William Grant & Co to become Highland Distilleries Co five years before going into liquidation, when the assets were transferred to the new company. Bunnahabhain was used almost entirely for blending up until the late 1970s when the 12 year old malt was launched, its label showing a Scottish sailor at the helm of his ship westering home.
OWNERS
Burn Stewart Distillers plc ?
REGION
Islay
PRODUCT
Bunnahabhain 12 year old single malt 40% vol
NOTES
A light and fresh aroma with a smooth peaty taste and a fruity refreshing finish.

BURLEIGH CASTLE
PERTH & KINROSS

Located to the E of Milnathort on the

Burleigh burn near Loch Leven. A Balfour seat from 1446 when its oblong tower was built. An additional west wall with round tower and gateway were built in 1582 probably by James Balfour of Mountquhanie, who married Margaret Balfour the Burleigh heiress. In 1606 Balfour was elevated to Lord Burleigh, while his descendent Robert, the 4th Lord who murdered a school master at Inverkeithing in 1707, periodically concealed himself from justice in an ash tree on the estate before taking part in the 1715 Rebellion. He subsequently suffered attainder, which was lifted in 1869 for Alexander Hugh Bruce heir to the estate.

BURNTISLAND
FIFE

Coastal town situated 10 miles NW of North Queensferry. So named because fishermens' huts were once burnt on the nearby island. While heading north the Romans probably landed here before camping on nearby Dunearn Hill. The land was held by Dunfermline Abbey for which it served as a supply port for coal, while above the harbour, and also owned by the Abbey, is Rossend Castle started by Durie of Durie in 1382 and substantially added to by the family in the 16th and 17th centuries. In 1563 it was occupied by Mary Queen of Scots, whose room, now known as Mary's room, ranks second only to the castles most interesting architectural feature, the large wing, with drawing room and bedroom with walls so thick that they included chambers within. The Queen later granted it to Sir Robert Melville who tried to negotiate her release during her captivity in England. Used by the Fife Covenanters in the 17th century when it was also taken by Cromwell, it was later owned by Sir James Wemyss of Caskieberry who became Lord Burntisland in 1672. A Royal Burgh in 1541, its good natural harbour which was in effect the town's reason for being, exercised a trade in fish, with the Baltic and the Low Countries long before it became the HQ for the herring fishing by 1793. In the 19th and 20th centuries, when its trade in coal thrived, it served as a busy railway town and ferry port, something that was undermined by the opening of the Forth Bridge in 1964. The post-Reformation church of St Columba was preceded by an earlier church (now gone) at nearby Kirkton. See Golf Club

BURNTISLAND GOLF CLUB
FIFE

Despite being one of Scotland's older golf clubs which was inaugurated in 1797, from an early date the select group of members played on the town's links before they reinstituted the club in 1828. With the tailor providing the feathers and the shoemaker the leather, the members had a ready supply of traditional feather balls but were forced to share the common land with fishermen drying their nets, housewives hanging out the washing, animals grazing and the local cricket club. The members were further restricted by the railways post-1800, and with the increase in numbers between 1870-90, the committee were compelled to find land in a new area known as the 'High Bents', providing them with six holes, that was used for up to ten years. Meanwhile the ladies were confined to the links. By 1897 the land adjacent to the 'High Bents' became part of the course, which was extended to 18 holes and laid out to suggestions by Willie Park when the Burntisland Golf Company was formed. In the same year the company planned to form The Burntisland Golf House Club and The Burntisland Golf Club were given playing rights over the course on payment of a per capita fee. This was one of the first clubs to allow ladies to play and to enjoy golf on Sundays. The House Club later built its own clubhouse by the Ist tee of the new course, and by 1924 nearly all members of the Burntisland Golf Club were part of the House Club when the per capita fee was abolished. Though the club has no written rules or constitution, plans are afoot to remedy this. Among the club's more distinguished members, Mr George Ferrier is of some renown. A professional in 1920, he later became well known in America's golfing administration, became president of the USPGA Seniors and served on the Ryder Cup Committee. In 1969 he presented the club with the Ferrier Trophy.

BUTTS, BATTLE OF, 1544
CITY OF GLASGOW

Taking place during the minority of Mary I when after going over to the English cause the Earl of Arran marched on Glasgow's Bishop's Palace causing death and destruction. To counter the threat, the Earl of Glencairn, with around 800 men attacked Arran's forces at the Butts, where the untimely arrival of reinforcements brought about Glencairn's defeat followed by reprisals exacted on the burghers and in Arran holding the Regency until 1554.

C

CAELRAVEROCK CASTLE
DUMFRIES & GALLOWAY

Situated at the mouth of the River Nith 7 miles SE of Dumfries. Defended by a moat, this triangular structure, built around 1310 and preceded by the original castle on or close to the site of an ancient Roman Fort, was added to up to the 17th century and comprises a gatehouse flanked by hugh drum towers, linked to corner towers by walls with adjoining internal buildings. Occupied by William Wallace in 1296 and taken by Edward I in 1300 who met the Archbishop of Canterbury here. It served as a base for a Eustace Maxwell from 1312 but was demolished and rebuilt after a second siege. By Maxwell's son it was held for the English in 1347 and was firmly established as a Maxwell seat by the time Robert Lord Maxwell Earl of Nithsdale developed it in a Renaissance style in 1620. During the time of Solway Moss, 1542, James V stayed here. Besieged and taken by the Earl of Sussex (1570) when it was partly destroyed. Following its capture after a 13-week siege by the Covenanters, led by Lieutenant Colonel Home, it lost its strategic importance and passed to the Maxwells of Terregles after 1716.

CAIRNBULG CASTLE
ABERDEENSHIRE

This oblong Keep with enclosing wall and round tower was built 2 miles S of Fraserburgh in 1475 by the Fraser family, who had acquired the land through marriage from the Earl of Ross in 1375. Formerly called Philorth Barony until the lands and castle were sold by Alexander Fraser to Fraser of Durris in 1619, probably to assist the former in funding the continued development of Fraserburgh harbour and town. It was restored in the

CAIRNBURGHMORE CASTLE
ARGYLL & BUTE

Situated on the Treshnish Isles, 5 miles NW of Staffa, west of Mull. The site of a Norwegian fort in 1249, followed by a fortalice of the Macleans. At the Reformation it became a receptacle of books and records from Iona, which were partly damaged after a siege by Cromwell's forces in 1652. During the 1715 Rebellion it was the scene of repeated conflicts and is now ruinous.

CAKEMUIR TOWER
MIDLOTHIAN

Standing in a valley 14 miles SE of Edinburgh. A tower house with battlements and a circular stair with square capehouse, it was built by Advocate Adam Wauchope by 1565. Its long- standing tradition as a place of refreshment for pilgrims and travellers between Edinburgh and Melrose Abbey was aptly captured in an old ballad:

See the way is long and drear.
Empty flasks and sorry cheer.
At Cakemuir there is bread and beer.
In the name of every saint, let not weary pilgrims faint

The scene of a meeting between Queen Mary and Bothwell after her escape from Borthwick Castle 13th June 1567, before they rode through the night to Dunbar Castle. In 1761 its tower was added to by Henry Wauchope whose family occupied it until 1794.

CALDER. SEE MID CALDER

CALLANDER
STIRLING

Town situated on the River Teith 8 miles

NW of Doune. While the origins of its name are uncertain there is some evidence to suggest it may derive from the Gaelic 'calladh' meaning 'hard' and 'dobhar' meaning 'water'. For a long time associated with the military owing to the area's abundance of timber and stone and its proximity to a river and hills which often marked the boundary between the Highlands and the Lowlands. The west of the town was thought by Skene (historian) to be the site of a Roman Fort possibly built by Agricola during his campaigns of 80-85 AD. Chiefly consisting of a long street intersected by two side streets, the present town, which developed from forfeited Jacobite estates and a soldier's station, in 1763 grew on the back of its cotton manufacture and the allure created by Sir Walter Scott's 'Lady of the Lake' (1810) extolling the area's scenic beauty. With the pacification of the Highlands, the town's strategic importance to the army was supplanted by its value as a station for the Callander & Oban Railway, which when completed in 1880, established Callander as a stopping place for visitors en route to the Central Highlands, a legacy which still endures to this day.

CAMBUSKENNETH ABBEY
STIRLING

Four miles east of the Royal Burgh of Stirling near the River Forth are the ruins of an Augustinian Abbey founded in 1147 by David I. Built on fertile land in an Early English style its closeness to Stirling gave it strong political associations and many royal favours throughout the building's development which took place between the 13th and 19th centuries. In keeping with tradition its plan included a cruciform church by the north wall of the cloister which was bordered by domestic buildings, including its sacristy, chapter house and refectory to the east and south

side respectively and an orchard opposite to the west. Its Abbot swore fealty to Edward I who was here in 1303 and 1305, but on its High Altar in 1308 the Scottish Barons swore to defend the claim of Robert the Bruce, and his son David's right to hold the Crown after him was upheld by a Parliament held here in 1326 before the Kings death. It was to Cambuskenneth that Bruce and his party journeyed after their victory at Bannockburn in Sir Walter Scott's poem 'The Lord of the Isles':

Our will be to the Abbot known,
Ere these strange news are wider blown
To Cambuskenneth straight ye pass,
And deck the church for solemn mass,
To pay for high deliverence given,
A nation's thanks to gracious heaven.

Following his flight from Sauchieburn, the murdered James III was interred here along with his Queen, Margaret of Denmark. Amongst its abbots were Abbot Henry who was High Treasurer of Scotland, 1493, while the accomplished scholar Abbot Patrick Panther, 1470-1519, was Secretary to James IV and Ambassador to France. Although the bell tower collapsed on the choir of the church in 1378 most of the destruction took place during the upheavals of the 16th century when James VI conferred the property on the Earl of Mar, with whose family it remained until 1709 when it was bought by Stirling Town Council. In 1865 the corpses of King James and Queen Margaret were uncovered but were re-interred and an altar was built over them by order of Queen Victoria. Today's remains include a substantial four storey-tower and some foundation stones.

CAMERONBRIDGE DISTILLERY
FIFE

The property of the Haig family from its

beginnings in 1824, it was built on the site of an earlier distillery owing, to the situation of the River Leven and services of the town. Starting as a producer of Malt whisky, with the advent of the new patent continuous stills in the 1830s, the Haigs switched to grain whisky and now use wheat and other cereals with malted barley to produce a spirit that is popular for blending with older malts. The family were active in promoting co-operation, and in the formation of the Distillers Co Ltd in 1877. Known to dwarf malt distilleries in size; with its sister grain distillery in Glasgow in 1995 it was producing one third of all Scottish grain whisky and was in famous blends like Johnnie Walker, Bells, Dewars and White Horse. With investment from the new owners United Distillers its output then trebled. Its water source, the Leven River, with its salmon ladder, was raised to Salmon grade status, restocked with brown trout and the environs made a conservation area.

OWNERS
Diageo plc ?

REGION
Lowland

PRODUCT
Cameronbridge 12 year old single grain whisky 40% vol

NOTES
Soft and smooth with a warm bouquet and hue.

CAMPBELLTOWN
ARGYLL & BUTE

Town situated 35 miles SW of Tarbert. The area was once the ancient seat of the Dalriadan Kingdom then called Dalruadhain until St Kieran landed here in the 6th century and named it Kilkerran, and built churches throughout Kintyre. This also served as the capital of the Lords of the Isles until the land was granted to the Campbells of Argyll by James IV (1488-1513) after his expedition to subdue the rebellious lords and in 1667 was created a Burgh of Barony for the Earl of Argyll, elevated to a Royal Burgh in 1700. The town played a significant part in east coast trade when its economy was supported by its herring fishing, distilling and by its shipbuilding, all of which brought overcrowding and an enlargement of the burgh that now benefits from travellers visiting the Mull of Kintyre. The oldest object of interest is the 14th century 'Campbelltown Cross' near the harbour whilst on the nearby Island of Davarr is the saint's cave, which has a painting of the Crucifixion by an inspired Archibald Mackinnon, 1817.

CANONGATE KIRK
CITY OF EDINBURGH

The church is situated in the Royal Mile near the Palace of Holyrood. The original building sprang from the needs of the Canongate inhabitants who had previously used the Abbey Church of Holyrood. Built in 1688 to plans by James Smith as a quasi-cruciform edifice after James VII had reintroduced the Catholic Mass at the Abbey Church. It played an integral part in the life of the burgh and witnessed most of the incidents of note, along with successive generations of citizens, with its proximity to the Tolbooth Prison. The present structure is in the shape of a Latin Cross but the more poignant reminders of the country's history are to be found in its graveyard where its residents include Adam Smith 1723-1790, David Allan 1744-1796, Robert Fergusson 1750-1774 and Dugald Stewart 1753-1828.

CAOL ILA DISTILLERY
ARGYLL & BUTE

Overlooking the Paps of Jura from the shores of the Sound of Islay, Caoila is one of the eleven island malts and began in 1846 as a venture of Hector Henderson, a distiller from Dumbarton. With a plentiful supply of stone and water from Loch nam Ban, a small distillery village grew by the shore and became a model working community in a healthy environment. Sadly Henderson's venture endured longer than his position: and in 1854 Norman Buchanan took over the running until 1863 when it was acquired by the whisky traders Bulloch Lade & Co, helping Caol ila to firmly establish itself in the market. This hastened further developments in 1879, including a pier from which it ferried its whisky by steamer to the railway lines. By 1880 as much as 147,000 gallons were being produced annually, particularly for blending. After enduring the usual austerity affecting other distilleries during the First World War, in 1920 Bulloch & Lade were replaced by new owners, a group of businessmen who formed the new Caol ila Distillery Co Ltd, bringing increased efficiency and lower production costs before eventually being bought by the Scottish Malt Distillers Ltd in 1927. To reach to its main port for distribution the whisky was transported by the Pibroch puffer which left the pier to travel around the Mull of Kintyre, bound for Glasgow, a route used down to this day. However, in the 1970s the Pibroch was taken out of service and the distillery rebuilt by the then new owners United Distillers.

OWNERS
Diageo plc ?

REGION
Islay

PRODUCT
Caol ila 15 year old single malt 43% vol

NOTES
A light peaty nose with a rich well rounded flavour.

CAPERDONICH DISTILLERY
MORAY

In the town of Rothes stands the legacy of Major James Grant, who in 1897 built the distillery which was known as Glen Grant no 2 owing to its predecessor which stands nearby. It derives its name and water source from the 'Caperdonich Spring' which is from the Gaelic 'Tobar Domnaich' meaning 'The Sunday Well '. Though a single malt in its own right, the two distilleries were linked by a pipe over the town's main street giving rise to the saying "Rothes streets flowed with whisky". Following the slump in the industry in the 1890s, the distillery closed in 1901 and remained in slumber throughout most of the political and economic uncertainties of the 20th century, while its neighbours experienced varying degrees of success. Production resumed, however, in 1965 when it was upgraded, modernised and named after the Caperdonich Well which supplies water to Glen Grant. Today the whisky is used for blending.

OWNERS
Chivas Brothers Ltd ?

REGION
Speyside

PRODUCT
Now only used for blending.

CARBERRYHILL, BATTLE OF, 1567
EAST LOTHIAN

Two miles SE of Musselburgh. In the hope of placating the rebel Lords' disquiet over Queen Mary's marriage to the Earl of Bothwell, both parties met after the Queen had intimated her compliance with the demands of the nobles. The stand off which ensued was mainly due to the reluctance of the Lords for conflict, the hope of Bothwell for reinforcements and the hesitancy of Mary's forces to support Bothwell. All of which ended in the

Queen surrendering to the rebels and her imprisonment in LochLeven Castle. The result of these events was to further erode the power base of the Queen, even after her escape when she sought refuge in England where she was again imprisoned and eventually executed.

CARBISDALE, BATTLE OF, 1650
HIGHLAND

The battle took place near the town during the Covenanting Wars. When the Marquis of Montrose sailed with 1200 men and munitions to Orkney, to lead the Royalists of Orkney against the Covenanters under General Strachan, the numbers of the latter of around 700 no doubt instilled confidence of victory. Despite this, through sheer force and surprise Montroses men were routed and two thirds of them killed or captured, including Montrose who was later executed at Edinburgh Cross, robbing Scotland and in particular Charles II of one of their finest soldiers.

CARDHU DISTILLERY
MORAY

It stands on the uplands above the River Spey about 8 miles SW of Craigellichie. Started in 1871 when John and Helen Cummings set up a still in an isolated farm near the Mannoch Hills, which provided an abundant source of peat and fresh soft spring water. Its name is from the Gaelic meaning 'black rock'. In an area teeming with illicit stills, the couple were at first leading figures in opposing compliance with the exciseman but eventually obtained a licence in 1824. The first major expansion began when their daughter-in-law, Elizabeth, rebuilt the distillery on its present site in the 1880s, and continued after 1893 when it was acquired by the whisky dynasty John Walker & Sons. Production increased steadily over the years despite the onslaught of recessions and wars in later decades, and in 1960 the distillery was rebuilt again.

OWNERS
Diageo plc ?

REGION
Speyside

PRODUCT
Cardhu 12 year old single malt 40% vol

NOTES
A round mellow nose, slightly sweet, with a delicate peaty taste.

CARDONESS TOWER
DUMFRIES & GALLOWAY

On a ridge overlooking the River Fleet 1 mile from Wigtown Bay, is a late 15th century oblong tower built by the M'cullochs, a notable Galloway family from whom it passed to the Gordons. With walls 12ft thick and standing 4 storeys high with attic, it was garrisoned by the English in the 16th century but was uninhabited by 1750 before it was acquired by Sir William Maxwell Bart.

CARDRONA TOWER
SCOTTISH BORDERS

Located 3 miles below Peebles, its name aptly means camp or castle on a ridge. A ruined L plan tower of the Governs, who occupied it between 1358 and 1685 when it figured in their feuds with the Stewarts of Traquair. It passed to the Williamsons who were distinguished burgesses of Peebles and whose descendants built the house on the right bank of the Tweed in 1840, near where Roman remains were found in the 1830s.

CARDROSS
ARGYLL & BUTE

Village situated 4 miles NW of Dumbarton. Name derived from the Gaelic 'cerdin ros' meaning 'rowan tree promontory'. On a wooded knoll at Castlehill on the Cardross to Dumbarton road once stood the castle where Robert the Bruce spent his last few years fishing, hawking and building ships before dying here in 1329. His heart was later taken by Sir James Douglas on a mission to the Holy Land but after his death at the hands of the Saracens in Spain it was retrieved and eventually buried in Melrose Abbey. A 17th century church was later built by the castle site. Although essentially a rural community, with Dumbarton the nearest Market Town, Cardross had strong links with Port Glasgow that were to provide a ready market for its sandstone and limestone in subsequent years. Despite its main street forming part of the high road from Edinburgh to Lanark, the area's coal mining, which lasted up until 1842, and its shale mines which peaked in 1904, failed to establish it as an industrial town. Apart from the Parish Church being bombed during World War II (1939-45) its location and size has spared it the agitation from events of national importance.

CARHAM, BATTLE OF, 1018
SCOTTISH BORDERS

It was fought just north of Coldstream and said to have been presaged by a comet. When the armies of Malcolm II of Scotland and Owen the Bald King of the Strathclyde Britons defeated Eric the Danish Earl of Northumberland, the Lothians became part of Scotland with the proviso that the customs and laws of the Anglo Saxons and Normans be preserved.

CARNWATH
SOUTH LANARKSHIRE

Village situated 10 miles SE of Carluke. Name derived from the Brythonic 'carn gwuydd' meaning 'cairn' or 'mound in wood', which was thought to be a place of worship for the ancient Druids. Originally belonging to the Sommervilles, who, from their seat at Cowthally Castle,

(of which very little remains), presided over the Burgh of Barony created for Lord Sommerville, 1451 until the 17th century when the lands passed to Sir George Lochart (Lord President of the Court of Session). With its Gothic windows and arched stone roof the ruined Church of St Mary, which once housed the Sommerville family vault, was built by Thomas, Ist Lord Sommerville, in 1424, close to the present church which was erected in 1867 with seating for 1000 people. Although not as old as the burgh, the Red Hose Race, which dates from the 16th century, is thought to be the earliest foot race in Britain and culminates in an award given by the laird on pain of forfeiture of his estate.

CARSLUITH TOWER
DUMFRIES & GALLOWAY

Overlooking Wigtown Bay 3´ miles SE of Creetown. Lands were held by the Brown family from the 14th century who started the 15th century oblong tower which became an L plan keep when a stair was added in 1568. A fervent Catholic, Gilbert Brown of Carsluith, became the last Abbott of Sweetheart Abbey (1565), before being exiled to France by James VI. The building is now a preserved ruin.

CASSILLIS, HOUSE OF
SOUTH AYRSHIRE

Occupying ground above the River Doon 4 miles from Maybole. The land became a Kennedy seat after Lady Marjory Montgomerie (heir) was rescued by Sir John Kennedy of Dunure from the threatening impositions of marriage by the Laird of Dalrymple in 1373, when the original tower was built. In 1509 David, 3rd Lord Kennedy, became the Earl of Cassillis, while Gilbert the 4th Earl, the so called 'King of Carrick', was notorious for his cruelty and torture of the Commendator of Crossraguel Abbey. A ballad by Johny

Faa, King of the Gypsies, describes how at the castle gate in 1643 he is said to have charmed the Lady and her maids away into obscurity. Its 17th century alterations included tower with stairway, making it an L plan structure, with a remodelled upper part which was followed by a large extension in 1830. In the 19th century the castle gave up evidence of its more macabre history when the clearing of a subterranean passage led to the removal of a cart load of human bones.

CASTLE CAMPBELL
CLACKMANNAN

It stands on a hill with an extensive view over the Forth valley 1 mile N of Dollar. The castle developed out of a late 15th-century oblong tower, built by Colin Campbell, Ist Earl of Argyll, who in 1493 changed its name from Gloume, which came from the nearby Gloume Hill where a wizard was reputed to have been burnt in the late 16th century. Forming a courtyard structure in the 16th century with enclosure and living quarters, it was here in 1556 that John Knox resided and dispensed the Lord's Supper with the 4th Earl of Argyll. Burnt by Montrose in 1645 following his victories at Auldearn, Alford and Kilsyth. To improve links with the tower in the early 17th century the eastern range was added. In 1805 the castle and Lordship was purchased by Crawford & Tait.

CASTLECARY
FALKIRK

Located 7 miles SW of Falkirk is a late 15th century tower house built by the Livingstones on the site of one of the forts of the Antonine Wall. Passing to the Baillie family in 1640, its eastern section was added in 1679 but was burnt along with the rest of the castle by Highlanders in 1715, later passing to the Dundas family who restored it. The excavation of its

grounds in 1902 gave up some Roman urns, coins and weapons.

CASTLE COEFFIN
ARGYLL & BUTE

The site was once occupied by a stronghold of a Danish Prince who gave it its name. It commands a position on the west side of Lismore Island in Loch Linnhe. Although this is a 15th century oblong keep with barmkin wall, it was built by Colin Campbell of Glenorchy on the site of a Macdougal stronghold after Colin, Ist Earl of Argyll, acquired the Lordship of Lorn in 1470. It remained a Campbell possession until the 18th century, when it fell into ruin.

CASTLE CRAIG
HIGHLAND

The castle holds a coastal position on the Black Isle 8 miles S of Cromarty. Built by the Urquharts (Barons of Ross) as a tower with defensive wall probably in the 16th century. Following the family's censure by the Catholic Church when they were deprived of the castle and their land, it became the principal residence of the Bishops of Ross but was later acquired by the Williamsons.

CASTLE DOUGLAS
DUMFRIES & GALLOWAY

Market Town situated 18 miles SW of Dumfries. Anciently called 'Causeway End' which may have come from the causeway that was built through the marsh by the community that existed here as early as the 14th century. It was renamed Carlinwark after the nearby Loch which provided the marl (fertiliser) from which the village prospered. The present name comes from the nearby castle of Threave, once held by the Douglases and a William Douglas of Gelston (merchant), for whom it was made a Burgh of Barony in 1791. It was rebuilt in 1792 with neatly laid out streets and a cotton factory that later failed. When a new charter was granted in 1829 handing the burgh's business affairs over to the Town Council, this was a busy coaching town, with mail and passengers being transported daily to and from Dumfries, Kirkcudbright and Portpatrick. Possessing many natural advantages, the fixing of the burgh boundaries in 1861 was followed by the building of the Town Hall in 1861, at a time when its post office was the busiest in SW Scotland and its trade thriving. From an open air market in 1819 to an enclosed one on Markethill by 1857, the reputation of Castle Douglas grew on the back of its Ayrshire and Galloway cattle as a commercial centre and main cattle market for SW Scotland.

CASTLE FRASER
ABERDEENSHIRE

Located in a meadow 5 miles SE of Monymusk. In 1454 the lands were acquired by Thomas Fraser who built the original tower called Muchal in Mar. Consisting of an oblong block with towers at two diagonally opposite angles, its lower north front with towers was built in 1576 by Andrew Ist Lord Fraser who changed its name and gave it a Z plan form. In 1617 the wings were added by a J. Bell. Consistent with the precarious climate of the times is the castle's remarkable contrivance for secret espionage with its spy holes and lugs (ears) within its walls.   These reflect the clandestine practices of the 2nd Lord Fraser, who was a zealous Covenanter, and the 4th Lord, a Jacobite whose stepson Charles Fraser (Old Inverallochie) commanded the clan at Culloden (1746), where he was murdered in the aftermath. Sold by the family in 1921, it is now owned by the National Trust.

CASTLE GRANT
HIGHLAND

Just N of Grantown on Spey is the ancestral seat of the Grants who started its central oblong tower in the 16th century, enveloping the old tower where extensive enlargements were made by Ludovic Grant, 1743-73, who also designed the plan of Grantown. It passed to the Earls of Seafield in 1811 and was held by Francis the 10th Earl in 1860 during an incognito visit by Queen Victoria and Prince Albert when it was described by the Queen as ' a plain looking house like a factory'.

CASTLE STUART
HIGHLAND

Positioned near the Moray Firth 6 miles NE of Inverness. Once a fine example of Baronial architecture, it was built by the Earl of Moray around 1625 with a main block fronted by two large towers creating a symmetry that is enriched by its battlements and pepper pot turrets. Figuring in the conflicts with the Mackintosh Clan, the previous landowners, much of the interior was used for the building of Darnaway Castle in 1812, when this functioned as a hunting lodge but has now returned to domestic use.

CATHKIN BRAES GOLF CLUB
CITY OF GLASGOW

Located in the town of Rutherglen. Since its founding by Adam Rodger in 1888, its members have enjoyed and endured the fresh air of the 700 ft high Braes around which the original course of nine holes was situated. One of the more majestic courses away from the Ayrshire coast, using hickory clubs (a variant of walnut) and gutsy balls (made from hard rubber, and replaced feathery balls) the players were left with an indelible impression of the course and what may have been a Roman encampment with its panoramic view of Ben Lomond, Ben Ledi and Ben Venne. After running its first major competition in 1889 for the Westwood Trophy (replaced by the Windyhill Cup), the club quickly established itself, and by 1897 plans were under way to enlarge the clubhouse and in 1904 extend the course to 18 holes. In 1907 its men, ladies and junior members totalled 400. Despite the difficulties the club had with the tenant farmers, the landowners, the Stuart Stevenson family helped resolve the issue by 1909 when a 15-year lease was concluded and the club settled into some years of stability helped by its most generous benefactor Mr William Stirling Stuart Stevenson. The club endured the usual shortages in members and materials during the 1914-18 War, when the club lost 19 men and much of the members' time was taken up with charitable initiatives. In 1919 its membership soared, prompting more upgrading work in future years, when the advent of the motor car and golf's rising profile was reaching an all-time high. So by 1934 when its course was improved, the committee resolved to build a modern clubhouse which was funded by £1,000 from the Laird. Meanwhile between 1925 and 1935, a William Tulloch of Cathkin Braes was emerging as a dominant figure in West of Scotland amateur golf, winning the Arrol Trophy and Tennant Cup between 1924 and 1926. In March 1938 the club was dealt a heavy blow when the Laird died, but before his death he had indicated his willingness to sell the land and this was carried out by his daughter. During the war of 1939-45, the Lady Members' Work Party played a charitable role while the course was defended against air-borne invasion and in 1941 Deputy Fuehrer, Rudolf Hess landed ten miles away at Eaglesham after his solo flight from Germany in a bid to get a negotiated peace through the Duke of Hamilton. The post-war period saw the introduction of synthetic balls, the continued success of Willie Tulloch in the West of Scotland Professional League and the strengthening of ties with the Laird's grandson Mr James Stuart Stevenson. To secure its future through efficiency, a more business-like policy was adopted but the casualties of this were the low subscription rates which had made the golf culture less class-based than in England. Nevertheless by 1968 it had 863 members and in 1973 the clubhouse was extended. The year 1977 saw the Queen's Jubilee Medal being awarded to Jimmy Heggarty, a long-standing professional of the club who had completed his half-century. Over a decade later in 1988, the club marked its centenary, a year which saw the men's and women's captaincy being held by Fraser Rae and the club champion Graham Haugh.

CESSFORD TOWER
SCOTTISH BORDERS

This large L plan tower, once protected by a moat and outer and inner wall was built 6 miles S of Kelso as the manorial residence of Sir Robert Ker, Warden of the Scottish Middle Marches in 1446. The Kers' descendants include the Earls of Roxburgh. Besieged by the Earl of Surrey in 1523, when in exchange for rights of passage the warden surrendered it to a thankful Earl, who had considered lifting the siege. It was later destroyed by the Earl of Hertford in 1545. Recorded in the Peerage as Lord Roxburgh in 1606, Robert Kerr's family occupied it until 1640, but by 1666 it was used as a prison for Covenanters and is now a large ruin.

CESSNOCK HOUSE
EAST AYRSHIRE

On top of a wooded bank 1 mile from Galston is a 16th century keep with additional courtyard mansion. When John Campbell built this tower around 1520, the land, then held by the church, was called Towre of Galstone. Although extended by George Campbell who held the estate between 1578 and 1597, it was Sir Hew Campbell who made considerable additions. Imprisoned in Edinburgh Castle (1662-65) for being obnoxious at court, he was forfeited in 1686 and the estate was briefly gifted to the Duke of Melfort until restored to Sir George Campbell after the Revolution of 1690. Cessnock was modernised in the 19th century when it was the property of the Duke of Portland.

CLACKMANNAN
CLACKMANNAN

Town situated 6 miles NW of Kincardine. The present name is derived from the Gaelic 'clach' meaning 'stone' and 'manau' an old Gaelic name for the district between the River Forth and Stirling. The stone in question now surmounts the plinth at the town cross. Ostensibly growing around its tower, as a Royal Burgh which later declined, it was granted by Malcolm IV (1153-65) to the monks of Cambuskenneth Abbey, with the grant being reaffirmed by Papal Bulls in 1164 and 1165. In spite of the fact that David II granted the barony and castle to a Robert Bruce (an illegitimate family member) in the 14th century, the town's history mainly began in the 15th century when the tower's pre-eminence had passed. The main shaft of the Mercat Cross predates 1551, when a mounting trefoil with the Bruce arms was added to mark the old town's erection into a Burgh of Barony for Bruce of Clackmannan. In the former mansion house (now gone), Robert Burns was knighted by Lady Bruce. As a Sheriffdom and County Town its old Tolbooth with the original bell tower and ogival spire was built in 1592 and once housed the trial court, which, as legend has it was formerly held on the Mercat Cross, to which the accused was chained. The building had ceased to function by 1830. Notwithstanding its trade in brick, timber and wool, its reversal of fortunes by 1880, when it was County Town in all but name, was primarily due to the growth of nearby Alloa. The view up the High Street today with its crow-stepped gables is typically 19th century. See Tower

CLACKMANNAN TOWER
CLACKMANNAN

Standing on a hill above the town is an old keep started by a member of the Bruce family who were granted the land by David II in 1359. The present structure is a 14th century rectangular keep which incorporated a larger south wing in the 15th century and was topped with a corbelled parapet with rounded angles and Renaissance arch. The eastern entrance doorway and belfry on the watch turret date from the 17th century as does the forecourt with moat and drawbridge in front, and enclosing walls around the keep. Its last historical high point came when the last Bruce to occupy the keep, Lady Bruce of Clackmannan, the last Laird's widow and a zealous Jacobite, knighted Robert Burns in 1787 with Robert the Bruce's sword.

CLAYPOTTS CASTLE
DUNDEE CITY

Situated 3 miles E of Dundee. The land which was originally the property of Lindores Abbey had passed to John Strachan by 1512 and was owned in 1560 by Gilbert Strachan, who with his son John built this peculiar oblong keep with its circular towers and square tops at diagonally opposite angles between 1569 and 1588. Stories regarding it being the residence of Cardinal Beaton's mistress are unfounded, as the Cardinal died in 1546. Later passing to the Earls of Dundee and Sir William Graham of Claverhouse in

1620, on the death of John Graham of Claverhouse at the battle of Killiecrankie in 1689 it was forfeited by William II and bestowed on Archibald Douglas Earl of Forfar. By the 19th century it was the property of the Home family.

CLEANSE THE CAUSEWAY, 1520
CITY OF EDINBURGH

Fought on the streets of the Capital over the position of Governor of Scotland during the minority of James V. Owing to the ascendancy of the Earl of Angus, his rival the Earl of Arran and Cardinal Beaton's party set upon Angus and his friends near the Netherbow Port. The engagement brought about the death of 250 people and the defeat of Arran and Beaton. Despite this Arran was to achieve more recognition after the return of the Duke of Albany and Angus's exile to France in 1522.

CLEISH CASTLE
PERTH & KINROSS

Located 4 miles SW of Kinross. The lands were acquired by Sir James Colville of Ochiltree in 1530, who bestowed the barony on his son Robert in 1537. Another Robert Colville, 3rd Baron Cleish built this large L plan tower house in 1600 amongst ancient Scottish yew trees and probably on a base started by his predecessor. A ruin before 1840, it was completely modernised in the 20th century.

CLOSEBURN TOWER
DUMFRIES & GALLOWAY

On land in the Nith Valley 12 miles N of Dumfries is a late 14th-century keep built by the Kilpatricks, after Ivo de Kilpatrick was granted the land by Alexander II in 1232. A descendant named Roger de Kilpatrick was involved with Bruce in the slaying of the Red Comyn in Dumfries, 1306. The mansion, built in the 17th cen-

tury was burnt down in 1748 when the castle again became the family home but in 1783 the estate was sold to James Stuart Menteith, whose daughter Polly was often visited here by Robert Burns in 1788.

CLUNIE CASTLE
PERTH & KINROSS

A ruined L plan structure, it was erected on an islet originally occupied by an ancient lake house in Loch Clunie. Built by George Brown, Bishop of Dunkeld, between 1485 and 1514, near the conjectured summer house of Kenneth Macalpine. As the home of the Earls of Airlie it was bought by the Crichtons of Eliock and was where the famous Admirable Crichton (1560-1585), one of Scotland's most precocious scholar travellers, spent some of his boyhood.

CLYDEBANK
CITY OF GLASGOW

Town situated 10 miles NW of Glasgow by the River Clyde. The one time village in Old Kirkpatrick Parish that was surrounded by farmland called 'barns o Clyde' developed as a great shipbuilding area from the 19th century onwards, following James and George Thomson's purchase of land at the mouth of the Cart from a Miss Hamilton of Cochno in 1871. They built what became known as Princess Dock where their first ship, The Braemar Castle, was completed in 1873. A new boiler works opened in 1881, an engineering works in 1883, and the opening of an additional yard by Napier Shanks and Bell at the East Barn's o' Clyde took place in 1877. Clydebank fast became a New Town with a church and school built in 1876, to the New Clydebank School which opened in 1888, and by 1891 there were eleven places of worship. The successful setting up of the American Singer Sewing Machine Factory in 1884 (producing hundreds of thousands of machines by 1913) later brought the boilermakers Babcock & Wilcox, who were followed by other industries that were to set the stage for a century of industrial innovation. The town was created a Police Burgh in 1886. The acquisition of Thomson's by John Brown's of Sheffield (owned briefly by Clydebank Engineering and Shipbuilding Co) linked the industries of ships and steel by 1899, a year which also saw a take-over by Clyde Navigation Trust of Napier Shanks & Bell, when the Rothesay Dock was built. The constant demand from the Admiralty for ships to police the British Empire led to the setting up of Beardmore's Dalmuir Naval Construction Works in 1906 which at times employed up to 10,000 people, producing naval craft, liners and, with an eye on the future, they also built airships including the R34, the first airship to fly the Atlantic twice. On the domestic front, the founding of The United Co-operative Banking Society of Glasgow in 1881 spawned a food industry that was to benefit the local population during periods of relative prosperity, as well as showing charity during the slumps of 1884, 1893 and 1909. The prosperity, brought by the war of 1914-18, made Clydebank one of Scotland's most flourishing industrial burghs by 1921, with shipbuilding and engineering employing over 14,000 people. It was in the last year of the war that the world's largest battleship HMS Hood was launched here. This figure was to decline steadily with the coming of the World Depression in 1930 when all the Clydebank's eight berths were empty, and work was suspended and Beardmore's Dalmuir Yard closed. In the midst of this was the prevailing squalor of its housing, which figures like David Kirkwood (MP,1922) had politicised in previous years, during the period of unrest when what became known as Red Clydeside

entered into the history of the Scottish Labour Movement. Continuing to benefit from the age of the cruise liner, the launch of the Queen Mary in 1934, built in John Brown's Yard and the Queen Elizabeth in 1938, marked a turning point in the industry of Clydebank and the industries of the river as it moved from civilian to military production in the run up to World War II. This included hundreds of vessels and the battleships King George V and Duke of York. As the site of the Royal Ordnance factory, Clydebank's contribution to the war effort during 1939-45 brought about heavy bombing which destroyed or damaged up to 4,300 homes and consigned a large part of the old town to the past. Attracted by the space for development, the newly arrived firms and expanding older firms had by 1955 provided employment to 10,000 people in Clydeside, making passenger ships and naval craft, later followed by oil super-tankers (post Suez Crisis 1956). Faced with increasing competition from newer ship yards in the Far East and the advent of Britain's decline as a maritime power, its shipbuilding adapted to the current demands of the home market, like the burgeoning North Sea oil industry in the 1960s which has provided a market which has since shrunk. The year 1967 saw the launch of the another of the Queens, The Queen Elizabeth II, which reinforced Clydebank's distinct reputation in the history of British shipbuilding.

CLYNELISH DISTILLERY
HIGHLAND

On the Sutherland coast near Brora NE of Dornoch. The distillery began life in 1819 when the future Duke of Sutherland saw how a purpose built distillery with a water source at the Clynemilton burn and supplies of grain from his tenant farmers, could undermine illicit distilling, which, according to contemporary sources had "nursed the people in deceit and vice". A model distillery of its day, the by-products such as its spent grain fed the adjoining piggerys, whose manure fertilised reclaimed land on Brora Moor. The moor also supplied the barley for distilling; while local coal scorched its one wash still and one spirit still to produce 10,015 gallons (45,527 litres) in 1821-22. Substantial improvements were carried out after 1846 by the new leaseholder and brother of the local bank agent, George Lawson, whose son's reputation for breeding livestock helped promote its whisky to a niche market for private customers at home and abroad, while trade orders were refused. It was bought by blenders Ainslie & Co of Leith in 1896; who increased production through enlargement to supply wholesalers as well, after replacing the Pelton Water power wheel in 1897 with the horizontal steam engine. But in 1912 the company was bought out by a trustee, John Risk, who with the Distillers Co Ltd formed The Clynelish Distillery Co Ltd which operated until 1930, when its shares were transferred to Scottish Malt Distillers. Closed periodically during the 1930s and 1940s, Clynelish saw the instalation of electricity in the 1960s when burning furnaces were converted to internal steam heating and an adjacent, more modern distillery was built combining tradition with efficiency. Renamed the Brora Distillery in 1975, its whisky is primarily used for blending, with only selected outlets for bottles.

OWNERS
Diageo plc ?

REGION
Highland

PRODUCT
Clynelish 14 year old single malt 43% vol

NOTES
A slightly briney nose with a rich, full-bodied flavour.

COATBRIDGE
NORTH LANARKSHIRE

Originally a mining town situated between Edinburgh and Glasgow. The name is either derived from the Middle English 'cote' meaning 'cottage' or from the Old Welsh 'coed' meaning 'wood'. Therefore 'wood' or 'cottage by a bridge'. In 1745 it was the scene of the 'Canter of Coatbridge' when the Jacobite army advanced on fleeing Government forces. The coming of the Industrial Revolution and the building of the Monklands Canal in 1790 provided its coal and ironstone trade with direct access to the Glasgow market, that by 1840 had sparked a profusion of hot blast furnaces with which the town excelled, until the exhaustion of local supplies and competition from England in 1900 sounded the death knell for the iron trade. Its end was delayed only by the discovery of processes for the extraction of by-products like sulphate, ammonia and tar. Started in 1844 by William Baker (patentee of lapwelding process), The Caledonian Tube Works made tube making the principal industry here and was later controlled by A.J Stewart and The Scottish Tube Co. The removal of the Union plant to Corby in England (1955) robbed the town of its heartbeat that is increasingly given over to more leisurely pursuits as the age of heavy industry passes.

COCKBURNSPATH
SCOTTISH BORDERS

Village situated 10 miles SE of Dunbar 1 mile inland. Formerly called Coldbrandspath which may have derived from a Danish chief called Coldbrand. The area was once dotted with Danish and British forts and Roman relics have been found here. In 1072 the lands were held by the Earls of Dunbar, on whose forfeiture in 1435 they were administered by the Homes of Wedderburn until 1465, and then held by a number of owners for over a century until they were granted by the Crown to Sir John Arnot in 1594. Housing the Earls of Home's burial vault, the nearby Dunglass Church, which probably dates from the 14th century, witnessed many a border calamity, for in 1544 the Earl of Hertford's forces passed through here, as did Somerset's in 1547. Boasting a harbour market and yearly fair when created a Burgh of Barony for Arnot of Cockburnspath in 1612 from when its Mercat Cross dates, the town's 16th century church has a remarkable sundial projecting from the corner of the SW wall. Situated overlooking the sea is the ancient Parish Church of St Helen, dating from 1163 and restored in 1876. See Tower

COCKBURNSPATH TOWER
SCOTTISH BORDERS

Conveniently situated by a stream on the Berwick road 1 mile SE of Cockburnspath village. The land was granted to Gospatrick Earl of Dunbar by Malcolm III in the 11th century after they had neutralised the area's lawlessness. It passed to the Earls of March (descendants) who probably built and occupied this tower by 1400 but on their forfeiture it reverted to the Crown in 1435 and along with the lands formed part of the dowry of James IV's Queen Margaret in 1488. Much later it became the property of the Earls of Home.

COCKENZIE & PORT SETON
EAST LOTHIAN

Fishing villages situated 15 miles SE of Edinburgh. In the 12th century the lands were granted by David I to the Saytons (Setons), the oldest titled family in the area, and in Medieval times the rocky coast provided three natural harbours for light craft, earning its elevation to a Burgh of Barony for Lord Seton, 1591 and Burgh

of Regality for the Earl of Winton, 1686. Located on an ancient trade route, Port Seton was once the site of salt works, and in 1722 its neighbour Cockenzie had one of the earliest horse drawn railway lines in Scotland. The Setons' 15th century Collegiate Church, which remains unfinished, retains a fine vaulted chancel and apse. Built in 1834 and improved in 1880, in its heyday Port Seton harbour sheltered up to sixty boats mainly for fishing, which, along with its coal mining, was the main source of employment in the 19th century. In the 20th century the area's coal reserves made it an ideal site for Cockenzie Power Station which faces the Forth Estuary.

COLDINGHAM
SCOTTISH BORDERS

Village situated 20 miles SE of Dunbar. Name derived from 'Colud' and 'ham' meaning 'Coluds people' or 'Coluds hamlet'. Rich in ecclesiastical history, the 7th century nunnery founded by the Northumbrian Princess Ebba on St Abbs Head was visited by St Cuthbert on more than one occasion before its total destruction by the Danes in 870. Its Cruciform Priory founded by King Edgar (son of Malcolm III) in 1098 once held jurisdiction over one eighth of Berwickshire and was plundered by the English in 1216, 1430, 1455 and in 1650 by Cromwell. Partly owing to its transference to Dunfermline Abbey by Robert III in 1378, the priory's wool trade gave birth to a considerable town which had surpassed all others in the Sheriffdom of Berwick by 1350. Under the control of the Home family in the 15th century, the priory is now a ruin. By the time it was created a Burgh of Barony for Stewart of Coldingham in 1638, the village traded mainly in farm foods and fish with the latter employing up to 35 families when its harbour was built at Northfield in 1833. During churchyard excavations in 1854, the priory's original foundations were exposed, along with some interesting relics, while in the area near St Abbs Head traces of early British Forts have been identified.

COLDSTREAM
SCOTTISH BORDERS

Town situated 9 miles NE of Kelso on the north bank of the River Tweed. The area was once known as Lennel after a village while the name Coldstream came from a tributary of the Tweed. Though nothing remains of the 12th century priory founded by Gospatrick Earl of March for Cistercian nuns from England, it was described as a house of black nuns by Gervase of Canterbury, and despite grants of protection from Edward III in 1333, the priory suffered greatly in succeeding centuries of border strife. A large number of bones dug up in 1814 were thought to be those of the slain from Flodden, an event now marked by the Riding the Marches procession in early August which ends with a service on the battlefield. A popular route for invading armies from the north and south, Edward I passed through here in 1296 as did Robert the Bruce, James IV on his way to Flodden (1513), and the Marquis of Montrose in 1640. The Coldstream Guards, whose former headquarters is now a museum, were raised by General Monck and marched from here to London to restore Charles II to the throne in 1660. The town also served as a chapel of ease for runaway couples on route to Gretna Green. The entrance to Coldstream is marked by an obelisk monument to Charles Marjoribanks, MP for Berwickshire in 1834. Among its mainly 19th century buildings are its Parish Church of 1908, which retains the original tower of 1716 and Smeatons five arched bridge which connects Berwickshire with Northumberland, dating from 1766.

COLLISTON CASTLE
ANGUS

A Z plan castle built 2 miles N of Arbroath. In 1545 the land was conveyed by Cardinal Beaton to John Guthrie who built this castle for his wife Isabella Ogilvie in 1553, both of whose initials were carved with the Falconer Arms above the doorway. It was altered considerably in 1621 as indicated by the inscription of the date and the Scottish shield on the wall of the central block, but by 1670 it had passed to new owners before being acquired by John Chaplin in 1721.

COMLONGAN TOWER
DUMFRIES & GALLOWAY

This 15th century tower was erected midway between Dumfries and Galloway by the Murrays of Cockpool, whose ancestor Wiliam de Moravia was granted a charter for the land by his uncle, Thomas Randolph, in the 14th century. The castle was occupied by their descendant the Earl of Mansfield in the late 15th century and was seen as a place of considerable strength before 1707. Its adjoining house was built by the Earl of Mansfield in the 19th century.

COMRIE TOWER
PERTH & KINROSS

By the River Lyon 3 miles NE of Kenmore is a small ruined L plan keep. Built as a Menzies stronghold it was burnt in 1487 when they moved to Castle Menzies but was later repaired and occupied by a younger branch of the family.

CORBETT TOWER
SCOTTISH BORDERS

Sited near a modern mansion 2 miles S of Morebattle on land that was probably owned by Melrose Abbey. The land was later held by the Corbett family and then the Kerrs, whose original tower was burnt by the English in 1522 in retaliation for a plundering expedition by the Scots into Northumberland, of which Lancelot Kerr was a leader. It was burnt again in 1544 during the Earl of Hertford's invasion but was rebuilt by the next generation of Kerrs in 1572 and repaired in 1820 by Sir Charles Kerr.

CORRICHIE, BATTLE OF, 1562
ABERDEENSHIRE

About 3′ miles SW of Echt is the site where the rivalry between the Earl of Huntly with 500 men and the Earl of Moray with the army of Queen Mary reached its climax, after both had jostled for positions of power and privilege from the Queen. The battle ended in a rout for the Earl of Huntly, who suffocated in his armour during an apoplectic fit. Following his demise a sentence of forfeiture was pronounced over his bones.

CORSTON TOWER
FIFE

The ruined remains of this 16th century tower are located 1 mile W of Strathmiglo. Originally the property of John Ramsay in the 15th century and held by his descendants until 1669, when it passed to the Colquhouns. In 1882 the main structure fell, leaving its east wall, which the new owner, the Marquis of Bute, rebuilt and preserved.

CORTACHY CASTLE
ANGUS

About 5 miles from Kirriemuir, on a triangular piece of ground, are the remains of the Earl of Airlie's baronial seat. Developing from the Laird of Clova's Tower in the early 16th century, large additions were made when it became the Earl of Airlie's possession in the 17th century. On the 4th of October 1650 Charles II stayed here after his defeat by Oliver Cromwell at Dunbar, which precipitated his defeat at Worcester and exile to Hol-

land. In revenge for the cordiality shown by the Earl the castle was rendered ineffective by Cromwell's forces and slid into a period of decline. However, additions were made by David Bryce around 1872, which blended well with the divergent styles of earlier times, some of which still remain.

COUPAR ANGUS
PERTH & KINROSS

An old Market Town situated 12 miles NE of Perth. Its name is derived from the Gaelic 'comh-pairt' meaning 'common land' while the county name was added to distinguish it from Cupar in Fife. Reputed to be the site of a 1st century Roman Camp probably built by Agricola, it was later chosen by Malcolm IV in 1164 as the site for a Cistercian Abbey (only the gatehouse survives) around which the town grew. Richly endowed by the Crown and the Hays of Errol it passed to the Balmerino family at the Reformation and was erected into a Lordship and then Burgh of Barony for James Elphinstone Lord Coupar in 1607. Although known for its cattle and horse fairs, weaving was once the main occupation here. Architecturally its Tolbooth dates from 1769 and its Parish Church, though from 1681, was rebuilt in 1859.

COVENANTERS' RISING, 1638-80

The roots of the religious dissent in the 17th century had their origins in the turmoil left by the Reformation, when the established church with its extensive property passed to the Crown and the nobility, thus serving to undermine the authority of the established institutions and leaving many to question what had once been accepted as sacrosanct. With the crowning of the infant James VI (1567-1625) came the enmity between the dominant nobles, gorged with church plunder, and the fledgling Presbyterian

Church, something that would inevitably undermine the Crown itself. In 1582 this manifested itself in the Ruthven Raid when Protestant nobles attempted to kidnap the King, and in 1600 with the Gowrie Conspiracy when the Earl of Gowrie sought to kidnap and possibly murder the King. The result of these events was to cast a shadow over the King's reign until he ascended the English throne in 1603 on the death of Queen Elizabeth when he presided over the Union of the Crowns, and in 1610 introduced Episcopacy into Scotland, aggravating matters further. Consequently, for the rest of his reign, the King tried to establish some sustainable religious tolerance and power-sharing between the Crown, the nobility and the newly established Presbyterian Church, which refuted James's belief in the divine right of kings while seeking to advance a less hierarchical doctrine. In 1625 Charles I ascended the English throne as King of Great Britain and Ireland, but was not crowned in Scotland until 1633 when he gave offence by his Episcopal ceremony and subsequently alienated the nobles who were convinced he hoped to retrieve church land and property. His introduction of the Laud's Liturgy or prayer book in Edinburgh's St Giles incited riots and provoked the signing of The National Covenant, 1638, in Greyfriars Churchyard, leading to Civil War. During that time (1644-45), his lieutenant in the north, the Marquess of Montrose, won several victories over the Covenanters at Tippermuir, Inverlochy, Auldearn, Alford and Kilsyth, but in 1645 the King himself was defeated by Cromwell at Nesbey, leading to his execution in London in 1649. Though Prince Charles was proclaimed King at Edinburgh's Mercat Cross in 1649, it was not until 1651, after his defeat by Cromwell at Dunbar and his acceptance of the Covenant that he was crowned King at Scone in the presence of the Earl of Argyll. His defeat at Worcester, however, led to his exile on the Continent. Losing some of its momentum under Cromwell's Protectorate, hostilities re-ignited in 1660 with the Restoration of Charles II. While appearing to exercise some degree of equanimity to stabilise the situation, the King wasted no time in getting Parliament to sanction the Act of Indemnity, 1662 the Act of Uniformity, 1662, and the Act of Indulgence, 1662. In later years Scotland witnessed the rise of Conventicles, where the Covenanaters were instructed in the open air by field preachers like Donald Cargill, but after the murder of Archbishop James Sharp on Magus Moor, most of the movement was defeated at Bothwell Brig, 1679. This left some extremists under Richard Cameron (Cameronians) who attempted to depose the King in the Sanquhar Declaration, 1680, a month before Cameron's death at Airds Moss. Along with his ardent followers, he had been ruthlessly put down in the east by Tam Dalyell of Binns during the Pentland Rising, 1666, and in the west by John Graham of Claverhouse, ending in what became known as the Killing Times (1681-87). His successor, James Renwick, made a second Declaration in 1685 but eventually became the last martyr of the Covenant executed in Edinburgh in 1688.

COVINGTON TOWER
SOUTH LANARKSHIRE

A landmark in its own right, it stands in the Clyde Valley between Carstairs and Thankerton. In the 14th century the lands were granted by Robert the Bruce to the Keiths, Hereditary Marshalls of Scotland. Later held by the Lindsays of Covington who in 1442 built this tower that was to pass out of the family's hands, and by the 17th century was the property of George Lochart, President of the Court of Session.

COWDENBEATH
FIFE

Village situated 7 miles NW of Burntisland. Its name derives from the Gaelic 'coilltean' and 'Beith' meaning 'at the back of the hill and birch'. Once an Agricultural Township, the place was firmly put on the industrial map by large scale mining developments in the 19th century when, with its ever growing population doubling every ten years, it achieved burgh status by 1890. This also gave rise to a vibrant social culture. The burgh enjoyed the high points and low points of the industry, but, like much of the area, from the 1920s onwards it witnessed a gradual decline that was compounded by the more recent fall in demand for fossil fuels and the opening of the M90 from Inverkeithing to Perth. This reversal has brought a return to some of the tranquillity of its early years.

COWDENKNOWES TOWER
SCOTTISH BORDERS

The defensive structure built on the bank of the Leader, 1 mile S of Earlston, is a 16th century Border pele which was once the seat of the ancestors of the Earls of Home, who probably started it in 1554. The date is inscribed on the SE tower, while on a lintel above the SE doorway are the letters S I H V K H and the date 1574. Their feudal cruelties in its underground pit and hanging tree outside called forth the rhyme ' Vengeance when and where ? upon the house of Cowdenknowes, now and forever mair'. The tower now forms part of the mansion built by the Earl's descendant.

COWIE
ABERDEENSHIRE

Fishing village situated on Stonehaven Bay SW of Aberdeen. Name derived from the Gaelic 'coille' meaning 'a wood'. Once strongly linked to King Malcolm Canmore, who is thought to have built a castle here. The land that was granted by Robert the Bruce to Sir Alexander Fraser for his services at the battle of Bannockburn (1314), and for subduing the area's unruly bands, passed through marriage to William de Keith and was created a Burgh of Barony for Keith the Earl Marischal in 1541. A good example of the early pointed style is the ruined church and burial ground on the Stonehaven road which once served as a chapel for the Earls Marischal and their retainers before being granted to Aberdeen Marischal College in 1593. Modern Cowie is closer to a quaint 19th century coastal community, characterizing a traditional way of life.

COXTON TOWER
MORAY

Occupying land 2 miles ESE of Elgin is a tall square turreted tower, built by the Inneses of Invermarkie in 1644. Four storeys high, with each floor vaulted and walls five feet thick, the tower was designed to resist sudden attacks from marauding local bands rather than a full scale onslaught. Later sold to the Earls of Fife, by the 19th century it functioned as a gardener's house.

CRAGGANMORE DISTILLERY
MORAY

In 1870, when John Smith built this distillery about 10 miles SW of Aberlour, on land held by the Macpherson Grant family, its closeness to the rail line was a determining factor. Taking its name from Cragganmore Hill, the source of its spring water, this was the first Speyside distillery to use the railway system whereby regular 'whisky specials' would leave the private siding, laden with thousands of gallons of whisky for markets in the south. An experienced distiller and manager, Smith removed the swan neck stills and installed the flat-topped stills which are an enduring legacy at Cragganmore to this day. Rebuilt in 1902 by his son Gordon, it remained with the family until 1923, when, like many other small family-run distilleries, it was sold to a consortium and became part of United Distillers. Its capacity increased from two to four stills in 1964 and more recently the former cooperage was converted into a late 19th century distillery owner's drawing room. This was officially opened by the Japanese Ambassador in 1994, when Cragganmore's Old Par blend was the best-selling whisky in Japan.

OWNERS
Diageo plc ?

REGION
Speyside

PRODUCT
Cragganmore 12 year old single malt 40% vol

NOTES
A flowery nose with a very complex taste that's slightly smoky, slightly nutty and slightly peaty, a real sipping whisky.

CRAIG TOWER
ANGUS

Perched overlooking the town of Montrose is a ruined tower with enclosing wall. The first Craig Castle was held by John Ogilvie but was destroyed by King James VI in 1595. Today's ruin was built around 1637 by a branch of the Earls of Southesk. His descendant David Carnegie, Dean of Brechin, was created Earl of Southesk after attending the coronation of Charles I at Holyrood Palace in 1633, and played an active role in ecclesiastical affairs. Conforming to the L plan, its inner courtyard and main buildings adjoin an outer courtyard accessed by the main gateway which is flanked by massive towers and double corbels.

CRAIGCROOK CASTLE
CITY OF EDINBURGH

Positioned on the E slope of Corstorphine Hill W of Edinburgh. In the 14th century, the lands belonged to John de Allyncrum, who gifted them to St Giles Church, but it was not until the 16th century when it was the property of the Adamson family, that the original Z plan tower was built. After a number of owners and further additions it was bought by Archibald Constable, Sir Walter Scott's publisher, and in 1812 was the birthplace of his son Thomas Constable two years before it was vacated, after the death of Mrs Constable. It continued to be associated with the leading figures of the day; while occupied by Francis Jeffrey (1773-1850), the celebrated critic and lawyer, Sir William Playfair was hired to make extensive alterations. More recently the building was used as an office.

CRAIGELLACHIE DISTILLERY
MORAY

About 13 miles SE of Elgin is one of Speyside's model 19th century distilleries. In 1888, Peter J Mackie of Mackie & Co of Glasgow, who were soon to launch a new blended whisky, White Horse, joined with Alexander Edward, owner of Benrinnes distillery, to build on the site close to Craigellachie Station. From here supplies of barley coal and empty cases came in on goods wagons that left with filled casks of whisky. The distinct flavour of the whisky owes much to the spring water from the hill of ' little conval ' and the Allachy burn. Known to his staff as restless Peter, Mr Mackie continued as chairman after the departure of Alexander Edward in 1900, eventually taking over the company in 1915. Later expanding south with warehouses in Campbelltown by 1922, Mackie was knighted by George V in 1924 before his death when his obituary in 'The Times' read "Sir

Peter had the restlessness of a vigorous mind, and was constantly planning fresh enterprises, most of which he succeeded in carrying out". One of the main changes he made in his last years was to change the name of the company to White Horse Distillers; which later made the company synonymous with his most enduring legacy, the 'White Horse' brand. Under Scottish Malt Distillers Ltd in 1930, Craigellachie was first lit by electricity in 1948 and underwent the redevelopment, albeit in some areas delayed, that affected most of the industry in the post-war period. Until 1964 its water wheel was being used to drive the wash still rummager, the year that also saw the rebuilding of the new stillhouse, mash house and tunroom, and the pot stills increased to four. Drawing its water for cooling from the River Fiddich, as the symbolic embodiment of its early history Craigellachie has now adopted the Spey Salmon, which represents the tenacity and vigour of its founder.

OWNERS
John Dewar & Sons Ltd ?

REGION
Speyside

PRODUCT
Craigellachie 14 year old single malt 43% vol

NOTES
A fresh aroma with a long, sweet, slightly spicy finish.

CRAIGIE CASTLE
SOUTH AYRSHIRE

About 5 miles S of Kilmarnock on Craigie Hill is a ruined courtyard keep. The lands were originally owned by the Lindsays until 1371 when John Wallace of Riccarton married the Craigie heiress and later built this early 15th-century tower. It was occupied by the Wallaces until 1600 when the family moved to

Newton-on-Ayr, after which time the castle fell into ruin.

CRAIGMILLAR CASTLE
THE CITY EDINBURGH

In the southern environs of the city is one of Edinburgh's more distinguished defensive structures. Started by Simon de Preston on the site of an earlier structure after he purchased the land from Sir John de Capella in 1374. His L plan tower, which had an inner court with walls, corner towers and adjoining buildings added by 1478, was to become a favoured out of town residence of the Stuarts. It was here that James III imprisoned his upstart brother the Earl of Mar, whose subsequent death in 1479 at the hands of a physician was shrouded in mystery, and also where James V took sanctuary during his minority with his tutor Gavin Douglas when Edinburgh was infected by the plague. Burnt by the Earl of Hertford in 1544 when an extensive outer wall / courtyard was built enclosing the gardens and including two chapels. The frequency of Queen Mary's visits with her French retinue contributed to the nearby land being called Little France. Mary's son James VI is said to have planned his matrimonial excursion to Denmark from here in 1590. Additions to the west range were made in 1661 by the then owner Sir John Gilmour, the Lord President of the Court of Session, but by the close of the century it had declined in importance and now stands as a substantial ruin.

CRAIGNEIL TOWER
SOUTH AYRSHIRE

The ruined 14th or 15th century tower is perched on a hill 1 mile S of Colmonell village by the River Stinchar. Legend has it that Robert the Bruce used the earlier castle on this site as a hiding place. Afterwards the present tower was used as a place of execution and as a feudal prison which later became a picturesque ruin, commanding a view of the Stinchar Valley.

CRAIGNETHAN CASTLE
SOUTH LANARKSHIRE

Situated in the Nethan Valley 6 miles WNW of Lanark. Lands belonged to the Douglases, on whose forfeiture they were acquired by Lord James Hamilton in 1455. The castle developed from a keep with surrounding wall about this time and was further enlarged in 1550 with surrounding walls and towers around the keep by Sir James Hamilton of Fynart, architect and superintendent of Royal Palaces under James V. Before the battle of Langside in 1568 Queen Mary stayed here. A house in the SW enclosure is the most enduring part of the castle, and was built by Andrew Hay, who purchased Craignethan from the Duchess Ann in 1665. In the 19th century it was identified as the Tillietudlem in Sir Walter Scott's 'Old Mortality'.

CRAIL
FIFE

A quaint little fishing port situated 8 miles SE of St Andrews. Called Caraile in 1153, according to some sources it's from the Gaelic 'Carr' and 'Cathair a'ille' denoting 'fort on the cliff'. A burgh of some antiquity, it was mentioned in the 9th century as having trade links with the Netherlands and in the 12th century was the site of a royal castle (east of harbour, now gone) of David I whose daughter-in-law, the Countess Ada, is said to have granted property here to the monks of Dryburgh. Although preceded by a 12th century burgh charter, also from the Countess Ada, a Royal Burgh Charter was signed by Robert the Bruce (1314-29), with privileges from later monarchs including the right to trade on Sunday; which greatly encouraged the enterprise

of the monks, particularly their fishing skills. Still retaining some 12th century work is the Parish Church of St Mary that was built by the monks around 1175 and made collegiate in 1517. In 1647 it was held by the Cistercian Nunnery at Haddington and was the charge of the Rev James Sharp (Archbishop of St Andrews 1660). It was here in 1559 that John Knox's idolatrous sermon to the townsfolk led to considerable destruction in and around Crail before the mob descended on St Andrews. The subsequent erosion of Crail's jurisdiction had as much to do with the turbulence of the times (notably the Union of 1707) as with the rise of neighbouring towns, leaving it a small trade in coal, grain and potatoes by 1860. The lasting legacy of Crail's early trade can be seen in its architecture, particularly its Tolbooth, which dates from 1517 but has a Dutch style roof of 1776 that houses a bell cast in Holland in 1520. All this blends with Crail's more traditional crow-stepped gables, pantiled roofs and cobbled causeways. In the Parish Churchyard are a number of mural monuments including a 16th century cross slab with Celtic designs and a 13th century tombstone. See Crail Golf Club.

CRAIL GOLF CLUB
FIFE

Near the town which gives it its name is situated the course of the Crail Golfing Society which was formed after a meeting of local worthies in 1786. Although this is Scotland's seventh oldest golf club, some accounts state that there was a golf club here in 1760 when golf was played on the town's links. In the tradition of golf in Scotland the members were from a broad spectrum of the community, but one of its more distinguished members was David Monypenny, who later became Lord Justiciary and one of the judges who tried William Burke, the famous grave robber and murderer in 1828. After setting in place the rules and regulations and all the other trappings of a club, with a course on Sauchope Links the members enjoyed a number of years' play, but due to a breakdown in discipline the society was dissolved in 1812 and was not re-established until 1824. Granted its first trophy, The Lindsay Medal, in 1830, the club played an integral part in golfing in Fife and in the wider issues of the day, for in 1835 the Silver Medal Competition was postponed when some members were obliged to join troops of cavalry at Cupar. Like many other Scottish golf clubs at the time Crail had to contend with intrusions on the town's common land by the tenant farmers of Sauchope Farm and the numerous breaks in the club's continuity. After these ruptures, in 1857 a competition was played on the Balcomie Links before another break in 1859-72, but by 1880 there were 29 members plus the Thistle Club for boys playing on the links' two eight-hole courses before the centenary in 1886. After this the club witnessed an increase in membership which was partly due to the rising popularity of Fife as a retreat for summer visitors. The closing years of the century saw its amalgamation with the East Neuk Club (1894), thereby providing a reserve of talent as the society became increasingly centred at Balcomie Links, which was extended to 18 holes. In addition the Balcomie Links were re-opened, the purchase was made of the pavilion for a clubhouse, and the Balcomie Golf Club was formed to run the clubhouse. To cope with the ever increasing demand, a new clubhouse was built in 1903 and The Crail Ladies' Golf Club was formed in 1901. But due to the austerity measures of World War I (1914-18) the club encountered financial difficulties and in 1917 the clubhouse and Links were taken over by the Town Council. In 1935 the Balcomie

clubhouse was extended. The club was affected again by war between 1939-45 when the Links were mined, trenches dug and barbed wire fitted for civil defence. Meanwhile the clubhouse was used by the Polish Brigade. Restoration work began in earnest in 1944, and in 1946 with the help of The Balcomie Links Management Committee play resumed, and the chapter was marked by the presentation of the Victory Cup. Celebrating the society's 175th anniversary in 1961, the decade's subsequent developments included a waterway system for the green (1963), an extension to the clubhouse (1968) and the purchase of Balcomie course and clubhouse for £30,000 in 1973. This year also saw the presentation of the Balcomie Cup and the emergence of the club's youth section in the local matches. Since then many improvements and developments in the course clubhouse and social fabric have set the club in good stead for the 21st century.

CRAMOND TOWER
CITY OF EDINBURGH

The tower is 5 miles NW of Edinburgh City Centre near the mouth of the River Almond, which was once the site of a Roman Camp. The lands belonged to the Bishops of Dunkeld during the reign of William the Lyon (1165-1214), when it was called Bishops Cramond, and were probably the site of an earlier structure where two bishops died. In 1409 the then Bishop exchanged his lands of Cammo for John de Nudre's earlier tower here, around which the church already had land. So it must therefore be assumed that the bishops built the four-storey oblong tower of today some time afterwards as an addition to the original Bishops' Palace. After the Reformation the tower was occupied by an English merchant named Ingles who vacated it in

1680 and whose descendants still owned it in the 19th century. The building is now in a well preserved state.

CRANSHAWS TOWER
SCOTTISH BORDERS

Among the Lammermuir Hills 9 miles NW of Duns is a well preserved 16th-century pele tower. Built on the former Douglas stronghold by the Swintons who held the land between 1400 and until 1702 when it reverted to the Douglases. King James VI is said to have attended mass here. Later held by the Earls of Morton (descendants), it was subsequently inherited by the Earl's son Lord Aberdour.

CRATHES CASTLE
ABERDEENSHIRE

On the left bank of the Dee 14 miles WSW of Aberdeen. Appearing as a chateau-like structure, Crathes is picturesquely situated in fine grounds which once formed part of the Royal Forest of Drum and, as the Land of Leys, were granted in a charter by Robert the Bruce to his erstwhile supporter Alexander de Burnard in 1324. The present four-storey L plan castle with its pepperpot turrets was started in 1553 and completed in 1596 by Alexander Burnett of Ley, whose initials, along with those of his wife Jean Gordon, are inscribed above a doorway in the east wall. Second only to its traditional exterior are the embellishments of its distinctive interior, which include its painted ceilings depicting the nine nobles, the nine muses, and the green Lady ceiling dating from 1600. In the 19th century a plain wing was added which was reduced in size following a fire in 1966.

CRAWFORD CASTLE
SOUTH LANARKSHIRE

Advantageously sited by the River Clyde opposite Crawford village, 44 miles SW of Edinburgh, is a baronial stronghold that was once defended by a moat. The seat of the Lindsays from 1178 who received the Crawford Earldom in 1398. From the accession of James IV in 1488 it was held by Archibald, Earl of Angus, whose attempt at renaming it Crawford Douglas was interrupted in 1528 when it was annexed to the Crown and became a favourite hunting seat of James V until reclaimed by the Angus Earls in 1542. It later passed to the Hamilton branch of the family, who made some 17th century additions, before being purchased by Sir George Colebrook in the 18th century.

CRAWFURDLAND TOWER
EAST AYRSHIRE

About 3 miles NW of Kilmarnock is a 16th century tower which adjoins a 17th century mansion. For a long time the stronghold of the Crawfords, a distinguished Ayrshire family who were descended from a Reginald de Craufurd, Sheriff of Ayr in the 13th century. A John Wilkinshaw Crawford was Colonal in the Hanoverian army (1745), who, although disgraced after he befriended the Jacobite Earl of Kilmarnock, became Falconer to the King in 1761.

CREICH TOWER
FIFE

A ruined L plan courtyard tower situated 6 miles N of Cupar. The original 13th century castle belonging to Macduff, Earl of Fife, was replaced in the 16th century by the present structure that was built by the Bethunes who acquired the land from the Liddles in 1502 and were confirmed in a charter of 1533 for Robert Betoun of Creich.

CRICHTON CASTLE
MIDLOTHIAN

Commanding a position at the head of the River Tyne 5 miles SE of Dalkeith is a former Crichton stronghold. With its oldest part consisting of a 14th century tower this was the property of Sir William Crichton in 1450, when as Chancellor to James I he added two wings. In 1488, the year of James V's accession, the lands were conferred on Patrick Hepburn, Ist Earl of Bothwell. The family's continued, though sometimes tenuous ties with the Royal Stewarts led to a visit in 1562 by Queen Mary I and her royal retinue to attend a wedding reception and in 1576 her son James VI bestowed it on his favourite, Sir Francis Stewart, 5th Earl Crichton. After his tour of Italy in 1581 he arcaded its north wing, which formed the distinctive part of the courtyard structure. The property of Hepburn of Humbie in 1649, it later passed to numerous owners and although in a ruinous state by the 19th century, its former strength still managed to inspire Sir Walter Scott when he eulogised it in his 'Marmion' of 1808:

The tower in different ages rose;
Their various architecture shows
The builders various hands;
A mighty mass, that could oppose,
When deadliest hatred fired its foes

The castle is presently cared for by Historic Scotland.

CROMARTY
HIGHLAND

Town situated on the Cromarty Firth 10 miles NE of Fortrose. Name derived from the Gaelic 'crom' and 'ard' meaning either 'crooked cape' or 'point' owing to the irregular shoreline of the Firth. Naturally the site of an early settlement, Cromarty had associations with Macbeth, who was Thane of Cromarty, and it later served as an important part of the Crown's administrative centre in the north, something borne out by the many charters granted by successive kings. A Royal Burgh from 1264, it was reduced to a Burgh of Barony in 1672 and by 1685 was expunged from the Burgh Roll. In the 13th century this was the site of a Trinitarian Priory and for a long time was a Sheriffdom of the Urqurarts, whose castle was burnt prior to 1772 when Cromarty House was built. Despite its official decline in former years its physical features and proximity to Inverness were guaranteed to restore its fortunes and official standing in the 18th century when its Court House and Tolbooth (1782) were built by the Ross family, along with much of the present town. The oldest antiquity is its 14th century cross. Also the birthplace of the renowned geologist, Hugh Millar (1802-1852); his thatched cottage has been restored and now houses some of his work and personal effects. With the development of its harbour by Thomas Ross, Cromarty switched from its staple trade in fish to industrial enterprises in iron, brewing and linen production, industries now largely replaced by the seasonal tourist trade. Architecturally the Parish Church, built around 1590 and one of Scotland's earliest Protestant churches, incorporates the laird's loft to the east and the scholar loft to the west. In 1740 an aisle was added, and renovations were carried out in 1952.

CROMDALE, BATTLE OF, 1690
HIGHLAND

West of Grantown-on-Spey. During the war between James VII and William of Orange, the Jacobite army under Viscount Dundee and led by General Thomas Buchan were routed by General Mackay's troops under Sir Thomas Livingstone near the Cromdale Hills. The combination of surprise and the quick deployment of cavalry won the day for Livingstone and effectively put an end to the resistance of the clans.

CROMWELL'S INVASION, 1650-52-60

The last of Scotland's wars of Independence was fought out after the death of Charles Ist but had its roots in the reign of James VI. Though disenchanted by Charles I reluctance to sign The Solemn League & Covenant, in recognising royal authority the Covenanters were opposing the republican principles sweeping England that culminated in the execution of their King Charles I and the rise of Oliver Cromwell. Unable to force the Stewart's claims on the English throne, the Scots declared the Prince of Wales King Charles II of Scotland in 1649 from Edinburgh's Mercat Cross. From his exile in the Hague before his landing in Scotland in June 1650, the King promised to uphold the Covenant and Presbyterianism along with the supremacy of the church in ecclesiastical matters and the Scottish Parliament in civil matters. Meanwhile after recently subduing Ireland and seeking to consolidate his power, Cromwell advanced north with General Lambert, crossing the Tweed with 16,000 men in July. To counter this, the Royalists under General David Leslie and numbering around 23,000 men laid waste to the surrounding countryside, forcing Cromwell to fall back on Dunbar for supplies from the sea, with the Scots at his rear anxious to block his route south. The victory by Cromwell in the ensuing battle brought about the break up of the Scottish united front, his occupation of Edinburgh and the eventual subjugation of Scotland by his adjutant General Monck. But in January 1651 south of the Forth was Cromwell's by conquest or alliance and north of the Forth was the recently crowned Charles II with his adviser the Earl of Argyll running the govern-

ment from Perth and Stirling and David Leslie their chief soldier. Cromwell failed to take Stirling owing to the larger Royalist force and so ordered his forces round by Inverkeithing and then to Perth, which was taken on 3 August, thus enabling him to get to the enemy's rear, blocking their retreat to the Highlands. As a counterblast to this, Leslie and the King, disenchanted by the betrayal of Argyll, resolved to march south to raise the English Royalists but in doing so sealed the fate of the Scots, they were followed in a chase by Cromwell, who left General Monck as Commander and Chief in Scotland. On 3rd September 1651, along with the King, they were routed at Worcester which was followed by a slaughter in the aftermath and forced the King to flee to France. Though the mechanics of Government introduced in Cromwell's Commonwealth, with new law courts and a council of state modelled on Republican lines, were a burden on the people, the free trade with England was of enormous benefit to Scotland, helping to expand commerce and industry through the development of trading ports. Retrospectively this proved to be like a trial run for the Treaty of Union in 1707. But with Cromwell's death in 1658 the Commonwealth lost its heartbeat, so when General Monck withdrew his forces in 1660 the link was finally broken, leaving the Scots to embrace the Restoration of Charles II in 1660, which was marked amidst much rejoicing.

CROOKSTON CASTLE
RENFREWSHIRE

Built on a hill 3 miles S of Paisley. In the 12th century the land was owned by a Walter de Croc but in 1330 was purchased by Sir Alan Stewart and granted to J Stewart of Darnley in 1361. A simple central keep, it was built in the early 15th century by the Stewarts and held by

Henry Lord Darnley between 1546-1567. Fortified by the Duke of Montrose in the 17th century, it later fell into ruin until it was saved by 19th century restoration work.

CROSSRAGUEL ABBEY
SOUTH AYRSHIRE

Located 2 miles SW of Maybole. The substantial remains of this once proud Abbey were began in the early 13th century when it was founded by Duncan Earl of Carrick and dedicated to the Virgin Mary. A dependent of Paisley Abbey, whose Cluniac monks it housed, it was lavishly endowed, particularly by the founder's descendants, notably Robert III, who granted it the right of regality, giving it control over most of Southern Ayrshire. Damaged during Edward I's invasion of 1296. The wayward ways of its monks brought an inspection by the Abbot of Paisley in 1370 and the resignation of its Abbot, leaving the place to fall into ruin. In the 15th century its church was rebuilt and was later visited by James IV while on one of his many visits to Whithorn, in the 16th century, after which the last of its abbots, Quinten Kennedy, was engaged in a famous dispute with John Knox at the Reformation. After being torturously roasted in 1570 Alan Stewart its Commendator signed over the property to Abbot Quintin's nephew Gilbert, 4th Earl of Cassillis, whose descendant preserved its remains after the rise of the Reform Church signalled the Abbey's decline. These remains now include a church with an outer court and gatehouse and an Abbot's House and Chapter House to the east.

CULLEN
ABERDEENSHIRE

Coastal town situated 40 miles W of Fraserburgh. Once called Invercullen, the present name is either derived from the Gaelic 'cuileann' meaning 'holly' or from 'cuilean' meaning 'little nook'. Erected into a Royal Burgh by William I between 1189-98, a charter was also granted by King Robert the Bruce, who endowed the chaplaincy in the Church of St Mary after his second wife Elizabeth died here in 1327. Once consisting of a single street with houses set gable to street, its lack of expansion brought it immunity from burgh commitments by 1618. And although its subsequent decline was briefly reversed with the introduction of flax and linen manufacture by the Earl of Seafield around 1750, it failed to prevent the demolition of the Old Town and the building of the present town to plans by George Williams between 1820-30. Described in 'Chambers Gazetteer' of 1832 as "a place enjoying genteel society, consisting of persons of moderate income attracted by cheap living", Cullen later grew as a family holiday resort which, with the limited revival of its herring fishing, brought great prosperity in the 20th century. About 1′ miles to the south, near Cullen House, stands the Auld Kirk with its 12th century work and additions made in 1536, prior to being made collegiate in 1543, for Alexander Ogilvie, whose sculpted effigy is housed within. See Cullen House, Cullen Kirk & Golf Club

CULLEN HOUSE
MORAY

Standing above Cullen Burn 6 miles W of Buckie. The original castle was the conjectured home of Martha, Countess of Carrick and mother of Robert the Bruce, whose consort Elizabeth de Burgh died here in 1327. The present structure was started around 1550 with additions by Sir Walter Ogilvie of Deskford and Findlater in 1616. Although sacked by Montrose in 1645, while under the Earls of Seafield, occupants from 1711, it was restored and had developed into a Scottish Baronial edifice when visited by the Jacobites in 1746. Much of the interior designs were by Robert Adam, while its exterior was remodelled and enlarged by David Bryce in the 19th century. More recently a fire brought about its sub-division into flats.

CULLEN CHURCH
MORAY

To the SW of the town centre stands the Kirk of Cullen, the centre of the Old Town of Cullen, which was rebuilt after 1645. This was preceded by an earlier foundation that was attributed to Robert I, who endowed a Chaplaincy here for the soul of his Queen, Elizabeth, who during a visit north in 1327 died nearby and was interred here. Today's church was founded in 1543 as a Collegiate Church by Alexander Ogilvie of Findlater whose memorial stone is housed within. Cruciform in shape, while predominantly 14th century with 16th and 17th century additions and 19th century alterations, the church was badly damaged in the Wars of Montrose in 1645 but still retains the original structure. Consequently the oldest portion, of today's structure is the east end and the south aisle. Along with the church's elaborately heraldic memorials to the noble families of Gordon and Ogilvie who were associated with it over the centuries, the sacrament house, or ambry, in the north wall ranks as a popular feature among visitors and local parishoners alike.

CULLEN GOLF CLUB
MORAY

The west of Cullen town, on the common links overlooking Cullen Bay, has been the site of a golf club since 1879. When the celebrated Tom Morris was invited to comment on the course in 1872, he recommended several changes which were augmented in 1907 when Charlie Neaves

extended the course to 18 holes. Today's course is a legacy of these two contributions and provides the perfect ambience for an evening stroll, with its coastal view and fresh air. In 1904 the players were somewhat restricted by the road crossing the fairway and the railway to the left of it. The first hole known as the Farskane was named after the Laird's manor house overlooking the links that has since 1921 been the Cullen Bay Hotel. In 1886 the club resolved to build a clubhouse which now stands on the part of the links near the bathing shelters. Though marginaly altered in later years, today's course still retains eight of the nine original Morris greens and three of the holes are almost untouched. For decades, however, the most enduring impressions left on visitors after visiting one of Banfshire's more distinguished clubs is its setting amidst the sea stacks and beach which in some ways reflect the challenging nature of the course itself.

CULLODEN, BATTLE OF, 1746
HIGHLAND

The final blow during the last rising in the cause of the Stewarts took place NE of Inverness. Against the advice of his General Lord George Murray, Prince Charles Edward deployed his army of beleaguered Highlanders, numbering around 5000 men, on ground more suited for English cavalry and artillery than the Highland mode of attack. Consequently in the face of English grapeshot the Jacobites were defeated by the Duke of Cumberland with a force almost double in size, better equipped and better fed. The carnage which followed the defeat marked the beginning of the pacification of the Highlands through the destruction of the clan system and the end of the Stewart dynasty in Scotland.

CULROSS
FIFE

A town situated on the coast 7 miles SE of Kincardine Bridge. Name derived from the Gaelic 'cuileann' and 'ros' meaning 'holly wood'. In keeping with Fife's religious and commercial traditions, with its coal mine and salt pans Culross developed around its Abbey. From a Burgh of Barony for the Abbot it was elevated to a Royal Burgh in 1592, but notwithstanding its earlier burgh status, the town's golden age was the 17th century when it exercised a brisk trade in coal, salt, wool, fish and girdles. But this prosperity suffered with the opening of the Carron Iron Works and the Dunfermline linen factories. Renowned for its buildings, especially its palace built by George Bruce between 1597 and 1611, Culross is a traditional Scottish burgh, with the archetypal cobbled causeways and old domestic fisher buildings, with their crow-stepped gables and pantiled roofs. Many of these serve as reminders of its former prosperity and owe much to the restoration by the National Trust of Scotland from the 1940s onwards. Once forming part of Perthshire, in 1891 it became part of the County of Fife by order of The Boundary Commission. To the east of the town is the site of the chapel which was built by Archbishop Robert Blackadder in 1503 and dedicated to St Mungo. See Abbey

CULROSS ABBEY
FIFE

Situated near the shore to the north of the town. Founded in 1217 by Malcolm, Earl of Fife, and dedicated to the Virgin Mary and St Serf was built in an English Gothic style and added to over a period of 500 years, during which time a vibrant trade was developed by its Cistercian monks. This stimulated the local economy and often attracted over a hundred ships to the Forth Estuary. In 1539 the Abbot pledged its land to finance badly needed repair work, but by the Reformation its revenues were controlled by Secular Abbots from the Colville family. After a visit by James VI in 1609, following his accession to the English throne it became a Temporal Lordship for James Colville Lord of Culross. In 1608 its stone was used for the now modernised Abbey House by Edward Bruce Lord of Kinloss, whose ornate family vault is on the north side of the church. Continued shrinkage in size owing to stone pillaging left its Abbey church being used as the Parish Church by 1633 with additions of 1824 facilitating further use which continues to this day. In contrast to the town buildings, little remains of the Abbey's domestic buildings save the foundations.

CULZEAN CASTLE
SOUTH AYRSHIRE

Commanding a view over Culzean bay 5 miles W of Maybole. The original 16th century castle was built by Thomas Kennedy, the younger son of Gilbert, 3rd Earl of Cassillis before his murder near Ayr in 1602. However, the credit for today's castellated mansion, into which the old castle is incorporated, goes to Robert Adam, who designed what some would regard as his masterpiece for David, 10th Earl of Cassillis, in 1777. The structure's predominantly classical Georgian style which permeates through to its interior with its fine plaster ceilings, the round drawing room, and the oval staircase in the courtyard, are in harmony with its richly cultivated gardens that extend into one of Scotland's original country parks. In 1831, Thomas the 12th Earl became Marquis of Ailsa. During the Second World War the castle accommodated its most famous guest, General Eisenhower, the Supreme Allied Commander, who was granted a life rent of one of its flats after the war.

CUMNOCK
EAST AYRSHIRE

A mining village situated 16 miles E of Ayr. The name may derive from the Old Gaelic 'cumnan' meaning 'a shrine' or from the Celtic 'comunn' meaning 'confluence of the stream' (the Lugar and the Glaisnock). Once belonging to the Dunbars, Earls of March, the lands which were raised to a Burgh of Barony for Dunbar of Cumnock in 1509, show evidence of its involvement in the religious strife of the 17th century. In its churchyard, the burial ground of two Covenanters, is where the ashes of one of their leading figures Alexander Pedan (1626-86), were interred after being exhumed from his grave at nearby Auchinleck. Cumnock's main claim to fame is its ties with Keir Hardie, the father of Scottish Socialism, whose time as a journalist here after uniting the Scottish Miners in 1888, is remembered by a bust of him in the local hall. While modern Cumnock is strongly linked to coal mining, in former times it was known for weaving and the making of snuff boxes.

CUPAR
FIFE

Town situated 10 miles NE of Markinch. Name derived from the Gaelic 'comhpairt' meaning 'common land' 'a partnership'. As a Royal Burgh in 1328 it was a suitable centre for judicial administration owing to its favourable position astride established routes of travel. Its castle, which once occupied the site of the school at Castlehill, was the seat of the Macduffs Earls of Fife, and where the Earl's wife and children were thought to have been murdered by Macbeth. An assembly was held here in 1276 and the town was later visited by a number of monarchs down through the centuries. No stranger to dramas at Castlehill,

David Lindsay (1486-1555) played out some of the first enactment's of 'The Three Estates' under the royal gaze of James V and Mary of Guise, whose daughter Mary I ironically visited here, as did her chief protagonist John Knox to give a sermon to the Lords of the Congregation at the Reformation, 1560. Given its former function as a County Town surrounded by rich farmland and centres for handloom weaving, Cupar sadly lacks older buildings other than the Parish Church with its tower of 1415, and the 17th century Mercat Cross. Three miles to the south is Scotstarvit Tower, built in 1579 and once home to John Scot (scholar), while in the locality is the Hill of Tarvit, an Edwardian mansion designed by Robert Lorimer.

D

DAILUAINE DISTILLERY
MORAY

Three miles SW of Aberlour, in a hollow near the River Spey is the fulfilment of local farmer William Mackenzie's endeavours, which began in 1851. Taking its name from the Gaelic word for 'the green vale', Dailuaine was started in the age of innovation and linked to what was known as the 'whisky railway' and the ever expanding markets in the industrial cities to the east and south. On Mackenzie's death in 1865 the distillery was let until 1879, when his son Thomas rebuilt it and took its output to 160,000 gallons annually, making it one of the largest distilleries in the Highlands. In 1891 Mackenzie & Co became a limited liability company called The Dailuaine-Glenlivit Distillery Ltd, but in 1898 changed its name again to Dailuaine Talisker Distilleries Ltd. An ambitious entrepreneur with other distilling interests, Mackenzie became chairman and Managing Director of the new company and expanded its blending and distilling business while setting up agencies for their brands at home and abroad. Sadly, before his death in 1915, the Company suffered a number of setbacks, including lost sales lawsuits and a fire, resulting in his widow selling out to a consortium including James Buchanan & Co Ltd, John Dewar & Sons Ltd, and John Walker & Sons Ltd. Dailuaine was rebuilt after the fire of 1917 and production was resumed in 1920. For forty years its four engines and two water wheels linked to overhead pulleys provided a unique source of power for its lighting and machinery, until Dailuaine was linked to the national grid in 1950. Between 1959-65 the building was rebuilt and modernised.

OWNERS
Diageo plc ?
REGION
Speyside
PRODUCT
Dailuaine 16 year old single malt 43% vol
NOTES
A full-bodied fruity nose with a smoky finish.

DALCROSS CASTLE
HIGHLAND

Occupying a commanding position on a hill 8 miles E of Inverness. Conforming to the L plan structure, it was built by the 8th Lord Lovat in 1621, and later became a possession of the Mackintoshes. Between 1703-1704 their 19th chief Lachlan lay in state here for 40 days, before 2000 men of Clan Chattan followed his remains to Petty Church. The castle's north wing was added in 1720, and in 1746 the Royal troops marshalled here before Culloden. Although externally plain, it remains a good example of a 17th-century tower house.

DALGATIE CASTLE
ABERDEENSHIRE

Mansion house situated 2 miles E of Turriff. At one time a 15th century L-plan keep, built by the Hays of Errol, a distinguished family of long-standing. In the 14th century a William de Haga of Errol held the office of Hereditary Constable of the Realm. Added to at various later dates: its 7- foot thick walls rise over 60 feet to its battlements, from which can be seen the town of Turriff, which may derive its name from the Gaelic 'turach' meaning 'tower place' owing to the area's numerous family seats. Its most notable feature, however, is its groined vaulted ceiling which was done during the ecclesiastical revival in the early 17th century. Sold in 1762 to Peter Garden of

Troupe, it was bought by James, 2nd Earl of Fife, in 1798, whose nephew General Sir Alexander Duff (1776-1851) resided here.

DALHOUSIE CASTLE
MIDLOTHIAN

Suitably positioned on the N bank of the River Esk 3 miles SW of Dalkeith. In the 12th century the lands were held by Simon de Ramsay whose descendant, a William Ramsay, swore fealty to Edward I of England in 1296 and 1304, while his son was prominent in the Wars of Independence. Developing from a motte and bailey, in 1400 Sir Alexander Ramsay successfully defended it against Henry IV of England. Consisting of an L plan tower in the 15th century, by 1619 Sir George Ramsay was created Lord Ramsay of Dalhousie and added an entrance, while the modelling of its tower was carried out by his son William whom Charles I made Earl of Dalhousie in 1633. Occupied by Cromwell, who corresponded from here in 1648. The soldiering traditions of the 5th, 6th, 7th and 9th earls resulted in the title being changed to Baron Dalhousie of Dalhousie in 1815, by which time it had developed into the stately castellated pile in wooded grounds that we see today. The family's continued elevation came, when, following a visit in 1842 by Queen Victoria and Prince Albert, Sir James Andrew Ramsay was elevated to Marquis of Dalhousie, 1849. Avoiding destruction by fire in 1867, the building is now used as a hotel.

DALKEITH
MIDLOTHIAN

A former Market Town situated 7 miles SE of Edinburgh. Its name derived from the Brythonic 'dol' and 'coed' meaning 'field in a wood'. The lands belonged to the Grahams in the 12th century when its castle was built, but passed through mar- riage to the Douglases, becoming a Burgh of Barony for Sir James Douglas in 1401. St Nicholas's 14th century church, which was made collegiate in 1406 for James de Douglas, has a chequered history. After being damaged at the Reformation (1560), and by Cromwell's Ironsides in the 17th century, it was later restored, but more recently by David Bryce in 1851, and now houses the tomb of James Douglas, the Ist Earl of Morton. Dalkeith was made a Burgh of Regality for Douglas of Lochleven in 1540. Its castle was restyled by James Douglas 4th Earl of Morton in 1575: but was sold to the Earl of Buccleuch in 1642 before being occupied by General Monck (1654-59) and by the Duke of Monmouth (1663). The Duke's wife, the Duchess Anne, hired James Smith to redevelop it into the classical structure now known as Dalkeith Palace (private house). Among its most distinguished guests were Prince Charles Edward, 1745, George IV, 1822, Queen Victoria, Prince Albert, 1824 and Edward VII. In the 18th century additions were made by Robert and William Adam but after having lost much of its glory and fine collection of artefacts (now housed in the Buccleuch's other residences), the palace was later used as a training centre, and its extensive grounds are now open to the public. Surrounded by cornfields and coalfields, Dalkeith's grain market once the most important in Scotland, provided the mainstay for the local economy, and along with lesser trades like the ropery, tannery, cork, nail, hat and tobacco suppliers, helped build a thriving rural burgh which still manages to retain some of its quaintness long after their demise.

DALMELLINGTON
SOUTH AYRSHIRE

Town situated 15 miles SE of Ayr. The name probably derived from the Gaelic 'dail meallan' and the English 'ton' therefore 'field and hills by the village'. A village from the 11th century, SE of the town is the site of an ancient moat which was once the seat of feudal justice and had strong associations with the Covenanters in the 17th century. Created a Burgh of Barony for Lord Cathcart in 1607, the village was industrialised in the 19th century as local coal fired its iron works, which later brought the railways.

DALMENY HOUSE
CITY OF EDINBURGH

Located 9 miles W of Edinburgh centre. In 1615 the Baronies of Barnbougle and Dalmeny were sold by Sir Robert Moubray to Sir Thomas Hamilton. Purchased by Sir Archibald Primrose in 1662, whose second son Archibald was created Viscount in 1700 and Earl of Rosebery, Lord Dalmeny in 1703. The house itself, built by William Wilkins in a Gothic style for the 4th Earl in 1815, is situated in wooded parklands and commands a fine view of the Forth. While visiting with Prince Albert in 1842 and 1847, Queen Victoria described it in her journal as 'beautiful, with trees growing down to the sea'. Presently the house with its fine grounds provides a perfect setting for its impressive display of artefacts.

DALMORE DISTILLERY
HIGHLAND

Taking its name from the Gaelic Norse word meaning 'the big meadowland', it sits on the shore of the Cromarty Firth near the town of Alness that was named after the river, now Dalmore's water source. As its name suggests, the fertile land and the Black Isle opposite were the main factors in Alexander Matheson's decision to build the distillery in 1839. The distillery was acquired by the Mackenzie family in 1867. Although in close proximity to the sea with road and rail links (Highland Railway, 1874) to the

north and south, it retained its ambience of timeless tranquillity until production ceased and it was closed during the First World War (1914-18), when it was used for the production of mines. After returning to making whisky it became one of the main ingredients in the White & Mackay brand, whose producers acquired Dalmore in 1960.

OWNERS
Kyndal International Ltd ?
REGION
Highland
PRODUCT
Dalmore 12 year old single malt 40% vol
NOTES
A malty nose with hints of sherry and a rich, mellow, fruity taste.

DALQUHARRON CASTLE
SOUTH AYRSHIRE

Overlooking the Girvan Water 8 miles SW of Maybole. The lands granted by Edward Bruce Earl of Carrick to the Abbey of Crossraguel in 1324 had by 1474 become the property of the Laird Gilbert Kennedy who subsequently built the original oblong keep. After being purchased by the Culzean family it was sold in 1536 to the Kennedys of Girvan Mains, whose descendant made large additions in 1679, but by 1790 a new mansion nearby had replaced the family house.

DALRY, BATTLE OF, 1306
STIRLING

SE of Tyndrum. Though crowned at Scone in March 1306, King Robert the Bruce had to win his kingdom through force of arms. But at Dalry his army was surprised and defeated by the Lord of Lorne, the husband of the aunt of Comyn, whom Bruce had murdered at Dumfries in Feb 1306. With the defeat for Bruce came his fugitive status and the period of his wanderings in the Western Highlands, where he found the resolve to continue the struggle.

DALSWINTON
DUMFRIES & GALLOWAY

Village situated 8 miles NW of Dumfries. Called Bale-swyn-toun in 1295, the name derived from the Gaelic 'baila' meaning 'village' and the Old English 'Sveins farm' ; therefore 'Village of Sveins farm'. Anciently the area was dotted with Iron Age hillforts that may have been occupied by the Romans, but by the 13th century it was a barony belonging to the Comyns that was later held by the Stewarts and Maxwells. The original Comyn Castle was replaced by a mansion built by Patrick Millar (1731-1815) Robert Burn's landlord and an inventor who landed his first steamboat on Dalswinton Loch in 1788. Also a farming pioneer, he introduced the iron plough, thrashing mill and the first turnip into Scotland. After his death the estate passed to James Macalpine of Lenny.

DALWHINNIE DISTILLERY
HIGHLAND

Located 6 miles SW of Aberlour. Originally known as Strathspey Distillery, it was built near the highest village in Scotland in 1897 by a group of local businessmen convinced its height of 1073 ft (327 meters) above sea level would give ready access to the abundant supplies of pure mountain water fed by the distillery burn, the Allt ant sluic. Traditionally a producer of blending whisky with strong American links, Dalwhinnie has survived the market fluctuations since the turn of the century and was run by a number of owners before being acquired by the United Distillers. Dalwhinnie is the northern highlands' representative in the classic malts range, its two traditional copper pot stills provide one of the malt

whiskies at the heart of the Black & White and the Buchanan's blends of whisky. As a reliable provider of work for the villagers, the distillery is active in local initiatives such as the rebuilding of the village hall, and has for a long time served as the weather station for the meteorological office for whom its manager records daily weather readings. Later developments like the new visitor centre (1991), in the former warehouse, which is capable of welcoming 40,000 visitors a year, and the virtual rebuilding of the distillery's internal fabric have helped Dalwhinnie to plan for its future whilst remembering its past.

OWNERS
Diageo plc ?

REGION
Highland

PRODUCT
Dalwhinnie 15 year old single malt 43% vol

NOTES
A gentle aromatic malt with a light, fruity, heathery honey flavour and a delicate finish.

DARNAWAY CASTLE
MORAY

Little now remains of the age old seat of the Earls of Moray by the River Findhorn 6 miles SW of Forres. Started in the 14th century by Thomas Randolph, Earl of Moray, who was Regent during David II's minority. A hall was added by Archibald Douglas, Earl of Moray, in 1450 and completed to original designs on his forfeiture in 1455. Queen Mary held court at Darnaway in 1564. The present structure is predominantly from the rebuilding of 1810, when this castellated oblong pile was built adjacent to the original hall, of which only the dark oak roof survives.

DARNICK TOWER
SCOTTISH BORDERS

A Border pele tower positioned at the base of the Eildon Hills, 1 mile W of Melrose. The nearby tower was built and occupied by the Heitons around 1425, but was burnt during the Earl of Hertford's expedition in 1545. A new charter was granted by Queen Mary in 1566 to Andrew de Heyton, who built this tower in 1569.

DEAN CASTLE
EAST AYRSHIRE

Built 1 mile NE of Kilmarnock town. In 1316 lands were bestowed by Robert the Bruce on Sir Robert Boyd, whose descendant built the oblong keep in the mid-15th century. In 1466 Lord Boyd's brother Sir Alexander was instructor in chivalry to the young James III and as such exerted considerable influence which was to lead to his downfall. Sometime after the building of a courtyard and surrounding wall, Thomas Boyd (Earl of Arran, married Princess Mary) and Sir Alexander were tried for treason, and the latter was beheaded. However, between 1654 and 1661 more work was carried out before the family were reinstated as Earls of Kilmarnock. Destroyed by fire in 1735 due to the carelessness of a laundry maid. By 1746 the family had been forfeited for supporting the Jacobites.

DEER ABBEY
ABERDEENSHIRE

Positioned on the bank of the River Ugie WNW of the village. Legend has it that the nearby land was granted in the 6th century by Bede the Mormaer of Buchan to St Columba, who in turn left it to St Drostan with the words "whosoever should come against it let him not be many years victorious". Around 580 a monastery was founded by St Drostan which was recorded as being a successful establishment in 'The Book of Deer'. St Mary's Abbey of Deer was founded in 1219 two miles away by William Comyn, Earl of Buchan, for Cistercian monks from Kinloss whose farming skills turned the wasteland into a highly productive agricultural district, a legacy which still endures today. The present ruins were built in an Early English style with a cruciform church, but the rest of the Abbey was once regarded as being an inelegant structure. Although pillaged by Robert the Bruce, the Competitor for the Crown, after the Abbots' support for Edward I and his vassal John Comyn it was granted full restoration after Bruce became the King in 1306. Its decline in the 16th century when its dwindling number of monks came under the Temporal Lordship of its last Abbot Robert Keith (2nd son of 4th Earl Marischal) was seen as the beginning of Columba's prophecy, which was fulfilled when the Keith's castle of Dunnottar was dismantled in 1720. Attempts at restoration by the Ferguson family in the 19th century were continued by the new owners the Aberdeen Diocese of the Catholic Church, and so today's ruins include the outline of the church and parts of the domestic quarters.

DINGWALL
HIGHLAND

Town situated 10 miles NE of Beauly. Name derived from the Old Norse 'thing' 'vollr' meaning 'meeting field of the thing' (assembly). The original Norse settlement was followed by a 12th century castle which has now vanished. Benefiting from trade around the Cromarty Firth, it was created a Royal Burgh by Alexander II in 1226 and in the 14th century the land passed to the Earls of Ross, after whose forfeiture in 1476 the town declined in standing. Returning to its status as a mere burgh in 1497, Dingwall failed to prosper in succeeding centuries and in 1724 sent a petition to the Convention of Burghs appealing for investment. The High St Town House (museum) and the Tolbooth date from the 17th century and are fronted by the original Mercat Cross. Created a Police Burgh in 1862 with the Dingwall to Sky Railway line started in 1864. Although eclipsed by Alness as Ross-shire's largest burgh, it retains its position as the county's major market and service centre, while also hosting the offices of the North of Scotland Hydro Electric Board: a project that has affected the town in various ways over the years. See Castle

DINGWALL CASTLE
HIGHLAND

The fragmentary remains sited on ground 14 miles NW of Inverness belong to the age-old seat of the Earls of Ross (Earldom forfeited 1746). These passed to Alexander, Lord of the Isles, before reverting to the Crown, and by 1481 the land was held by James Stewart, the second son of James III. In former times it would have been strongly defended with ditches and moats owing to its proximity to the Cromarty Firth.

DIRLETON CASTLE
EAST LOTHIAN

Situated in Dirleton Village 3 miles NW of North Berwick is a coastal fortification which was started by the Norman De Vaux family as a 13th century enclosure with towers. In 1298 Edward I's invasion force was harassed by Scots from Dirleton, resulting in a siege and its surrender to Bishop Anthony Beck (Bishop of Durham), who partly demolished it. By 1350 the castle and lands had passed to the Halyburton family, from whom they were seized by William Earl of Douglas, in 1363 as an act of defiance against David II. Dirleton started to look like something resembling today's structure

when the eastern ranges and the south wall entrance were built in the 15th century, followed by the construction of the northern court with adjoining towers that was inspected by James IV in 1505. The estate passed to Lord Ruthven in 1506, who added a mansion, and whose descendant became the Earl of Gowrie. In 1600 the castle and lands were used by the 3rd Earl to bribe Logan of Restalrig into assassinating the King, who subsequently forfeited the Earl and granted the estate to Thomas Erskine, created Lord Dirleton in 1603 after saving the King from the Gowrie conspirators. In 1631 the property was held by Sir James Maxwell. Dirleton last saw conflict when in 1650 its Moss troopers surrendered to Cromwell's 1600-man force under Major General Lambert and Colonel Monck, who destroyed much of the structure leaving it like the ruin we see today. A mansion was later built nearby but is also ruinous.

DIRLETON CASTLE GOLF CLUB
EAST LOTHIAN

Taking its name from the castle and village, the club has strong ties with Gullane Golf Club since it was founded in 1854 during a meeting in the Golf Tavern. Indeed up until 1982 all prospective members were required to belong to Dirleton Parish. The six members at the inaugural meeting resolved to adopt the rules of Tantallon Golf Club but it was the landlord of the Golf Tavern George Stevens who as first secretary of the club enforced the rules, with a professionalism that got the club of to a good start. The fact that the meeting was convened in the tavern suggests that golf was already played on Gullan common land, as an association of farmers had already formed the East Lothian Golf Club. Having previously played on rough grazing land, the club's main concern was to improve and remodel the 13 hole course by removing the holes at the church gate, the table hole and the barn door. This led to the first hole being replaced near the smiddy, the second at the rabbit burrow and the third at the head of the pond, with additional holes being bored next to the race course. In 1882 responsibility for the course's maintenance was taken over by Gullan Golf Club, situated in the nearby village where 90% of Dirleton's members now reside, but up until 1982 all members of the latter had to live within Dirleton Parish. Among the clubs trophies "The Patron's Medal" donated by Mr John Grant in 1854 is the most prestigious while the Derby Cup is played for during the main inter-club matches.

DIRLOT TOWER
HIGHLAND

The ruins of this 14th century tower by the River Thurso, 15 miles S of Thurso town, were probably built by the powerful Donald de Cheyne, whose family had considerable influence in the area in the 13th century. In 1464 it was the property of George Gunn, a Crown representative and head of Clan Gunn, but was later held by a bold and daring freebooter named Sutherland.

DOLLAR
CLACKMANNAN

A rural town situated 16 miles NE of Stirling at the foot of the Ochil hills. Name derived from the Gaelic 'dail' and 'ar' meaning 'meadow ploughed land'. Once famous for Castle Campbell, a 15th century tower house in Dollar Glen, latterly the town grew in importance with Dollar Academy school, designed by William Playfair in 1819 with an endowment from John Macnab, a local shepherd who made good as a sea Captain. The original Grecian edifice with portico dome, upborne by fluted columns was extended periodically to accommodate the growing numbers of pupils, which totalled over 500 by 1882. By 1961, when the building was restored, it still ranked as one of Scotland's leading schools. See Golf Club

DOLLAR GOLF CLUB
CLACKMANNAN

Situated near the town. Since its founding in 1890 the club has been proud of its status as the oldest club in the Hillfoots. The original course consisted of nine holes and was laid out in Market Park, but in 1898 this was inherited by the ladies when the men established a new course on ground between Mill Green and Gloom Hill, which later became known as Jack's Park after the local landlord. In 1906, after a disagreement over rent, the club moved to the present site at Brewlands when Ben Sayers was engaged to complete the construction and design of the club. Dollar quickly established some status in the early part of the century by attracting figures like Ray, Varden and Duncan, but despite the rise of grander courses and its appeal slipping in succeeding decades, it still held an allure for those prepared for a stiff test challenge. It was the first 18 hole golf course in the county and the oldest club in Clackmannan-shire. One of the more memorable chapters in its history was played out when the caddies, imbued with trade union principles, went on strike for an increase from sixpence to ninepence, 1908. This was around two years before the opening of the present course, which has served to attract visitors ever since. The clubhouse, which is located within Dollar itself, is an impressive sandstone building at the top of west Burnside, and it was here that the centenary celebrations were held in 1990 which attracted some sporting celebrities.

DORNOCH
HIGHLAND

Coastal town situated on the Dornoch Firth NE of Tain. The name probably derived from the Gaelic 'dornach' meaning 'fist pebble place'. Once the site of an early settlement which was overrun by Norsemen, it was the likely site of a Culdee Cell by the 11th century and as such developed as an ecclesiastical community. That was firmly established by the building of Dornoch/Caithness Cathedral in 1224-45 by Bishop Gilbert de Moravia; this was burnt in 1570 by the Mackay Clan of Strathnaver, along with the adjacent Bishop's Palace and the rest of the town. The granting by Charles I of Royal Burgh status in 1628 with all its trading privileges probably had more to do with its Cathedral as an anchor of stability in the unruly north than the area's best natural resource, its stone (Caithness stone), for which it became famous after the development of its large freestone quarry. Retaining the charm and dignity befitting its long history, after its Cathedral in order of importance comes the 16th century Bishop's Palace, the Court House and the old Town Jail, which is now a museum. A silent witness to the Sutherland Clearances of 1807-21, the town's rise as a popular holiday destination was furthered by its fresh air, good sandy beaches and its long golfing tradition, which dates from 1616. Along with other towns, Dornoch claims to have burnt the last Scottish witch. In 1722, a Janet Horne, alleged to have transformed her daughter into a pony and had her shod by the Devil, was burnt in the market square on the site now marked by a stone. After the loss of its Royal Burgh status and its Town Council in 1975, most of the public services were run by the Highland Regional Council based in Inverness. See Cathedral

DORNOCH CATHEDRAL
HIGHLAND

The See of Caithness was founded by David I at Dornoch around 1150 on the site of an earlier Celtic foundation. Between 1224 and 1245 it was developed from a church dedicated to St Bar or Finbar by Bishop Gilbert de Moravia into the Cathedral of the Virgin Mary (later St Gilberts), which was burnt in 1570 by the Mackays of Strathnaver and damaged in a gale in 1605, so consequently the tower is all that remains from this period. Partially repaired in 1616 by the 13th Earl of Sutherland and used as a church. Between 1835-37 it was rebuilt in a Gothic style by William Burn at the behest of the Duchess of Sutherland, whose family burial vault it still houses. In 1924 the Cathedral was restored and continued to be used as a Parish Church. On the opposite side of the structure stands the Bishop's Palace, which was burnt in 1570, redeveloped in 1813 and used as a Court House but now functions as a hotel. See Town

DOUGLAS
SOUTH LANARKSHIRE

Town situated on the Douglas Water 9 miles NW of Abington. In the 12th century the lands were granted by Kelso Abbey to the Douglases, whose castle (now gone), was the key to the Western Counties during offensive and defensive actions, and gave the town its political importance. Named Castle Danger by the English it was taken and retaken over the years until the family's forfeiture in 1455, and became a Burgh of Barony for the Earl of Angus in 1458. Once a prebend (an allowance given by the bishop to an acting minister) of Glasgow Cathedral, St Bride's 12th century church (ruin) houses the Douglas Mausoleum where Sir James Douglas, who attempted to take Bruce's heart to the Holy Land in 1330, is interred. The Douglases death at the hands of the Moors and the caskets return along with the Earl's body was remembered in verse:

And Scotland, thou may'st veil thy head
In sorrow and in pain:
The sorest stroke upon thy brow
Hath fallen this day in Spain!
We'll bear them back unto our ship,
We'll bear them o'er the sea,
And lay them in the hallowed earth,
Within our own countrie.

Damaged during Cromwell's occupation, it was abandoned as a place of worship in 1780 but the chancel was magnificently restored in 1880 by Lord Home and now includes effigies of the good Sir James. However, more striking is that of Lady Lucy Elizabeth Douglas, whose effigy, carved of Alabaster and black marble, lies in the centre. Crowned with a tower and clock presented by Mary Queen of Scots in 1565, the chapel also houses in caskets the hearts of Sir James and of Archibald, Earl of Angus (Bell the Cat), along with Ist and 2nd World War memorials to the Lanarkshire Yeomanry. In 1689 the area provided shelter for Covenanters until their extirpation by a force led by the Douglases. After his visit of 1832, Sir Walter Scott included its castle in his 'Castle Dangerous' (pub. 1832). Built by Robert Adam in 1757 on the site of the earlier castle that was destroyed in 1755, Adam's castle was itself demolished when it was undermined by a coal seam in 1937.

DOUNE
STIRLING

An old Market Town situated 9 miles NW of Stirling. The name is derived from the Gaelic 'dun', meaning 'hillfort', owing to the Roman Fort that was once part of their northern supply line, and was probably preceded by an earlier defensive structure. The two-arched bridge over the River Teith was built in 1535 (widened 1866) by Robert Spittal (tailor to James IV) to spite the ferryman who had previously refused him passage because he lacked the money. Through the centuries Doune thrived as a town catering for soldiers, drovers and travellers from in and around the Central Highlands, who were drawn to its popular cattle fairs and its manufacture of pistols. And by the 19th century the town was greatly benefitting from the cotton mill at Deanston which provided work for up to 1,000 people. The Doune Motor Museum, which started as a hobby of the Earl of Moray, now houses a wide range of classic vintage cars. See Castle

DOUNE CASTLE
STIRLING

Positioned between the Rivers Teith and Ardoch near Doune town. The site of an early hill settlement, it later became the seat of the Earls of Menteith, though it was Robert, Ist Duke of Albany, who started the present structure. Developed into a courtyard keep by his son Murdoch when Regent of Scotland (1419-24), during James I's captivity. On the King's return, when Albany was beheaded nearby Doune became Crown property and functioned as a dower-house for successive queens like Mary of Guelders, 1451, and Margaret of Denmark, 1471, while James IV, a frequent visitor, bestowed it on his Queen, Margaret of England, in 1503. It later became the property of James Stewart, who became Lord Doune in 1581. His ill-fated descendant the Earl of Moray, who resided here before his murder in 1592, is referred to in this ballad, along with his yearning widow:

O lang, lang will his lady
Look ower the Castle Doune

Ere she see the Earl O' Moray
come sounding through the town.

With walls 10 ft thick and a 15th century square tower, with its round staircase the distinctive feature, it was used as a political prison and continued its associations with the Stewarts, for it was sometimes visited by Queen Mary in the 16th century and in 1745 was held for Prince Charles Edward by Rob Roy's nephew, Macgregor of Glengyle.

DOUNREAY
HIGHLAND

Originally a village situated 12 miles W of Thurso. The name is thought to derive from the Gaelic 'dun' meaning 'hillfort' and 'Urray' after a Pictish chieftain. The claim is borne out by the traces of Pictish Forts in the area and the accidental discovery in 1751 of the original village with its Mercat Cross that now stands in the town centre. In 1626 James VI erected it into a Burgh of Barony for Donald Mackay Ist Lord Reay. Ironically the town's isolation near the northern tip of Scotland meant it remained relatively obscure until the industrial age, when its harbour, built by a Major Innes in 1833, facilitated the export of the areas sandstone and limestone. But in the 20th century its position and its geology brought it notoriety when in 1969 it became the site of The UK Atomic Energy Authority's controversial fast breeder nuclear reactor. Its workforce who were housed in the nearby town of Thurso were known locally as the Atomics.

DROCHIL CASTLE
SCOTTISH BORDERS

Overlooking the Tweed 7 miles WNW of Peebles is a 16th century Z plan castle with diagonally opposite towers. Designed as a palace more than a defensive structure around 1581, for James Douglas

Earl of Morton (Regent of Scotland), whose pleasure was short-lived due to his involvement in the Darnley murder in 1567. In the name of James VI (Darnley's son), he was executed by the Maiden (guillotine) at Edinburgh Cross in 1581.

DRUMCLOG, BATTLE OF, 1679
SOUTH LANARKSHIRE

SW of Strathaven. Subsequent to the assassination of Archbishop Sharp by the Covenanters on Magus Moor during their extirpation by John Graham of Claverhouse (bloody Claverse) in the west, his men advanced against a Conventicle meeting held by Balfour of Burleigh accused of Sharp's murder. Having lost the element of surprise due to superior numbers, and due to the marshy ground, Claverhouse's dragoons were unable to charge, affording the Covenanters a short-lived victory. This bolstered their belief in providence and the justness of their cause.

DRUMCOLTRAN TOWER
DUMFRIES & GALLOWAY

Located 14 miles SW of Dumfries. An L plan tower, it was built by Sir John Maxwell in 1550 after he married Lady Agnes, the Drumcoltran heiress whose family had held the land since 1368. It was held by the Irvings, Hynds, and Herons successively from 1668 until 1875 when it reverted to Maxwell ownership.

DRUMELZIER CASTLE
SCOTTISH BORDERS

This ruined L plan tower stands near the Tweed, 4 miles SW of Broughton. In the 14th century the land passed through marriage from the Frasers to the Tweedies, who built the tower in the 16th century before it passed through indebtedness to John, Lord Hay of Yester later Ist Earl of Tweeddale.

DRUMLANRIG CASTLE
DUMFRIES & GALLOWAY

The castle commands a fine view down the Vale of Nith 17 miles NW of Dumfries. From 1356 the barony was held by the Douglases and in 1388 Sir William Douglas was created Ist Baron of Drumlanrig. His 11th descendant, the celebrated Ist Duke of Queensberry and Earl of Drumlanrig in 1684, built this quadrangular courtyard mansion on the site of an older castle between 1676 and 1689 after retiring from public life. The Renaissance arcade, with its groined and ribbed Gothic vaulting, flanks the double circular staircase that leads to the main entrance, which is centred in a neo classical facade crowned with towers and turrets. Clearly the castle's design is indicative of the more relaxed and inspired spirit of the age, which, although leaving its history somewhat uneventful has assured the cultivation of its beautiful grounds, while enabling the Dukes of Buccleuch (Queensberry descendants) to establish the castle with its artefacts as one of the most distinguished architectural gems in South West Scotland.

DRUMMINOR CASTLE
ABERDEENSHIRE

On the banks of the Kearn burn 3 miles S of Kennethmont are the remains of the former Forbeses castle built in 1456. Now incorporated into a relatively modern Baronial mansion built in 1577, six years before, this was the scene of the murder of several Gordons at a banquet given by the Forbes's, with whom the family were bitter rivals. It was sold in 1770 and left to decay until some work was carried out in the 19th century, and in the 1960s it was restored by a Mrs Margaret Forbes Sempill.

DRUMMOND CASTLE
PERTH & KINROSS

Built on a rock 3 miles from Crieff. The land was purchased by Sir John Drummond in 1487 when the original tower was built. In 1605 the family acquired the title of Earls of Perth, and shortly after, the adjoining southern keep was built. The frequent visits made by James IV and later by Queen Mary in 1566 marked the high points of its history before it was shattered by the damage wrought by Cromwell's cannons in 1651, resulting in a modern mansion being erected to the east in 1689. Though strengthened in 1715 by Royalist troops, in 1745 the Jacobite dowager Duchess caused its walls to be levelled to prevent a repetition. Partially rebuilt in 1822, it is presently renowned for its fine gardens.

DRYBURGH ABBEY
SCOTTISH BORDERS

About 5 miles SE of Melrose are the substantial ruins of the Abbey founded by Hugh de Morville in 1150. Possibly built on the site of St Modan's 6th century church, which may have been built on the site of a Druidical Temple, as some sources claim the name is from the Celtic 'durach-bruach' meaning 'bank of the grove of oaks'. It was dedicated to St Mary and developed in a Norman Gothic style for Premonstratensians from Alnwick, with generous grants from later monarchs also making it a rich prize for invading armies who despoiled its once proud church. In 1322 it was burnt by Edward II's retreating army but its subsequent restoration by Robert the Bruce fell short of its former standing. This was consistent with the disobedience of its monks, who were censured by Pope Gregory for frequent lapses in discipline during the 14th century. Future attacks by Richard II, 1385, Sir Brian Latoun, 1544, and by the Earl of Hertford in 1545 left the Abbey in a ruinous state and in 1587 the lands were annexed by James VI, who erected them into the Lordship of Cardross, 1604, for John Erskine Earl of Mar. In 1700 the ruin was purchased by Thomas Haliburton, Walter Scott's grandfather, later becoming a favourite haunt for the young novelist, whose burial here in 1832 evoked the rhyme:

So there in solemn solitude,
In that sequestered spot
Lies mingling with its kindred clay
The dust of Walter Scott !
An where is now the flashing eye
That kindled up at Flodden field,
That saw in fancy onsets fierce,
and clashing spear and shield.

Though its once proud church still retains some of the nave transepts and choir with north and south aisles of two bays, the ruins of the cloister buildings to the south east take pride of place. While the south range is one of the best of its type, the east side includes its library on the site of St Modan's Chapel and the well preserved Chapter House with its stone barrel-vaulted roof. Next to this was the warming room which was linked to the day rooms, above which were the dormitories. Of the additions that were made up to the 16th century most are 12th and 13th century.

DRYHOPE TOWER
SCOTTISH BORDERS

Situated near the S end of St Mary's Loch 16 miles SW of Selkirk. The Scott's earlier oblong tower that was the birthplace of Mary Scott, 1550 (The Flower of Yarrow) was partly demolished in 1592 after its owner Walter Scott of Harden (bastard son of James V) was party to the attempted assassination of James VI at Falkland Palace. Today's structure is the result of the rebuilding work of the 17th century.

DUART CASTLE
ARGYLL & BUTE

At the eastern entrance to the Sound of Mull is the long-standing stronghold of the Macleans. The site was first occupied by a defensive structure in order to repel incursions by Norsemen from their base on the Isle of Man, but in 1366 Duart was started by Lachlan Maclean after marrying Lady Margaret, daughter of the Lord of the Isles. First recorded in 1390, its prominent oblong keep dates from the 14th century and was often the scene of feuds between the Macdonalds and the Macleans. Lachlan Maclean of Duart exposed his wife on a tide-swept islet (Lady's Rock) in 1523 until she was rescued by a passing boat. Added to in the 16th century, its strategic importance during James IV's attempts to subdue the Macdonald Lords of the Isles eventually resulted in its surrender in 1608 by Hector Maclean, who promised to give it up for use by the Crown whenever required. His son, also Lachlan, who attended court in 1631, was created a Nova Scotia Baronet and built the mansion at the north range before dying here in 1669. In the 17th century the estate passed to the Argyll family but in the 19th century was reacquired by the Macleans and restored.

DUCHAL TOWER
EAST AYRSHIRE

About 2 miles SW of Kilmarnock are the ruins of a late 13th century keep. The land belonged to the Lyle family from the 13th century for whom it was erected into a Lordship in 1446. The property later passed to the Porterfield family in 1544 who held it for 300 years.

DUCHRAY CASTLE
STIRLING

The land on which the castle stands by the Duchray water, 3 miles SW of Aberfoyle was purchased by John Graham of

Downance in 1569 from John Drummond. Essentially a tower with round turrets, it was built around 1600 by William Downance whose family were cadets of the Earls of Menteith. In 1653 the castle was the rendezvous point for the Royalist force under the Earl of Glencairn and in the subsequent victory over Cromwell's forces near Aberfoyle, the Laird Graham of Duchray's foot bore the brunt of the battle. For this and for subsequent acts of bravery James VII acknowledged his services in 1685. The tower was still held by a Graham in 1875.

DUDHOPE HOUSE
DUNDEE CITY

Overlooking Dundee are the remains of the Scrymgeours' castellated mansion. In 1298 the land and the hereditary office of Constable was granted by William Wallace to his lieutenant Alexander Scrymgeour, after he aided the successful ejection of the English from Stirling Castle. The present quadrangle, started by 1600 on the central courtyard plan, is four storeys high with three round corner towers and an arched gateway. In 1641 a knighthood was bestowed by Charles I on Sir James Scrymgeour, who also elevated the tower and fortalice to the principal Messuage (Manor House), and as such it was visited by Charles II in 1650 after his defeat by Cromwell at Dunbar. Further additions were made in the 17th century and it was converted into a Woollen Mill in the 18th century, before being adapted for use as a barracks in the 19th century when much of the interior was altered.

DUFFTOWN DISTILLERY
MORAY

Taking its name from its home town and the whisky capital of the north. It began as a sawmill and mealmill that were converted in 1896 by Peter Mackenzie,

Richard Stackpole, and John Symon, founders of the Dufftown Glenlivit Distillery Co Ltd. Drawing its water from Highlandman Jock's Well in the Conval Hills, the partners received generous approval from local farmers, merchants and Inn keepers and order books quickly filled. In 1898, on Mackenzie's move to Edinburgh, the company changed to P. Mackenzie & Co Distillers Ltd, which was eventually run by Mackenzie's son John and a new partner, the grain merchant and wines & spirit broker George Stoddart, who had replaced Symon and Stackpole on the board. Its jealously guarded water supply was frequently redirected in the dead of night by the neighbours, landowners and distillers until a mutual agreement was reached. However, misfortune was to overcome Mackenzie, when, after establishing it as successful blenders in the United States, the company failed to recover from the Prohibition law of 1920-33, forcing the sale of P. Mackenzie, including Dufftown-Glenlivit and Blair Atholl distilleries, to Arthur Bell for just £56,000. The return to full production (1934-41) was interrupted by the war but resumed in 1947 and continued throughout its expansion in 1968, producing 3,000,000 litres of alcohol throughout the 1970s, and enjoyed a further increase with new stills, mash tun and malt mill. In 1985 Arthur Bell's was acquired by Guiness Plc.

OWNERS
Diageo plc ?

REGION
Speyside

PRODUCT
Dufftown 15 year old single malt 43% vol

NOTES
Light, with a medium nose with a sweet slightly fruity taste.

DUFFUS
MORAY

Village situated 7 miles W of Elgin. Its name probably derived from the Gaelic 'dubh' and 'uisg' meaning 'dark water', a reference to Loch Spynie (now drained). The former fortification to the west of Duffus on Burghhead once marked on a Roman map in 86 AD and later occupied by the Picts, is one of the area's earliest settlements. This is interwoven with the history of the land, which was held by the De Moravia family before being granted by David I to a Fleming in the 12th century, when the castle was built. Created a Lordship (1650) for a descendant, Nicholas, son of the Earl of Sutherland. Apart from its castle the main antiquity is the nearby church of St Peter (ruin) which, dating from 1226, once housed a chapel dedicated to St Peter and an altar to St Catherine. Medieval remains include the basement of a tower and a porch built by Alexander Sutherland, its Rector, in 1524. Having 900 parishioners in 1649, the old church was replaced in 1782, but much of today's village is 19th century. See Castle

DUFFUS CASTLE
MORAY

On the top of a mound 4 miles NW of Elgin are the substantial ruins of what was once a 14th century stronghold that was preceded by a more primitive fort built by a Fleming who held the land in the 12th century. Used as a residence of David I, 1150 it was built by the De Moravia family, including a tower with enceinte walls 5ft thick and with drawbridge. It later passed to the Sutherlands who bore the title of Lord Duffus. Thought to have been visited by Claverhouse in 1689, like many other places in the far north of the country, the castle's location has severely curtailed its involvement in any historical dramas of note.

DUMBARTON
WEST DUMBARTONSHIRE

Town situated 15 miles NW of Glasgow on the east bank of the River Leven. Name probably derived from the Gaelic 'Dun Breatainn' meaning 'hill' or 'fort of the Strathclyde Britons'. This had much to do with its status as Capital of the Kingdom of Strathclyde from the 5th century. After being elevated to a Free Royal Burgh by Alexander II in 1222, it received fresh charters from successive kings that were confirmed by James VI in 1609. Although boat building was the main industry here from the 15th century; Dumbarton rejected proposals by Glasgow in 1685 for harbour developments, which led to the building of Port Glasgow and to Glasgow purchasing the rights to levy dues on Clyde shipping in 1700. Following the introduction of glass manufacture by the late 18th century which had ceased by 1850 owing to cheaper imports from Austria, and despite its decline to a Sub Port by the deepening and widening of the River Clyde in 1770, it emerged in the 19th century as a centre for shipbuilding. Its oldest yards, Archibald Macmillan's and William Denny's formed the nucleus of the industry. Along with the ancillary industries, these gave birth to modern Dumbarton and a revolution in shipbuilding design. this included launch of The Premier (1846) the world's second oldest steamship, The Peter Stewart , (1867) Scotland's largest iron sailing ship, the tea clipper 'The Cutty Sark' (1870) , the first steel liner at Dennys Yard in 1879 and the Hovercraft in the 20th century. See Castle & Golf Club

DUMBARTON CASTLE
WEST DUMBARTONSHIRE

Situated on Dumbarton Rock by the River Clyde. Once the site of a Roman naval station followed by a fort belonging to the Strathclyde Britons until the 8th century. It was besieged by the Vikings in the 8th and 9th centuries and was the seat of Duncan I from 1018 until 1034 when he became King of Scotland. As a strategic stronghold of Edward I it was captured by Robert the Bruce in 1309 and was later the departure point for his son David II en route to France after his defeat at Halidon Hill in 1333. Besieged by the fleet of Edward IV in 1481 and taken by James IV in 1489, it also provided a period of sanctuary for Mary I after the battle of Pinkie before her departure for France in 1548 and continued to be held for the Queen during her absence. In 1581, Esme Stewart, Duke of Lennox, was made Governor here. In the following century it was seized by the Covenanters in 1639 and garrisoned by Cromwell in 1652. The present building is mainly 18th century and was visited by Queen Victoria in 1847, when it served as a barracks which continued to function into the 20th century.

DUMBARTON GOLF CLUB
WEST DUMBARTONSHIRE

Following a holiday at Saint Andrews, the Mecca for golfers, the Sons of the Rock, W Craig, a writer, and John and Archie Denny, of shipbuilding fame, returned to their home town with a golfing fever. Before long a Provisional Committee was formed and a lease of the Broadmeadow secured, making the club a reality by June 1888. Under its first Captain, Chief Constable Charles Mcardy (1888-91), its first telephone was installed. Acquiring its first trophies, the gold and silver medals in 1889, from 1891, when the nine holes of the course were named, it was the scene of many inter-club matches as the sport's rising popularity in the town and elsewhere prompted the building of a new clubhouse (May 1891). This increasingly showed the need for the

course extension from 9 holes to 18. With the first Honorary President, Peter Denny LLD, who had been Provost of the town (1852-53), the club was assured a good hearing in its dealings with the Town Council who granted four ten year leases between 1887-1917. But it proved to be the railway companies who threatened the course up to 1892, a year before it was lengthened from 1,928 yards to 1,430 yards. Though the club had lady members from its early days, in 1911 the Ladies' Secretary requested her members be allowed to play unaccompanied on the course one evening a week, but it wasn't until 1920 that the first Ladies' Committee was formed. During the First World War the club received officers serving at Dumbarton Castle and in 1915 the course was extended with seven new greens that in 1921 became part of the full 18 hole course. The year also saw the granting to the club of the Shanghai Cup by the Marine Engineers Institute Shanghai. In 1934 the Gordon Shield was presented by a local worthy. During World War II the Scottish Command requisitioned the land for anti-aircraft guns; and the clubhouse was used to billet soldiers when it sustained damage from air raids during the Clydebank blitz. It was during this period that golf was played here on Sundays for the first time. The clubs ongoing problems with drainage and pressure from the Agricultural Committee to continue cattle grazing in the 1950s led to plans for a new course which eventually came to nothing, and in 1957 the lease was again extended. In 1961 The Ballantines Quaich 4 Ball was given by Distillers George Ballantine & Sons. As one of the oldest golf clubs in the country and for a long time one of the best in the west of Scotland, the club celebrated its centenary in 1988 by which time after six variations of the 18 hole course the final layout was possible.

DUMFRIES
DUMFRIES & GALLOWAY

Town situated 70 miles SE of Glasgow. Originally spelt Dumfres, which came from the Gaelic 'dun-phres' meaning either 'hillfort among the shrubs' or 'fort among the Frisians'. The area was once inhabited by Caledonian tribes who resisted Roman rule, but was later held by the Scots of Dalriada whose settlement gave rise to a village which sprang up around the fort on the mound in the 10th century. Eventually it became a town and Royal Burgh (1168) and a seat of justice for Galloway by 1200, with growing trade links and a population of 2,000 by 1300. During the wars of the 14th century the castle was held by Edward I prior to taking Caerlaverock, and in 1306 its Greyfriars Friary was as a consequence of his treachery, the scene of the murder of Red Comyn by Robert the Bruce, prior to his crowning at Scone. In Sir Walter Scott's 'Marmion' the Bruce's justification did somewhat vindicate him:

"Abbot ! " The Bruce replied, "thy charge
This much however I bid ye know,
No selfish vengance dealt the blow,
For Comyn died his country's foe
Nor blame I friends whose ill-timed speed
Fulfilled my soon-repented deed"

The towns closeness to the border brought Edward II here to receive homage from the Scottish Lords, and led to its burning by an English force in 1488 and 1536, which continued to leave it vulnerable until Mary Queen of Scots ratified a peace treaty here in 1563. Despite being destroyed again in 1570, this time by the Earl of Sussex, the burgh had recovered enough by 1617 to receive James VI, and continued to witness the fluctuating fortunes of the Stewarts. In the 1745 Rising, from his headquarters in the County Hotel, Prince Charles Edward penalised the town for £2,000 and 1,000 pairs of shoes before leading his army south. In 1633 it was erected into an Earldom for the 7th Baron Crichton of Sanquhar. Depicting a winged figure of St Michael with staff trampling on a dragon, the town's armorial bearings include the motto 'A loreburn', a war cry which comes from the gathering point at the Lower Burn. The cattle fair which started on the sands in 1659 and once sold over 20,000 head annually had declined by 1865 with the coming of the railway, when the town's mainstay became the hosiery trade started by R Scott & Son in 1816. Industrially, from Mckinnels Foundry around 1900, The North British Motor Manufacturing Co was formed, which produced 125 Drummond Cars between 1905 and 1908. The firm was replaced by Arrol-Johnston (1911) whose production of the prestigious Arrol Astor car employed up to 500 men before 1914. Later merging with Astor Engineering Co, making Arrol Astor stationery engines, the legacy left by the firm's closure in 1931 was applied to farm machinery. The Burns statue on the High Street is a reminder of the visits made by the poet between 1791 and 96, when he frequented the nearby Globe Tavern and occupied the house to the south where he died. St Michael's 18th century church witnessed the simple burial service of the bard who was later interred in a purpose-built mausoleum. Near the remains of an Iron Age fort is the Burgh Museum which was designed like a windmill with a Camera Obscura and opened in 1836.

DUNAVERTY GOLF CLUB
ARGYLL & BUTE

During a meeting at the Argyll Arms Hotel, Campbeltown, in 1889, ten men undertook to found the Dunaverty Golf Club. Among them was the Duke of Argyll's Chamberlain and the local Minister, while its first President was Lord Lorne the Duke's heir, after whom the Lorne Medal is named. After recruiting the Machrihanish Golfers to help with the course, a committee of managers was formed and in the first year the club boasted 42 members who convened at the Argyll Arms before and after any game until the clubhouse was built in 1893. As early as 1897 the club bosted the inclusion of lady members. One of Dunaverty's early champions and personalities in 1898 was Jimmy Lyon whose relish for liquor often moved him to boast "when I'm sober I can see the hole like a flower pot. Give me two drams and I can see it like a bucket." His name was later used jointly in the Macallan Lyon Trophy. According to some sources the members were offered the land by the Duke of Argyll for £100˙00 in 1912, which had it been accepted would have prevented the acrimony in later years over rent of the site. Dunaverty experienced the usual shortages during the Great War 1914-18. After the return to normality in 1922, the Glasgow engineer Charles Mcneil presented the Mcneil Cup, and in the following year the committee named the course's 18 holes. The Mcneil Cup was added to with the Amod Mcneil Quaich by the latter's father in 1924, the year the ladies' section was formed, giving urgency to the building of a new clubhouse in 1925. The club's continued popularity brought about the building of a new course in 1935 which, particularly on the Machribeg side, was remodelled and compressed into its present shape after World War II, (1945). The course was measured in 1965 by the Scottish Golf Union and given the standard scratch score of 63, but in 1973 was extended 787 yards to its present length of 4597 yards. One of the club's more distinguished ladies is Bella McCorkindale, who was runner-up in the Ladies British Open and in 1981 at last won the British Championship.

DUNBAR
EAST LOTHIAN

Coastal town situated 26 miles SE of Edinburgh. Name derived from the Gaelic 'dun-bar' meaning either 'fort on the height' or 'fort on the point'. The fort around which the town grew was burnt by Kenneth I in 856, and became the seat of the Northumbrian Prince Gospatrick in 1072, and castle of the Earls of Dunbar in the 12th century. A strategic prize for defensive and offensive campaigns down through the centuries, as in 1296 when Edward I defeated the Scots here. After the Countess of Dunbar (Black Agnes) successfully repelled an assault by the Earl of Salisbury in 1339, apart from its occupation by French troops between 1516 and 1537, the castle remained in Scottish hands up until its destruction by an Act of Parliament in 1567 (now a fragmentary ruin). Its important position both geographically and historically moved Sir Walter Scott to describe the construction and strength of its storm-batterd seaward side in 'Marmion':

That the wild clamour and affray of those dead artisans of hell,
Who laboured under Hugo's spell,
Sounded as loud as the ocean's war,
Among the caverns of Dunbar

The town was created a Burgh of Barony by David II (1379-71), who granted it, with a Free Port at Belhaven, to the Earl of March in 1370. Despite its elevation to a Royal Burgh by James II (1445), and its subsequent rise in importance, frequent attacks from England hampered the burgh's growth, which did not get under way until the 18th century. Burnt by the Earl of Hertford in 1544 and by German mercenaries under the Earl of Shrewsbury in 1548, the town also suffered at the hands of Cromwell (1650), who, after defeating the Scots here, stole its ships and damaged its harbour, crippling its trade. Other than as the point of arrival of General Sir John Cope before the battle of Prestonpans, 1745, a visit to its coast by the American pirate John Paul Jones, 1779, and its status as a garrison town during the Napoleonic Wars, Dunbar's history is concerned with trade. As headquarters of the Fall family, Scotland's premier merchants, it became an important market for wheat, timber and fat stock, with trade links to Baltic Ports. A Sub Port of Leith by 1842, the construction of its harbour in 1844, covering five acres, aided its flourishing fishing industry and a prolific trade in potatoes with London from 1850. But after the contraction of both by 1914, Dunbar's pre-eminence was as a district centre and sea-side resort on the east coast route from Edinburgh to London. Although the site of a Collegiate Church in 1342, the present Gothic church, by Gillespie Graham with its large tower, often served as a landmark to mariners. At the north end of the High Street stands the 17th century town House and former Tolbooth of 1620, near Robert Adam's Lauderdale House. Dunbar was also the birthplace of John Muir (1839-1914) who helped develop the American National Parks; an example of his work is located nearby. See Battles

DUNBAR, BATTLE OF, 1296
EAST LOTHIAN

Taking its name from the town, it was fought during the Wars of Independence when the English under Edward I responded to a Scottish assault by advancing from Berwick. The main objective of his army under John de Warenne, Earl of Surrey was to bring into line the King's vassal John Balliol, who had renounced his fealty and whose noble's the Earls of Buchan, Mar and Lennox had occupied Dunbar with a large army. The premature advance of the Scots from their superior positions and the disorder which followed brought about their defeat by the

Earl and his 12,000 men along with the taking of the castle and town. This paved the way for the seizure of Scotland's main strongholds, Edinburgh and Stirling.

DUNBAR, BATTLE OF, 1650
EAST LOTHIAN

This was one of the many battles fought by the Scots in support of Charles II, compelling Oliver Cromwell and General Monck with around 16,000 men to confront 23,000 Scots under General David Leslie. The prelude to attack by the Scots involved a descent from the hillside, giving Cromwell the opportunity to seize the offensive, which ended in defeat for General Leslie, 10,000 taken prisoner and 3,000 slain. The consequence of this was to facilitate the advance of Cromwell's Protectorate to the north and contributed to the King's exile to the Continent.

DUNBEATH CASTLE
HIGHLAND

Its position on a cliff 1 mile S of Dunbeath village has long been the site of a defensive structure which was probably built to repel attacks from the Danes. The present Baronial fortalice, started by the Sinclairs around 1630, was captured by General Hurry for Montrose in 1650. In the 19th century it was incorporated into a mansion.

DUNBLANE
STIRLING

Town situated 6 miles NW of Stirling. Name derived from the Gaelic 'dun' meaning 'hillfort' while Blane is from St Blane. Therefore 'hill of Blane'. An ancient landmark, Dunblane was burnt by Kenneth Macalpine, 844-60, and later by the Britons and Danish pirates. In 1150 its bishopric was established by David I when its Cathedral was founded on the site of St Blane's 6th century church. As an Episcopal See it was made a Burgh by the 14th century, and a Burgh of Barony for the Earl of Kinnoull, before declining along with its Cathedral after the Reformation. In 1712, a Peregrine Osborne was created Viscount Dunblane. No stranger to the Jacobite cause the outskirts of the town was where the Duke of Argyll's forces encamped in 1715 prior to their inconclusive engagement with the Earl of Mar's forces at nearby Sheriffmuir, and in 1745 the town was visited by Prince Charles Edward. Notwithstanding a visit from Queen Victoria in 1844 and its subsequent status as a Victorian tourist destination it failed to rival Bridge of Allan as a Hydropathic centre. The town's rural economy also benefited from wool production, notably from the Springbank Mills founded in 1857 by the Wilson family, and the cotton mill at Ashfield built by Robert Pullar & Sons in 1865. See Cathedral

DUNBLANE CATHEDRAL
STIRLING

The site of a church from the 6th century, the bishopric founded by David I in 1150 had one of its earliest prelates, Bishop Maurice bring it into the centre of Scottish affairs when he served as Bruce's Chaplain at Bannockburn, 1314. The lower part of the tower is all that remains of King David's Norman Cathedral. Despite being strongly connected and endowed by the Earls of Strathearn and its Bishop Ochiltree crowning the young James II at Holyrood Abbey in 1437 its remoteness and size left its history limited and its maintenance neglected. Remaining vacant for over a century, its 13th century nave was built by Bishop Clement but most of the original Gothic structure was destroyed by the Reformers and thereafter the roofless nave was used as a Parish Church. During this time the building frequently lost many of its fit-

tings, fixtures and its books up until the restoration work began in 1873. The Leighton Library, which contained 1400 volumes but is now enlarged was bequeathed by Bishop Leighton for use by the church after his transfer to the Glasgow Archbishopric in 1671 ?. Though finally regaining its former Gothic splendour in 1893 when its nave was restored by Rowand Anderson, the Cathedral forms a blend of beauty and simplicity, with its west door's deep mouldings in a Second Pointed style and the west widow distinct features. More substantial are the square tower, and aisle-less choir, with Chapter House and Lady Chapel to the north. In 1914 its choir was restored by Robert Lorimer. These features are further enriched by the effigies of its bishops and members of the Strathearn family. See Town

DUNDARVE CASTLE
ARGYLL & BUTE

Occupying land on the shore of Loch Fyne 5 miles NE of Inveraray is the Macnoughtons' 16th century L plan tower house. Inscribed above the doorway is the date 1596 and the admonition " Behold the end: be not wiser than the highest " with the family motto "I hope in God ". As one of the few well preserved castles in the West Highlands, it is a good example of the 16th-century style practised in these parts.

DUNDAS TOWER
CITY OF EDINBURGH

On Dundas Hill 8 miles W of Edinburgh centre stands an L plan fortalice with later additions built in 1416 by the Dundas family, who held the seat here from the 12th century. In 1424 a wing was added by James Dundas. After sustaining a siege in 1449, later generations of the family made some additions in the 16th and 17th centuries. Then in 1623 Sir

Walter Dundas erected a sundial and fountain that must have been seen by Cromwell, who was here in 1651. Though fitted out as a distillery in the early 19th century, in 1875 it was purchased by the trustees of the late James Russell and now stands beside a mansion house.

DUNDEE
DUNDEE CITY

City situated on a hill on the north bank of the Tay, 22 miles NE of Perth. The name either derived from the Gaelic 'dun' and probably 'deagh' meaning 'fort of the fire', or perhaps from the Latin 'Don-dei' meaning 'hill of God'. The site of a Stone Age settlement, due to the security it offered and the ready access to water. This undoubtedly made it just as important during the Roman occupation and it was the scene of much strife after their departure. Here in 834 the Scottish King Kenneth Macalpine is said to have based himself here prior to being defeated by King Brude of the Picts on Dundee Law, and in the 11th century Malcolm II concentrated his forces here before his victory over the Danes at Barrie. Elevated to a Burgh by William I in 1190, and a Royal Burgh by 1195, its rapid growth made it one of the most important burghs in the Kingdom by 1200. The churches of St Mary, St Clement's and St Paul's are adjoined by a tower on the site of a chapel built by the Earl of Huntingdon (1169-1200), and later burnt by Edward I in 1291, 1296, and 1303. Owing to Dundee's position as a significant supply point on Scotland's eastern seaboard, in 1297 the town was besieged by William Wallace, who demolished its castle, and it was later the scene of the Great Council Meeting at Greyfriar's Monastery when Robert the Bruce was acknowledged as King (1307). He subsequently ordered the castle's rebuilding and visited it in 1314, but it was again burnt along with the

town during Richard II's invasion in 1385. St Mary's Church, although burnt repeatedly over the centuries, it still retains its 15th century steeple. It also bore witness to affairs of church and state during the six day visit in 1528 of James V and his Queen, when they were lavishly entertained by numerous prelates, nobles, and gentlemen. It was during the reign of Jame's daughter Mary, while under the ministry of George Wishart, Dundee was the first town in Scotland to receive the broad doctrines of the Reformation. During later conflicts, its strategic coastal position continued to provide a convenient supply port during military campaigns and as such was fortified for Henry VIII after the battle of Pinkie, 1547, occupied by Montrose in 1645, taken and burnt by Cromwell, 1651, and in 1715 was visited by the Old Pretender, whose son Prince Charles Edward occupied it during the Jacobite Rebellion. One of its more distinguished sons was the soldier John Graham of Claverhouse (Bonnie Dundee) (1648-89), who became Viscount Dundee in 1688 before his victory and death at the battle of Killiecrankie. Like many parts of Scotland, the city's industrial era was ushered in with the construction of the railways like The Dundee Newtyle Railway line (10 miles), 1831, and the Tay Railway Bridge in 1844. This occasioned a visit to the city by Queen Victoria and U.S General Grant, along with lesser vips after the opening ceremony. With its growing industrial base, Dundee earned a reputation for the construction of whaling ships and the manufacture of jute. These led to a population explosion and the Improvements Act of 1871 which helped restore and improve its roads, harbours, domestic, commercial and civic buildings (designed with the foresight that was sadly lacking in the city fathers of the 1960s). Between 1871 and 1881 around 160 ships were launched here with an average tonnage of 13,000 tons. Known in the popular imagination as a centre for jute, jam and journalism by the 20th century, latterly, despite witnessing the usual urban decline associated with heavy industry and the folly of its capricious town planners, the city still manages to retain some vestiges that serve as reminders of its golden age.

DUNDONALD CASTLE
SOUTH AYRSHIRE

About 5 miles SE of Irvine is a 14th-century tower that was probably built by Robert II on the site of a previous structure. A favourite residence of Robert II and Robert III, in 1390 the former died here. It became the property of Sir William Cochrane (1639), who was created Baron in 1647 and Earl in 1669 but as a result of stone pillaging it gradually declined into the ruin we see today.

DUNDRENNAN ABBEY
DUMFRIES & GALLOWAY

On the banks of a burn 5 miles ESE of Kirkcudbright are the substantial ruins of the Abbey founded in 1142 by David I for Fergus Lord of Galloway. Built in a Norman and Early English style for Cistercian monks from Rievaulx in Yorkshire, with endowments from David I the monks became industrious farmers whose enterprise gave birth to the village to the SE. Possibly owing to the grants of trading rights from Henry III in 1223, the monks swore fealty to Edward I in 1296 but reverted to the Scottish cause after being burnt and raided in 1299 and 1385. Like the civil service of the Middle Ages, its abbots often held political posts, as in 1433 when Abbot Thomas Livingstone represented the Scottish Church at the Council of Basle and advocated the deposition of Pope Eugenius IV. In a state of near collapse during the 16th century, when from 1523 it was held by the

Maxwells who were its Commendators, it was here Queen Mary spent her last night in Scotland after her defeat at Langside,1568, and before her imprisonment, trial and execution in England. In 1587 her son James VI annexed it to the Royal Chapel of Stirling and in 1606 had it erected it into a Temporal Lordship for John Murray, later Earl of Annandale. It suffered the fate of many abbeys which were pillaged for their stone by the local people while serving as a Parish Church (until 1742) but in the 19th century its total collapse was arrested by the Earl of Selkirk and in 1841 it was handed over to the Government. The present remains are of the north and south transepts of its cruciform church, along with the facade of the adjacent Chapter House facing the cloister garth. In the Abbey grounds are some interesting sculpted stones that include the gravestones of its former abbots.

DUNFERMLINE
FIFE

Town situated 5 miles NW of Inverkeithing. Its name is probably a Gaelic expression for 'fort on the hillock' or 'the castle by the winding stream'. Secured a prominent place in history due to its proximity to St Andrews, from a fort to a church which had been augmented by 1072, Dunfermline continued to grow and by the early 12th century was a Royal Burgh. Apart from its Royal Palace built after 1304 and its occupation by Richard II in 1385, much of its history up until the Reformation is concerned with its Abbey, which gave the town royal connections for over four hundred years. Created an Earldom for the Seton family in 1605, it was burnt in 1624 and later became a centre for weaving while trading in coal and linen. Encouraged by the French Revolutions of 1789 and 1830, amongst its weavers who sought political reforms were the Carnegie family, whose son Andrew Carnegie (1835-1910) went on to amass a large fortune in the U.S steel industry after immigrating in 1848 to America. There he furthered his ethical blend of hard work, a sense of humanity and civic pride before he endowed many towns and cities around the world with educational institutions. The town benefited from the Improvement Scheme of 1875 and by 1880 was the centre for table linen and had up to 20 collieries in the area while its peripheral industries included rope tan, dye and soap works along with its bleachfields, iron foundries and flour mills. After 1900 the benefits received from its native son included a library, swimming baths, a public park (Pittencrieff) and numerous public and social institutes. The completion of Rosyth Naval Dockyard by 1915 provided employment for many of its townsfolk and latterly the decline of its traditional industries was tempered by the through trade from the new Forth Road Bridge in 1964 which has helped it maintain its position as one of Fife's principal burghs. See Abbey & Golf Club

DUNFERMLINE ABBEY
FIFE

Situated in the town. The Abbey developed from the Church of the Holy Trinity founded by Queen Margaret (1069) who is buried here along with her husband Malcolm III. At one time one of the richest and largest abbeys in Scotland, the ruins of today's Norman Gothic structure were founded by David I in 1128 for Benedictine monks from Canterbury and quickly became a favoured resting place for royalty en route north. From this period the nave is all that remains. Following its burning and occupation by Edward I (1303-4) restoration work was ordered by Bruce and a palace was built that was to be strongly linked to the Stewart line

when it became the birthplace of David II, James I and Charles I, and the frequent residence of James IV and Queen Mary, followed by her son James VI. Consequently it became a prize of war which was burnt by Richard II in 1385 but was restored and enlarged in 1540. It followed the usual course of decline in the 16th century when it was damaged by the Reformers, resulting in its church being used by the local parishioners who still use it today. The Abbey's extensive property was held by Commendators until 1589 when it became the property of Ann of Denmark, Queen consort, and its other lands were eventually granted to court favourites. Owing to its eclipse of Iona as the site of the Royal Sepulture between 1093 and 1401, up to fifteen monarchs were interred here. Its cruciform church with its mainly 12th century nave includes additional side aisles, transepts choir with Lady Chapel, two western towers and a great central tower, most of which were added between the 14th and 17th centuries. Its conventional buildings were built on two levels and now comprise 13th century dormitories to the east, with 14th century dining hall in the adjacent range and parts of the refectory pend and guest house extending to the south west.

DUNFERMLINE GOLF CLUB
FIFE

Due to its ties with the ancient Burgh of Dunfermline, with its royal palace, the practice of golf at Golf Hill to the north of the town gained an ascendancy over other sports due to its popularity with James VI of Scotland and his son Charles I who were followed by the numerous royal courtiers. Its appeal declined after James VI ascended the English throne in 1603 and it wasn't until 1887, mainly due to its rising popularity in the country as a whole, that the Dunfermline Golf Club was founded. Up and running by 1889, its first trophy, the Lockart Medal; was presented by a founding member, Robert Lockart, who after moving to the United States inadvertently helped raise the game's profile after he was reported by two old ladies for practising his game playing in New York's Central Park, and arrested. In later years he, along with his friend John Reid, came to be regarded as the fathers of American golf. Owing to the condition of the course, membership had fallen by 1890 and the course was relocated at Ferryhills above North Queensferry, with its fresh air and spectacular views across the Forth. In the same year a clubhouse was erected and the Forth Rail Bridge was opened, with a new station at North Queensferry that opened up the area further. Extended to 18 holes in 1892, the club slowly established itself in the run up to World War One. During that time it served as the Royal Artillery HQ when trenches were dug and barbed wire put over the course, while the club forged strong ties with the Royal Navy Grand Fleet and the United States' Navy Sixth Battle Squadron. Reminders of this period are The Grand Fleet Cup and the US Navy Cup. Sadly, due to encroachments by the nearby quarry company with dangers from explosions, suffocation from dust and members falling into the quarry, ground was earmarked on the Estate of Torrie. For centuries this was the home of the Saxon Wardlaw Family who moved north with other Anglo-Saxon nobility after 1066. Including 150 acres and a mansion house, the 18 hole course was designed by James Braid in 1928 and was to facilitate a breed of players in the 1930s like Ian Anderson & Bill Dale, contenders for the British Open Championship, while the ladies' section received the Lady Victoria Wemyss Cup from a cousin of the late Queen Mother. The course was partly used for crop cultivation during World War II (1939-45) when it suffered bomb damage, and the clubhouse was partly used by the army. The state of the clubhouse in the post-war period forced another move in 1953, two miles to the west of the town at the Pitfirrane Estate, for centuries the home of the distinguished Halkett family of Norman descent. Since then the clubhouse and course of 18 holes has frequently been praised for its quality turf and individual characteristics, whilst helping to spawn champions like Joan Lawrence, six times Fife Champion and winner of the Scottish Championship in 1962, 1963 and 1964. The year 1970 saw the granting of the Pitfirrane Cup and the J.T. Smith Cup which are played for annually. In 1987 the club celebrated its centenary year and held a celebrity tournament which has since become an annual fixture that raises thousands of pounds for charity. At the Annual General Meeting in 1997 the granting of equal rights to ladies took the club firmly into the 20th century while preparing it for the 21st.

DUNGLASS CASTLE
ARGYLL & BUTE

Located 20 miles NW of Dumbarton. In 1480 the life rent of the lands and fortress were held by Lady Luss, whose descendant, a Humphrey Colquhoun of Luss, built a more modern house nearby before his murder at Bannachra in 1592. The castle was dismantled in 1735 when the Commissioners of Supply ordered its stone to be used for rebuilding the quay.

DUNKELD
PERTH & KINROSS

Town situated 15 miles NW of Perth on the bank of the Tay. Name derived from the Gaelic 'dun-chailleann' meaning 'fort of the Culdees' or possibly 'Caledonians'. The Culdee Church, founded by the Pictish King Constantine, became the seat of

Columban supremacy in Scotland by 824 and encouraged King Kenneth Macalpine to favour Dunkeld as joint capital with Scone in 850. Constantly in fear of attack from all directions owing to the riches of its Cathedral, an old Dunkeld litany read 'From Caterans and robbers, from wolves and wild beasts, Lord deliver us'. Notwithstanding attacks by the Danes in 865, the transference of the Primacy to Abernethy and the burning of the town in 1027, the bishopric was revived under Alexander I by 1124 with the refounded Cathedral being visited by William I in the 12th century, James V in 1529 and Queen Mary in 1564. The basis for its economy was the age old farming and forestry, in particular the Birnam Wood, where oaks were felled for King James IV's 240ft long ship 'The Great Michale' in 1511. Having a chequered history during later upheavals, it was created a Burgh of Barony for the Bishop in 1512, and spared the destruction its Cathedral suffered at the Reformation (1560), but was burnt after the battle of Killiecrankie, 1689, when 1200 Cameronians prevented the advance of 500 Jacobites, crushing the hopes of James VII's adherents. Although rebuilt it was ineffectively a Royal Burgh in 1704 under the Dukes of Atholl. Connected to the nearby village of Birnham by Telford's seven-arched bridge built in 1809, the cultivation of the forests in the surrounding area by the Duke of Atholl continued a tradition which since 1938 has involved the Forestry Commission. Covering an area of 9,000 acres, the three main forests of Craigvinean, Murthly, Strathbrann and also the Balnaguard Estate are now home to species of larch, pine, spruce, Scots fir, douglas fir, beech, oak and grey alders. Dunkeld Little Houses, built after the fire of 1689, were restored by the National Trust in the 1950s along with other town buildings. See Cathedral & Battle

DUNKELD CATHEDRAL
PERTH & KINROSS

By the river in the town stands the partly ruinous Cathedral that was originally founded in 815 by King Constantine to replace Iona as the Episcopal Capital. Refounded by Kenneth I, who in 850 housed St Columbas' relics here, it was richly endowed and was later pillaged by the Danes. On the death of Bishop Fortrenn, 865 (its first bishop), the primacy was transferred to Abernethy but was revived by Alexander I (1107-24). Started in the early 13th century in a late Norman style, today's building includes a nave which dates from 1406 and was begun by Bishop Cardney, who also built its Bishop's Palace and a massive NW tower to repel hostile neighbours. In 1450 Bishop Lauder, its major benefactor, completed the nave, started its belfry and built its Chapter House, 1457. Extensively damaged at the Reformation, its choir was re-roofed to serve as a Parish Church, which it still is today. In 1689 the Cathedral witnessed the celebration of prayers after the Cameronian Regiment, along with the townsfolk, held out against 500 Highlanders flush with victory after the battle of Killiecrankie. Its restoration by 1815 by the Duke of Atholl gave its parishioners the capacity for over 600 seats. Among its memorials are statues of Bishop William Sinclair, Bishop Robert Cardney and a large stone effigy of Alexander Stewart, Earl of Buchan (The Wolf of Badenoch).

DUNKELD, BATTLE OF, 1689
PERTH & KINROSS

Fought outside the town during the Covenanting Wars, between the Highland army of 5,000 men led by Colonel Cannon and 1200 Cameronians under the Covenanting Colonel Cleland. A veteran of Drumclog, Cleland's death during the early part of the fighting, which was concentrated around the Marquis of Atholl's mansion, only strengthened the resolve of his men, whose opponents, unable to dislodge them from their strong position, retreated to the hills and abandoned their campaign.

DUNNICHEN, BATTLE OF
SEE NECHTANSMERE

DUNNING
PERTH & KINROSS

Village situated 10 miles SW of Perth. Name derived from the Gaelic 'dunan' meaning 'small fort on hill' which was probably part of the Roman's northern defensive network. The Church of St Serf, who is thought to have died here, still retains its 13th century tower. Created a Burgh of Barony for Rollo of Duncrab in 1511, the village was burnt by the Earl of Mar in 1715. Its Parish Church which was enlarged in 1810 had by 1880 revealed its fine Norman arch which is now in a preserved state.

DUNNOTTAR CASTLE
ABERDEENSHIRE

Built on a rock 1 mile S of Stonehaven, probably on the site of an earlier Pictish settlement which was followed by a fort. The land and castle were obtained by Sir William Keith, the Earl Marischal, from Lord Lindsay by 1392 prior to the original L plan tower being built on sacred ground. The Earl's subsequent excommunication by the Bishop of St Andrews was revoked by a Papal Bull of 1394 on condition a church was built nearby, and the Marischal stronghold then settled into a period of calm. The keep had an east range with stables, servants' quarters and a smithy added followed by a priests' house and enlarged visitor accommodation in the late 16th century. Besieged by Montrose in 1644. The Earl entertained Charles II here in 1650 and in 1651 it was selected as the safest place in

Scotland for the Scottish Regalia, which during Cromwell's siege in 1652 was skilfully extricated by the Rev Granger's wife and hidden in Kinneff Church. An additional quadrangle of buildings to the north, added in the 17th century, comprised a chapel and brewery, bakehouse and storehouse. Used as a prison for Covenanters who were housed in the notorious Wigs Vault. It was finally destroyed by the Duke of Argyll in 1716 due to the Earl's Jacobite sympathies and was sold to the York Building Co in 1720. Although repurchased, it finally passed out of the Keiths' hands in the 19th century and is now a ruin.

DUNOLLY CASTLE
ARGYLL & BUTE

Standing on top of a rock overlooking the sea, 1 mile N of Oban. The site of a fortalice from the 7th century, and principal seat of the Macdougals, Lords of Lorn from the 13th century. Today's ruins are of an early 15th century L plan courtyard keep, with walls 9ft to 11ft thick that were poetically described in Brydson's poem:

The breezes of this vernal day
Come whispering through thine empty hall
And stir instead of tapestry
The weed upon the wall
And bring from out the murmuring sea
And bring from out the vocal wood
The sound of nature's joy to thee
Mocking thy solitude

The estate was forfeited because of the Macdougals' support for the Jacobites in 1715, but was restored before 1745. The new house of Dunolly to the north houses the famous Brooch of Lorn, taken from Robert the Bruce by the Lord of Lorn at the battle of Dalry in 1306.

DUNROBIN CASTLE
HIGHLAND

Overlooking the Dornoch Firth 1´ miles from Golspie Town. The seat of the Sutherland family from the 12th century, when Robert Thane founded the house. It developed from a 13th century square keep which was surrounded by numerous later additions, including a 17th century courtyard mansion built to the south west by John, 13th Earl of Sutherland. In 1746 the Sutherland Militia imprisoned the Jacobite Earl of Cromartie here, after whom the Cromartie Rooms are named. Since the greater portions were added to the north east by the 2nd Duke between 1845 and 1851, the castle's contrast of oriel windows, battlements, turrets, and pinnacles form a blend of features ranging from a German Schloss, a French Chateau and a Scottish Fortalice. Dunrobin was visited by Queen Victoria in 1872 to found a monument to her late 'Mistress of the Robes', the 2nd Duchess.

DUNS
SCOTTISH BORDERS

Market town situated 15 miles W of Berwick Upon Tweed. Its name is derived from the Gaelic 'dun' meaning 'hillfort'. Developing from an ancient settlement on Duns law which by 1489 was a Burgh of Barony for Home of Ayton. It was granted to the monks of Newbattle in 1316, while Duns park was often used as a staging post for attacks on Berwick. In 1318 Bruce's forces gathered here under Randolph and James Douglas, whose relative Archibald Douglas led another assault from here in 1333. In 1650 Cromwell's forces occupied the town after their victory at Dunbar. Like many of the east coast towns Duns's fate was determined by Anglo Scottish politics that constantly thwarted growth following attacks and counter attacks. The for-

mer town, burnt by the English in 1544, 1545 and 1548, and later known as Brunton (from burntown), was rebuilt on the site of the present burgh in 1588. The Covenanting Stone, or ' Duns Stone', is thought to mark the site where in the Civil War the standard was raised by the Covenanters under General Leslie, whose forces encamped here while facing Charles I's army at Berwick. The stand-off eventually led to the pacification of Berwick. The birthplace of the theologian Duns Scotus (1265-1308) is marked by a cairn at Castle Pavilion Lodge donated, along with his bust in the town park, by the Franciscan Order in 1966. The main County Town of Berwickshire between 1661-1696 and also 1903 to 1975, after the Local Government Scotland Act in 1975 Duns kept its District Council but lost its Regional Administration to Newton St Boswells. Like many border towns Duns has kept the traditional summer riding festival which since 1949 has included the crowning of the wynsome Maid o' Dunse. The architectural history of the place revolves around Thomas Boston's House, where Duns Scotus was born, Cockburn's Town House, once occupied by Cockburn of Langton, Superior of the Burgh until 1698, the Tolbooth Cells under the Town Hall, built in 1817 and the Mercat Cross first erected in 1792. See Duns Tower

DUNS TOWER
SCOTTISH BORDERS

To the NE of the town are the remains of a tower built by Thomas Randolph, Earl of Moray in 1320. Constantly ravaged in border warfare between Scotland and England, in 1545 the Earl of Hertford's invasion force burnt and occupied the castle, while during the Covenanting Wars in 1639, General Leslie had his headquarters here. Additions were made by William Hay of Drumelzier when his family acquired the lands in the late 17th century and a western portion was added by a descendant, Alexander or Robert Hay. Sadly the structure was greatly altered in 1820 when the old tower lost its original battlement.

DUNS, HOUSE OF
ANGUS

The house and grounds are to be found 4 miles W of Montrose Town which has for a long time had strong though somewhat tenuous ties with its builders. The lands were owned by the Dun family in the 14th century when the progenitor of the family, a Robert Erskine, bestowed them on his son Thomas in 1376 when the first castle was built. The family's influence greatly increased in the early 15th century after obtaining the rights to the customs of the local ports, which led to much conflict with Montrose Burgh. The loss of two sons and one brother at the battle of Flodden, 1513, and the murder of the priest Thomas Foster at the hands of James Erskine of Duns, led to the latters sojourn on the Continent: where he adhered to the Lutheran doctrines and on his return promoted the Reformation and the first school in Scotland for the Greek language under Pierre de Marsiliers in 1534. Seriously damaged in the Civil War of the 17th century, the tower was replaced in 1730 by the present house, built by William Adam in a Palladian style for Erskine, Lord Dun. As relatives of the Earl of Mar the family were pro-Jacobite in the 1715 and 1745 rebellions.

DUNSCAITH CASTLE
HIGHLAND

Remotely positioned on a rock on the W side of Sleat, Isle of Skye. The site of a very early castle that was mentioned in the poems of Ossian. The scant ruins of today are of an oblong courtyard keep that was the principal seat of the Mac-

donalds. In 1515, as Crown property, it was besieged by Lachlan Maclean of Duart and Alaister Macleod of Dunvegan, but was vacated by the Macdonalds in 1596 when James VI granted the family Duntulm Castle.

DUNSKEY CASTLE
DUMFRIES & GALLOWAY

Overlooking the sea at the head of Castle Bay SE of Portpatrick are the ruins of an L plan courtyard tower. The earlier structure which once stood here, recorded by the Sheriffs of Galloway in 1303, was plundered and burnt in 1489 by Sir Alexander Maculloch of Myrtoun and others for which they received a respite (suspended sentence) in 1503. Bearing a resemblance to some of the castles on the east coast, particularly Ravenscraig in Fife, the present ruins, built around 1510 by William Adair, are fronted by a moat with the sea on its other three sides, while the main building consists of an unbroken front of 100ft on the landward side. Passing to the Montgomerys, Viscounts Aird in the 17th century, it was later held by the Rev Blair, Minister of Portpatrick, but by 1684 had fallen into ruin.

DUNSTAFFNAGE CASTLE
ARGYLL & BUTE

Strategically sited at the entrance to Loch Etive 5 miles NE of Oban. Once the site of a Pictish Fort and later stronghold of Dalriadan Kings, until the 9th century this was the resting place of the Stone of Destiny before its removal to Scone. Including a 13th century keep with a 16th century gatehouse and enclosing wall, the castle was started by the Macdougals of Lorn and Alexander II as a strategic stronghold against the Norsemen. King Robert the Bruce captured it in 1308 after his victory at the Pass of Awe, and conferred it on Sir Arthur Campbell of Lochawe. A place of refuge for James

Earl of Douglas after his forfeiture in 1455, and was visited by James IV, 1490. It served as a military post with an English garrison during the rebellions of 1715 and 1745 and was where Flora Macdonald was imprisoned in the summer of 1746. The castles subsequent ruinous state was arrested by some restoration work and it is now cared for by Historic Scotland. According to some records the burial place of Dalriadan Kings and Alexander II is in the vicinity.

DUNTREATH CASTLE
STIRLING

Built on ground by the Blane River 8 miles W of Crieff. Formerly owned by the Earls of Lennox. The land was conferred on William Edmonstone by James I in 1434, and has remained in the family ever since. Originally a 15th century tower house, it was uninhabited from 1740 but was rebuilt as a castellated mansion by Archibald Duntreath in 1857.

DUNTRUNE CASTLE
ANGUS

Located on the N side of Loch Crinnan 4´ miles NE of Dundee. At one time the site of a 12th century fortress with enceinte wall, this 16th century L plan tower house was for a long time the seat of the Campbells of Duntroon. In 1644 it was besieged by Alastair Macdonald (Colkittoo) for Montrose but by the 18th century had been sold to the Malcolms of Poltalloch. Today it functions as a dwelling house.

DUNTULM CASTLE
HIGHLAND

It overlooks a small bay 9 miles N of Uig Isle of Skye. At one time called Dundavid after a local king or a Viking. The land belonged to the Macdonald Lords of the Isles and then the Macleods, before being granted by James VI to the Macdonalds

of Sleat. It was on a ship in the bay that James V received the submission of the island chiefs during his expedition to subdue the Western Isles in 1540. When confirmed by the Privy Council in 1616 as the residence of Donald Gorm of Sleat who built the keep he was permitted six gentlemen in his household, four tuns of wine and required to exhibit three principal kinsmen before the council yearly.

DUNURE CASTLE
SOUTH AYRSHIRE

This ruined 15th century Kennedy keep, stands on a rock 7 miles S of Ayr. The land was acquired by Earl Gilbert Kennedy of Cassillis who after forging the necessary signatures proceeded to imprison and torture the Abbot of Crossraguel. In the late 17th century the castle and lands were purchased, along with Dalquharron Castle, by Sir Thomas Kennedy of Kirkhill whose descendant still owned it in the 19th century when it was ruinous.

DUNVEGAN CASTLE
HIGHLAND

Built on a rock by Dunvegan Loch on the Isle of Skye. The castle forms a blend of styles from the 14th to the 19th century. Probably the site of a Danish fort, it later developed from a fortified enclosure and seat of the Macleods, who were descended from Leod, son of Olaf the Black, and have held the site for over 700 years. Its distinctive feature is the 16th century fairy tower built by the chief Alastair Cotach, which was followed by a long edifice by Rory More who was knighted by James VI for maintaining order in this unruly region. The hostile culture of grievance rivalry and bad blood and the internecine struggles it engenderd among the island clans was recalled in Sir Walter Scott's poem 'The Lord of the Isles':

Brave Torquil from Dunvegan high,
Lord of the misty hills of Skye
Macneil, wild Barra's ancient thane,
Duart, of bold Clan Gillian's strain,
Fergus of Canna's castled bay,
Macduffith, Lord of Colonsay,
Soon as they saw the broadswords glance,
With ready weapons rose at once

Additional southern and northern sections were added in the 17th and 18th centuries, and by the 19th century it looked like the castellated mansion of today. In 1773 it was visited by Dr Johnson, followed by Sir Walter Scott in 1814. It contains many historical artefacts, including the Fairy Flag, thought to have been captured by a Macleod from a Saracen during the Crusades, and Rory More's drinking horn which was traditionally used as a test of manhood for the Macleod heir.

DUPPLIN MOOR, BATTLE OF, 1332
PERTH & KINROSS

Taking place on Miller Acre near Forteviot after Edward Balliol, flush with victory over the Earl of Fife, engaged a numerically superior Scottish force led by the Earl of Mar, then Regent of Scotland. Mar's subsequent defeat due to a surprise attack by Balliol's forces, led to much slaughter, his own death and paved the way for the seizure of Perth, and ultimately Balliols crowning at Scone.

E

EARLSFERRY
FIFE

Fishing village situated 1 mile SW of Elie. Its name is thought to derive from Macduff, Earl of Fife, who, during his flight from Macbeth in the 11th century, hid here in the nearby cave at Kincraig Hill before being ferried to Dunbar. Legend has it that the village then obtained a privilege confining pursuers to the shore until escapees were halfway across the River Forth. It was probably constituted a burgh following a request from Macduff to Malcolm III (1058-93). After the loss of its original charter in a fire it was confirmed as a Free Royal Burgh by James VI (1589), when it was described as being of 'old past memory of man'. With two weekly markets, two annual fairs and the right to levy dues and customs it seems to have been a place of considerable trade. But the loss of its MP before the Act of Union in 1707 left the burgh unrepresented in the Westminster Parliament and in future decades it lost out to its neighbour Elie.

EARLSHALL CASTLE
FIFE

Located 1 mile E of Leuchars village. Built for comfort rather than defence, this is a fine example of a 16th-and 17th-century L plan courtyard mansion house, and stands on the land that once formed part of the estate belonging to the Earls of Fife after they vacated Leuchars Castle. In 1497 it was acquired by Alexander Bruce and his wife Janet Stewart of Rosyth. The present building was started by Sir William Bruce, 1546 and completed by his great- grandson, who was also William, for his wife Lady Agnes Lindsay in 1617. Its remarkable coved timber ceiling that was completed in 1620, with its

200 panels depicting numerous coats of arms and animals taken from the natural history of the time, was preserved in 1892 when R.W. Mackenzie financed the house's reconstruction under R.S. Lorimer, the distinguished Edinburgh architect.

EARL'S PALACE
ORKNEY

Conveniently built on level ground near Birsay Bay NW of Kirkwall, and near the first seat of the Earls and Bishops of Orkney. In 1564 a charter was granted to the brother of Mary I, Lord Robert Stewart, who started this oblong courtyard edifice with towers in 1574. Its similarities to Holyrood Palace are due to the fact he was once Commendator of Holyrood Abbey. Its north wing was added by his son Patrick who succeeded him around 1600 and was also known for his tyranny while trying to destroy the Norse Odal system (freehold land tenure without superior). In the face of mounting criticism of his brutality the Earl was imprisoned and then executed in Edinburgh, 1615. See Bishop's Palace

EARLSTON
SCOTTISH BORDERS

Town situated 8 miles NW of St Boswells in the Leader Valley. Formerly called Ercildoun from the Cambro-British 'Arcwl-dun' meaning 'prospect hill', a vantage point to the south of the town. Growing around its church which was often visited by the pious David I in the 12th century, it was granted by Walter de Lindsay to Kelso Abbey and later to Coldingham Priory in exchange for Gordon. Its name changed around this time when its manor passed to the Earls of Dunbar. Best known as the home of the 13th century poet and prophet Thomas the Rymer, whose tower stands to the south of the town. The year 1590 saw its elevation to a

Burgh of Barony for John Home of Cowdenknowes and the building of Cowdenknowes House, which ranks with the three 18th century family seats Mellerstain, (open to the public), Carolside and Kirklands as the principal mansion houses in the area. Earlston's trade was traditionally concerned with agricultural produce, wools and tweeds. In its local churchyard is Rhymers stone inscribed 'old Rhymers race lies in this place' along with a cross slabstone.

EDINBURGH
CITY OF EDINBURGH

The metropolis of Scotland was built on three elevated hill ridges from east to west on the south bank of the Forth Estuary. The central hill to the west is terminated by a rocky precipice which is surmounted by Edinburgh Castle, where the city began in the pre-Christian era. The site was continually fought over by rival tribes until the Castle was built in the early 7th century by the Northumbrians, and though spelt 'Eidden' long before, which is from a Gaelic word meaning 'hill slope' it was later linked to their late King Edwin, as by 1130 it appears as a castle and village recorded as Edwinesburgh. It was occupied by the Scots under King Indulf (954-962), when it was called 'Dunedin' from the Gaelic meaning 'fort on hill slope', but the Dun was dropped and the English burgh added. The village castle and church became a town of some importance after David I constituted it a Royal Burgh 1124-27, and founded Holyrood Abbey in 1128 to the east of the castle, both helping to establish the two points between which the city's spinal column developed. In the course of this some of what became the lower levels of the thoroughfare were sealed up and forgotten. During its occupation by Edward I in 1291 and 1292 the authorities yielded to Eng-

lish rule until 1313 when Randolph, Earl of Moray, retook its castle that was later destroyed by King Robert the Bruce (1313), in keeping with his scorched earth policy. The castle was rebuilt and reinforced by Edward III who resided here until it was secured for Scotland by William Douglas, 1361. The optimism and confidence subsequently enjoyed was later dashed when in 1385 during Richard II's invasion the town was burnt. Following James Ist last Parliament in 1436, Edinburgh formally became Scotland's Capital due to the security it offered royalty from upstart nobles, and the frequency of the parliaments held here which brought a number of privileges for fairs, markets and the levying of customs during the reign of James II (1427-1460), when the town's defences were reinforced. The optimism felt by the townsfolk on the accession of James III (1460-1488) and his marriage to Ann of Denmark proved short-lived when the burgh was infected by the plague of 1475 that was to recur in 1497 and 1513. Along with the nearby Mercat Cross, St Giles Church, which was made collegiate in 1466, served as the main meeting place for the towns people, who were to witness much factional fighting when Edinburgh was occupied by the King's brother and rival the Duke of Albany, ending in the King's murder, and the hurried crowning of James IV (1488-1513). The royal pageant celebrating the King's marriage to Margaret Tudor in 1503 was the first of many such festivities the town witnessed during James IV reign. But his more enduring legacy was the Royal College of Surgeons which was founded in 1505 and later grew into one of Scotland's finest institutions. However, it is in the country's military history that the King made his most honourable contribution, when he led the army mustering on the Borough-moor to Flodden field where the

King himself fell. The gathering was remembered in verse by Sir Walter Scott in his poem 'Marmion' when Lord Marmion approached one of Edinburgh's surrounding hills:

They passed the glen of Scanty rill,
And climbed the opposing bank until
They gained the top of Blackford Hill ...
But different far the change has been
Since Marmion for the crown
Of Blackford saw that martial scene
Upon the bent so brown:
Thousand pavilions, white as snow,
Spread all the Borough-moor below.

The double calamity of the plague and the defeat at Flodden in 1513 where the King was slain led to the building of the City Wall (Flodden Wall) and the formation of the City Guard, who failed to prevent danger on its streets during the numerous conflicts between the Douglases and the Hamiltons (Cleanse the Causeway, 1520) throughout the reign of James V (1513-1542). With the establishment of the less fortified Holyrood Palace as the royal residence in 1525, the founding of the College of Justice (Court of Session) in 1532 and investment from affluent merchants, there followed a period of calm that was shattered when the town was burnt in 1542 during the Rough Wooing of Mary I by Henry VIII of England. Edinburgh was burnt again by the Earl of Hertford in 1544 and pillaged after the battle of Pinkie in 1547. Its later occupation by a friendly 6,000 man French force sent by Henry II of France to facilitate the marriage of Mary Stewart to the young Dauphin highlighted the religious divide between Protestant and Catholic which had first become apparent with the death of James V in 1542. The conflict was exacerbated by the arrival of the Reformer John Knox in 1559, when the burgh became the HQ for the Reform Party, the establishment of Presbyterianism by 1560,

with the arrival of Queen Mary I at Leith in 1561 polarising the people further. Her marriage to Lord Darnley in 1566 was followed in quick succession by the murder of her Italian secretary Rizzio, Darnley's murder, her marriage to Bothwell, and her exile in 1567, leaving the city in a state of unrest. This continued up until the accession of her son James VI, who, with a donation from Robert Reid, founded Edinburgh University in 1583 that was to provide the burgh with a corner-stone of stability. Much of his reign was fraught with trials, executions and disputes with nobles over personal liberties and royal prerogatives which often drained the royal coffers until he assumed the Crown of England in 1603. During the reign of Charles I (1633-1649) several parliaments were held here and St Giles was created a Cathedral. His introduction of the Liturgy (prayer book) to curb Presbyterianism was resisted by the Town Council and troops of citizens, who became the first signatories to the National Covenant in Greyfriars Kirkyard in 1638. This made the city a hotbed of resentment throughout the Covenanting Wars when it was the seat of executive power that was to continue up until Charles I's execution in 1649. The High Courts of Justiciary with their large courtrooms were built in 1639 in the shadow of St Giles Cathedral, housing the High Court, first and second courts of the Courts of Session, the courtrooms of the Lords Ordinary and the Great Hall of Parliament House. Its building completed the nucleus which was devoted to the town's trade, law, business, religious and civil administrative needs. However, in the mid 17th century the bustle on its streets was somewhat muffled by the resounding news that the plague had returned, forcing the authorities to seal of certain parts of the medieval streets that included Mary Kings Close and what became the foundations of the City Chambers. After being impoverished by the Civil War, the burghers welcomed the proclamation of Charles II as King from the Mercat Cross in 1649 but displayed some ambivalence towards the execution of Montrose at Edinburgh Cross, 1650. James Graham Marquis of Montrose was one of Scotland's foremost military tacticians who won victories for Charles I against the Covenanters at Auldearn, Alford, Inverlochy, Kilsyth and Tippermuir. In his poem 'The Execution of Montrose', William Aytoun paid tribute to the unswerving loyalty he had shown for the King:

They set him high upon a cart
The hangman rode below
They drew his hands behind his back
And bared his noble brow ...
Then as the Graham looked upwards,
He saw the ugly smile
Of him who sold his king for gold
The Master fiend Argyle'

Despite a period of calm during Cromwell's occupation 1650-60, the city rejoiced at the Restoration of King Charles II in 1660, which was followed by the trial, torture and execution of numerous Covenanters (1663), many of whom were buried in Greyfriars Kirkyard. The reign of James VII (1685-1689), which saw the blatant promotion of Catholics whilst instilling in the citizens a taste for public spectacles like the humiliation of Magistrates, was cut short when the Convention of Estates, held here in 1689, dismissed the King and offered the Crown to William and Mary. Sensing prosperity, the citizens invested heavily in the Darien Expedition which in 1698 sailed from Leith, but its failure cost the city around £400,000 and hastened the Union with England in 1707, when the Parliament voted itself out of existence. Its removal to London caused widespread rioting until the rioters occupied the city, sowing the seeds of unrest throughout the country that Jacobitism

would later harvest. In the 1715 Rising, Edinburgh foiled an attack by 1500 Jacobites who were later deterred by a 6,000 man Dutch force. In 1736 it was the scene of more unrest when during the hanging of Andrew Wilson, a popular smuggler, Captain John Porteous of the City Guard fired into the crowd, causing the carnage which provoked the lynching of Porteous by a mob (Porteous Riots). Although taken by surprise by the Jacobites in 1745 who proclaimed James VII as King and Prince Charles Edward as Regent from the Mercat Cross, the castle held out for the Government. The Royal Exchange (now the City Chambers), built in 1753 by John and Robert Adam forms a square, with open court surrounded by archways adorned with balustrade and vases. Although at first used by traders, it later became the permanent Council Chambers. The influx of large numbers of Scots and Irish migrant workers to Edinburgh's mills, factories and breweries in the 18th and 19th centuries added to an already bad housing shortage, causing them to form political movements promoting the ideals of the French Revolution (1790). The contribution to the city's northern expansion was the southern section of James Craig's New Town, which began in 1767 and was followed by St Andrews Square, started in 1771, Charlotte Square, begun in 1791 to designs by Robert Adam, South Bridge, built in 1788, and the Nor Loch, drained in 1816, followed by the development of Princes Street Gardens, 1816-30. The visit made by George IV in 1822 at the insistence of Walter Scott reaffirmed the city's status as the Capital of Northern Britain. Also the classical architecture of its New Town, with its sandstone squares, streets, crescents, circuses, monuments and institutions earned Edinburgh the accolade 'The Athens of the North', making it a centre for the Scottish Enlightenment, while helping to promote the city as the publishing capital of the country. In 1834 the cramped conditions of the old University gave way to a new building near South Bridge which was begun in 1789 and designed by Robert Adam and William Playfair in a Greco-Italian style. By 1882 its library contained up to 140,000 books and 2,000 volumes of manuscripts, while its many professorships included 34 in the faculties of law, the arts, divinity and, more importantly, medicine. The city's reputation for medical excellence, and in particular anatomy had prompted the underworld activities of the body snatchers William Burke and William Hare, and their paymaster Dr Robert Knox, which ultimately led to the hanging of Burke in the Grassmarket in 1829. First incorporated in 1505, the Royal College of Surgeons, built near the University by William Playfair, 1883, in a Grecian style offered a wide range of courses pertaining to physical and mental health, and further enhanced the city's pre-eminence in the field of medicine. The construction of the Dean Bridge by Thomas Telford in 1831, and George IV Bridge by John Henderson in 1837, aided further expansion to the north and south of the city. This provided housing for its growing professional class, who, with their spiritual sensibilities, were a captive audience during the General Assembly of 1843, when the Disruption Debate prompted the founding of the Free Church of Scotland, the college of which was built on the Mound by David Cousins in the 1850s. Sometimes called a Medieval space rocket, the Walter Scott Monument on Princes Street was designed by George Meikle Kemp and built in 1855 in honour of one of the city's more notable worthies, who did much to reaffirm the Scottish identity (after the 1745 Rebellion and the Treaty of Union 1707), while also putting Edinburgh on the Victorian tourist trail. His statue by Steel sits centred at its base. Amongst Edinburgh's other sons were Alexander Graham Bell (inventor of the telephone), who was born in 1847 in Charlotte Square, and Robert Louis Stevenson (writer) who was born in 1850 at Howard Place in the New Town. The latter grew up in an Edinburgh of stark contrasts, as its enchanted past in the underworld squalor of the Old Town sat uncomfortably with the promising middle class respectability of the New Town, a fact which undoubtedly coloured some of his writing, most notably 'Dr Jekyll and Mr Hyde' (pub 1886). It was to be less than a century later that the subterranean parts of the Old Town in which the plague victims had been incarcerated were opened up, and continues to offer Edinburgh citizens a unique insight into one of the darker periods in the lives of their forefathers. The Old Town skyline was further improved in 1859 by William Playfair's New College and Church of Scotland Assembly Hall, built in the vicinity of Mary of Guise's old Palace. Between this and the Bank of Scotland (by David Bryce and Richard Crichton) is the Free Church of Scotland College and the offices by David Cousins. Also by Playfair is The National Gallery by the Mound, built in 1854 in a neo-classical style and flanked by east and west Princes Street Gardens. Inspired by the advances made in medical science, the old Infirmary at the bottom of Infirmary Street, which was opened in 1729, was replaced by the then new building overlooking The Meadows, that was designed by David Bryce in a Baronial style and opened in 1880 with the help of public subscription. As a teaching hospital it worked in unison with the nearby Medical School and Graduation Hall, built by Rowand Anderson by 1898, and provided a steady stream of graduates for Britain's burgeoning colonies. The Waverley and Haymarket railway stations, built between 1840 and 1898, coupled with the completion of the Forth Rail Bridge in 1889, ushered in the era of rail travel as symbolised by the North British Hotel (now Balmoral), built in 1902 by W. Hamilton Beattie, and the Caledonian Hotel, built in 1902 by J.Peddie and G.W Brown. Both of these served as barometers for the city's tourist trade that has continued to thrive ever since. At the turn of the century Edinburgh's main industries were publishing, brewing and confectionery, while from its institutions came a high number of doctors, engineers, lawyers and administrators. Suffering little damage during the war years, despite the attempted bombing of the Forth Rail Bridge by a Zeppelin in the Ist World War (1914-18), and the slight bombing of Leith in the 2nd World War (1939-45), Edinburgh was a popular place for service personnel to spend their leave. Built in 1939 by Thomas Tait, St Andrews House on Regent Road had for decades served as Scotland's administrative centre, while housing the office of the Secretary of State for Scotland. On the same road, overlooking the Royal Mile, is the Old Royal High School which grew from a 16th century Grammar School of 1519, which itself sprang from a 12th century school at Holyrood Abbey. Built on a terrace cut into the rock of Calton Hill, it was designed in a Grecian Doric style with influences from the Temple of Theseus in Athens, and with accommodation for over 500 pupils. After coming under the City School Board in 1872 its popularity declined and it was eventually vacated, but after the ambiguous devolution referendum of 1979 it provided the central focus for the Scottish Independence Movement and came to symbolise a parliament in waiting. With the enactment of the Scotland Act, 1998 the plans for a parliament building were implemented and paved the way for its construction at Holyrood Road. Post-war Edinburgh witnessed the same inner city renewal as did many other European cities, prompting a movement of people

to the outskirts. The first Edinburgh Festival of 1947 had by 1997 mushroomed into a dynamic blend of international music, theatre and dance, staged during the month of August, culminating in a firework display by Edinburgh Castle. See Castle, Holyrood Palace, St Giles & St Mary's Cathedral

EDINBURGH CASTLE
CITY OF EDINBURGH

Perched on a volcanic rock of the basaltic variety that rises 383ft above sea level and was once protected by the Nor Loch. This was the site of a stronghold from earliest times, for in the 5th century it was held by the Votadini tribe, Ancient Britons who fought the Northumbrians for possession up to the 11th century. The Northumbrian King Edwin rebuilt it in the 7th century as a fortress surrounded by a wooden stockade which was used by successive Scottish monarchs and underwent many changes in the process. Occupied by Malcolm III (1058-93) and his Queen, Margaret, it was besieged by his brother Donald Bane at his death during a failed attempt to capture the young Prince Edgar. The castle was increasingly used as a royal residence by the reign of Alexander I (1107-1124), and later by William the Lyon, Alexander II and by Alexander III in the 13th century, when it was the depository of national records and the regalia. Built in the 12th century in a Norman style, its oldest building is Queen Margaret's Chapel, which despite being the scene of the marriage of Alexander III to Margaret, daughter of Henry III of England, in 1251, has borne witness to most of the major conflicts between the two nations down through the centuries. After being taken by Edward I in 1291, the castle frequently changed hands during the Wars of Independence, when it was an English possession between 1296 and 1313 until retaken by the

Earl of Moray, the nephew of Robert the Bruce, and then destroyed in accordance with the King's scorched earth policy. Rebuilt by Edward III in order to hold Southern Scotland but captured by William Douglas in 1361, after which David II built a tower (Davies Tower, stood until 1573). In 1385 it withstood a siege by the Duke of Lancaster compelling Robert II to allow the townspeople to build houses within its walls, when it continued to serve in the middle of the nation's chain of resistance after Berwick and before Stirling. Though the accession of the Stewarts and the emergence of Edinburgh as the chief burgh in the kingdom brought about the building of the Great Hall, Royal Apartments, and the Crown Room at the SE corner during the reigns of the five James's between 1406 and 1542, it had ceased to be a full-time royal residence by 1488. With more stability came the desire for less fortified accommodation like Holyrood Palace, which was started in 1501. One of the castle's more macabre episodes was the Black Dinner held here in 1440, when the 6th Earl of Douglas, friend of James II, was dragged from the feast and executed after the ominous Black Bull's head was placed on the table. In 1560 this was the scene of the death of Mary of Guise and in 1566 the birth of her grandson James VI. Following the siege of 1573, when the castle was held for Queen Mary, most of the old buildings were swept away and replaced with the half moon battery and the arched gateway erected by the Regent Morton. In continuing to determine the fate of the Stewarts, it was occupied by Charles I before his coronation at Scone, 1633, was plundered by one of the dynasty's chief adversaries Oliver Cromwell, in 1650, who seized Scottish records and the Black Kist, a chest of jewels which belonged to James III, and stayed in government hands throughout the 1715 and 1745 rebellions. Subsequent to which it

has been garrisoned by Scottish Regiments, whose valour displayed during later conflicts is remembered throughout the fortress. At the behest of Sir Walter Scott, the 19th century saw the discovery (1818) of the Crown Jewels hidden in a chest in the upper Crown Room, and in 1829 the return from England of that substantial piece of ordnance Mons Meg. Used as a prison during the Napoleonic Wars. The castle's main areas of interest are St Margaret's 12th century Chapel, the Scottish Crown Jewels, its fine collection of arms and armour, the Scottish National War Memorial designed by Robert Lorimer in 1924 and the Stone of Destiny (Stone of Scone) returned in 1996. Extending from its drawbridge is the castle esplanade that was formed with the rubbish removed from the Royal Exchange in 1753 and with the Witches Well where 300 witches were burnt between 1479 and 1722. It is now used to stage the Edinburgh Festival's Military Tattoo.

EDRADOUR DISTILLERY
PERTH & KINROSS

Located about 2′ miles E of Pitlochry. Among all Scotland's distilleries Edradour is the smallest and in many ways the most traditional. While displaying the simplicity that's consistent with the style and scale of its period, it forms a cluster of whitewashed buildings in the hill above Pitlochry. Taking its name from the Gaelic 'Edred dobhar' meaning 'stream of King Edred', who was a local warrior King, the distillery takes its water from under the Moulin Moor and in the 1990s was getting 37 inches of rain every year. As a byproduct of farming, whisky distilling was an indelible part of the Highlands' culture, but became increasingly outlawed after 1644 when the Scottish Parliament levied 2s 8d on a Scots pint of liquor. After this came the Malt Tax, following the Union of 1707. Nevertheless the area's dense woodland made it perfect for illicit distilling, which continued in the face of the minimum legal requirement of 500 gallons per still until an Act of Parliament in 1823 reduced it to 40 gallons. The year 1825 marked the founding of Edradour as a co-operative by a group of local farmers whose building work still stands. And, like the weavers of their day, they took their skills in what was at first a cottage industry and built a major industry, that has grown relentlessly ever since. By 1841 the success of their venture moved the local farmer to develop the co-operative into a permanent distilling enterprise, involving eight individuals headed by John MacGlashan & Company of Edradour in the Parish of Moulin. The enterprise greatly benefitted from the growing popularity of Pitlochry as a Spa Town and its proximity to Blair Atholl, where the frequency of Queen Victoria & Prince Albert's visits inevitably brought the fashionable members of society, thus encouraging the railway companies. The distillery was run by one of the original farmers, William McIntosh, and his son John, whose endeavours concentrated the malting process which had previously been done at local farms and has continued to be done in this time-tested way. After the slump in sales in the 1920s, the distillery was bought in 1922 by a Glasgow distiller and pioneer blender, William Whiteley, whose 'House of Lords' blend found a ready market in royal households, luxury liners, and first class hotels, not to mention the countless Speakeasies in prohibition New York of the 1930s. Another of his blends was the 'King's Ransom' which in 1945 found its way on to the menu at the Potsdam Conference attended by Churchill, Truman and Stalin. Until 1947 the distillery relied on the wooden paddles and the Edradour Burn for power, making it one of the last distilleries to switch to electricity. In 1982 Edradour was acquired by

The House of Campbell, among whose directors was the 12th Duke of Argyll and 26th Chief of Clan Campbell.

OWNERS
Andrew Symington ?

REGION
Highland

PRODUCT
Edradour 10 year old 40% vol

NOTES
A slightly sweet cherry nose which continues through to its rich and smooth taste with its smokey, peaty, Highland characteristics.

EDWARD I INVASION, 1296

During the period of uncertainty following the crowning of John Balliol as King of Scotland in 1292, after he had sworn fealty to Edward I the arbitrator in the struggle for succession, the latter tried to assert his right as supreme overlord with a view to assimilating both nations. The reality became all too clear however in 1294 when Edward's attempts to recruit support from the Scots for his war with France, after King Philip had seized Gascony, sparked a wave of nationalist fervour in Scotland and the expulsion of many English figures. Anxious to anchor themselves to their natural ally, in 1295 an alliance was forged between Scotland and France, obliging the Scots to invade England. Forced to take action, in 1296 Edward invaded Scotland with 3,000 horse and 30,000 foot, capturing Berwick and its castle, massacring its inhabitants. The first major opposition came at Dunbar when the Scots were worsted, leaving Edward to drive home his advantage in an open country. Securing Edinburgh after an eight day siege, when its castle surrendered, the King then marched to Stirling which he took without resistance before heading north and taking Perth, where he received the surrender of Balliol. The army eventually reached Aberdeen and Elgin, while accepting the submission of the people as he went and on his return south Edward took the coronation stone or Stone of Scone as a poignant symbol of his victory. This he consummated by his Parliament at Berwick on 28th August 1296, where he received the fealty of the clergy, barons, and gentry whose names filled the skins of parchment known as the Ragman Roll. In restoring the land to the clergy, and preserving the rights of feudal barons, Edward preserved the ancient jurisdictions while taking care that the key castles were in English hands and the chief executive posts of Governor, Treasurer and Justiciar were held by the Earl of Surray, Hugh Cressingham, and William Ormsby respectively. The main feeling prevailing Scotland at that time was that of anger at the lack of dialogue, which gave way to the rising popularity of William Wallace necessitating a second invasion shortly afterwards.

EDWARD I INVASION, 1297

Among Edward I ministers administering Scotland in 1297, non more than William Ormsby the Justiciar aroused as much discontent, which increased to reach every area of Scottish life. With spring growing into summer an unknown figure named William Wallace showed himself as a leader of national resistance. The son of Sir Malcolm Wallace of Elderslie in Renfrewshire, he belonged to a family of knightly landowners but was by no means in close contact with the great magnates of the realm. In May he slew Heselrig the Sheriff of Lanark who was responsible for the murder of his lady love Marion Bradfoot, heiress of Lamington, and so began his military career. Of the many who flocked to his banner, which he raised in the name of King John Balliol, most were from the smaller gentry rather than the powerful magnates. His consummate skills at turning a

multitude into a regular army involved the first four men having a fifth as leader and every multiple of ten thereafter having a leader over them, enforcing absolute obedience under pain of death. In resorting to guerrilla tactics Wallace drove the English out of Perth, (ejecting Ormsby at Scone), Stirling and Lanarkshire and in so doing incited pockets of revolt to flare up in various parts of Scotland, while securing most of the strongholds in the process. Thus challenging the more prominent figures of the land like the Bishop of Glasgow, Sir Andrew Moray and Bruce the young Earl of Carrick to join him. Alarmed at the rapidity of his advance, Edward I dispatched the Earl of Surray with Henry de Percy at the head of an army but after Wallace had laid siege to Dundee and threatened Stirling their advance was halted as Wallacs's descent from the north prevented them crossing the River Forth by Stirling Bridge, where in 1297 he dealt a decisive blow to Surrey's invasion force. After consolidating his position in Scotland, Wallace led an invasion into northern England and was made Guardian of the Kingdom on his return. In June, Edward arrived at Roxburgh with, a large army and defeated Wallace on his own ground, forcing him to resign the guardianship over to Comyn. But in the wake of his victory the English King sought to pacify the Lowlands, and in order to subdue the whole country he had to return every year. During this time Wallace's attempts at petitioning King Philip of France and soliciting the Pope for help resulted in a Papal Bull dated 1300 claiming dominion over all Scotland, that was followed by a contradictory request urging the Scottish Bishops to make peace with England. In Scotland war continued apace as Wallace's forces defeated the English at Roslin, 1303, but with Comyn and the principal barons submitting to Edward and the gradual recapture of the main strongholds, the country capitulated with the capture of Stirling Castle in 1304. With his power base eroding by the day Wallace was relentlessly hunted until he was captured in Glasgow with the help of some Scottish Barons and taken to London, where he was hung drawn and quartered.

EDWARD II INVASION, 1314

In the wake of the struggle for overlordship of Scotland in the late 13th century, a parliament was held in London that framed a system of government for Scotland which advanced feudal law at the expense of the ancient customs of the Celts, Scots and Brets or Britons. Present at this, along with other Scottish nobles, was Robert Bruce, Earl of Carrick and contender for the crown, whose secret alliance with William Lamberton, Bishop of St Andrews and friend of Wallace, gave continuity to the events past and present, while also giving Bruce a chance to redeem himself after his support for Edward in previous years. Removing himself from court disguised as a groom, Bruce rode to Scotland and arrived at Dumfries where he met with Comyn, the Guardian of the Kingdom, in the Church of Greyfriars. A dispute then arose which ended in Comyn's murder and Bruce's excommunication for defiling hallowed ground. On being outlawed by Edward I, Bruce was propelled into instant decision-making and with the help of his brother dispatched appeals for support to his friends, adherents and sympathisers among the church and the nobility, in particular Sir James Douglas his erstwhile supporter. On the 27th of March 1306 he was crowned at Scone by Bishop Lamberton in the presence of the Bishops of Glasgow and Moray, thereby unravelling all Edward's statecraft. Losing his first battle at Methven in June to the recently dispatched Earl of Pembroke and his second at Dalry in August to the Lord

of Lorn, his victory at Louden Hill over Pembroke in 1307 marked a sea change for the Scots. Fortunately for Bruce, the year also marked the death of Edward I and the succession of his inexperienced son, crowned King Edward II, who was imbued with his fathers hatred of Scotland, that was now being secured through force of arms by Bruce, who in 1308 won over the clergy. In England King Edward II was distracted by his squabbling nobles but made some fruitless marches north, probably to escape the strife at court. It was however the capture by the Scots of Perth, Roxburgh, Edinburgh and the Isle of Man by 1313 that compelled him to march north with a vast army in the hope of saving Stirling Castle, then under siege. It was in the poem 'The Lord of the Isles' by Sir Walter Scott that the young Kings first major confrontation is described:

To that lone island's shore,
Of all the Scottish conquests made
By the first Edwards ruthless blade
His son retained no more,
Northward of Tweed, but Stirling's towers,
Beleagured by King Roberts powers
And they took term of truce,
If England's King should not relieve
The seige ere John the Baptist's eve
To yeild them to the Bruce.

Assembling at Berwick, they spent the 22nd June at Edinburgh before reaching Stirling on St John's Day, 24th June. Against the advice of his nephew the Earl of Gloucester, the King's refusal to delay the engagement resulted in a total disaster at the battle of Bannockburn, that forced Edward to flee the field and his army to follow. Stirling then surrendered and all Scotland acknowledged Bruce as King. The culmination of Bruce's struggle, the defeat of Edward II army Sir Walter Scott extolled in another stanza in his

'The Lord of the Isles':
And well did the Stewart's actions grace
The sire of Scotland's royal race !
Firmly they kept their ground;
As firmly England onward pressed,
And down went many a noble crest,
And rent was many a valient breast,
And slaughter revelled round.

Despite the victory, Edward made some vain attempts at invasion and refused to accept Bruce as an equal sovereign, but in 1328 his son Edward III signed the Treaty of Northampton acknowledging Scotland's sovereignty.

EDZELL CASTLE
ANGUS

Built near the West Water 6 miles NW of Brechin. The ruins of this magnificent castle are matched only by those of Dunnottar. Originally belonging to the Glenesks and later the Stirlings, the estate passed through marriage around 1350 to the Lindsays, Earls of Crawford, who built this keep in the late 15th century. Enlarged by David the 9th Earl of Crawford into a quadrangle castle with a large garden and ornamental wall as such gardens were fashionable in the time of Queen Mary, who visited here in 1562. It was occupied by Cromwell's forces in 1651, was bought by the Earl of Panmure in 1715 and partly demolished by Argyll's Highlanders in 1746. Sadly some storm damage added to its destruction.

EILEAN DONAN CASTLE
HIGHLAND

Positioned on an island on Loch Alsh, E.Skye. This 13th century castle and enceinte wall built on the site of a vitrified fort were reinforced as a bastion of royal authority in 1266 after the battle of Largs, when Colin Fitzgerald was appointed its Constable. Its 14th century keep was built by Thomas Randolph Earl of Moray,

who adorned its walls with fifty human heads to tame the local inhabitants. In the 15th and 16th centuries it was a stronghold of the Mackenzies of Kintail who built a tower, but was taken by the Earl of Huntly in 1504 for James IV and in 1539 was attacked by Donald Gorm of Lewis who died in the fray. William Mackenzie the Earl of Seaforth held it with Spanish troops in 1719, until it was battered into a ruin by three English Men of War, but more recent restoration work has made it the archetypal Scottish castle in its picturesque setting.

ELCHO CASTLE
PERTH & KINROSS

Built on a rock near the River Tay 5 miles NE of Perth. The site of an earlier castle which Blind Harry referred to as ' A place of retreat for William Wallace in the 13th century'. It developed from a 16th century keep with square and round towers, and like many castles of this period it was built for residential and defensive purposes. Elcho was for a long time the home of the Wemyss family, for whom it was a barony in 1628, but had in the 19th century begun to decline before it was re-roofed in 1830.

ELGIN
MORAY

Town situated 67 miles NW of Aberdeen. Name derived from 'elgga' meaning 'little Ireland', as it was once a mythical name for Ireland. Although consisting of a fort on Ladyhill before and during the time of the Celtic Mormaers of Moray, later followed by a castle and royal hunting seat up until the 16th century, it was its erection into a Royal Burgh by David I, 1136, and the building of its Cathedral in 1224 that provided the catalyst for the burgh's growth. In 1234, Alexander II, who often hunted here, granted the town a charter and introduced the orders of the Blackfriars and Greyfriars. Marking the turning point for Edward I's forces in 1296 after they stayed two days in its castle, Elgin was also visited by James II in 1457 after regaining possession of its Earldom from the unruly Douglases. The town was partly burnt along with the Cathedral by the Wolf of Badenoch in 1390. After the rebuilding work of 1538, Elgin comprised a High St from Ladyhill to the Cathedral with plots of land for grazing, and two main streets linked by narrow wynds and boundary walls, with entrance ports facing all four directions. The period of conflict fought out on its streets between the Earl of Gordon and the Earl of Moray, from two of the area's leading families, gave rise to the proverb 'Half done as Elgin is half burned'. Although on the margins it was affected by the Reformation, 1560, when its Cathedral was wrecked, marking the decline of the church's influence and the rise of the Merchant's Guild, whose monopoly was eventually ended by an Act of Parliament. With its trade in fish, wool, and agricultural produce it was granted the right by James VII to build a harbour at Elgin Head, Lossiemouth in 1687 which facilitated the expansion of foreign trade when the burghers enjoyed wines, spirits, silks and general merchandise from France, Holland and Germany. The trade flourished up until the Treaty of Union in 1707. As capital of the County and head of six burghs, Elgin served as the ecclesiastical, administrative and commercial centre of Moray, with its inevitable redevelopment in the 19th century attracting many merchants, professionals and artisans from in and around Moray to its woollen mills, sawmills, distilleries and tourism trade. Consequently these developments secured its status and prosperity well into the 20th century. Apart from its Cathedral the main places of interest are the Natural History Museum and the Moray Motor Museum. See Cathedral

ELGIN CATHEDRAL
MORAY

Standing in the town are the ruins of the Highlands most important Cathedral. It was built on the site of the Church of the Holy Trinity founded by Alexander II in 1224 as the centre for the Bishopric of Moray, which had been founded by his forefather Alexander I by 1120. Largely built by Bishop Andrew de Moravia and known as the Lantern of the North, its Early English architecture was once described as being inferior to few in Europe, with its vast dome overshadowing much of the town and its history. This once extended from the western entrance to the high alter with its richly ornamented arches flanked by massive pillars. Burnt in 1270 when some of the present ruins were built, it was again burnt in 1390 by the Wolf of Badenoch (Alexander Stewart, 4th son of Robert II) following his excommunication by the Bishop. Its reconstruction in a Gothic style by Bishop Innes before 1414, with a Chapter House added by 1500, followed by its nave choir and transepts replaced between 1507 and 1538, culminated in the building of the Bishop's Palace around 1557. The destruction inflicted in 1560 by the iconoclasts, who dismantled its roof, was added to by Cromwell's forces in 1650, resulting in the collapse of its central tower, 1717, nave and part of the transepts which invited stone pillaging until the building of the Keeper's House in 1807. Today the building retains its two distinctive western towers flanking its western entrance, substantial parts of the nave's north and south wall, its north and south transepts and a fine Gothic choir with extended north wall and adjacent octagonal Chapter House. Parts of the east wall extend from the choir. Amidst the ruins is a curious 6th century Pictish Cross-slab. See Town

ELIBANK HOUSE
SCOTTISH BORDERS

The ruins of this L plan house stand on a site by the S bank of the Tweed 5´ miles E of Innerleithen. Probably built on the site of a Border pele by Sir Gideon Murray, a cadet of the Darnhall family and eminent lawyer. In 1643 his son Patrick was created Lord Elibank.

ELIE
FIFE

Fishing village situated 10 miles W of Leven. The name either derived from the Gaelic 'ealadh' meaning 'grave' or from the Old English 'Eligh' meaning 'eel Isle'. Once a place of some importance, it was created a Burgh of Barony for Scott of Grangemuir in 1599, which later formed part of Kilconquhar Parish, until it came into its own in 1639 when its Parish Church was built. Added to in 1726 and repaired in 1831, it still retains some of its original work. With its natural harbour affording shelter in gales, and its fishermen's cottages contrasting with 17th century buildings, it typifies the traditional Scottish fishing village. After the successful rescue of 300 royal troops in 1696, it was recommended to the Government by General Wade (charged with pacifying the Highlands) as being suitable for naval ships. Although his advice was not acted upon, a harbour and pier were later built and Elie continued to thrive as a fishing village until the decline of the port, when it became a residential village with facilities for pleasure sailing and golf. Contrary to some pessimistic forecasts after the joining in 1929 of the Police Burgh of Elie and the Royal Burgh of Earlsferry, Elie retained its distinctiveness, making it popular with summer sea bathers, but has more recently regained some of its former tranquillity.

ELIE GOLF CLUB
FIFE

Extending from the town, with a view of the sea stretching out before it, is the Elie Golf Course. From the early days of the 15th century on the Earlsferry Mure, golf has played a significant part in the local people's recreation, despite a decision by the military "that fute-ball and Golfe be utterly cry'ed downe" in an attempt to increase the popularity of archery. Although officially approved by 1589, it was not until 1858 that the Earlsferry & Elie Golf Club was formed when the Golfers Tavern (now known as the 19th hole) was used for meetings after play on the 9 hole course. In 1875 The Earlsferry Thistle Club and The Golf House Club were formed. For the latter a clubhouse was built in Melon Park in 1877, and the course extended, but the biggest transformation in the locality happened in 1884, when the Elie & Earlsferry Ladies Golf Club was founded by a Mrs Anderson. In the face of ongoing encroachments by the farmer of the Grange Estate, developments continued and in 1887 the premier award, the Baird Gold Medal, was presented by Mr William Baird, the club's first captain, and in 1898 the Club Challenge Cup was awarded to the ladies. With the opening of an 18 hole course in 1895, largely at the behest of Col. Glover, the stage was set for a century of play. In the early part of the 20th century, which saw the tumult engendered by the war of 1914-18 when men enlisted (twelve of whom were not to return) and women joined the Red Cross, congestion on the course prompted the plans for a relief course, but this came to nothing and the club continued to strive for security of tenure from the Grange Estate. Meanwhile the ladies sought to expand their operation, but to no avail, and remained under the umbrella of The Golf House

Club, leading to a proposal in 1936 for amalgamation, which The Golf House Club turned down. Nevertheless, a practical fusion of sorts took place slowly before, during and after the war of 1939-45 which naturally led to a stronger emphasis on junior membership and the reduction in age of entry in 1949. With the opening of the Forth and Tay Bridges and the threat of land purchases for housing developments, the club renewed its efforts to secure its tenure in 1961, but it was not until 1974 that it came in part by Miss Baird's offer of Melon Park (to be renamed Baird Park). Appropriately she was invited to mark the club's centenary celebrations in 1975 by lighting the bonfire. Among the club's more distinguished players, W.D.Smith stands as the seven times winner of the Baird Gold Medal.

ELLON
ABERDEENSHIRE

Town situated 16 miles N of Aberdeen on the bank of the Ythan. Its name is derived from the Gaelic word 'Eilean' meaning 'island'. Once the seat of the Comyns, Earls of Buchan, its Kirk lands were owned by the Cistercian Abbey of Kinloss which gave it its former name of Kinlossellon. In the vicinity of Ellon Bridge was the old Earls Head Court of Ellon. First called 'Moot Hill of Ellon' (meaning hill of assembly) and in later times 'Earls Hill' it was here that the Earl and Dempster sat to dispense judgement in the open air, a tradition remembered on the Burgh Arms with its azure, three garbs and the motto "judge nocht quhill ye end". In 1707 it was erected into a Burgh of Barony for the Earl of Buchan and in 1780 Ellon Castle was built by the 4th Earl of Aberdeen. Its cattle and grain markets that once made it a thriving centre for local trade, encouraged merchants and bankers to form a Town Council in

the 19th century (constituted 1901) and a Police Burgh in 1893. The sale of the castle estate and town by the Gordons enabled many residents to buy their homes, shops or farms, and gave Ellon a newfound sense of pride which has expressed itself in its fine town parks, while more recently it has benefited from the investment brought to its larger neighbour Aberdeen during the 1970s oil boom. Standing on high ground at the entrance to the town is the old but beautiful cruciform Church of St Mary on the Rock, which was bestowed on Kinloss in 1310, replaced in 1777 after its destruction during the 1745 Rebellion and rebuilt in 1871 by George E. Street R.A .

ELLON CASTLE
ABERDEENSHIRE

Located 20 miles NE of Aberdeen. Originally called Kermuchs when a Kennedy possession, it later passed to the Forbeses of Watterton. A castle built in 1780 by George Hamilton Gordon, 4th Earl of Aberdeen (Prime Minister 1852-55), was followed by a Gordon castle in 1851, which was in turn replaced in the 20th century.

ELPHINSTONE TOWER
EAST LOTHIAN

It occupies a site 2 miles S of Tranent on land that was held by the Elphinstones from the 13th century. The death of Sir Alexander Elphinstone at the battle of Piperdean in 1435 led to the marriage of Agnes Elphinstone (heiress) to Gilbert Johnstone, who built this oblong tower. In 1545 George Wishart (martyr) came face to face with his arch enemy Cardinal Beaton here, before Wishart's subsequent trial and execution at Saint Andrews. A wing added in 1600 was demolished in 1885 and more recently the structure was undermined and has since suffered more damage.

ELSHIESHIELDS TOWER
DUMFRIES & GALLOWAY

This simple turreted L plan keep is positioned 2 miles N of Lochmaben. A seat of the Johnstone family from the late 16th century, its most remarkable feature is its turret, which served as a signal tower for the area. In 1602 the house of William Johnstone of Elshieshields was burnt by Maxwell of Kirkhouse.

ERCHLESS TOWER
HIGHLAND

Standing near the bank of the River Beauly 10 miles SW of Beauly town is an early 17th century L plan tower which was the seat of the Chisholms from the 15th century. As zealous Jacobites they garrisoned it after Killiecrankie in 1689 and fought at Sheriffmuir in 1715 and Culloden in 1746.

ESSLEMONT CASTLE
ABERDEENSHIRE

This L plan tower 2 miles SW of Ellon town was built under king's licence by Henry de Chayne in 1500. Uninhabited in 1625, when it passed to the Errol family. In 1728 it was the property of the Gordons who partially occupied it until 1766 when another mansion house was built.

ETHIE CASTLE
ANGUS

Built 5 miles N of Arbroath. Probably developing from a 15th century keep or an L plan which was inhabited by the Abbott and subsequently Cardinal Beaton between 1530 and 1546. It passed to Sir John Carnegie of Ethie in 1549, whose grandson became Earl of Ethie in 1647, a title he exchanged in 1662 for Earl of Northesk.

EVELAW TOWER
SCOTTISH BORDERS

Occupying high ground 6 miles SW of Duns. This 16th century L plan keep later became a castellated house, which was common in the Borders region when stability returned prior to the Union with England in 1707.

EVELICK CASTLE
PERTH & KINROSS

About 5´ miles ENE of Perth is a ruined tower which was a former stronghold of the Lindsays, who were descendants of the Earl of Crawford and Knights of Evelick. Sir David Lindsay of Leroquhy assumed the title of Evelick in 1497, Sir Alexander Lindsay who obtained the estate in 1663 was created a baronet by Charles II in 1666. Later Sir Thomas Lindsay (heir) was murdered on the nearby Braes of Gowrie by his stepbrother James Douglas, resulting in the latter being executed at Edinburgh Cross in 1682. It ceased to be occupied by the family in the 18th century and passed to the Murrays of Murrayfield in the 19th century.

EYEMOUTH
SCOTTISH BORDERS

Fishing village situated at the mouth of the River Eye NE of Ayton. The river name is derived from the Old English 'Ei' meaning 'water' or 'stream'. As a dependent of Coldingham Priory, this was a busy port from the reign of Alexander II (1214-1249), trading in fish, wool and hides, and later became a favoured port of call for smugglers. Encouraged by its status as a Free Burgh of Barony, with Free Port conferred by James VI on Sir George Home of Wedderburn in 1588, the fruits of this illicit trade were often hidden in the deep hiding holes in some of the older town buildings. Described in 'Chambers Picture of Scotland', 1827, as being 'dark and cunning of aspect, full of curious alleys, blind and otherwise, and having no single house of any standing but what could unfold a tale of wonder'. Apart from a visit from Cromwell, 1650, and from Burns, during his tour of 1787, chief among its historical events is the Great Disaster of 1881 when 24 boats, nearly half the fleet, sank with 129 men leaving 107 widows, 60 adult dependants with 351 children, for whom a relief fund of £50,000 was raised. A memorial stone depicting a broken mast stands in the old cemetery while the Eyemouth Museum, opened at the centenary in 1981 in the Old Kirk (former Parish Kirk, built 1812), displays the Disaster Tapestry and other reminders of Eyemouth's past. Started by Smeaton in 1768, improved in 1887 and altered in 1962, its harbour helped expand its staple trade which has declined drastically after the ban on east coast herring fishing in 1976. Hertford's Fort, built above the village during the 1544-45 invasion, ranks with Gunsgreen House by Robert Adam (1773), as the main place of interest.

EYNHALLOW CHURCH
ORKNEY

On an island between Rousay and the mainland of Orkney are the ruins of what was once a monastery, probably founded in the 12th century as a Benedictine House. The name itself is taken from the Gaelic Eyin-helga meaning Holy Isle. The island figures in the 'Orkney Saga' in 1155 when it was recorded as being occupied by monks. Undoubtedly its location spared it the instability many of its southern brethren would have suffered, but the effects of the weather have taken their toll. More recently the building was converted and used as cottages, but in the 19th century a fever broke out and the four families who lived here vacated their homes. It was during the unroofing of the buildings by the owner Mr Balfour that the church was discovered. Essen-tially from two periods; although altered to suit both functions, the porch and part of the chancel walls are 12th century while most of the nave and some of the chancel walls are 16th century.

F

FAIRBURN TOWER
HIGHLAND

Located above the River Orrin 4 miles S of Strathpeffer is a late 16th century oblong tower which was once a stronghold of the Mackenzie family.

FALKIRK
FALKIRK

Town situated between Edinburgh and Glasgow. Formerly called 'Varia Capella' in Latin, 1298, the present name is derived from 'fawe-kirk' which in Middle English means the same: 'speckled church of mottled stone'. Long after the Romans occupied the nearby strategic station on the Antonine Wall (ruin) to the east, St Modan founded a church here around 717, but it was Malcolm III's church, built in 1070 on the same site, that gave the place its name. In 1080, William the Conqueror's son was reputed to have been here. Figuring in the Wars of Independence and in the Civil War, in 1298 Edward I routed the forces of William Wallace nearby, which led to much slaughter, and prior to the battle of Sauchieburn in 1488, the discontented nobles occupied the town. After its erection into a Burgh of Barony for Lord Livingstone, 1600, it witnessed in quick succession the solemn subscription to the Solemn League and Covenant in its old church, 1643, its decimation by the plague (1645), which was particularly virulent in the area and its elevation to a Burgh of Regality for the Earl of Callander, 1646. The second battle of Falkirk was fought in 1746 when the retreating Jacobites defeated a Hanoverian force advancing from Edinburgh. The forfeiture of the Jacobite Earl of Linlithgow after the 1715 Rising left baronial and burgh control in the hands of a Stentsmaster (tax assessor) and the Feuars Committee. Both encouraged growth until its elevation to a Parliamentary Burgh with a Municipal Constitution in the Reform Acts of 1832 and 1833. Though the capital of SE Stirlingshire with Falkirk Trystes (cattle markets), which were among the largest in Scotland after being transferred from Crieff in 1770, it was the Falkirk Iron Industry that spurred the town's growth and secured its position in Scotland's industrial belt linking Glasgow and Edinburgh by railways and waterways like the Forth and Clyde Canal, 1790, and the Union Canal, 1822. The Falkirk Iron Works were begun in 1819 by a colony of workmen from Carron. Initially supplying the domestic market, its 900-man workforce produced 16,000 tons of shell and shot during the Crimean War, 1854-56. The town's peripheral industries included distilleries, chemical and dynamite works, fire brick and tile yards and a leather factory. With its 20 independent family foundries by 1900, some of which were taken over by Allied Iron founders and Federated Foundries, the town played a predictable role during both World Wars, and during the Second World War, The British Aluminium Company started a rolling mill here. With the collapse of the Falkirk Iron Co and the Carron Co in the 1980s came much needed investment that helped revitalise the town's commerce. The recently restored Callander House, which dates from the 14th century, gives visitors an interesting insight into Falkirk's past, while the cruciform Parish Church, which dates from 1070 but was burnt in 1810, and rebuilt in 1811, houses effigies of the early Lords of Callander. See Battles 1 & 2

FALKIRK, BATTLE OF, 1298
FALKIRK

One of the earlier battles fought during the Wars of Independence. In order to secure the back door to England before retrieving his lands in France, Edward I marched north with a force some exaggerated estimates put at 80,000 foot and 7,000 horse. Opposing the army was a guerrilla leader named William Wallace. The latter's numerical disadvantage of around three to one determined the outcome, despite a valiant stand by the Scottish infantry with their pikes, whose ranks were finally broken by English archers, leading to considerable slaughter. Falkirk was the last battle fought by Wallace for Scottish Independence, and hastened his retreat to the Continent, where he solicited the Pope for support.

FALKIRK, BATTLE OF, 1746
FALKIRK

To prevent the capture of Stirling Castle by the Jacobites during their retreat north, General Hawley marched north with 8,000 men. After much manoeuvring, the Jacobites, numbering around 8,000, crucially beat Hawley's men to the hill SW of the town. Overtaken by rain, the Royal Dragoons' failed assault from their position by a ravine forced a retreat which caused widespread chaos in the ranks behind and a full scale retreat. The victory was the last one achieved by the Jacobites before their final defeat at Culloden. See Jacobite Rebellion

FALKLAND
FIFE

Village situated by the Lomond Hills 6 miles NE of Leslie. Originally called Kilgour, which was thought to mean 'yellow church' (beds of yellow sandstone have been found nearby), the present name probably comes from the Old English 'falca' meaning 'a falcon', from the practice of falconry. In 1160 the land formed part of the dowry of Malcolm IV's niece, Ada or Ela, on her marriage to Duncan, 5th Earl of Fife. As a community of retainers, the barony and hamlet owed its existence to the royal hunting seat which was popular with prelates, peers and noblemen for falconry and boar hunting, ultimately leading to the building of Falkland Palace in the 15th century and to the town's elevation to a Royal Burgh by James II in 1458. The renewal of charters in 1595, allowing weekly markets and four public fairs annually, set the seal on the town's dependency on the palace and its subsequent decline after 1603 when James VI ascended the English throne. In 1652 its forest was cut down by Cromwell to build a fort at Dundee. Occasionally visited by royals, the town's privileges were overlooked at the Treaty of Union in 1707 and it was occupied by Rob Roy's forces after the battle of Sheriffmuir, 1715. The legacy left by its royal ties, which later gave rise to the old adage 'Falkland bred', was in stark contrast with a group of Falkland vagrants who once inhabited these parts, but, treated like untouchables and better known as Scrapies, their only visible means of existence was a horse or a cow which covered their nocturnal activities of plunder around the Lomond Hills. Apart from agriculture, linen weaving for the manufacturers of Dundee became the main trade here and was expanded in the 1920s. Still retaining traces of its former status in its street names, Falkland later became a haunt of artists attracted by the old red roofed 17th and 18th century houses that are now preserved by the National Trust. See Palace

FALKLAND PALACE
FIFE

One of Scotland's premier palaces, it stands at the base of the Lomond Hills 8 miles SW of Monimail. A royal hunting seat from the 12th century and later the residence of royal courtiers. In 1160 the lands were obtained from Malcolm IV by Duncan, Earl of Fife, whose descendants sold the Earldom and estates in 1371 to

Robert Stewart, Earl of Menteith, later Duke of Albany before they reverted to the Crown in 1425. The 13th century Falkland Castle was replaced by Falkland Palace nearby which, although developed by earlier monarchs, was completed by James V in a Renaissance style around 1537. Once consisting of buildings on the south east and north side of the quadrangle, with the west side enclosed by a wall, today's remains include the south and east side of the square. After the rout at Solway Moss the King lay sick here, when after receiving the news of the birth of his daughter Mary he uttered the famous Stewart prophecy " It cam wi a lass, it will gang wi a lass" before dying here on 14 December, 1542. A favourite residence of Mary of Guise, and where she consented to the armistice with the Lords of the Congregation in 1559. It was regularly visited by Mary I between 1561 and 1566, when she spent her mornings hunting and her afternoons reading Greek and Latin classics, or playing chess and music. In 1582 it was the place of retreat for James VI after the Ruthven Raid (attempt by rebel lords to kidnap the King). In the 17th century it was visited by Charles I, (1633), followed by his son Charles II on his return from Holland in 1650 and after his coronation at Scone in 1651 but it suffered a fire during Cromwell's occupation. This resulted in the ruinous building which Rob Roy occupied in 1715. Its decay continued until the 19th century when it was restored by the Marquis of Bute and since 1952 has been held by the National Trust.

FALSIDE TOWER
CITY OF EDINBURGH

Favourably positioned on a hill 7 miles E of Central Edinburgh is a 15th century oblong tower with an adjoining 16th century L plan house. Lands belonged to the De Such family and then to the Setons in the early 14th century, when a "John of Fausyde" was a prisoner of the English (1307), and in 1371 a William De Seton granted the lands to his armour-bearer. Mentioned by the Earl of Hertford in 1544, it served as a vantage point for the the Scottish snipers in 1547 during the battle of Pinkie, resulting in its burning by the English. It was later restored and added to in 1618 by a John of Falside before Robert Falside sold the estate in 1631 to an Edinburgh merchant named Hamilton.

FARNELL CASTLE
ANGUS

The original structure built 3 miles SE of Brechin as the residence of the Bishops of Brechin was visited by Edward I of England in 1296. However, the Farnell of today is a 16th century tower built by Bishop Campbell in 1566, which later became the property of the Earl of Southesk. In the 19th century it was used as an almshouse for estate workers.

FAST CASTLE
SCOTTISH BORDERS

A ruinous sea fortress keep situated 4 miles NW of Coldingham. Used as a base by the English for raiding the surrounding land until captured in 1410 by Patrick, son of the Earl of Dunbar. It became the property of the Home family in 1467 who rebuilt it in 1521 but it passed through marriage in 1580 to Logan of Restalrig who had a sentence of forfeiture pronounced over his bones (1609), when his part in the Gowrie Conspiracy (see Perth) was revealed. The setting was thought to have been used for Sir Walter Scott's Wolf Crag in his 'Bride of Lammermoor'. Now a ruin.

FEARN ABBEY
HIGHLAND

Located 12 miles north of Alness. Originally founded at Edderton in 1221 or 1277 by the Earl of Ross. In 1238 it was moved to Fearn owing to the unruly neighbouring clans and its richer soil. Of its twenty one abbots its fifteenth was Patrick Hamilton who was burnt at St Andrews as a heretic in 1528. Architecturally its cruciform abbey church included a nave, choir, Lady Chapel and two transeptal chapels, but of the Abbey and the church which was rebuilt in the 14th century in a First Pointed style and completed by Abbot James Cairncross in 1545, little remains. The church became a Parish Church after the Reformation until 1742, when its roof collapsed, killing forty four people. Basically rebuilt in 1772 as a Parish Church retaining some of its original structure, it now houses a number of memorials to the Ross Family of finely carved stone and monumental effigies.

FENTON TOWER
EAST LOTHIAN

Standing on a hill 2 miles S of North Berwick. The lands once belonged to Patrick Wytelaw but on his forfeiture they passed to Sir John Carmichael who as Warden of the West Marches built this ruined L plan tower in 1577. His presence at the Raid of Reidswire in 1575, one of the last Border fights, led to his murder by some Borderers in 1600.

FERNIE CASTLE
FIFE

Erected 3 miles W of Cupar on land which anciently belonged to the Earls of Fife. In the 15th century this was the property of the Fernie family who built the original 16th century oblong tower, and in 1527 it was part of a barony for an Andrew Fernie. An additional round tower was added later, making it an L plan. Passing through marriage to the Balfours in the 17th century, the castle

was forfeited in 1715 after John Balfour's pro-Jacobite stance. Several additions have been made since and it now functions as a hotel.

FERNIEHERST CASTLE
SCOTTISH BORDERS

The original keep built in 1490 in the Jed Valley 2 miles SE of Jedburgh belonged to the Kerrs who were of Anglo-Norman stock and settled in Teviotdale around 1350. Burnt by the Earl of Sussex in 1570 and destroyed by Lord Ruthven in 1571 due to Sir Thomas's sympathies for Queen Mary. It was rebuilt in 1598 by Andrew Kerr as an L plan tower and minor additions have been made since. Visited by Sir Walter Scott and Wordsworth in 1803, it was later adapted as an information centre.

FETTERCAIRN DISTILLERY
ABERDEENSHIRE

In the village of the same name 11 miles NW of Montrose is one of Scotland's oldest distilleries, which owes everything to the fertile land of Mearns and the foresight of Alexander Ramsay. The grain mill that he converted in 1824 to the east of the North Esk that flows below the Braes of Angus, was further developed by James Stewart, who, along with fellow smugglers outside the village, took advantage of the more liberal climate for whisky production and acquired a licence in 1824. It gained respectability by its proximity to the Gladstone family (of political fame) estate and a visit from Queen Victoria, when a large stone archway was erected. Apart from a chimney, today's building shows all the traditional features of a 19th century distillery, with its pagoda roof with Doig vent rising above the whitewashed outbuildings and black slated roofs, that are the result of the 1887 expansion of its more modest predecessor. These developments enabled it to adapt to changes in production methods owing to increased demand, particularly for the blending market, and have been preserved by successive owners including Whyte & Mackay who acquired Fettercairn in 1973.

OWNERS
Kyndal International Ltd ?

REGION
Highlands

PRODUCT
Fettercairn 10 year old single malt 40% vol

NOTES
A pungent robust bouquet with subtle tones of oak and peat and a complex of flavours that are spicy and firm, resulting in a well balanced finish.

FIDDES CASTLE
ABERDEENSHIRE

This L plan tower stands 2 miles SW of Dunnottar on land which once belonged to the Arbuthnotts from the 13th century. With features including pepper pot turrets, circular towers and crow-stepped gables, it dates from the 16th century and was recently restored.

FINDLATER CASTLE
ABERDEENSHIRE

Perched on a rock 2 miles E of Cullen. The property of the St Clairs (Sinclairs) in the 14th century and then of the Ogilvies. In 1445 Sir Walter Ogilvie (Knight), was permitted by the Crown to fortify the castle and in 1638 his descendants were made Earls of Findlater. On her visit north in 1562, Queen Mary was refused entry here. The property of the Earls of Seafield in the 18th century, it is now partly ruinous.

FINGASK CASTLE
PERTH & KINROSS

Located 12 miles NE of Perth. Consisting of a late 16th century tower and central addition with pepper pot turrets from 1675. This one-time stronghold of the Thrieplands was built on the site of an earlier structure which was a place of strength and withstood a siege in the Civil War of 1642. Stalwarts of the Stewart cause: in 1674 a Patrick Thriepland was knighted for his services against the Covenanters, his son John joined the Earl of Mar in 1715 and the castle was later visited by the Old Pretender, 1716. Ransacked by the Hanoverians in 1746, after the family's forfeiture it was owned by the York Building Co until 1783 when it was repurchased by the Thrieplands who made some additions. It was sold to outsiders in the 19th century but eventually returned to the family, who restored it.

FINHAVEN CASTLE
ANGUS

The fragmentary remains of this 14th century tower with 16th century additions stand 6 miles NE of Forfar. Once the property of the Bruces, it passed to the Crawford family, 1375. In 1453 it was the scene of a banquet given for James II, and of a marriage ceremony for Master Crawford and the daughter of Cardinal Beaton in 1545. Finhaven was later held by Lyndsay of the Byres when the present structure was built by Lord Lyndsay, who sold it in 1629 to Lord Spynie. As the property of the Carnegies, in 1775 it was purchased by the Earl of Aboyne.

FINLARIG CASTLE
STIRLING

Standing at the bottom of Loch Tay NE of Killin are the ruins of the Earls of Breadalbane's seat built on the site of an earlier fort. Conforming to a Z plan, it was built in 1609 by Sir Duncan Campbell, 7th Laird of Glenorchy, near the family chapel and burial ground. For a long time the scene of conflict between the

Campbells and the Macdonalds, the castle's stone water tank and overflow drain was known as the scaffold within.

FLODDEN, BATTLE OF, 1513
SCOTTISH BORDERS

Twenty miles SE of Coldstream. One of the most ignominious defeats in Scottish history. Following an invasion of Northumberland by King James IV, the Scots, numbering what some accounts put at around 80,000, having lost a march on the Earl of Surrey retreated north to the area around Flodden. In his haste to prevent the enemy's march into Scotland, the King left his vantage point on Branxton Hill and began the battle on level ground with his artillery and six divisions. Responding in kind, after some hours, victory over the Scots was total, with the death toll of 10,000 men, including the flower of Scottish chivalry and their King. The closing stages of the battle evoked the rhyme:

Still rose the battle's deadly swell,
For still the Scots, around their king
Unbroken fought in desperate ring,
The precious hour has passed in vain,
And England's host has gained the plain;
Wheeling their march, and arching still,
Around the base of Flodden Hill

The catastrophe was to engender much fear and insecurity in future generations of Scots whose leadership ranks were considerably depleted, and for a time encouraged a more defensive policy.

FLOORS CASTLE
SCOTTISH BORDERS

To the NW of Kelso town in extensive grounds stands a large castellated mansion built for the Ist Duke of Roxburgh to designs by Sir John Vanbrugh but with a considerable contribution from William Adam. From its beginnings in 1718,

Floors' development spanned two centuries and was indicative of the desire of the landed aristocracy to display their wealth and power in a less fortified and more relaxed setting which was consistent with the stability of the age. Starting with the central oblong block with four corner towers, its interior still retains fine examples of Adam's work, who completed the first stage of its development by 1725. Although described by Sir Walter Scott as 'the largest inhabited mansion in Britain' it underwent further developments between 1838 and 1849 when it was remodelled by William Playfair including the east and west pavilions. This gave it the symmetrical grandeur with its castellated embellishments that we see today. As one would expect of such a grand design it houses many interesting 18th and also 19th century artefacts that more than compensate for its historical deficit. In the grounds is the spot where James II died after the bursting of a cannon at the siege of Roxburgh Castle in 1460.

FORDELL CASTLE
FIFE

Built a suitable distance of 2 miles E of Dunfermline. The barony was granted to Sir James Henderson on his resignation as Lord Justice Clerk in 1511. Consisting of two L plan towers that almost form a Z plan, it was started by the Hendersons in 1567 but after suffering a fire it was rebuilt by James Henderson and his wife Jean Murray in 1580. Fordell was visited by Queen Mary to attend the marriage of her maid of honour Marion Scott to George Henderson, Laird of Fordell. Noted for its brazier on the battlement, intended for a signal tower. The nearby chapel of Therotus was rebuilt in 1650 and used as a family vault. Fordell House, the new family home, was built by John Fordell in 1721.

FORDYCE TOWER
ABERDEENSHIRE

Located 2´ miles W of Portsoy. Essentially a tower house, it was built in 1592 by Thomas Menzies, whose family were Provosts of Aberdeen. A wing containing a separate house was added later.

FORFAR GOLF CLUB
ANGUS

Although the history of golf in Forfar is obscure, the game was practised in the late 18th century, when Rev Andrew Eadie played on the older course to the north of the town. In 1871 Colonel Dempster of Dunnichen permitted the playing of golf over fifty acres of ground to the east, and under the auspices of James Brodie, began the formation of the Forfar Golf Club, which had its 18 hole course laid out by Tom Morris of Saint Andrews. After negotiating the whins, broom and dykes and the characteristic undulations of "rig and furrow", the players would return to the rented room at Lochhead Farm until the club's improved prosperity funded the building of the clubhouse in 1889, to which ladies were admitted in 1894. Most of the inter-club matches were played between the neighbouring clubs of Montrose Mercantile, Grange, and Carnoustie Caledonia in the golfing season, though the club did have a Winter League from 1926. With members coming from beyond Forfar, during the First World War (1914-18) many garrison soldiers became Honorary Members and after it, in 1920, the club was able to purchase the course for £700 when its membership stood at 541. In 1926 the proposals made by James Braid were implemented. Suffering the usual constraints during World War II (1939-45), activity resumed after the war and in the 1960s membership increased rapidly and during the 1970s the figure reached 850. Among the club's more celebrated personalties is Sandy Saddler, who, after being champion here seven times, went on to represent Scotland no less than ten times, and Britain fourteen times, between 1959 and 1967. In the last year he was the only player to win two singles in the Walker Cup. Among the clubs oldest trophies are The Lowson Challenge Cup, received from Agnes Lowson in 1901, The Brodie Younger Shield, presented by Dr James Lowson in 1898, The Coronation Commemorative Quaich given by Mrs A Wright in 1902 and The Bruce Medal presented by Robert Bruce in 1869.

FORRES
MORAY

Town situated 4 miles SE of Kinloss near Findhorn Bay. Its name either derives from the Gaelic 'Foras', meaning 'little shrubbery' or from 'faruis' meaning 'brink edge or border', a reference to its proximity to the river. The 10th century Sueno's Stone to the east of the town is 23ft high and depicts a battle either between the Danes and the Scots or the Picts and the Scots. Identified with Ptolemy's (2nd century Egyptian Geographer) Varis Chart after the charting of Moray by the Romans, Forres was a place of importance from earliest times and a vibrant trading settlement in the 6th century, which later became a member of the Hanseatic League (a trading group of German, Baltic and European ports), with royal connections down through the centuries. As described in this ballad:

Forres in the days of yore
A name many Scotias cities bore
And there her judges oer and oer
Did Scotland's law dispense;
And there the monarchs of the land
In former days held high command
And ancient architects had planned
By rules of art in order grand,
The royal residence.

Once the site of a castle where King Duffus was murdered in 966, Forres was immortalised by Shakespeare as the place where King Duncan held camp whilst Macbeth and Banquo, attempting to join him, were met by three witches. Malcolm I is also thought to have resided here in the 10th century, as did David I, who rebuilt its castle in the 12th century, followed by his grandson William I, when a Royal Charter was granted which was confirmed by James IV in 1496. By that time Forres had lost out to its neighbour and rival Elgin as the administrative centre for the area. Near Sueno's Stone are the Witches Stones where three witches, accused of plotting the death of King Duffus, were burnt in the 10th century after being rolled down Cluney Hill in barrels. Its Gothic-styled Mercat Cross, erected in 1844, is an imitation of the great crosses of the Middle Ages, and, like the town's other objects of interest, dates from the 19th century. On Castlehill stands an obelisk built to the memory of James Thomson, an army surgeon who saved 400 Russian soldiers after the battle of Alma in 1854. The Falconer Museum, built in 1870 in an Italian style with a bequest from Alexander Falconer (natural historian, botanist and geologist), houses the many interesting relics from the area's past.

FORSE TOWER
HIGHLAND

On a peninsula 2 miles N of Latheron stands a 14th century courtyard keep. In 1400 Kenneth Sutherland, a descendant of William Earl of Sutherland, married Lady Keith, the Forse heiress. A grant of half the lands and its castle was made by James V to the family in 1538 and with their descendants it remained until the 19th century.

FORT AUGUSTUS
HIGHLAND

Village and fort situated in the Great Glen at the SW extremity of Loch Ness. The land was originally held by the Lovats, after whose forfeiture in 1716 a barracks was built to subdue the Highland Clans. In 1730 it was strengthened and enlarged by General Wade, who named it Fort Augustus after William Augustus, Duke of Cumberland. Although capable of housing 300 men with 4 corner bastions and 12 six pounder guns, it was captured by the Jacobites in 1746 and dismantled, but later served as a prison and headquarters for the Duke of Cumberland after Culloden, 1746. Ironically, it was here that the Jacobite Lord Lovat was brought as a prisoner. Occupied until sold in 1857 to Lord Lovat it was later presented by his son to the Benedictine Fathers, who in 1870 opened it as a school, which operated until recently.

FORTEVIOT
PERTH & KINROSS

Village situated 7 miles SW of Perth. First appearing as 'Fothuir tabaicht' in a Pictish chronicle of 970, while the origin of this is unclear it may derive from the Irish ' fothar' meaning 'woodland'. After the Roman withdrawal it became the Capital of the Pictish Kingdom of Fortrenn, with a royal palace probably at Halyhill, in which King Kenneth Macalpine resided prior to dying here (858) in a church founded by the Pictish King Fergus. Relics of this foundation include the Dupplin Cross that stood above Bankhead Farm, the Dornochy Cross shattered in the 18th century and now housed in the church (built, 1778), along with the 10th century Forteviot Celtic hand bell. The palace that was once occupied by Malcolm I (943-954), Kenneth II (971-995) and Duncan I (1034-1040) has now disappeared. On Miller Acre near

Halyhill, Edward Balliol's army encamped before the battle of Dupplin Moor in 1332. Down to the 20th century the original village suffered a steady decline in importance until it was demolished and rebuilt in 1926 by Lord Teviot of Dupplin as a model village with school, village hall and smithy.

FORTINGALL
PERTH & KINROSS

Village situated 4 miles W of Kenmore. Although the derivation of its name is unclear it may come from the old Gaelic 'fothir' and 'cill' meaning either 'fortified church' or 'wooden church'. The possible birthplace of Pontius Pilate, whose father, a legionnaire during the Roman occupation, was involved with a local girl. This was thought by Skene to have been the site of a Roman Camp or fort in 208 AD, with a rich and varied landscape that harbours numerous memories and monuments of antiquity, like monolithic circles, forts and burial sites. Dating from the 7th century, and probably founded by St Adamnan, the Parish Church, built in 1902 on the foundations of a pre-Reformation building, houses pieces of Celtic crosses, a 7th century hand bell and an ancient baptismal font. In the churchyard is the 3,000 year old Yew tree. Often the scene of clan conflicts between the Stuarts, Macivor, Mackintoshes and Camerons, the nearby Rannoch Moor was where William Wallace rallied supporters and where Bruce took refuge in the 14th century. During the 1745 Rising, the village was ransacked by the Hanoverians.

FORTROSE
HIGHLAND

Town situated 10 miles NE of Inverness. Name derived from the Gaelic 'Foterrois' meaning 'under' or 'beneath the promontory'. Once consisting of two towns, Chanonry (or Fortrose) and Rosemarkie. The original name of Rosemardkyn was derived from the Gaelic 'ros' meaning 'cape' and 'marc' meaning 'horse'. This may have been a Royal Burgh from the 13th century, but it was the site of a church from a very early period which had grown into a Cathedral and Bishopric founded by David I in 1124 which until the Reformation in 1560 dominated much of the town's history. Fortrose and Rosemarkie were united under James II and constituted a Free Burgh in favour of Bishop Ross in 1455, but, after lapsing to the Crown at the Reformation, with the addition of Chanonry in 1592, were reunited as the Royal Burgh of Fortrose. Unfortunately the destruction of the town and its Cathedral by Cromwell's forces in 1652 marked the beginning of its decline as an Episcopal See. The Cross of Rosemarkie, now in the west of the town, was taken from the market place of Fortrose where the last witch in Scotland was said to have been burnt. In the 19th century the area was popular with the geologist Hugh Millar (1802-1856) who, in his ' Rambles of a Geologist', complimented it on its vast beds of bolder clay. By this time Fortrose had no trade other than that generated by summer visitors to its sandy beaches, and today it is becoming increasingly residential. See Cathedral & Golf Club

FORTROSE CATHEDRAL
HIGHLAND

The Bishopric of Ross was founded by David I by 1131 in the town of Fortrose / Rosemarkie on the site of a church which according to legend was built around 712 by St Curitan, also known as St Boniface. Its schools of divinity and law flourished under its educated clergy and by 1300 its Cathedral was erected and dedicated to St Peter and St Boniface. Considerably larger than today's remains and built of red sandstone in an English Gothic style, it incorporated a nave of four bays with aisles and round-headed windows. In addition it had a choir with aisles, Lady Chapel, west tower, quasi-transepts, rood turret and vaulted Chapter House over a crypt. The damage inflicted at the Reformation by the Earl of Morton did not impede a visit in 1562 made by Queen Mary, who was received by her ardent supporter the distinguished Bishop Elphinstone who was later imprisoned in the Tower of London. Damaged by Cromwell's forces in 1652 to provide stone for his fort at Inverness. In the 17th century its ruins were partly used as a prison and in the 19th the Town Council met here. Its sole remains are the south aisle of the chancel nave and a detached Chapter House which shows some fine examples of Gothic vaulting. In 1880 a hoard of silver coins from Robert II's reign were found in the Cathedral Green.

FORTROSE & ROSEMARKIE GOLF CLUB
HIGHLAND

The Chanonry Peninsula, protruding into the Moray Firth, was deemed the ideal location for a golf course when Fortrose was founded in 1888 at the insistence of Mr Kennedy, a former businessman from Shanghai and consummate sportsman. In the following year the six hole course was opened. So popular was the area for recreational pursuits, with its fresh sea air, that it wasn't long before members from a cross-section of the community, not least the young, reached fifty. Employing most of its resources to clear the prospective course, in 1895 a wooden clubhouse was built and in 1900 the course was extended. The club's patron J D Fletcher (Barrister) of the Rosehaugh Estate played a prominent role in the club's development while bringing an enterprising zeal that brought some fi-

nancial security which diminished owing to the onset of war in 1914. It was not until 1919, after the clubhouse had been used as a Guardhouse by the Highland Cyclist Battalion, that the full material damage of the war was assessed. After the armistice of 1918 came ambitious plans to extend the course to 18 holes to designs by James Braid, and in 1924 the new course was opened. Despite this it was to be another ten years before the new clubhouse was built. While lady members had existed here since the early days, it was in the wake of the Suffragette Movement and the freedom experienced during the war years that engendered the first Ladies' Committee in 1922. The club was suspended in a state of limbo during the Second World War, (1939-45), when the course and clubhouse were used by a multinational combat force training for D-Day. The recompense from the War Department for damage suffered during this period was £4,000 which helped restore all 18 holes by 1947. After introducing Sunday play in 1949, membership was to swell forcing the building of the new clubhouse in 1959, funded by a Miss Isa Ross on the condition that no alcohol was sold on the premises. Presently the club bar is housed in an extension. By 1970, membership stood at 200, and apart from a small piece at the 4th fairway and the 5th green, all the course belonged to the club with a membership that continued to grow, so that in 1977 the granting of the liquor licence and an extension were well received. This was augmented by a further extension to the clubhouse in 1990 and by 1999 the membership had reached 700.

FORT WILLIAM
HIGHLAND

Town and fort situated at the foot of Ben Nevis SW of Inverness. Dating from the mid 17th century, the wooden fort built by General Monck in 1655 during Cromwell's Protectorate, and known as the Garrison of Inverlochy, was replaced in 1690 by General Mackay's stone structure, with its bomb proof magazine, two bastions for twelve pounders, and accommodation for 104 men. Renamed Fort William after William III, with the surrounding land named Maryburgh after the King's consort, the fort resisted sieges by the Jacobites in 1715 and 1746 but was sold by the Government in 1860 to a Mrs Campbell of Monzie, and later dismantled to make way for the railway. Furthered by General Wade's road link and lifeline to Inverness, the capital of the Highlands, the town that sprang up, originally called Gordonsburgh, became a burgh in 1874 and was linked to the south by the West Highland Railway Line in 1894. Basically Victorian in appearance, the town eventually established itself as the Gateway to the Highlands with facilities and information for the many travellers, which is still much sought after today. The West Highland Museum, housed in an 18th century building, exhibits many Jacobite and Stone Age relics.

FOUNTAINHALL CASTLE
EAST LOTHIAN

Situated 1´ miles SW of Pencaitland. The lands once belonged to the Pringles of Woodhead, who built the original house that was developed into an L plan castle in 1638 by Robert Pringle (Writer to the Signet) after receiving the estate from Charles I in 1636. It was constituted a barony in 1685 for John Lauder of Fountainhall, an Edinburgh merchant who became Lord Fountainhall, Lord of Session, in 1689, prior to making further additions.

FOWLIS EASTER
ANGUS

Village situated 5 miles NW of Dundee. Name derived from the Gaelic 'fo-ghlas' meaning 'sub stream' or 'burn'. The lands were granted by David I to William Maule after the battle of the Standard in 1138 but later became the property of Sir Roger Mortimer and Sir Andrew Grey in 1377 until purchased by Murray of Ochtertyre in 1669. Built on the site of an earlier 12th century church that was dedicated to St Marnock, Fowlis's 15th century church, erected and made collegiate by the 3rd Lord Gray, is of Hewn stone, while the interior includes some finely carved wood panels and a curious wood screen with a painting of the crucifixion and numerous biblical figures, most notably the Virgin Mary, St John the Baptist and St Peter.

FOWLIS WESTER
PERTH & KINROSS

Village situated 6 miles SW of Methven (see previous entry for name derivation). The site of the castle once occupied by the Earls of Strathearn is now marked by a mound. Although the original church is now gone, its 13th century replacement was found to contain an ancient Pictish stone, while an additional stone probably from the same period stands in the village and depicts a wolf chase on the one side, with a joug (neck collar) on the other. Although the building later fell into decline it was restored in the 20th century.

FRAOCH EILEAN CASTLE
ARGYLL & BUTE

Positioned on a small island on Loch Awe 25 miles SW of Dalmally. In the 13th century Alexander III granted the island to Gilbert Macnaughton who started this structure. The castle figures in a Gaelic poem which describes how the hero of Fraoch, while trying to gather fruit for his lady love Mengo, engages a fiery dragon that guards the island, leading to a combat fatal to both.

FRASERBURGH
ABERDEENSHIRE

Town situated 18 miles NW of Peterhead, occupying the southern slope of Kinnairds Head on Fraserburgh Bay. The evidence of pre-historic kitchen middens at nearby Phillorth (found in the 20th century) suggests the site was occupied by early Pictish and Danish settlers who, as tradition states, were converted to Christianity by St Modan. Originally called Faithlie, the village was developed into a town by Alexander Fraser of Phillorth, for whom it was erected into a Burgh of Barony in 1546, which became Fraserburgh. Attempts to establish a university foundered after the prospective principal lost royal favour. The town is symmetrical in plan and extends to the south of the harbour, which started with a small pier built in the 16th century by Alexander Fraser. Thus prompting James VI to grant two charters erecting it into a Free Port in 1588 and a Burgh of Regality in 1592. On Kinnairds Head (nearby) is the old Fraser Castle built in 1570, while below it stands the family's square tower. Between 1807-37, while under the guidance of Lord Saltoun, its harbour extension made it one of the main herring fishing ports on the north east coast, along with Aberdeen and Peterhead, with a fleet of 192 boats by 1834 giving work to over 2,400 people between June and September. The proximity of the town to the best fishing grounds in the North Sea and the introduction of the steam drifter secured decades of growth for Fraserburgh and the industry which supplied 1,000,000 barrels to Russia in one year alone. In 1930 the introduction of the seine net helped replace herring with white fishing which has itself declined drastically.

FRENCHLAND TOWER
DUMFRIES & GALLOWAY

It stands by a burn 1 mile E of Moffat. In the 13th century the land was granted by the Bruces to a Frenchman named Roger Franciscus. However, it wasn't until the 16th century that an oblong tower developed, which was altered to make an L plan mansion, probably by Robert Frenchie who succeeded his father in 1610.

FRENDRAUGHT TOWER
ABERDEENSHIRE

A fragment of a tower situated 7 miles E of Huntly was built as a Crichton stronghold in the heart of Gordon country after James Crichton obtained the Lordship in the late 15th century. In 1630, after a skirmish with the Leslies of Pitcaple, it suffered a mysterious fire and six men died, including the Laird of Frendraught and the Marquis of Huntly's son. Using his court influence, Crichton had a John Meldrum of Pitcaple hanged but a later inquiry revealed it had started internally, leading to Crichton's temporary imprisonment. In 1642 Sir James Crichton was created Viscount Frendraught.

FRESWICK TOWER
HIGHLAND

Perched on a rock overlooking the sea 5 miles S of Duncansby Head. The land was granted by Robert the Bruce to the Mowat family who built the original tower which was visited by Cromwell's forces in 1652. The estate was sold to Sinclair of Ratter (1661), who built the present mansion house nearby shortly after.

FYVIE
ABERDEENSHIRE

Town situated 25 miles NW of Aberdeen. Name derived from the Gaelic 'fiamh' meaning 'track' or 'path'. The Priory of St

Mary that once stood here was founded by Fergus Earl of Buchan in 1179 for Benedictines from Tiron, and was subordinate to Arbroath Abbey. A Royal Burgh and Sheriffdom when visited by Edward I in 1296, the land granted to Sir James Lindsay in 1390 by the Earl of Carrick was after a number of owners bought, along with the castle, in 1597 by Sir Alexander Seton, who became Lord Fyvie in 1598 and Ist Earl of Dunfermline in 1605. Having its status as a burgh revoked in 1690 after the 4th Earl of Dunfermline supported Viscount Dundee in 1689, the Lordship and estate was bought by the Earl of Aberdeen by 1734. The period of unmatched prosperity enjoyed by its staple farming trade between 1860 and 1878 was reversed by the collapse of the Glasgow City Bank in 1878 and since then this essentially Victorian town has had a chequered history. See Castle & Church

FYVIE CASTLE
ABERDEENSHIRE

Situated by the River Ythan 30 miles NW of Aberdeen. Originally a royal hunting seat visited by William the Lyon in 1211, Alexander II in 1221 and Edward I in 1296. Its development was under way by the late 14th century, when it was referred to as King Robert's Park, which in 1380 the Earl of Carrick (later Robert III) granted it to his cousin Sir James Lindsay. It was besieged by a nephew of Robert Keith in 1395 before it passed to Sir Henry Preston (1397), who built the oldest part, the south-east tower of 1400. Passing to the Meldrums (1440), who built the Meldrum Tower in the south west corner, with adjoining ranges to the west and south. It owes its greatest splendour to the Meldrums' successor Alexander Seton, (Ist Earl of Dunfermline) raised to Lord Fyvie in 1598, who built the main entrance (Seton Tower) between the other two, thereby creating a splen-

did south front resembling a French chateau. In the 17th century it was occupied by Montrose (1644), before he engaged a force under the Earl of Argyll (Skirmish of Fyvie), was held by Lord Aboyne for Charles I, 1646, and by Puritans in Cromwell's time, but in 1690 the Earl of Dunfermline was outlawed and forfeited. Purchased in 1726 by the Earl of Aberdeen, whose son General Gordon built the Gordon tower around 1750, by 1889 it had been sold to a Mr Forbes of Leith. Today the castle exhibits a fine collection of paintings and armour.

FYVIE CHURCH
ABERDEENSHIRE

Near the town of the same name are the remains of the Parish Church of St Peter, which William Ist granted to the Abbey of Arbroath along with the lands, tithes, obligations, pasturage and other pertinents in the 12th century. Today the church boasts a number of Tiffany stained glass windows and Celtic stones.

G

GALASHIELS
SCOTTISH BORDERS

An old Market Town situated 34 miles SE of Edinburgh on both sides of the River Gala, which, with its shepherds huts, or sheilings from the Old Norse 'skjol' meaning 'a shelter', gave the town its name. With traces of a Pictish and Roman presence at Catrail and Rink Hill, by 1340 Galashiels had become a hamlet for huntsmen and guardians of the nearby royal hunting seat in Ettrick Forest. The town's armorial bearings show two foxes looking up at a plum tree and recall the surprise attack by local men in 1337 on an English raiding party while they were eating plums (Soor Plooms Raid). The event is also marked by the 'Braw Lads Gathering' when a Braw Lad and lass ride the town's marches. Originally belonging to the Douglases, on their forfeiture in 1455 the land passed to the Pringles, who built Gala Tower in 1457, and in the 19th century Gala House, which was designed by David Bryce in a Scottish Baronial style since 1946 this has housed the Gala Art Club. A Burgh of Barony for Pringle of Galashiels in 1599, and a weavers' village by 1666 with an agrarian economy and markets in Melrose and Selkirk, the modern town owes much to the spirit of manufacture in the 19th century, a time which saw its river powering woollen mills built by the Scott and Pringle families. By 1868 it was constituted a Parliamentary Burgh, and by 1882 the 17 mills and 5 spinning mills produced blankets, plaids and shawls, along with its chief products, its tweeds, which were marketed worldwide. The town held its position well into the 20th century amidst competition from mills in Hawick, Selkirk, Dumfries and Innerleithen, and in 1909 the South of Scotland Technical College was founded, which later became The Scottish College of Textiles. Following the floods of 1880 and 1881 many of the older buildings were demolished, leaving the Mercat Cross, dated 1695, as its oldest antiquity, which now stands near the Cloth Hall founded by Robert Douglas.

GALDENOCH TOWER
DUMFRIES & GALLOWAY

In a hollow 7 miles NW of Stranraer is an L plan ruin that was built between 1547 and 1570 by Gilbert Agnew, 2nd son of Andrew Agnew of Lochnaw. However the family have long since abandoned it.

GARDYNE TOWER
ANGUS

The house stands on a sloping bank above the Lunan water 9 miles S of Brechin. The tower, built in 1580 with shot holes and turrets, was inscribed with the shield of the Gardynes of Ley, while over the door in the west front additions of 1740 there is the Lyal of Dysart crest. The short and dumpy towers, that are capped with imitation battlements with short mock gargoyles like guns suggest the architect's playful fancy was a reaction to the long restrained need for serious defensive designs.

GARGUNNOCK HOUSE
STIRLING

This was once the site of a fort on Keir hill 6 miles W of Stirling, from where William Wallace attacked and ejected the English from Gargunnock Pele below before crossing the Forth. The present 17th century mansion, which incorporates an older wing, was built closeby and belonged to the Grahams and then the Stirlings.

GARMOUTH
MORAY

Seaport and village situated at the mouth of the River Spey 9 miles NE of Elgin. The name is probably derived from the Gaelic 'gearr magh' meaning 'a short plain'. Dating from Medieval times, the village later rose in importance owing to the salmon fishing and smuggling trade, and by 1587 had become a Burgh of Barony for Innes of that Ilk. It played an important role in the Civil War when it was burnt by Montrose in 1645 and also as the scene of Charles II, arrival from Holland in 1650 after he had signed the Solemn League and Covenant. The village derived much of its income from the timber cultivated in the forests of Glen More, Abernethy, Rothiemurchus and Glenfeshie. Consequently the use of this resource meant the timber-built town was dangerously exposed to the havoc wrought by the flood of 1829, leading to the cutting of the river mouth in the 20th century.

GARTH TOWER
PERTH & KINROSS

A simple keep, it stands on the bank of the Lyon 7 miles W of Aberfeldy. Although its age is uncertain, in the 14th century it belonged to the Earl of Buchan (The Wolf of Baddenoch) and was known as the castle of the fierce wolf. This unruly chief was imprisoned here by the orders of his father Robert II, until released by Robert III. It later passed to their descendants, the Stewarts of Atholl, who were raided by the Menzies of Weem in 1504 and vacated it in 1577. After a number of owners its ruinous state was restored by Sir Donald Currie MP in the 19th century and was further improved in the 20th century.

GASK HOUSE
PERTH & KINROSS

Located 10 miles SW of Perth. With the land, bearing traces of Roman fortified posts, it was granted by Robert the Bruce to Sir William Oliphant, who was active in the Wars of Independence and became Lord Gaskness. It was in 1625 to the Oliphants cousin, who was the first Jacobite Laird. In 1745 Prince Charles Edward stayed here and in 1746 it was ransacked by the Hanoverian forces. The present house, built in 1801, was occupied by the ballad writer Caroline Oliphant, Lady Nairn (1766-1845), who was famed for her songs ' Laird o' Cockpen ', ' The land o' the Leal ', ' The Auld House ' and ' Charlie is my darling ' .

GATEHOUSE OF FLEET
DUMFRIES & GALLOWAY

Town picturesquely situated on the River Fleet, 7 miles NW of Kirkcudbright. The first part of its name owes its origins to a solitary house at the gate of an avenue leading to the Caley Mansion. Formerly known as Kalecht, it was held by the Stewarts and then the Lennoxes before passing to the Murrays, whose descendant built the present house in 1763, and for whom it became a Burgh of Barony in 1795. As landowner he oversaw the village's development into a town which became dominated by its cotton mills, started by the Yorkshire firm of Birtwhistle in 1793 and 1794. Although once seen as the Glasgow of the south, its similarity to a miniature Edinburgh New Town reflects its former prosperity which by 1900 had irreversibly declined. The old Caley Estate has since been taken over by the Forestry Commission and cultivated as a nursery forest.

GIGHT TOWER
ABERDEENSHIRE

Situated on the bank of the Yethan 5 miles NE of Fyvie, are the ruins of an L plan tower built after 1479 by William 3rd, son of the 2nd Earl of Huntly. Plundered by the Covenanters in 1644, it remained a Gordon possession until 1787, when Catherine Gordon, mother of the poet Lord Byron, sold it to the 3rd Earl of Aberdeen.

GIRNIGOE CASTLE
HIGHLAND

Dominating a coastal promontory 3 miles NE of Wick is the ruined stronghold of the Sinclairs, Earls of Caithness. The extensive courtyard developments added to the west and east sides of the original 15th /16th century keep, combined with the rocks, moat and ditches to the south and the ocean to the north to make it one of the most important towers in the north. Because of the leniency the young master had shown towards the local people, John, 4th Earl of Caithness imprisoned his son here between 1576 and 1582 when, after being starved for some time, he was fed salted meat then, withholding all liquids, was left to die of raging thirst. The building was vacated in the 17th century.

GIRVAN
SOUTH AYRSHIRE

Town situated 22 miles SW of Ayr. Originally called Invergaven owing to its position at the mouth of the Girvan Water (formerly Gaven), which is probably derived from the Gaelic 'garbh allt' meaning 'rough stream'. This has been the site of a village from the 11th century, which became a Burgh of Barony for Boyd of Penkill who occupied the nearby Barganny Castle. Despite receiving a charter in 1696, it did not enjoy burgh privileges until 1785, when it was still an insignificant village. Described by Robert Heron in his 'Journey through the Western Counties of Scotland' (1793), as having "houses so low as to seem at the south end of the village, rather like caves dug in the earth than houses built upon it". The introduction of cotton weaving attracted many Irish migrant workers (prior to the potatoe famine, 1847) and by 1836 it had countless handlooms supplying the Glasgow factories. Also known for its smuggling activities, the extension of its harbour in 1881 and the advent of rail travel furthered its fishing and farming trade, which was followed by tourism for people from the built-up industrial centres attracted by the coastal pursuits.

GLAMIS CASTLE
ANGUS

Built on the left bank of the Dean NE of Glamis village. The site of a royal residence from the 11th century, where Malcolm II is thought to have died in 1034. The land and barony was granted by Robert II to his secretary John Lyon on his marriage to the King's daughter in 1372. It was however, his successors, the Ist Lord Glamis in 1445 who built the 15th century tower, and the 9th Lord Glamis (Ist Earl of Kinghorn, 1606), who greatly improved the structure and lived here between 1578 and 1615. The castle also figured in Shakespear's 'Macbeth'. A charter of 1677 obtained by Patrick, 3rd Earl of Kinghorn, declared his heirs to be titled Earls of Strathmore. Under the guidance of such eminent figures as Inigo Jones, Jacob De Wit and Capability Brown in the 17th and 18th centuries, the family brought the castle closer to its familiar sculptors, corbellings, pepper pot turrets and pinnacles. In 1716 during the Jacobite Rising, the Old Pretender met his advisers here and declared he " had not seen its designs matched on the Continent ". Visited by Sir Water Scott, 1793; in the early 20th century the late Queen Mother grew up here. Presently the castle is a very popular attraction and houses a large collection of artefacts.

GLASCLUNE CASTLE
PERTH & KINROSS

Standing above a burn 3 miles NW of Blairgowrie is the Blairs of Glasclune's Z plan castle. Built around 1600 with round towers it was once a place of considerable strength but is now a ruin.

GLASGOW
CITY OF GLASGOW

The city is situated on the River Clyde to the west of Edinburgh. After the Roman retreat, the district became part of the British Kingdom of Strathclyde but by the 4th century St Ninian, who was trained in Rome, founded a church on the site of Glasgow Cathedral, giving rise to two villages called Glesche and Cathures, the former giving the city its name. This may come from the Gaelic 'glas cau' meaning 'green hollow'. Once the site of a Culdee Cell, a bishopric was founded in 543 AD by St Kentigern (Mungo), who as legend has it, gave the city its armorial bearings after finding the Queen's wedding ring inside a fish. For centuries, the area was overrun by tribal barbarism until the reign of Alexander I (1107-1124) who restored the land to his brother David, who revived its bishopric, thus prompting the building of a timber Cathedral by Bishop John Achaius, along with a bishop's castle. The former was rebuilt in 1233, and in 1246 a Dominican Friary was founded, with a church that rivalled the Cathedral in grandeur. Figuring in the Wars of Independence, its streets were the scene of Earl Percy's defeat at the hands of William Wallace before the latters capture here in 1305, provoking the Bishop of Glasgow to support his successor Robert the Bruce after absolving him of Comyn's murder. The charter of 1189 and the privileges of an annual fair (forerunner of the Glasgow Fair) brought with it the enmity of Dumbarton and Rutherglen, whose merchants sought to protect their trading rights. Although these privalages were curtailed in the 13th century Glasgow secured free trading rights in Argyll and Lennox. This competition continued to cause bitter rivalry down through the centuries when Glasgows status as a University Town by 1451 and an Archbishopric by 1492 did much to further growth while providing the catalyst for change at the Reformation, when its population numbered around 4,500. In 1544 during the minority of Mary I, the Earls of Glencairn and Arran fought out the battle of the Butts here and it was around this time that the Gorbals was the site of a leper hospital founded by Lady Lochow, daughter of Robert, Duke of Albany. While its representation in Parliament (1546) and its elevation to a Royal Burgh (1611) served as milestones for its pre-eminence and later status as the commercial capital of the country, the city was transfixed by struggle and strife during later decades. It was after being affected by famine and pestilence, 1649 that it suffered the great fires of 1652 and 1677, and during the former one third of the city was burnt. Occupied by Cromwell in 1650 and by Claverhouse in 1679, Glasgow supported the Government in 1715 and gave token support to the Jacobites during their ten day occupation in 1746. The Malt Tax and Shawfield Riots of 1725 were symptomatic of the deep mistrust of the Treaty of Union of 1707 and led to a mob occupying the city, the death of several citizens and the wounding of 17 others. Like Edinburgh, its industrialisation, coupled with bad housing for its migrant workers from Ireland and the Highlands, caused many social problems that continued despite increased prosperity marked by the establishment of the Glasgow Arms Bank in the 1750s, and later by the deepening and widening of the Clyde. This was funded by the revenue from its growing trade in cotton and tobacco, moving the citizens to form a regiment to oppose the American War of Independence in 1770. Its observatory, built on Garnet Hill in 1808, was relocated due to the volume of smoke from its diverse and innovative industries. These included the manufacture of chemicals, 1786, the introduction of steam power loom weaving by J.L Robertson, 1793, the starting of a dye company by Charles Mackintosh at Pollokshaws, 1795, the trial run of Bell's Comet on the Clyde in 1812, and the introduction of Neilson's hot blast furnace at the Clyde Iron Works in 1824. Though small by later standards, when gas lighting was introduced in 1818 there were thousands of looms, scores of cotton mills and numerous printing works contributing to a burgeoning industrial base. This precipitated the founding of the Glasgow City Bank in 1839 that greatly stimulated its other major industry, shipbuilding, which was being concentrated on the Clyde in Govan and in Partick. The relentless expansion of its textile trade, which by 1854 gave employment to 1500 people who operated its spinning factories, cotton weaving factories, and its weaving and spinning factories, took the number to almost 100 factories. The odium of its poor housing and bad sanitation which contributed to the cholera epidemic of 1832, in which 3,000 people died, eventually led to an official report which stated that in some cases up to 600 persons lived in one tenement stair alone. Basic living standards continued to elude its citizens with the City Improvement Act of 1866, when some of its streets were redeveloped and widened, but overall it sacrificed basic domestic needs for commercial expediency, despite a population increase of around 71,000 to 487,000

between 1801 and 1881. From a harbour covering four acres at the Broomielaw in 1860 it had stretched two miles along the Clyde by 1880, and handled ores from Spain, wine from France and Portugal, oil and ivory from Africa, teas, spices, cotton and jute from India, cotton, cattle, tobacco, corn flour, beef and timber from America, sugar, teak and mahogany from the West Indies, and meats, wool and gold from Australia. The city's main exports were cotton, tobacco, coal, iron, silk rope, chemicals, glass, machinery and ships, helping to establish its reputation as the Second City of the Empire. Most of Victorian Glasgow was built by Alexander Thomson or Greek Thomson (1817-75), who was so called because of his Grecian designs. His many churches and tenements may have influenced Charles Rennie Mackintosh, who was a schoolboy at the time of Thomson's death. Although founded in 1450 by Bishop John Turnbull and richly endowed, the Glasgow University of today was built between 1870 and 1891 at Gilmorehill, in a Gothic style, by Gilbert and Oldrid Scott. For many Glaswegians, the attraction of a weekend's sport provided a healthy outlet from labour intensive work in its factories, yards and docks, and this ultimately gave rise in 1873 to the founding of Rangers F.C, followed in 1888 by Celtic F.C, and so began a long-standing football tradition which continues to this day. Chief among its ten railway stations was the Glasgow Central which was started in its more basic form in 1841. The Glasgow School of Art, designed by Charles Rennie Mackintosh, was opened at a time when many of the city's artists were being inspired by a group now known as The Glasgow Boys. These included Edward Hornel, James Park, George Henry, William Guthrie, Stuart Park and Edward Walton, whose rejection of the established media of expression through religion and literature has influenced generations of

Scottish artists. In 1912 Govan was annexed to Glasgow. The takeover of the shipbuilders Swan Hunter by Barclay & Curle & Co in 1913 helped co-ordinate the city's impressive war effort, 1914-18, in men and materials, and after the war Lithgows was established on the Clyde. The impact of its industrial contribution on the country as a whole, was second only to the influence of the political reform movements that it spawned. Its members, fired with enthusiasm after the Russian Revolution of 1917, incited the Red Clydeside Riots of 1919, which gave birth to the Scottish Socialist Movement, and precipitated the election of ten MPs to serve in Britain's first Labour Government, 1924-29, headed by Ramsay Macdonald. Rebuilt in 1927 after being damaged by fire, the Kelvin Hall, the city's main cultural venue, survived the heavy bombing during World War II (1939-45), which was followed by the city's postwar reconstruction including large housing developments, and an exodus from the inner city slums. A blight on the citys landscape these had been so aptly described in Alexander Macarthur's 'No Mean City', published in 1935. Despite the move away from heavy industry Glasgow still retains its position as the commercial capital of Scotland and numerous reminders of its golden age, which undoubtedly influenced the granting of the European City of Culture Award in 1994. See Cathedral

GLASGOW CATHEDRAL
CITY OF GLASGOW

Standing on Castle Street, this has been the site of a religious community from the 6th century and is strongly associated with St Kentigern (Mungo). After a gap of 500 years the bishopric was refounded by Earl David, (1115), later David I, in whose presence the wooden Norman-style Cathedral was consecrated in 1136.

Burnt in 1192, it was rebuilt and reconsecrated by Bishop Jocelin in 1197 and dedicated to St Mungo. Although developed over centuries, its architecture dominated the city skyline in one form or another up to the 17th century, while its bishops played a central role in affairs of state. Bishop Wishart absolved Bruce of Comyn's murder and shortly after provided him with coronation robes, thus signifying the church's support for the Scottish cause. The present structure, started in a Gothic style probably by Bishop Bondington (1233-58) who completed its Gothic crypt and choir, was augmented in the 15th century by the steeple, began by Bishop Lauder along with the vestry, Chapter House, and the north east corner of the choir, which were continued up until 1447 by the influential Bishop John Cameron. Under his reign the see was at the the height of its power with over fifty prebendaries with manses near the Cathedral forming an Episcopal Court said to rival that of the Kings. Its northern aisle was reroofed by Bishop Muirhead between 1455 and 1473. Following Glasgow's elevation to a Metropolitan See by James IV in 1492 with suffragans (subordinate bishops) of Dunkeld, Dunblane, Galloway and Argyll, its development continued up to the Reformation, 1560. Archbishop James Beaton then carried off its records and saintly relics to France, and its other property including sculpted figures and its leaden roof were removed. After being saved from total destruction by the citizens and repaired by Bishop Spottiswood and Archbishop Law, it was the scene of the General Assembly held in 1638 when bishops were deposed, Episcopacy abolished and the new church formed. At the east end of St Mungo's Crypt are two stone coffins, one of which is thought to date from the 6th century, while in the south east corner is St Mungo's Well where the saint was thought to have been baptised. The Cathedral afforded few remarkable incidents from 1650 onwards. Its maintenance continued to occupy the minds of councillors until 1829 when a subscription was set up resulting in its full restoration by 1860, albeit without its two western towers and Consitory House. Today's essentially oblong structure, with its north and a south transepts and the remarkable Blackadder Aisle joined by Rood Screen below the central tower, is less of a landmark to shipping and more of a fine example of Medieval Gothic architecture. The Cathedral houses memorials to the military and the sacrifices of distinguished individuals and in its grounds are a number of curious stones.

GLENBUCKET CASTLE
ABERDEENSHIRE

Situated 13 miles SW of Rhynie on the bank of the Don. A Z plan tower house and a former stronghold of the Gordons, who were once the most powerful family in the area. The inscription above the doorway reads "John Gordon, Helen Carnegie, 1590. Nothing on Earth remains bot faime". Supporters of the Stewarts, the last laird John Gordon fought at Sheriffmuir in 1715 and at Culloden in 1746, before escaping to Norway and then to France when his estates were forfeited and later passed to the Earls of Fife. Although ruinous it still retains some of its original features

GLENCADAM DISTILLERY
ANGUS

Built in 1825 by the River Esk near the town of Brechin. It wasn't until 1885 that a licence was acquired by Mr George Cooper, and the distillery was thereafter run by various owners until bought by the blenders Gilmour Thompson & Co in 1891. Greatly benefitting from the Caledonian Railway from 1845, which provided access to markets in Dundee and beyond, under the new owners it grew in future decades to become an integral part of the whisky industry and was bought by Hiram Walker & Sons in 1954. Modernised in 1959, it was under George Ballantine's banner in 1987 and was taken over by Allied Lyons, who later formed Allied Distillers. An excellent Highland Malt in its own right, it is mainly used for blending, most notably in the Stewarts Cream of Barley.

OWNERS
Angus Dundee Distillers plc ?

REGION
Highland

PRODUCT
Glencadam is primarily used for blending

NOTES
A delicate fruity bouquet with a full-bodied sweetish flavour and a good finish.

GLENCAIRN RISING, 1653-54

During the exile of Charles II, when Scotland had fallen under the Cromwellian Protectorate enforced by General Monck, an approach was made by William, 8th Earl of Glencairn, to Charles II for a commission to lead a force in his support. As Royal Commander and Chief he raised an army at Loch Earn consisting of several clans, including Glengarry with 200 men, Cameron of Lochiel and Lord Athole with 100 horse and 1200 foot. The Earl's failure to win the confidence of his men and the Highland Chiefs who had been out with the masterly Montrose, 1644-45, weakened the leadership from the outset and at Dornoch brought about his replacement by General Middleton, a veteran of the Thirty Years War and the original contender for the post. During a banquet given on his arrival, a quarrel erupted between Glencairn and Middleton's, lieutenant Sir George Munro, leading to a duel in which Munro was wounded, weakening the cohesion of the command structure further. Before marching to Strathspey, the army consisted of around 3500 foot and 1,500 horse, but failed to capture Ruthven Castle, and were now being challenged by two forces totalling 3600 men under Monck and General Morgan, with orders to secure Inverness and Perth along with other gates to the Highlands, with its terrain totally unsuited for his troops. Fortunately, in February 1654 the rebels marched south and were defeated at Dunkeld by Morgan and at Lochgarry in July were put to flight, resulting in Middleton returning to Charles II on the Continent. The campaign was finally concluded when Glencairn sued for a truce with Monck, securing his disbanded and disarmed army safe passage home. In 1654 the Earl was left out of the Act of Grace (conciliatory policy introduced by Cromwell) but after the Restoration of Charles II received the office of Chancellor.

GLENCOE, MASSACRE OF, 1692
HIGHLAND

Following James VII forfeiture of the throne of Britain, 1689 partly due to his pro Catholic stance, his successor William II sought to establish his authority in the north. In the hope of bribing the Highland Chiefs into submitting to William II, a plan was implemented by the Earl of Breadalbane and the Earl of Stair, resulting in a decree being issued, imposing an oath of allegiance to be taken by all chiefs by 31st December 1691. With the failure of Macian, Chief of the Glencoe Macdonalds to meet the deadline, came the murder of his kinsfolk at the hands of Captain Campbell of Glenlyon's men. In the poem by William Aytoun 'The widow of Glencoe' is a poignant reminder of the aftermath:

Weep not children of Macdonald !

Weep not thou, his orphan heir
Not in shame but shameless honour,
Lies thy slaughtered father there.
Weep not but when years are over,
And thine arm is strong and sure,
And thy foot is swift and steady
On the mountain and the muir

The attack was all the more barbaric because it was inflicted after they had enjoyed two weeks of hospitality in the glen before receiving instructions for the massacre of their hosts. This intensified the enmity between the Macdonalds and the Campbells which had begun when the Macdonald Lords of the Isles lost much of their influence to the Campbells of Argyll in the 15th and 16th centuries.

GLENDEVON CASTLE
PERTH & KINROSS

Between Auchterarder and Clackmannanshire is a 15th-century Z plan castle that was the property of the 8th Earl of Douglas, who was slain by James II at Stirling Castle in 1452 after refusing to stop conspiring with the 4th Earl of Crawford (The Tiger Earl) against the King. Still held in the 16th century by the Crawfords, who restored most of it, in 1766 it became the property of the Rutherfords but recently became a hotel.

GLENDRONACH DISTILLERY
ABERDEENSHIRE

In a peaceful rural setting in the Forgue Valley about 5 miles NE of Huntly is one of Scotland's old traditional distilleries, founded by James Allardes & Partners in 1826. Glendronach takes its name from the Dronac burn which runs through the middle of the distillery. The time tested methods of Glendronach includes the use of the old malting floor, one of the few left in Scotland, and the spirit being matured in sherry oak casks. From September to June the kiln's tall pagoda roof is wreathed in plumes of peaty smoke as the spirit is processed, and the building blends into the pastoral setting with an air of timeless tranquillity. Purchased in 1920 by Charles Grant and Son, the founder of the Glenfiddich Distillery, it was sold to WM Teachers & Sons Ltd in 1960, becoming part of Allied Breweries in 1976 and later Allied Distillers in 1987.

OWNERS
Allied Distillers Ltd ?

REGION
Highlands

PRODUCT
Glendronach 15 year old sherry matured 40% & 43% vol

NOTES
A sherry aroma with a creamy Brazil nut taste, traces of sherry sweetness and a crisp sherry finish.

GLENDULLAN DISTILLERY
MORAY

Just SE of Dufftown by the River Fiddich, is Speyside's seventh oldest distillery. Founded in 1817 by the Earl of Fife next to the River Fiddich to relieve unemployment after the Napoleonic Wars, its building gave rise to the local saying "Rome was built on seven hills, Dufftown on seven stills". Its powerful water source was piped about half a mile down to an overshot water wheel, generating 16 horse power to drive all the machinery, which, according to contemporary sources, was "a great saving compared with steam engines". The first owners, William Williams & Sons of Aberdeen, spared no expense on rebuilding work. Spending an estimated £20,000 by 1898 to create one of the most modern distilleries in the region, with a capacity to make 150,000 gallons of whisky a year. Glendullan was spared the cost of road transportation and shared with the neighbouring Mortlach Distillery the

Great North of Scotland Railway sidings, which for years served as a direct link to the main northern conurbation's of Inverness, Fraserburgh, Aberdeen and beyond. But due to the insecurity felt throughout the industry after World War I, the company merged with Greenlees Brothers Ltd of Glasgow in 1919, which had already merged with Alexander Macdonald of Leith, later becoming Macdonald Greenlees Ltd. Surviving under the wing of Distillers Co Ltd, during the inter-war years and throughout World War II Glendullan retained its water power until shortly after reopening in 1947, when it changed over to electricity. The infra structuring started in the 1960s included a new distillery completed in 1972, with a capacity for one million gallons a year with a stillhouse built with a glass front to enable visitors to see the copper stills creating their magic. Working in tandem, both distilleries made the same product in the time honoured way that became an essential contributor to the blends of Old Par until 1985, when the old distillery was converted into a workshop.

OWNERS
Diageo plc ?

REGION
Speyside

PRODUCT
Glendullan 12 year old single malt 43% vol

NOTES
A full fruity bouquet with a smooth malty lingering taste.

GLENEAGLES CASTLE
PERTH & KINROSS

Situated just SW of Auchterarder. From the 12th century until 1799 the land belonged to the Haldanes, who had a castle here which served as a quarry in 1624, during the building of the present Gleneagles Mansion House that was the property of Admiral Lord Duncan by 1799. In the 20th century the adjacent land was developed as a centre for golf by a Mr Donald Matheson after spending a holiday here in 1910. The King's and Queen's courses designed by James Braid and opened in 1919 were followed by Gleneagles Hotel in 1924. Other than the interruption of World War II, when it was used as a convalescent home, it gradually built a reputation as an attractive venue for golf and now functions as a premier centre for international golf tournaments, attracting the good and the great.

GLEN ELGIN DISTILLERY
MORAY

When built in 1898 by the Glen burn SE of Elgin Town, it was correctly predicted by its architect Charles Doig, who as the designer of numerous distilleries gave his name to the characteristic Doig roof ventilators, that this would be the last built in Speyside for at least fifty years. Caught at the end of the whisky boom, its owners William Simpson of Rothes, a former manager of Glenfarclass, and James Carle, a local agent for the North of Scotland Bank, were shaken by the failure of Pattisons of Leith, Scotch whisky blenders with whom the market for malt whisky fillings used in blended whisky collapsed. From an investment of £13,000 came only five months of production at around 2,000 gallons a week, albeit of a first class Highland Malt. Sold at auction in 1901 to an anonymous buyer for £4,000, Glen Elgin's future remained uncertain even after its purchase by the Glen Elgin Glen Livit Distillery Co, whose best intentions came to nothing, and in 1906 it was sold again to Glasgow distiller & blender J J Blanche. Glen Elgin was later acquired by Scottish Malt Distillers in 1936 and closed throughout

much of the war (1941-45). The distillery's problems with water supplies were made worse by transport costs, owing to the absence of a railway siding, leading to a rundown of the plant and machinery until it was given a new lease of life in 1964. As part of a medium-to long-term plan to increase production, its mashhouse, tunroom and stillhouse were rebuilt and re-equipped. Production of Glen Elgin in 1998 reached two million litres a year and it became an essential part of the famous White Horse blend.

OWNERS
Diageo plc ?

REGION
Speyside

PRODUCT
Glen Elgin 12 year old single malt 43% vol

NOTES
A slightly fruity nose and a soft smooth heather honey sweet taste.

GLENFIDDICH DISTILLERY
MORAY

Founded by William Grant, the one time shoemaker and cattle herder, outside his home town of Dufftown. With the help of his children, the spirit that flowed from the stills on Christmas Day in 1887 was to establish itself as the best dram in the valley. Glenfiddich in Gaelic means 'valley of the deer'. As former book-keeper and manager of Mortlach distillery, Grant made Glenfiddich with its adherence to age-old methods, a quality Highland Malt; a standard upheld by the family to this day. Fiercely independent and far-sighted, Grant opened Balvenie Distillery next door in 1892 in order to secure water rights from the Robbie Dhu spring's which splashes down the Conval hillside to make that unique spirit that is the only Highland whisky to be distilled, matured and bottled at its own distillery. Latterly the family have bought 1200 acres of the surrounding land to secure their water source. Enduring the ups and downs of subsequent decades, over a century later the family's international reputation owes much to their belief that making whisky is more of an art form than a science, with a healthy regard for modern methods. Consequently, the methods still involve the old process of spring water and malted barley being turned into wort in the mash house and then fermented with yeast in wooden wash buckets made of Douglas Fir. It then goes to the still house, its traditional copper pot stills fired by coal, before the spirit is run through the spirit safe where the middle cut, or heart of the distillation, is retained prior to being matured in oak casks. Finally, unique to Glenfiddich is the marrying process whereby the spirit is united in wooden marrying tuns.

OWNERS
William Grant & Sons Ltd ?

REGION
Speyside

PRODUCT
Glenfiddich classic single malt (no age given) 43% vol

NOTES
A fresh fragrant aroma with a crisp, dry, fruity, slightly sweet taste and smooth lingering finish.

GLENFRUIN, BATTLE OF, 1603
ARGYLL & BUTE

Three miles SE of Gairlochhead. As a consequence of a long running clan feud between Sir Humphrey Colquhoun of Luss, chief of the clan, and Alister Magregor of Clan Gregor with his Royal Commission, the latter deployed 400 men at the head of the glen and another division in ambush. The subsequent victory for the Macgregors, however, gave way to large scale plundering and rein-forced the clan's outlaw status, which continued up until the 18th century.

GLENGARNOCK TOWER
NORTH AYRSHIRE

By the Garnock water 2 miles NW of Kilbirnie village are the ruins of a 15th-century courtyard keep with 16th century additions. The barony was held by the Riddles until the mid 13th century and then the Cunninghams until 1725, when it fell into ruin. Continued stone pillaging weakened the structure further and in 1839 a storm overthrew its missing wall.

GLENGOYNE DISTILLERY
STIRLING

Located 4 miles SE of Killearn village and NE of Glasgow. Under licence in 1833, after Hugh Lang set up business on the Broomielaw importing rum and exporting whisky, it wasn't long before the company, headed by his three sons Gavin, Alexander and William, saw Glengoyne's potential and purchased it in 1876. Although on the border of the Highland and Lowland producing regions, its water coming from the Dumgoyne Hills, flows into the Glengoyne burn and over the Glengoyne waterfall, and the distillery's temperate atmosphere, created by the Gulf Stream, which combine to produce a unique Highland Malt with some Lowland similarities. Located about fifteen miles N of Glasgow, since the days of the railways, the area's scenic beauty, notably the sleepy glen itself, the Campsie Fells, and nearby Loch Lomond have often been rivalled by the whisky itself in attracting visitors from Glasgow and elsewhere over the years. After the usual process of malting, mashing, fermentation, distillation and maturation, the Glengoyne single malt is produced; a distinctly unpeated malt that is also used in blending.

OWNERS

MacLeod Ian & Co Ltd ?

REGION
Highland

PRODUCT
Glengoyne 10 & 17 year old single malt 40% & 43% vol

NOTES
Its malty aroma with hints of oak apple and sherry produce a smooth unpeated oak and apple flavour with a clean fruity finish.

GLEN GRANT DISTILLERY
MORAY

Founded in 1840 by the brothers John and James Grant on six acres of land in Rothes, the distillery was supplied with fresh water from the Caperdonich Well on the hillside above. In 1872 after the death of James Grant, one time lawyer, banker and Provost of Elgin, his son Major James Grant took over the management. Installing refrigation, electric lighting and a hydraulic lift by 1900, when not acquiring a reputation as a sportsman and intrepid explorer, he was in fact the archetypal Victorian gentleman. In the nearby family house hung the trophies of his travels, including a fine collection of plants that fill the distillery's woodland garden with its apple orchards, ponds and flowers. Built into a rock nearby is the whisky safe, used by the Major during his afternoon strolls with guests, until his death in 1931. The distillery then passed to Douglas Mackessack, who gradually built up the international reputation which has continued to this day. Its appeal to whisky blenders has given Glen Grant that dual quality, helping to raise its standing further from 1978 onwards, its later owners Seagram Distillers plc taking it to the number one brand of whisky in Italy by 1996.

OWNERS

Chivas Brothers Ltd ?

REGION
Speyside

PRODUCT
Glen Grant, usually no age given but is available as a 10 year old single malt 43% vol

NOTES
A subtle fruity sweet nose and a distinctive dry character that is enhanced by fruity flavours and a delicate sweetness.

GLEN KEITH DISTILLERY
MORAY

Housed in the Old Keith Mills SE of the town until 1958. The new distillery on the same site by the Isla Waterfall was the first built in Scotland by Seagram (Canadian Distillers) and was crafted in local stone. As a result Keith stands as a testament to the Scottish stone-masonry that has skilfully created a traditional design to blend with the neighbouring distilleries around the River Isla. The attention paid to its form was as keenly applied to its function, which heralded new standards of innovation for the industry, particularly the whole Chivas Glenlivit Group. Constant laboratory testing ensures that the water, malted barley and spirit are maintained to a high standard, with the traditionally tall stills adding even greater refinement, while combining with computerisation since 1970 (the first used in Scotland's distilling process) and the micro-processors in the mash house (since 1980) to ensure the same standard is present in every dram.

OWNERS
Chivas Brothers Ltd ?

REGION
Speyside

PRODUCT
Glen Keith 10 year old single malt 40% vol

NOTES
A smooth toasted aroma with an aromatic sweetness that gives a soft, dry, fruity taste and a warm finish.

GLENKINCHIE DISTILLERY
EAST LOTHIAN

Its rural setting 15 miles SE of Edinburgh has provided a ready source of raw materials since it was established by two farming brothers, John and George Rate, in 1837. Drawing the water from the Kinchie burn fed by springs in the nearby Lammermuir Hills, they produced a unique kind of malt which put Glenkinchie on the map but bankrupted the brothers in the process before 1853 when the plant was closed. In 1890 it was bought by a consortium of brewers, blenders and wine merchants who rebuilt it and in 1914 the company was one of five Lowland Malt whisky distilleries to form the Scottish Malt Distillers Ltd, later United Distillers. Its closeness to the metropolis and distribution centre gave Glenkinchie an advantage over some of the more remote distilleries started at that time, and this has continued up to the present day. One of its more unique feature is the world's only museum of malt whisky production, which includes a scale model of a distillery that was made for The British Empire Exhibition in the 1920s. Marketed as the Edinburgh Malt, Glenkinchie is the Lowland representative in the classic malts range which typify Scotland's malt producing regions. The two large copper pot stills also provide one of the main malts at the heart of the famous blends of Bells Haigs and the deluxe blend 'Dimple'.

OWNERS
Diageo plc ?

REGION
Lowland

PRODUCT
Glenkinchie 10 year old single malt 43%

vol

NOTES
This is the smokiest of the Lowland Malts; it has a light and delicate nose with a smooth pleasing taste.

GLENLIVET, BATTLE OF, 1594
MORAY

Ten miles SW of Dufftown. In response to the rebel earls of Huntly and Errol, a royal force was dispatched headed by the young Earl of Argyll. Though advised to wait for reinforcements from the King, Argyll, brimming with confidence due to his vastly superior numbers, resolved to risk battle which surprisingly commenced with an attack by Huntly's artillery, followed by well trained cavalry. In the ensuing confusion came defeat for the Royalists followed by the loss of royal favour for the Earl. Consequently the battle strengthened the hands of the Catholic northern earls.

GLENLIVET DISTILLERY
MORAY

About 13 miles SW of Dufftown in the foothills of the Cairngorm mountains is one of Speyside's foremost distilleries, built in 1824 near its water source Josie's Well. Its founder, George Smith, whose great-grandfather Thomas had been a local farmer and illicit distiller after settling in this part of the Highlands in 1715, was encouraged by the Duke of Gordon's eagerness to relieve unemployment in the glen, and obtained a licence in 1824 to distil on his farm in Upper Drumin. This was encouraged by the new spirit of openness engendered by the Act of Parliament of 1823, which reduced taxes on whisky in order to discourage illicit distilling. Due to increased demand, Smith, along with his son John as partner, opened a new distillery on the present site at Minmore Farm in 1858. Caught at the crossroads between the old days and new ways, Smith's habit of keeping a pair of hair trigger pistols lest his erstwhile smuggling companions carry out a threat to put the building to the torch won him respect and popularity among the progressive distillers in the Highlands. His reputation later won him the approval of such leading figures of the day as Sir Walter Scott (one of Edinburgh's 18th century critics on good spirits) Charles Dickens, James Hogg and George IV. At the time of his death in 1871 his product was being exported abroad through his Edinburgh agent Andrew Usher & Co. Inherited by his son John, the firm grew in strength with each generation and in 1921 it was inherited by Captain Bill Smith Grant, under whose guidance it retained the pre-eminence which was enhanced in 1978, when as part of the Canadian company Seagram Distillers plc, it became synonymous with Scotch whisky in more than a hundred countries, and the leading 12 year old malt in the USA.

OWNERS
Chivas Brothers Ltd ?

REGION
Speyside

PRODUCT
Glenlivet 12 & 18 year old single malt 40% & 43% vol

NOTES
A light, fruity, slightly sweet nose with a floral, slightly malty palate
A nose that is sweet with a subtle fragrance leading to a sweet, fruity and floral flavour.

GLENLOSSIE DISTILLERY
MORAY

Situated near the River Lossie 3 miles SW of Elgin. When John Duff, a local publican, proposed plans for Glenlossie to his prospective partners HMS Mackay, a burgh surveyor, and Alexander Allan, a local Procurator Fiscal, much attention

was given to the use of the distillery's sloping site and the large dam of water that would force a water wheel of eight horsepower to drive the machinery. The water that forms the essential ingredient in Glenlossie comes from the Bardon burn which flows from the Mannoch Hills. Managed by Duff from the outset, in 1887, when the Glasgow whisky blender John Hopkins joined the trio, production ran at 90,000 gallons (409,000 litres) a year. After Allan's death and John Duff's departure in 1896, the Glenlossie Glenlivet Distillery Co was formed by HMS Mackay as senior partner and J H Hair (nephew) as Managing Director, under whose auspices new warehouses, a rail link and other improvements to the building were carried out prior to its closure caused by war-time austerity measures (1914-19). A fire in 1929 caused severe damage despite the efforts of its 1862 horse-drawn fire engine (now housed in distillery) and paved the way for a take-over by Scottish Malt Distillers, in 1930. Production was resumed and its fortunes revived during the post-war period with increased storage space, a new warehouse (1950), and further improvements in the 1960s and 70s. The Mannochmore distillery, built alongside Glenlossie in 1971, draws its water from the same source, while managing to produce its own distinctive Highland Malt.

OWNERS
Diageo plc ?

REGION
Speyside

PRODUCT
Glenlossie 10 year old single malt 43% vol

NOTES
Fresh with a medium dry flavour and a slightly spicy finish.

GLENLUCE ABBEY
DUMFRIES & GALLOWAY

The ruins situated near the village are of an abbey that was once described as one of Southern Scotland's most beautiful. Founded in 1191 by Roland Lord of Galloway for Cistercian monks from either Dundrennan or Melrose, it covered more than one acre of ground and had a garden orchard and nine acres of farmland. Once called 'Vallis Lucis' meaning 'place of herbs'. Its traditional plan included a cruciform church with the adjacent central cloister garden surrounded by various other buildings. In 1235 the Abbey was plundered by the soldiers of Alexander II who were dispatched against the Galloway rebels. Notwithstanding visits by James IV (1488-1513) with Queen Margaret while on their many pilgrimages to Whithorn, its ecclesiastical status began to be challenged by temporal vested interests when the Gordons of Lochinver and the Earls of Cassillis laid claim to Glenluce (with its decaying fabric), which was halted by a Papal Bull of 1560 when Thomas Hay was made its Commendator. After his death in 1580 the property was acquired through forgery and murder by Gilbert, 4th Earl of Cassillis, but by 1602 it was erected into a Temporal Barony for Laurence Gordon. Though by 1619 it was annexed to the See of Galloway, by the close of the century it had become the property of Sir James Dalrymple (later Earl of Stair). Its English Gothic Church stands prominent amongst the other ruins which are mainly 13th century but have some 16th and 17th century work, while its Chapter House still retains its ribbed vaulted roof.

GLENMORANGIE DISTILLERY
HIGHLAND

Meaning 'glen of tranquillity' in Gaelic. One of Scotland's most sought after spirits is distilled on the shore of the Dornoch Firth NW of Tain. The area was known for distilling from at least the 17th centu-

ry and a brewery from 1820. The land of Morangie was held in 1567 by Abbot Thomas Ross but it was a great-grandson, George Ross, who left the first written evidence of distilling here when an Aquavitie pot with fleake and stand was mentioned in his will of 1703. In 1815 the land passed out of the family's hands. Attracted by the time-tested quality of the mineral-rich water from the Tarlogie Springs, the Matheson Brothers acquired its first licence in 1843. The family's tendency to grow and adapt rather than rebuild helped the distillery retain the original character that is still apparent today. After reaching 20,000 gallons in 1849 and making use of the Tain Railway line, by 1864 vast opportunities opened up for the producers, with reports in the 'Inverness Advertiser' in 1880 stating that a consignment of Glenmorangie was seen en-route to San Francisco and another to Rome, envoking the idea that the Vatican had learnt of its virtues. Reconstructed in the 1880s, Glenmorangie grew unabated with the export boom of 1897, and its purchase by Macdonald & Muir of Leith in 1918 reaffirming its position as a market leader that survived closure during the Great Depression (1931-36) and the war years of 1941-44. Quickly returning to normal, during the surge in demand between 1976 and 1990, the stills doubled to four and then to eight. Overseen by the famous 16 men of Tain, the climax of the operation comes when the essence spirit is matured in air-dried casks, made with wood from the Ozark mountains of North Carolina USA, that have been seasoned with Kentucky bourbon for four years.

OWNERS
Glenmorangie plc ?

REGION
Highland

PRODUCT

Glenmorangie 10 and 18 year old single malt 40% and 43% vol

NOTES

A sweet malty nose and a smooth fruity honeyed taste with a trace of nuts.

A perfumed nose with nutty caramel overtones and a mellow sweet taste with a trace of mint.

GLEN MORRISTON, BATTLE OF, 638
WEST LOTHIAN

Fought near Mid Calder when the Scots under Donald Bree or Breac, King of Dalriada, sought to wrestle the territory between the River Avon and the Pentland Hills from the Angles, but was utterly routed, provoking the siege of what is now Edinburgh. The battle was part of the ongoing process in which the ethnic, geographical, and ideological elements fused together to form what became the Lowlands of Scotland.

GLEN ORD DISTILLERY
HIGHLAND

Sharing the motto of the local Mackenzie Clan, 'I shine not burn', Glen Ord was built in 1838 at the Muir of Ord, 15 miles NW of Inverness, and indirectly draws its water from the River Orrin, which runs from the mountain of 'sgurr a'choi re Ghlais'. Like many Highland Malts, it has some of the characteristics of the landscape with its rugged terrain and its ever-changing climate; these no doubt enhanced its appeal with the indigenous population of Inverness and Nairn, who were linked to it by the railway by 1815, and provided its main markets until recently. Glen Ord became part of the famous whisky firm John Dewar & Sons Ltd in 1923. Its six traditional copper pot stills provide one of the Malts at the heart of Dewar's 'White Label' blend, the top-selling whisky in the USA by 1994, and since recent expansion from its local base new markets have been established in

Europe. The need for the centralised processing of barley into malt prompted the building of the drum maltings at the distillery in 1968, which now provides malt for many of the company's distilleries which like Glen Ord have broadened their appeal.

OWNERS

Diageo plc ?

REGION

Highland

PRODUCT

Glen Ord 12 year old single malt 40% vol

NOTES

A dry nose with a smooth, slightly peaty taste and a long-lasting, rich aftertaste.

GLENSHIEL, BATTLE OF, 1719
HIGHLAND

Some 10 miles SE of Stromeferry. Near a stream and bridge was the scene of a battle where the Jacobites, 1500 in all, including Spanish mercenaries, were led to defeat, under the Earl Marischall and Marquis of Tullibardine, at the hands of 1600 Hanovarians headed by General Whightman. Following the defeat, the bulk of the Spanish force surrendered while the Jacobites dispersed to the hills and their leaders to exile on the Continent, further weakening the chance of a Stewart restoration.

GLENTROOL, BATTLE OF, 1307
DUMFRIES & GALLOWAY

Near Loch Trool N of Minnigaff. After his defeat at Carrick with his party and some additional followers, Robert the Bruce fooled the English force settled in their camp, of his numerical superiority with the noise of the local livestock, thus discouraging their movement and bringing about their defeat and flight. The victory had the effect of eclipsing Edward II's olive branch policy towards the Scots with the rising popularity of Bruce.

GLENTURRET DISTILLERY
PERTH & KINROSS

The oldest Highland Malt distillery in Scotland, is located just outside Crieff. Founded in 1775 but dating from 1717, when there were at least five illicit stills on the site owing to the area's rich distilling tradition and the essential water from the Turret burn. In 1887 the writer and traveller Alfred Barnard noted "I could see the chimney stack 120 feet high as I turned into the Glen. Here are no fads, appliances, or patents, but like the buildings the vessels are all of the ancient pattern", a description that still holds true today. Displaying the familiar farmsteading look, with pyramid-shaped roof capped with a ventilator, by 1906 its 16-man work force followed the age old process of 1) Malting; the barley is malted 2) Milling; the malt is milled, grist is obtained 3) Mashing; the grist is mixed with hot water-this extracts the fermentable sugars into a solution called wort 4) Fermentation; wort is filtered off and cooled-yeast added. Wort ferments producing wash 5) Distillation; the wash is distilled twice in pot stills 6) Spirit Sample Safe; malt spirit is obtained 7) Maturation; the spirit is matured in oak casks. Dismantled in 1920, the distillery was opened again in 1959 when re-development work began that has continued to the present day.

OWNERS
Edrington Group Ltd, The ?

REGION
Highland

PRODUCT
Glenturret 12 year old single malt 40% vol (also available in 15 21 & 25 year old)

NOTES
A light delicate nose and a full body with a creamy maltiness and a hint of sweetness.

GOLDIELANDS TOWER
SCOTTISH BORDERS

On the right bank of the Teviot 2 miles S of Hawick are the ruins of an oblong tower which was built as a watchtower for nearby Branxholm Tower and as a family seat by Sir Walter Scott of Buccleuch, before he was slain by the Kerrs in Edinburgh, 1552. Another of the name was Sir Walter Scott the writer who gave it some historical resonance in his 'The Lay of the Last Minstrel' which was set around the middle of the sixteenth century:

And soon the Teviot side he won
Eastward the wooded path he rode,
Green hazels o'er his basnet nod
He passed the peel of Goldielands,
And crossed old Borthwick's roaring strand;
Dimly he viewed the moat-hills mound,
Where Druid shades still witted round;

Additions were made by his son, also Walter, in 1596, who was the first Laird of Goldielands and was involved in the Raid of Reidswire in 1575. The last of that line of the Scotts died out in the 17th century when it reverted to the Buccleuch family.

GORDONSTOUN
MORAY

Originally called Plewlands, which in Lowland Scots means 'ploughed land', the village is situated 2 miles W of Lossiemouth. Held by the Bishops of Moray from the 12th century, the land was later bought by Sir Robert Gordon, 3rd son of the 11th Earl of Sutherland in 1636 when its name changed to Gordonstoun. His grandson, the scientist Sir Robert Gordon, known as 'the warlock' took great pleasure in frightening the villagers, who believed him to be educated in the black arts. In 1795 the estate passed to Alex Cumming Esq, who became a baronet in 1804. This was once the site of a 15th century tower with 17th century additions built by the Marquis of Huntly, which, apart from the wings, were mostly swept away during later developments. Gordonstoun School was founded in 1935 by a Mr Kurt Hahn (its first headmaster), who restarted his project after his first attempt by Lake Constance was banned by Hitler. Having limited success in the early days, by 1950 its popularity increased as it became known for its royal connections. Between the 1930s and 1970s it was attended by Prince Philip (now Duke of Edinburgh), Prince Charles, Prince Andrew, and Prince Edward. While focusing on the development of character and intelligence the school places an emphasis on training for life rather than intellectual eminence.

GOSFORD HOUSE
EAST LOTHIAN

Occupying land 6 miles NW of Haddington, is the late 18th century home of the Earl of Wemyss and March. The main section, built by Robert Adam in 1800, had some alterations and additional north and south wings added by William Young in 1890. Standing in finely cultivated grounds, the house is noted for its marble hall and other fine features and exhibits.

GOUROCK
INVERCLYDE

Town and Ferry Port situated on the Firth of Clyde, 2 miles W of Greenock. Name derived from the Gaelic 'guireoc' meaning a 'pimple' or 'hillock'. The land was held by the Douglases before 1455 and it served as the departure point for James VI's expedition to suppress the Western Isles in 1494. The Kempoch Stone also known as Granny Kempoch is an ancient monolith and talisman 6ft high and 2ft in diameter which was often used by fisher-

men and married couples for good luck. It was held in such awe that in 1692, Mary Lamont, a local teenager, was burnt, along with other women, after confessing to an attempt to throw it into the sea to destroy boats and ships. With its Court House, markets and fairs, long after being created a Burgh of Barony in 1694 for Sir William Stewart of Castlemilk, the land was bought by Duncan Darroch, a poor Inverkip herd boy who became a successful West Indian merchant. Failing to realise the potential of its natural harbour and its fishing stocks, Gourock remained an unimportant fishing village until 1858 when it became a Police Burgh. First started in 1736, the Gourock Rope Works was to become the biggest of its kind in Scotland until its removal to Port Glasgow in 1851. Functioning as a dormitory town for the nearby industrial centres in later decades, between July and August Gourock served as a watering place for Glasgow families attracted by its sandy beaches and latterly by its marina for pleasure sailing.

GOVAN
CITY OF GLASGOW

Town situated on the outskirts of Glasgow. Its name derivation is uncertain but probably comes from one of the following, the Saxon 'God-win' owing to its excellent ale tasting like wine, the Gaelic 'amhan' meaning a 'ditch', or from the Gaelic 'gobheinn' meaning 'little hill'. The likely site of a monastery founded in the 10th century by King Constantine, who resigned his crown to become a follower of St Columba. Reminders of this period are the 40 or so 10th and 12th century Christian Stones in the Parish Church that include hogback tombstones, cross slab shafts, upright crosses, recumbent slabs and a Druidical sun stone. In 1136 David I bestowed the land on Glasgow Cathedral but despite the transfer of the revenues to Glasgow University after the Reformation in the 16th century, the community remained a country village until the 18th century when their population, numbering 1500, saw most of their traditional farming and fishing trade being supplanted by weaving. However, through the enterprise of the Dixon and Reay families, Govan became a large centre for iron and coal supplies in the late 19th century, which aided its shipbuilding, making it an integral part of the industrial base of Glasgow, to which the town was annexed in 1912. In contrast with this has been the more recent decline of its shipbuilding that has adversley affected the area.

GRANDTULLY CASTLE
PERTH & KINROSS

Built in finely wooded grounds near the Tay, 3 miles NE of Aberfeldy. The lands once belonged to Sir John Stewart of Innermeath and Lorn who occupied the original castle nearby in the late 14th century. The present structure developed from a 16th century keep when the land was erected into a Free Barony in 1538 for John 4th Lord Innermeath. The additions of 1626 by Sir William Stewart (Sheriff of Perth) included gables and pepper pot turrets, ultimately making it a Z plan castle and was later augmented by a chapel with vestry added in the 19th century. St Mary's chapel nearby to the south was the burial place of the Barons of Grandtully until the 17th century.

GRANGEMOUTH
FALKIRK

Seaport situated on the south bank of the River Forth. Its name derived from its location at the mouth of the Grange burn which once flowed around the grange of the Abbey at Abbotshaugh. The town was started by Lawrence Dundas in 1777 during the Forth & Clyde Canal develop-

ments and by 1810 ranked as a Head Port with through trade from the Carron Iron Works and from undercutting the shore dues levied at Leith. It played a significant part in Scotland's industrial supply line by the time its dock was built in 1843. Apart from its supply industries the main activity here was shipbuilding, which produced up to 500 ships between 1879 and 1952. The towns primary function was complemented by the nearby navel base at Rosyth during both World Wars and the Cold War. The oil refinery that was started in 1924 mushroomed to become a large petro-chemical terminal plant by 1965, with a crude oil pipeline linked to the Finnart terminal on Loch Long, and a pumping capacity of 3" million tons yearly. Reminders of the town's rich industrial history can be seen in its museum.

GREENAN CASTLE
SOUTH AYRSHIRE

Perched on the edge of a cliff 3 miles S of Ayr. Lands were held by the Davidson family who had a previous fortalice here in the 15th century, but the present ruins are of an oblong tower which was built by John Kennedy of Baltersan in 1603.

GREENKNOWE TOWER
SCOTTISH BORDERS

Erected 12 miles NE of Earlston on land that once belonged to the Gordons but passed through marriage to the Setons of Touch early in the 15th century. The stone on its wall is inscribed with the names and family shields of Jane Edmonstone and James Seton, who built this L plan tower in 1581. Purchased by the Pringles of Stitchel in the 17th century, it was later occupied by Walter Pringle of Stitchel, a zealous Covenanter.

GREENLAW
SCOTTISH BORDERS

Coastal town situated 7 miles SW of Duns. Its name derived from the position of the older village near green law now Greenlaw House. Once the site of two religious houses that were subordinate to Kelso Abbey. In the 12th century the land was held by the Homes, Earls of Dunbar, but by 1598, when it became a Burgh of Barony for Home of Spott (descendant), New Greenlaw had began to emerge in the valley. Imbued with civic pride, by 1696 it became capital of Berwickshire, when its Mercat Cross was erected by Sir Patrick Hume of Polwarth (later Earl of Marchmont). The town's 19th century buildings are a reminder of a time when it competed with Duns for the status of capital of the area until a bill passed by Parliament in 1903 favoured the latter as County Town. Built on Medieval foundations in 1712, and possibly predated by an 8th century building, the Parish Church ranks first amongst its oldest buildings, which also include the Gaol, built in 1824, and the Grecian style County Hotel of 1831.

GREENOCK
INVERCLYDE

Industrial town situated on the River Clyde 24 miles NW of Glasgow. Its name probably derives either from the Gaelic 'greannach' meaning 'rough and gravely' or 'grian-aig' meaning 'a sunny bay'. Under the guidance of the Shaw family, Greenock grew as a village when John Shaw received permission from James IV (1488-1513) to erect a church, which became a Burgh of Barony in 1635 and a Parish shortly after. Its inhabitants were described in 1656 by one of Cromwell's customs officials as being 'all seamen or fishermen trading with Ireland and the Isles in small boats'. Although opposed by Newark (now Port Glasgow),

Greenock succeeded in removing restrictions to foreign trade by 1681, owing to the loyalty of one of the Shaws at the battle of Worcester, 1651, when Cromwell defeated Charles II. With its large fishing fleet it exported thousands of barrels of herring to La Rochelle, besides other quantities to Danzig, and Swedish and Baltic ports. Despite the combined opposition from Clyde Royal Burghs it later succeeded in building its harbours and quays in 1710. Escaping much of the political instability of the 18th century, apart from an anti Jacobite stance in 1715 and a brief encounter with Rob Roy Macgregor, who seized its fishing boats to transport stolen cattle to Loch Lomond, the burghers' preoccupation with trade led to the Shaws granting over burgh affairs to the community between 1741 and 1751, and in 1785 the Greenock Banking Co was founded. Its most famous son is James Watt (1736-1819), the inventor of the steam engine, while in the town's West Kirk (built 1592, restored 1864) is buried Mary Campbell, Burns's 'Highland Mary'. Notwithstanding the reduction in trade with the deepening and widening of the River Clyde in 1770, its revival following the building of a railway terminal and five harbours between 1782 and 1881, where electric light was used in Scotland for the first time, inspired the 'Celebration Ode'

Thus have we come by leaps and bounds
To hold the vantage nature gives,
'Spite the veiled darts of feigned friends
Let it be known that Greenock lives.

Also serving as a transit point for immigrants between 1821 and 1830, around 46,000 people left its shores for Canada, the USA and Australia. Started in 1780, its shipbuilding had expanded by 1840 to produce 7,000 tons annually, which mainly consisted of steamers, but later diversified after steel had replaced iron by 1900, and continued to supply Britain's shipbuilders until well after World War I. During the slump in the 1920s and 30s, the town witnessed much social unrest, mainly due to its squalid housing and the Depression, but by 1939 the industry had revived with the return to war production. This brought with it the heavy bombing that luckily failed to destroy its port, which served as a base for the Free French Navy, and as such was visited by General De Gaulle in 1941. In the post-war period Greenock gradually lost out to the more modern European and Japanese yards which forced the closure of its peripheral industries. It was at this time that its town planners experimented with the current ideas in social engineering. The Custom House, built with a fine Doric portico by William Burn in 1818, serves as museum along with the Maclean Museum and Art Gallery, founded in 1876 by James Maclean, a local sawmiller.

GREYFRIARS KIRK
CITY OF EDINBURGH

Taking its name from a monastery founded in the 15th century by James I and located outside the city wall between the Grassmarket and the present kirkyard. The building was destroyed at the Reformation, (1560) and in 1562 Queen Mary granted the yards as a burial ground. The main entrance of today's church is from Candlemaker Row and incorporates a number of periods but was begun in 1612. It was in the church and outside on a tombstone that 'The National Covenant' was signed in 1638. Now known as the Old Church which was thought by some to have an ungraceful form, its steeple which rose from its west end was accidentally blown up in 1718 after the local authorities had lodged gunpowder in it for safe keeping. A second church was annexed in 1721 during the repairs of the

old building and although both were destroyed in a second fire in 1845, before long it was providing services for the local parishioners. Among these was a local shepard named John Grey whose death and burial in the kirkyard in 1858 gave rise to the legendary Greyfriars Bobby, a Skye terrier whose loyalty to his master was to involve an ongoing vigil beside his grave for fourteen years, until his own death and burial alongside him in 1862. This chapter was marked by a statue erected outside the kirk at the behest of Baroness Burdett-Coutts. After becoming serviceable again in 1857 the kirk acquired its distinguished stained glass window and was reputed to be the first Presbyterian church to adopt the use of an organ. Among the many other Edinburgh worthies buried in its graveyard is the famous Gaelic poet Duncan Ban, the architect of the New Town James Craig, the scholar and tutor to James VI George Buchanan, the poet Alan Ramsay, and the one time Regent of Scotland James Douglas, Earl of Morton.

GYLEM CASTLE
ARGYLL & BUTE

Kerrera Island 4 miles to the SW of Oban has been the site of a castle from the 12th century and for a long time the stronghold of the Macdougals of Lorn who built the late 16th century L plan tower. In 1647 it was besieged by the Covenanters under General Leslie and in the tumult, the Brooch of Lorn (See Dunolly Castle) was stolen by Campbell of Inverawe, but was later restored to its hereditary keepers.

H

HADDINGTON
EAST LOTHIAN

Town situated on the River Tyne 20 miles E of Edinburgh. The name is thought to derive from a Saxon chief called Haden who settled here while the 'ton' is from the Old English meaning 'village' or 'farm'. A Royal Burgh by 1130, the land was granted by David I in 1139 to Ada, daughter of the Earl of Surrey, on her marriage to his son Prince Henry. A convent founded here for Cistercian nuns around 1159 by Ada, Countess of Northumberland, was once the largest in Scotland. After reverting to the Crown in 1178, the burgh witnessed a number of events of national importance, including the birth of the King's son, later Alexander II (1198-1249), its burning by King John of England in 1216, the assassination of the Earl of Atholl, 1242, and its destruction by Edward III to avenge the seizure of Berwick, 1355. Started in the 14th century, and built in an English Gothic style with Norman features, the Parish Church of St Mary later acquired the title Lucerna Laudoniae or 'lamp of Lothian', which is thought to have derived from the original Franciscan Abbey Church founded in 1242 but demolished at the Reformation. Staying with matters spiritual, Haddington's most famous son was the religious reformer John Knox (1505-1572), who attended the local Grammar School. The town's capture by the English, under Sir James Milford after the battle of Pinkie, 1548, led to a Franco-Scottish force encircling the town and to the signing of the Treaty of Haddington, 7th July 1548. After a prolonged siege, the English force was beset by the plague, resulting in a 6000 man relief force under the Earl of Rutland entering the town by night (10th October 1549), and providing a protective corridor for men and supplies to Berwick. Apart from its elevation to an Earldom for Thomas Hamilton in 1627, and a visit from Cromwell in 1650, its later history was concerned with its own internal affairs. The once famous Grammar School, founded in the 14th century, was incorporated into the Knox Memorial Institute, established in 1880, which became the Knox Academy in 1948. Haddington was the first place in Scotland to be visited by cholera in 1831, which originated in Hindustan and killed 58 people. Although its growth was impeded by the wars of the 17th and 18th centuries, the town's tweed mills and maltings greatly benefited from the Industrial Revolution and despite a population increase in the 20th century, it still manages to retain the human scale of a Medieval burgh. Haddington's most famous female worthy is Jane Welsh Carlyle (1801-1886), whose marriage to Thomas Carlyle (historian) in 1826 gave the town a literary past that is now displayed in the family home in Lodge Street, now the Jane Welsh Museum. The Town House built by William Adam in 1748 had an additional Town Hall added in 1831, with a large ornamented spire by Gillespie Graham. Once the seat of a circuit Justiciary Court until that was removed to Edinburgh, its local Court House was built in 1833 in a Tudor style by William Burn, and to the east of this is the Corn Exchange, built in 1854 by Robert Billings. Outside the town to the SE is Traprain Law, which was once the site of an extensive Iron Age settlement which was held in the 5th century by the Votadini tribe, whose endeavours at holding a defensive position are still visible. In 1919 a large amount of ancient silver ware was discovered here which is now in the National Museum of Antiquities in Edinburgh.

HADDO HOUSE
ABERDEENSHIRE

Situated 20 miles N of Aberdeen. The original " House of Haddo " or " House of Kellie ", the traditional home of the Gordons of Methlick was besieged by the Covenanters under the Earl of Argyll in 1644, resulting in its destruction and Sir Gordon of Haddo being taken to Edinburgh and beheaded (Raid of Kellie). In 1731 the Palladian edifice of today was built by John Baxter to designs by William Adam for William, 2nd Earl of Aberdeen. Suffering a fire in 1887 just after its interior was decorated with designs by Robert Adam, the building is now fully restored and proudly sits in its fine gardens.

HAGGS CASTLE
CITY OF GLASGOW

This L plan tower house was built 2 miles SW of the city centre by Sir John Maxwell, 12th Baron of Pollock in 1585 for his wife Margaret Cunningham. It served as a jointure house (property granted to a bride to be enjoyed after her husband's death) but is of little historical note. In the 17th century it acquired a reputation for its ties with religious dissenters when it was used as a refuge for Covenanting preachers around 1640, and a Conventicle was held here in 1667 and 1676, when the sacrament was administered. It fell into ruin in the 19th century but is now restored and used as a museum.

HAILES CASTLE
EAST LOTHIAN

The rock by the River Tyne 4´ miles NE of Haddington has been the site of a Hepburn castle from the 13th century. Today's structure is essentially a courtyard keep with 15th and 16th century additions which was visited by the Earl of Somerset's invasion force in 1547, who described it as a place of some strength. Occupied by Lord Grey of Wilton in 1548 and subsequently held for the English by Hugh Douglas with 50 men from Longniddry. Hailes was also a stronghold of the Earl of Bothwell and was where he brought Queen Mary after seizing her in Edinburgh, 1567. Later passing to the Dalrymples of Hailes, in 1835 it was used as a granary and is now a ruin.

HALIDON HILL, BATTLE OF, 1333

A decisive engagement fought during the Wars of Independence, when in an attempt to take Berwick Edward III invasion force took up the superior position on the hill and awaited the larger Scottish relief force under Sir Archibald Douglas. Though essentially fought on foot, the Scots failure to recover from the opening shower from the English archers brought total defeat. This enabled Edward to restore his puppet king Edward Balliol to rule Scotland and return south.

HALKIRK
HIGHLAND

Village situated 7 miles SW of Thurso. Name derived from the Norse 'Ha Kirkiu' meaning 'High church'. Its early religious significance was due to the visits made to the area by St Fergus, the Pictish Bishop of Ireland, in the 8th century, to whom the first church was dedicated. The tower which once stood here was occupied by the Bishops of Sutherland and Caithness but was burnt in 1222, causing the death of Bishop Adam. Opposite the site stands Brall Castle (see castle), stronghold of the Harolds and Sinclairs, the Earls of Caithness who, as feudal overlords of the area, probably instigated the act of arson, owing to the levying of a land tax by the Bishop. Halkirk was joined to the Parish of Skinnet soon after the Reformation, and up until the 17th century the area continued to figure in feudal conflicts, to which the relics of its towers, castles and forts testify. Its church, once its reason for being and built in 1743, was enveloped by the village of today, which was started by John Sinclair in 1803 and was supported by the area's rural economy, which was later supplanted by quarrying and whisky distilling. The former was founded by the Caithness Quarrying Flagstone Company, which until 1905 exported its flagstone to Aberdeen, Glasgow, Newcastle and overseas. Between 1845 and 1930, like many other places in Scotland, Halkirk witnessed an exodus of people to Canada, America, Australia, New Zealand and Argentina.

HALLFOREST TOWER
ABERDEENSHIRE

Originally a hunting seat built by Robert the Bruce 1´ miles SW of Kintore. In the 14th century it was bestowed by the King on Sir Robert de Keith, the Great Earl Marischal of Scotland who probably built it shortly after. Consisting of an oblong keep, it was visited by Queen Mary in 1562, occupied by the Earl Marischal in 1639 and frequently attacked in the wars of that period, to which some of its present ruinous state testifies.

HALLGREEN CASTLE
ABERDEENSHIRE

Built by the sea near Inverbervie. Although the site of a castle in 1376, the present ruined L plan courtyard structure was built by the Raits of Hallgreen in 1687 and would seem to have been defended by a moat and drawbridge with portcullis at one time. While held by the Farquhar family in the 19th century it was incorporated into a mansion.

HAMILTON
SOUTH LANARKSHIRE

Town situated 9 miles SE of Glasgow. The site of a settlement from a very early pe-riod, and originally called Cadzow after its castle. The land was held by the Hamildon family in the 13th century and was created a Burgh of Barony in 1475, when its name changed to Hamilton. Continuing to rise in importance along with the family, it was created a Royal Burgh in 1548-49 and in 1668 a Burgh of Regality in a charter from Charles II. Built in 1591 and added to later, Hamilton Palace, the family seat, and in its heyday one of the largest palaces in Scotland, was a place of refuge for Mary Queen of Scots after her escape from Loch Leven (1569), and the headquarters for Cromwell's forces in 1652. The Hamilton Declaration asserting the rights of the Covenanters was signed here by the dissenters on 13th June 1679, while Hamilton Woods provided them with a place of sanctuary after their defeat by the Duke of Monmouth at Bothwell Bridge. A Collegiate Church founded here in 1451 by Lord Hamilton, but demolished in 1732, was replaced by the present church, designed by William Adam in 1734. Once a producer of lace fabrics introduced from France by the Duchess of Hamilton; though there were well over a thousand looms in the town by 1810, the trade was eventually overshadowed by mining following the development of its coal reserves throughout the 19th century. By 1926 these had undermined the palace foundations and brought about its demolition. The decline of the towns coal mining industry from then on raised its profile as the administrative centre for Lanarkshire by 1948, at a time when its lack of industry was making it a dormitory town for Glasgow.

HARLAW, BATTLE OF, 1411
ABERDEENSHIRE

Two miles NNW of Inverurie. The battle was fought when the Lord of the Isles, in trying to reclaim the Earldom of Ross, overran Ross-shire. To prevent the fulfilment of his threat to burn Aberdeen, the Earl of Mar, with his quickly assembled force, repelled an initial assault by the rebels and compounded his advantage with the advance of his well armed knights. Their success in breaking the enemy's ranks proved decisive in bringing victory. The defeat dealt a blow to the many families who were left without fathers and heirs for a generation and to the invincible reputation of the Highland Charge.

HARTHILL CASTLE
ABERDEENSHIRE

Standing by a stream one mile S of Oyne. This Z plan courtyard castle was built in 1638 by Patrick Leith who was a cadet of the Leiths of Edingarroch. Noted for its massive sturdy walls, round towers, bartizans and arched gateways, it was once occupied by a local freebooter who, after being confronted by local opposition, prudently burnt Harthill and emigrated. It later passed to the Erskines of Pittodrie and has lately been restored.

HATTON CASTLE
ANGUS

The castle's position at the base of Hatton Hill gives it a commanding a view of Sidlaw hill pass to Strathmore. The lands were granted by Robert the Bruce in 1317 to Sir William Oliphant (Knight) whose descendant Laurence, 4th Lord Oliphant, built this Z plan tower in 1575. The lands and castle were acquired by Sir James Halyburton of Pitcur (Knight) by 1627 and during the Covenanting Wars it was garrisoned by their supporters under Earl of Crawford (Lord Lindsay) in 1645, narrowly escaping an attack by Montrose. After passing to the Mackenzies of Rosehaugh it became ruinous but is now restored.

HAWICK
SCOTTISH BORDERS

Town situated 18 miles SW of Galashiels. Name derived from the Old English 'heah wic' meaning 'high dwelling' or 'village'. The land once belonged to the Lovel family and was probably a Burgh of Barony from an early date as its Church of St Mary (rebuilt 1763, restored 1880) was consecrated in 1214. Either before or after the lands were burnt by Sir Thomas Umfraville in 1418, the barony was conveyed by James I to Sir William Douglas of Drumlanrig, but was later resigned to the Crown in 1452 and passed to the Scotts of Buccleuch in the 16th century. An earlier charter granted to the people of Hawick by Sir James Douglas was confirmed by Queen Mary in 1545. Burnt by Sir Ralph Evers and Sir Brian Latoun in 1544, Hawick was completely destroyed by the townsfolk in 1570 to prevent its use by the Earl of Sussex but was rebuilt along with nearby Branxholm Tower (see castle) in a more fortified style. After being re-erected a Burgh of Barony in 1669, the town grew steadily and by the 18th century John Hardie, a merchant and baillie of the town, founded the hosiery trade that was furthered by the Laing, Pringle, Elliot, Watson and Laidlaw families and was to provide the mainstay of the towns economy in future decades. The Common Riding tradition which is held here between May and June celebrates the time after Flodden, (1513) when the English standard was captured from a group of English soldiers. Recently the town became very popular with tourists wanting to witness the production of its internationally renowned mill products. Another of Hawick's abiding passions is the recreational Rugby Club which has produced numerous international players over the years.

HAWTHORNDEN CASTLE
MIDLOTHIAN

Overlooking the Esk Valley 1 mile below Roslin are the remains of a Drummond seat. The land belonged to the Abernethys, the Douglases and then the Drummonds, who built the 15th century keep with screen wall on the cavernous rock that had once been used as a place of refuge for Robert the Bruce. By the southwest courtyard wall is a subterranean chamber in the rock that was once used as a pit or prison. Home to Sir John Drummond, who was Gentleman Usher to James VI. His son William Drummond (poet and writer) was born here and it was here in 1618 that the poet and writer Ben Johnson, having walked from London was received by Drummond with the words: 'Welcome welcome Royal Ben ' to which Johnson replied 'Thank ye, thank ye Hawthornden'. He added a mansion house in 1638 which completed the enclosure, before dying here brokenhearted at Charles I's execution in 1649. Further improvements were made by Rev William Abernethy Drummond (1720-1809), later Bishop of Edinburgh, but latterly it ceased to be a Drummond seat.

HELENSBURGH
WEST DUMBARTONSHIRE

Town picturesquely situated on the River Clyde 8 miles NW of Dumbarton. Once comprising the lands of Milrigs or Malrigs owned by John Shaw of Greenock, in 1776 they were sold to Sir James Colquhoun, under whose patronage the New Town grew. Named Helensburgh after the latter's wife Helen Sutherland, daughter of Lord Strathnaver, it was often regarded as an early example of good town planning and was probably influenced by Edinburgh's New Town. Shortly after being erected a Burgh of Barony for Colquhoun of Luss, 1802, it

was used by Henry Bell (steam navigator and Provost of the town 1807-09) as a watering place during his steam navigation trials, which led to the creation of Bell's Comet in 1812. The inventor retired here and was buried nearby in 1830. Later an obelisk was erected to his memory and stands overlooking the sea. After the opening of its rail link with Glasgow in 1857, its growth accelerated and the town became a popular residential district for Glasgow's professional and merchant classes. Although of little commercial importance, its weavers were once known for their bonnets and stockings which they sold to the many summer visitors who flocked here from in and around Glasgow. In 1886 John Logie Baird, the inventor of television, was born here and in succeeding decades it became a popular haunt of artists and writers, notably Neil Munroe and Colin Hunter. The most enduring legacy from this period however is Charles Rennie Mackintosh's Hill House. Built in 1903 with a commission from the publisher W.W Blackie, it still serves as a testament to the artist's design skills.

HERMITAGE CASTLE
SCOTTISH BORDERS

Situated by the Hermitage Water 6 miles NE of Newcastleton. It was begun by Nicholas de Soulis in the 13th century to replace the family's 11th century seat nearby. Comprising two massive oblong blocks joined by a middle section, almost giving it an H shape, Hermitage has been one of the Borders strongest and best-preserved baronial fortalice. Consequently its erection angered Henry III into assembling an army in 1243, claiming its closeness to the border posed a threat to England. Rebuilt by the Dacres in the 14th century, it was granted by David II to William Douglas, known as the Knight of Liddesdale, who in 1342 imprisoned

Alexander Ramsay here before starving him to death. In 1398 it became the property of the Earl of Angus (Red Douglases), who developed it into the structure we see today, before it was exchanged for Bothwell Castle on the Clyde (1492), with the Earls of Bothwell. As bankrupts, the Douglases had frequently used it as a bargaining tool with the English. It was here in 1566 that James, 4th Earl of Bothwell, met Queen Mary, who rode 40 miles from Jedburgh and back in one day, a feat that led to a fever. Hermitage was acquired by the Scotts of Buccleuch in 1594, in whose possession it remained until the 20th century.

HERTFORD'S INVASIONS, 1544-45

During the remaining years of King Henry VIII reign the English court, anxious to weaken the alliance between Scotland and France, appointed the Earl of Hertford Lieutenant General in the north, ordering him to declare Henry guardian of the infant Scottish Queen Mary and Protector of the Realm. With the compliance of Scotland's Regent the Earl of Arran, a peace treaty was signed at Greenwich in 1543 whereby the young Prince Edward was to marry the young Queen Mary. In response, Henry's main opponent Cardinal Beaton strengthened the alliance with France by repudiating The Treaty of Greenwich, and shortly after, the Regent Arran defected to the Beaton Party, compelling Henry in 1544, during his war with France to order an invasion by the Earl of Hertford. The army embarked by ship at Berwick and in May the fleet appeared in the Firth of Forth before landing 10,000 men at Leith. Hertford then proceeded to burn much of Edinburgh along with Holyrood Palace, and was further assisted by Sir Ralph Evers who had recently arrived from Berwick with 4,000 men. The army subsequently fell on Leith, from

where they returned to Berwick to rendezvous with the land forces who had pillaged towns to the south of Edinburgh. After leaving forces near the border to man occasional raids, Hertford returned to London where he was made Lieutenant of the Kingdom by the Queen in Henry's absence. Ironically the policy strengthened the Franco-Scottish alliance, and with his assistance requested in France only served to fan the flames King Henry had hoped to dampen. The havoc wrought in 1544 by Sir Ralph Evers and Sir Brian Latoun in the Borders region was brought to a halt in 1545 when the Regent Arran defeated them at the battle of Ancrum Moor, where both leaders fell. The victory was significant in that it encouraged King Philip of France to commit troops as a precursor to his own invasion of England. This was overtaken by the internal strife that erupted in Scotland, with the burning of the heretic and martyr George Wishart and the murder of Cardinal Beaton in retaliation, 1546, distancing Scotland from Catholic France and closer to the Reformers in England. In the wake of the deployment of French galleys in the Forth, there then ensued a race for the capture of St Andrews Castle, held by Beatons murderers, until its capture by the Franco-Scottish force in 1547. After the death in 1547 of King Henry and King Francis I of France, Hertford, now Duke of Somerset resumed his attempt to consummate the marriage between the monarchs while trying to advance the long outstanding claim of Edward I for feudal suzerainty. Reaching Berwick in August and crossing the Tweed in September, he defeated the Scots at the battle of Pinkie at Musselburgh and burnt Leith, but with his army only provisioned for a month was forced to return south.

HIGHLAND PARK DISTILLERY
ORKNEY

The most northerly Scotch whisky distillery in the world is located in the town of Kirkwall. It was founded in 1798 on the site of a smuggler's bothy by Magnus Eunson, a church Elder by day and a smuggler by night who hid the contraband under the pulpit, safe from excisemen. It takes its water from the pool at Cattie Maggies Well at Greenvale and Crantit Spring. Located amidst the green fertile islands battered by majestic Atlantic waves, its thought that Highland Park's character comes from peat beds that have absorbed the salt spray of centuries, giving a heather honey quality to the whisky that distinguishes it from all other malts. Bought by the Grant family in 1908 it continued to be run throughout World War I (1914-18), during the presence of the Grand Fleet at Scapaflow, but was sold by the family to Highland Distilleries in 1937. Like its exterior which typifies a distillery of its period the production methods are in keeping with tradition, as it is one of the few remaining distilleries where barley is still malted on the malting floor.

OWNERS
Edrington Group Ltd, The ?

REGION
Highland

PRODUCT
Highland Park 12 18 and 25 year old single malt 40% 43% & 53.5% vol

NOTES
A heather honey, balanced smokiness with a rounded smokey sweetness and a rich, full taste.

HILLSLAP TOWER
SCOTTISH BORDERS

Positioned 2 miles above Melrose is an L plan tower built by the Cairncross family in 1585. Hillslap's main claim to fame is as the prototype of Glendearg Castle that figured in Walter Scott's 'The Monastery ' in 1820. The tower now functions as a dwelling house.

HODDAM CASTLE
DUMFRIES & GALLOWAY

The castle stands on the bank of the Annan, 4 miles SW of Ecclefechan. From the 14th century this was the seat of the Herries family, who had strong ties with the Bruces, who occupied the first Hoddam Castle nearby, which was demolished in accordance with one of the many border treaties. The present L plan structure was built in 1627 when Richard Murray of Cockpool acquired the estate from the 6th Lord Herries. In 1653 it was purchased by David, Ist Earl of Southesk, but by 1690 the castle and barony were sold to John Sharpe, whose descendants sold it to Edward Brook in 1878. It is now in a ruinous state.

HOLYROOD PALACE
CITY OF EDINBURGH

The principal palace of Scotland is situated at the bottom of the Royal Mile in the NW corner of the Queen's Park, a former deer forest. The legend that claims the name and the erection of the Abbey of Holyrood resulted from divine intervention when David I was confronted by a stag while hunting on Holy Rood day is probably spurious. The Abbey was probably built to protect a piece of Christ's true cross bequeathed to the King by his pious mother Queen Margaret. In 1128 he founded the Abbey of Holyrood for Augustinians and built it in the grandest manner with royal apartments. Following its burning by Richard II in 1385, the Abbey's double function waned and in 1501 the Palace of Holyrood was built by James IV as the seat of royal power. The progress and gratitude that came to characterise the reign of James IV, gave the

King an almost celebrity quality, which climaxed in his death at the battle of Flodden, 1513. The Kings last evening in the Capital is remembered in Sir Walter Scott's 'Marmion':

Old Holyrood rung merrily,
That night, with wassell, mirth, and glee:
King James within her princely bower,
Feasted the chiefs of Scotlands power,
Summoned to spend the parting hours;
For he had charged that his array
Should southward march by break of day.

Enlarged by James V in 1528, it was mostly destroyed by the Earl of Hertford in 1544 and by Somerset in 1547, but was rebuilt after the return from France in 1561 of Queen Mary, who held court here during most of the remaining years of her unfortunate reign (1542-67). It was here that she had some of her most acrimonious meetings with John Knox and where her upstart Italian secretary David Rizzio was murdered by the Scottish nobles, led by her jealous husband Lord Darnley, 1566. Although occupied by her son James VI, after his accession to the English throne following the death of Queen Elizabeth in 1603, it was temporarily neglected until improvements helped set the stage for the crowning of Charles Ist in 1633, which ultimately led to Cromwell's occupation in 1650, when it suffered a fire. The present edifice was commissioned by Charles II in 1671 and designed by William Bruce (Surveyor General) and built by Robert Mylne (Master Mason). Retaining the James IV tower of 1505, it was built three storeys high around an arcaded quadrangle, with turreted towers at each end of the facade connected by a platform roof and balustrade, with the central doric portico and clock tower with crown as the main entrance. The design is typical of the Scottish Renaissance style which emphasises the front at the expense of the sides

and back. Designed to give special attention to state apartments, its interior by William Bruce (Master of Works) consists of a richly embellished blend of panelled rooms, Italian marble mantelpieces, tiles and marble pavings from Holland and ornamental plaster work, all of which provide the background for many rare paintings, tapestries, furniture, and other works of art. Continuing to figure in the dynastic struggles of the Stewarts, after the Reformation, during the reign of James VII (1685-89), the palace was rife with rumours of Popish plots and counter-plots. During the city's occupation by the Jacobites in 1745, Prince Charles Edward held state here to the delight of the Highland Chiefs, and after his defeat at Culloden (1746) the victorious Duke of Cumberland en route south occupied the very same sleeping apartment. In the 19th century, the palace precincts provided sanctuary for debtors, while the apartments served as a haven for Charles X of France in 1830, when he was driven from his throne. Between 1850 and 1861 it was often used by Queen Victoria and Prince Albert as a stopover point en route to Balmoral, and in 1859 their son Edward Prince of Wales stayed here during a short attendance at Edinburgh University. The Queen's Park, once a richly cultivated Royal Demesne (estate), was repurchased by the Crown in 1844 and was the scene of the review of 20,000 volunteers by Queen Victoria in 1860. Since then both palace and park have provided a relaxed setting for successive monarchs during their annual sojourns in Scotland's Capital. In a commanding position in the southern section of the Queen's Park is Arthur's Seat an extinct volcano that rises 822 ft above sea level. Resembling a lion in slumber, it sits majestically high above the parks other natural features including the Salisbury Crags, Hunter's Bog (a former rifle range), St Margaret's Loch, Dunsappie Loch and

Duddingston Loch. The nearby village of Duddingston was the site where an Anglo-Norman Knight named Dodin settled in the reign of David I, 1124-53. Over the centuries the park has been used for primitive settlements, a hunting ground, military camps and of course recreational pursuits. See Holyrood Abbey.

HOLYROOD ABBEY
CITY OF EDINBURGH

Founded in 1128 by David I for Augustinian monks, probably to house a piece of the rood from Christ's true cross which belonged to his mother Queen Margaret. No expense was spared on its cruciform church, built in a Norman Gothic style but which was sadly replaced by William I's mainly Gothic structure, incorporating two western towers and a great central tower intersecting the nave and transepts. It was burnt by Richard II in 1385. The royal apartments to the south of the Abbey were sometimes used by the Stewart Kings from Robert III until they were supplanted by the present palace in 1501. Following further attacks by Hertford in 1544 and Somerset in 1547, the Abbey passed into secular hands, but after the repairs and elevation of its church to Chapel Royal and Order of the Thistle by James VII it witnessed further destruction in 1689 when the King was replaced by William and Mary (Glorious Revolution). In 1768 the roof collapsed with some of the walls but thanks to the preservation work of 1816 these now form part of the ruins which include the outline of the Abbey, the nave and the most interesting part, the French doorway. The ashes of Mary of Guelders, David II, James II, James V and Lord Darnley were interred here. See Holyrood Palace

HOMILDON HILL, BATTLE OF, 1402
The series of incursions into England in the Spring of 1402 proved detrimental to Anglo-Scottish relations and culminated in the Earl of Percy's victory over the Scots under Archibald, 4th Earl of Douglas, during their retreat north. After his wounding and capture, Douglas broke the conditions of his release and allied himself with Charles VI of France, who granted him the Duchy of Touraine.

HOPETOUN HOUSE
CITY OF EDINBURGH

By the Firth of Forth 12 miles NW of Edinburgh is the ancestral home of the Hope family, who are descended from the Norman family of de Hope. In 1678 John Hope purchased the Baronies of Abercorn and Niddry, and his son Charles was created Earl of Hopetoun, Viscount Airthrie and Baron Hope in 1703. Today's neo-classical structure, originally designed by William Bruce between 1699 and 1702, was transformed into a Palladian edifice in 1755 by William and Robert Adam's north and south wings with their octagonal domes connected to the main block by sweeping colonnades. Its interior shows that convenience was sacrificed for its grandeur which contrasts with Adam's decor, the Chippendale furniture and the complement of paintings and artefacts. Designed by William Bruce and Alexander Edward, its grounds include a deer park, along with clusters of oak, chestnuts and yew trees that border the avenues, gardens and orchards to form a symmetry that provides the perfect setting for what is seen as Adam's masterpiece of Georgian architecture. Its later associations with the Royal Family included a visit by George IV in 1822, and later by Queen Victoria and by the Queen Mother who both slept here.

HORSEBURGH TOWER
SCOTTISH BORDERS

The ruins of this pele tower of uncertain

age stand on a hill 2 miles below Peebles. From the 13th to the 17th century the land belonged to the Horseburghs of Horseburgh, who sold it to Robert Stewart of Shillinglaw. The ruined rectangular keep of Nether Horsburgh nearby was built by the same family, who were Sheriff Deputes of Peebles under Lord Yester.

HOUSTON
RENFREWSHIRE

Village situated 6 miles NW of Paisley. The lands of St Peter, so called after an 8th century church dedicated to St Peter, were granted by Baldwin, Sheriff of Lanark to Hugh Padvinan in the 12th century and later took the name of Hughs-Town, which was corrupted into Houston. Created a Burgh of Barony for Houston of that Ilk in 1671, which the family held until 1740, it was eventually acquired in 1782 by Alexander Spiers of Elderslie who built the new village. Houston was for a long time subordinate to the neighbouring Parish of Killellan, and although the uniting of both in 1717 led to the building of cotton mills, both missed out on Scotland's heavy engineering boom in the 19th century due to bad communication links. Cotton production continued well into the 20th century when agriculture was Houston's economic backbone and when many of the 19th century buildings were swept away. The relatively modern Mercat Cross in the centre of the village stands on a plinth thought to date from the 14th century. The Parish Church, built in 1874 by the Spiers family, houses the 17th century effigies of John Houston and his wife Ann, who died in 1456.

HUNTERSTON TOWER
NORTH AYRSHIRE

Situated between Largs and West Kilbride is an early 16th century tower with a 17th century wing. Built by the Hunter-ston family, who held the land from the 13th century and who were Venators (hunters) of the King's lands from an earlier period. In the 19th century a mansion was built nearby to replace the old family house. A silver broach found on the estate in 1826 is thought to have been lost by a Norseman at the battle of Largs, 1263. Latterly the castle was surrounded by a nuclear power station.

HUNTLY CASTLE
ABERDEENSHIRE

On a sloping site 1 mile NE of Fochabers stand the remains of a keep that was once incorporated in a 13th century motte and bailey. Then called Bog of Gight, the original structure was built by the Strathbogie Earls of Atholl whose land was granted by Robert the Bruce in the 14th century to the Gordon family. In 1445 Alexander Seton became the Ist Earl of Huntly and built the castle shortly after. The family's support for the church of Rome frequently brought the enmity of the Presbyterian Church and its more prominent adherents while also helping to define them as one of the most noble families in the north. The structure erected by the first Earl was destroyed in 1594 by the King after Huntly defeated the Earl of Argyll at the battle of Glenlivit, but was rebuilt in 1602 by George the 6th Earl and Ist Marquis of Huntly whose popularity at the Court of James VI had won him a reprieve from forfeiture for his part in a Jesuit Conspiracy. This also brought him the post of King's Lieutenant and Justiciar in the North until 1607 when it was bestowed on the Earl of Argyll. Huntly's influence waned during the reign of Charles I but he played an important role in the Covenanting struggles as their northern opponent until his castle was besieged several times and captured by General Middleton and later fell into ruin.

I

INCH HOUSE
CITY OF EDINBURGH

In the south of Edinburgh 2´ miles from the town centre stands a 17th century mansion house. Developing from an L plan tower which was originally surrounded by water, Inch was built in 1617 by James Winram of Nether Liberton, who was Keeper of the Great Seal in 1623. Further additions were made in 1634, and by 1760 the land had been completely drained. A family of considerable property in Liberton, his son James Winram possessed the Baronies of Liberton, which included Nether and Over Liberton. More recently it was surrounded by a housing development and the mansion functions as a community centre.

INCHAFFRAY ABBEY
PERTH & KINROSS

Positioned on rising ground on what was once an island 6 miles E of Crieff. The name is thought to derive from the Latin 'Insula Massarum' meaning 'island of the masses'. Founded as a priory in 1200 by Gilbert 3rd Earl of Strathearn. Its Augustinian monks received a number of royal grants down through the centuries but comparatively little is known of the building's history before it was pillaged for its stone and demolished in 1816. One of its abbots, Maurice, blessed Bruce's army at Bannockburn in 1314, and another was slain at Flodden in 1513. Possessing great influence down to the Reformation when in 1565 its Commendator was James Drummond, later Lord Madderty, for whom it was erected into a Temporal Lordship in 1609. It later became the property of the Earl of Kinnoul and in 1816, during the building of a turnpike road through the ruins, several stone coffins were discovered. Today's limited ruins include a western gable and a single arched apartment.

INCHCOLM ABBEY
FIFE

On the Island of Inchcolm on the River Forth is a well preserved Augustinian Abbey. The site of a very early religious settlement which later figured as St Colms Inch in Shakespeare's 'Macbeth', where Sweno the Norwegian King was buried. In 1123 when Alexander I founded a priory here it was inhabited by a hermit and follower of St Columba who lived on shellfish and the milk from one cow. Built in a mainly Early Pointed style and created an abbey in 1235, its present church, to the north east from which extends the 12th-century nave of the original church, later Abbots House, dates from the 13th and 15th centuries. Plundered and burnt several times between 1385 and 1547, the last time was after the battle of Pinkie when the Duke of Somerset, while harrying shipping in the Forth, used it as a purpose-built fort which was demolished by order of the Privy Council in 1550. Though granted to Sir James Stewart in 1544, its revenues passed into secular hands and the buildings later fell prey to pirates who used it as a base until 1581, when its stone was used for the Edinburgh Tolbooth. Repaired periodically, it continued to be used for defensive purposes, for in the 19th century it served as a naval battery and then as a hospital for the visiting Russian Fleet. Later used for coastal defence during the 1st and 2nd World Wars. The remaining buildings are the 13th century octagonal Chapter House next to its south transept, with a 14th century cloister walkway (later dormitory) on its west side which accessed the central cloister gardens. From the garden's SE corner extend the dormitories and the infirmary range and on the west and south side of the cloister is the 14th-century guest house.

INCHDREWER CASTLE
ABERDEENSHIRE

On high ground 3 miles S of Banff is a former stronghold of the Ogilvies, who acquired the estate from the Curror family in the mid-16th century. Sir Walter Ogilvie and his son George remodelled and enlarged the castle while expanding their property interests around 1557, and a descendant made Inchdrewer his chief residence when he was made Lord Banff in 1642. After the murder of Lord Banff by his servants in 1713, the house was burnt to destroy the evidence and fell into decay for a long period until its subsequent restoration.

INCHGOWER DISTILLERY
MORAY

Conveniently sited near the town and the port of Buckie. When built as a model distillery in 1871, its founder, Alexander Wilson, a member of a prominent family of factors, was on his second attempt. The first was Tochieneal Distillery near Cullen, which closed in 1870 after 46 years when the Earl and Countess of Seafield doubled the rent. Its high quality water from the Menduff Hills and cooling water from the Buckie burn combine with Inchgower's modern interior to create a model distillery with its carpenter's shop, cooperage, smiddy and warehouses built around a courtyard with workers' cottages separate, preserving the aesthetic qualities that have changed little over the years. The by-products of draff and pot ale which fed over 300 animals on the nearby farms are still used in animal feed today. Flourishing between 1910-29 under the management of Walter Wilson, a keen breeder of Aberdeen Angus cattle, in the 1930s the family's fortune declined when the family home of Arradoul House and the distillery were bought by Buckie Town Council, who sold it to Arthur Bell & Son in 1936.

Ceasing to make its own malt in the 1960s, the distillery chose to use its kilns to expand output which has doubled since. Inchgower later became an important element in the blending of Bell's, Britain's most popular whisky.

OWNERS
Diageo plc ?

REGION
Speyside

PRODUCT
Inchgower 14 year old single malt 43% vol

NOTES
A distinctive nose with a rich, full, slightly spicy flavour.

INCHINNAN
CITY OF ABERDEEN

Village situated 6 miles NW of Glasgow. Name derived from the Gaelic 'innis' meaning 'island' or 'pasture meadow'. The Inan part is thought to derive from Saint Finnan. Once the site of a church dedicated to St Conval, who taught Christianity here in the 7th century, the lands were granted by King Malcolm IV to Walter, High Steward of Scotland in 1158 while its church was held by the Knights Templars until transferred to the Knights of St John of Jerusalem in 1312. They were later held intermittently by the High Steward's descendants, and the Earls of Lennox until sold to the Duke of Montrose in the 18th century. As one would expect, much of the village's history revolves around its church, which was rebuilt in 1828 but replaced in 1902 by a later church gifted by Lord Blythswood (Lord Lieutenant of Renfrewshire), the then landowner. Today this houses some 10th and 12th century Christian stones. The decline of the villages mainly rural economy in the 19th century, causing an exodus of people to the neighbouring towns was reversed between 1911 and

1921 owing to the building of Beardmores hangars for the construction of airships.

INCHOCH CASTLE
HIGHLAND

Near the bank of the Moray Firth 1´ miles NE of Auldearn are the ruins of the Hays of Lochloys' 17th century baronial keep. Starting from an L plan castle, an additional wing was added later.

INDUSTRIAL REVOLUTION

Though unlike the revolutions which preceded it, the Industrial Revolution was the culmination of centuries of internal strife and engendered a more collective and dynamic transformation which was to combine and extend its influence far beyond the British Isles. The two elements that were central to the industrial development of 18th and 19th century Scotland were agriculture and industry. With improvements in farming came a large exodus of rural peoples to the urban industrial centres. Though these changes had their roots in the late 17th century tobacco trade from the Virginian market, the foundations for growth were firmly set in place with the Treaty of Union in 1707, when the great expansion in Britain's trade with the rest of the world brought a ready supply of raw materials, helping to facilitate innovation and development. Scotland's premier industry in 1727 was the linen trade. The locally obtained flax used in the industry grew along-side its staple crops, that were tended by the very people who spawned the cottage industry. These were the same people who were to flock to the growing industrial centres of Edinburgh, Glasgow, Aberdeen and Dundee with the advent of spinning machinery. A central part of the emerging commercial capital of Scotland, Glasgow's tobacco barons just managed to survive the instability caused by the American War of Independence (1775-83) with the detrimental effect it had on trade. It was around this time that a new era dawned with Richard Arkwright's water frame and the development of James Watt's steam engine, while in literature Adam Smith published 'The Wealth of Nations' ,1776, laying the foundations of modern liberal economics. By 1799 Glasgow had built a burgeoning cotton trade on the basis of its linen trade, with its major showpiece being the New Lanark mills: started in 1785 by David Dale and continued by Robert Owen, whose endeavours secured main markets in Germany, Italy, France and Switzerland. With the many handloom weavers in the south and east of Scotland now switching to cotton, the stage was set for rapid expansion by the manufacturers of Paisley and Glasgow. However, with the invention of the flax power spinning weel in 1825, the production of flax was becoming increasingly concentrated in Forfar, Fife and Perth. In 1759 Dr Roebuck of Sheffield founded the Carron Iron Works (the largest in Europe by 1840) for the smelting of iron with coal instead of wood, that was later followed by the Clyde Iron Works in 1787. Both helped establish a smelting industry for the west, while smaller foundries and forges made agricultural implements, machine parts and domestic utensils. The industry's strong but slow growth was quickened by the advent of Blackband ironstone in 1801, and the hot blast furnace created by James Neilson in 1828, which produced three times as much iron with the same amount of fuel, resulting in over 50 hot blast furnaces being established by 1839 and more than doubling by 1853. Coupled with this industrial growth was the extensive infrastructuring taking place as the era of the railway enabled Scotland's mineral wealth to be exploited which had began with the building in 1790 of Smeaton's

Forth & Clyde canal from Port Dundas and Grangemouth and was followed by the Union Canal between Edinburgh and Glasgow in 1822. This broke the monopoly of the Midlothian coal barons with cheaper coal from the western fields. By the mid 19th century, the country's rocky coast had been made safe by the endeavours of Robert Stevenson, designer of a network of lighthouses that guided the country's prolific maritime trade that was furthered by the steam engine. With the West Indian sugar trade came an export market for Glasgow's machine makers, supplying the sugar-producing countries of the world by 1850. From the ports on the Clyde, famed for their marine engines, had come the Comet in 1812, invented by Henry Bell (1767-1830), but it was the linking of shipbuilding and engineering by the Scotts of Greenock that led to the first iron steamer launched on the Clyde in 1839. Contiguous to this was the career of Robert Napier who became one of the leading lights in the history of Clyde engineering after founding his shipbuilding yard at Govan in 1842, before entering into building iron ships powered by his own engines. Meanwhile, the cotton trade had slowed down owing to the disruption caused by the American Civil War (1861-65). The revival of the linen trade with the arrival of jute combined with flax in 1867 to make Forfar the hub of activity, with its 18 mills co-ordinating the efforts of the other 72 in Dundee and 18 in Arbroath. All of which were part of a national total of nearly 200 flax, jute and hemp factories with over 70,000 employees, making Paisley the main centre for its production. By 1870, iron was replacing wood in shipbuilding, but was itself overshadowed by the lighter mild steel being developed by Siemens and Thomas Gilchrists in 1878, which facilitated the launch of the first steel liner at Denny's yard at Dumbarton the following year. Further improve-

ments in boiler and engine production were to make the steamer the heartbeat of Britain's merchant fleet, bringing raw materials and foodstuffs that were often re-exported to overseas markets which continued to stimulate innovation in the country's industrial base during future decades.

INGLISMALDIE CASTLE
ABERDEENSHIRE

About 6 miles SW of Laurencekirk stands the Livingstones 16th-and 17th-century L plan mansion with its angle turrets and crow-stepped gables. A long plain wing added later was converted into a mansion. In the 17th century it was held by the Carnegies and then became the residence of the Lords Falconer of Halkerton, ancestors of the Earls of Kintore.

INNERLEITHEN
SCOTTISH BORDERS

Mill Town situated 6´ SE of Peebles. Name derived from the Gaelic 'inbhir', therefore 'confluence of the River Leithen'. The land was granted to Kelso Abbey by Malcolm IV (1153-65) who also granted its church the right of sanctuary after his son's body rested here, following a drowning accident in the river. A mere Kirk hamlet from the 12th century which was held by the Stewarts of Traquair from the 16th century, after Burns's visit in 1787 its development was under way with a woollen factory started by Alexander Brodie in 1790. Around the same time its medicinal saline spring became a popular attraction and was thought to be the 'St Ronans' in Sir Walter Scott's romance of 1824. Innerleithans growth meant that by 1845 it boasted five woollen mills, making it an integral part of Scotland's woollen industry. The original printing works, built by Robert Smail, are now a museum. See Golf Club

INNERLEITHAN GOLF CLUB
SCOTTISH BORDERS

Regardless of the failed attempt to found a club in 1884, a meeting was convened in the Traquair Arms Hotel in 1886 which was chaired by the original driving force, Mr Kidd Brown, whose tenacity finally got the plan off the ground. The annual subscription was set at 5 shillings and an approach was made to Mr Park of Musselburgh to lay out the grounds, which had been let to Mr William Tait of the Kirklands. Innerleithan quickly acquired all the trappings and paraphernalia of a club, including the Silver Golf Club trophy presented by a Mr Thorburn in 1889. The year before, the first hut had been erected for maintenance equipment, but doubled as a pavilion until the clubhouse was built in 1896 with facilities for both sexes. Experiencing the usual disputes with the farmers, by 1905 the course had been further perfected, despite the flooding from the Leithan Water in 1896 and the whistle of bullets from the nearby firing range, it was frequently praised for its turf, greens, and the scenic beauty of the Leithan Valley. All of which endured the Great War 1914-18 when the course was used by officers and men billeted in the town, but during World War II the course was closed and in 1942 the pavilion mysteriously burnt down. After this moves were afoot to use the clubhouse. Consequently, after the end of hostilities, sights were set on an improved 9 hole course and land was leased from Mr Stewart of Caberston Farm which became the Ist, 2nd and 3rd holes or rather the round loop, now the most appealing part of the course. Between 1956-1985 the distinguished figures on the course were Ian Turnbull, nine times club champion and latterly Norman Smith who won it seven times.

INNERMESSAN
DUMFRIES & GALLOWAY

Once a proud burgh but now a mere hamlet situated 2´ miles NE of Stranraer. The name is derived from the Gaelic 'inbhir' and 'Messan' meaning 'mouth of the River Messan'. In keeping with its pattern of development and decline most of Innermessan's historical high points are confined to the more remote past. Thought to have been the site of the Caledonian Novantae settlement recorded by Ptolemy (Egyptian Geographer) in the 2nd century. Skirting the coastline on a high bank is the Moat of Innermessan, where the settlement may have stood. Once surrounded by a fosse from which it rises 30 feet high, its level top measures 95 from east to west by 98 from north to south.

INNERPEFFRAY
PERTH & KINROSS

Town situated on the River Earn 3 miles SE of Crieff. Name derived from the Gaelic 'inbhir' meaning 'river mouth' while Peffray is probably from the Welsh 'pefr' meaning 'bright and sparkling'. An established river crossing during the Roman occupation, the community later had strong associations with the Drummond family, who are interred in the old church, which was founded by John Drummond and made collegiate in 1508. The nearby library, founded by Sir David Drummond, Ist Lord Madderty, in 1691, contains up to 3,000 books, mainly on divinity, while its French Bible of 1632 bears the autograph of the Marquis of Montrose. See Tower

INNERPEFFRAY CASTLE
PERTH & KINROSS

The ruins of this L plan tower house stand on the bank of the Earn 4 miles SE of Crieff. Built around 1610 by James Drummond, Ist Lord Madderty, the Innerpeffray Chapel close by was the burial place of the Drummonds from 1508. In 1691 the estate of David, 3rd Lord Madderty, helped found the library of the local school.

INNERWICK
EAST LOTHIAN

The village is situated 4 miles SW of Dunbar. The name either derived from the Old Norse 'eng-rvik' meaning 'close or narrow bay' or from the Gaelic 'inbhir bhuic' meaning 'confluence of the Buck' (back burn). In the 12th century David I bestowed the Manor of Innerwick on Walter Stewart but by 1380 it had passed through marriage to Alexander Hamilton, whose family built the 15th century castle around which the village grew. Taken by the English after the battle of Homildon Hill in 1402, but retaken and destroyed by the Regent Albany. In Medieval times the Parish was divided between the Baronies of Innerwick and Thornton, (stronghold of the Homes) whose respective castles, with their natural defences on either side of the Thornton burn, witnessed their own destruction, along with the village, during the invasion by the Duke of Somerset in 1548. The church and its revenues, which Walter Stewart granted to Paisley Abbey in the 12th century, passed into secular hands at the Reformation and by 1670 were held by Sir Patrick Wedderburn. Recovering enough to be made a Burgh of Barony for Maxwell of Innerwick in 1630, the village's later history was mainly concerned with the local rural economy.

INVERALLOCHY CASTLE
ABERDEENSHIRE

Occupying land 4 miles SE of Fraserburgh are the early 16th-century ruins of a Comyn stronghold. The family were granted the land by Margaret Hay in 1504 when the Great Seal was bestowed on William Comyn who was knighted in 1507 and built this castle shortly after.

INVERARAY
ARGYLL & BUTE

Town situated on the NW of Loch Fyne. Name derived from the Gaelic 'inbhir' therefore 'mouth of the River Aray'. Its position between the heart of Argyll and the Lowlands made it the site of an early settlement which later developed around its castle. Consequently the town had strong links with the Campbells, who have resided here since the 14th century when the Old Town on the north side of the bay was establishing itself as the County Town. Created a Burgh of Barony in 1472, a Royal Burgh in 1648, and a Parliamentary Burgh from 1661, its period as a Sheriffdom in the 17th century is remembered in some of the buildings used in the due process of law. In 1650, a Grammar School was founded here. During one of his descents into Argyll in 1644, Inveraray was partly burnt by Montrose, the Duke of Argyll's arch enemy, but was later to recover enough to function as a ferry port, and, like most coastal towns it was dependent on herring fishing and farming, the former being represented on the burgh shield. It was rebuilt in the 18th century along with the castle by the 3rd Duke of Argyll, who introduced linen manufacture in 1748. As with its peripheral trade, this was supplanted by tourism. For a long time renowned for its natural rugged beauty, the area was well suited to its function as a military training ground during World War II, when it was visited by King George VI, King Haakon of Norway and General Eisenhower. After the war the town received favourable grants from the Historical Buildings Council of Scotland which helped save many of its 19th-century buildings. Among these, the All Saints Episcopalian Church, which dominates the town and provides a perfect vantage point, was built in the 1860s. Its large tower and peal of ten bells were added by the 10th Duke of Argyll in 1920. The Parish Church, also founded by the Argyll family and built in 1804, once accommodated English and Gaelic worshippers separately. The oldest antiquity in the town is the sculptured stone cross on the main street, which is thought to date from 1400, while nearby stands an obelisk erected to the memory of four Campbells who were executed without trial after Argyll's failed rebellion in 1685. The Jail House and Courtroom (1820) building is now a museum. See Castle

INVERARAY CASTLE
ARGYLL & BUTE

By the bank of the Aray on the NW side of the town is the land that was for a long time held by the Argyll family who settled here in the 14th century. The first castle was built in the mid 15th century by Sir Colin Campbell, the first laird and progenitor of the Earls of Argyll, 1457, who acquired the Lordship of Lorn in 1470. Between 1744 and 1761 the 3rd Duke of Argyll built this quadrangular, two-storied pile with four round corner towers to the 18th century Gothic designs of R.Morris, but its interior owes everything to the work of John Adam and Robert Mylne. The fire of 1877 gutted the central tower but by 1880 the building was restored to more than its former magnificence with a new upper floor that is complemented further by the backdrop of its fine grounds with its oaks, larches and spruces. Although damaged again by fire in 1975, the castle's full and skilful restoration provides the appropriate ambience for its works of art while also housing a genealogical records service.

INVERBERVIE
ABERDEENSHIRE

Town situated 10 miles SW of Stonehaven. Name derived from the Gaelic 'inbhir' therefore 'mouth of the River Bervie'. In 1341 it was the scene of the arrival of David II and his English Queen after journeying from France, and in 1342 the King granted the town a Free Burgh Charter. The place owes its distinction as a Royal Burgh to the same King, who was treated kindly by the inhabitants after being shipwrecked nearby at Craig David in 1361. Stented as a Royal Burgh by James III in 1483, apart from being known for its Carmelite Friary, which stood near the old bridge from 1433, it figures little in the country's history until the 18th century. In 1788 the Haughs of Bervie introduced the first spinning linen machine in Scotland, which with the water from its river, spawned its flax mills which continued into the 20th century.

INVERGARRY CASTLE
HIGHLAND

On a rock (Ravens rock) near the shore of Loch Oich 8 miles SW of Fort Augustus are the ruins of a late 16th century L plan tower. For a long time this was the seat of the Jacobite Macdonalds of Glengarry, whose chief occupied it until 1746. It was visited by Prince Charles Edward in 1745, a week after he raised the standard at Glenfinnan, and again in 1746 a day after Culloden, when he slept on its bare floor prior to its burning by the Duke of Cumberland.

INVERGORDON
HIGHLAND

Coastal town situated 13 miles NE of Dingwall. Originally called Inverbreackie due to its position at the mouth of the River Breakie, the then village grew around its castle, for which it served as a supply port. The village was rebuilt and renamed by William Gordon of Embo in the 18th century, when it developed a largely marine based economy. This led to the building of its harbour, followed by a dockyard with its deep water facilities that made it ideal for naval ships during the Ist and 2nd World Wars, when it witnessed a considerable population increase. The town's industrial initiatives following 1945 met with varying success, the most notable being its aluminium plant, and latterly the use of its deep water facilities for oil rig construction, while its naval dockyard facilities, a central feature and employer of the town though now somewhat limited included large underground storage tanks for vessels.

INVERKEITHING
FIFE

Town situated 4 miles SE of Dunfermline. The name is derived from the Gaelic 'inbhir' and from 'Keith' meaning 'mouth of the River Keith'. Its Royal Burgh status, which was confirmed by William I in 1165, superseded the granting of an earlier charter, which suggests this was a place of some importance from an early period, probably owing to its coal reserves and its ferry port status, something that was subject to Dunfermline Abbey. By a Papal Bull of 1196, a hospital was confirmed here as the property of Dryburgh Abbey, and in the 14th century a Franciscan Friary was founded. The town often bore witness to events of national importance by virtue of its proximity to St Andrews and Dunfermline. In 1303 it was occupied by Edward I, was witness to the death of Robert III's widow, Annabella Drummond in 1403, her family shield being inscribed on the Old Mercat Cross, and was the scene of the battle of Inverkeithing in 1651 when Cromwell defeated the Scot's Royalist

Army. From 1511 to 1615 the Moubrays were the area's chief landowners. Two of the town's most famous sons are Samuel Greig (1735-1788), who helped develop the Russian Navy, and the Rev Robert Moffat (1797-1883) the African missionary. The original Parish Church of St Peters was bequeathed by Waldeve, son of Gospatrick, while its successor of 1440 was burnt in 1825 but rebuilt in 1826 in a Gothic style, retaining its original tower. See Battle

INVERKEITHING, BATTLE OF, 1651
FIFE

Fought during the Civil War when, while attempting to restore Charles II to the throne and push back Cromwell's Protectorate, a Royalist force under General David Leslie failed to defeat Cromwell's force under General Lambert advancing to the relief of Perth. The latters assault of Leslie's rear left the road to England open for the Royalists, who tried to exploit the opportunity which ultimately ended in Charles II's defeat at Worcester and his exile 1651-60.

INVERKIP TOWER
INVERCLYDE

Perched on a rock near Inverkip on the Firth of Clyde are the ruins of a late 15th-century tower which was the site of a castle in the time of Robert the Bruce.

INVERLOCHY CASTLE
HIGHLAND

Situated by the River Lochy 2 miles NE of Fort William. The possible site of a Pictish Town where Pictish Kings occasionally resided. With the help of English engineers, in the 13th century the Comyns built a tower here which in the 15th century was developed by George, 2nd Earl of Huntly into a quadrangular courtyard castle with walls 9ft thick and four round corner towers, which now make up the ruins. The north west tower is Comyn's tower. On Inverlochy's shores in 1645, the Royalists, under the Marquis of Montrose, en route to Inverness, surprised and defeated a force twice their size under the Earl of Argyll, whose forces sought sanctuary here. The event is recalled in William Aytoun's poem:

Twas I that led the Highland host through wild Lochabers snows,
What time the plaided clans came down to battle with Montrose
Ive told thee how the southerns fell beneath the broad claymore
And how we smote the Campbell clan by Inverlochy's shore

Modern Inverlochy Castle to the north east was began by the Ist Lord Arbinger in the early 19th century as a shooting lodge. Enlarged in 1861 in a Scottish Baronial style, it was visited by Queen Victoria in 1873. See Battle

INVERLOCHY, BATTLE OF, 1645
HIGHLAND

NE of Fort William. During the campaigns of Montrose, who sought to crush the Covenanters and establish Charles I on the throne, his Highland army, after ravaging Argyll, were followed by a force twice their size under the Earl of Argyll. The decision to turn around in the Great Glen and march towards Inverlochy Castle proved fortutous for Montrose, whose Highlanders attacked and routed Argyll after breaking his right wing which led to much slaughter. The news of the victory in the north moved Charles I to recklessly break off negotiations at Uxbridge, as it helped bring about his final defeat at Nesby in 1645.

INVERNESS
HIGHLAND

City, seaport and capital of the High-

lands, situated by the Moray Firth at the mouth of the River Ness, which with the Gaelic 'inbhir' is how its name translates. As the Capital of the Pictish Kingdom and site of the court of King Brude, St Columba travelled here in 565 before converting the King and his people. The original castle of Inverness was the property of Shakespeare's Macbeth who was Mormaer of Ross and Moray in the 11th century long before its strategic importance prevailed over its size, and David I held his Justicar Court here, which aided its later elevation to a Sheriffdom with authority over the whole of the north. Similarly, as a thriving trading community living around its castle, its central location brought exclusive trading privileges for its main exports wool, fish, hide and cattle and the granting of a Royal Burgh Charter 1153-65 but also exposed it to attack from all sides by unruly clansmen, which became apparent when the town was burnt in 1229 by chief Gilespick M'scourlane. In the the 13th century a Dominican Friary was founded here by Alexander II. The town and castle were occupied by the English in 1296 and 1303 but after being liberated by King Robert the Bruce in 1310 were held by the Royal Stewarts until the 15th century. It was here in 1312 that Robert I and King Haakon of Norway signed the Treaty of Inverness. The castle and town were burnt by Donald, Lord of the Isles, while en route to his defeat at Harlaw, 1411, were burnt again in 1455 by a descendant and its castle was occupied by James III in 1464 and by James IV in 1499, who made the Earls of Huntly its hereditary keepers in 1508. The meeting of the Convention of Estates held here by Mary of Guise in 1555 was later followed by the area's pacification and the taking of its castle by the forces of Mary I in 1562, thus bringing the stability that enabled her son James VI to grant the Great Charter of 1591 that was later ratified by

Charles II. The fort (citadel) built by Cromwell as one of the most northerly outposts of his Protectorate was destroyed in 1685 by the local people, who used its stone for town buildings. Inverness was held by the Mackintosh Clan for the Jacobites in 1715 and regarded as the Jacobites' Capital City between 1745 and 1746. Prior to their withdrawal and subsequent defeat at Culloden, the castle's destruction was in keeping with their order of no quarter issued against the Hanoverian forces. Suffering limited inconvenience after the earthquake of 1815, the town greatly benefited from communication links like the opening of the Caledonian Canal in 1822, the Inverness and Nairn Railway in 1855 and in the 20th century the first aerodrome in Britain (1933), providing the first inland mail service in 1934. The spirit of optimism in its fishing and farming industries from 1820 onwards brought the feuing of land and the burgh's rapid expansion with wide new streets, harbour facilities, hotels and public services which helped shape much of the town we see today. Owing to the Cabinet meeting held in a Bridge Street Town House by Lloyd George in 1921, the town's position as capital of the Highlands was reaffirmed, and as such it oversees a large share of the area's education, agricultural, commercial and tourism projects. Concentrated around Bridge St and Church St are the town's most historical buildings, erected between the 16th and 19th centuries. These include; Abertarff House, built in 1593 as a Town House for Colonel Archibald Fraser, Bridge St Town House occupied by Mary I, 1562, the remaining clock tower of Cromwell's Fort (1657), Dunbar's Hospital and Weigh House, built 1668 (now a community centre), and the Court House, built 1792, repaired in 1828 and 1923. See Castle and St Andrew's Cathedral

INVERNESS CASTLE
HIGHLAND

Owing to the town's history, this must have been the site of an early defensive structure. The castle which stood in the town in the 11th century was probably the property of Shakespeare's Macbeth, who was Mormaer of Ross and Moray. The present structure was an important fortalice during the Wars of Independence when Robert the Bruce ordered its destruction, it was rebuilt in 1412 by the Earl of Mar to counter the threat from the unruly Lords of the Isles, who were summoned here in 1427 to a Parliament held by James I. About this time the Mackintoshes, its Hereditary Keepers, led by their chief, strengthened it. Occupied by James III (1464), and by James IV (1499), who made the Earls of Huntly its Constables, the castle was captured by Queen Mary's forces when the Governor, a retainer of the rebel Earl of Huntly, was hanged. Repaired and then destroyed during the Covenanting struggles, in 1718 it was occupied and enlarged by the Hanoverians, so much so that by the 1745 Rebellion it posed a formidable threat to the Jacobites, for whom Inverness was the Capital City, and was subsequently captured and destroyed. In 1834 the present castle was started, followed by an additional part in 1846 which was used as the Court House, a Prison and was later adapted for use as the the Council Buildings. The discovery of the old castle well in 1899 owing to subsidence was followed ten years later by the erection of a statue to Flora Macdonald which fronts the castle and was designed by Andrew Davidson, a local sculptor.

INVERQUHARITY CASTLE
ANGUS

It stands on a steep bank 4 miles NE of Kirriemuir. The land was held from 1420 by the Ogilvies, who built this 15th century L plan tower. The family distinguished themselves in local and national history when an Alexander Ogilvie was smothered at Finhaven Castle in 1446, his descendants received a Baronetcy in 1626, another Alexander Ogilvie was captured at the battle of Philliphaugh and executed in Glasgow, 1646: and a Captain Ogilvie followed James VII to the battle of the Boyne in 1690. The castle later became ruinous but is now restored.

INVERUGIE CASTLE
ABERDEENSHIRE

Situated 2 miles NW of Peterhead overlooking the River Ugie. Between 1165 and 1214 the lands were granted by William the Lyon to Bernard La Chayne, who built a tower which passed through marriage in 1350 to the Keith family, later becoming the principal seat of the Keith Earls Marischal. The present fragmentary ruins are from a tower of 1600, built by the 5th Earl Marischal, who founded Aberdeen's Marischal College in 1593.

INVERURIE
ABERDEENSHIRE

Town situated 17 miles NW of Aberdeen. Spelt Inverury until 1866, the name is derived from the Gaelic 'inbhir' meaning 'confluence of the river' and 'urie' which itself means 'abounding in Yew trees'. Dating from remote antiquity the area had a strong Pictish presence, traces of which include stone circles and sculpted stones along with the discovery of pottery, stone axes and flints. The Bass Hills in the vicinity of the River Urie, once the site of a Norman earthwork, was served by the Bailey on the nearby little Bass. On Conyng Hill to the south, the site where proclamations were read, is the legendary burial site of the Scottish King Aodh, or Ethus, who died in 881. Established by William I in 1195 as a Royal Burgh, Inverurie later became the property of the Earl of Gairoch, whose great grandson King Robert the Bruce, lay sick here on the eve of his victory over Comyn at Barra in 1307. With the nearby confluence of the Rivers Urie and Don, a concentrated trading point and the central feature of the local economy, the town's trade continued to inspire confidence, which was reaffirmed in a charter of Novodamus granted by Mary Queen of Scots in 1558. The scene of a victory for Lord Lewis Gordon and 1200 Jacobites over the Laird Macleod and 700 loyalists in 1745. With the return to stability the town's prosperity grew, and in 1807 it became a terminus for the Aberdeen Canal, through which it was able to trade its coal, lime, iron, timber and agricultural produce up until the canal's closure in 1852. Built in 1863, the Town Hall is a neat Italian edifice with clock tower, while the adjacent Andrew Carnegie Library, added in 1911, is now used as a museum. Transformed in 1902 by the coming of the Locomotive & Carriage Works (now gone) , by 1921 the burgh had expanded enough to include Port Elphinstone, prior to serving as a garrison town during World War II. See Battle

INVERURIE, BATTLE OF, 1308
ABERDEENSHIRE

Fought between the armies of Robert the Bruce and his arch rival John Comyn, Earl of Buchan and ally of Edward II. The routing of the latter's troops enabled Bruce to devastate the Earldom of Buchan with fire and sword and move against his other principal enemy in the west, the Lord of Lorne. The victory marked the beginning of Bruce's return to power after a period in the wilderness and was to culminate in his victory at Bannockburn.

IONA ABBEY
ARGYLL & BUTE

The Abbey stands on the islands east

coast near the village. The original timber monastery, founded in 563 by St Columba as a base during his conversion of local Picts to Christianity, was for 150 years the National Church of Scotland north of the Forth and Clyde and a beacon of stability on the margins of Western Europe, following the chaos left by the fall of the Roman Empire. Built near the site of the present monastery, it incorporated a monastery, church, small court, guest chamber, dormitory, dining hall and St Columba's cell. After the saint died here in 597, the monastery retained its influence, but owing to the frequent raids from Norsemen it was replaced by Dunkeld as the ecclesiastical centre. In 1203, after the ejection of the Norsemen, the Lord of the Isles carried out rebuilding work for the Benedictines which make up today's ruins. From a very early period Iona was the last resting place for monarchs from Scotland Ireland and Norway. It was Sir Walter Scott who gave a token reminder of this tradition of privilage that was also awarded to the chiefs of the island clans, in 'The Lord of the Isles':

For when on Coolin's hills the lights decay.
With such the Seer of Skye the eve beguiles;
Tis known amid the pathless wastes of Reay
In Harris known, and in Iona's piles,
Where rest from mortal coil the mighty of the
Isles.

Under the Bishop of Dunkeld in the 15th century and the Bishop of the Isles, 1506, it served as the Cathedral of the Isles until 1560, but in the 17th century was granted by Charles I to the Argyll family. Dating mainly from the 13th and 15th centuries, its Romanesque church (Cathedral) houses its nave, transepts, choir and sacristy on the north side and chapels on its south side, with St Columba's shrine near the entrance. This adjoins the cloister garden which from east to west includes the 13/15th century Chapter House with the library and dormitory above. In addition there is the recently restored Abbots House outside the courtyard, the 13th-century dining hall on its north side, and the west range with the early Christian Chapel (restored). Fronting the church is a well and nearby this are the 12th-century crosses of St Matthew, St John and St Martin.

IRVINE
EAST AYRSHIRE

Seaport town situated 7 miles W of Kilmarnock on the River Irvine. Formerly written 'urwyn' the exact derivation is unclear but is probably Gaelic for 'Green River'. One of Scotland's oldest Royal Burghs, it had received its charter from Alexander II by 1249, which was confirmed and enlarged by Robert Bruce in 1308 in gratitude for the town's support during the Wars of Succession. A Carmelite Friary founded here around 1293 by Fullarton of Fullarton was visited by Edward III in 1335 and was dependent on Kilwinning Abbey until the Reformation, while the ruined Seagate Castle, built in the 14th century, was the seat of the town's overlords, the Earls of Eglinton. Re-erected a Royal Burgh by Robert II in 1372 it was created a Parliamentary Burgh, 1429. Like much of Scotland the town suffered from the plague in 1546, witnessed the witchcraft trials in 1640 and was affected by the Covenanting struggles in 1650. Handling imports for Glasgow until the building of Port Glasgow in 1670, Irvine ranked as the third busiest port in Scotland in 1760, with a contraband trade chiefly confined to whisky from Arran by 1845, an export trade in carpeting, tanned leather and coal: while importing timber from America and butter from Ireland. In 1781 Robert Burns worked as a flax dresser here, and it was here, after the destruction of his lodgings during New Year celebrations, he described himself as being "left like a true poet not worth a sixpence". Today Irvine boasts one of the original Burns Clubs. Another of the town's literary figures was the novelist John Galt (1779-1839), who received much of his inspiration from life on Scotland's south west coast that is best exemplified in his 'Annals of the Parish' (pub. 1821). For centuries this was the main trading link between Scotland and Ireland and though at one time rivalling Ayr, its port was undermined by the development of the Clyde, and by 1882 ranked as a Sub Port of Troon. Gradually its traditional weaving industry was replaced by the Mackie & Thomson shipyard by 1911, the Royal Ordnance factory prior to 1939, and more recently by the service industries.

ISLE OF JURA DISTILLERY
ARGYLL & BUTE

Jura's only distillery stands in the SE of the island at Craighouse above the harbour and takes its water from Loch 'A Bhaile Mhargaidh' meaning 'market loch'. The rich tradition of distilling on Jura dating back to 1502 was augmented by the building of a distillery in 1810 which flourished in later years and was rebuilt as the most efficient in Scotland by its new owners Messrs James Ferguson & Son in 1876. Partly owing to the recession in the industry but primarily due to a dispute with the landlord over rent, from 1900 its doors remained closed for fifty years. During this time the island was used as a retreat by George Orwell, who was no doubt moved by its tranquillity when he wrote part of '1984' here in the 1940s. In contrast with its stillness is Jura's bounty of wildlife which includes over 100 species of bird, among which are the Golden Eagle and on a more down-to-earth footing 6,000 red deer. The name Jura is thought to mean island of Red deer. Rebuilt in the late 1950s to designs by Delm Evans, since 1963 Jura's long-neck stills have produced a light, clean spirit that has been an important part of the Mackinlay blend and was later acquired by Invergordon Distillers Plc, which was taken over by Whyte & Mackay in 1994.

OWNERS
Kyndal International Ltd ?

REGION
Highland

PRODUCT
Isle of Jura 10 year old single malt 40% vol

NOTES
A dry, slightly sherry nose with a hint of butter and malt on the palate; sweetish with a hint of Island dryness and saltiness.

J

JACOBITE REBELLION, 1708

On the death of James VII, 1701, an attempt was made in England to proclaim his son James Francis Edward as King by those desirous of the return of the old faith, notwithstanding the Act of Settlement, 1701, when the male line of the Stuarts was excluded from succession. In response to this, at the behest of the French King, lieutenant Nathianiel Hooke undertook a reconnaissance mission in 1705 and reported favourable circumstances for a Jacobite rising, moving King Louis to order the fitting out of an expedition at Dunkirk, including five men of war, two transports, and twenty frigates with 4,000 troops. But the arrival of the Prince at Dunkirk alerted English agents, whose masters mobilised a larger English fleet in the Channel on the day of their departure. From there on the endeavour went from bad to worse as the main part of the fleet was dispersed and the Prince's ship, after reaching the Scottish coast, was unable to land owing to bad weather and the advance of the English ships, forcing it to return to Dunkirk.

JACOBITE REBELLION, 1715-16

Following the death of Queen Anne in 1714, the exiled James Francis Edward Stewart the Chevalier St George, also known as the Old Pretender, asserted the claim of the Stewart Kings from the Court of St Germain in a bid to prevent the passing of the Crown to the Hanovarian dynasty. Meanwhile in Scotland the Earl of Mar raised his standard at Breamar, 1715, proclaiming James King before marching southwards and reaching Dunkeld with around 2,000 men. Shortly after, the Prince received the erroneous news of the Earl of Mar's victory over the Earl of Argyll at Sheriffmuir, 1715, while the failed attempt of the Duke of Ormonde extin-

guished any hope of raising the English Jacobites. Hampered in his progress by the death of King Louis XIV of France, and without material aid, Prince James travelled incognito to Dunkirk. Setting sail in a small privateer with some attendants, he landed at Peterhead and with George Keith the Earl Marischal proceeded to Fetteresso where they met the Earl of Mar. Before long the Prince had established his court at Scone and though assured of the support of their local chiefs, he failed to inspire the common soldier. More alarmingly Jame's chief adjutant the Earl of Mar, with his grave reservations about the success of the enterprise, secretly sought to extricate himself and the Prince. The opportunity arose when news reached the Jacobites of the Duke of Argyll's approach with a superior force. The army then retreated to Montrose, where after being informed of Argyll's two day's march to their rear the Prince was persuaded of the futility in continuing the campaign, bade farewell to his supporters and boarded a ship with the Earl of Mar for France. Finding his situation untenable after his return he eventually removed himself to Rome, where in 1719 he married Clementina Sobieski who bore him two sons, Prince Henry Benedict and Prince Charles Edward Stewart.

JACOBITE REBELLION, 1719

While the Jacobite court at St Germain was rife with intrigues the Earl of Mar, chief minister to Prince James Francis Edward, hatched a plot in 1718 to solicit the support of Charles XII of Sweden, from whom George I of England had seized the Duchy of Bremen and Verden. After failing to be realised due to King Charles untimely death, the Prince left secretly for Madrid in response to an offer of support from Cardinal Aberloni, who, with the backing of the Spanish King, was preparing an expedition at Cadiz. At the head of the main expedition, which consisted of 5,000 men, and arms and substantial amounts of ammunition, was the Duke of Ormonde, while the second expedition comprised only two frigates, a battalion of men and 3,000 stands of arms under the Earl Marischal, who was to head for Scotland and raise the clans. Though the Duke of Ormonde's force was driven back by a storm, the smaller force reached Stornoway in Lewis. Judiciously the Chevalier Prince remained behind in Madrid, for no sooner had the rebellion begun than it ended, when the Jacobites were defeated at Glenshiel. It was at this point that the Prince married Clementina Sobieski, niece of the King of Poland and later mother to Prince Charles Edward Stewart. Another attempt was planned in 1722 but failed owing to lack of material support and divisions among English Jacobites.

JACOBITE REBELLION, 1745

In 1745, over a generation after the attempt by James VII to restore the Stewarts to the throne, his son Prince Charles Edward, also known as the Young Pretender, sailed on 13th July from Belleisle in France in the Doutelle with limited funds from pawning his jewels and 180,000 borrowed livres. The consort ship, 'The Elizabeth', which carried the ammunition, was severely damaged after an encounter with the Lion, an English man of war, forcing the former to make for Brest and enabling the Doutelle to head for the Outer Hebrides, off Scotland's NW coast. On 2 August the Prince landed on Erisky, the possession of Macdonald of Clanranald. While meeting with some scepticism, Charles won the support of most of the local clans, whose enthusiasm spread through the Highlands, challenging more chiefs to rally to the cause, and on the 19 August the royal standard was raised at Glenfinnan to the jubilation of the clansmen. Amongst

these were Cameron of Lochiel, Macdonald of Glengarry, Clanranald, the Keppoch Macdonalds, Stewarts of Ardshiel, Macleans of Duart and the Macgregors. Meanwhile to the south the Government Committee of Six put a bounty of 30,000 L on the Prince's head and ordered John Cope to secure the forts and garrisons in the Highlands. After out manoeuvring Cope's forces, the Prince entered Perth on 25 August amidst much rejoicing. It was here that Lord George Murray joined the Prince who made him Lieutenant General, but who also shared command with the Duke of Perth. After staying a week to discipline his men, the army advanced towards the Capital, which was taken without bloodshed after the expiration of an ultimatum, when the Netherbow Port was seized during the exit of a coach. Though failing to take the castle, before long to the W Prince Charles Edward was holding court at Holyrood to the delight of the Highland Chiefs and many of the ladies whose hearts and minds he had won, along with many of the burghers. Alarmed at the Jacobite victory over General Cope at Prestonpans (21 September) and their march south, the London Government recalled troops from the Continent including a 6,000 man Dutch force, so by late October 14,000 men under General Wade had assembled at Newcastle. On 18 November, the Jacobites, numbering around 5,400, took Carlisle. Confident of reaching London quickly after giving Wade the slip at Carlisle, so swift was their march south that they gradually lost control of their positions in the north, so that by their arrival at Derby they were cut off, ridden with low morale, hunger and disappointment at the lack of support from a hostile populace. To add to their problems the Duke of Cumberland was marching north with around 8,000 men. Unaware of the panic in London with a run on the banks, the Jacobites retreated on Black Friday, 6th

December. Re-entering Scotland on 20th December, the army experienced a few minor encounters during their speedy retreat north, during which time the acrimony that had begun at Derby between the Prince and his adjutant Lord George Murray increased. In spite of this, with additional French troops the army defeated Wade's successor at Falkirk and continued their retreat north with the Duke of Cumberland's force to the south slowly closing the gap. With desertion rife and morale low on April 15 the Jacobites attempted a night attack at Nairn on Cumberland's birthday, but fell back on Culloden where they were finally defeated by the Hanovarians on the 16th April 1746. The Prince then spent five months hunted as a fugitive in the Highlands and Islands until he boarded a ship for France at Loch nan Uamh. In 1748, in accordance with the Treaty of Aix-la-Chapelle, he was forced to leave France for Rome where he died a drunkard, a habit he had acquired during his time as a fugitive.

JEDBURGH
SCOTTISH BORDERS

Town situated on the Jed Water 46 miles SE of Edinburgh. Called Jedworth in 1251 meaning 'town on the Jed'. The name may derive from the Old Norse 'gedda' meaning 'pike', (the Jed Staff was once used to stir up fish), while Worth is from the Old English meaning 'hamlet' or 'village'. Its position by the river suggests it was the site of a settlement from an early period and by the 9th century was the site of a church built by the Bishop of Lindisfarne, which moved the pious David I to found a priory in 1138 which became an abbey in 1147. Although better known for its Abbey, it was once the site of a 12th century castle that was popular with Scottish Kings, including David I, Malcolm IV, William I, Alexander II, and Alexander III, before being ceded to the English under the Treaty of Falaise, 1174. As a Royal Burgh of David I (1124-53), along with its Abbey it was attacked by the English periodically who, after occupying its castle for 63 years, were ejected in 1409 when it was destroyed by the men of Teviotdale. The town was occupied by the Earl of Surrey in 1513 and the Duke of Somerset in 1547. In a bid to remove unruly local chiefs, Queen Mary held a Justice Court here in 1566 and during the minority of her son James VI the town held out against the forces of the Regent Lennox, 1571. As a Sheriffdom and Market Town, between 1603 and 1707 Jedburgh benefited from the trade in contraband arising from the unequal taxes levied in England and Scotland before adjusting to the changes brought about by the union with England in 1707, when farming and tweed mills (later under the Laidlaw and Stewart families) bolstered its economy. Known as the Raid of Reidswire, in 1575 a dispute between the Scottish and English Wardens of the Middle Marches over the liberty of a Henry Robson led to a battle in which the townsmen were saved by men from Tyndale with the Jeddart Axes and Staffs, a 7ft-8ft pole with iron head figuring prominently. In the 18th century the town was occupied by the Jacobites twice, was visited by Robert Burns in 1783 and by Walter Scott who served as an Advocate here in 1793. Jedburgh 'hand ba', an old custom celebrated on 'Fastern's Een' or Shrove Tuesday in February following the first new moon after Candlemas, involves a ball being thrown by the 'uppies' and the 'doonies' teams towards an appointed goal. The groups are so named because they consist of those who were born in the appropriate parts of the town. Apart from its Abbey the Castle Jail Museum and Queen Mary's House take pride of place amongst its architectural gems and helped win the town the Europa Nostra Medal for the Protection of

Cultural and natural heritage in the 1970s. See Abbey

JEDBURGH ABBEY
SCOTTISH BORDERS

In an attractive setting by the Jed River near the town are the ruins of an Augustinian House founded in 1138 by David I as a priory which was raised to an abbey by 1147. One of the many Border abbeys that helped develop the rural economy while bringing stability, most of the remains are of 12/13th century work. Richly endowed by David I, Malcolm IV and William I, in 1285 the ill-fated Alexander III married Joland (daughter of the Count of Dreux) here. During the Wars of Independence it was rendered uninhabitable but after some repairs its monks enjoyed a period of prosperity exporting wool to England, with a hospital being granted by Robert III (1390-1406). But it suffered the fate of most Border abbeys as it bore the brunt of many invasions when it was damaged by repeated attacks in the 15th century. After returning to a semblance of normality, it was pillaged and burnt by the Earl of Surrey, 1513, followed by Sir Ralph Evers in 1544 and the Earl of Hertford in 1545. Consequently there was little for the Reformers to destroy in 1560 when its revenues went to the Crown and it became a Temporal Lordship for Alexander Grey Lord Home in 1606. It was at this time that the nave of its church was still used for worship. The continued use of its ruins as a shelter in future border conflicts is apparent by its present state. Now a Parish Church built in 1875, the Abbey was repaired by the Marquis of Lothian so while the visitor centre skilfully recreates its past, much can be gleaned from the ruins. The roofless cruciform church which retains its doorway, nave, central tower, choir and both transepts was built in a Norman Gothic style, while its three levels of lanced arch windows are kept subordinate to the rose window and central tower to the east. Among its conventual buildings surrounding the cloister garden were the store to the west side, a dining hall and infirmary to the south side, but its Chapter House with dormitory above to the east are the chief remains.

JERVISTON TOWER
SOUTH LANARKSHIRE

Overlooking the Clyde Valley 1 mile S of Motherwell is the one time seat of the Baillie family, who occupied the site from an early period. The present L plan tower house dates from the late 16th century.

JERVISWOOD TOWER
SOUTH LANARKSHIRE

Located 1 mile from Lanark. Once the exclusive site of the Livingstone's quadrangle tower until around 1650, when it was acquired by George Baillie, ancestor of the Earl of Haddington. The present house with its traditional crow-stepped gables was erected by the Baillies shortly after.

K

KAMES CASTLE
ARGYLL & BUTE

At the base of a hill near Bute bay is a 16th century keep. The seat of the Bannatynes, who held the land from the 13th century and who were Chamberlains to the Stewart Kings when Bute was Crown property. The present house was built around 1800 by Sir William Macleod Bannatyne, who became Lord Bannatyne in 1799. The castle was the birthplace and home of the critic and essayist John Stirling (1806-1844). Once described by Thomas Carlyle as a dilapidated baronial residence, it is now fully restored.

KEISS CASTLE
HIGHLAND

It occupies ground near Sinclair Bay 9 miles N of Wick. The ruins of this 16th-century Z plan castle were once a stronghold of the Sinclairs, who were cadets of the Earls of Caithness. Alas its geographical position put enough distance between it and the country's historical upheavals to deprive it of any notable incidents.

KEITH
MORAY

Town situated 18 miles SE of Elgin. Consisting of Old Keith and New Keith on the right bank of the Isla and Fife Keith on the left, its name derived from the Gaelic 'coed' meaning 'wood'. In 1177 William I granted the land to Kinloss Abbey which oversaw the old town's creation as the principal seat of jurisdiction for the area with its capital punishment administered from the Regality Courts on the hill where New Keith now stands. As a prisoner on route to Edinburgh and his eventual execution, in 1650 the Marquis of Montrose was forced to listen to a sermon here by William Kininmouth, chaplain to his arch enemy General David Leslie. In the 1750s the New Town was built by the Earl of Findlater to the SE with a large Market Square surrounded by a spacious symmetrical street plan with proportionately sized houses and links to Old Keith by road. On the north bank of the Isla stands Fife Keith, built by the Earl of Fife in 1816 and linked to Keith by two bridges built in 1609 and 1790, while below the newer bridge witches were once drowned in a pool called Gauns Pot. The Catholic Church of St Thomas, erected between 1816 and 1831 and modelled on the Sta Maria della Vittoria Church in Rome has an altar piece that was presented by King Charles X of France along with a statue of St John Ogilvie who was born in Milton Tower, the town's oldest building. Although a producer of flour, wool and corn, the distilling of whisky which was once the chief product here totalled 20,000 gallons annually by 1856 but was replaced by the woollen trade by 1956.

KEITHHALL
ABERDEENSHIRE

About 1 mile E of Inverurie stands a ruined 16th century Z plan castle. Originally called Caskieben, the estate was held by the Johnstones, who started the present structure. Purchased by Sir John Keith in 1662, who was created Earl of Kintore and Baron Keith of Inverurie and Keithhall in 1677. The additions of 1700 included a front and east wing which greatly transformed the structure.

KEITH HOUSE
EAST LOTHIAN

Occupying a site between Pencaitland and Blackshiels, it was built by the Keiths, Earls Marischal, among whom was George, the 5th Earl who journeyed to Denmark to escort Princess Ann to Scotland to marry James VI. For this the Danish King granted him the original timber roof of 1589. In the 17th and 19th centuries the house was repaired in a Gothic style at the expense of the original features.

KELBURN CASTLE
NORTH AYRSHIRE

At the base of Largs Hill S of Largs town stands a 16th century Z plan tower house, in grounds once noted for their orchard and gardens. It was built in 1581 by John Boyle whose ancestors had held the land from the 13th century. The adjacent house, added around 1722 by the Ist Earl of Glasgow, contrasts well with the older building and is a good example of a Scottish mansion house of the period.

KELLY CASTLE
ANGUS

Built on the bank of the River Elliot, 2 miles SW of Arbroath. Held between 1444 and 1630 by the Auchterlonies who built the 15th century keep. In 1679 it came to the Earl of Panmure, an ancestor of the Earls of Dalhousie. After suffering the vicissitudes of Scottish history it was uninhabited in the 19th century when a new house was built nearby, but the original castle has since been restored.

KELSO
SCOTTISH BORDERS

Town situated on the River Tweed, 42 miles SW of Edinburgh. Originally called Calkou meaning 'chalk height', it developed out of the village that surrounded its Abbey which was founded by David I in 1128. Often figuring in the affairs of state Kelso was a burgh by 1237 with its closeness to the Scottish Border making it a strategic point for offensive and defensive positions. In 1255 Kelso was visited by Henry III of England, and in 1296 by his successor Edward I, who with a vast army crossed the Tweed here en route to North Berwick and his victory over the Scots at Dunbar. In 1380 and 1391 the embassies of both countries arrived here to sign a truce in its Abbey which was at the centre of the town's affairs up until the 16th century. Kelso was occupied by the forces of Lord Hume after the battle of Flodden in 1513 and suffered greatly during the Rough Wooing of Queen Mary by Henry VIII, when it was plundered in 1544, and again in 1545 by the Earl of Hertford who destroyed its Abbey (ruin). The lawlessness of the surrounding countryside, no doubt encouraged by the chaos, led to Queen Mary I holding a council meeting here in order to pacify the area. In the 17th century it was erected into a Burgh of Barony for Lord Roxburgh, 1614, repulsed the armed attempt by Charles I to force Episcopacy on Scotland, 1639, and was the headquarters of General Leslie's army, 1644, in the continuing struggle. As a staging post for large armies, Kelso was also exposed to different diseases, and in 1645 was ravaged by the plague. Although a rendezvous point for the Jacobites in 1715, its occupation by Prince Charles Edward's forces in 1745 marked the end of its strategic importance, and the burghers then settled into a period of stability amidst its rural calm. One of the earliest Scottish newspapers, 'The Mail ', was printed here in 1797 by James Ballantyne, who in 1802 commissioned the first two volumes of Sir Walter Scott's 'Border Minstrelsy', Scott being a figure who had strong associations with the town. Apart from its agriculture, which had been well developed by the monks,

Kelso also had a small trade in tobacco, leather and linen that prospered with the through trade from coaches travelling between Edinburgh and London, which in turn gave rise to its many Georgian and Victorian buildings, including the oldest from 1750, and its Town Hall from 1816. See Abbey & Golf Club

KELSO ABBEY
SCOTTISH BORDERS

Overlooking the town are the remains of a 12th century Tironesian Abbey that are as much a testament to war as they are to peace. After a move from Selkirk it was refounded in 1128 by David I for Benedictine monks from Tiron Picardy and dedicated to St Mary and St John, becoming one of the largest abbeys in Scotland through royal grants and the monks building skills and enterprise. At its peak it controlled the tithes (10% of annual land or labour production) of thirty-three Parish Churches, all forfeitures within Berwickshire, several manors, and a vast number of farms, granges, mills and fishing rights. Owing to its prize status most of the structure was destroyed during centuries of strife, leaving the west end of its cruciform church the chief ruin. The Abbey and its graveyard, where in 1150 Henry, the son of David I, was buried has a number of interestingly inscribed tombstones. Mitred in 1165, its abbots played a prominent role in statecraft and consequently played host to royal personages, for in 1255 it was the scene of a banquet given when Henry III and his Queen visited their son-in-law Alexander III and their daughter Margaret. Its reputation for hospitality also made it a popular refuge for those who sought food and shelter but its Abbot's conciliatory response to Edward I lost it the royal favour of King Robert the Bruce. In 1460 Prince James was brought here on the death of his father at Roxburgh. Its

decline in the 16th century was marked by its seizure by Lord Hume in 1513 and its demolition by the English in 1523, forcing its monks to beg for food and shelter. Plundered and damaged during the Rough Wooing of 1544 and by Hertford in 1545, this culminated in its spoilation by the religious zealots during the decline of Popery when its monks were expelled and its property divided amongst court favourites. It became a Temporal Lordship for Robert Ker in 1607. The ruined church was used by the community in the 17th century and as a prison in the 18th century, but by the 19th century the Duke of Roxburgh had preserved its 12th century remains. These are in a Norman Gothic style and include the church's west front with Galilee Porch, central tower, with north and south transepts and two bays of the nave. Its domestic buildings, of which the parlour survives, conformed to the traditional central cloister garden plan.

KELSO GOLF CLUB
SCOTTISH BORDERS

The history of golf in Kelso had an ignominious start when in 1632 Thomas Chatto received a fatal strike from a ball while spectating in the kirkyard. All records ceased for almost two hundred years until 1887, when at the request of J D Crichton Smith, Provost of Kelso, the Duke of Roxburgh consented to its playing on Friars Park. After a meeting in the ante room of the Corn Exchange, an excellent course of eleven holes was laid out for the use of the 15 members who first played here on Saturday 8th October. Mentioned in the Golfing Annual of 1887-88 as being surrounded by history and immersed in scenic beauty, the first competition was held on Friars Haugh, while the first golf match took place between Kelso and Hawick. The clubs' longstanding ties owe much to Kelso's founder who joined the latter prior to 1887. Under the guidance of Ben Sayers, a native of Leith, and player in every Open Championship from 1880-1923, a new private club course was laid out in 1913 at Berrymoss by the racecourse, to a standard that reflected Sayers' skill and experience, which he also imparted to royalty and noblemen keen to improve their playing technique. After World War One the club had a marked effect on the town as people adjusted to normality and in 1926 the course was visited by the Prince of Wales and the Duke of Roxburgh en route from Floors Castle. On realising the need for course alterations owing to the expansion of the Kelso Race Course, James Braid was called in and playing commenced in June 1930. The numerous competitions with their neighbours Jedburgh in the 1930s produced some club crackshots like Jack Scott and Hugh Murray, whose standards were upheld during the 1950s when an increasing number of young people joined the club. And in 1958 Kelso was host to a golf exhibition attended by 500 people including the Duke of Roxburgh and some star players. The club's development continued apace and in 1972 Her Grace the Duchess of Roxburgh became a member. In 1975, after much wrangling, the committee resolved to extend the course to 18 holes but it wasn't until the 1980s that the new course was completed with a new clubhouse, so in 1987 Kelso marked its centenary with a confidence that reflects the quality of its course and its motto 'far and sure'.

KENMURE CASTLE
DUMFRIES & GALLOWAY

At the head of Loch Ken is a 16th century L plan structure with 17th century additions. The age-old stronghold of the Lords of Galloway, it was held by the Gordons of Lochinver from 1297. Once a favourite residence of John Balliol in the 13th century, it was burnt in 1568 after Queen Mary's defeat at Langside and by Cromwell in 1650. Although Sir John Gordon was created Viscount Kenmure in 1633, by 1837 the peerage was extinct. The castle now stands as a ruin.

KENNEDY CASTLE
DUMFRIES & GALLOWAY

Between Loch White and Loch Black to the W of Stranraer is a site that was occupied by a castle at various periods. The building was started in 1607 by John Kennedy, 5th Earl of Cassillis, to replace an older keep once held by John Kennedy (Keeper,1482), and passed in 1677 to Sir John Dalrymple, later Earl of Stair. Sited on what was once an island in Lochinch, it included a main block with square central towers at each end but was left a ruin after being destroyed by fire in 1716, and a new castle was built in the 19th century.

KILBARCHAN
EAST RENFREWSHIRE

Town situated 5´ miles SW of Paisley. The name is thought to derive from the Gaelic 'cill' meaning 'church' or 'cell' while 'Barchan' is probably derived from the holy man who either built the church or to whom the church was dedicated, which gave the place its early religious significance. Barnhill, to the east of the town, was either the site of a Danish Fort or an ancient observation post. Although its importance grew under the monks of Paisley Abbey, who were granted the land in the 12th century by Walter Fitzalan, Steward of Scotland, it was the nearby Ranforlie Castle which gave the town its place in the country's religious chronicles. Standing on land once called Preiston, it was the seat of the Knox family from whom John Knox the Reformer is descended. Elevated to a Burgh of Barony for Cunningham of Craigends in 1704, through the market in Paisley the town thrived from 1740 on the weaving of silk and cotton for the merchants of Glasgow. An example of this cottage industry is best preserved in the weaver's cottage which houses William Meikle's loom on which he wove tartan for the Royal Family in the 1930s.

KILBIRNIE
NORTH AYRSHIRE

Town situated 11 miles SW of Paisley. Name derived from the Gaelic 'cill' meaning 'church' and from Birnie or Birnus or even Brendan after the titular saint of the Parish, who founded a church here that was later subordinate to Kilwinning Abbey. The lands once belonged to the Barclays of Ardrossan, but in 1470 passed through marriage to Malcolm Crawford of Greenock, for whose descendant Crawford of Kilbirnie, it became a Burgh of Barony in 1642 before passing to the Lindsays in 1661. By the late 18th century it had a small but thriving trade in flax, iron, linen, thread and limestone which later gave way to its staple industry, net and rope making. Between 1843 and 1930 there was a prosperous iron and steel industry here. Its Parish Church, dating in part from the 15th century, but restored in 1855, has a pre-Reformation nave, and rich Renaissance wood carvings with heraldic symbols. See Tower

KILBIRNIE TOWER
NORTH AYRSHIRE

About 20 miles SW of Glasgow near Glengarnock hills, is the Barclays' ruined 14th century tower with 17th century additions. The barony was held by the family until 1470 when it passed through marriage to Malcolm Crawford of Louden, who was progenitor of the Crawfurds of Kilbirnie. John Crawfurd of Kilbirnie built a two storied addition in 1627 but after passing to the Lindsays in 1661 it suffered a fire in 1757.

KILCHURN CASTLE
ARGYLL & BUTE

Positioned at the N end of Loch Awe 2´ miles SW of Dalmally. Once the site of a Macgregor stronghold it later passed to Sir Duncan Campbell of Loch Awe, whose nephew Colin Campbell of Glenorchy built the original keep around 1440. As founder of the Breadalbane family and a Knight of Rhodes he distinguished himself in the Eastern Wars before dying in 1498. Additions were made in 1615 and it was besieged by the Covenanters in 1650. The work done by the Ist Earl of Breadalbane (of Glencoe notoriety) in 1693 transformed it into a courtyard castle designed to accommodate a large garrison, while its round towers would suffice to defend it from sudden attack from Highlanders. It was inhabited by the Breadalbane family until 1740 and garrisoned by the Hanoverians until 1749. Although it became derelict it is still one of the grandest baronial ruins of the Western Highlands.

KILCOY CASTLE
HIGHLAND

Erected 8 miles NW of Inverness. In 1618 Alexander Mackenzie, the 4th son of the 11th Baron of Kintail, acquired the land and built this Z plan castle shortly after. Alterations were made in 1679 and in the 18th century it was the birthplace of Lieutenant General Alexander Mackenzie. A ruin by the 19th century, it has recently been restored.

KILDRUMMY CASTLE
ABERDEENSHIRE

Located 39 miles W of Aberdeen. A 13th-century Baronial courtyard castle, it was built by Gilbert de Moravia, Bishop of Caithness, to guard against the southern approaches. But in 1306 it was captured by the Prince of Canarvon (Prince of Wales), later Edward II of England, resulting in the imprisonment of King Robert I's Queen and the murder of his brother Nigel. It later passed to the Lords Erskine, Earls of Mar, who entertained David II here in 1361. In the 15th century it was bestowed by James III on his favourite, Robert Cochrane, who was hanged over Lauder Bridge by jealous nobles. Damaged by Cromwell's forces and burnt by John Graham of Claverhouse in the 17th century. It was here that John, 11th Earl of Mar, hatched the Jacobite Rebellion of 1715 after which the property was forfeited before being acquired by the Gordons of Wardhouse in 1731, but is now a ruin.

KILKERRAN TOWER
SOUTH AYRSHIRE

About 1 mile from Dalry on the Girvan Water stands the ruins of a 15th century keep which was built by the Fergusons, who held the land from the 14th century.

KILLIECRANKIE, BATTLE OF, 1689
PERTH & KINROSS

NE of Pitlochry. The combination of natural features and unbridled valour secured for Viscount Dundee with his troop of cavalry and 2,500 foot a victory over King William's forces numbering 3,000 foot and 1,000 horse led by General Hugh Mackay. On reaching the pass Mackay was surprised by the Highlanders positioned above, and despite trying to establish a more elevated position his forces were broken by the first Highland Charge. The ferocity of the charge resonated through Scotland's military history, and in the 19th century William Aytoun extolled it in 'The Lays

of the Scottish Cavaliers':

Like a tempest down the ridges
Swept the hurricane of steel
Rose the slogan of Macdonald
Flashed the broadsword of Lochiel !
Vainly sped the withering volly
Mongst most of our band
On we poured until we met them
Foot to foot and hand to hand

Their victory was tempered by the death of Dundee, which marked the beginning of the end of King James' cause.

KILLIN
STIRLING

Village situated at the southern base of Loch Tay, 23 miles SW of Aberfeldy. Its name is partly derived from the Gaelic 'cill' meaning 'church' but the second half is more obscure. Probably the site of a church from an early period, the picturesque setting which undoubtedly drew early settlers still attracts visitors today. Although created a Burgh of Barony for Campbell of Breadalbane in 1694, the place had strong links with the Macnab clan, who were persecuted by the Campbell lairds before their eviction in the 19th century. Their burial ground can still be seen below the Falls of Dochart. See Finlarig Castle

KILLOCHAN CASTLE
SOUTH AYRSHIRE

This substantial structure is sited 3 miles NE of Girvan. From the 14th century the Cathcarts possessed lands here. The present L plan mansion house was built in 1586 by Ihone Cathcart of Carltoun, whose descendants occupied it until the 20th century.

KILMAHEW CASTLE
WEST DUMBARTONSHIRE

About 1 mile E of Cardross stands a former seat of the Napiers who held the land from the late 13th to the early 19th century. A distinguished family in the history of Scotland, the Napiers of Kilmahew were related to the Napiers of Merchiston (of mathematical fame) in Edinburgh. Essentially a 16th century tower house, it was developed between 1540 and 1700 into the shape of a parallelogram 40ft by 25ft. The Kilmahew branch of the family married into the noblest families in the kingdom, for in the early 17th century Sussana, daughter of the 5th Earl of Glencairn married John Napier of Kilmahew, and by 1695 Margaret Napier of Kilmahew married John 10th Earl of Glencairn. In the 19th century the land was bought by James Burns Esq who built a Gothic style mansion nearby.

KILMAICHLIE CASTLE
MORAY

About 3´ miles above Ballindalloch on the bank of the Avon stands a 16th century oblong tower. Built by the Stewarts, whose ancestor Alexander, 4th son of Robert II, originally owned and first developed the estate in the 14th century. Considerable additions were made in the 18th century and it was the property of George Matheson in the 19th century.

KILMARNOCK
EAST AYRSHIRE

Town situated 13 miles NE of Ayr. The first part of the name is from the Gaelic 'cill' for 'church' while the second half, once thought to have derived from St Marnoc, is probably from Eman, or Maemanoc, a holy man who built a church here, giving rise to the name Kilmaernanog, which was corrupted into Kilmarnock. The lands were held by the Boyd family from the 14th century and were made into a Burgh of Barony for Thomas, 5th Lord Boyd, in 1591, owing to the wealth procured from its coalmines. A centre for bonnet weaving at the beginning of the 17th century, when Timothy Pont, an early traveller and writer described it as being 'a large village and of great repair with a weekly market and fairstone bridge over the River Marnock'. The town figured in the Covenanting Wars when it was the headquarters for General Dalziel and was later burnt. In 1661 it was erected into an Earldom for William, Lord Boyd, whose family's failed attempt to have it elevated to a Royal Burgh resulted in the burgh privileges being passed to the townsfolk, which no doubt determined their loyalty to the Government during the Jacobite Rebellions of 1715 and 1745. Strongly connected with Robert Burns, who published the Kilmarnock Edition here in 1786, while many of his early patrons lived in and around the area. In the local Kay Park, granted by Alexander Kay and opened in 1879, stands the Burns Memorial Statue. During that period, the town was a thriving commercial centre thanks to the dexterity of its weavers and cobblers, which, along with the fire of 1800, the Improvement Act of 1802, and the abolition of feudal superiority in 1832, laid the foundations for the Kilmarnock of today. With names like Glenfield and Kennedy Ltd (engineers), Blackwood & Morton (carpet makers), Smith Brothers (printers), Clarks (shoe co) and Johnnie Walker (whisky blenders), the town's commercial status climbed and the population swelled. From 6,000 in 1800 it had increased to 45,000 in 1950, when it ranked as the regional centre for North Ayrshire. The Dick Institute donated by James Dick (inventor) and opened in 1901, houses a library and museum with antiquities and a natural history section. See Golf Club

KILMARNOCK BARASSIE GOLF CLUB
NORTH AYRSHIRE

The reason for the club's founding was in part due to the travelling time required by local men desirous of a game on the Prestwick and Troon courses. So with its beginning in the town's George Hotel on 25th November 1887 after a meeting of the town's distinguished worthies came the positive influence of golf on the young who were precluded from playing in the neighbouring towns due to the travelling costs. At the end of the year land had been leased from Mr Morton of Holmes Farm for a nine hole course and on 12th January 1888 'The Ossington Golf Club' was constituted. The name came from the Ossington Coffee Tavern, a popular meeting place for local merchants, and from where they conducted their business. Opening for play on 10th March 1888, for accommodation the members used a tool shed. The prodigious nature of the ground with almost overnight re-growth led to playing being confined to winter months, leaving cattle to deal with the growth during the rest of the year. The gift from Alexander Walker, the club's president, of a medal, led to the first medal competition held on 23rd March 1889. Not to be outdone, in 1893 the ladies were given playing rights exclusively on Saturday, but owing to ongoing conflict with local tenant farmers, golfing activities were transferred to the lands around Hillhouse and Barassie Mill, part of the Hillhouse Estate that had been recently acquired by the Duke of Portland. Though the old hut had been transferred from Holmes Farm, the main social gathering point was Mrs Howie's Farm until the building of the novel bungalow-style clubhouse in 1903, which provided commodious facilities in subsequent decades. The event was marked by a match be-

tween the celebrated golfing figures Harry Vardon and James Braid, who were both at the height of their careers. After failing to purchase land for a nine hole ladies' course between the Glasgow Ayr Railway line in 1904, and with membership numbers rising, the course was altered and extended, which, with the clubs growing prestige, made it the venue for 'The Evening Times' Trophy Competition in 1905, the first event of any significance. After the 1914-18 war during which time the course was enjoyed by the officers and cadets at Army camps at Gailes and Troon, the overall membership reached 400 (1919). Significantly, the name was changed to Kilmarnock Barassie in 1926 and within ten years the course was further improved by Mr Mathew Monie. Like many courses in Scotland, during World War II between 1939-45 it provided recreation for troops and grazing for sheep, thus making a contribution to the home front. Though the venue for the men and boys' championships, after the war the club saw a steep upturn in its popularity and between 1952-88 was the venue for no fewer than 28 junior and senior championships. Among the clubs more distinguished members in the 1990s were Gordon Sherry and Jim Milligan both members of winning Walker Cup Teams.

KILMARTIN HOUSE
ARGYLL & BUTE

The ruins of a 15th century Z plan mansion stand 8 miles NW of Lochgilphead. Originally occupied by the Rector of Carsewell, who later became Bishop of the Isles in 1566. After finding the place too mean for his dignity, he erected the much more splendid Carnassary Castle on the opposite side of the Glen.

KILMAURS
EAST AYRSHIRE

Town situated 2 miles NW of Kilmarnock. Formerly part of the old hamlet of Cunningham, the name changed in the 13th century when the church was dedicated to the French Saint Maurus, though there is also evidence to support the claim that it means 'hill of the great cairn'. This is borne out by the area's many traces of hillforts and tumuli. In the 12th century the land of Cunningham was granted by Hugh de Morville to a fellow Norman named Wernebald whose descendants assumed the name Cunningham and received additional land from Robert the Bruce, and the title Earl of Glencairn that was bestowed on Sir Alexander Cunningham (Lord Kilmaurs) in 1488. In keeping with its rich ecclesiastical history, Sir William Cunningham founded a Collegiate Church here in 1403 with land and revenues and a mill that were acquired by William 5th Earl at the Reformation. On its elevation to a Burgh of Barony for the 3rd Earl in 1527, a grant of 280 Scots acres was made to the local tradesmen. Among these were its cutlers, who, although at one time dominant with their expert produce surpassing that of Sheffield and Birmingham, were later supplanted by shoe and bonnet factories, followed by coalmining and the hosiery trade. The house rebuilding between the 1920s and 30s marked the disappearance of some of the old burgh, which subsequently lost its administrative and judicial functions to the District and County Councils. Its council building or Tolbooth, however, still stands as a reminder of its importance in Ayrshire in former times.

KILRAVOCK CASTLE
HIGHLAND

It stands on a bank above the River Nairn 3 miles SW of the town. In the 13th century the lands were acquired by Hugh Rose of Geddes, whose descendant Hugh, the 7th Baron built the present 15th century tower before, according to one account, he was hanged by some noblemen over Lauder Bridge. Visited by Queen Mary in 1562 and enlarged into a courtyard castle in the 17th century. Just before the battle of Culloden (1746), Prince Charles Edward was here, followed by the Duke of Cumberland, who on his arrival exclaimed to the Laird: "You have had my cousin with you". Visited by Robert Burns in 1787. Further additions were made in the 19th century.

KILSPINDIE GOLF CLUB
EAST LOTHIAN

Originally known as Luffness Golf Club, which was founded at the instigation of Peter Brown in 1867 but was relocated in 1897 as a nine hole course on the present site on the west side of Aberlady Bay at Kilspindie Links. Since then the Wemyss family have proved to be reliable landlords from their home at nearby Gosford House. Sharing part of the land with the Volunteer Rifle Range, a year after the opening of the course and clubhouse by Lord Wemyss in 1898, the name was changed to Old Kilspindie, which continued to benefit from the support of Lord Wemyss, and by 1903, in concert with other East Lothian clubs, it prevailed over the North British Railway Co to provide an improved timetable and a special golfer's ticket. The year 1908 saw the course lengthened, a telephone installed in the clubhouse, the admission of lady members, and the final withdrawal of the Volunteer Rifle Brigade. One of its more distinguished club captains 1909-12 was Arthur Balfour who was Prime Minister between 1902-05. The club boasted nearly 380 members and 1600 visitors every year but this soon fell to 133 and 200 respectively. Despite this a 20 year lease was taken out in 1925 when membership returned to their pre-1914 levels and subscription levies increased. Thereafter, the club went from strength to strength under figures like J. Guild, Captain in 1927 before going on to international level and Presidency of the Scottish Golf Union in 1933. With the installation of electricity, the club was firmly in the 20th century, but despite ongoing improvements it was the gathering storms in Europe that suspended activity between 1939-45, when the sacrifices already anticipated were experienced in all quarters. This later gave way to a new found optimism post-1945 when German POW's broke up the anti-tank obstacles on the beach. It was, however, the gales and high tides of 1948-49 that damaged the course turf and in later years the long-standing barrage of feathers and seagull's droppings from hundreds of birds, along with the eradication of daisies, that proved a more formidable obstacle. The club's gradual acceptance of sexual equality, no doubt hastened by the war, brought about the first woman Captain, Miss Philips, in 1949, and though holder of ladies' championships since 1927 it was not until 1958 that the first tangible award, the Mrs S.G. Rome Trophy, was played for. Among the men's trophies, the H.W Hope medal is the oldest (1867), and for the boys, The Boys' Challenge Trophy from 1972.

KILSYTH
NORTH LANARKSHIRE

Town situated 12 miles NE of Glasgow. Formerly called Monaeburgh, the name of the present town built around 1665 is derived from the Gaelic 'cill' meaning 'church', while Syth could be from St Sytha, an Italian saint, or from Oswith, an English female saint. Among the area's forts, which included Roman and Cale-

donian structures, is Colzium Castle, the one time stronghold of the Edmonstones. Kilsyth was the scene of a battle in 1645, in which Montrose defeated the Covenanters. In 1661 it was made a Viscountcy for Sir James Livingstone. The town's importance was primarily due to its central position between Glasgow, Edinburgh and Stirling, which aided its principal industry, weaving, and the supplying of Glasgow mills until its own mill was built in 1845. See Battle

KILSYTH, BATTLE OF, 1645
SOUTH LANARKSHIRE

To the west of Falkirk. The last victory secured during the campaign of Montrose, who with a force numbering 4,400 foot and 500 horse confronted 6000 foot and 1000 horse under the Covenanting General William Baillie. The disadvantage of Montrose's numbers was counterbalanced by his superior position which facilitated the total rout of the enemy. Though victorious, Montrose's failure to hold together his army of clansmen, who mainly fought for sectional interests, brought defeat at Philiphaugh and robbed him of his chance to subdue Scotland and aid Charles I in England.

KILWINNING
NORTH AYRSHIRE

Town situated 16 miles NW of Ayr which takes its name from the 'church of St Winning', the 8th century Irish Saint who landed near here around 715. While much of its early history is tied to its Abbey, its standing as the home of Scotland's first mother lodge has given it a rich tradition in Freemasonry. Also known for the practice of archery; from 1488, with royal approval , it was promoted in the town as the principal art of war, which probably had some correlation with the success of the English archers at Agincourt in 1415. During the annual competition in July, the archer who shot down the Popinjay from the church steeple would be known as the master of ceremonies for the succeeding year. When erected into a Temporal Lordship for Hugh Earl of Eglinton in 1603, the town's main produce was gauzes and shawls which were sold at the Glasgow and Paisley markets, but by 1845 most of the townsmen were employed at the New Eglinton Iron Works (now gone). The effects of the decline of its Abbey after 1560 were alleviated by its position at a crossroads on the old north road from Ayr, providing a lifeline that brought further expansion in the 20th century, virtually making it a suburb of Irvine. See Abbey

KILWINNING ABBEY
NORTH AYRSHIRE

Located NW of Irvine by the River Garnock are a few fragmentary remains of this once proud Abbey. Thought to be the cradle of Free Masonry in Scotland and built as a priory by the Fraternities of Architects, formed to uphold the principles of Gothic architecture, and whose travelling privileges gave rise to the name Freemasons. By 1189 Richard or Hugh de Morville founded the Abbey for Tironesian Benedictines on the site of the 8th century cell of the Irish monk St Winnan or St Finian. According to another legend Sir Richard was an English Knight who founded the Abbey as an act of repentance after being involved in the murder of Thomas a Becket at Canterbury Cathedral. Rising to become the most opulent religious house in Ayrshire with grants and gifts confirmed by various monarchs from Robert I to James IV, (1306-1513) by 1550 the Abbey was held by a Commendator, but its last Abbot, a Gavin Hamilton, an opponent of John Knox, was killed in a skirmish at Restalrig in Edinburgh, 1571. Rocked by the

Reformation, which resulted in its tithes of sixteen parishes being erected into a Free Temporal Lordship for Hugh, 5th Earl of Eglinton, in 1603. Its old church was used until 1775 when a new one was built and further repairs were carried out by Archibald 11th Earl of Eglinton in 1789. Although bearing traces of some Norman work, most of the 13th century Gothic remains include the large south transept, part of the Chapter House and the south wall of the nave.

KINCARDINE
ABERDEENSHIRE

Village situated 2 miles NE of Fettercairn. Name derived from the Gaelic 'ceann' and the Brythonic 'cardden' meaning 'head of the wood' or 'thicket'. The castle which once stood here was thought to have been the scene of Kenneth II's murder in 995 and was also known as the residence of William I (1165-1214), Alexander III (1249-1286) and Robert Bruce in 1283. It was here in 1296 that John Balliol resigned as Scotland's overlord to Edward I of England, who took the Stone of Destiny as a trophy after failing to capture the Crown. Created a Burgh of Barony for the Earl Marischal in 1531, in the following year it became the capital of the County but its status waned after 1600 when the Sheriff Court was moved to Stonehaven, which, with its 18th century development, almost completely eclipsed Kincardine. In the locality above the main road and railway is a 6ft blue granite monolith called the Court Stone, thought to mark the site of the old Baron Courts.

KINCLAVEN CASTLE
PERTH & KINROSS

Situated on the bank of the Tay 8 miles N of Perth are the remains of a square enclosure that was once a royal residence of Alexander III in 1264. William Wallace's forces stayed here in 1297 after engaging the forces of Edward I nearby. Though later becoming ruinous it was rebuilt and garrisoned by Edward III's forces in 1335 but eventually became a stronghold for Scottish garrisons.

KINGHORN
FIFE

Coastal town situated 4 miles SW of Kirkcaldy. Called Kingornum in 1140 and Kingorny in 1654, the name probably derives from the Gaelic 'ceann' and 'gronn' meaning 'head of the marsh' , or literally 'kings horn', which would have been blown when he sallied out for the chase. This must have been the site of a settlement long before it was elevated to Royal Burgh status by William I around 1170, when its castle was an established resting place for royalty travelling to and from Saint Andrews. One of the more prominent memories of its royal connections however, is as the place where King Alexander III died in a riding accident in 1286 while en route to his Manor House, an event now marked by a cross on the Pettycur road. In the late 14th century the lands were granted by Robert II to Sir John Lyon, for whose heirs it was raised to an Earldom in 1606. Kinghorn's virtual decline into obscurity in later years was arrested by its flax spinning and later its shipbuilding, which was itself undermined when the railway bought and subsequently neglected its harbour, causing the emphasis to switch to leisure in the 20th century, due to its rising popularity as a seaside retreat.

KINGUSSIE
HIGHLAND

Town situated 40 miles SE of Inverness. Name derived from the Gaelic 'ceann giuthseich' meaning 'head of the fir wood'. As capital of Badenoch, the land was held from the 13th century by the Comyns, Lords of Badenoch, who ruled from their seat at Ruthven Castle, which was to become a stronghold of Alexander Stewart, the 'Wolf of Baddenoch', in the 14th century. After passing to the Earls of Moray, who granted it to the Huntlys in the 15th century, the town and castle were made a Burgh of Barony in 1464 for Alexander Seton, Ist Earl of Huntly. A Carmelite Friary, founded by George 2nd Earl of Huntly by 1501, stood within the boundaries of today's town which was itself developed by a descendant, the 4th Duke of Gordon, for the tenantry of the local feu holders whose lease had been terminated. In 1738, James Macpherson, the translator of the controversial poems of Ossian, was born here. The castle was burnt by the Marquis of Montrose in 1689 but was rebuilt as Ruthven Barracks in 1718 and stood until it was burnt by the Jacobites in 1746. Kingussie's location also enhanced its appeal as a supply point for hill walkers visiting the Cairngorms and anglers fishing in the Spey, along with more famous visitors like Robert Louis Stevenson, who had a book, 'The Graver & the Pen' , published here in 1883. The Parish Church, built in 1792 and known as Tom a Mhoid, 'the little hill of court', stands on the site of the old friary. A former manse and shooting lodge, the museum in Duke St offers a broad view of Kingussie's folk culture.

KININVIE HOUSE
MORAY

Occupying land in Glen Fiddich 3 miles SE of Craigellachie. While the original structure was probably built in 1480 the present house was erected by the Leslies after John, 3rd Earl of Atholl, granted the land in 1521 to Alexander Leslie after whose death in 1549, his statue was preserved in Mortlach Church. Additions were made in the 19th century when it was still a Leslie possession.

KINKELL CASTLE
HIGHLAND

It stands on high ground about 6 miles S of Dingwall. Essentially a 17th century T plan mansion built by the Mackenzies of Gairloch. It was occupied by a farmer by the 19th century but owing to some thoughtful restoration work now resembles something closer to its former state.

KINLOCHALINE CASTLE
HIGHLAND

Favourably sited in a picturesque setting by Loch Aline, just NE of the Sound of Mull. It was built for a Lady of the Macinnes Clan as a 15th century oblong keep with additions made in the 16th century. Legend has it that the builder was paid with butter. It was captured in 1644 by Colkitto, the lieutenant of the Marquis of Montrose, and burnt on his departure. Presently the castle is wind and weather proof.

KINLOSS
MORAY

Village situated by Findhorn Bay 3 miles NE of Forres. The name is either derived from the Gaelic 'ceann' and 'loch' meaning 'head of the loch' or 'cinn luss' meaning 'head of the herbs'. Most of the village was once part of a hunting fief and developed around its Abbey, which was founded by David I in 1150 and was raised along with the village into a Burgh of Barony for the Abbot in 1497. The lands were annexed to the Crown after the Reformation in 1581 and were erected in 1601 into a Temporal Lordship for Edward Bruce, who became Lord Bruce of Kinloss in 1604. After being sold to Alexander Brodie of Lethan in 1643, the Abbey was pillaged for its stone while also serving as a church that continued long after Kinloss was constituted its own Parish separate from Forres in 1657, and long before the building

of its Parish Church, 1795 (restored, 1830). More recently this rural burgh has given its name to the nearby RAF base. See Abbey

KINLOSS ABBEY
MORAY

Once a far-flung outpost of Christendom that gave rise to the village, the Abbey is 12 miles to the west of Elgin. It was founded in 1150 at the behest of an inspired David I following the King's near fatal encounter with a stag after losing his way during a hunt in the nearby wood. He oversaw its construction during his summer sojourns at Duffus Castle but later conferred it on his favourite order, the Cistercian monks from Melrose Abbey. The Abbeys' accumulated wealth by the time of visits from Edward I, 1303, and Edward III, 1336, included lands in Strathisla, Burgie, Inverern, and tofts (plots of burgh land) in Inverness, Nairn, Forres, Elgin and Aberdeen. The most distinguished Abbot here (1526-41) was the lawyer Robert Reid who became Bishop of Orkney. Later the property of Edward Bruce, who became Lord Bruce of Kinloss in 1604, and oversaw the building in its entirety before its stone was sold by Brodie of Letham for use in Cromwell's citadel in Inverness, 1650. Consequently its ruins are somewhat limited and show the usual emphasis placed on its church with the south side of the nave and parts of the north and south transepts. Parts of the Abbot's House also remain.

KINNAIRD CASTLE
ANGUS

Situated on a hill 3´ miles SE of Brechin. Lands were acquired by Duthac de Carnegie by 1409, who probably built the original castle that was burnt in 1452 by the Lindsays. The later structure, built by Sir Robert Carnegie, the Ambassador to France, in 1550, was elevated in importance during the 16th and 17th centuries, when it was visited by James VI, Charles II and the Chevalier St George. The building was later incorporated into a mansion.

KINNAIRD TOWER
PERTH & KINROSS

The 15th century oblong tower which stands on a hill 10 miles NE of Perth was built by the descendants of Randolph Rufus who held the barony in the 12th century and whose son adopted the name Kinnaird. Visited by James VI in 1617, it was occupied by the Livingstones by 1649 but was purchased in 1674 by Sir Patrick Thriepland, who restored it. In the 19th century his descendant, also Patrick, thoroughly renovated it and made it a museum.

KINNAIRDS HEAD. SEE FRASER-BURGH TOWN

KINNEFF
ABERDEENSHIRE

Town situated 9 miles SW of Stonehaven. The name may have derived from the hunting lodge built here by Kenneth II (971-95) or from the Gaelic 'ceann' meaning 'a head' referring to the the towns coastal position which has meant that its rocks have become a valuable building material. Kinneff Castle which is now rubble and was probably begun by Kenneth II figured during the minority of David II 1329-39 who after being persued by an English force landed nearby at what was later called Craig David. The castle was later held by an English garrison. Near the castle St Adamnan had a cell near a spring in the 7th century. This testifies to a long religious tradition. However, it is Kinneff Church that occupies a proud place in the country's historical annals because

in 1651 during Cromwell's occupation it became a hiding place for the Scottish Crown Jewels, Sword and Sceptre. See Church

KINNEFF CHURCH
ABERDEENSHIRE

In the village of the same name stands the church that superseded the original church that was strongly associated with the Scottish Crown Jewels during Cromwell's occupation in 1651, when the local Minister and his wife Christian Grainger concealed them in the church. The regalia were removed in 1660 at the Restoration of Charles II who rewarded Mrs Grainger with 200 Merks after the death of her husband in 1663. The present building was erected in 1738 and restored in 1876 with 424 sittings, and contains a number of monuments including one to its most celebrated ministers Mr Grainger and his wife. See Town & Dunotter Castle

KINNEIL
FALKIRK

Village situated on the Firth of Forth, SW of Bo'ness. The name either derived from the Old Gaelic 'cinnfhabhail' meaning 'at the end of the wall' or 'cinn alla' meaning 'at the head of the crag'. The land and barony were granted to Sir Walter Hamilton by Robert the Bruce before 1329 and in the 19th century were owned by his descendant the Duke of Hamilton, whose seat was Kinneil House. Part of Boness Parish in 1669, the last Minister of Kinneil was William Wishart who was persecuted during the Covenanting Struggles' with which the village had strong associations. Largely depopulated in 1691 due to migrant working practices, the cycle was reversed with the agricultural innovations of 1750 before the village received another boost when James Watt invented the first steam pumping engine in the workshop of Kinneil House between 1764 and 1768. See Kinneil House

KINNEIL HOUSE
FALKIRK

Situated near the River Forth just S of Boness. In the 14th century the lands were granted by Robert I to the Hamiltons, whose descendant the Earl of Arran built a 16th century feudal keep, referred to as a palace before being blown up by James Douglas 4th Earl of Morton, in 1570, but was rebuilt with an L plan house and occupied by the Regent Arran in 1579. William Douglas, Earl of Selkirk, was created Duke of Hamilton in 1661. Enlarged and embellished by William the 3rd Duke and Duchess Ann in the 17th century, around 1764, James Watt (inventor) developed his steam engine here. Vacated by the Hamiltons in 1809, it was then occupied by Dugald Stewart, writer and friend of Sir Walter Scott and Robert Burns. Before his death in 1828 Stewart wrote some of his most celebrated works here. Today Kinneil is held in trust for the nation.

KINROSS
PERTH & KINROSS

Town situated 25 miles NE of Stirling on the western side of Loch Leven. The name is derived from the Gaelic 'ceannrois' meaning 'head of the promontory'. Treated as a capital by Alexander III, from where he and his Queen were forcibly taken to Stirling Castle by the Comyn faction in 1257. As County Town it was once the property of the Douglas Earls of Morton and became a Burgh of Barony for Douglas of Kinlochleven in 1541. For William Bruce, who built Kinross House on the site of an earlier house of the Mortons, it became a Burgh of Regality in 1685, but much of the town's history is connected with Lochleven Castle.

Though losing some of its former importance after the removal of the Morton's seat, in 1723, as capital of the County, it consisted of a main street criss-crossed by lanes conforming to a grid plan, and in the 19th century boasted a Court House, while its council was replaced by a Magistrate under the General Police Improvements Act. Once a manufacturer of cutlery, this was replaced by cotton weaving that flourished between 1836-45 until it in turn was supplanted in 1867 by the town's three woollen mills, which supplied some of the Glasgow merchants. Notwithstanding the demolition witnessed during the town's westward expansion, Kinross still retains some interesting structures such as its Old Tolbooth, built around 1600, repaired by Robert Adam in 1771, and Kinross House, built in 1685 in a Renaissance style, while in the locality are some imposing monoliths which stand as reminders of a more remote period in history.

KINTORE
ABERDEENSHIRE

Town situated on the bank of the Don 12 miles NW of Aberdeen. The name is probably Gaelic for 'head of the forest'. The land was once part of a royal hunting ground located around the nearby Hall Forest Castle (ruin) and was granted by Robert Bruce in 1309 to Robert de Keith, Great Marischal of Scotland. Although a mere village, its royal connections led to its elevation into a Royal Burgh by William I (1187-1200) but it was not until much later that it developed a sound mercantile system with its timber, farming and the conveyance of granite which it channelled through Port Elphinstone, the canal link with Aberdeen. In 1506 James IV granted a new charter and in 1677 it was erected into an Earldom for Sir John Keith. Its most famous worthy was Sir Andrew Mitchell

(1708-1771), who went to school here and later became Ambassador to Prussia in the time of Fredrick the Great. Once consisting of a main street, Kintore's architectural gems are somewhat limited but its Town Hall dates from 1740 and its Parish Church from 1819.

KIRKCALDY
FIFE

Coastal town situated 25 miles SW of St Andrews. Its original name was thought to be 'Keldei' due to its conjectured status as the site of a 6th century Culdee Cell. But it was later known as 'Langtoun' after its long street and reverted to Kirkcaldy which is either Gaelic for 'church' or 'fort on the high hill' or 'harbour of refuge'. Rising from relative obscurity in the 12th century, by 1329 in a charter from Robert I it was a burgh dependent on Dunfermline Abbey, and in 1450, when Kirkcaldy was a thriving port trading in coal and salted fish with England and the Continent, it had its land and property conveyed to the Baillies and Town Council. Despite the ratification of its original charter of 1644 and its creation as a new Royal Burgh and Free Port for services rendered, its trade declined due to losses incurred during the Civil War of 1689 and the Act of Union in 1707, and remained sluggish until the 19th century. On a more creative note, the town's historical high points are concerned less with actual events and more with individual characters like the economist Adam Smith (1723-1790) who was born here, attended the local Grammar School and wrote 'The Wealth of Nations' here, writer Thomas Carlyle (1795-1888) who between 1816 and 1819 taught Mathematics at the Burgh School and the architect Robert Adam (1728-92), who was born here the son of William Adam, builder. The revival in trade in 1772 boosted the iron works that made marine engines, boilers plus sugar and rice mill equipment which it exported to Holland, Baltic Ports, America and the West Indies. By 1876 its linen trade had spawned the production of linoleum, of which, under the Nairn family it became the world's largest producer, with seven factories employing 1300 people by 1833. Continuing to prosper well into the 20th century, linoleum was still being produced here in the 1990s, albeit on a smaller scale, as the town adjusts to the demands of its lighter industries in the technological revolution. Much of the burgh's pre and post-industrial heritage can be seen in its Museum and Art Gallery.

KIRKCONNELL TOWER
DUMFRIES & GALLOWAY

Located 2 miles NE of New Abbey. In 1410 the lands belonged to Aymer de Maxwell, husband of Janet de Kirkconnel whose descendants started this L plan tower in the 10th century. With its four feet thick barrel vaulted ground floor walls, it rises 3 storeys high to its battlements with adjoining capehouse. Additions were made by the pro-Jacobite James Maxwell in 1780 on his return to Scotland, from where he had fled after the 1745 Rebellion.

KIRKCUDBRIGHT
DUMFRIES & GALLOWAY

Town situated 32 miles SW of Dumfries on the left bank of the River Dee. Once the site of a 12th century church dedicated to St Cuthbert, from whom the town takes its name. Traces of the land's occupation by the British Selgovae tribe, who were ousted when the Romans invaded the area in 82 AD, are to be found in the place names to the west of the town, where an ancient fort with mound and deep fosse once stood. This defensive structure was followed by a 13th century castle at Castledykes where Edward I and his Queen probably stayed during their ten day visit in 1300. As County Town, it was a Royal Burgh by 1330 and after Balliol's (Edward I's vassal) forfeiture it became a Burgh of Regality held from 1369 by the Douglases, Lords of Galloway until their fall in 1455. In the same year it was visited by James II who made it a Free Royal Burgh. The church of the 15th century Greyfriars Friary (damaged at the Reformation) served as a Parish Church between 1564 and 1730 when it was replaced by St Mary's Church, which was rebuilt in 1838. During its somewhat chequered history Kirkcudbright was nearly destroyed by a force of Manxmen led by the Earl of Derby, 1507, was visited by James IV while on a pilgrimage to Whithorn, 1508, opposed the National Covenant, 1666, and harboured the fleet of William II while en route to Ireland in 1689. Favouring the Status Quo as the guarantor of trade and stability, the townsfolk opposed the Union of 1707, sent a force to assist the Hanoverians despite being the preferred landing place for the Old Pretender in 1715, and in 1778, during the American Wars, Privateer John Paul Jones, who was born at Kirkbean, sailed into Kirkcudbright Bay and raided the Earl of Selkirk's residence. Although a traditional Market Town thriving on supplies from land and sea, its port ranked as a creek in Dumfriesshire in the 19th century and served more as an import distribution centre for the area. Later becoming the haunt of artists, led by the first local artist to gain international fame, Edward Hornel (1864-1933) whose work is well displayed in his former home Broughton House in the town centre. Up until 1925 this was a centre for Clydesdale horse breeding and with the extension of the burgh boundary in 1950 the custom of Riding the Marches

was revived. Erected above the harbour in 1583, Maclellans Castle (ruin) was built by Sir Thomas Maclellan of Bombie whose descendant, a Robert Maclellan of Bombie, was created Lord Kirkcudbright in 1633. The 16th century Tolbooth was built with the stones from Dundrennan Abbey while its present Parish Church of 1838 with its nave, transepts, clock tower and spire occupies the site of the old friary.

KIRKHOPE
SCOTTISH BORDERS

This oblong tower stands on a hill 7 miles W of Selkirk. Probably built after 1535 when an Act of Parliament required the building of Border towers as part of James V's defensive strategy. While the property of the Scotts of Harden, a wealthy Border family, in 1543 it was attacked during an English incursion. The laird's son, Walter Scott of Harden, lived here when he wooed and won the heart of Mary Scott ('The Flower of Yarrow'), and they were married in 1576. Purchased by the Duchess of Buccleuch in the early 18th century, it later fell into ruin but is now restored.

KIRKINTILLOCH
EAST DUMBARTONSHIRE

Town situated 8 miles NE of Glasgow on the Forth & Clyde Canal. This was probably a place of some importance during the Roman occupation as its name is derived from the Gaelic 'caerpentulach' meaning 'fort at the end of the ridge'. It was around this fort at the end of the Antonine Wall, which was replaced by a 13th century Comyn castle (now gone), that the town grew. Created a Burgh of Barony for William de Comyn 1211-14; this was later granted by Robert I to Malcolm Fleming (1306), but passed in 1373 to Gilbert Kennedy. Apart from being re-erected a Burgh of Barony (1526) after losing burgh status, suffering at the hands of the Jacobites in 1745, and being the first place in Scotland to be visited by Asiatic cholera in 1832, the burghers focused mainly on enterprises like its trade in coal, cotton and whisky which it channelled through the Forth & Clyde Canal from 1826 until well into the 20th century. Electing its first Provost in 1871, the town was governed by a dual administration, incorporating the old and new Town Councils, until the former's abolition in 1908.

KIRKLISTON
CITY OF EDINBURGH

Village situated on the River Almond 9 miles W of Edinburgh. Originally called Templeliston after the Knights Templars who settled here and built a church in the 12th century, the second part of the name is either a family name or is from the Celtic 'lioston' meaning 'an enclosure by the riverside'. Held by the Knights of St John of Jerusalem from the 14th century up to the Reformation, in 1298 on the site now called Newliston, the army of Edward I encamped while en route to Falkirk and victory over the Scots under William Wallace. When created a Burgh of Barony for the Earl of Winton in 1621, the village's economy was essentially agrarian but was later stimulated by the area's shale deposits which found ready markets in Scotland's southern industrial belt. Dating from the 12th century, the Parish Church was redeveloped in the 19th century and contains the burial vault of the Stair family including the ashes of the Countess 'Lady Ashton' who figured in Scotts 'Bride of Lammermoor' of 1814. Today's village was built in the late 19th and early 20th century with the benefits derived from the building of the Union Canal 1811-21, the Forth Rail Bridge in 1890 and the setting up of the Shale Oil Industry, 1901-11.

KIRKTON
FIFE

About 2´ miles S of Newport are the remains of a mansion house that was built by David Balfour and Cathrine Crichton in 1585. The estate passed to the Young family in the early 17th century and was acquired by a John Gillespie around 1700.

KIRKWALL
ORKNEY

Capital city of Orkney situated on the SE of the island. Name derived from the Old Norse 'Kirkiuvagr' meaning 'church bay' after the Scandinavian Earls built a church here dedicated to St Olaf. Although a Norse settlement from the 7th century the present town developed around its Cathedral which was built in 1138 when the island served as a base for marauding Norsemen and as the winter quarters for King Haakon, who, after his defeat at Largs, 1263, died here in the Bishops Palace. In 1379 the St Clairs became the Earls of Orkney and later built Kirkwall Castle from where they ruled like despot kings until 1470 before Orkney and Shetland served as part of the dowry for James III's wife, Margaret of Denmark. Its Royal Burgh Charter of 1486 ratified all rights and privileges of previous charters including the right to hold courts with the power of pit and gallows, markets and annual fairs. An onlooker at the Reformation, Kirkwall did witness the trial of witches who were burnt at Gallowhill to the south of the town. Owing to its support for Charles II this was the departure point for 2,000 men under Montrose in 1650 and was occupied in 1651 by Cromwell's forces, who built a fort east of the harbour that served as the most northern bastion of his Protectorate. Represented in Parliament in 1670, while the town's distant island status precluded it from the political upheavals of the 18th and 19th centuries this was to become its best natural asset when large numbers of Kirkwall's sons became merchant seamen and so further enriched the island's seafaring tradition while also bringing a strong cosmopolitan dimension to the islanders' understanding of the outside world. Kirkwall benefited from the Naval Base at Scapaflow, 1914-18, and by the allied occupation during World War II, 1939-45, and latterly received an added boost from North Sea Oil exploration. Tankerness House, a 16th century merchant's Town House in Broad St, provides a far reaching view into the life of this ancient community. See St Magnus Cathedral & Bishop's Palace

KISIMUL CASTLE
WESTERN ISLES

On Castle bay on the S of the Island of Barra is a Macneil stronghold. In 1344 the land was restored by David II to Ronald, son of Rodrick Malan, in order to secure his support in his wars with England. Although the date of the structure remains uncertain, its enclosing wall, the only part of the island that remained dry at high tide, is probably 14th century, but at a later date a keep was built near two fresh springs. Owing to the charter of the island being obtained by Rodrick Macmurchan from the Lord of the Isles, it remained a Macneil possession down through the centuries, when more additions were made. Repairs started in 1938 by an American architect and lineal descendant were eventually completed in the 1970s.

KNOCK CASTLE
ABERDEENSHIRE

Advantageously situated on a hill 2 miles SW of Ballater are the ruins of a courtyard keep that was built by the Gordons around 1600.

KNOCKANDO DISTILLERY
MORAY

Deriving its name from the Gaelic 'cnoc-an-dhu', meaning 'little black hill'. It enjoys a favourable position by the River Spey 8 miles SW of Craigellachie. In 1898 John Tytler Thomson, a spirit broker and whisky merchant from Elgin, bought part of the Dalbeallie Farm from James Grant, but it was however his subsequent rent of the land of Cardnach Farm, which included Cardnach Spring, that provided the main ingredient in Knockando's success. After appointing the architect and engineer Charles Doig, the distillery was built in a pinkish granite stone that was quarried locally. On the 2nd June 1899, following its completion, 'The Elgin Courant' and 'The Elgin Courier' reported : "Mr Thomson has selected the most beautiful site and one in which every convenience can be obtained". Though getting favourable acclaim for its product, the slump in the market sounded the death knell for Mr Thompson's operation, and in 1903 it was purchased by the successful wine and spirit merchants W & A Gilbeys Ltd. Under the prudent and dynamic Walter and Alfred Gilbey, Knockando's prospects were revived, with further developments including its own railway siding by 1905, which helped establish its place in the market, and production that continued throughout most of World War One (1914-18) until 1917 when it stopped for two years. During the 1920s and 1930s sales were steady but stagnant, owing to the rise in excise duty, and in 1939 The Ministry of Food ordered production to stop to conserve barley. The return to production after 1945 marked a deceptively low period, but was to give way to a prosperous era for Knockando in the 1950s. In 1962 Gilbeys merged with United Wine Traders and was renamed Distillers &

Vitners, who included Justerini & Brooks, later acquired by Diageo plc. Despite the gradual contraction of operations from then on, including the closure of the railway in 1971, Knockando has concentrated on its time-tested quality production methods, which include its season dating. This is a process that includes the year of distillation, the seasoned year of bottling on the label. All of which helps to facilitate the unique method of production, which, unlike other malts that are bottled after a set period of time, takes place after reaching a level of perfection usually 12 or 14 years.

OWNERS
Diageo plc ?

REGION
Speyside

PRODUCT
Knockando Season distilled 1989 and bottled in 1998 43% vol
Knockando Extra Old distilled 1997 and bottled in 1998 40 & 43% vol

NOTES
A delicate flowery aromatic nose, slightly smokey and fruity with a slight underlying sweetness that gives way to a dry finish.

KNOCKDHU DISTILLERY
MORAY

Built NE of Keith in 1894 by the Distillery Co Ltd following the discovery of several springs on the southern slopes of Knock Hill. It was surrounded by fertile farmland with its quality barley, an inexhaustible supply of peat and the crofting communities that were a reliable source of labour during the winter months, after working the land in the summer. With power being supplied by a 16 horsepower steam engine, its two pot stills could turn out 2500 gallons of spirit per week, while the cottages built around the distillery for its workforce formed a little community. For decades its distinctive taste made Knockdhu very attractive to blenders, prompting the building of additional warehouses in 1898 and forming its main markets for decades later. Connected to the national grid in 1940, in the 1960s it eventually parted company with its horse and cart, and its pot stills were converted to mechanical stoking, which proved to be an attractive feature when it was taken over by Inver House Distillers Ltd in 1988. Shortly after, the whisky was relaunched as the An cnoc, which is Gaelic for The Knoc.

OWNERS
Blairmhor Ltd ?

REGION
Highland

PRODUCT
An Cnoc 12 year old single Highland Malt

NOTES
A distinctive aroma with a hint of dryness, a mellow, nutty, smooth taste with a long finish.

KNOCKDOLIAN TOWER
SOUTH AYRSHIRE

The ruins of this tower are situated on the bank of the River Stincher 2 miles SW of Colmonell village. The lands of Knockdolian were originally held by the knightly Graham family, one of whom Sir John Graham married Dame Helen Kennedy daughter of the Laird of barganny. Their tower was further developed into what became the ruins of today around 1650 by Fergus M'Cubbins for his spouse Margaret Kennedy. In the 18th century a mansion house was built nearby.

KNOCKHALL CASTLE
ABERDEENSHIRE

At the mouth of the River Ythan near
Newburgh stands a ruined L plan tower
built in 1565 and held by the Udney family. Partly damaged in 1639 when taken
by the Earl Marischal for the Covenant.
In 1640 a foraging party from Aberdeen
assailed Knockhall and were admitted
by Lady Udney in her husband's absence. Since the accidental fire of 1734 it
has remained in a ruinous state.

L

LADYBANK GOLF CLUB
FIFE

The club was formed at a meeting in the one time Royal Hotel in 1879. Numbering 26 members, at the first Annual General Meeting, the first Captain was Sheriff Maitland Herriot, and the Rev George Johnstone was the Secretary. The original 6 hole course designed by Tom Morris of Saint Andrews was extended to a circular 9 hole format in 1910. With the game's growing popularity in the area and the country as a whole, the course at Annsmuir became an appendage of the town, and in 1925 a new clubhouse was built at a cost of £400 with the opening ceremony being performed by Mrs Crichton, wife of Ladybank Provost. The course was maintained by a group of volunteers during the 2nd World War. In 1950, the land, which formed part of the Ballantager Estate owned by the Earl of Leven and Melville, was bought outright for £850 with donations made by generous individuals. This enabled the club to accommodate a growing number of visitors, with the surplus land providing a further 9 holes, making for an 18 hole course opened in 1961. Since then further additions have been made including a new clubhouse (1971), which was extended in 1975. And in the late 1970s the course was selected for the opening qualifying stages for the British Open at Saint Andrews; the leading qualifier on 139 was Rodger Davis, and other qualifiers included Sam Torrance Bernhard Langer and Jack Newton, the young Ian Woosnam was unsuccessful. In 1983 the conversion of the old course hotel into a country club was marked by a match between the world-famous Jack Nicklaus and Severiono Ballesteros. Naturally both players have been awarded Honorary Membership while the club's own offspring have included George Will of Ryder Cup fame and Dale Reid, a prominent figure among the lady golfers. In 1995 Ladybank's members numbered 770 and since 1970 all female members have enjoyed total equality.

LADYKIRK
SCOTTISH BORDERS

Village situated 6 miles up river from Coldstream and derives its name from a church built and dedicated to the Virgin Mary by James IV. For centuries it was used as a crossing point from north and south for invading armies in which its old bridge between Ladykirk and Norham played a central part, and in the 19th century was still in use. In the 13th century Ladykirk was the scene of a meeting between Edward I and the Scottish nobles to decide on the successor to the Scottish Crown. The land was held by Kelso Abbey up until the Reformation, 1560, when the then Parishes of Horden and Upsettlington became Ladykirk Parish. The old parish derived its name from the Anglo Saxon 'Horn' and 'Den' which means 'curved wooded valley' near which once stood a monastery. See Kirk

LADYKIRK
SCOTTISH BORDERS

It stands on the north bank of the River Tweed across from Norham Castle 6 miles NE of Coldstream. According to tradition it acquired its name after being dedicated to the Virgin Mary following its founding around 1500 by James IV, who had been spared from a drowning accident in the Tweed. Cruciform in plan, the building displays many examples of Gothic architecture in Scotland in the late 15th century. Although built without aisles it has apsidal terminations to the choir and transepts while the west end is terminated by a square tower. The exterior shows the usual arched windows punctuated by buttresses that extend to the flagstone roof which is overshadowed by the tower, of which the upper part was the work of William Adam around 1743.

LAG TOWER
SOUTH AYRSHIRE

Just W of Dundonald are the ruins of a large 16th century tower built by the Griersons of Lag, who held the land from the 14th century. A Gilbert Lay Grierson married one of the heiresses of Sir Duncan of Kirkpatrick in 1412. The last occupant, a Sir Robert Grierson, was a well-known enemy of the Covenanters in the 17th century.

LAGAVULAN DISTILLERY
ARGYLL & BUTE

Known as an island malt owing to the building's location on the Island of Islay. The art of distilling was said to have been introduced to Scotland's whisky Isle by St Columba in 573 AD. Lagavulan, which is from the Gaelic 'Lag A 'Mhuillin' meaning 'mill in the hollow', lies by the natural harbour that is guarded by Dungvey Castle, a former stronghold of the Lords of the Isles. The site of at least ten illicit stills in 1740, the first legal distillery was begun in 1816 by John Johnston, who was attracted by the pure water from the Lochs at Solan that flows over almost 100 waterfalls before reaching the distillery. The business was taken over by a spirit merchant who made several improvements. It then merged with a company headed by Peter Mackie, or 'Restless Peter' owing to his dynamic energy, who later became the driving force behind the White Horse Distillers. Lagavulan's pear shaped copper pot stills provide one of the malts at the heart of the famous 'White Horse' blend. Among the changes in the 1960s re-development was the closure of the old malt mills and the building of a new stillhouse

OWNERS
Diageo plc ?

REGION
Islay

PRODUCT
Lagavulan 16 year old single malt 43% vol

NOTES
A distinctive robust malt with an intensely dry, peaty aroma and an exceptionally long, balanced finish.

LAMINGTON
SOUTH LANARKSHIRE

Village situated 12 miles SE of Lanark. Name derived from a Flemish man called Lambin and the Old English 'ton' denoting 'town or village'. Although granted to Lambin by David I (1124-53), it was later erected into a barony in 1368 for William Baillie (whose 17th descendant became Lord Lamington in 1880) until Charles I (1625-49) granted it in a charter to the Douglases, with the right to hold two weekly markets and annual fairs. In the 19th century three Roman Camps were identified in the area close to where William Wallace's camp was sited. Alas, the tower associated with the hero was destroyed in the 18th century. The Parish Church, of Norman design, has a bell dating from 1647.

LAMLASH GOLF CLUB
NORTH AYRSHIRE

The club is located on the Isle of Arran overlooking the picturesque bay of Lamlash, a natural harbour which through the centuries has been affected by many events of national importance. These include the battle of Largs, 1263, the Sutherland Clearances in the 19th century and its use by the Royal Navy and Scottish Commandoes before and during both World Wars. Founded by the men of Lamlash in 1889, although the original eight hole course had no actual designer in 1896 W. Auchterlonie extended the course to 18 holes, some of which extended the farmhouse. The ship's cabin which was the original club house was replaced in 1903-04 with a stylish square building complete with all the proper facilities and front entrance porch and pitched bungalow-style roof. In 1908 Willie Fernie a professional golfer at Troon and winner of the British Open in 1883 was instrumental in adding five new holes which formed the course being played today. Along with the ladies' section, Lamlash has played a prominent role in the life of the island over the years while extending itself to visitors from the mainland. The clubs awards reflect its associations with distinguished individuals, and include The Hamilton Bowl presented by the Duchess of Hamilton after opening the original clubhouse in 1904, The Fleet Cup Staff gifted by John Martin Staff Surgeon of HMS Magnificant in 1909 and the Thomson Cup given by Mr Thomson of London.

LANARK
SOUTH LANARKSHIRE

Town situated 10 miles SE of Motherwell. Name derived from the Welsh 'llanerch' meaning 'a forest glade'. With its early Roman connections the town was a place of some importance and the site of a 12th century castle built on the mound at the Castle Gate by David I, who had also made it a Royal Burgh by 1159. Frequently visited by kings when its castle doubled as a royal hunting lodge, it often figured in the Wars of Independence when the town was burnt (1244), and was the scene of Wallace's victory (1297) over the English Sheriff of Lanark. In 1150 the church of St Kentigern (now a fragmentary ruin NE of the town) was granted by King David to Dryburgh Abbey, but in 1777 was replaced by the Parish Church of St Nicholas, which now houses a bell dating from 1110. The town and castle was held by Edward I until 1310. The once Franciscan Friary which was initiated by Robert the Bruce, 1314, who made a grant of a manor and orchard, was founded by his son David II in 1346 and was where the meeting of the whole Franciscan Order was held in 1496. A hospital dedicated to St Leonard which appears in 1327 evidently held some land here, probably around St Leonards Street, which was granted to the burgh before 1792 when the ruins were demolished. Lanark's political ascendancy took place in the 14th and 15th centuries when in 1369 it was a member of The Four Courts of Burghs and in 1469 was represented in Parliament. No stranger to the turbulence witnessed during the reign of the Stewarts, on the Common Muir of Lanark encamped the armies of James II, 1452, of Charles II in 1682 after having been occupied by 4,000 English Horse, and before their defeat at Rullion Green in 1666 about 3,000 Covenanters set out from here. In the 1780s its age-old weaving industry provided a ready made workforce for the endeavours of David Dale in the New Lanark Mills that undermined its homespun products. The Lanimars Festival which is probably rooted in the old Corpus Christi procession and the summer solstice, held in early June, involves the traditional Riding of the Marches and a procession of lorries displaying literary, historical and fanciful subjects designed by the children of the local schools. Also involving the local children is the Whuppity Stoorie Festival held on Ist of March at 6pm when under the chiming bells the children run around the church three times beating each other with paper balls attached to string, exorcising the evil spirits which come in the whirl of stour

(March dust) to destroy the crops. See Golf Club

LANARK GOLF CLUB
SOUTH LANARKSHIRE

The site chosen for the course by the founding fathers in 1851 was Lanark Moor, about a mile from the town. The decision was contiguous to the earlier state of affairs, when there were four members and four holes while the trees provided shelter from the rain and their branches were used for hanging clothes. This was alleviated by the cramped conditions of Moor cottage. At the first Annual General Meeting, the 21 members who were enrolled were assured a good game of golf on the six hole course. After acquiring the trappings of a club and experiencing some set backs, the full 18 hole course arranged by the celebrated Tom Morris was realised by 1897. Under the Captaincy of the dynamic W.J Carmichael Anstruther, the permanent clubhouse was opened in 1862. The ongoing contention over the use of the course by the local militia who encamped here yearly was eventually resolved in 1909 when the club took out a 25 year lease and purchased the last part of Elliots Fields. This was followed by a new plan overseen by Ben Sayers, and so the form of today's course began to emerge. While the lady members were recognised in 1895, in the wake of the Suffragette Movement in 1909 they broke away to form their own club and weren't reunited with Lanark until 1947, the year the juniors were integrated. As in many other clubs after 1918, the members were forced to raise prices in 1924 to fund the remodelling of the clubhouse and extensive interior work in 1933. In the interim the 13th and 14th holes were added to the course by James Braid between 1926-27, followed by other improvements that continued before and during the Second World War, 1939-45. In

1951 Lanark marked its centenary, confident of its record at providing recreation for the local population while playing a distinguished role in the golfing culture of the Scottish Lowlands. Central to all of this was its collection of trophies that include the oldest, 'The Claret Jug' bought in 1857 with club funds, and the championship Quaich given by R B Dick in 1949.

LANARK, NEW
SOUTH LANARKSHIRE

Town situated 1 mile SW of Old Lanark on the bank of the Clyde. The site was developed in 1783 by the philanthropist David Dale and Richard Arkwright as the seat of cotton manufacture, which began with the opening of the first mill in 1785 and the second in 1788 followed by two subsequent mills. Carried on by the founder's son-in-law, Robert Owen, between 1799 and 1827 it was a model social experiment with each mill built 160ft long, 40ft wide and 7 storeys high. In addition the spacious village close by, which accommodated up to 200 families, was located in a healthy rural setting with its fresh air and the Falls of the Clyde providing the main attractions. In 1881 the works were bought by the Lanark Spinning Co which doubled its size and introduced new machinery. Today the town stands as a fine example of an 18 / 19th century industrial town with a strong social element.

LANGHOLM
SOUTH LANARKSHIRE

An old Market Town situated 23 miles SW of Hawick. Name derived from the Old Scots 'lang' and the Old Norse 'holm-r' therefore 'long meadow'. The town developed around a border fortress belonging to the Armstrongs. It was near here in 1455 that the forces of the Crown dealt a final blow to the Douglas Dynasty. Although created a Burgh of Barony for the Earl of Nithsdale in 1621 and a Burgh of Regality for the Duchess of Buccleuch in 1687, the town remained in relative obscurity and as such was marginalised by the building of New Langholm in 1778. The land that had previously been leased by the Duke of Buccleuch had become a centre for cotton and tweed manufacture by the 19th century, with a library started in 1800 with donations from a native son, the engineer Thomas Telford (1757-1834), and the Town Hall built in 1811. Above the town stands an obelisk statue of Sir John Malcolm, an 18th century civil servant, but it is the celebrated poet Hugh Macdiarmid (1892-1978) who was born here, who stands as the most distinguished figure in the town's more recent past. See Golf Club

LANGHOLM GOLF CLUB
DUMFRIES & GALLOWAY

The club owes its existence to Mr Alex Scott of woollen mill fame, whose family's love of sport started a rich sporting tradition in the town, starting with the founding of Langholm Rugby Club in 1871. So it was in 1892 at a meeting in the Eskdale Temperance Hotel that a decision was made to form a club that had its ground selected and its clubhouse opened by 1894 under Mr Alex Scott the first president. The club played its first inter-club game with Carlisle and the first ladies medal was played for in 1895. Like many clubs in Scotland, Langholm had to tread carefully over the land, which was either common land under lease or private land owned by a farmer and inevitably bordering working farmland. The year 1912 marked an important stage in the club's development for on 14th September the new clubhouse was opened, with an extended 9 hole course that was followed a year later with the right from the town council to tap the main underground water supply. Play was interrupt-

ed by the war, 1914-18, but resumed in 1919 with the ranks of its membership depleted by six. Despite this the 1920s saw a colourful mix of personalities and skill, engendering a new era for the club which for a time was at odds with the lady members. This undoubtedly had much to do with the number of members, which in 1925 totalled 88 men, 102 ladies and 31 juniors. With such a wealth of talent Langholm was one of the more dominant clubs in the Borders Tournaments in 1933, but membership dropped in the run up to and during World War II, 1939-45, when the course was requisitioned by the army. In 1948 Langholm became a member of The Scottish Golf Union. In a bid to improve membership levels, Sunday playing was voted for in 1950, which provoked an outcry from older Langholm burghers led by the Rev Burnside, whose draconian black and white perspective was in contrast with the younger members and one time combatants who argued they had killed men on Sundays. Failed attempts to initiate the building of an extensive sports complex, known as Manson's dream, was followed by the purchase of the land in 1954 that was to usher in an era of confidence symptomatic of the mood of the nation as a whole, which produced such champions as Bert Weatherstone. However, this mood was dashed in the 1960s when the club's resources sank to new lows and the course was let for grazing during the winter months when not being dominated by figures like David Latimer. The upturn witnessed in the 1970s was later augmented by the new clubhouse opened in 1982 and the extension of the course to 18 holes in 1986, less than ten years before the centenary.

LANGSIDE, BATTLE OF, 1568
CITY OF GLASGOW

To the S of Glasgow. Following Queen Mary's escape from Lochleven with her powerful nobles the Queen gathered her 6,000 supporters at Hamilton, thus provoking her brother James Stewart, Regent Moray to muster the forces of the rebel lords which numbered over 4,000 men. From nearby Mary witnessed the failure of her forces to capture Langside Hill from the Regents troops, who were reinforced at a critical moment, giving way to a torrent and the flight of the Queen's army. The defeat marked the beginning of the end of the Queen who then sought sanctuary in England where she was eventually executed in 1587.

LANGTON
SCOTTISH BORDERS

Village situated 2 miles SW of Duns. The name is derived from the length of the main street. The lands that had once belonged to Kelso Abbey, passed to a William de Vipont in the 12th century. Witnessing the usual instability of a border village, on the nearby hills of Raecleugh head and Campmuir were built military stations, of which the former was possibly Danish, and was where the burning of the village by Henry Percy in 1558 was later witnessed, while the latter was built following the 1715 Rising. In 1760 Langton was peacefully razed to the ground and substituted for nearby Gavinton, named after the new landowner David Gavin Esq who found the old village an obstacle to improvements.

LAPHROAIG DISTILLERY
ARGYLL & BUTE

The most southerly distillery on Islay and the Western Isles has weathered the full rage of the Atlantic storms since the brothers Donald and Alex Johnston first distilled whisky here in 1815, giving rise

to the present distillery in the 1820s. The name Laphroaig, pronounced 'Lafroyg', in Gaelic means 'the beautiful hollow by the broad bay'. Its rich tradition in distillation involves its peaty water, which comes from its own peat beds, and the malted barley, germinating on a traditional malted floor before being dried by the smoke from the peat fire (which enhances the peaty character) prior to being distilled twice then left in oak casks. Laphroaig remained in the family for generations despite repeated sabotage attempts by neighbouring distillers, long before its sale in the 1950s its somewhat uneventful history enabled the Johnstons to skilfully perfect the art of encapsulating the different elements of the rain, peat, barley and granite that mature in its warehouses.

OWNERS
Allied Distillers Ltd ?

REGION
Islay

PRODUCT
Laphroaig 10 & 15 year old single malt 40% vol

NOTES
A peaty, sweet nose with a palate that is peaty, slightly salty but with an undertone of sweetness.

LARGO
FIFE

Consisting of Upper and Lower Largo the villages are situated on the SE coast of Fife. Name derived from the Gaelic 'leargach' meaning 'steep sloping'. The land belonged to the Lundins in the 12th century and passed through marriage to Prince Robert, son of William I (1165-1214). For bravery at sea a Barony Charter was granted by James III to the celebrated Naval Commander Andrew Wood in 1482, thus enabling Largo to develop a considerable trade with Holland in coal, salt, iron and sandstone. Staying with its seafaring past, its most famous son was Alexander Selkirk (1676-1721) who accidentally acquired fame after he was shipwrecked off South America on the Island of Juan Fernandez for four years, providing Daniel Defoe with the prototype for 'Robinson Crusoe' (pub. 1719). In 1670 the land was held by the Drummonds. Among its buildings of interest are its 17th century church, incorporated in 1817 and enlarged in 1826, while the roofless ruin of Largo House, built in 1750, stands near the ruins of Sir Andrew Wood's 16th century tower. The nearby Norries Law where local tradition claims a Celtic Chief was buried, was in 1817 the scene of the discovery of Celtic silver which is now in The National Museum of Antiquities in Edinburgh. The barony, held by the Erskines in the 19th century, had an economy sustained by fishing and a flour mill but latterly Largo has become popular with tourists while still managing to retain its original character and size.

LARGS
NORTH AYRSHIRE

Coastal town situated 15 miles SW of Gourock. Name derived from the Gaelic 'Learg' meaning 'hillslope' . Once the site of an ancient fort, possibly Roman, the present town, which grew around a church dedicated to St Columba, gave its name to a battle in 1263 when Alexander III defeated King Haakon of Norway. The land, held by the Balliols until 1296, was granted by Robert the Bruce in 1314 to his son-in-law Walter Stewart, who shortly after bestowed the church on Paisley Abbey; the latter held it up until the Reformation when the church lands were made a Temporal Lordship for Lord Claud Hamilton as Lord Paisley. In 1629 the town became a Burgh of Barony for Alexander Menstrie. Following its devas-

tation by the plague in 1644, Largs witnessed a number of cases of witchcraft before lapsing into a long period of inactivity up until 1834 when its harbour opened. Though it quickly became a hub of activity with its steamboats transporting people and goods to and from Glasgow, later Largs functioned as a seaside resort for the railway-travelling public from the industrial centres in the north east. See Battle

LARGS, BATTLE OF, 1263
NORTH AYRSHIRE

Fought in the town during the Norse invasion, when the Scots led by Alexander III gained an advantage over the Norse invasion fleet of King Haakon. The damage suffered by their fleet in a storm the day before forced the Norsemen to effect an early landing which the Scots exploited to the full and secured a victory. The defeat effectively put an end to the Norwegian claim to sovereignty over Scotland's Western Isles.

LASSWADE
MIDLOTHIAN

Town situated 6´ miles SE of Edinburgh. The name is either derived from the Old English 'Loes woed' meaning 'ford on the meadow' or perhaps the Anglo Saxon 'Laeswe' and the Old English 'weyde' which jointly mean 'a well watered pasture of common use'. In the 12th century its Parish Church became a Mensal Church of the Bishop of St Andrews and in 1478 a hospital was founded here by Robert Blackadder (later Archbishop). Although the area was once the site of a Roman Camp and of Wallace's Cave, in the 13th century the chief defensive structure was the nearby Melville Castle, whose owners had strong connections with the area. However, the town acquired more fame from its literary associations during the 18th and 19th centuries, for between 1798 and 1804 Lasswade served as a rural retreat for Sir Walter Scott, who was visited here by James Hogg and William Wordsworth. And from 1840 until his death in 1859, Thomas de Quincy, author of ' Confessions of an English Opium Eater' (pub. 1821), stayed outside Lasswade at Polton. Essentially a sleepy village until the 18th century with Edinburgh and Dalkeith as the nearest Market Towns, Lasswade acquired a reputation for its paper mills, carpet factory and flour mill while its other industry, coalmining, brought it to the country's attention in 1770 when the Parish was the scene of a coalmine fire which lasted 20 years. Replacing a much older church (ruin), the Parish Church that was built in 1793, and where Henry Dundas, Viscount Melville, known as the uncrowned king of Scotland, was interred in 1811, was itself replaced by 1956.

LAUDER
SCOTTISH BORDERS

Town situated 12 miles NW of Coldstream. Name derived from the River Leader which is from the Gaelic 'dobhar' meaning 'water'. In the 12th century David I bestowed the land on Hugh de Morville and between 1175 and 1189 a Richard de Moreville founded a hospital here; the land later passed to the Douglases who held it until their fall from grace in 1455. The original Lauder Fort, now thought to be incorporated in Thirlestane Castle, was built by Edward I before 1307. In its old church (now gone), in 1482, the Scottish nobles led by the Earl of Angus resolved to murder King James III's low born favourites Roger and Cochrane who were hanged from Lauder Bridge. Claiming Royal Burgh status from the 12th century, its charter firmly comes on record in 1502 when as a Market Town with a rural economy it frequently traded its corn for lime and coal

with the merchants of Kelso and Dalkeith. The cruciform Parish Church built in 1673 by Sir William Bruce and funded by the Duke of Lauderdale was repaired in 1820 and contains a large number of sittings and a bell dating from 1683.

LAURENCEKIRK
ABERDEENSHIRE

Town situated 14 miles SW of Stonehaven. Originally called Conveth it was renamed Kirktown of Conveth when its church was dedicated to St Laurence of Canterbury in 1244, and later became Laurencekirk. The property of the Barclays in the 12th century, the land later passed to the Falconers of Haulkerston on whose estate a small hamlet was built but in 1765 it was sold to Lord Gardenstone who built a village that had become a thriving town by 1772 and a Burgh of Barony by 1779. Mainly a producer of linen, along with its cattle and grain markets it later acquired some renown for the making of snuff boxes, which, under the guidance of Charles Steven & Son, were sent by steamer to Aberdeen, Montrose and Dundee. The present Church of St Laurence was built in 1873.

LAURISTON CASTLE
CITY OF EDINBURGH

Situated 4 miles NW of Edinburgh centre. The land was purchased from the Forester family of Corstorphine by Sir Archibald Napier of Merchiston in 1587. A master of the Scottish Mint in 1576 and the father of John Napier, the inventor of logarithms, he built this oblong tower before 1608. Purchased in 1683 by William Law, an Edinburgh Goldsmith whose son John Law resided here. In 1845 it was enlarged by the then owner Lord Rutherford, but was sold to Thomas Crawfurd in 1871, before being entrusted to Edinburgh Corporation.

LAW CASTLE
NORTH AYRSHIRE

Built on an eminence overlooking the village of West Kilbride. This 15th century tower was thought to be the matrimonial home built for James III's sister on her marriage to Thomas Boyd, later Earl of Arran. In 1670 it became the property of Major Hugh Bontin.

LEADHILLS
SOUTH LANARKSHIRE

Village situated 30 miles SW of Lanark. A mining area since 1239 and probably during the Roman occupation as Roman roads and camps have been found in the vicinity. As one of the highest villages in Scotland it stands 1300 feet above sea level and on a clear day can be seen the Pentland Hills to the north, the Isle of Man to the south and the Isle of Arran to the west. After a period of slumber the village was awakened in the 16th century to the bustle of gold prospecting, some of which was of a high enough quality to be included in the Scottish Crown. As a Burgh of Barony for the Duke of Hamilton from 1661, its isolation spawned a literary legacy that began in 1686 when the poet and artist Alan Ramsay was born here the son of a mine superintendent. This continued with the village's circulating library, dating from 1741, thought to be the oldest in Britain, and in 1803 it was visited by William Wordsworth and Samuel Coleridge. At its height in 1810, its mines produced up to 1400 tons of lead, and along with their sister mine at Wanlockhead Village were considered the richest in the country. Although it continued to thrive under the Lead Hills Mining Co from 1861, the industry declined after the 1914-18 war.

LEITH
CITY OF EDINBURGH

Seaport situated on the Firth of Forth.

Once called Inverleith from the Gaelic 'inbhir' and 'liath' meaning 'mouth of the grey river'. The land belonged to Holyrood Abbey in the 12th century but in 1329 Edinburgh obtained a grant of its port and mills in a charter from Robert I, while south Leith was held by the Logans of Restalrig. After the burning of its harbour by the English in 1313 and 1410, which was the scene of the arrival of James I and his Queen, 1423, the King introduced a harbour toll in 1428 for its reconstruction. In 1449 Mary of Guelders disembarked here, as did Margaret of Denmark in 1469. Constantly engaged in a trade war with Edinburgh Council, in 1485 it was decreed that 'No merchant of Edinburgh presume to take into partnership any indweller of the town of Leith under pain of forty pounds to the Kirkwark and to be deprived of the freedom of the city for ane zear'. Burnt by the Earl of Hertford, 1544, and again by the Duke of Somerset, 1547. Although held by the Lords of the Congregation in 1559, it was the scene of the celebrated arrival of Mary Queen of Scots in 1561, which occasioned the verse:

There rode the Lords of France and Spain,
of England Flanders and Lorraine;
While serried round them thousands stood,
From the shore of Leith to Holyrood.

In 1589 Ann of Denmark arrived here after her marriage in Norway to Mary's son James VI. Notwithstanding Leith's obvious prosperity as the main fish market on the Firth of Forth by 1584, leading to its creation as a Parish in 1609 and a Burgh of Barony in 1636 with Edinburgh as superior, within fifteen years it had subscribed to The Solemn League & Covenant; and in 1643 it was ravaged by famine and the plague, when half the population died, many of whom were buried in Leith Links. The port was occupied by Cromwell's forces under General

Monck, 1650, who built Leith Citadel to secure his supply line. Its continued function as Edinburgh's sole trade link with Continental ports and the wider world was reaffirmed in 1698 when it became the departure point for the Darien Expedition, which came to be looked on as Scotland's first attempt at empire building. On its 1500 men and 5 frigates were pinned the hopes of the Leith and Edinburgh merchants, who greatly suffered from its subsequent failure. The scene of much piracy and treason in the 18th century; in 1715 its Citadel was held by the Jacobites who robbed its Customs House and though a mutiny of the Seaforth Highlanders in 1778 was resolved without bloodshed, during a later mutiny in 1799 twelve Highlanders were killed and twenty wounded. In 1764 Leith was the birthplace of Sir John Gladstone (merchant) whose son William was to acquire some political fame when he became Prime Minister in 1868. The founding of Leith Bank in 1792 reflected the confidence of the Leith merchants and served as a milestone for the port's 19th century prosperity, which was well under way when Queen Victoria and Prince Albert landed here in 1842. Displaying all the trappings of a port Leith became the haunt of the writer Robert Louis Stevenson (1850-94) who scorned the hypocrisy of middle class Edinburgh and warmed to the character and honesty of the burghers of Leith, with their bohemian attributes. A Parliamentary Burgh in 1833, to handle the increasing volume of trade in subsequent decades its port facilities were considerably upgraded, starting with the opening of the Victoria Dock in 1852, followed by the Albert Dock in 1869, the Edinburgh Dock in 1881 and the Imperial Dock in 1910. Continuing to grow unabated, its industrial prosperity in the 1880s was such that it boasted a large number of shipyards, sawmills, flouremills, engi-

neering works, breweries and distilleries, making it one of the premier trading ports on Scotland's eastern seaboard by the 20th century prior to its amalgamation with Edinburgh in 1920. The port made a positive contribution during both world wars when it was slightly bombed by a Zeppelin in 1916 and by a plane in 1940. Its prosperity declined after 1945 and finally containerisation sealed Leith's fate as a bustling port. As one would expect, Leith retains some architectural gems that reflect the port's golden age. The Sailors' Home by the shore was built in 1883 in the Scottish Baronial style with accommodation for up to 115 men. Built in 1817 in a classical style, Trinity House, which now stands off the Kirkgate, was originally founded as a seaman's charity, possibly around 1380, and later sought to promote safety measures at sea and in harbour. On Commercial St, the Customs House, built in 1812 in a Grecian style, is adorned in front with two fluted pillars that support a pediment and flank the doorway, which is accessed by a central platform with balustrade and steps on either side. The Court House or Town Hall (now a Police Station) off Constitution Street was built in 1827 to a classical design for a relatively small sum of £3,300. Among its more individual buildings is the Corn Exchange in Baltic Street built in a Romanesque style in 1862 with a distinguished octagonal tower.

LENNOX CASTLE
CITY OF EDINBURGH

Near the village of Currie on the outskirts of the Capital is a 15th century tower built by the Earls of Lennox and the occasional residence of Queen Mary and the Regent Morton in the 16th century. It was the favourite hunting seat of James VI who is said to have granted it to his Goldsmith George Heriot, the founder of Edinburgh's George Heriots School . Also known as Lymphoy, the castle is now a ruin.

LENNOXLOVE TOWER
EAST LOTHIAN

Built about 1´ miles S of Haddington on land that was originally called Lethington. From 1345 the land belonged to the Maitlands, who played a leading role in the affairs of state while building the 15th century L plan tower as the family seat. The birthplace of John Maitland (1616-1682), who was Commissioner of the Solemn League and Covenant 1643-46 and was imprisoned by Cromwell after the battle of Worcester, 1651, becoming Secretary for Scottish Affairs (1660-80) on his release. In the 18th century it passed to Lord Blantyre who made some additions and renamed it Lennoxlove in honour of the Duchess who assisted in its purchase. The castle is presently the home of the Duke and Duchess of Hamilton and houses some interesting works of art.

LERWICK
SHETLAND

Seaport and capital of Shetland situated 27 miles NE of Sunburgh. Once occupied by the Picts and then the Vikings, the name is derived from the Scandinavian 'Leir-vik' meaning 'mud bay'. Other than being the scene of the assembly of King Haakon's fleet before the battle of Largs in 1263, its geographical position frequently left it a distant observer of many of the country's historical milestones. In 1470 however, it become a Crown possession after Orkney and Shetland were ceded to Scotland by Norway, as part of Princess Margaret's dowry on her marriage to James III. And by an Act of Parliament in 1625, the town was partly destroyed after greatly aiding the Dutch Herring fishermen. In keeping with its

seafaring history, its bay, often visited by naval forces, was the scene of a battle between ten Spanish and four Dutch ships in 1640, provided safe anchorage for a fleet of Commonwealth ships during Cromwell's occupation in 1653 and was used as a supply point during the building of Fort Charlotte, 1665, to repel a Dutch assault. Despite this, within ten years it witnessed the burning of the fort and town, 1673. Rebuilt and redesigned along with much of the present town, on its completion in 1781 it was used as a naval base which became a base for the Royal Naval Reserves in the 19th century. In 1778 the bay was visited by the American Pirate John Paul Jones who was said to have been frightened away after confusing the red petticoats of the women going to market with English soldiers. From 1818, when the town was created a Burgh of Barony for its citizens, until the 1920s the burgh boundary covered roughly half a square mile, but in 1938 it expanded to accommodate its growing herring fishing industry and was extended again in 1965 before the oil boom of the 1970s. The festival of 'Up Helly Aa' is a Viking fire festival which takes place on the last Tuesday in January to mark the end of the holy days (Yule tide) and the return of the sun six months hence.

LESLIE
FIFE

Village situated 10 miles NW of Kirkcaldy. Originally called 'Fetty kil', the area was once fought over by the Caledonians and the Romans for the Passage of Leven and later became a popular royal hunting ground. In 1283 the Norman de Leslie family obtained the lands from Alexander III and its name changed. Leslie Green was erected into a Burgh of Barony in 1457 for George Leslie of Rothes, whose descendant, the Ist Duke of Rothes and Lord Chancellor of Scotland, built Leslie House in the 17th century, which, following a fire in 1763, was rebuilt as a dwelling house and later became a residential home. Supported by its flax spinning works, paper mills, bleachfields and annual fairs, for a long period Leslie had strong trade links with the Market Towns of Cupar and Kirkcaldy, but the decline of its wool and tweed production by the 1950s left its Jute Mills and Fettykill paper mill forming its industrial base.

LESLIE CASTLE
ABERDEENSHIRE

It stands by the Gadie burn 3 miles NW of Insch. Land belonged to the Leslies from the 12th century, when it was occupied by a timber fort with moat and drawbridge. After passing to John Forbes through marriage, today's L plan castellated mansion was built by his son William in 1661. Acquired by the Leiths of Leithhall in the 18th century. The castle is now in a well preserved state.

LESMAHAGOW
SOUTH LANARKSHIRE

Town situated 20 miles SE of Glasgow. Its name may derive from the Gaelic 'leas' meaning 'enclosure, garden' and St Machute who may have built a church here in the 6th century. The priory founded here in 1144 by David I for Tironesian Benedictines as a dependency of Kelso Abbey was richly endowed by Robert I and William I before being burnt by an English invasion force led by John of Eltham (brother of Edward III), for which the King killed him at Perth. Burnt again, at the Reformation, 1560, when, along with Kelso Abbey, it passed into secular hands, being conferred on the Earl of Roxburgh and later the Marquis of Hamilton, 1623. The Priory Church served as a Parish Church until 1803 when the present church was built. Fig-

uring again in future conflicts, when many of the town's menfolk died at Bothwell Brig, 1679, while in support of the Covenant, it was the scene of the arrest of Colonel Rumbold, a chief conspirator in the Rye House Plot (attempted assassination of Charles II) in 1685, and in 1745 of Macdonald of Kinloch Moidart the Aide-de-camp to Prince Charles Edward. See Craignethan Castle

LETHENDY TOWER
PERTH & KINROSS

On the bank of the Tay 4 miles SE of Blairgowrie is the Herrons L plan house which bears the date 1678, although it is thought to pre-date the introduction of artillery a century earlier. The building is now close to a mansion house built in the 19th century.

LEUCHARS
FIFE

Village situated 8 miles NE of Cupar. Originally called Loughyards owing to its low and level ground the present name is from the Gaelic 'Luachair' meaning either 'rushes' or 'marshy flat'. The land once belonged to the Earls of Southesk and the Bruces of Earlshall, but the original Castle of Leuchars (now gone) was once the stronghold of a Celtic Chief and was later rebuilt as the seat of the DeQuincies before being demolished by the Earl of Pembroke in the year 1327. Leuchars main building of interest is its 12th century Norman Church, which was built by Seyer De Quinci and incorporates a 17th century tower and belfry. For generations the chief trade here was weaving, which was later expanded to supply export markets in America and the West Indies through the merchants of Dundee and Cupar. From World War II an RAF airfield has operated from here and today provides a civilian rescue service. See Earlshall Castle

LEVELLERS' RISING 1724

In late 17th century Galloway, the wide open expanse of farmland was increasingly being encroached upon by the cattle being taken from place to place by drovers seeking to capitalise on the quality cross breeds that resulted from the initiative of Lord Basil Hamilton, who imported scores of cows from Ireland to supply the English market. In Galloway, conflicts between farmers and drovers became inevitable, forcing commissioners to fence off roadsides and thereby increase the distance for travellers, cattle herders and shepherds, while affecting the runrig system of cultivation and common pasturage. Coupled to this were the wider land reforms taking place as small crofters became part of larger farms. Though generally accepted by the 18th century, bands of Levellers emerged who scoured the countryside at night tearing down fences led by the celebrated Billy Marshall, an army deserter from the royal family of gypsies. Frequent riots ensued and at Culquha in the Stewartry the Levellers were defeated by soldiers under the sheriff bringing the death of some and the imprisonment of 200, while others were banished to the plantations. So high was the general feeling that it evoked the following rhyme:

Against the poor the lairds prevail in all their wicked works,
Who will enclose both hill and dale and turn cornfields to parks.
The lords and lairds they drive us out
From mailings where we dwell ;
The poor man cries, where shall we go?
The rich say go to hell .

LEVEN
FIFE

Seaport town situated 12 miles NE of Kirkcaldy at the mouth of the River Leven which may take its name from the Gaelic 'leamhan' meaning 'elmwood' or from the Gaelic 'lean' meaning a 'swampy place'. With its natural harbour and its river, a rich source of food, it was probably the site of a settlement from an early period but later became part of the Durie family estate until 1554 and by 1614 was the property of Sir Alexander Gibson, Lord President of the Court of Session. On becoming a Burgh of Barony for Lauder of the Bass in 1609 Leven began to thrive as a Market Town and port and by 1641 it gave the title of Earl of Leven to the Covenanting General Leslie. The town continued to prosper in future decades under successive landowners as the only Market Town in the area. In 1867 it was made a Police Burgh with harbour developments by 1876 so that despite the lessening of trade with the building of new docks at Methil in 1890, it still imported steady amounts of flax, barley, timber and pig iron, some of which supported its main industry, flax spinning, which has all but disappeared.

LEVEN CASTLE
INVERCLYDE

By the River Clyde near Gourock. The castle was developed from the usual 16th century L plan keep built by the Mortons, who held it until 1547 when it passed to the Sempills, who remodelled it. By the 18th century it was the property of the Shaw Stewarts and is now completely intact.

LICKLAYHEADS CASTLE
ABERDEENSHIRE

Positioned at the base of Glenochie near Oyne. This was formerly the seat of the Leiths but was acquired by the Forbeses of Leslie and built in 1629 to an L plan design. In the 18th century it passed to the Duff family, by whom it was extended, but it became the property of the Lumbsdens in the 19th century.

LINCLUDEN ABBEY
DUMFRIES & GALLOWAY

At the junction of the Cluden Water and the River Nith 1 mile N of Dumfries was the site chosen in the 12th century by Uchtred, son of Fergus Lord of Galloway, for a Benedictine Nunnery. In 1296 the Prioress swore fealty to Edward I and within a hundred years the house was suppressed on the petition of Archibald Douglas Lord of Galloway who was patron of the priory. According to some sources this was either on account of their irregularities, insolence or for financial expediency. Nevertheless the Earl showed his allegiance by building a Collegiate Church with a Provost and twelve canons. Building work continued into the 15th century and included richly decorated architecture with ribbed arch-work and the customary armorial bearings of its founders who were both buried here. So fine was its architectural attributes that it became a favourite residence of the Douglases, Wardens of the West Marches, moving William 8th Earl to hold a parliament here for local chiefs to help improve border warfare tactics. Although probably the scene of some interesting events due to its closeness to the border, the building is distinguished for its connections with historical figures like Robert III whose daughter Margaret, and wife of the Earl of Douglas, was buried here. Among its Provosts in the 15th century are included John Cameron who became Lord Privy Seal, and Chancellor of the Kingdom; John Methven who became Secretary of State and Ambassador of the Court; and James Lindsay who was Keeper of the Privy Seal and Ambassador to England. Gradually falling into decline after the Reformation, today's ruins include the south transept, part of the choir and sacristy, much of the north range, the distinctive Princess Margaret's tomb and a former moat in the grounds.

LINDORES
FIFE

Village situated 2 miles SE of Newburgh. Name derived from the Gaelic 'linn' meaning 'pool loch' and 'dorus' which translated means 'at the opening' which no doubt comes from the nearby loch of the the same name. The land was anciently held by the Macduffs, Thanes of Fife, and in 1800 revealed traces of their castle. Nearby, William Wallace's forces defeated the Earl of Pembroke in 1298. Its Abbey, around which the village developed, was founded in 1191 by David, Earl of Huntingdon, and was at the centre of its affairs up until the Reformation, 1560, after which, along with the land, it was erected into a Lordship for Sir Patrick Leslie in 1600. Some of the present village was undoubtedly built with the stone from the Abbey ruins. See Abbey

LINDORES ABBEY
FIFE

To the east of Newburgh are the scant ruins of a once prosperous Abbey and centre of activity for the area. Founded in 1191 by David Earl of Huntingdon, the grandson of the pious David I, it was built in an English Gothic style with a cruciform church to the north side of the cloisters and domestic buildings on the other three sides. Through the thrift of its Benedictine monks it grew gradually in size and riches with its abbots attending to their prominent positions in the Catholic Church when not receiving guests like Edward I, 1291, John Balliol, 1294, William Wallace, 1298, and David II. It was here that the rebellious James, 9th Earl of Douglas retired after spending thirty years opposing the rule of James II and James III. A regality for the Abbot by 1510 and frequently attacked by parties from Dundee in 1543. Following the monks expulsion at the Reformation John

Knox wrote "they were all reformed, their mass books and missals burnt as well as their idols and vestments of idolatry". In 1600 Sir Patrick Leslie was made Lord Lindores. The measure of its destruction can be seen around the groined arch of the porch which formed the entrance to the Abbey through the cloister court and part of the tower.

LINKWOOD DISTILLERY
MORAY

A secluded leafy corner of the Highlands and a pretty dam outside Elgin provides the backdrop for one of Speyside's oldest distilleries. Started in 1825 by the factor of the Seafield Estates, Peter Brown, who among other things improved the productivity of his land, and provided the the final link in the agrarian cycle with his barley used in whisky and its draff by-product used to feed cattle. In 1825, Customs & Excise records show Linkwood produced 1000 gallons (4,500 litres) from two stills. Influenced by the proposed North of Scotland Railway line linking Elgin to Aberdeen (built, 1875), following his father's death in 1869, William Brown Junior built new premises in 1873 that were mentioned in a local journal as being "conveniently planned, with enduring qualities and a fine appearance". Weathering the slump in the 1880s and Mr Brown's death in 1893, as the Linkwood Glenlivet Co it was floated in 1897, and the premises enlarged, doubling its capacity at a time when a good price was to be had in the markets of the south. The company's success between 1902-32 under Innes Cameron, an Elgin whisky broker, later made it an important part of Scottish Malt Distillers, and continued under another remarkable figure, Roderick Mackenzie, who became manager following its re-opening in 1945. Mackenzie's near obsession with maintaining its uniqueness, arguing that the basic character of a malt is determined by the vessels and the immediate environment, sometimes objecting to the removal of cobwebs, helped preserve its quality through to the re-development's in 1962, which he oversaw before his retirement. After proving inadequate by 1971, a new distillery was built to satisfy the upsurge in demand of whisky blenders.

OWNERS
Diageo plc ?

REGION
Speyside

PRODUCT
Linkwood 12 year old single malt 43% vol

NOTES
A slightly smokey nose with a palate that is full-bodied with a hint of sweetness.

LINLITHGOW
WEST LOTHIAN

Town situated 20 miles W of Edinburgh. Name derived from the Brythonic 'llyn llyth cau' meaning 'lake of the broad hollow'. This is at variance with some claims that the name is Gaelic for 'lake of the Grey Dog', owing to the town's armorial bearings showing a dog tied to a tree in a loch with the inscription 'My Fruit is my fidelity To God And the King'. Once the site of a Roman Station followed by a castle, it was around the latter and the 15th century Linlithgow Palace that the town developed. With their preceptory at nearby Torphichen from the 12th century much of the land was occupied by the Knights of St John who lived under the wing of the Royal Court. This did inevitably brought the town Royal Burgh status in 1138 and a chapel founded by David I (1124-53), followed by a Carmelite religious house established by the inhabitants in 1290. Subsequent to this the town swore fealty to Edward I, 1298 when his army encamped here before defeating William Wallace at Falkirk, was the site of a castle built by the King in 1302, north east of the Palace, and witnessed their ejection in 1313, resulting in the town and castle being traded by John Balliol to Edward III, 1334 in a bid to gain some support for his usurpation of David II. The townspeople developed an executive body with parliamentary representation in 1367 and membership of The Four Courts of Burghs in 1369, when it was the second richest burgh in the kingdom, with its palace, one of the main royal residences, and its castle facilitating events of national importance from the 14th to the 19th century. During the Regency of Albany the town was burnt in 1411 and in 1424, prior to the building of the present palace in 1425. At Linlithgow Bridge in 1526 the Earl of Lennox was killed by the Earl of Angus while trying to free the young James V, and at the Reformation, 1560, John Knox and his followers descended on the town and burnt its religious buildings. While Regent to the infant James VI in 1570, James Stewart, Earl of Moray was murdered here by Hamilton of Bothwellhaugh. Its once vibrant trade, which arose from its charter rights along the coast, failed to recover after the Reformation and in 1599 it was raised to an Earldom for Alexander 7th Lord Livingstone. Amidst the uncertainty of the 17th century the burgh was often used as a place of refuge, for in 1606 and 1608 the Linlithgow Convention was held here when the Presbyterian Church curbed the powers of Episcopacy, during the Covenanting War, 1637 the Privy Council and Law Courts assembled here and while the plague was raging in Edinburgh in 1646, the University moved here. For losses incurred during Cromwell's occupation in 1651, the burghers received funds from Charles II which went to build the original Town Hall in 1670 to designs by John Mylne (King's Master Mason). Occupied by the Jaco-

bites during the 1745 Rising and by the Hanoverians after their defeat at Falkirk in 1746, when the palace suffered a fire. Despite the rise of neighbouring towns its commerce had recovered by 1724 when during Defoe's journeys through Scotland it was described as 'having a good face of business'. Further expansion in trade during the Industrial Age making it a supplier of shoes, whisky, linen, glue and agricultural produce owed much to the building of the Union Canal in 1818-22 (closed, 1965) and its central location, raising it to sixth in order of Scottish Burghs in 1856. Also benefiting from the through trade from Scotland's principal towns and cities, in 1914 it was visited by Queen Mary, followed by Winston Churchill in 1945 and Queen Elizabeth in 1955, but in 1975 its autonomy was undermined by the abolition of the County Councils and their replacement by regional bodies that were based in the principal cities. Started in 1541, the Festival of Common Riding, held on the first Tuesday after the second Thursday in June involves the menfolk marking the town's boundaries by riding the marches to commemorate the time when common land had to be distinguished from Crown land. After the 17th century West Port House, built by the Hamiltons of Westport, the next object of interest is the Cross Well. Possibly dating from 1538 but later repaired, it is remembered in the old adage 'Glasgow for bells, Lithgow for wells', when the town was celebrated for its water. See Palace

LINLITHGOW PALACE
WEST LOTHIAN

On the southern shore of Linlithgow Loch is a promontory which has provided a secure position for habitation from earliest times. With traces of a Roman presence, by the 12th century it was the site of a church and a royal manor house that was incorporated into a pele tower by Edward I in 1302 but was retaken by William Wallace in 1303 and later served as a residence of Scottish Kings. Following much construction work it was destroyed along with the church by a fire in 1424 which in turn gave rise to the structure of today, started in 1425 by James I (1406-37) and continued by James II (1437-60) until the completion of the south west corner. A popular place for James III (1460-1488) and his Queen; he greatly added to the surrounding grounds. The north side may be attributed to the reign of James IV (1488-1513). It was the King's absence at the battle of Flodden and the distress of his Queen, Margaret Tudor, (daughter of Henry VII of England) that Sir Walter Scott was to give expression in his poem 'Marmion':

His Queen Margaret who in Lithgow's bower
All lonely sat and wept the weary hour.
The Queen sits lone in Lithgow pile,
And weeps the weary day,
The war against her native soil,
Her monarch's risk in battle broil:

However, it was the reconstruction work of James IV and of James V, who was born here in 1512, that established it as the well embellished symmetrical structure. Their labours were rewarded when in 1538 James V's Queen Mary of Guise declared she had never seen a more princely palace, and in 1542 their daughter Mary was born here. During a visit by James VI in 1617, he was so moved by its ruinous north side that he ordered reconstruction work that included sleeping accommodation and banqueting hall, with Renaissance fireplaces, above which was the parliament hall. Its similarities to Heriot's Hospital suggest it was the work of William Wallace, who was the King's Master Mason in 1620. The removal of the Royal Court to London left it entrusted to the Earls of Livingstone, when its walls periodically bore witness to the affairs of state. In 1646 when Edinburgh was infected by the plague it housed the Scottish Parliament, in 1651 and 1659 it was occupied by Cromwell, who dated some of his letters from here, and in 1745, while in the care of Mrs Glen Gordon, a staunch Jacobite, Prince Charles Edward visited here. Its next visitors were General Hawley's Dragoons in 1746, when either by accident or design it was set on fire and left in the state we find it today. St Michael's Church, adjoining the palace and consecrated by Bishop Birnham of St Andrews between 1240 and 1249, is a fine example of a Medieval Parish Church built in a Scottish Decorated, style and is predominantly 15th century. According to some sources (Buchanan, historian) it was here before St Catherine's altar that James IV had an apparition warning of his impending death at Flodden, 1513. Visited by James V 1528-36, after suffering damage at the Reformation, 1559 and by Cromwell who used it as a stable, it was repaired after the Education Act of 1646 and used by Edinburgh University to house classes. Restored in the 19th century when its crown tower was removed (1812). In the 20th century Linlithgow was visited by King George and Queen Mary, 1914 and by Queen Elizabeth and the Duke of Edinburgh in 1955. The First World War memorial was built by Chalmers while its aluminium crown by Geoffrey Clarke was added in 1964.

LITTLE DEAN TOWER
SCOTTISH BORDERS

Above the Tweed 2 miles E of St Boswells is a ruined tower of the Kers of Cessford. Probably built in the 16th century in the shape of a D, its north side, which rises on the right bank of the Tweed, gave it protection from the north while a nearby ravine gave it a similar defence from the east side. Two storeys high, as one would expect its walls, which are six foot thick, contain shot holes.

LIVINGSTONE
WEST LOTHIAN

Town situated 15 miles SW of Edinburgh. Name derived from 'Levings tun' (town) after an Englishman or Fleming who settled here in the 12th century and whose descendant James Livingstone of Callander, was ennobled Lord Livingstone by James II in 1455. The church around which the original village of Kirkton grew was granted by David I to Holyrood Abbey in the 12th century. Although lacking its own objects of interest, one mile east of the village stood the peel tower of Linlithgow which was defended by an earthen rampart and fosse and garrisoned by Edward I in 1302, while one mile north east of the village was the site of a tower down to the 18th century which was thought to have been a royal hunting seat. In 1670 Sir Patrick Murray of Livingstone, the most promising botanist of his time, left a large selection of plants, which helped stock Edinburgh's first Botanic Gardens (Old Physic Gardens). Livingstone Parish, which once included Whitburn, was disjoined in 1730, while its barony was purchased by the Earl of Rosebery in 1812. Notwithstanding its erection into a Burgh of Barony for the Earl of Linlithgow in 1604, it remained a sleepy village until the 18th / 19th century when, through its roads and rail links, the town enjoyed over a century of industrial growth, when the area's coal shale and lime reserves found ready markets in Glasgow and Edinburgh. The decline of its mining, and population growth in Glasgow after 1950 led to the building of the New Town in the 1960s which later adapted to the technological revolution as well as Old Livingstone embraced the Industrial Revolution.

LOCH-AN-EILEAN CASTLE
HIGHLAND

Isolated on a small islet 3 miles E of Aviemore are the remains of a fortalice once held by the Wolf of Badenoch, the unruly son of Robert II, who burnt Elgin Cathedral and town in 1390. Its walls once surrounded the whole island and incorporated a square tower but now provide a sanctuary for birds.

LOCH DOON CASTLE
EAST AYRSHIRE

The castle stands on a small rocky islet surrounded by Loch Doon just S of Dallmellington. A ruined courtyard structure, it was started in the 13th century by the Bruces, Lords of Carrick. After Robert the Bruce's defeat at Methven, 1306, it was occupied by the English, who despite fortifying it with a gateway which contained a portcullis, were ejected when it was retaken and held by the supporters of David II, Bruce's heir when Scotland was controlled by Balliol in the 14th century. Figuring in the feuds between the Kennedys and the Crawfords, in 1510 it was reported to have been destroyed by fire during James V's attempts to subdue the feuding barons, but shortly after, further additions were made.

LOCHINDORB CASTLE
HIGHLAND

The remains of the Comyns, Lords of Badenochs' 13th century courtyard castle are sited on an island 7 miles NW of Grantown. In 1303 Edward I stayed here for a month during his incursion into Badenoch, and received the submission of the northern barons. The extended English occupation led to its enlargement with an outer wall which prevented the Scots gaining a foothold. Despite a seven month siege by the Regent Andrew Murray between 1335 and 1336, when it was held for the Duke of Atholl (vassal of Edward III), Murray was forced to lift the blockade owing to the approach of King Edward's forces. In 1372 it became a stronghold of Robert II's son "The Wolf of Badenoch". Although strengthened by Archibald Douglas in 1455, it was destroyed by order of James II in 1456 after the Douglas's fall. In the 19th century it belonged to the Earl of Seafield.

LOCH LEVEN CASTLE
PERTH & KINROSS

On an island in Lochleven W of Glenrothes are the substantial remains of a courtyard keep probably from the 13th century. Held for David II by an Alan de Vipont against John de Strivilin (a vassal of Edward Balliol) before the land and loch were acquired in 1353 by Sir Robert Douglas. His descendants used it to imprison Mary Queen of Scots on 17th June 1567, and with their allies the Confederate Lords forced her to sign her abdication in favour of her infant son James VI. On the 2nd May 1568 the Queen effected her escape with the help of the young Willie Douglas, who stole the keys while Sir Robert Douglas was sleeping. These were later found in the loch in the 19th century. An additional four-storey round tower with six foot thick walls was built in the 16th century, when the castle was again used as a prison, this time for the Earl of Northumberland (1569), after his failed rebellion and prior to his trial and execution in London. After a period of neglect, in 1840 the courtyard was cleared of accumulated rubbish and weeds, giving ready access to all parts of the castle. Its garden was later cultivated and the surrounding land planted with trees.

LOCHMABEN
DUMFRIES & GALLOWAY

Town situated 10 miles NE of Dumfries. The name is either Gaelic for 'loch of the maidens' due to an ancient nunnery on one of the nearby lochs, or from 'Maponos' meaning 'the sun God of the Ancient Britons'. With traces of British and Roman Forts in the area it was probably the site of an early settlement that later grew up around its 12th century castle, the ancestral home of the Bruces. The granting of its oldest charter by the Crown in 1296 helped facilitate its eclipse of Annan as the main Burgh of the Bruces Lords of Annandale and as such, with a castle and its proximity to the border, it suffered severely down the centuries when many of its records were lost. It was occupied by the English from 1298 until their ejection in 1384 by the Douglases, who held it until their attainder in 1455. As part of the agricultural supply line to Dumfries, the town was burnt by the Earl of Warrick in 1463 but resisted an attack by the dejected Earl of Douglas and the Duke of Albany in 1484 (battle of Lochmaben). The charter granted by James VI in 1612 ratifying previous charters made Lochmaben a Parliamentary Burgh which was later bestowed on John Murray Earl of Annandale in 1625 as Lord Lochmaben. In 1745, the Jacobites, heading for Dumfries, marched through here and though the year also saw the restoration of its Town Hall with steeple and clocktower added, much of today's town was built during later decades in the 18th and in the 19th centuries with the profits from its considerable trade in linen and permian red sandstone. See Castle

LOCHMABEN CASTLE
DUMFRIES & GALLOWAY

Standing on a peninsula at the S end of the Loch, 1 mile SE of the town is the ancestral residence of the Bruces, who were granted the land by David I in 1124 when the earlier castle was built. Essentially a 13th century parallelogram structure it was once surrounded by a moat with reinforced drawbridge. In 1295 Robert the Bruce's grandfather, the Competitor to the throne, died here. Its commanding position at the entrance to south west Scotland gave it a strategic importance that made it an important prize for Edward I in 1298 when it was strengthened, and while a Competitor for the Scottish Crown (1304) a place of sanctuary for Robert the Bruce, who subsequently bestowed it on Randolph the Earl of Moray. While constantly finding its fate decided by the pendulum of Anglo-Scottish politics, the lands and castle were handed over to Edward III by his vassal Edward Balliol, then retaken in 1346 by David II and held until occupied again by the English, who after raiding the Douglas lands were besieged, captured and effectively expelled from Annandale by the Earl of Douglas. However, it became a royal castle after the fall of the Douglases in 1455, for between 1503 and 1506 James IV made repairs and improvements which included a large hall. In 1565 during the suppression of the rebellion against her marriage to Lord Darnley, Queen Mary visited Lochmaben, then in the keeping of the Maxwells, whose subsequent quarrel with her son James VI led to a two day siege before it surrendered to the Crown. Passing to the Murrays in 1612, who later became Earls of Annandale, by the 18th century the castle was abandoned.

LOCHNAW CASTLE
DUMFRIES & GALLOWAY

Overlooking the White Loch 5 miles W of Stranraer are the remains of a 16th century tower incorporating 15th century work with 17th and 18th century ranges. The land and castle once belonged to the Agnew family, who were hereditary Sheriffs of Galloway from 1330 to 1747. During this time they were briefly expelled from the area when Archibald the Grim besieged and burnt the earlier castle in 1390. After their return in 1426, Sir Andrew Agnew built the tower for his wife Dame Anna Stewart, daughter of the Ist Earl of Galloway. Additions were made at later dates followed by further developments in 1820.

LOCH RANZA CASTLE
NORTH AYRSHIRE

Situated at the N end of the Island of Arran are the remains of a 16th century L plan structure. The site of a castle from a very early period and of a hunting seat of Scottish Kings in 1380. Although associated with the Bruces, in the late 14th and early 15th century it was held by John Menteith, Lord of Arran, who in 1433 conferred it on Sir Duncan Campbell of Lochawe, from whom the Argyll Earls are descended. Held in the 15th century by Alexander Lord Montgomery, who was an ancestor of the Earls of Eglinton, the castle figured in James IV's expedition to tame the Western Isles in 1493. A chapel was added by the Duchess of Hamilton in the 18th century, but by the 19th century the structure was a roofless ruin.

LOCHWINNOCH
RENFREWSHIRE

Town situated 10 miles SW of Paisley. The latter part of the name is either from the Gaelic 'innis' of which the genitive is innise and means 'an island' or from St Winnoc' to whom a chapel was dedicated close by. Although the area was littered with early defensive structures when Strathclyde was occupied by the Britons, it was around its church and the later Castle Semple (now gone) that the original village grew. The former became a Collegiate Church founded by John Lord

Semple in 1504, while the latter was the seat of the Semples until the 18th century. Of the mansion house which replaced it in 1735, only fragments remain. Distinguished figures in the struggles and strife of the nation: in the 13th century Robert and Thomas Semple fought for Bruce, in 1424 a John Semple helped negotiate the release of James I from England, for which he was made a Knight, 1430, John the Ist Lord Semple founded the Collegiate Church, 1504, before dying at Flodden in 1513 and his son Lord Robert Semple fought for Queen Mary at the battle of Pinkie in 1547. The castle and land was purchased in 1727 by the Macdowalls of Garthland, who greatly developed the village, which prospered from its cotton and woollen mills, supplying the merchants of Paisley but by 1808 the land was broken up and the house sold (burnt down, 1924) to a Colonel Harvey, later acquired by the Department of Agriculture. Latterly Castle Semple Loch became a popular place for curling during the winter months. Spared the status of a dormitory town for Glasgow, the area's natural setting blends well with Castle Semple Country Park and the nearby Macneil Regional Park which was opened in 1970. See Barr Castle

LOCHWOOD TOWER
DUMFRIES & GALLOWAY

The fragmentary ruins of the Johnstones' 15th century tower stand 6 miles S of Moffat. Although burnt in 1593 by the Maxwells, the Johnstones retained possession of it and in 1633 were created Lords Johnstone of Lochwood. Known for the strength of its structure and situation, it was restored and occupied until 1724.

LOGIERAIT
PERTH & KINROSS

Village situated 10 miles NW of Dunkeld on the north bank of the Tay. Name derived from the Gaelic 'lag-an-rath' meaning 'hollow of the circular fort'. Once the site of a castle and hunting seat used by Robert III. In 1671 it was created a Burgh of Regality for the Earl of Atholl and for a long time the place was the seat of the Earl of Atholl's Regality Courts which wielded despotic power over its wide jurisdiction. Another part of the aparatus of feudal justice is the site outside the village where a farmhouse once stood and known as 'Clais an deoir' meaning 'the place of weeping' was where in times past the bodies of the accused were handed over to their families. One of the village's more famous sons was Adam Ferguson (1723-1816), Professor of Moral Philosophy at Edinburgh University and author of 'Principles of Moral and Political Science'.

LONGMORN DISTILLERY
MORAY

In 1894, a year after forming the Longmoran Distillery Co Ltd with Charles Shirres and George Thomson, John Duff built the distillery SE of Elgin on the Longmorn Farm, on the site of an ancient chapel dedicated to Saint Marnoch, from whom its name is derived. A distiller of some experience, Duff saw the potential of the site, with local springs and ready supply of peat from the Mannoch Hills, and a nearby railway station with links to four points of the compass. Building Benriach Distillery nearby, Duff failed to see the shrinking market and the coming recession, forcing the transference of the distillery into public ownership in 1897.

In 1914 the management was taken over by J R Grant, whose family, the famous Longmorn Grants, were linked to the company until 1979. The same building that Duff erected houses the distillery of today, where the malting process produces that distinctive character that is much sought after by blenders and connoisseurs alike.

OWNERS
Chivas Brothers Ltd ?

REGION
Speyside

PRODUCT
Longmorn 15 year old single malt 43% vol

NOTES
A rich aroma and delicate fragrance with a complex balance of floral flavours and sweetness.

LORDSCAIRNIE TOWER
FIFE

This simple ruined L plan courtyard keep stands on level ground surrounded by hills 3 miles NW of Cupar. Built in the mid 15th century by Alexander Lindsay, 4th Earl of Crawford, known as " Earl Beardie " or " Tiger Earl " owing to his fierce personal appearance and disposition. The Great Hall was later fitted out and used as a church by a Minister of Monzie when he was ejected from the Parish Church at the Reformation, 1560. Despite falling into decay it has resisted climatic forces and human attempts to pull it down.

LOUDOUN HILL, BATTLE OF, 1307
SOUTH AYRSHIRE

To the E of Darvel. One of the early victories of Robert the Bruce during the Wars of Independence. His opponent was the Earl of Pembroke whose forces included John, 2nd Baron of Hastings and claimant to the Scottish throne through his grandmother, daughter of David Ist. The near-miraculous defeat of 3,000 English by 600 Scots owed everything to the square formation of the spearmen, who repelled the attack by heavily armed cavalry.

LUFFNESS HOUSE
EAST LOTHIAN

Commanding a view over Aberlady Bay is the Luffness Mansion House. Originally occupied by a fort built in 1549 by a French General named Des Thermes to prevent the landing of provisions for the English garrison at Haddington. In the 14th century the land belonged to the Bickerton family before passing to the Hepburns, who built this T plan mansion house in 1584, incorporating the original tower. In 1739 the estate was bought by the Ist Earl of Hopetoun, who, like his great grandson John, 5th Earl, in the 19th century made further additions.

LUMPHANNAN
ABERDEENSHIRE

Village situated 25 miles SW of Aberdeen. Its name is derived from the Gaelic 'lann' meaning 'church' and 'Finain' after St Finain. Made famous as the site of Macbeth's Cairn, 1 mile north of the church, where in 1057 Macbeth was defeated and slain by Malcolm Canmore. The one time timber castle named Peel Bog may have been where Macbeth made his last stand but it was where Edward I received the submission of Sir John de Malaville in 1296 after his victory at Dunbar. Of the stone castle which replaced it around 1400, little remains. As part of the Barony of Oniel in the 13th century, the land was held by the Durwards, who were patrons' of its church, but in 1487 the village was granted by James III to Thomas Charteris of Kinfauns, and later figured in James VI's witch trials, 1596-97. See Battle

LUMPHANNAN, BATTLE OF, 1057
ABERDEENSHIRE

South of Alford. The murder of Duncan I at Dunsinane by the usurper Macbeth, Mormear of Moray, provoked the defeat of Macbeth in Cumbria by Siward, Malcolm III's uncle. While giving Malcolm control of Cumbria, the Crown of Scotland was not secured until Malcolm defeated, pursued and killed Macbeth at Lumphannan in Strathbogy. The Macbeth of Shakespeare was taken from Holinshead's Chronicle of Scotland which originally came from Wyntoun's Chronicles.

LUNCARTY, BATTLE OF, 993
PERTH & KINROSS

Located near the village north of Perth. According to Boece, after the invasion by the Danes of the coast of Angus around 990, Kenneth II marched from Stirling with a quickly assembled force. Despite the Danes' formidable onslaught, the Scots rallied and launched a counter attack with reinforcements led by the Hays, resulting in the rout of the invaders. The rewards for the valour shown by the Hay family on that day gave rise to the Hays of Errol dynasty.

LUSS
ARGYLL & BUTE

Village situated on the west side of Loch Lomond 10 miles NE of Helensburgh. The name is derived from the Gaelic word 'lus' meaning 'herb plant'. Renowned for its picturesque beauty and wild shrubbery, the area was originally associated with the 6th century missionary St Kessog, who later suffered martyrdom and is remembered in the nearby Parish Church. At the beginning of the 12th century the Earl of Lennox conferred the lands on the Dean of Lennox and by 1263 Luss was important enough to be plundered by the forces of King Haakon of Norway during their descent on Loch Lomond. In the 14th century it passed through marriage to the distinguished Colquhoun Family who held it down to the 19th century. Sir John Colquhoun was Lord High Chamberlain of Scotland in 1474. Once of a considerable size the Parish was reduced in the 17th century when the present village became a Burgh of Barony for Colquhoun of Luss, 1642, but by the 19th century, when much of the present village was built, it incorporated part of Inchcailloch Parish. Around 1790 the family house of Rossdhu was built to replace their earlier castle. Standing at the head of Glen Luss overlooking Loch Lomond, Luss still retains the allure of a quaint Scottish village.

M

MACALLAN DISTILLERY
MORAY

In the heart of Speyside NE of Aberlour stands the Macallan distillery that developed from a farm-steading in 1824 near the drovers road that once linked the rural north with the industrial south. In 1892 it was bought by Roderick Kemp, an Elgin merchant and owner of Taliskar Distillery on the Isle of Skye, who was eager to exploit its closeness to Inverness, with its rail links to ready markets in Scotland's growing industrial towns and cities. Drawing its water from private bore holes sunk deep into the Morayshire countryside, Macallan's quality owes much to the fact that its much smaller wash stills are matched by two spirit stills unlike other distilleries this is less than normal and of course its maturation in sherry oak casks from Spain. This process ensured its survival in later decades before and after 1968, when it was listed as a private limited company 'Macallan & Glenlivet Ltd' on the London Stock Exchange. The stability and continuity of the company, as symbolised by the 17th century Laird's House at Easter Elchies, now used as the company headquarters, is best reflected by the fact that the two daughters of the Harbinson and Shiach families, descendants of the Kemps, formed the largest shareholding group in 1994. The year also saw Macallan ranked the third most popular whisky in the United Kingdom, and amongst the top five in the world with Glenmorangie and after Glenfiddich, Glen Grant, and Glenlivet. Limited to markets in Scotland and Italy in 1969, today Macallan's is sold in seventeen countries throughout Europe, America and Asia while also being used in blends like Cutty Sark, The Famous Grouse, J & B, Chivas Regal, Bells, Ballantyne's and the liqueur Drambuie.

OWNERS
Edrington Group Ltd, The ?

REGION
Speyside

PRODUCT
Macallan single malts 10, (40%) 12, 18 and 25 year olds 43% vol

NOTES
Slightly sweet, fruity sherry aroma with a smooth well-rounded sherry wood taste
A sherry bouquet with a flowery currant calvados taste and a rounded finish
A wine-like sweet nose with a hint of almonds and pears, and a sherry wood taste
A heathery honey nose with a rich and full sherry oak taste that is smooth and mellow.

MACDUFF
ABERDEENSHIRE

Seaport town situated 2 miles E of Banff. Originally known as Doun or Down from the Gaelic 'Dun' meaning 'hillfort', in 1783 James, 2nd Earl of Fife, changed the name of this hill town to Macduff (the family name being Duff) and in the same year it was elevated to a Burgh of Barony. A small fishing hamlet prior to 1732, it was later developed under the fosterage of the Earl of Fife whose harbour (bought by the Town Council, 1898) developments enabled it to undercut the harbour dues at Banff by half in 1877. Its export trade in herring, live cattle and grain to Leith, London, Holland and Baltic ports was significantly increased along with its import trade, following the opening of a rail link in 1860. The ports shipwrights responded positively to increased demand for fishing boats and nets as techniques improved and markets expanded in the 19th and also in the 20th century, when the benefit from harbour extensions in the 1960s enabled the port to retain a fleet engaged in seine net fishing.

MACDUFF'S CASTLE
FIFE

Positioned on a sandstone cliff just outside East Wemyss are the ruins of a courtyard tower. The land was originally part of the Wemyss Estate but was disjoined and occupied by the Livingstone family for three generations who probably built the first tower, and passed to the Hamiltons and then the Colvilles in 1530 before again becoming part of the Wemyss Estate. Its towers date from the 15th and also the 16th centuries when an outer and inner court were added, but by the early 18th century it had fallen into ruin.

MACHRIHANISH GOLF CLUB
ARGYLL & BUTE

Located in the SE of the Kintyre west of Campbeltown. Like many of Scotland's golf clubs its founding was the result of a meeting held in a hotel, namely The Argyll Arms Hotel in Campbeltown where a local banker, two ministers and two doctors gathered to prepare for its inaugural opening. Though initially viewed by some as a pastime peculiar to the east coast, after a short time the club grew from a 10 hole course in 1876 to an 18 hole course in 1879, which was designed by the renowned Tom Morris after the ground on the west side of the river had been secured. In 1887 a new clubhouse replaced the former hut. With favourable reports from players and local papers such as 'The Campbeltown Courier', its popularity increased and in 1896 the doors were opened to the ladies, albeit subject to some restrictions up until 1897. With improved modes of travel like the steamers plying the Kilbrannan Sound, and the opening of the rail line from Campbeltown in 1906, the club became a popular venue for the Scottish Ladies Championship, held here in 1909 and 1913, but did not return until 1921. The appointment in 1920 of Archie Thomson, the club's first professional, brought an invaluable source of skill that was imparted to many members, particularly the ladies, up until 1926, when he left to open a golf school in Glasgow. The legacy left by Thomson was carried on by his brother Hector who won the West Coast's prestigious Tennants Cup in 1933, The Scottish Amateur Championship in 1935, and the British Amateur Championship in 1936. Turning professional in 1940, by 1953 he had won the Scottish Professional Championship and during the postwar years Hector's son Arthur upheld the tradition. As a result of its use as a training centre by the Royal Navy Fleet Air Arm and later by the RAF Coastal Command, the club recruited the services of the architect Sir Guy Campbell whose work makes up most of what we see today. This has been described as a compromise between a holiday course and a serious test of golf, and blends strikingly with the seascapes and landscapes which provide the abundance of fresh air. Latterly suggestions were mooted to provide a second 18 hole course. Of the club's 24 awards, the Gold Medal, presented in 1876 by Captain Stewart, is the oldest, while 5 of its 13 cups serve as reminders of the club's strong ties with the armed forces.

MAINS CASTLE
SOUTH LANARKSHIRE

Located 1 mile N of Kilbride is the recently renovated tower of the Lindsays, probably dating from the early 15th century. In 1382 the land became the property of the family whose descendants lived at Mains in great wealth and splendour until forced to sell the estate in the late 17th century. Once surrounded by a fosse with drawbridge, the castle became roofless and by 1792 was a complete ruin.

MARNOCH CHURCH
ABERDEENSHIRE

About 2 miles SW of Aberchirder on the bank of the Deveron stands the old church of Marnoch. The site's early spiritual significance stems from its position by the Caledonian stone circles some of which remain in the churchyard, with the latter being superceded by a later church. Today's building was erected in 1792 with seating for over 800, when it was described as a plain, barn-like edifice, but was replaced by a more commodious place of worship. The Parish of Marnoch came to prominence in the 19th century during the Disruption Debate when the imposition of an unpopular minister led to the new Marnoch Free Church.

MAUCHLINE
SOUTH AYRSHIRE

Village situated 12 miles NE of Ayr. Name derived from the Gaelic 'Magh linn' meaning 'field in the pool'. The site of a battle in 681 when the Picts under Cruithne were defeated by the Strathclyde Britons. In 1165 the lands were granted to Melrose Abbey by Walter Fitzalan, the Steward of Scotland, who also founded the original Parish Church, which remained under the Abbey's extensive jurisdiction until the Reformation, 1560. The Kirktown of Mauchline prospered from the monks' enterprising farming skills and in 1510 was made a Burgh of Barony by James IV for the Abbot. Witnessing the religious strife of the 16th and 17th centuries at first hand, in 1544, two years before being burnt as a heretic, George Wishart preached here, and in 1585 five dissenters were executed here. As a Temporal Lordship with the right to hold a market, 1608, it passed to

Hugh Campbell of Loudon but was frequently distracted from trade owing to its position at the heart of the West Country Covenanting district, for in 1647 it was the scene of the battle of Mauchline Moor when the Covenanters defeated the King's troops. On the same moor in 1666 the Covenanters gathered before their defeat at the battle of the Pentland Hills or Rullion Green. Mauchline's chief claim to fame however, is its ties with Robert Burns, who lived at Mossigel Farm nearby during some of his most prolific periods of writing between 1784 and 1793. The Old Mauchline Kirk (now rebuilt) witnessed the funeral services of Burn's daughters, with the Kirkyard providing the setting for 'The Holy Fair', and the town's Changehouse (Possie Nanceys Tavern, still a public bar) was used as the setting for 'The Jolly Beggers' , while his 'Holy Willie's' poem was based on a member of the Kirk of Session. Regardless of its later reputation as a centre for weaving, the making of snuff boxes and curling stones, today the eminent bard is its main attraction. In 1829 the Parish Church was rebuilt with Mauchline red sandstone and now stands near the castle in the town centre along with its other old buildings. See Castle

MAUCHLINE CASTLE
SOUTH AYRSHIRE

By a stream in Mauchline village stands a 15th century tower house. The site of a priory in the 12th century when the land was granted to the monks of Melrose by Walter Stewart, the High Steward of Scotland. In 1606 the land was acquired by Hugh Campbell of Louden, who had been supported in his appointment as Bailie of Regality by the Abbot of Melrose before the Reformation. Consequently the layout is typical of a good civil and ecclesiastical dwelling house. In the 18th century the property was acquired by a

Gavin Hamilton, an early patron of Robert Burns who in a ground floor room was married to his ' bonny Jean Armour ' on 5th August 1788.

MAXTON
SCOTTISH BORDERS

Village situated 6 miles SE of Melrose. The name would seem to derive from Maccus, a man who owned the manor here in the 12th century which was known as Maccusston from the Old English 'ton' meaning 'farm', 'village' or 'settlement'. While the monks of Melrose held some of the surrounding land in 1200, the forfeited land of Makerstun formerly held by a William de Soulis had by 1328 been granted by Robert I to Walter the Steward of Scotland, who bestowed its 12th century church of St Cuthbert on Dryburgh Abbey. The church lands were later broken up at the Reformation. To the NE of the town stands the ruined Little Dean tower which was the home of the Kerrs' a notable border family for whom Maxton was created a Burgh of Barony in 1588. A very popular village prior to the Treaty of Union in 1707, for many years it served as a rendezvous point for men at arms responding to attacks from the south.

MAXWELLTON
DUMFRIES & GALLOWAY

Town situated on the River Nith opposite Dumfries. Originally called Bridgend it was renamed in 1810 on becoming a Burgh of Barony for Maxwell of Terregles. Its long standing reputation as a squalid and disorderly place that served as a sanctuary for criminals gave rise to the saying 'you might trace a rouge all over the kingdom, but were sure to lose him at Bridgend'. Under the Maxwells, changes were augmented through infrastructuring which was greatly aided by its closeness to Dumfries, of which it eventually became a suburb, before being incorporated into the burgh in 1929.

MAXWELLTON HOUSE
DUMFRIES & GALLOWAY

On the bank of the Cairn 3´ miles SE of Moniave is a considerably modernised 17th century courtyard mansion house. The land was sold by the Earl of Glencairn to Stephen Lawrie, whose son stayed here with his wife Agnes Greirson, both of whose initials and family arms appear on a lintel with the date 1641. An additional panel is inscribed with the names of Sir Robert Lawrie and Dame Jean Riddel, but its main claim to fame, however, is as the 19th century home of Annie Lawrie, who figured in the famous Scottish ballad. Although the house's interior was completely rebuilt, it still retains its original courtyard appearance.

MAYBOLE
SOUTH AYRSHIRE

Town situated 9 miles SW of Ayr. The name probably derived from the Gaelic 'magh boaghail' meaning 'moor of danger'. This was the capital of Carrick and stronghold of the Kennedys of Cassillis, who were known as the Kings of Carrick, when the place had more baronial mansions than Edinburgh. The land was held by Melrose Abbey in 1200 but most of the town land was later owned by the Collegiate Church of St Mary (ruin) founded by Kennedy of Dunure in 1371 and one of the earliest of its kind in Scotland. Elevated to a Burgh of Barony in 1516 for the Earl of Cassillis while trading in wine, wax, woollen and linen cloth. After the printing of the 'First book of Discipline' in 1561, its Provost's House was the scene of the inconclusive Reformation Debate between Quentin Kennedy (Abbot of Crossraguell) and John Knox, when the

Catholic mass was attacked and defended in front of 80 witnesses. A rural community from earliest times, its sheep farming tradition established by the Cistercian monks was later highlighted by the Lammas Fair at the foot of the Eildon Hills, which, as one of the biggest in Scotland before 1880, once sold up to 70,000 lambs in one day. It was at one of Maybole's annual market fairs that Robert Burns's parents Agnes Brown and William Burnes met for the first time. The decline of its weaving, which had for a long time attracted Irish migrant workers, spurred Charles Crawford and John Gray to begin the production of footwear along with Jack and Thomas Hunter's enterprise in agricultural implements. The legacy of this is the former workers recreational facilities of which its golf clubs, particularly Turnberry and Ayrshire, are pre-eminent. Concentrated in its High Street are its chief buildings; its Town Hall, once the Town House of the Kennedy lairds and later the Tolbooth, while near by its 16th century castle are the remains of the Collegiate Church. See Castle & Church

MAYBOLE CASTLE
SOUTH AYRSHIRE

Occupying land in Maybole village 9 miles SW of Ayr is a 16th century L plan tower house. Built by the Earl of Cassillis, who was the hereditary chief when Maybole was the capital of the district of Carrick. Additions were made in the 17th century by John, 5th Earl of Cassillis, who was deeply involved in local feuds in Ayrshire and Galloway. In 1615 he was succeeded by John, 6th Earl, who was created Extraordinary Lord of the Court of Session by Charles II, 1649 and was primarily responsible for the castle's distinctive features, which have survived the enlargements of the 19th century, when it was occupied the factor of Lord Ailsa.

MAYBOLE CHURCH
SOUTH AYRSHIRE

Located on the side of a hill 9 miles S of Ayr. In 1371 Sir John Kennedy of Dunure founded the Chapel of St Mary with one clerk and three chaplains, which further added to the area's rich ecclesiastic tradition with its closeness to Crossragual Abbey and the area's numerous estates, giving it a contrasting mix of churchmen and barons. A little over ten years later a college had been founded by Kennedy with a confirmatory mandate from Pope Clement VIII in 1382. Later becoming the burial place for the Earls of Cassillis and some of the other local nobility who would have benefited from its decline at the Reformation, 1560. The building was entire at the end of the 17th century but today's old church which stands near the site of a 12th century Parish Church consists of the original 15th century unroofed oblong shell with the familiar arched windows, mouldings and carvings.

MEGGERNIE CASTLE
PERTH & KINROSS

Near the head of Glenlyon 22 miles W of Aberfeldy is a 16th century square tower built by the Campbells of Glen Lyon and incorporating an earlier structure. It is five storeys high with square towers, turrets at angles and ornamental dormers. In the 19th century it was bought by W. G Stewart Menzies.

MEGGINCH CASTLE
PERTH & KINROSS

In the Carse of Gowrie 12 miles E of Perth stands an oblong mansion house. The inscription on its north front indicates it was built by the Hays of Megginch in 1575 when the house was surrounded by finely wooded parks. In 1640 it was sold to the Drummond family, whose descendant John Murray Drummond changed its interior from a 16th-century to a 19th century house.

MELGUND CASTLE
ANGUS

Positioned on a bank 8 miles NE of Forfar are the ruins of a 16th century L plan hall tower which was developed out of a square keep. The latter provided the family with a refuge in times of danger while the retainers and strangers were left out in the common hall. Built by Cardinal Beaton (1494-1546), whose name and that of his wife were carved on the wall. Its uncertain if it was church property before the Reformation (1560), but afterwards it was occupied by David Bethune of Balfour, a near relative of Cardinal James Beaton. The estate then passed through the hands of the Lyons, the Maules and the Murrays. In 1868, Agnes Murray, the Melgund heiress, married Sir Gilbert Elliot, to whose son the Earl of Minto it gave the title of Viscount. Now partly ruinous.

MELROSE
SCOTTISH BORDERS

Market Town situated at the north base of the Eildon Hills 3 miles SE of Galashiels. The name is derived from the Gaelic and British 'maol' meaning either 'bare moor' or 'bare promontory'. The Old Melrose which stood up river was once the site of a 7th century monastery founded by St Aidan, but was burnt by Kenneth I in 839 when the name was transferred to the then village of Fordel where David I founded an abbey in 1136. The town which developed witnessed the triumphs and disasters of a border town, with an abbey that overshadowed its affairs up until the Reformation in 1560. Burnt by Richard II in 1385 after a fruitless Scottish expedition, and during Hertford's invasions in 1544 and 1545. The town was long famous for its Mel-

rose land linen that provided its main source of revenue, with an export market in London and on the Continent until the mid 18th century, when it was supplanted by Galashiels. For John Ramsay, Viscount Haddington, it was created a Burgh of Barony, 1605, a Temporal Lordship with Abbey, 1609, and a Burgh of Regality, 1621, which was later acquired by the Buccleuchs. After the publication of Walter Scott's 'The Abbey' and 'The Monastery' in 1820, which brought the town into prominence, Melrose became popular with tourists who were followed by permanent residents from in and around the prospering southern industrial belt, thus reviving the burgh's flagging fortunes. A Police Burgh in 1895 with a Town Council in 1901, the latter was abolished in the local government reorganisation in 1975. Apart from its Abbey its other interesting structures include its Mercat Cross of 1642 surmounted by the Unicorn of the Scottish Arms with the mallet and the rose, its railway station, opened in 1849, the Motor Museum and the Melrose Museum. As a premier borders tourist destination with a rugby club founded in 1877, the town is still assured a season in the public gaze. See Abbey & Battle.

MELROSE ABBEY
SCOTTISH BORDERS

Located in the vales of the River Tweed in the town. The original foundation which stood up river was begun by a disciple of St Aidan in the 7th century, but today's extensive ruins are the legacy of David I, who ordered its building and housed it with Cistercian monks from Rievulxe in Yorkshire, 1136. Formerly called Fordel after the place, its Norman styled church, dedicated to the Virgin Mary and consecrated in 1146, had an adjacent dormitory and oratory. Possessing considerable portions of land in many parts of Scotland and England, the Abbey's destruction in the crossfire of Anglo-Scottish politics led to a distinguished breed of abbots who built and rebuilt it over the centuries. Such was their political/financial status that in 1222-24 Henry III granted Abbot Adam's men safe conduct through his domains with their revenue and it was at this time that the Abbey was developed further. With the Wars of Independence came the political vagaries and the wanton destruction, when the Abbey was burnt and the Abbot petitioned Edward I in 1307 for timber for rebuilding work. Attacked again in 1322 by the troops of Edward II when its Abbot William Peebles and some monks were slain, provoking Robert the Bruce to grant £2,000 for its rebuilding. Though exempt from military service, the monks were often engaged in the cause of the Stewarts from the time of Robert I, whose heart was finally buried here after a failed attempt by Sir James Douglas to take it to the Holy Land in 1330. In 1385 the retreating Richard II stayed here for a night before burning it in the morning prior to despoiling Newbattle and Dryburgh Abbeys. Its ongoing royal connections meant its Abbot Andrew Hunter was the confessor of James II, and Lord High Treasurer, 1449-53 and Ambassador to France, 1488. Of the Abbey's former grandeur Sir Walter Scott was moved to write:

And far beneath, in lustre wan,
Old Melrose' rose, and fair Tweed ran:
Like some tall rock with lichens grey,
Seemed dimly huge, the dark abbey.
When Hawick he passed, had curfew rung,
Now midnight lauds were in Melrose sung.

In the 16th century the administration and revenues were invested with the Crown but the Abbey failed to recover after the attacks by Brian Latoun, 1544, Earl of Hertford, 1545, and was held by the Lords of the Congregation in 1558. Later passing through the Stuarts, Douglases, Ramsays, and the Scotts of Buccleuch whose descendant funded repair work which was overseen by Walter Scott in 1822. The parts of the church still standing are of the mainly 15th century structure built on 12th -and 13th century foundations. Its richly embellished sculpting was indicative of the Decorative period and of the Abbey's wealth. Todays ruins include the distinctive vaulted nave with part of its north aisle, chapels and a considerable part of the south aisle with its eight arcaded chapels, a branch of the north and south transepts, with nearby choir with two chapel bays, from which extends the altar and the large east window. Of its domestic buildings the Chapter House is the most entire.

MELROSE, BATTLE OF, 1526
SCOTTISH BORDERS

As a consequence of the Regent Earl of Angus's attempts to retain his position as ward of the young King James V, and the intrigues of the Queen, an attempt at rescue was made by Walter Scott of Branxholm with around 1,000 men in Melrose. The failure of this endeavour delayed the King's escape for two years, when in 1528 open war ensued between the Crown and Angus who eventually retired to England.

MENSTRIE CASTLE
STIRLING

Situated 2 miles E of Stirling in a modern housing estate are the remains of a courtyard mansion house. In 1568 Sir William Alexander, poet to James VI and later appointed Lieutenant of Novia Scotia by Charles I, was born here. The house was burnt in the 17th century by Montrose during his revenge raid on Castle Campbell but was later refitted and in 1734 was the birthplace of Sir Ralph Abercromby, the hero of Aboukir during the Egyptian Campaign. The castle was again ruinous in the 19th century when its gateway was dated as being of 17th century work.

MENZIES CASTLE
PERTH & KINROSS

One mile W of Aberfeldy between Weem Hill and the Tay stands a restored Z plan mansion of the Menzies. The site was once occupied by the Menzies' House of Weem which was burnt by the Stewarts of Garth before the present house was built in 1577. Its construction marked the end of the deadly conflict between the families when James Menzies married Barbra Stewart of Atholl. Above the vaulted ground floor are the main rooms while on the second floor are the bedrooms, while its attic is provided with pepper box angle turrets and dormers, one with the epigraph '1577 IMB IN OWR TYME' and on the lintel 'PRYSIT BE GOD FOREVER'. The building shows the progress made at the end of the 16th century towards open mansions instead of enclosed defensive structures and in 1840 much of the interior was altered at the behest of the 6th Baronet and was saved from dereliction by the family clan society.

MERCHISTON CASTLE
CITY OF EDINBURGH

Occupying land to the SW of Edinburgh off Colinton Road stands the 15/16th-century L plan mansion house of the Napier family, who played a distinguished role in the running of the city. In the 15th century three members of the family were Lord Provosts and in 1550 John Napier, the inventor of logarithms, was born here. Its situation on the southern and western approaches to the city meant it figured in the Douglas Wars and in the civil strife during Queen Mary's reign, 1567, when William Kirk-

caldy bombarded it, and it suffered more fire attacks in the same year. Some additions were made in the 19th century when it became a boarding school and today it still serves as a part of the educational establishment.

METHIL
FIFE

Seaport situated 2 miles SW of Leven. Name derived from the Gaelic 'Maoth-coill' meaning 'soft boggy wood'. For the Archbishop of St Andrews it was constituted a Burgh of Barony in 1662 when its wooden harbour was replaced by a stone structure built by the 2nd Earl of Wemyss. This laid the foundation for its long-standing trade in coal, which was greatly expanded in the 19th century by the Fife Coal Company, resulting in extensive harbour developments in 1877. The nearby village of Buckhaven, thought to have been inhabited from the 16th century by Netherlanders noted for their oddities, formed the Burgh of Buckhaven, Methil and Innerleven in 1891. Methil served as a collection point for convoys during both world wars but by 1950 its coal trade was in decline and today has all but disappeared.

METHVEN
PERTH & KINROSS

Village situated 7 miles NW of Perth. The name is either derived from the Brythonic 'medd faen' meaning 'mead stone' or from 'maid' and the Old English 'fenn' meaning 'boundary fen'. Prior to 1323 the lands were held by the Moubrays, who came over with William the Conqueror, but were later confiscated by Robert the Bruce and bestowed on his son-in-law Walter, the 8th Steward of Scotland, whose son became Robert II in 1371. The battle of Methven was fought here in 1306 when Robert the Bruce's band was surprised and defeated by the Earl of

Pembroke. Its traditional weaving and farming based economy was undoubtedly encouraged by its long-standing ties with the church, for as early as the 13th century it was the site of a religious community followed by a Collegiate Church in 1433, founded by Walter Stewart, Earl of Atholl. In 1549 a hospital was founded here by David Haliburton. After its castle, around which most of its history revolves, comes its church buildings, including today's structure built in 1783 with a spire and clock erected in 1826 by public subscription, and the nearby remains of the old church aisle of 1516 added by the Crown, and once the burial place of the Smythes of Methven. See Castle & Battle

METHVEN CASTLE
PERTH & KINROSS

Sited 1 mile E of the village is a good example of a 16th century Scottish mansion. In the 11th century, the lands were held by the Mowbrays but were given to Walter, High Steward of Scotland, by Robert Bruce in the 14th century. For a long time the residence of James IV's widow Queen Margaret, who died here in 1541 when the property passed to Henry Stewart, her third husband. In 1664 Patrick Smythe purchased it and his descendants still occupied it in the 19th century.

METHVEN, BATTLE OF, 1306
PERTH & KINROSS

The battle marked an unlucky start to Bruce's campaign to win his kingdom following his crowning at Scone. At Methven near Perth, he was defeated by the Earl of Pembroke and forced to retreat into the mountains where, excommunicated and outlawed, he remained until 1307, when he returned to win a victory at Louden Hill.

MID CALDER
WEST LOTHIAN

Town situated 12 miles SW of Edinburgh. Name derived from the river which probably comes from the Gaelic 'Caled' and 'dobhar' meaning 'hard stony water'. In the 12th century the lands of Calder were granted to Randolph de Clere, who built a church here in 1215, but were renamed Calder-Clere to distinguish them from the adjoining Calder Comitis held by the Earl of Fife, which included today's Mid and West Calder. Granted by Robert the Bruce to his erstwhile supporter James Douglas for whose descendant James, 4th Earl of Morton its title was confirmed by James V and Mary I long before his execution in 1581. They passed through marriage to James de Sandislands in 1349, an ancestor of the Torphichen family, who built its pre-Reformation Gothic church, 1542 (enlarged 1863), and Calder Castle, which was later replaced by Calder House. It was in the latter that John Knox celebrated Communion according to Protestant rites in 1566. After the forming of Mid and West Calder in 1643, the latter growing around its Kirk, the towns faded into the background of history until the rise in importance of Mid Calder as a stopping place for coaches travelling between Edinburgh and Glasgow in the 18th century. Among the area's subsequent industrial developments, including the extraction of shale, ironstone, coal, limestone, sandstone and other minerals, its shale was unique in that it started a trade in petroleum which thrived until after 1918, when it was undermined by cheap oil imports from America. In 1929 the nearby Pumpherston Works (still operating in 1980) became the main shale oil refinery in Scotland.

MILLPORT GOLF CLUB
NORTH AYRSHIRE

The land on which the club was developed on the Isle of Greater Cumbray, west of the Isle of Bute, was once held by Norsemen but was much later the property of the Marquis of Bute, who became the first Honorary President on its founding in 1888. As capital of the island, with its well maintained harbour and pier the town of Millport was a popular destination for the sea bathers on the ferries and steamers from Glasgow and Greenock. With an eye on the future, the meeting chaired by Provost Brown of Millport in the Religious Institute on Buchannan St in Glasgow sought to increase the town and island's appeal and form a club with a view to encouraging better facilities and infrastructuring. Consequently, over the years a growing number of people lived off the island. Forming 9 holes, laid out at Damhead Farm (now Upper Kirkton) the course's setting amidst beautiful sea views and mountain scenery, and its fine green turf owes a great deal to the diplomacy of Mr John Windsor Stuart Factor of the Bute Estate. The ladies held its first female competition in 1891, and by 1892 membership totalled 63. Winning its first match against Rothesay by 41 holes, the two clubs quickly built up strong competitive ties which have provided challenge and experience to aspiring enthusiasts ever since. In 1909 a new clubhouse was built. Millport's first trophy, the Arthure Cup was granted by Mr Arthur of Carlung and gave rise to one of the most important challenges, the Bi-annual Competition. The need for expansion and the opening of a second course in 1914 proved short-lived as during the Great War of 1914-18, playing was greatly reduced. Nevertheless further expansion was planned when hostilities ceased, and in 1920 the extension of the no2 course to 9 holes was drawn up. This was later encroached upon by the construction of the upper reservoir in 1924 and the rest given over to cattle grazing. The decision to develop the Ist course was carried out in 1933, the year of the first Open Amateur Competition to be held here for the major prize the Cumbrae Challenge Cup, first won by the club in 1955 by George Macgregor. The competition was discontinued in 1956 but revived in 1965. In later years the club buildings were augmented by facilities for members, particularly in 1975 with a loan from the Town Council, while the course continued to remain under lease from the Bute Estate. The renovations carried out with a grant from The Highland & Islands Development Board were consummated by refurbishment's to the clubhouse in 1987, a year before the centenary. In the rolls of the club champions J G Stewart has been the most pre-eminent, winning six times between 1979-87.

MILNGAVIE
DUMFRIES & GALLOWAY

Town situated 8 miles NW of Glasgow. Name derived from the Gaelic 'Muileann gaoithe' meaning 'a wind mill'. Although there has been a community here for centuries, which appeared on Bleaus Atlas in 1654 as Milgay, the present town is mainly 19th century but with some 18th century buildings. Once the main village in the area, its rapid growth in later decades owed much to its cotton production, its elevation to burgh status and its proximity to Glasgow and the River Clyde, for which its Clober Estate, a former bleachfield, served as a transit camp for bomb victims from Clydebank during World War II. During the post-war period Milngavie became an overspill town for its larger neighbour when the estate became part of a 1300 house building project by Milngavie Town and County Councils in

1957. The Lillie Art Gallery, built in 1962, exhibits 20th century Scottish works which include The Glasgow Boys, Francis Cadel and Leslie Hunter.

MILTON DUFF DISTILLERY
MORAY

To the SW of Elgin in the Glenlivet area is the site that was chosen in 1824 for the building of the first legally established distillery under the name Milton Duff. The area's long-standing reputation as the garden of Scotland had allot to do with the dexterity of the Benedictine monks from Pluscardine Priory whose ale, once said to be the finest in Scotland, played a significant part in establishing the area's long-standing tradition in the production of alcohol. Central to this has been the water supply for Milton Duff which comes from the Black burn after permeating the mossy uplands of the Black Hills. During the distillery's first 60 years of production, many of the smugglers' tools were used for production, while its location fuelled claims that the still and mash house were built within the monks' original brew house. When the renowned whisky historian Alfred Barnard visited here in 1877 he stated: " in this well known establishment, some of the oldest fads and methods are in use, and the ancient style of stills and utensils, as carried on by the smugglers, have also been continued". Like many of the neighbouring distilleries, Milton Duff combines the key elements of water, barley, peat and the shape of the pot still to produce the liquid that is matured in casks in the atmosphere of the distillery grounds. Outwith the distillery, the clean air and fertile farmland overshadowed by the granite peaks, and irrigated by the rivers Spey, Livet and Lossie make it a haven for a wide range of wildlife including 200 species of bird, among which are osprey, eagles, and buzzards. Today's buildings are a contrast between the old and the new, giving it the capacity for efficient production levels whilst accommodating the needs of the public.

OWNERS
Allied Distillers Ltd ?

REGION
Speyside

PRODUCT
Milton Duff 12 year old single malt 43% vol

NOTES
A flowery nose with hints of peat, vanilla and heather with a palate that is lightly peated with traces of almond, honey and floral.

MINGARRY CASTLE
HIGHLAND

The castle is isolated on a rock on the N side of Loch Sunart NE of Tobermory. With rocks on its south side which gave access to and from ships and a ditch on its north side, the structure takes the form of an irregular hexagon and has occupied this strategic position at the mouth of Loch Sunart since the 13th century. For a long time the stronghold of the Macians, who were descended from the Lords of the Isles. As the most south westerly bastion of Macian territory, and bulwark against incursions by the Macleans of Morvern and Mull, it figured in Sir Walter Scott's 'The Lord of the Isles':

From Hirt that hears their northern roar,
To the green Ilay's fertile shore;
Or mainland turn, where many a tower
Owns thy bold brother's feudal power,
Each on its own dark cape reclined,
And listening to its own wild wind,
From where Mingarry, sternly placed
O'er awes the woodland and the waste

It was occupied by James IV in 1493 and 1495 during his successful expedition to subdue the Western Isles. Partly demolished in 1517 by a Knight of Lochalsh, and during a siege by the Macleans in 1588, when its occupants were eventually saved by the arrival of Government forces. In 1644 it was captured by Alastair Macdonald (Colkitoo) and used as a prison for Covenanters. Although it was added to in the 18th century it soon became a ruin.

MINNIGAFF
DUMFRIES & GALLOWAY

Village situated 1 mile NE of Newton Stewart. Name derived from the Gaelic 'Monadh dubh' meaning 'dark mountainous region'. The area's neolithic remains and its hilly terrain suggest it was the site of a number of early hill fort settlements. In 1263 the land was granted by Alexander III to Alexander the Hereditary Steward of Scotland, whose descendants, the Earls of Galloway, built the nearby Garlies Castle (ruin) in the 15th century, 1 mile to the north. At Loch Trool to the north, Robert the Bruce defeated a 1500 man force under the Earl of Pembroke in 1306, and at the foot of the Loch in 1685 a party of Covenanters were slain by a troop of dragoons. A Burgh of Barony for Mckie of Larg from 1619, and described in 1684 as having a substantial weekly market where the moor men of Carrick and elsewhere bought large quantities of meal and malt, Minnigaff was gradually overshadowed by Newton Stewart and today is virtually a suburb with farming and forestry (Glentrool National Forest Park) dominant since 1950.

MINTO
SCOTTISH BORDERS

Village situated 1 mile N of Denholm. The name is of very questionable origin but may come from the Old Welsh meaning a hill. Once forming part of the Parish of Hasendean the lands were granted by David I to the Bishop of Glasgow in the 12th century. On Minto Crags, which form its chief natural feature, is Flatlips Castle. Restored in the 15th century, this was a stronghold of the Turnbulls of Barnhills, whose family held the land in the 14th century, and whose descendant, a well known Borders freebooter, used a small platform below the castle known as Barnhills bed as a lookout that featured in Walter Scott's 'Lay of the Last Minstrel' when it was published in 1805:

Mid cliffs from whence his eagle eye
For many a league his prey could spy;
Cliffs, doubling, on their echoes borne
The terrors of the robbers horn

It rises three storeys high from its vaulted ground floor, with its first floor having lookout windows all round. The castle's top storey with attic and roof added by the 3rd Earl of Minto in 1857 now houses a family museum. In 1390 the land passed to the Stewarts and in 1705 was held by Gilbert Elliot as Lord Minto, whose descendant built Minto House in 1814. The village church, built in a Gothic style by William Playfair around 1830, with a number of improvements made over the years, still stands as a fine example of its period.

MITTON, BATTLE OF, 1319

In response to the siege of Berwick, the Scots, under the Earl of Moray, invaded England with around 5,000 men and were opposed near Swale by the Archbishop of York with around 20,000 men. In the engagement which followed, the latter were defeated with over 4,000 dead, many of whom were ecclesiastics which gave rise to the title 'The Chapter of Mitton'. The knock on effect of this was the raising of the siege of Berwick and a two-year truce signed between the two nations.

MOCHRUM
DUMFRIES & GALLOWAY

Village situated 9 miles SW of Wigtown. Name derived from the Gaelic 'maghdhruim' meaning 'ridge of the plain'. In the 14th century the land was bestowed by David II on Patrick Dunbar, Earl of March, whose descendants the Dunbars, Sheriffs of Morayshire, built the Keep by Mochrum Loch around 1475 to replace the much earlier castle at Castle Loch. With a late 16th century tower close by it served as the family seat until it passed in the 19th century to the Countess of Dumfries, and later the Bute family, who restored it with an adjoining courtyard by John Patrick, 3rd Marquis, in 1911. The Parish Church, built in 1794 as the direct successor of a 12th century church dedicated to St Malachy, who is thought to have passed through here around 1140, had galleries added in 1835. Among the reminders of the area's forts or entrenchments, which number around twenty, Barsalloch Point, Doon of May and Chippermore are the most substantial, while the closest, Druchtay, near the village, is an Anglo Norman structure dating from 1190.

MOFFAT
DUMFRIES & GALLOWAY

A Border town situated 23 miles NE of Dumfries which derives its name from the Gaelic 'magh fada' meaning 'a long plain'. The town comes on record in the 11th and 12th centuries and later appears in charters from King Robert the Bruce and David II. While trying to recruit the support of the Annandale Lords, and before his defeat by the Earl of Douglas at Annan, 1332, this was the scene of the encampment of King John Balliol and his army. Moffat's rise to prominence in the 17th century followed its elevation to a Burgh of Regality for Johnstone of Corehead in 1648. During his extirpation of the Covenanters, 1678, who frequently held Conventicles in the area, the Black Bull Inn, the town's oldest building, was used as a headquarters by John Graham of Claverhouse and his dragoons. The Moffat House Hotel, built in 1767 by one of the Adams family for the Earl of Hopetoun, was where James Macpherson compiled his controversial Poems of Ossian in 1759. In 1704 Moffat was described as a small straggling town, where people went to drink the waters. Along with its position on the mail coach route, this soon brought a rapid rise in its popularity, with visits from David Hume (philosopher), James Macpherson (poet), James Boswell (biographer), and Joseph Black (chemist), all of whom helped promote the town as the Cheltenham or Baden of Scotland, leading to the building of the Moffat Hydropathic Hotel in 1877 (burnt down, 1921). Amongst the town's residents throughout this period were John Rogerson (1741-1823), the physician to Catherine, Empress of Russia, and John Loudon Macadam (1756-1839) the road engineer, who died here. The area's traditional sheep farming led to the building of its woollen mills, which, since the trade was revived in the 1950s, have made a significant contribution to Scotland's woollen industry which is now remembered in the Moffat Museum. See Golf Club

MOFFAT GOLF CLUB
DUMFRIES & GALLOWAY

The club was founded in 1884 when playing began on a field of the Chapel Farm. In 1904 a suitable site was leased from Mr William Younger, MP, on the Auchen Castle estate known as the Coatshill land situated some 670 feet above sea level. Since the designing of the 18-

hole course by Ben Sayers, players have enjoyed a commanding view of the town and much wider countryside, moving many to describe it as one of the most attractive inland courses in the country. The cost of the original clubhouse was £800. In 1905 the course was officially opened and orchestrated by Major Mackenzie-Grieve in front of 300 people; Mrs Younger played the first ball. From ten members in 1884, the numbers have increased gradually over the years to 59 in 1904, 107 in 1907, reaching 350 by 1995, which included the country and junior members. In the early 1970's the club purchased the land on which the course was built and in later years bought the grazing rights before engaging in extensions to the course and alterations to the clubhouse. In 1973, the course record was established by Mr G J Rodaks with a score of 60 (less 2,58). The club has come a long way, since the early days tees have been extended, landscaping has been carried out, and trees have been planted. In 1984 the centenary dinner was given an added boost by the presence of professionals like Jessie Valentine and Jimmy Murray with the toast to the club being proposed by Charlie Green, former Scottish amateur champion and Walker Cup player.

MONIFIETH
DUNDEE CITY

Coastal town situated 6 miles NE of Dundee. The name is either from the Gaelic 'Monadh feidh' meaning 'hill of the Deer' or from 'moin foide' meaning 'moss-muir with the peats'. The obvious signs of early settlers are the undulations left by a vitrified hill fort on Monifieth Law, while to the SW of this is the Gallow hill of Ethiebeaton, where much later settlers held Baron Courts in feudal times. A Culdee Cell which stood here in the 6th century still functioned in the 12th centu-

ry and was probably used by the pious David I, who is thought to have had a hunting seat here. The land and church, granted by the Earl of Angus to Nicholas Lay Abbott of Monifieth in 1220, was acquired shortly after by Arbroath Abbey and held right up to the Reformation, but the Grange of Monifieth, bestowed by King Robert the Bruce on his supporter William Durham in the 14th century, was for 400 years held by the Durhams, who played an important role in the affairs of state. A William Durham was one of the deputation of five who submitted the Five Articles of Perth to James VI in 1618, and his grandfather was a friend of the Reformer John Knox. Monifieth's later development was a reflex response to its neighbour Dundee which provided a ready market for the produce of its foundries, mills and carpet factory, resulting in the village being constituted a burgh in 1895. Like many Victorian industrial towns Monifieth had a rich social culture which was traditionally comprised of choral, dramatic, literary and musical groups that were adversely affected by its larger neighbour from the 1950s onwards.

MONIMAIL
FIFE

The village situated 5 miles SW of Cupar probably derives its name from the Gaelic 'moin mil' meaning 'moss moor with hill'. The lands of Monimail once belonged to the Archbishop of St Andrews, whose summer palace, which stood to the north of Melville House, was built by Bishop Lamberton before his death in 1328 and improved by Cardinal Beaton in the 16th century. The village is also known as the home of the satirical poet David Lyndsay (1490-1555) who was Lord Lyon King of Arms to James V and whose house, which once stood on Mount Hill, is now replaced by a pillar erected to the memory of the Earl of Hopetoun. The community's rural economy was transformed during the move from small holdings to larger farms between 1900 and 1914 when the area saw a significant migration of its people to Canada. See Castle

MONIMAIL CASTLE
FIFE

Built in the grounds of Melville House 3 miles W of Cupar. Essentially a tower house that was preceded by the country residence of the Archbishop of St Andrews from the 14th century. It was greatly enlarged by Cardinal David Beaton who in 1539 became Archbishop. In 1564 Archbishop Hamilton granted the house and land to James Balfour of Pittendreich who later became Lord President of the Court of Session and whose name appears on a parapet with the date 1578. Its derelict state in 1627 led to its purchase by the 2nd Lord Melville who also acquired the title of Lord Monimail, but in the 19th century the tower was used as a bothy by the gardeners of Melville Castle.

MONK CASTLE
NORTH AYRSHIRE

In a wood 2 miles N of Kilwinning stand the ruins of a traditional 17th century Laird's House, with two storeys and a vaulted ground floor. At the time of the Reformation, the land, which once belonged to the Abbey of Kilwinning, was acquired by the Duke of Chatelherault, 1552, who bestowed it on his son Claud Hamilton, the Commendator of Paisley Abbey. The son of the latter, who was created Earl of Abercorn and Baron of Monk Castle, probably built the ruins that we see today which attest to the roof decay in the 19th century.

MONKLAND HOUSE
NORTH LANARKSHIRE

Standing on a high bank in the Calder Valley 2 miles S of Airdrie is an L plan mansion house. The land was originally owned by the monks of Newbattle, who held it from the 12th century (1153-65), but after the Reformation in 1587 it passed to Mark Ker, Commendator of Newbattle Abbey who became Lord Newbattle in 1591. In the 17th century the house was built; which although provided with modern conveniences its design was in keeping with a defensive structure with a strong basement and small ground floor windows.

MONS GRAPIUS, BATTLE OF, 84 AD
PERTH & KINROSS

During his campaign of conquest the Roman General Agricola advanced north with an army of 8,000 men, 3,000 horse and auxiliaries while his fleet harried the coastline. After crossing the River Isla, on Mons Grapius the Romans encountered around 30,000 Caledonians encamped with their chief Calgacus. Though bringing defeat to the Caledonians, ironically with their victory, came their own defeat and retreat before the great barrier of the Grampian Mountains, which obstructed their forward movement.

MONTROSE
ANGUS

Coastal town situated 30 miles NE of Dundee at the south end of the River Esk. Originally called Celurca, its present name is probably derived from the Gaelic 'moine rois' meaning 'moss on the promontory'. The site of a town as early as the 10th century and of a settlement long before. The estuary was a favoured point of anchorage for Danish sea rovers, who in 980 massacred its inhabitants during one of their coastal raids. In the 12th century, when it was erected into a Royal Burgh by David I (1124-53), the town derived a significant source of revenue from its salt pans and mills. A Dominican Monastery was founded here in 1230 by Alan Durward and although the town was burnt in 1244, it retained its importance, as did its castle where Edward I resided in 1296 when he received the news that Balliol had resigned the Scottish Crown. In the following year the castle was destroyed by William Wallace but the town continued to figure in the struggle for Scottish Independence when it became the conjectured departure point for Lord James Douglas on his mission to take Bruce's heart to the Holy Land in 1330. Montrose was visited by David II in 1369 after the burghers sought his release from England. Although it suffered at the hands of the Erskines of Dun in the 15th century, by 1534 a John Erskine founded a school here for the study of Greek which was later attended by the Reformers George Wishart and Andrew Melville, who were taught by Pierre Marsillers. In 1548 an English naval assault on the town was successfully repelled by Erskine. During the religious strife of the 17th century James VI convened a General Assembly here to advance the cause of Episcopacy and in 1644 and 1645 its most famous son, James Marquis of Montrose, held the town for the King against the Covenanters four years before it was blighted by the plague. Continueing to figure in the struggles of the times, this was the planned point of arrival for the Old Pretender in 1715 and was occupied by the Government forces in 1745 until their ejection in favour of the Jacobites who were in turn replaced by an occupation force of Cumberland's troops. As Scotland's premier tobacco port for much of the 18th century, when it also had a reputation for the import of French Claret, which owed much to the Franco-Scottish Alliance, it was described as being 'well built and airy' by Dr Samuel Johnson during his visit here with James Boswell in 1773. The Ship Inn on the High St where they both stayed still stands. The burghers outward looking trading practices in fish, grain, sailcloth, and flax with Baltic, Mediterranean and European ports during later decades is best reflected in its architecture, most notably its gable ends (gable endies) which show a direct influence from the Low Countries. These contrast with the wide open High Street and its fine 18th and 19th century buildings which typify the Scottish Burgh. Later enjoying some popularity as a seaside destination, more recently its economy has been supported by the revenues from whisky and oil. See Golf Club 1&2

MONTROSE MERCANTILE GC
ANGUS

Formed in 1879 by a Mr D J Donald, who became its first Captain. The club was affectionately known as "the Merky", and witnessed a marked increase in membership with Saturday play and the closure of both the Union G.C. and the Mechanics G.C. One of the enduring strengths of the club has been its all-inclusive policy which took its diverse membership to 240 by 1898. Originally meeting in the Star Inn, the members erected their first custom-built clubhouse in 1891 facing the Links. Gradually getting involved with other fledgling clubs in fund raising activities, while further developing their club, the members installed gas lighting in 1898. It was, however, a donation by Mr Paton, a local philanthropist, of the new clubhouse that opened in 1904, that was to prove a more enduring legacy of the founding spirit. In the same week, the other attractions taking place on the Links were the Ladies' Annual Tournament, which drew much attention, and the Wild West Show, headed by Bill Cody (Buffalo Bill). The year 1902 saw five holes being added to the course to compensate for the abandoned five holes at the East Links, which was bordered by a mix of common and private land. In 1904, Willie Park (a prominent course designer in Britain, USA and Canada) designed a new course, and many of its holes form part of the present course. The club saw much contraction and expansion in its course and in its membership in subsequent decades, when names like Cobb and Keillor became established in its championship records. Although the droppings left by sheep, who were used to keep the grass short, proved an inconvenience, it was the air raids during World War II (1939-45) that proved a more formidable challenge, as they did to other Montrose clubs when part of the Links was hit. The post-war period saw the pre-eminence of names like Cobb and Richmond, but latterly the need for a more collective response, due to rising running costs, saw the other Montrose clubs merge while the Mercantile stayed independent. In 1992 the first Lady Captain, Mrs A. Murray was elected.

MONTROSE, ROYAL, GOLF CLUB
ANGUS

While the history of golf on the town's Links dates from the 16th century (one of the world's earliest golfers, James Melville, played here before 1562), its development was delayed by the periods of instability in the country's history. Consequently, it was not until much later that it was freed from the constraints imposed by the meddling Town Council. In 1785, one of the earliest records of its progress was of a petition submitted to the Town Council protesting at the encroachments by shepherds and gardeners on part of the links. The present Royal Montrose GC was formed in 1810, as the Montrose Golf Club, but in 1818 the members were still meeting in the Star Inn, before playing on the 17 hole course for a medal, then returning to the Inn for dinner. In 1825, the members had 14 dif-

ferent holes to play, and with the help of William Gladstone (PM four times 1868-94), the club acquired the patronage of Prince Albert and became the Royal Albert Golf Club in 1845. The course was augmented by a new course of 6,120 yards after 1849, owing to the intrusion by the Caledonian Railway, which cut across the old course in two places. Enjoying 25 holes to play by 1866, a year after the first clubhouse was built, the members also relished the fresh sea air which increasingly attracted visitors from the built-up industrial centres, of which Montrose was to become one after the course was altered by order of the Town Council to ensure the expansion of the Caledonian Railway Station and the Wet Dock. In 1888, after seeking advice from Tom Morris, the new circular course was opened with a tournament open to all. The Montrose Ladies Golf Club, formed in 1889, began with a putting course, but was to become one of Scotland's premier clubs by 1900. In 1909 the Montrose golfers mourned the passing of the club's first professional golfer, Robert Dow. Like much of Scotland, Montrose was a magnet for generations of the railway travelling public from Glasgow and the West, who flocked to the sandy beaches and free golf course, along with the locals who sought solace and space from the clattering of the town's cramped mills. Between 1918-21, the course was enlarged. Such was its popularity that in 1927 the North Links Ladies Golf Club was formed for the purpose of competitive play, resulting in a clubhouse being built in 1929 with a membership of 76, plus 38 juniors by 1935. One of the more memorable events during the war years 1939-45 occurred on 25th October 1940, when two Heinkels, in their attempt to bomb the nearby aerodrome, dropped four bombs on the course, prompting the Air Ministry to requisition a section of the land. Since the post-war years, the club has continued to play an active part in the life of the town, along with the neighbouring clubs, and in 1986, the ninth oldest golf club in the world changed its name to Royal Montrose Golf Club, after amalgamating with the Victoria GC and the North Links Ladies GC.

MONYMUSK
ABERDEENSHIRE

Village situated 20 miles NW of Aberdeen. The name is derived from the Gaelic 'moine musgach' meaning 'muddy peat moss'. The legacy left by the main 6th century northern Culdee mission which sought to convert the Picts is the 12th century Norman church with some 20th century additions that once housed the Monymusk Reliquary (now in the Museum of Antiquities, Edinburgh). Consisting of a richly decorated Pictish box called The Brecbannoch, it once contained the bones of St Columba and after 1211 was carried before the Scottish army before engaging in battle, the most notable being the battle of Bannockburn in 1314. In 1245 the Earl Mar founded an Augustinian Priory here which replaced the Culdee Cell and continued to give the area some religious significance up until the 16th century when it became ruinous. The place was also the scene of Malcolm I's military camp in 1078, prior to his suppression of the rebels of Moray, and at the nearby Campfield Robert the Bruce's army lay before their victory at Inverurie in the year 1308. In the 16th century, prior to the building of Monymusk House, the land was purchased by the Forbeses of Monymusk, becoming a Burgh of Barony in 1589 and in 1612 a Burgh of Regality for the family who occupied the house and held the land until 1712, when it was acquired by Francis Grant who made some additions. Following the opening of the railway station

Monymusk grew gradually with its housing, built in the style of an English village. Latterly the surrounding land has been cultivated by the Forestry Commission, who have also built accommodation for foresters. See Castle

MONYMUSK CASTLE
ABERDEENSHIRE

Located near Monymusk village 7 miles SW of Inverurie. The castle built by William Forbes who succeeded to the estate in 1587 has as its nucleus a lofty L plan structure to which wings were added on both sides. In 1712 it was purchased by Sir Francis Grant of Cullen whose, descendants made some additions and who still lived there in the late 20th century.

MORAY GOLF CLUB
MORAY

Since its beginnings in 1889 the club has remained at its present site on the Links at Lossiemouth by the west of the beach. Though formed by the men of Elgin, the driving force behind it was the Rev Alexander Lawson M A who was Collegiate Minister of Elgin from 1882, and became the club's first Captain. Recently a copy of his instruction book, entitled 'Letters on Golf by a Parish Minister' was sold at Philips Auction for £8,400. Comprising the old and new course, both of 18 holes, the former was designed in part by the renowned Tom Morris but has been periodically altered in the 20th century, while taking pride of place is the clubhouse, designed in a Scottish Baronial style. One of the club's more eventful gatherings was the meeting held in 1916 that voted to expel Ramsay Macdonald MP for his pacifist views, which were completely at odds with the general mood towards the war raging in Europe. But in 1929, five years after the first attempt, the vote was carried to reverse the decision, by which time he was Prime Minister and preferred to remain a member of the Spey Bay Golf Club 12 miles away. The club has been host to many national tournaments over the years and upholds the general rules by which other clubs are governed.

MORTLACH
MORAY

The village situated just SW of Dufftown may derive its name either from the Gaelic 'Morthulach' meaning 'a big hillock' (hill) or from the Gaelic 'morlag' meaning 'a great hollow'. Once the seat of a Columbian Church dedicated to St Moluag who also started a school and farm in the 6th century. Shortly after his victory over the Danes, King Malcolm II founded a bishopric here to further promote Christianity, which in the 12th century was transferred to Aberdeen by David I. Consequently the central role its church had played has meant that the rest of its history has taken place on the margins of the village. There is the site of a Fort on Conval Hill to the west, Balvenie Castle to the north, Auchindoun Castle to the south east and standing stones to the south. Fluctuations in its farming industry in its more recent history led to numerous illegal whisky stills which were the forerunners of the area's many distilleries, among which Mortlach, founded in 1823, is the oldest. See Church, Battle & Distillery

MORTLACH CHURCH
MORAY

The church and village of Mortlach SW of Dufftown has had some religious significance from an early period, for in 1157 a Bull of Pope Adrian mentions a monastery and five churches which probably developed from its connections with St Moulag who assisted St Boniface during his missionary work in the north. The story concerning the inspired Mal-

colm II, whose success in clinching victory over the Danes, 1014 due to divine intervention moved him to extend the church of St Moulag by three lengths of his spear, is not without foundation. This is probably one of the last high points associated with the church, as its location precluded it from playing a more integral role in the country's history, of which it is consigned to an early period. The present cruciform church consists of some of the earlier structure, along with a north wing added in 1826 and extended in 1876. In the churche's east end are two lancet windows and part of the walls that may date from the 13th century, while nearby in the north wall is the mid 16th century recumbent effigy of a knight in armour, purported to be that of Alexander Leslie a local nobleman. The oldest objects it houses are The Pictish Battle Stone and the Elephant Stone that date from the 6th and 11th centuries respectivly.

MORTLACH, BATTLE OF, 1014
MORAY

South of Dufftown. Fought when the forces of Malcolm II of Scotland sought to stem the advance of the Norsemen under Sigurd the Stout, who had overrun the province of Moray. According to the legend of Boece, on seeing the Scots' pending defeat the King looked towards the chapel dedicated to St Moluag and sought divine intervention, which came in the form of victory for the Scots and the death of the Norse leader at the hands of King Malcolm. Malcolm's victory in the north left the King space to consolidate his position in the south.

MORTLACH DISTILLERY
MORAY

One of the first distilleries to be built on the seven hills around Dufftown, and reputed to stand on an illicit still which drew its water from Highland man

John's Well. Its founders James Findlater, Donald Mackintosh and Alexander Gordon leased the land from the Earl of Macduff and were licensed in 1823 during the Government's attempts to stamp out illicit distilling by reducing taxes on spirits. A new owner, John Gordon, who had previously brewed beer here, had attained some celebrity in Leith and Glasgow by 1862 with his new product ' The Real John Gordon'. Running it in conjunction with the adjoining farm, in 1853 a land surveyor George Cowie, who helped plan the railway lines in Banffshire, became a partner and eventually the owner when John Gordon died in 1867. Prominent in business and active in public life, he became Provost of Dufftown before handing over the business to his son Dr Alexander Cowie, who became a leading Highland Distiller of his time and Deputy Lieutenant of Banffshire. He is also credited with installing three new stills and a railway siding for direct links to markets in the south. Mortlach was bought by John Walker & Sons of Kilmarnock in 1923. Apart from a short period in 1944 it continued production during World War II. To satisfy the ever growing demand, in 1964 a new distillery, mash house and tun room were completed in an open-plan style, while retaining the original stills. Today Mortlach's triple form of distillation on three wash, and three spirit stills produces whisky for blending, and a by-product pot ale and daff used in animal feedstuffs.

OWNERS
Diageo plc ?

REGION
Speyside

PRODUCT
Mortlach 16 year old single malt 43% vol

NOTES
A creamy nose with a sweet slightly fruity flavour.

MORTON CASTLE
DUMFRIES & GALLOWAY

Amidst the hills of upper Nithsdale 3 miles N of Thornhill, stand the ruins of a courtyard keep with D shaped angle towers. Although the site of a stronghold from the 12th century, when the barony belonged to the Earl of Nithsdale, the present structure is predominantly 15th century. By the 14th century it was held by Thomas Randolph, Earl of Moray and nephew of Robert the Bruce but passed through marriage to the Earls of March and then the Douglases, (1440), who became Earls of Morton. Despite its gradual decline after the Douglas's fall (1455), it still remains a substantial ruin.

MOUNTQUHANIE CASTLE
FIFE

About 2 miles W of Cupar are the ruins of a late 16th century keep. The building bears the arms of the Balfours, with the initials A.B and the date 1597, which are an abbreviation for Andrew Balfour of Strathor and Mountquhanie whose mother was the daughter of Patrick, Archbishop of St Andrews. Held by Sir James Balfour who was a leading figure in the reign of Mary Queen of Scots (1542-67). The castle was occupied by the Crawfords in 1683, when an additional west wing with turreted doorway was built and lived in until the early 19th century, when it was owned by the Gillespie family.

MOY CASTLE
ARGYLL & BUTE

This old keep was for a long time the residence of the Macleans. Standing on rocky foundations at the N end of Loch Moy on the southern side of the Island of Mull, the structure is of an early type but there are few features by which its date can be accurately determined. The walls probably date from the 14th century while the upper part seems to have been modified in the 17th century.

MUCHALLS CASTLE
ABERDEENSHIRE

With a view of the North Sea from a site 5 miles NE of Stonehaven is a well preserved 17th century Scottish courtyard mansion, started by a Burnet of Leyis in 1619 and completed by his son Sir Thomas Burnet in 1627. Though the exterior is essentially Scottish the interior has a distinctly foreign influence as the figures on the ceilings are not of national heroes but of Classical and Biblical figures, a common practice throughout Europe during the Renaissance period.

MUCKRACK CASTLE
HIGHLAND

Located on a steep bank 4 miles SW of Grantown is a recently restored 16th-century keep. Originally the seat of the powerful Grant family of Rothiemurcus, it was built in 1598 by the 2nd son of John Grant of Freuchie, who was one of Queen Mary's party present at the murderof Rizzio at Holyrood Palace, 1566. Developing from a simple keep that was extensively rebuilt with courtyard added later, by the 19th century, when it was the property of John Dick Peddie, it became ruinous.

MUGDOCK CASTLE
EAST DUMBARTONSHIRE

Occupying land near Strathblane 7 miles N of Glasgow is the old stronghold of the Grahams. The family held the lands from the early 13th century and built the original towers with enceinte wall in the 14th century. The massive quadrangular tower was once defended by a deep broad ditch (fosse) drawn around it from the lake, and in the 16th or 17th century a modern mansion was added within its original walls, which was a common

practice at that time. The high point of the castle's history was as the birthplace of John Graham, 5th Earl and Ist Marquis of Montrose, 1612, during whose imprisonment in Edinburgh Castle, 1641, the Committee of Estates ordered Lord Sinclair to 'Violently brak up the gates and doors of the place of old Montrose'. Rendered open and insecure when the Marquis occupied it again prior to his famous campaign in 1644, the house fronting the loch and the north tower was partly damaged by the Buchanan Clan. From the ruins of this, another house was erected in 1655, which was used as a dwelling house until 1774, when it was replaced by a third house.

MUIRFIELD GULLANE GOLF CLUB
EAST LOTHIAN

The home of The Honourable Company of Edinburgh Golfers, who were descended from the Gentlemen Golfers Golf Club of Edinburgh in 1744, first saw life in 1891 after the club's removal from Musselburgh. The course was laid out by David Plenderleith to plans by Tom Morris. In 1892 it was host and winner (H Hilton) to the first Open Championship. Over the years the course has undergone some extensions and alterations while continuing to host championships well into the 20th century. Up to 1992 the Open has been played here 14 times with post-war winners including Henry Cotton, 1948; Gary Player, 1959; Jack Nicklaus, 1966; Lee Trevino, 1972; Tom Watson, 1980; Nick Faldo, 1987 and 1992.

MUIR OF ORD GOLF CLUB
HIGHLAND

Located near the village of the same name 6 miles west of Dingwall. The club was instituted in 1875 and laid out on old arable and rough grazing land by James Baird, one of the more distinguished architects of the day. Basically a hard, heathland-type course, though home to few natural trees, extensive plots of Scots pine and larch have been planted that divide the 6th and 13th fairways. Alas the Wick and Inverness Railway line divides the course into 9 holes each.

MUNESS CASTLE
SHETLAND

One of the most distinctive of Britain's castles is to be found on the remote Island of Unst. It was built in 1598 by Laurence Bruce of Cultmilindie, who took refuge here after murdering someone in an affray. His mother was the daughter of Lord Elphinstone, and mother, by James V, of Robert Stewart, Abbot of Holyrood and Earl of Orkney. Oblong in shape, it was three storeys high and has two large round towers projecting at diagonally opposite angles, which makes it a Z plan castle. Above the main entrance is the rhyme which reads:

List ye to know this building quha began ?
Laurance the Bruce he was that worthy man,
Quha earnestlie his arris and offspring prayis,
To help and not to hurt this work alwayis
The zeir of God 1598

The castle's remoteness has spared it the impact from the precarious fluctuations of Scotland's history but the constant attacks from the weather have gradually undermined its structure.

MURTHLY CASTLE
PERTH & KINROSS

Erected on level ground near the River Tay 4´ miles SE of Dunkeld. Developing from a small 16th century keep thought to have been a royal hunting seat, it was greatly extended when Murthly became the property of the Stuarts Barons of Grandtully in 1615, and thereafter took the form of an L plan courtyard castle. In the 19th century

the 6th Baronet commissioned Gillespie Graham to build a new mansion which was left unfinished and later demolished.

MUSSELBURGH
EAST LOTHIAN

Coastal town situated at the mouth of the River Esk 6 miles ESE of Edinburgh. While the original name of Eskmouth came from its position on the river, after the burghers refused a reward for honouring the body of Robert Ist's nephew the Earl of Moray, who died here in 1332, it acquired the name 'Honest Toun', but the present name is from its 'mussel bank'. With traces of a Roman presence, this has been the site of a village since the 7th century, and was granted with the surrounding land to Dunfermline Abbey in the 11th and 12th centuries by Malcolm III and David I. The scene of an assembly of Scottish Barons who swore fealty to Alexander II in 1201. The King granted the town privileges which later led to Robert the Bruce raising it to a burgh 1315-29, called Mucchellburg and in later years it acquired some spiritual significance when it became the site of a leper hospital in 1418 dedicated to Mary Magdalene. It was 1530 when James V made a pilgrimage here on foot to the Chapel of our Lady of Loretto at Pilgrims Well. Owing to its coastal position and its proximity to the Capital, the burgh was often used as a stepping stone for invading armies from the south, for in 1544 it was burnt by the Earl of Hertford and in 1547 by Lord Grey after the battle of Pinkie. Although a Burgh of Regality for Dunfermline Abbey in 1562, at the Reformation it was conferred on John Maitland Lord Thirlestane who held it until 1709, when it was bought by the Duchess of Buccleuch. Traditionally a fishing port, the town had trade links with Holland as early as the Middle Ages before Leith attained its dominance and in 1632 briefly enjoyed the privileges of a Royal Burgh until their erosion by the Edinburgh merchants. Musselburgh Links, for a long time the town's recreational area, was for centuries at the centre of its historical high points. Used by James IV (1488-1513) for playing golf, from 1676 it was where the Silver Arrow Competition for the Royal Company of Archers (Royal Bodyguard) was held. In 1638 the Marquis of Hamilton with a Royal Commission to destroy the Covenanting movement was confronted here by thousands of its adherents, and in 1650 Cromwell's army encamped here. Its position on one of Scotland's most ancient trading routes assured its involvement in future upheavals, as in 1715 when the burghers gave men and money to defend the Capital against the Jacobites, and in 1745 when they placated the rebel army on their route to victory at Prestonpans. In continuing its long sporting tradition the townsfolk witnessed the setting up of the The Edinburgh Golfing Society in 1735, the Royal Musselburgh Golf Club in 1774, and the starting of the Musselburgh Races in 1817. The latter decision no doubt being influenced by the building in 1792 of a 2,000 man military barracks. Sir John Rennie's five arched bridge, built in 1807, over the Esk, linking the town to Fisherrow, is thought to have been built on or near to the site of an earlier bridge from Roman times. Severely affected by the cholera epidemic of 1832, in the following year its representation in Parliament helped further its trade, which by 1880 was mainly concerned with sail cloth, fishing nets, fish, golf clubs and balls. Amongst its buildings are included the Old Tolbooth, built in 1590 with stone from Loretto Chapel but altered in 1875 with a much earlier clock tower, the Town Hall built in 1762, while outside is the Mercat Cross with a unicorn holding the Burgh Shield. Although

started in the late 16th century, its Grammar School was eclipsed by the more famous Loretto Boarding School dating from 1778 and modelled on an English public school. The steady decline of the town's industry throughout the 20th century was tempered by the through trade from the A1 road link between Edinburgh and the south which has continued to make Musselburgh the southeastern gateway to the Capital, of which it is now virtually an extension.

MUTHILL
PERTH & KINROSS

Village situated 3 miles SE of Crieff. Name either derived from the Gaelic 'maothail' meaning 'soft spongy ground' or from the Old English 'moet hill' meaning 'hill of justice'. The site of a Culdee Community in the 12th century that later became the residence of the Deans of Dunblane and for some time after the Reformation, 1560, the seat of the Presbytery. The legacy of its former status is its 15th century church, built by Bishop Ochiltree on much older foundations and incorporating a 12th century tower, but sadly it has been pillaged for some of its stone. The area's main defensive structures are the 15th century Drummond Castle to the west, and to the south west on the Roman road are the extensive remains of the Roman Camp at Ardoch, built by Agricola in the 1st century. The village which replaced the one burnt by the Jacobites in 1715 was described in 'a late 19th cenury guide 'as one of the best built and pleasantest villages in Scotland'. See Drummond Castle

MYRES CASTLE
FIFE

Situated outside Auchtermuchty on what was probably a marsh (which its name implies) is a Z plan castle comprising two blocks with angled round towers. The land and office of Claviger (Key bearer or Macer), originally connected with the nearby Falkland Palace, was held by John Scrimgeour, 2nd son of the Counstable of Dundee, in 1484. His grandson, also John Scrimgeour, who was Master of the Kings Works and held the charter in 1531, built the original lower section shortly after. The south west tower which was the watchtower was erected along with the south west front in 1616 by Stephen Paterson after acquiring the land in 1611. Although a John Paterson succeeded his father to the Office of Claviger and Sargent of Arms in 1628, in the 19th century, when the castle was enlarged, the Office of Claviger was given to the Court of Session. Presently the building is privately owned.

MYRTON CASTLE
DUMFRIES & GALLOWAY

Situated slightly inland 3 miles SE of Lendalfoot. In the 14th century the lands were held by the Maccullochs who built the original keep during the period when James IV made numerous pilgrimages to the shrine of St Ninian at Whithorn between 1488 and 1513. The frequency of the King's sojourns at the tower led to it being called the King's chamber. In the 16th century an additional L plan structure was added. After being occupied by the Maxwells from 1682 to the late 18th century the old tower was converted into a dovecote in the 19th century and is now covered in foliage.

N

NAIRN
HIGHLAND

Town situated 16 miles NE of Inverness at the mouth of the River Nairn. Name derived from the Gaelic 'uisge an fhearna' meaning 'water of Alders'. Formerly called Invernairn meaning 'mouth of the river Nairn' which undoubtedly made it the site of an early settlement. In the 9th century Sigurd Earl of Orkney built his burgh here around Nairn Castle (now gone), which often figured in raids by Danish sea rovers. Erected into a Royal Burgh, 1190, by William I, whose successor Alexander II granted the castle and lands to the Bishop of Moray in 1226. As Sheriff Constables, the Cowder family were Hereditary Keepers of its castle from the 14th to the 18th century when hereditary jurisdiction was abolished. In the interim, when Nairn thrived as a Market Town and supply port for the area, the town enjoyed long standing links with with the Stewarts, for in 1312 the lands were conferred by Robert the Bruce on his brother-in-law Hugh the Earl of Ross, whose descendants held it until it was forfeited to the Crown in 1475. When challenged about the inferiority of Scottish towns following his accession to the English throne in 1603, James VI was heard to remark 'he had a toon (Nairn) in Scotland sae lang that the inhabitants of one end did not understand the language spoken at the other end'. They included the English speaking fishermen in the south east and the Gaelic speaking Highlanders in the south west. Mainly confined to the margins of Scottish history, other than its burning by Montrose after the battle of Auldearn in 1645, the creation of the Nairn Lordship, 1681, for Robert Nairn of Strathard, the main event in its historical records came in 1746 when before the battle of Culloden the Duke of Cumberland's forces encamped here. On the Duke's birthday, 15th April, the Jacobites attempted a surprise night attack, which failed when they were overtaken by the dawn, adversely affecting the outcome on Culloden Moor the following day, when the cause of the Stewarts perished. Described by Samuel Johnson in 1773 as being 'in a state of miserable decay'. After some setbacks its harbour, built by Telford in 1820, revitalised Nairn's commercial base with trade in timber, freestone, farm foods and fish until the decline of the latter when the burgh, then rebuilt, became a popular holiday destination. Expanding further in the 1920s, Nairn still derives most of its income from seasonal trade along with the additional oil-related prosperity. See Golf Club

NAIRN GOLF CLUB, THE
HIGHLAND

A traditional Scottish Links course in Nairn town. In 1797 records of the Town Council show that the Magistrates had gathered to roup the grass of the links so as not to prevent the gentlemen or others of the town from playing golf. It was, however, the railway in the 19th century that put the game of golf on a sound footing, with links to Inverness in 1854 and Aberdeen in 1858. Mentioned in 'The Field Magazine' in 1875, it wasn't until 1887, following a meeting of the committee, that a suitable ground was marked out by the professional, Andrew Simpson, to 18 holes. Among the seventeen founding fathers there was one Lord Provost, three solicitors, one barrister and two doctors. Under Robert Finlay QC the later friend of James Balfour PM and Attorney General (1900), the club benefited from his experience of the country's best courses which brought the widening of the course in 1888, its extension by Tom Morris in 1890 and in 1892 the funding of the new clubhouse building. Along with Balfour he did much for the advancement of the sport as a whole and often brought colleagues to Nairn from Westminster. Another of his lasting reminders is the Finlay Cup. Since 1890 the junior members of the club have played for the Lawrence Boys' Challenge Cup presented by Mr Justice A T Lawrence. The plans for improvements drawn up by James Braid in 1909, including a new green, were continued with later work in the 1920s to keep pace with improvements at Lossiemouth and Dornoch while being overseen by the landlord Viscount Finlay. On the completion of the course in 1923, with many of its enduring hallmarks, Braid's assertion that it would maintain its position as a first class links has been borne out. With politicians and celebrities outnumbering golfing champions, Nairn became a popular bolt hole for people like Ramsay Macdonald (PM 1924-35) , Lt Col Herman Cyril Mcneil (author of Bulldog Drummond novels), Field Marshall Earl Haig and later Harold Macmillan (PM 1957-63). Between the wars, 1918-39, the clubs elitist policy was replaced by more openness, which has engendered a stronger community spirit. Since the holding of the Scottish Ladies Close Amateur Championship in 1910, moves were afoot to get a parity between the sexes, so in 1925, after the founding of the Ladies Committee, facilities for ladies improved, which no doubt helped decide the venue for the competition in 1929, 1938, 1951, 1959, 1965, and 1974. For the men the highlight of the golfing calendar used to be the Northern Open Tournament which in 1925 was the initiative of Jack Bookless, Scottish Amateur Champion and Nairn player. Up to 1986 the club has won no fewer than nine times. Among the club awards, the Cowder Cup (1888) is the oldest and the K.M Cameron fouresomes

Trophy (1997) the most recent. With the new clubhouse of 1990, Nairn looked forward to hosting the 37th Walker Cup in 1999.

NECHTANSMERE, BATTLE OF, 685
ANGUS

South east of Forfar near Dunnichen Hill. Fought to stem the tide of Egfrith King of Northumbria, anxious to reassert the rule of the Britons and Angles. In feigning a retreat the Pictish King Brude or Bredei drew the enemy into inaccessible country and slew Egfrith along with much of his army. The victory was significant in that it re-established Pictish territory and broke the yoke of Angle supremacy.

NEIDPATH CASTLE
SCOTTISH BORDERS

Strategically built on a hill guarding the approaches to Peebles town, this has been the site of a fortalice from a very early period, when it was the chief residence of the powerful Fraser family who were Sheriffs of Peebleshire. Sir Simon Fraser, who twice defeated the English forces in one day at the battle of Roslin Moor in 1303, used Neidpath as part of his daughter's dowry in 1312, when it passed to the Hays of Yester. Built to an L plan, with additions made in the 15th century, it was visited by James VI in 1587, and in 1650 Lord Yester held it for the King against Cromwell until he was forced to surrender after a fierce bombardment. In 1654 the Earl and Marquis of Tweeddale, descendants of the Hays of Yester, added a new portion. Sold to the Duke of Queensberry in 1686 and inherited by his son, who like his descendants used it as a summer home until 1750, when it passed to the Earl of Wemyss. In 1810 it was occupied by the philosopher and writer Professor Adam Fergusson, who entertained Sir Walter Scott here.

NETHER HORSBURGH TOWER
SCOTTISH BORDERS

About 3 miles SW of Peebles stand the ruins of a rectangular keep built by the Horsburgh family, the Sheriff Deputes of Peebleshire, and were considered one of the oldest territorial families in the country. Their principal seat was the nearby Horsburgh Castle.

NEVILLES CROSS, BATTLE OF, 1346

At the request of Philip of France David II launched an invasion of England which was repelled at Nevills Cross near Durham, when his 2,000 men at arms and 13,000 lightly armed troops were routed by the Archbishop of York and the northern barons. The King and his many nobles were captured and not released until 1357, after the Treaty of Berwick, which included a ransom of 100,000 merks, which almost bankrupted the country.

NEWARK CASTLE
SCOTTISH BORDERS

Situated 4´ miles NW of Selkirk above the River Yarrow. The lands were held from 1423 by the Douglases, who had built this castle to replace Auldwourk Castle which has now disappeared. Although essentially a fortified oblong keep with surrounding walls 10 feet thick, its more leisurely function as a royal hunting seat for Ettrick forest in times past is indicated by the royal arms carved on a stone in its west gable, a reference to it becoming Crown property in 1455 on the Douglas's fall. It later passed to the Scotts of Buccleuch. Often caught in the midst of Anglo Scottish hostilities, it was taken by the English under Lord Grey in 1548, after the battle of Philiphaugh in 1645 it witnessed the massacre of 100 prisoners by Sir David Leslie, later made Lord Newark (1661), and after their victory at Dunbar (1650)

the castle was occupied by Cromwell's forces. Its reputation for hospitality while the residence of the bereaved Duchess of Monmouth and Buccleuch, after the execution of her husband, the Duke of Monmouth in 1685, was romanticised in the following part of Sir Walter Scott's 'The Lay of the Last Minstrel' in 1805:

The Duchess marked his weary pace,
His timid mien, and reverend face,
And bade her page the menials tell,
That they should tend the old man well:
For she had known adversity,
Though born of such a high degree;
In pride of power, in beauty's bloom,
Had wept oer Monmouths bloody tomb!

In 1831, a year before his death, the poet visited Newark with William Wordsworth. Today it stands as a substantial ruin.

NEWARK CASTLE
INVERCLYDE

Occupying land on the southern bank of the Clyde at Port Glasgow, originally called Newark, stand the remains of a quadrangular courtyard keep, built by the Maxwells after they acquired the land from the Danyelstounes through marriage in 1402. King James IV visited here in 1495 on his way to suppress a rebellion in the Western Isles. Above the doorway in the NE section of the courtyard is the inscription 'Blessingis of God be heirin 1597'. This section shows how the Renaissance influenced old Scottish design, as the traditional angle turrets, crow-stepped gables and stair turrets blend with the new detail on the doors and windows. Occupied until the early 18th century before being acquired by Michael Shaw Stewart, it is now in a preserved state.

NEWBATTLE ABBEY
MIDLOTHIAN

Situated near the River Esk about 8 miles SE of Edinburgh is an education centre which today incorporates the former Abbey. The legacy of the pious David I, from 1140, as an appendage of Melrose Abbey the Benedictine monks aspired to the self-sufficiency of their superior house by acquiring property throughout the area and beyond. This included large tracts of land, saltworks, rights of pannage, privileges for cutting wood in royal forests, rights of pasturage and the revenues of several churches. A favourite residence of Alexander II (1214-1249), whose wife was buried here. It was burnt by Richard II in 1385 but was rebuilt with a donation from Edward Crichton in 1419 and enjoyed over a century of stability before it was burnt again by the Earl of Hertford in 1544, leaving less for the Reformers to vandalise in 1560. The son of its first Commendator became Lord Newbattle in 1591 and Earl of Lothian in 1606. The remains uncovered between 1878 and 1895 revealing all the usual layout of a cruciform church and conventional domestic buildings around the cloister are now incorporated in the 19th century castellated mansion. Built by the Marquis of Lothian, his descendant donated it for adult education in 1936.

NEWBURGH
FIFE

Town situated on the south shore of the Firth of Tay. Deriving its name from the time when burghs were too few and new, it was developed by Lindores Abbey (See Abbey) after Alexander III made it a Burgh of Barony for the Abbot in 1266. After the extensive land grants were made in 1457 by Abbot John to the local residents, who paid homage, common service and 40 bolls of barley, the town prospered from the dexterity of its fishermen and weavers and in 1593 was raised to a Royal Burgh by James VI. In 1631 its status was confirmed in a charter from Charles I. Despite this, Newburgh never exercised its right to parliamentary representation, which evidently stifled its growth from a rural community to an industrial town in later years. To the south are the remains of Macduff's Cross or Stone which in days gone by gave any of the clan members immunity from justice after touching it, while Mugdrum House to the west, built in 1786, has in its grounds the Mugdrum Cross which is thought to be of Celtic origin.

NEWMILNS
EAST AYRSHIRE

Town situated 8 miles E of Kilmarnock, which was so named because of the production of muslin at its many mills. In a charter from James IV dated 1490, the place was made a Burgh of Barony for Campbell of Loudon. During succeeding centuries it functioned as a relatively unimportant weaver's village which in the 17th century gave shelter to Dutch Huguenot settlers who are thought to have introduced the drawloom for pattern weaving. This combined with its erection into a Burgh of Regality for the Earl of Loudon, 1707, was to usher in 200 years of prosperity derived from its cottage weaving tradition, which by 1790 made it one of the busiest centres for cotton production in north Ayrshire. Production increased with the new power loom and in 1876 a lace factory was built by the Morton family. Sadly in 1906 the last handloom weaver ceased production and by 1956 the place boasted nine lace factories. The Newmilns Council buildings, dating from 1739, are second in age to its oldest building the Newmilns Tower. See Tower

NEWMILNS TOWER
EAST AYRSHIRE

Standing in the town 7 miles E of Kil-marnock is the ruined 16th century tower of the Campbells of Louden. Though its early history is obscure, it was occupied by a Captain Inglis in the 17th century, when it was used as a prison for Covenanters. Its walls are five foot thick and three storeys high with an open parapet and shot holes. The castle was later used as a stable for the adjacent local inn which still operates.

NEWTON STEWART
DUMFRIES & GALLOWAY

Market Town situated on the River Cree 7 miles NW of Wigtown Bay. Name derived from William Stewart, its founding father, who as 3rd son of the 2nd Earl of Galloway obtained a charter from Charles II in 1677 erecting it into a Burgh of Barony. Owing to its former function as a ford across a river, unlike other 18th century towns Newton Stewart was not built on a regular plan and looked more like a straggling village, with many of its first inhabitants including the more transient members of society attracted by its liberal feu contracts. Within a few decades smuggling did much to promote the town's advancement in the Wigtown economy, taking its population to 900 by 1792. In 1778 the Castle Stewart Estate was purchased by Sir William Douglas whose attempt at changing the village name to Newton Douglas was tied to his vigorous efforts to develop the town with the introduction of weaving and carpet manufacture which soon failed and the name reverted to Newton Stewart. By 1884 the town had acquired a degree of respectability as its irregular shape with its thatched houses were being replaced with slated two-storey buildings along its main street, while above the town were built fine villas for families attracted by its excellent

schools. Owing to the low level of land and its proximity to the hills and the River Cree, much of the land has been drained to facilitate further expansion, bringing the town closer to Minnigaff with which it serves as a supply point for hillwalkers and anglers. The most interesting building is St Johns Church, York Road, which houses the museum.

NEWTON CASTLE
PERTH & KINROSS

Above the town of Blairgowrie commanding a view of the valley is a Z plan house, the exact age of which is unknown. The exterior is a good example of a 17th century Scottish house of this type and was the birthplace of the well known merchant George Drummond in 1687. He later became Lord Provost of Edinburgh six times and tenaciously promoted the building of the North Bridge, which linked the Old Town with the planned New Town.

NIDDRY CASTLE
WEST LOTHIAN

About 3 miles E of Linlithgow is a large L plan ruin. Originally called Niddry Seton after its builder George, 4th Lord Seton, who died at Flodden in 1513. After her escape from Loch Leven in 1568, Lord Seton conducted Queen Mary here and it was from here that she sent a messenger to her cousin Queen Elizabeth asking for assistance. The castle remained with the family until the reign of Charles II (1649-85), when it passed to the Hopes of Hopetoun, whose descendants became Earls of Hopetoun in 1703.

NORTH BERWICK
EAST LOTHIAN

Coastal town situated 12 miles NW of Dunbar. Name derived from the Old English 'bere' and 'wic' meaning 'barley farm' or 'village'. Easily identified by the

Bass Rock off its shoreline and Berwick Law in the town centre. In the 7th century the rock was occupied by St Baldred, an anchorite whose ruined chapel still remains, while Berwick Law, a 600 ft high mound topped by a whale's jawbone is an extinct volcano and probably the site of an early settlement, as prehistoric pottery has been uncovered in the vicinity. So distinct were they to travellers by land and sea down through the ages that they were sometimes woven into verse as in this stanza from Sir Walter Scott's 'Marmion':

And now close at hand they saw
North Berwick's town and lofty law
Fitz Eustice bade them pause a while,
Before a venerable pile,
Whose turrets viewd afar,
The lofty Bass, the Lambie Isle,
The ocean's peace or war.

During the Napoleonic Wars it was surmounted by a signal tower. In the 12th century the land was held by Duncan Earl of Fife who founded a nunnery which received land and two hospitals from his son Duncan with the proviso that poor folk and pilgrims were to be received as far as was possible. Developing on the narrow headland between two sandy bays, by the 14th century, when the burgh was held by the Douglases, its harbour's Free Port status made it a rich agricultural centre with some fishing and was frequently used as a supply port for invading armies who sought the strategic prizes of Tantallon and Dirleton castles. Probably created a Royal Burgh by Robert III in 1425, it was represented in parliament by 1480. The Auld Kirk by the harbour which may date from the 12th century but has 16th century additions was the place where in the famous witch trials of 1591 the devil was said to have appeared to 94 witches and 6 wizards who danced in the kirkyard to Geil-

lie Duncan playing on the Jew's Harp. Despite its status being confirmed in a charter of Novodamus by James VI in 1568, the burgh steadily declined and by 1691 was described in the Convention of Burghs as 'having no fairs or weekly markets ships or a ferry boat, except two fishing boats'. The present Parish Church, first built in 1670 and enlarged in 1770, houses an hour glass, a metal baptismal ewer and four silver chalices, two predating 1670. In later years the town fell into relative obscurity when its herring fishing disappeared. After 1860 the burgh fell back on its rich farmland (once known as the garden of Scotland) which supported the community in later decades when the present town was built with stone from the local quarry. Today the ambience of the place has an air of residential and recreational tranquillity with its golf club prominent.

NOTLAND CASTLE
ORKNEY

It occupies land at the N end of Westray Island 20 miles N of Kirkwall. Developing from an oblong keep, in the early 15th century the land belonged to the Bishops of Orkney, who built the first castle. In the year of 1560, Gilbert Balfour of Westray, a supporter of Queen Mary, obtained possession of the castle from Adam Bothwell, Bishop of Orkney, and under the Queen's orders Balfour prepared the castle for a visit from the Queen and her husband the Earl of Bothwell (Duke of Orkney) in 1565. It was around this time that most of the Z plan courtyard structure took shape. Besieged and taken by Patrick Stewart, Earl of Orkney in 1591 after his father had died while trying to curb the powers of the bishops, in the 17th century it provided a refuge for the officers of Montrose's army and was burnt and made ruinous by Cromwell's forces.

O

OAKWOOD TOWER
SCOTTISH BORDERS

Favourably sited on a steep bank overlooking the Ettrick valley 4´ miles SW of Selkirk. In 1541 the land was granted by the Crown to William Scott on condition he would build a house that would supply the armed horsemen serving in the King's wars. The present square tower was built in 1602 by a Robert Scott for his wife, a daughter of the House of Murray. Held by the Scotts until it became the property of Lord Polwarth in 1867, it is now a private dwelling house.

OBAN
ARGYLL & BUTE

Coastal town situated opposite the Isle of Mull. Name derived from the Norse 'hop' meaning 'a bay' or 'creek' which in Gaelic is 'ob' therefore 'small bay'. Once a fishing and farming community, when it was visited by Dr Johnson and James Boswell in 1773, the latter remarked favourably on how "the little hotel keepers in the little clachan (small village) of Oban have not lost their reputation". In 1786 a fishing station was established which was followed in the 19th century by the erection of a Militia HQ in 1809, it being raised to a Burgh of Barony for the Duke of Argyll, 1811, its elevation to a Parliamentary Burgh, 1832, and to a Police Burgh in 1862. The publication of Sir Walter Scott's 'The Lord of the Isles' in 1814 (the year of his visit) hastened Oban's development, which was further enhanced by a visit from Queen Victoria in 1847. By this time its reputation as the gateway to the Western Isles and an important point on the Victorian tourist trial won it the appellation the 'Charing Cross of the Hebrides' in the popular imagination. From its main streets extend its quays, hotels and railway station which, as the terminus for the Edinburgh-Glasgow line, also made it an attractive residential summer retreat. Despite this its strongest link is with the sea for which it has acted like a magnet for mail boats, passenger ferries, fishing boats, steam boats and pleasure craft plying the waters from places in and around Argyllshire. Dominating the horizon from Oban hill is McCaig's Tower, an imitation Roman Colosseum built of granite in 1897 for Norman McCaig, a local banker who sought to relieve unemployment and erect a memorial to his family, but after his death it was left unfinished and was renamed McCaigs Folly. St Columba's Catholic Cathedral to the NW was built of granite to designs by Giles and Oldrid Scott in 1922. Witnessing much house building in the 1930s, for generations of young people from the islands Oban was their first impression of a mainland town and as such it provides educational and recreational facilities. In the 1990s two of its main attractions included its glassworks and distillery.

OBAN DISTILLERY
ARGYLL & BUTE

Situated in the town is one of Scotland's oldest distilleries which grew up alongside the town after being founded in 1794 by the prestigious Stevenson family. Their tireless efforts established Oban as one of the premier towns of Argyll, and the gateway to the Western Isles, thereby providing a ready market. A West Highland representative in the classic malt, Oban operates the traditional batch process of a malt whisky distillery, at the heart of which is the two copper pot stills, supplying markets in the United Kingdom and overseas, and was visited by Her Royal Highness the Princess Royal in 1991.

OWNERS
Diageo plc ?

REGION
Highland

PRODUCT
Oban 14 year old single malt 43% vol

NOTES
A fresh, delicate, slightly peaty aroma with a smooth fruity taste and a long inspiring aftertaste.

OLD BISHOPTON HOUSE
RENFREWSHIRE

Commanding a view over the Clyde 1 mile W of Bishopton village is a 17th century L plan mansion house. Built by the Brisbanes, who held the estate from the 14th to the 17th century, when it was acquired by John Wilkinshaw of that ilk, later becoming the property of Hugh Dunlop. It then passed through marriage to Lord Sempill who sold it to Sir J. Maxwell of Pollock.

OLD MELDRUM
ABERDEENSHIRE

Town situated 18 miles NW of Aberdeen. Although once called Bethelnie Parish from the Hebrew meaning 'house of God', owing to the creation of an early church, it was changed in the 17th century to the present name which is from the Gaelic 'meall-droma' meaning 'hill ridge', as the area was reputed to be the site of a Roman Camp. The church already mentioned was dedicated to St Nathalin and gave its name to the January Fair where the local farmers had sold their produce since 1672, when Charles II granted the town a Burgh of Barony Charter in favour of James Urquhart. The Parish Church, which dates from 1684, was rebuilt in 1767 and enlarged in 1954. North east of the village stands Meldrum House (hotel). A 17th century Grecian edifice which was built on the site of a family seat formerly held by the Setons from

the 13th century, the house passed to the Urquharts of Meldrum in 1610 and was enlarged in the 19th century. Meldrum became an Agricultural Township supplying the main markets in Aberdeen when its farming supplanted its distillery, brewery and cotton manufacture.

OLD SLAINS CASTLE
ABERDEENSHIRE

On a rock facing the North Sea 7 miles SSW of Peterhead is a large ruinous keep of the Hays of Errol, probably built in the 16th century on the site of an earlier structure. Though noted as an extensive stronghold protected by a deep ditch with drawbridge, it was demolished by James VI in 1594 after the victory at Glenlivet which was the culmination of the Earl of Huntly's rebellion, which the 8th Earl of Errol was party to. Much of today's ruins are a reminder of that fateful day.

ORCHARDTON TOWER
DUMFRIES & GALLOWAY

Located in a field 6 miles SE of Castle Douglas. The land of Orchardton was the property of Alexander Carny, once the Provost of Lincluden, who died in 1422. But it was a John Carny who was probably a grandson, who built this tower around 1450.

ORKNEY GOLF CLUB
ORKNEY

The club owes its existence to Angus Buchanan, a keen sportsman from Edinburgh who in 1884 was appointed Manager of the National Bank of Scotland in Kirkwall. With fellow enthusiast Sheriff Armour and others they founded The Orkney Golf Club in 1889, playing the first Armour Medal Competition on the scenic 9 hole course on Birsey Links, which brought them recognition in the 'Orkney Herald' and the wider public. After carrying out improvements, the second and third competitions were held in May and June, but with gales the cumulation of seaweed and the acceptance that the club must cater for a growing number of followers, a site closer to the burgh, at Pickaquoy, was developed. Such was the passion for the game that players would come from far and wide to play for the Armour Medal, and compete with golfers from Shetland who often sailed over in their private boats to play for the Gold Medal, acquired from Birsey, and the Silver Star Medal, presented by Sheriff Thomas. After the lease of land from the Dundas Estate, the course was extended to 9 holes in 1895, increasing its appeal further. The closing years of the century saw the presentation of the Lady's Cup, (1897) by the wives of the players, while in the wider picture golf had become so popular that clubs now existed in Stromness, Sanday, and Stronsay, when Orkney boasted 111 members including 95 males, 4 ladies, 6 boys and 6 country members. With the termination of the lease from the Dundas Estate in 1901, the club was relocated at the 41 acre site at Grainbank and so began a frenzied period of activity to prepare the land for a 9 hole course that was duly opened with new pavilion in 1902, amidst a festive atmosphere. The club's association with naval personnel from the destroyer flotilla (remembered by the Flotilla Cup, gifted by officers & men in 1909) at Kirkwall and the Home Fleet at Scapaflow before 1914 brought an extension to the clubhouse and a stronger social element that continued during and after the war of 1914-18, when the lady members had achieved a greater acceptance among the men. In 1923 the extended 18 hole course was opened and by 1926 its members numbered 159 males, and 123 females. For much of the club's history, playing revolved around the Hamilton Cup, but during World War II the course was largely given over to the

war effort, particularly the military, whose deployment of anti-invasion defences were confined to the fairways, thus enabling some personnel to practice when not being obstructed by grazing sheep. The club was gradually brought back into something resembling its former state after the war when, in 1949, it hosted the competition for the Flotila Cup, three years before celebrating the 50th anniversary of the opening of the Grainbank Course. Attempts made in the 1960s to make the club more viable, including the selling of land and the encouragement for new players, met with some success. This was helped along by competitions for the Hamilton Cup, 1922; Cupal Cup, 1932; and the Heddle Cup, all of which took the membership to 125 by 1975 with the likelihood that it would exceed 250 by 1989.

ORPHIR CHURCH
ORKNEY

Situated on the south side of the island next to the Parish Church are the remains of a Romanesque church dedicated to St Nicholas. In the 'Orkney Saga' of 1136 it stated that 'There in Orfir, was a great drinking-hall, and there was a door at the east gable from the south in the side wall, and a noble church stood before the hall door, and one went down steps from the hall into the church'. The building has the unusual distinction of being the first circular Medieval church in Scotland. Owing to its proximity to the Earl Haakon's Palace, it was probably erected by a wealthy Norse nobleman in the time of Haakon's successor Earl Paul II with whom according to some sources he travelled to the Holy Land. This would place its construction between 1090-1137. Sadly, although the building was complete in 1757, by 1760 it had been robbed of some of its stone to build the Parish Church. So by 1760 it was described by

Bishop Pecocke as being "20 feet in diameter and 15 feet high, is vaulted with a hole in the top to give light, and there is a small window in the east end".

OTTERBURN, BATTLE OF, 1388

Fought in response to a massive raid across the border by the Earls of Douglas, March and Moray. During their return from harrying the land as far as Durham, the Scots were engaged but managed to defeat Sir Henry Percy's army, causing the death of the Earl of Douglas. The Earl's sacrifice was immortalised in verse by Sir Walter Scott:

These were the arms that once did turn
The tide of fight on Otterburn,
And Harry Hotspur forced to yield,
When the dead Douglas won the field

The later counter-assault by the Scots without their weak and recalcitrant King Robert II made the need for firm leadership more apparent, prompting the rise of his son, the Regent Albany.

OTTERSTON HOUSE
FIFE

It stands on ground 2 miles NE of Inverkeithing. The land was acquired in the 13th century by Philip de Moubray through marriage to the daughter of the Earl of Dunbar. Recognised as a distinguished statesman, he was Ambassador to England in 1215, but the property stayed with the family for a while after and was then held by numerous families for over 500 years until repurchased by Sir Robert Moubery in the early 19th century. Owing to the major alterations made in 1851, which greatly increased its accommodation but destroyed its antique character, the only part of the original structure remaining is the round tower and the doorway with its lintel inscribed with the date, 1589, and 'Welcome Friends. D.M' .

P

PAISLEY
CITY OF GLASGOW

Town situated 10 miles W of Glasgow. Name derived from the Brythonic 'Pasgell' and 'lledh' meaning 'pasture plain'. Once the site of a Roman Station and conjectured to be Ptolemy's (Egyptian geographer) Vanduaria. The lands were granted by Malcolm IV in 1157 to Walter Allan, High Steward of Scotland, who in 1163 founded Paisley Priory which became an Abbey by 1220, with a village for retainers. While sharing the fate of its Abbey, the village was burnt in 1307 during the Wars of Independence and did not recover until 1404, when the office of Heritable Sheriff was granted by Robert III. The town's advancement had as much to do with the Abbey resuming its functions following repairs as it had with its proximity to Glasgow, and in 1488 it was created a Burgh of Barony for Abbot Shaw, a staunch supporter of King James V who visited the town in 1498, 1504 and 1507. It was at Paisley that the Lords of the Congregation (opponents of Mary I's ties with France and Rome) met in 1556 before hurriedly moving to Hamilton. The Paisley Grammar School, founded by a Royal Charter in 1576, gave the town a rich educational tradition that was enhanced much later by the founding in 1848 of its Art School, which undoubtedly attracted its large community of poets, many of whom were of Irish and Scottish extraction. Severely affected by the plague in 1588, 1602 and 1645, when the town was sealed off. It was during this period that its first hospital was built, 1618, and the town was raised to a Lordship for Lord Claud Hamilton, 1591. Paisley was visited by the forces of Charles I in 1649 when the burghers raised a force for the Royalist cause, but after their defeat at Dunbar, 1650, it was occupied by Cromwell's troops, who laid a heavy burden on the burgh's resources. Always a supporter of Christian values, between 1677-97 the town saw the burning of numerous witches and also sent a force to the Edinburgh Convention in 1688 to support the crowning of William and Mary. Free trade with England at the Union of 1707 met with a mixed response, but after the transitional setbacks prosperity ensued, encouraging the burhers to support the Government in the 1715 and also in the 1745 Jacobite Rising when the town was fined £1000 by the rebels, £500 of which was paid. The introduction of white thread (Nuns thread) in 1722 by Christian Shaw eventually made Paisley the seat of its production and by 1791 the area had over 100 small thread mills, enriching an already thriving linen trade with America and Europe. The fruits of its dexterity helped to establish the Paisley Bank by 1787 and to conceive the Paisley Shawl, a design made up of the best patterns in India and France but with its own individual characteristics. Fierce competition from home and abroad plus the introduction of cotton thread in 1812 drastically reduced its thread mills to around 12 in 1812, but by 1830 most of the smaller firms had been absorbed by J & J Clarke or by John Coats who presided over the industry throughout the century and beyond. Created a Parliamentary Burgh in 1833 and a Police Burgh in 1862. The introduction of the printed shawl from England in 1870 sounded the death knell for the shawl trade and many of its ancillary industries including the production of bleach, machines, soap and dyes. Despite this the merger between the Coats and the Clark firms with their international concerns, by 1900 Paisley again became part of the wider industrial network in which its engineering industry which grew from its textile trade, made machinery for sugar refineries, sawmills, oil refineries and mining. The burgh's four stages of expansion were 1832, 1900, 1920 and 1957. While some of its traditional industries remain, albeit on a smaller scale, the emphasis is on lighter industries with the reminders of its golden age now consigned to its museum and Art Gallery. See Abbey

PAISLEY ABBEY
CITY OF GLASGOW

Located about 7 miles west of Glasgow. This well preserved Benedictine Abbey was started as a priory around 1163 by Walter, High Steward of Scotland, and was built near the site of the 6th century church of St Marinus. Owing to Crown privileges it quickly rose to the status of an abbey, with confirmation from Pope Honorius III in 1219, but its proximity to William Wallace's land at Elderslie brought much destruction, for in 1307 it was destroyed by the forces of Edward I. Built up under the care of the Stewart Kings, many of whom were buried here and by its last Abbot John Hamilton. It withstood the forces of reform and was created a Temporal Lordship for Lord Claud Hamilton, 1587. About this time its design conformed to the cruciform quadrangular plan with the church, its tower and spire, the cloister and conventual buildings, which essentially formed a blend of Gothic and Decorative styles. The oldest part of today's structure largely consists of the church, built by Abbot Thomas Fervas who died in 1459 and Abbot George Shaw before 1500, and was still used in the 19th century. This latter period also saw extensive rebuilding work, started by the celebrated Rowand Anderson and later continued by Robert Lorimer. All of which was colourfully illuminated by the fine stain glass windows. Amongst the tombs in the choir there is one of Marjory Bruce, daughter of Robert I, and her grandson

Robert III, but the oldest object of interest is the Celtic Cross of St Barochan. See Town

PARK CASTLE
DUMFRIES & GALLOWAY

Outside the village of Glenluce in view of the ruined Glenluce Abbey stands the fortified house of Park. Built by Thomas Hay, the epigraph above the door reads

'BLESSIT BE THE NAME OF THE LORD THIS VERKVAS BEGUIT THE DAY OF MARCH 1590 BE THOMAS HAY OF PARK AND IONET MAK DOVEL HIS SPOUS'.

Thomas Hays father, the younger son of the Hays of Dalgetty in Aberdeenshire was appointed Abbot of Glenluce in 1559 by Pope Pius IV but later joined the Reformation Party. The building is the traditional L plan fortified house with additions made at a later date which suffered with the rest of the house during a period of neglect, but are now both restored.

PEEBLES
SCOTTISH BORDERS

Town situated on the north bank of the Tweed, 23 miles south of Edinburgh. Name derived from the Brythonic 'Pebyll' meaning 'movable habitation, tents'. Probably due to the fresh supply of water that would have attracted early settlers. The area was once dotted with hillforts of the Ancient Britons and as tradition has it was thought to have been visited by St Mungo, the 6th century missionary, who may have built a church here. When David I created Peebles a Royal Burgh by 1153 it was already in the diocese of Glasgow, and its castle a popular royal hunting seat which was later visited by Malcolm IV, William I, Alexander II and Alexander III. This led to the erection of religious buildings like the Parish Church of St Andrew, founded by Bishop Jocelin in 1195 (replaced by the Holy Cross Church of St Nicholas, both ruinous), a Trinitarian Friary (now below the ruins of Cross Kirk) founded by Alexander III in 1260, and the poor hospital of St Leonard, founded at nearby Horsburgh and mentioned in 1395. The town was occupied in 1296 by Edward I, who bestowed it on Aymer Valence, Warden of Scotland. Shortly after Robert the Bruce granted it the right to hold a fair, and on his death in 1329, visits by his son David II led to a couple of the Burgh Commissioners helping to negotiate with the English for the King's release after the battle of Durham and ultimately to a confirmatory Royal Burgh Charter, 1367. During one of the many visits by James I (1406-1437) the King saw the sports of Beltane (May Ist) involving horse racing and archery which attracted large crowds from Southern Scotland and inspired him to write a poem entitled 'Peblis to the Play':

At Beltane, when ilk body bounds
To Peebles to the play,
To hear the singing and the sounds,
Their solace sooth to say,
By firth and forest forth they found,
They graithit them full gay,
God wait that would they do that sound,
For it was their feast day
They said of Peebles to the play;

The festival itself originated with the Ancient Britons who lit fires on hill tops in honour of their deity Ball. Peebles growing prosperity as a Market Town from the 14th century, from which its Mercat Cross dates, brought its destruction by the Earl of Hertford in 1545 and the building of a new town with a defensive wall. This proved more of a useless obstruction when the place was burnt accidentally in 1604. After his defeat at Philiphaugh, 1645, the Marquis of Montrose fled here to seek support from the local lairds, and five years later the town was occupied by Cromwell's forces during the siege of Neidpath Castle. The castle of Peebles, which dated from the 12th century, was by 1700 used as a quarry, when its last remains were used to build the town prison. Figuring little in the Covenanting struggles, it remained spectating during the 1715 Rebellion, and in 1745 was occupied by a division of Jacobites before their march south. Among its native sons were William Douglas, 4th Duke of Queensberry, or Old Q (1724-1810) whose family town house is now the Tweeddale Museum / Chamber Institute, Sir John Elliot who became physician to George Prince of Wales, the writer John Buchan (1875-1940) and the brothers Robert (1802-71) and William Chambers (1800-83), printers and publishers. Both did much for Peebles's 19th century development when as County Town it became popular for river fishing in the Tweed (now traversed by a 15th century bridge), tweed mills and a Hydropathic Establishment built in a Georgian style in 1878 but rebuilt in 1907 by James Millar after a fire. In 1897 the Riding of the Marches was revived, followed by the introduction of the Beltane Queen Festival in 1899. Despite the house building that was carried out between 1920 and 1950, visitors are still charmed by the quaint scale of this Border town. In the Tweeddale Museum housed in the Chambers Institute (donated by William Chambers in 1859) are displayed reminders of Tweeddale's rich and varied past. See Neidpath Castle

PENCAITLAND
EAST LOTHIAN

Village situated 15 miles SE of Edinburgh. Name derived from the Old Welsh 'Penchet-llan' meaning 'head of the wood and enclosure'. An ancient Parish with the River Tyne running through it dividing it into East and West Pencaitland which are linked by a bridge dating from the 16th century. The land was granted by William I (1165-1214) to Everand Pencaithlan who gifted its church to Kelso Abbey, but this was later acquired by the monks of Dryburgh Abbey who held it up to the Reformation. Standing in East Pencaitland is a pre-Reformation church with aisle housed in a mainly 16th century structure with a 17th century tower. The nearby Winton House, built in 1620 in a Scottish Renaissance style by George the 3rd Earl of Winton, whose descendant George the 5th Earl was forfeited in 1716 for supporting the Jacobites, later became the property of George Hamilton, who had been made Lord Pencaitland in 1712.

PENICUIK
MIDLOTHIAN

Town situated 10 miles SE of Edinburgh. Name derived from the Brythonic 'Penn-y-cog' meaning 'hill of the Cuckoo'. The area had links with St Mungo in the 6th century, but apart from the land of what is now Penicuik being held by a Hugh de Penicok in 1296 and sold by an Alexander Penicuik in 1746 to John Clerk, a prosperous Montrose merchant who had made a fortune in Paris, the town's pre-eminence was in the Industrial Age. The old family seat SW of the town, a large Grecian edifice built in 1761 by Sir James Clerk (arts connoisseur) was often visited by Alan Ramsay (poet and painter) but was severely damaged by a fire in 1899 and is now a shell. The paper mill built at Valleyfield in 1709 by a Mr Anderson, printer to Queen Ann, was used during the Napoleonic Wars (1810-14) to house prisoners and billet soldiers. But with the industry's expansion came the purchase of a nearby corn mill in 1803 that was used to print bank notes, and a

second mill in 1815, bringing production capacity to 2,500 tons of paper annually. In addition the building of Telford's bridge over the River Esk, 1812, furthered the town's growth and brought the railways, which opened up the area's trade in coal, shale and ironstone. Despite the introduction of liberal working practices by the Cowan family and increased competition, paper and coal remained the mainstay of its economy, causing an increase in house building and in 1933 an extension of the town boundaries. However, the steady decline of its paper manufacture from 1960 onwards, ending in the closure of its last mill in 1975, and the move away from fossil fuels resulted in the setting up of the Edinburgh Crystal Works between 1969 and 1974. The town's architecture, though limited, is dominated by the United Free Church building erected by William Pilkington in 1862.

PENKILL TOWER
SOUTH AYRSHIRE

Overlooking the Girvan Water 3 miles E of Girvan is a 16th century tower which was built by the Boyds after they acquired the land before 1530. More work was done in 1628 by Thomas Boyd after his marriage to Marion Mure of Rowallan. The castle was restored in 1857 by Alexander Thomson when he was employed by Spencer Boyd Esq of Penkill.

PENSHIEL TOWER
EAST LOTHIAN

It occupies ground 5 miles SW of Newtongrange near the Moorfoot Hills. The lands of Penshiel are referred to in a charter of 1200 granted by the Earls of Dunbar to the monks of the Isle of May but later became the property of the monks of Melrose. The ruins of this oblong tower once included a courtyard with surrounding wall. The site's strong religious connections point to the castle being built as a safe house by the Melrose monks, whose pre-Reformation chapel once stood below the castle in the Glen called Chapelhaugh.

PENTLAND RISING, 1666

Occurring in the middle of the Covenanting struggles. As Lieutenant Colonel for the SW of Scotland Sir James Turner, with a Royal Commission, resolved to crush the Covenanters by billeting soldiers on recalcitrant members and exerting fines for non-attendance at public worship. His measures fell short of those urged by Archbishop Sharp, amongst others, but evoked a lasting resentment which came to a climax when a homeless group of the persecuted came upon a party of soldiers haranguing an old man in the village of Dalry. After wounding one and the surrender of the other three the rebels were left with no option but to take their cause further. Seizing the instrument of their plight, Sir James Turner at Dumfries, they marched north east to Lanark with their prisoner and his revenue, with which they provisioned their growing band of supporters which some estimates put at 3,000. At the head of the group was Colonel Wallace. Coming within five miles of Edinburgh, where a force was being marshalled to oppose them, the rebels had to contend with the November weather, food shortages and diminishing numbers. So with around 900 men they retreated west and eventually took up positions on the ridge of a hill near the plain called Rullion Green, which became the scene of their defeat by Thomas Dalyell of Binns, their chief protagonist in the east. Though forming the hub of the Covenanting movement, the moderate peoples of Edinburgh and its environs persecuted the remnants of their army who they saw as extremists while the Government, vindicated by the outcome, stood back as the movement with-out its vanguard lay vulnerable to the coming oppression. With instruments like the boot and the thumb screw there followed mass torture and numerous trials and executions, while others were fined and deported until such measures gave way to a more charitable approach by the administration.

PERTH
PERTH & KINROSS

Town situated 22 miles SW of Dundee. The name either derived from the Gaelic 'Bartha' meaning 'height over the Tay' or from the Brythonic 'Perth' meaning 'a thicket' (a wood). Also known as St Johnstone after its 12th century church dedicated to John the Baptist. Though the likely site of a Roman Fort, as they occupied Old Perth in the 1st century AD, the place firmly comes on record in 1115 when the Augustinian monks were granted land here by Alexander I prior to it receiving Royal Burgh status from David I between 1124 and 1127. Appearing again in a charter from the King when some of its land was acquired by Dunfermline Abbey, its status was confirmed by William I in 1210 after the town's destruction by the Tay. Notwithstanding its proximity to Scone, where Scottish Kings were crowned, and the grandeur of its ecclesiastical buildings, giving it the character of a capital, with up to fourteen parliaments and numerous Scottish Church Councils being held here between 1201 and 1459, Perth remained a regional centre after 1482, when James III established Edinburgh as the Capital. In 1266 the Treaty of Perth was signed here when Norway ceded the Hebrides to Scotland. While providing a natural shelter for merchant ships, the River Tay was visited by German and Flemish traders prior to 1280 and was also used as a supply point for invading armies during the 13th and 14th centuries, when the town changed hands several times. Occupied by Edward I in 1296 when he carried off the Stone of Destiny after failing to get the Scottish Crown, the town was retaken by Robert the Bruce in 1312 but was seized by Edward Balliol after the battle of Dupplin Moor, 1332, and skilfully fortified by Edward III in 1336 until he was forcefully ejected by Robert High Steward of Scotland in 1339. Amongst its religious foundations were a Dominican Friary founded by Alexander II in 1240, where James I was murdered, 1437, a Carthusian Priory established in 1429 by the ill fated James I, and a Franciscan Friary started by Laurence Ist Lord Oliphant in 1460. The scene of a clan battle in 1396 between Clan Chattan and Clan Kay which Walter Scott graphically illustrated in his 'Fair Maid of Perth'. During the frequent attacks from the plague in the 16th and 17th centuries, its victims received only limited comfort in its declining religious houses which, like many others across the country, were damaged at the Reformation, when John Knox gave a sermon here in St Johns Church, 1559. The Gowrie House (now the site of the County Buildings) was the scene of the murder of the Earl of Gowrie in 1600 (Gowrie conspiracy), then Perth's Lord Provost, who it was claimed attempted to assassinate James VI after inviting him to his home. Perth was created an Earldom for James 4th Lord Drummond in 1605 and a Dukedom for the 4th Earl in 1696. Continuing to figure in the country's political upheavals, in 1644 the town was occupied by the Marquis of Montrose, it became the site of Cromwell's fort after his occupation in 1651, was held by Claverhouse in 1689, by the Earl of Mar for James VIII in 1716 and by his son Prince Charles Edward in 1745, when he stayed at the Salutation Hotel on South Street. During the replacement of its traditional linen trade by manufacture in the 19th century, much of the town centre was being extended with spacious Georgian terraces, crescents and streets, with the church of St John taking pride of place near the High Street. Divided into three churches in the 18th century, it was restored to its original form in 1923 by the distinguished Sir Robert Lorimer, when its First World War memorial was added. The six buildings which form the nucleus of the town are St Johns Church, already mentioned, the Sheriff Court on Tay Street, built in 1819, St Ninians Cathedral on Atholl St, built in a Gothic style and completed in 1890, the Fair Maids House, built on the site of the Blackfriars Monastery and once home to Simon Glover, father of the heroine in Sir Walter Scott's 'Fair Maid of Perth'. The City Hall on Tay St was opened in 1911, while the Art Gallery off George St opened in 1935. To the north of the town is Balhousie Castle, a former 15th century tower house built by the Hays, later Earls of Kinnoull, but transformed in 1863 into a Scottish Baronial pile by George 12th Earl, and now houses the museum of the Black Watch Regiment.

PETERHEAD
ABERDEENSHIRE

Coastal town situated 33 miles NE of Aberdeen. Once the site of a Pictish settlement, up to the 16th century the place was called 'Peterugie' after the church of St Peter and the River Ugie but changed to Peterhead when the land passed from the Abbey of Deer to Robert Keith (son of the 4th Earl Marischal) at the Reformation, 1560. A Burgh of Barony from 1587 for the Earl Marischal, Commendator of Deer Abbey, it later passed to George Keith the 5th Earl who while ruling as feudal overlord from the family seat at Inverugie Castle developed the town from a small fishing village, that became a thriving industrious community with harbours, Continental trade and a rising population by the 18th century. When the Old Pretender landed here for the 1715 Rising, when he received support from the Keiths and the townsfolk, who paid dearly for the family's Jacobite sympathies after the rebellion failed and the town was sold along with the Keiths' other estates to the York Building Company in 1720. The land was later purchased by the Edinburgh Merchant Maidens Hospital. A popular spa town in later decades with a harbour built by John Smeaton in 1793 and enlarged by Telford in 1818. Its continued growth as a merchant port made it the capital of British whaling until 1820 when the trade was replaced by herring fishing which at its peak in 1907 its 420 boats landed 291,000 crans (37´ gallons / 170 litres). A history of its maritime past is exhibited in its museum and art gallery in Peter Street. Its other buildings include the old Ugie Fish House built in 1587 by George Keith, and the Town Hall in Broad Street built in 1788 and fronted by a monument erected in 1869 to Field Marshal Keith. After his forfeiture in 1715 he became military adviser to the King of Prussia before dying at the battle of Hochkirchen in 1758. Its more notorious prison built in 1891 provided an abundant source of labour for its granite quarries and its harbour projects, which have latterly served as an operational base for many services linked to the oil industry. See Golf Club

PETERHEAD GOLF CLUB
ABERDEENSHIRE

The earliest endeavours to form a club in Peterhead were in 1841 when several prominent society figures instituted a club, drew up rules and formed a committee. For the first fifty years members played on the 4 but later 6 hole course on Cairntrodlie Links, matches originally being played over three rounds totalling 12 holes, but in 1891 Col Ferguson Laird of Pitfour Estate leased the ground at

Craigewon Links for a 9 hole course which was laid out by Willie Park and opened in 1892. Additional land was acquired in 1907 for the course to be extended to 18 holes. Like many other courses at this time its rising popularity before and during the Great War 1914-18 brought the need for extended facilities, so in 1923 more land was leased and an additional 18 hole course (New Course) was laid out by Laurie Auchterlonie of St Andrews. In 1929, some years after the distinguished James Braid was recruited to suggest improvements to both courses, the erosion by sand of the 16th fairway was becoming an apparent problem. His advice on bunkering on the old course and improvements to the new course layout was set out in a letter, but during World War II the latter was neglected owing to the shortage of Greens Staff, and it was reopened after the war as a 9 hole course. Concern over erosion by sand continued to be expressed at Committee meetings during later years right up to 1969, when it was almost engulfing the whole clubhouse and encroaching on the 15th, 16th, and 17th holes, prompting the building of the present clubhouse and the replacement of the first three holes.

PETTY
HIGHLAND

Village situated 7 miles NE of Inverness. Name derived from the Brythonic 'Pett' meaning 'a portion of land' or 'share of land'. Legend has it that in the 6th century St Columba took refuge in Petty Bay during a storm conjured up by Broichan the pagan priest which ironically led to the erection of a church in the saint's honour (later rebuilt). From their seats at Stuart and Moy castles (only traces remain), the land was held in the 12th century by the De Moravia (Murray) and Mackintosh families respectively until

1314, when Robert I erected the area into an Earldom for his nephew Randolph Moray. Held successively by the Ogilvies of Banff, 1512, George 4th Earl of Huntly, 1548, whose Castle Stuart figured in the conflicts with the Mackintoshes avenging the execution of their chief, and by King James V's son James Stuart Ist Earl of Moray, 1563. Petty played an integral part in the area's rural economy, and in 1611 it became a Burgh of Barony for the Earl of Moray. Its church, now unused, still houses the Mackintosh family vault. See Castle Stuart

PHILIPHAUGH, BATTLE OF, 1645
SCOTTISH BORDERS

To the SW of Selkirk. Fought during the Civil War, when Montrose, with his considerably reduced army of 1100 horse and 500 foot, after his victory at Kilsyth was surprised by General Leslie, who had returned from England with 4,000 horse. Following his defeat Montrose escaped to the Continent but returned in 1650 to avenge the death of Charles I and briefly became Governor of Scotland under Charles II.

PINKIE, BATTLE OF, 1547
EAST LOTHIAN

The site is located to the west of Musselburgh. In another attempt to force the marriage of Edward VI and Mary Queen of Scots, the Duke of Somerset marched north and crossed the border with 12,000 foot and 2,000 horse, while the Scots with their quickly assembled force of around 30,000 advanced to the site near Musselburgh. Though in a superior position on Edmonston Edge, the Scots' decision to attack proved fatal, as a large part of the army was galled by the English cannon shot before being routed by their main force, profiting from the Scots' lack of cavalry. This was the last battle fought between the two independent kingdoms and averted the marriage of their respective monarchs.

PINWHERRY CASTLE
SOUTH AYRSHIRE

Situated NW of Colmonell village in the Stinchar valley is a 16th century L plan tower which was built by a branch of the Kennedies. In 1596 it belonged to a John Kennedie of Balquharrie but after the death of John Kennedie the last Kennedie owner in 1644, the property passed to John Earl of Carrick in 1648.

PIPERDEN, BATTLE OF, 1436
With the ending of the truce between Scotland and England came an invasion by the Scots headed by the Earl of Angus, Warden of the Middle Marches, who gained a victory over Sir Robert Ogyl and Henry Percy, 2nd Earl of Northumberland. The success precipitated the attempted kidnapping of Scotlands' Princess Margaret while en route to France to marry the Dauphin.

PITCAIRLIE CASTLE
FIFE

Dating from the 16th century, it stands between Auchtermuchty and Newburgh. The land originally belonged in 1296 to Sir Alexander Abernethy who, after supporting the Bruce, changed his allegiance to Edward I. It then passed through marriage in 1312 to Sir Andrew Leslie, whose descendant, the 4th Earl of Rothes, bestowed it on his son Patrick (later Lord Lindores), who built the original vaulted tower in the 16th century and whose family occupied it until the mid 17th century. The family of its new owner, Colonel James Cathcart of Corbieston, greatly altered it, with the addition of a round tower at the S end, while a descendant, Sir Robert Cathcart, became Laird of Pitcairlie in 1857 and was appointed Vice Lieutenant of Fifeshire in 1886.

PITCAPLE CASTLE
ABERDEENSHIRE

On the right bank of the River Urie 5 miles NW of Inverurie stands a predominantly 17th century Z plan mansion with 16th-century work. From the 15th century it belonged to the Leslies of Balquhain, who were constantly engaged in feuds between Aberdeenshire families in the 16th and 17th centuries. Scene of the imprisonment of the Marquis of Montrose after his defeat at Carbisdale, 1650, and while en route to his trial and execution in Edinburgh. By 1820 it had fallen into a ruinous state when it was restored and enlarged by the architect William Burns.

PITCRUVIE TOWER
FIFE

In a field 1 mile NW of Upper Largo are the ruins of a rectangular tower. The land originally formed part of the Barony of Loudin but in 1498 was acquired through marriage by John, later Sir John Lindsay of Pitcruvie, son of the 4th Lord Lindsay of the Byres. Around 1500 he built this castle as a separate residence during the lifetime of his father, who resided at Struthers Castle and in 1517 became Sheriff of Fife. The family held the castle and land until 1650, when it was purchased by James Watson of Aithernie (Provost of St Andrews).

PITCULLO CASTLE
FIFE

A 16th century L plan mansion, it stands on a rocky mound 3 miles W of Leuchars. The land belonged to the Sybbalds in the reign of James III (1460-1488) but had passed to the Balfours by the 16th century, when the original L plan keep was built. In the 17th century an additional SE wing was added and further additions were made in the 19th century by the Trent family, who, along with the Hays, had their arms carved on the ceil-ing of a small room. However, by 1854 Pitcullo was completely covered with ivy and the SE wing was later removed, but more recently the castle was saved from total ruin and is now wind and weather proof.

PITFICHIE CASTLE
ABERDEENSHIRE

About one mile N of Monymusk stands a tower which once belonged to General Hurry or Urrie, a distinguished figure during the Covenanting Wars of the 17th century. He served with the Earl of Leven, and also with Montrose at the battle of Carbisdale, when he was captured, taken to Edinburgh and executed. It was the property of the Forbes family in the 18th century and unroofed and ruinous in the 19th century, but was fully restored in the 20th century.

PITFIRRANE CASTLE
FIFE

Two miles W of Dunfermline stands a castellated mansion. From 1399 the land belonged to the Halkett family, whose descendant George Halkett married Isobel Hepburn of Waughton prior to extending the early 16th century tower into an L plan mansion. Both of the families' arms and mottos appear on the tower which reads "Fides Sufficit" and "Go till it" 1583 and the initials G.H.I.H. The south and east sections were extended in the 17th century and further additions were made in the 19th century by the celebrated architect David Bryce.

PITHEAVLIS CASTLE
PERTH & KINROSS

This simple oblong structure occupies ground just W of Perth. With its angle turrets on the tower furnished with gun holes it is a good example of a 16th century Scottish house that appears in a charter of 1586 when a John Ross of Craigie confirmed the sale of the lands and Manor House of Pitheavlis to Robert Stewart. It was used as a farm house in the 19th century when it fell into a state of disrepair, but is now a private dwelling house.

PITKERRO CASTLE
DUNDEE CITY

About 3 miles W of Broughty Ferry is an oblong structure with turrets and an adjacent turret stair. In 1534 the land of Pitkerro was the property of John Durham, the second son of Alexander Durham of the Grange of Monifieth. Probably built by the son or one of his immediate descendants, it remained with the family until the early 18th century and was considerably modernised in the 19th century.

PITSLIGO CASTLE
ABERDEENSHIRE

Overlooking the North Sea 5 miles W of Fraserburgh are the substantial ruins of an L plan courtyard keep built in 1424 by Sir William Forbes, who acquired the land through his marriage to the daughter of Sir William Fraser of Philorth. Its walls, which rise to fourteen feet and are nine feet thick, bear some interesting inscriptions. A panel dated 1577 and bearing the Royal Coat of Arms appears on the oldest portion of the south wall tower, while on the east wall is the same shield quartered with the arms of Ireland and England to commemorate the accession of James VI to the English throne. In 1633 Alexander Forbes was knighted Lord Pitsligo but the title was forfeited by his great grandson, also Alexander, who took refuge here after the Jacobite defeat at Culloden in 1746.

PITLOCHRY
PERTH & KINROSS

Town situated 28 miles NW of Perth. The name either derives from the Gaelic 'Baile chloichridl' meaning 'village of the stones' or from 'Pet chioichreach' meaning 'stony place'. Once a little Highland village with mansion, in 1746 Prince Charles Edward stayed here before heading to his final defeat at Culloden. Though at one time spoken of as a centre for trade for Perthshire, today's town grew from the village built on either side of General Wade's High road between Dunkeld and Blair Atholl in 1845, when on recommending the quality of its air, the Royal Physician Sir James Clerk raised its profile, leading to the opening of a rail link in 1865 and the building of a Hydropathic establishment. However, the closeness of the River Tay, Loch Tummel (Hydro Electric Dam), Killiecrankie battlefield, Blair Castle, and Glen Garry did play a significant part in establishing its long-lasting popularity. In addition to this was the affluence afforded by its thriving tweed mill, distillery, cattle and horse fairs, which brought extensive rebuilding, completed by 1900, and made it the typical 19th century Market Town we see today. As late as 1947 the town became a burgh. The Pitlochry Festival Theatre which opened in 1951 was the inspiration of John Stewart who ran the Glasgow Park Theatre. Extended in 1981, it now ranks along with Pitlochry Highland Games as a popular public event.

PITTENWEEM
FIFE

Seaport situated 1 mile SW of Anstruther. Spelt Petnaweem in 1150, the name is derived from the Brythonic 'Pet-na-h-uam' meaning 'land' or 'village of the cave' which according to tradition was occupied by St Fillan in the 7th century. From the 12th century the land was the property of the Priory of May, which was it-self transferred to Pittenweem Priory in the 13th century, but the exact details of the transaction are unclear. Its proximity to one of Scotland's ecclesiastical centres gave Pittenweem royal favour down through the centuries, bringing it Burgh of Barony status in 1526, a Royal Burgh Charter in 1541, the granting to the town of the local priory by James VI who visit-ed here in 1593 and its elevation to a Lordship in 1606 for Fredrick Stewart. In 1650 the surrounding land was mined for its coal by Cromwell's forces, followed by the army of his arch enemy Charles II who were well received by the people and Magistrates. With a coastline that was often the haunt of smugglers, in 1736 the robbery of a town house by Andrew Wilson a popular local smuggler led to his conviction and his hanging in Edin-burgh, provoking the Porteous Riots which moved Sir Walter Scott to write his 'Heart of Midlothian' (pub.1818). Apart from a visit from John Paul Jones (Amer-ican Pirate) in 1779, its subsequent histo-ry was uneventful. Later becoming one of Fife's busiest fishing ports, a testimony to the port's civic pride is its 16th and 17th century buildings that include: the Gyles House, a 17th century sea captain's house near the harbour, Kelly Lodge, a late 16th century Town House, once the homes of the Earls of Kelly, and the 16th century Parish Church built on the site of an earlier church and now adjoining the Old Tolbooth.

PLUSCARDEN ABBEY
MORAY

Located 6 miles SW of Elgin. In carrying on the policy of his great grandfather, Alexander II founded a priory here for Valliscaullian monks, a branch of the Cis-tercian order, to counter the area's law-lessness. Despite being burnt in 1390 by the Wolf of Badenoch during his descent

upon Elgin, it was rebuilt and thrived under the authority of the Bishops of Moray until 1454, when its monks were replaced by the Benedictines from Urqu-jhart and it became a dependency of Dun-fermline. The last of its priors, Alexander Dunbar, who died in 1560, was replaced by the Lay Prior Lord Alexander Seton, whose father was a supporter of Mary I. After the last of the monks died in 1595 it was held by a number of owners includ-ing the Earl of Fife, and the Marquis of Bute, but remained derelict from 1890 until 1948 when a group of Benedictine monks began skilfully restoring it into the Abbey of today. Regranted abbey status in 1974, the buildings are laid out with a cru-ciform church to the north, and cloister garth with monastic buildings down its east and south sides, and functions like a modern abbey in an age-old setting.

POLLOKSHAWS
CITY OF GLASGOW

Town situated 2 miles W of Glasgow cen-tre. Spelt Pollock in 1150, the present name is derived from the Brythonic 'poll' and the Old English 'scaga' therefore 'a pool by a wood'. From a small hamlet by the Cart bridge in 1654 to a village by 1710, Pollokshaws was essentially an 18th century industrial town, boasting one of Scotland's first printing works started by Ingrim and Co in 1742 and quickly followed by bleaching and hand-loom weaving. From 1813 this was a Burgh of Barony for Maxwell of Pollock. Its continued expansion with iron foundries, paper mills and cotton mills gave the town an integral position in Scotland's industrial base and Police Burgh status in 1893, when its railway and electric trams were increasingly making it a suburb of Glasgow, with which it was amalgamated in 1912.

PORT DUNDAS DISTILLERY
EAST DUMBARTONSHIRE

Located on the north side of Glasgow near its water source at Loch Katrine. Functioning as a small operation producing Lowland Malt from pot stills under the Macfarlanes. The family combined with another local distillery in the 1860s after both had installed new continuous 'coffey' stills, which brought the large scale promotion of spirit, able to supply the cities of the southern industrial belt. The amalgamated Macfarlane & Co was one of the six whisky companies which formed Distillers Co Ltd, and with its sister distillery in Fife accounts for one third of the industry's total production of Grain whisky, that is also used in its blends such as Johnnie Walker, Dewars, White Horse and Bells. Now one of Britain's largest and most modern distillery's, it was rebuilt in the 1960s with the construction of the dark grains plant, one of the most advanced in the world, and a highly efficient heat and power plant unique to the industry and able to export surplus energy to the national grid. The plant has also pioneered the total utilisation of spent wash, the residue of distillation, and is now involved in local conservation initiatives.

OWNERS
Diageo plc ?

REGION
Lowland

PRODUCT
The whisky is primarily used for blending.

PORTEOUS RIOTS, 1736
CITY OF EDINBURGH

The last of the major upheavals in the Capitals historical annals occurred in 1736, when two smugglers, Andrew Wilson (merchant) and a youth named Robertson were condemned to death for robbing the Custom House at Pitten-weem in Fife. Following a failed escape from the Tolbooth prison, Wilson made a second attempt during the service in the Tolbooth Church by seizing the guard, thus enabling his junior partner to make good his escape and winning Wilson the sympathy of the congregation and the townsfolk. With rumours abounding of plans to effect his escape from the gallows, the City Guard under Captain John Porteous was reinforced. After Wilson's execution, the crowd, either saddened by the unfortunate end for a popular figure, or feeling cheated by the abrupt end to the excitement, began throwing missiles, and in the mounting tension, Captain Porteous ordered his men to fire into the crowd, killing six people. On being brought to trial, the prosecution refuted the claim by the defence that Porteous had ordered them to fire overhead, asserting the guards were compelled by Porteous to fire directly into the crowd, for which he was sentenced to death. On realising the likelihood of a Royal pardon at 10pm on the 7th September, a mob took control and eventually gained access to the prison and removed Porteous, who was found hanging from a signpost the next morning. The following parliamentary enquiry resulted in the Lord Provost being disqualified from holding any other office and in Porteous's widow receiving £2000' a year.

PORT GLASGOW
INVERCLYDE

The town situated 24 miles NW of Glasgow owes its existence to the rapid increase in the trade of its larger neighbour from the 17th century onwards. In 1668 the Magistrates of Glasgow bought the land of Newark from Patrick Maxwell and proceeded to build a port that could accommodate the larger ships its neighbour was unable to harbour. Constituted a Free Port with the many privileges that brought, by 1710 it had the first Custom House on the River Clyde, which handled most of its trade with America and the West Indies, from which the town derived much prosperity. Boasting the first graving (dry) dock in Scotland by 1762, the town was disjoined from Newark in 1775 and constituted a separate burgh. In its heyday the port was known for shipbuilding, sawmills, sugar, iron, brass, and sailcloth but its trade declined along with Glasgow during the American Wars of Independence (1775-77) and suffered further from the deepening and widening of the upper Clyde (1790). Despite this, its shipbuilding was revived with the advent of steam propulsion when in 1812 at Woods Shipyard Henry Bell's Comet was built. The town's union with Dumbarton, Renfrew, Rutherglen and Kilmarnock in sending a member to parliament brought continued growth throughout the 19th century and beyond but the traces of this are now to be found in its more recent industrial decline. See Newark Castle

PORTINCROSS CASTLE
NORTH AYRSHIRE

On the banks of the Firth of Clyde 2 miles W of Kilbride are the ruins of an L plan castle which developed from a tower house. A fine example of an early Scottish stronghold, it was designed with two kitchens to accommodate royalty. Portincross west belonged to the Barony of Arnel which King Robert the Bruce conferred on Sir Robert Boyde of Kilmarnock for his services at Bannockburn in 1314 and which remained with his descendants, the Boyds of Portincross, until 1737. Abandoned after the Restoration of Charles II when it was used by fishermen. During a storm in the winter of 1739 it was unroofed and later fell into ruin.

PORT PATRICK
DUMFRIES & GALLOWAY

The port and village situated 6 miles SW of Stranraer owes its name to the erection of a church to St Patrick which as mythical legend has it was where the saint set foot after traversing the Irish Sea in the 5th century. Its tower later served as a beacon for ships. The Barony of Port Logan to which the village belonged was held by the Adairs of Kinhilt until the 17th century when the land passed to Hugh Montgomery of Airds for whose descendant it became a Burgh of Barony, 1620. Unsuccessfully renaming it Port Montgomery, from their seat at nearby Dunskey Castle the family oversaw the port's development, which as the closest point of land between Scotland and Ireland (21 miles) it operated a postal and passenger ferry service between the two countries from 1662. For a long time Port Patrick was celebrated as the Gretna Green for runaway Irish couples, registering 126 marriages between 1774-1826 when the practice was curbed. The building of a pier in 1774 resulted in a considerable trade in coal, cattle and horses, prompting a harbour development built by John Rennie in 1821 and a lighthouse in 1835. A reversal of fortunes with the loss of its mail contract in 1849 and the dismantling of its lighthouse (rebuilt in Cylon) culminated in its improved communications with Stranrear and Belfast and the gradual rundown of its harbour and pier due to coastal erosion. With the railway link to Stranrear laid in 1861 and a branch line to its harbour in 1862 came its popularity as a holiday town for people attracted to its sandy beaches, golf course and other recreational pursuits that continued up to the 1950s. Even so its traditional maritime role was assured in 1921 when the Post Office began a radio station for shipping leading to its coastal communications system. The popular Port Patrick Hotel was built in 1905 at the behest of Mr Ewing, the owner of Dunskey Estate above the harbour. See Dunskey Castle

PORTREE
HIGHLAND

The capital town of the Isle of Skye is situated on the islands NE coast. Its name was thought to derive from the Gaelic 'Port-Righ' meaning 'Kings port' but latterly the 'Righ' or 'Ruigh' is interpreted as 'sloping hill'. The ancient territory of the Macdonalds who shared the island with the Macleods, Mackinnons, and Macdonalds of Sleat, when the land nearby was called Columkille after the much earlier Columbian Church that stood to the NW of the town. No stranger to royalty; King Haakon of Norway anchored his fleet here in 1263 prior to his defeat at the battle of Largs. During James V pacification of the Western Isles in 1540, the King's forces anchored in its bay, where they received the submission of the local clan chiefs, and over two centuries later a fugitive Prince Charles Edward visited Portree after his flight from Culloden, 1746. The town then being a cluster of black houses and an inn, the Prince stayed in a nearby cave before he bade farewell to Flora Macdonald at an inn (now the Royal Hotel). In 1773 during a visit by Samuel Johnson and James Boswell, the latter noted the intention of Sir James Macdonald to build a village which decades later, long after it was eventually started by the third Baron Macdonald, became the commercial and administrative centre for the Isles with its quay, 1819, market and fairs, Court House, 1867 and prison. The port later witnessed a large exodus of people to North America, many of whose descendants often contribute to modern Portree's main industry, tourism.

PORTSOY
ABERDEENSHIRE

Town situated 8 miles W of Banff. The last part of the name is from the Gaelic 'saoi' meaning 'warrior', therefore 'harbour of the warrior'. Although little is known of its early history, its feudal overlords were the Ogilvies of Boyne and in 1550 Queen Mary erected it into a Burgh of Barony for Sir William Ogilvie, whose seat was the nearby Findlater Castle (see castle). Its Royal Burgh Charter, dated 1554, remained dormant until 1692, when an inspired Sir Patrick Ogilvie (Lord Boyne) built its harbour, thereby laying the foundations of its 18th century prosperity, derived from its export trade in Portsoy's green serpentine marble, along with fish and agricultural produce. Of these its marble was frequently exported to France. Its merchant houses around the harbour reflect the benefits from its trade, which declined during the Napoleonic Wars due to extended tariffs on wines and other goods, later giving rise to smuggling. The harbour built in 1825 by the Earl of Seafield, but destroyed in a storm in 1835, was rebuilt in 1884 to advance the trade in herring at the turn of the century, by which time Portsoy ceased to be a seaport for trading vessels and later focused on the somewhat precarious holiday trade which continues to this day.

POWRIE CASTLE
ANGUS

Situated 3 miles NNE of Dundee. This large 15th century ruin was long the residence of the Fotheringham family who acquired the lands of Wester Powrie in the reign of Robert III (1390-1406). The family occupied it until the 16th century when it was burnt during the Duke of Somerset's invasion of 1547 and it was completely empty by the 18th century.

PRESTON
EAST LOTHIAN

A village situated $^1/_2$ mile SE of Preston-pans. The name is derived from 'Priests town' owing to the monks of Holyrood and Newbattle having land here for farming and the working of saltpans. Its position on an established trading route helped develop its trade, which revolved around its 17th century Mercat Cross where the Guild of Chapmen of the Lothians (travelling merchants) met annually at Jerome's Fair to sell their wares and elect office bearers. Originally the territory of the Earls of Home, the land here passed through marriage in the 14th century to the Hamiltons, whose seat the Preston tower house (see castle) was later replaced by Preston House, now itself a ruin, and was erected into a Burgh of Barony for the Commendator of Holyrood in 1652. Bought by Lord Grange before 1715, the house was later occupied by Dr James Schaw who bequeathed it for use as a boys' school which closed in 1832. The town's growth was positively affected during the Industrial Revolution and by the 1920s along with the village of Cuthill, virtually became one urban unit. Old Hamilton House, which stands in the main street, and was built in 1628 by John Hamilton, is a good example of a 17th century merchant's town house. Opposite this stands Northfield House, a 16/17th century L plan structure built by Joseph Marjoribanks, an Edinburgh merchant who acquired the land from George Hamilton. See Tower

PRESTON TOWER
EAST LOTHIAN

Between Prestonpans and Musselburgh stands a 15th century L plan fortalice on land that was once held by the Earls of Home, who held princely sway over the SE of Scotland. In the 14th century the circumjacent barony passed to the

Hamiltons who as the Hamiltons of Preston built the tower on top of an earlier structure but it was burnt by the Earl of Hertford in 1544, by Cromwell in 1650 and by accident in 1663. After which it was abandoned in favour of Preston House but was reacquired in the 19th century by Sir William Hamilton, a Professor of Logic.

PRESTONPANS
EAST LOTHIAN

Coastal town situated 8 miles E of Edinburgh. Like much of the area the land was held by the monks of Newbattle from the 12th century, who after giving it its name Priestown started its coal mining and developed its saltpans, making it Scotland's main supplier of salt, with a yearly average of 42,000 bushels (a dry measure of 8 gallons) before 1792. This was then carried to the neighbouring towns in creels by a group known as the salt wives. In addition, its thriving fishing community renowned for their oysters and a harbour built by the monks helped raise it to a Burgh of Barony for the Commendator of Holyrood Abbey in 1552. While witnessing the passing of many invasion forces down through the centuries, the main event of note was the Jacobite victory at the battle of Prestonpans, 1745. After the contraction of the salt trade post 1707 due to imports from the south, the town fell back on its fishing (netting 30,000 oysters in 1839) and its soap factory. However, it was the Prestonpans Co-operative Society, founded in 1869, that was to become the third largest employer in 1948 after brewing and coal mining, with 2,000 members and an annual turnover of £240,000. See Battle

PRESTONPANS, BATTLE OF, 1745
EAST LOTHIAN

The first victory for Prince Charles Edward Stewart's Jacobites during the 1745 Rising. The battle was fought near the town of the same name when the Jacobites advanced from Edinburgh to do battle in the open with Sir John Cope's government troops marching from Dunbar to the relief of the Capital. The decision to make a night attack by the Jacobites on their roughly equal enemy of around 2,000 was decisive and left the enemy little time to assemble or manoeuvre their forces, who were totally defeated. The outcome stiffened Jacobite resolve and left the way clear to England. See Jacobite Rebellion

PRESTWICK
SOUTH AYRSHIRE

Town situated 2 miles NE of Ayr. The first half of the name is from 'Priest' while 'wick' is from the Old English 'wic' meaning 'dwelling'. Although coming on record in 1174 when the land was bestowed on Paisley Abbey by Walter Fitzalan, son of the Great Steward of Scotland, apart from a brief association with Robert the Bruce it remained an obscure place until 1600 when James VI confirmed it as a Burgh of Barony governed by thirty-six Freemen. This was an archaic tradition of local government that pre-dated the Anglo Norman influence in the 12th century and hampered its growth until its abolition in 1903 when Prestwick was a small weavers' village on the Glasgow-Ayr road. The town's raison d'etre was as a coastal resort and premier golfing venue, with the founding of Prestwick St Nicholas in 1851 followed by Prestwick St Cuthbert and Routenburn, making it the St Andrews of the west. In 1935 its standing was enhanced further with the building of an aerodrome by Scottish Aviation Limited, providing an invaluable contribution to the war effort, 1939-45, when it operated as the HQ for RAF Ferry Command and the USAF Transport Command. This precipitated its post-war status as a civil, commercial and international airport with a new terminal built in 1964 which still operates today. See Golf Club

PRESTWICK ST NICHOLAS GOLF CLUB
SOUTH AYRSHIRE

Situated near the town overlooking Ayr Bay. Although the west of Scotland does not boast the same golfing tradition as the east coast, its development here in recent centuries has been no less apparent. Originally called the Mechanics Club, it was formed in 1851 with 28 members four months after the Prestwick Club. The development of the course owed much to the freedom of the town playing fields, which were liberties granted to the soldiers of Robert the Bruce, who along with their descendants were Freemen of the burgh. One of the moving forces behind its founding was Tom Morris who had come to Prestwick Club as Head Greenkeeper and whose aim was to form a club to cater for those who were not elected to the exclusive old club. Surprisingly the artisan nature of the club disappeared and it was renamed St Nicholas GC in 1858 after the patron saint of the town. Owing to the congestion felt by the players who had to share the course with Prestwick Golf Club, the membership successfully sought a new course and were poised to transfer when the title proved defective. Fortunately another site was found to the landward side of the town and a 12 hole course was laid out that would later become one of Scotland's first full-scale ladies' courses when Prestwick St Nicholas moved to the present links course in 1892, the year the clubhouse opened. Laid out by Charles

Hunter, it has changed little since then. One of the clubs early successes was James Robb in 1906, who represented Scotland against England five times and paved the way for internationalists like Gordon Lochart, John Wilson and Allan Stevenson. Hosting many Open Championships over the years, and though short by modern standards (5952 yards), the course still provides a good challenge to players today.

Q

QUEENSFERRY, NORTH
FIFE

Village located on the shore of the River
Forth opposite its royal neighbour. Like
South Queensferry it developed from the
royal and religious links between Edinburgh and Fife. As part of the Parish of
Dunfermline it appeared in a charter
from King Robert the Bruce 1315-28 and
later its chapel of St James was granted
by William Bishop of St Andrews to
Dunfermline Abbey. In the 18th century
it acquired a gun battery after the appearance of the American Pirate John
Paul Jones in the Forth Estuary. The description in the 19th century of North
Queensferry consisting from time im-
memorial, of operative boatmen, without
any admixture of strangers, is an apt description of the village's raison d'etre although it did enjoy some popularity as a
summer sea bathing destination in the
19th century with the building of the
Forth Rail Bridge. Like its neighbour
across the water its ferry service was
eroded by the Forth Bridges, the more recent of which was the Forth Road Bridge
in 1964. See South Queensferry

QUEENSFERRY, SOUTH
CITY OF EDINBURGH

Coastal town situated by the River Forth
and the Forth Rail Bridge. So called because the wife of King Malcolm III
Queen Margaret (later St Margaret) traversed the River Forth from here on her
many visits from Edinburgh to Dunfermline Abbey (1069-1093). In 1295 it
was recorded as Queneferie, in 1491
Queneferie, and in 1461 as Quenis Fery. It
was in the 12th century that Malcolm IV
great grandson of Queen Margaret gave

to the monks of Dunfermline a grant of
the right of ferry which was also given to
the monks of Scone, a free passage to the
abbot, the monks and their men. It was
the former grant which was confirmed
by Pope Gregory in 1294 that gave rise to
a small town, which although located by
one of Scotland's most important rivers
which provided opportunity for trade its
expansion was obstructed by the steep
hill on its southern side. Consequently it
continued to have a more transient function en route to the larger neighbouring
towns. Consistent with this was its links
with the various religious houses across
the water and the Abbey of Inchcolm on
the Island of Inchcolm. In 1333 a Carmelite Friary stood here that was founded
by Laird James of Dundas, the ruins of
which still stood in the 19th century. As a
burgh dependant on Dunfermline Abbey
it became a Royal Burgh in 1636 and had
parliamentary representation shortly
after which probably stimulated the
town's economy for it was during this
period that it had 20 ships on its register
and shipbuilding was carried out. However, it was in the 19th century that
Queensferry was firmly on the map with
the channels for trade and tourism when
its Hawes Inn figured in Sir Walter
Scott's 'Antiquary' and ironically with
the construction of The Forth Rail Bridge
which was to mark the beginning of the
end for its ferry service. Built by The
Forth Bridge Company to designs by
John Fowler, and completed in 1890, the
top of the structure is 360 feet above the
water while its cantilevers which span
1710ft made it one of the 19th century's
foremost endeavours in steel bridge construction. The 1,000 men resident in
South and North Queensferry during its
construction in the summer of 1884
would have no doubt enjoyed the various coastal attractions like its fresh air

and sea views during their daily breaks which continued to attract visitors during future decades. The opening of The Forth Road Bridge in 1964 hastened the end of its traditional ferry service which for centuries had served royalty and other dignitaries travelling to and from the Capital of which it is virtually an extension. See North Queensferry

R

RADICAL WAR, 1820

With the industrialisation of Scotland in the early part of the 19th century, came the driving force of change that was to transform the lot of the tenant farmer and their farm labourers, as they were increasingly drawn to the industrial centres of the south and ultimately the abiding urban squalor, something that caused much unrest throughout 18th and early 19th century Europe. In Scotland nowhere was this felt stronger than in the southern industrial corridor, but in particular Glasgow, with its channels for trade over the Atlantic and to the wider world. On 25th April 1820, a group of radicals left Germiston for Glasgow, where the plan of action was posted throughout the city. In convincing the more passionate members among the recently gathered supporters, of the assistance in men and munitions from the Carron Iron Works in Falkirk, their ringleader, named Turner, drew many to the cause. After resolving to march to Conderrat under the command of Andrew Hardie, a secret agent named King dutifully preceded them and with the help of a native named Andrew Baird tried to coax the villagers into rallying to the cause about to be visited upon them, but judiciously most of them refrained. This left the total force of 30 men armed with pikes to take on the might of the British Government. On nearing Bonnybridge, in a successful bid to decoy the party with the inducement of new recruits, King recommended they traverse the bleak moorland of Bonnymuir and rest. After a disappointing wait and no recruits from Falkirk, Carron or Stirling, on seeing the hopelessness of their cause both Baird and Hardie attempted to return home but were surprised by Lieutenant Hodgson's 10th Hussars and Lieutenant Davidson of the Stirlingshire Yeomanry. Both of them routed the rebels, who were imprisoned or transported to the colonies and their leaders executed. Although the rising was small by previous standards it served as one of the very early milestones in the Scottish Labour Movement.

RANFORLIE TOWER
RENFREWSHIRE

Positioned on high ground above the village of Bridge of Weir facing northwards. In the 15th century the original keep was built by the Knox family who held the surrounding land. A family of some distinction, their descendants included the Reformer John Knox and Andrew Knox who became the Bishop of the Isles in 1606 and were also distantly linked to the Irish branch from whom the Barons of Ranfurly sprang. Ranforlie passed in 1685 to the Dundonalds, who later sold it to the Hamiltons of Holmhead, but was later acquired by the Aikenhead family and is now a ruin.

RATHO
CITY OF EDINBURGH

Village situated 9 miles SW of the city centre. The name is thought to derive from the Gaelic 'Rath' meaning 'a fort' or 'artificial mound'. The forfeited Barony of Ratho was part of the dowry of Robert, Ist's daughter Marjory on her marriage to Walter, Steward of Scotland in 1315 (who shared command of the left wing at Bannockburn), and in 1404 was erected into a Principality for John son of Robert II. A Rectory until 1429, Ratho Parish became an appendage of Corstorphine Parish from 1444 until regaining its former status in 1633. During this time the property was acquired by Alexander Fowlis, 1563, who obtained a charter from James VI which the family held until it was bought in 1786 by a Thomas Macnight. Previously supported by its rural economy it also benefited from the Union Canal, built in 1822 to link Glasgow and Edinburgh, thereby drawing it closer to the Capital, for which it became a dormitory.

RAVENSCRAIG CASTLE
ABERDEENSHIRE

Overlooking the River Ugie 3 miles NW of Peterhead are the ruins of a 14th century L plan castle. Once known as Craig of Inverugie, it was defended by a moat and was probably started by the de Cheyne family, but around 1350 it passed through marriage to the Keiths, Earls Marischal, who built most of what we see today. They also built the Inverugie Castle nearby which became the chief residence of the elder branch of the family. In 1589 a charter records the transference of Ravenscraig to John Keith, son and heir of Andrew Keith of Ravenscraig, and in the same year James VI visited the castle for the marriage of the laird's daughter.

RAVENSCRAIG CASTLE
FIFE

Perched on a sea cliff 1 mile SW of Dysart. Protected by the sea on three sides and a ditch on its north front. It was built by David Boys (Master of Works) around 1450 for Queen Mary of Guelders as a courtyard keep with projecting semicircular towers, the designs probably being conceived by her husband James II before his death in 1460. The lands were held by the Ramsays before the Queen's death in 1463, when James III granted the castle and land to William Earl of Caithness, 1470, in recompense for the forfeited castle of Kirkwall and Earldom of Orkney. Parts of the upper front were added in the 16th century while parts of the southern range with sea wall date from the 17th century.

REAY
HIGHLAND

Village situated 10 miles SW of Thurso in a picturesque setting. Preceded by an earlier village, the present name is thought to derive from either the Gaelic 'reidu' meaning 'smooth level' a 'plain' or from the Old Norse 'rett' meaning 'a public fold', a cattle pen. Although once the site of an ancient fort and probably a place of some note that was subject to incursions by Norse sea rovers in the 8th and 9th centuries, thereafter Reay remained isolated from the country's tumultuous history. The original town which was rediscovered in a sandstorm in 1715, had been erected into a Burgh of Regality by James VI in 1616 for Donald Mackay, later made Ist Lord Reay in 1628. Its Mercat Cross, salvaged in a storm and now standing in the later village was at the centre of the community, which has traditionally been concerned with farming and fishing, the latter benefiting from its harbour built in 1875, as did its growing flagstone industry. In 1928 the skeleton of a Viking with the remains of his shield and battle axe in hand was discovered on Reay Links and presented to the Museum of Antiquities in Edinburgh. The fall in Reay's population in the early 20th century was alleviated by the building of the controversial UK Atomic Energy fast breeder reactor at Dounreay in 1958, which provided work for up to 1500 local men, and its operators are known locally as the Atomics. Contrasting with this legacy of its modern history are its more taditional historic buildings that include an 18th century church with a pre-10th century Celtic cross slabstone.

REDCASTLE
ANGUS

Looking out to the North Sea 2 miles E of Montrose are the ruins of a courtyard castle. The site of an early defensive structure which was a favourite point of attack for the Danes. This was followed by a hunting seat built by William I in the 12th century which the King Robert the Bruce conferred on a branch of the Campbells in 1316, but, was purchased by the Stewarts of Innermeath in 1366. Though taking its present shape in the 15th century, while occupied by Lady Redcastle, widow of John Lord of Innermeath, in 1579 it was burnt by the Protestant faction led by James Grey of Invergowrie (Black Jack) who was subsequently outlawed in 1581. Later held by the Ruthvens of Gardyne and then the Carnegies. By the 19th century it was in a ruinous state.

REDCASTLE
HIGHLAND

Positioned on the N side of Beauly Firth 6′ miles W of Inverness. To consolidate his influence, in the 12th century William the Lyon built the earlier fortress of Ederdour that belonged to Sir John Bysset in 1238 and to Sir Andrew de Bosco in 1278. Most of the present L plan castle dates from the 16th century and in 1562 was visited by Queen Mary shortly before it was acquired by the Mackenzies. Although modernised in the 19th century it was a ruin in the 20th century.

REDHOUSE
EAST LOTHIAN

The ruin situated just E of Longniddry is a fine example of a late fortified courtyard house. The lands of Easter Reidspittell were purchased in 1607 by John Laing, Keeper of the Royal Signet, who built the main block shortly after for his wife Rebecca, daughter of Lord Denniston. Their initials were inscribed on a lintel above the Renaissance doorway. The property was acquired by his daughter Lady Jean Laing and her husband Andrew Hamilton, whose brother was the

Earl of Haddington and his father-in-law a Supreme Court Judge. After confirmation of the title in 1612 came the building of the north west tower and in 1621 a charter of Novodamus erected the whole estate into a Free Barony. The last of the Hamiltons to occupy it was a Colonel George Hamilton who was executed for his part in the 1745 Rebellion, when it was forfeited to the Crown and later fell into the decayed state we see today.

RENFREW
RENFREWSHIRE

Town situated W of Glasgow on the River Clyde. Name derived from the Brythonic 'Rhynn Frwd' meaning 'headland of the flowing brook'. Associated with the Stewart line from the 12th to the 19th century. The land and Royal Burgh of Renfrew were granted by David I around 1147 to Walter Fitzalan, who as hereditary Steward of Scotland later moved and then elevated Renfrew Priory into Paisley Abbey, 1169. From their seat at Castle Hill (gone by 1775), the family established a power base and ties with Scotland's ruling families which led to a descendant, also Walter Stewart, marrying Princess Marjory Bruce in 1315, and the birth of their son, later Robert II. Confirmatory charters were granted by later monarchs, and in 1614, after prolonged conflict with Paisley over trading privileges, James VI assented to Renfrew's claim to be the chief port on the Clyde, and granted a ferry, Free Port status and the right to levy customs and tolls. The title of ' Baron of Renfrew', bestowed in 1404 by the burgh and district on the heir apparent to the Scottish Throne, is still held by the Prince of Wales today. Following the decline of its limited foreign trade by 1710, its commerce, mainly with Ireland, was supported by its traditional farming, weaving and fishing owing to the town's extensive and long-held rights to salmon fishing on the Clyde, which were exercised until the 19th century. However, the opening of the shipyards William Simons in 1860 and later Lobnitz & Co took the town into the industrial age, leading to the setting up of ancillary industries and an influx of migrant workers from Ireland and the Highlands. The boilermakers Babcock and Wilcox who operated from here by 1895, the Cartyne Steel Castings, 1907, and the Clyde Rubber Company from 1912 were undoubtedly attracted by the area's diverse industrial base with its good road, rail, and sea links. The bombing suffered during World War II owed much to the town's industry but primarily its airport, which started in 1914 and grew rapidly after 1945 to become the Scottish Headquarters of the British European Airways in 1965. Although Renfrew then bore the county name the administrative centre for the area was its old rival Paisley. The Town Hall, built in 1873 in a Gothic style on the site of the Old Tolbooth was burnt during an air raid in 1941 but is now restored.

REPENTANCE TOWER
DUMFRIES & GALLOWAY

Situated on a hill near Hoddam Castle 4 miles NW of Annan. It was built in a commanding position for seeing and being seen and served as a signal tower from the 15th century. This gave it extensive views over the Solway to the Cumberland mountains. The name is thought either to derive from the act of repentance shown by its builder, a chief who killed his prisoners after returning from a raid into England, or that it was built after the stones from the chapel which once stood here were used to build Hoddam House.

RHYNNIE
ABERDEENSHIRE

Village situated 38 miles NW of Aberdeen. The name is either derived from the Gaelic 'Rathan' meaning 'little fort' or from the Old Welsh 'Rhyn' meaning 'a point of land'. The scant remains of the vitrified fort on the summit of the Tap O'Noth are in stark contrast with the even fewer remains of the much later Lesmore Castle to the west. As part of the Lordship of Strathbogie, the land was bestowed by Robert the Bruce around 1320 on Sir Adam Gordon (ambassador) and stayed with the family for generations. Despite its elevation to a Burgh of Barony for the Duke of Gordon from 1684, with its closeness to the River Isla (Bogie) offering some opportunity to trade in the rural economy, the distance of its main market at Inverurie and to a lesser extent Banff restricted its economic development. The area boasts a number of ancient monoliths and Druidical remains that testify to an age-old tradition in quarrying, which over the centuries has yielded a large amount of sandstone, granite and slate, with which the village was built in the 19th century. At one time owned by the Duke of Gordon and Richmond, in 1926 when the Huntly Estates were sold, the Forestry Commission purchased much of the surrounding land at a time when the village was witnessing a housing development. See Druminor Castle

ROMAN INVASION, 78-84 AD

The invasion of Britain by Julius Ceaser in 55 BC had more to do with personal advancement than territorial gain for an already overgrown empire. Nevertheless it provided valuable information for his successors and ultimately a staging post for their advancement north. So when Julius Agricola arrived as Governor of Britain in 78 AD, the Romans northern territory stretched from the Humber to the north, covering most of the Brigante Kingdom up to their border at the Solway Firth in the north west, and the land of the Votadini below the River Forth in the south east. In the summer of 79 AD he subjugated the tribes north west of the Solway Firth, an area that now covers Dumfries & Galloway, and strengthened his hold by force and by the seduction of the natives with the pleasures of civilised life, while educating them in better building skills and writing, moving some to study the Roman language. In 80 AD he advanced into the hilly region between the Clyde and the Solway Firth, then on to Stirling and north east to the Tay, invading the land of the Picts and the Scots while building roads and forts at strategic points which were invariably captured when the legions dispersed to their winter quarters. This was eventually countered when Agricola reinforced them all the year round. Later using the natural boundary of the Rivers Forth and Clyde, thus establishing the most northerly frontier of the Roman Empire. These defences were later incorporated into the Antonine Wall. The patchwork of kingdoms to the south in what is now Lowland Scotland included those of the Dumnonii tribe, to the south and south west in Dumfrieshire was the Novantae and Selgovae while to the east was the Votadini. In resolving to go further, in 82 AD Agricola penetrated Kintyre to reach the western ocean, when he caught sight of the shores of Ireland: while using the navy to supply the army and chart Scotland's coastline, providing vital information on inhabited areas, numerical strengths and strategic points. This was to provoke more unrest and unity among the tribes when the fleet appeared in the Tay, leading to attacks on Roman Forts which were repelled and gave heart to the Romans who resolved to go further into the heart of Caledonia. The success

or failure of his plan to capture the whole island was decided in the year 84 AD after his victory at a battle called Mons Grapius described by Agricola's biographer Tacitus. Thereafter he abandoned his endeavours in the face of logistical difficulties then retreated over the Tay and to his winter quarters south of the Forth and Clyde. Agricola's last attempt at conquest before he was recalled to Rome by Emperor Domitian was to order his fleet to encircle the island.

ROMAN INVASION, 138-139 AD

In order to subdue the Brigantes, who had encroached on the territory set during the building of Hadrian's Wall, in 139 AD during the reign of Antonius Pius, Hadrian's successor Lollios Urbicus was dispatched to Britain to restore territory lost by the Romans and their neighbouring tribes during the Brigantes' threatened expansion. In marching northward to the Forth and Clyde to repel any future attacks from the north and to subjugate the southern tribes he erected a new wall which some records suggest was built on the lines of Agricola's construction. Measuring about 36 miles long, it consisted of a stone foundation with an earth wall 24ft thick and 20ft high, with 3 forts at each end, and intermediate forts at 2 mile intervals with watchtowers between them. Fronting this was a fosse 40 ft wide and 20 ft deep. The relatively quiet period during Lollius Urbicus's commission owes everything to the sophisticated network of defensive structures manned by a considerable body of well motivated troops and the consummate skills of the Roman engineers. This also explains the lack of records made of Urbicus's action in the field, leaving one focusing on his most enduring legacy, the Antonine Wall. However, with the rise of a new emperor in 162 AD came the usual resurgence of hostility from the native tribes, in particular the northern group who were subdued by Calpernius Agricola. In 182 AD during the reign of Commodus, a more formidable rising took place by the nations on the north side of the wall, who succeeded in breaking through the great barrier and slew the commander wreaking havoc in the neighbouring province. The event created enough alarm in Rome to hasten the arrival of Marcellus Ulpius, who quelled the unrest after two years' fighting.

ROMAN INVASION, 208-209 AD

By 204 AD the size of the Roman province in Britain was proving increasingly difficult to defend and so gave rise to the two provinces called Upper and Lower Britain. The former consisted, the land from the Humber to the Firths of the Forth and Clyde, containing mainly nations of the Brigantes, with their dependent tribes, and occupied by the 2nd and 20th Legions. With the collapse of the treaties made by Governor Albinus came open hostility from the indigenous population who wrought havoc by killing and looting while over-running the province. So to arrest the worsening situation, the ageing Septimius Severus travelled from Rome with his two sons and arrived in a litter in 208 AD. In concentrating his forces, Severus sought not merely to repel the enemy but to effectively prevent them from renewing their attacks by taking the war into their heartland. But by this time the various factional tribes had formed into a confederacy which combined into two nations, the Caledonii and the Maetae, both of which lay to the north of the wall. Sticking to his objective, Severus dismissed their ambassadors who sued for peace and led his forces past the fortresses and rivers towards Caledonia. Characteristically he overcame the natural obstacles of expansive woodland, extensive marches and formations of rock by building roads, and bridges, and clearing woodland. It is

to this campaign that many of Scotland's Roman roads north of the Forth and Clyde may be attributed. While building as he went, from Falkirk he proceeded to Stirling then skirting the River Forth to the west he headed for Menteith. From there he travelled east to Dunkeld, between the two stretched a thick wood. On crossing the Tay, he reached the camp at Grassy Walls then proceeded towards the large camp at Forfar, known as Battledykes, where he left a large force to secure his retreat. According to some historians, Severus is thought to have marched as far as the Moray Firth and to have entered Caledonia with a vast army, but apart from some guerrilla tactics from the natives there is no account of him having fought any battle. Nevertheless he secured a peace treaty with the Caledonii and the Maetae who ceded territory between the Forth and Clyde line and the Tay. It was about this time that the natives were recruited as mercenaries into the Roman Army, which under later Emperors and Governors continued to occupy the province until their final withdrawal in 410 AD.

ROSEHEARTY
ABERDEENSHIRE

Coastal village situated 8 miles SW of Fraserburgh. The name derives from the Gaelic 'ross' meaning 'cape' or 'wood' and 'ard' meaning 'headland' or 'height'. Said to date from the 14th century and to have developed out of a settlement of crofters and shipwrecked Danes, Rosehearty was created a Burgh of Barony in 1681 for Lord Forbes of Pitsligo whose family ruled from the castle of that name close by (see castle). Originally consisting of two parts, the sea town where the fishermen lived, and the New Town, where the merchants and farmers lived, the burgh's produce was often sold in the market of its larger neighbour Fraserburgh.

ROSEMARKIE
HIGHLAND

Coastal town situated 1 mile NE of Fortrose. Name derived from the Gaelic 'ros' and 'marc' meaning 'cape of the horse'. Serving as a base for missionaries from an early period, the church re-founded by St Curitan around 716 added to its religious significance and led to the development of a town in the 9th century which, although older than its neighbour Fortrose, failed to become as important. Its long association with the latter began in 1120; when David I founded the Bishopric of Ross here, a century before the choice of Fortrose as the site of the Cathedral sparked a conflict of interests. A Royal Burgh under Alexander II, 1214-49, Rosemarkie, along with Chanonry, was constituted a joint or united burgh under the common name of Fortrose in 1444 and in 1455 all three were created a Free Burgh for Bishop Ross by James II. The elaborately carved Pictish Stone found in 1821 during the building of the present Parish Church is tangible evidence of Rosemarkie's antiquity, reinforcing the claim that this was the site of St Curitan's 8th century church, and it ranks amongst the town's most ancient artefacts along with other Pictish carvings in the local museum. Originally 10ft high when found, but accidentally broken by workmen when unearthed, it is now housed in the church to the west of the door. Above the town stands the mound of Courthill which was thought to be the seat of feudal justice.

ROSENEATH
ARGYLL & BUTE

Fishing village situated on the Gare Loch 4 miles NW of Helensburgh. Called Neveth in 1199: and Roseneveth, 1477, the name may derive from the Gaelic 'ros' and 'neimhid' (churchland) therefore 'cape of the sacred meeting place'.

Part of the Lennox Lordship from an early period Roseneath's much earlier claim to fame is as the site of St Modan's Well, where the saint founded a 6th century church to which pilgrims travelled to take its healing waters and which was granted to Paisley Abbey in 1225. The precipitous rock called Wallace's leap where, as legend has it, the hero leapt on to his horse to escape his pursuers' is sited to the north of Roseneath Castle, a 17th century ruin once held by the Marquis of Argyll. His ancestor Colin Campbell 1st Earl of Argyll, acquired the land here in 1489, before developing the area's farming and fishing. The acquisition proved fortunate for the Covenanters in the 17th century, who were sheltered here by the friendly Archibald, 9th Earl of Argyll. At Campsie Bay to the SE are the ruins of the Argylls' castle which was used as a subsidiary residence to Inveraray, but after the fire in 1802 the then Earl replaced it with an Italian style mansion (now gone). The building of its pier in 1845 later brought trade from the many ferries and steamers that plied the Gairloch but more recently the town became popular with pleasure craft.

ROSLIN
MIDLOTHIAN

Also spelt Rosslyn, the town is situated 7 miles S of Edinburgh and derives its name from the Gaelic 'raisc' and 'linn' meaning 'marsh' or 'fen' and 'pool'. After coming to England with William the Conqueror, 1066, the St Clair family settled here and with grants from successive monarchs extended their territory to become the chief barons of Midlothian by the 13th century. Figuring in the Wars of Independence, on Rosslyn Moor in 1303, the English army under Sir Ralph de Manton were surprised and defeated by a Scottish force led by John Comyn. Apart from its castle NE of the town, its most important building is Roslin Chapel, dedicated to St Matthew. Founded in 1446 as a Collegiate Church by William St Clair, Earl of Orkney, and built to a cruciform plan but not completed, today's structure comprises a choir, four transepts of the planned nave and central aisle with pillars. The craftsmanship in its Gothic interior, once thought to be the work of foreign masons but now believed to be indigenous, is best exemplified by the apprentice's pillar, which local tradition claims was carved by the novice during the absence of his master who returned and killed him in a jealous rage. The arches between the central aisle pillars are adorned with carvings depicting biblical and rural scenes, including the seven deadly sins and the seven cardinal virtues. Later the chapel became the St Clair (Sinclair) family burial vault. It was to those recumbant nobles and to the death by drowning of the Earl's wife that Sir Walter Scott composed a lasting tribute in 'The Lay of the Last Minstrel':

Blazed battlement and pinnet high,
Blazed every rose carved buttress fair
So still they blaze, when fate is nigh
The lordly line of high St Clair
There are twenty of Roslin's barons bold
Lie buried within that proud chapel;
Each one the holy vault doth hold
But the sea holds lovely Rosabelle!

In 1456 the charter granted by James II erecting Roslin into a Burgh of Barony for the Earl of Orkney and Caithness with market and annual fair failed to halt its decline into a rural village by 1690. During this period it was occupied by Hertford's forces in 1544, by Cromwell in 1650, and though its chapel was only defaced at the Reformation it was severely damaged by a lawless mob in 1688. A favoured haunt for gypsies, who brought much theatre to the town in the 16th and 17th centuries, it also became popular

with 18th and 19th century celebrities like Samuel Johnson, Daniel Defoe and Sir Walter Scott. Erected into an Earldom in 1801 for Alexander Wedderburn, the chapel's restoration by the 4th Earl of Argyll in 1862 has made it one of southern Scotlands most venerable attractions. See Castle

ROSLIN CASTLE
MIDLOTHIAN

On a rock by the banks of the River Esk 8 miles SE of Edinburgh are the ruins of a massive courtyard keep with enclosing walls defended by a drawbridge and gatehouse. In the 12th century the barony was held by William de Clair whose descendant, also William, built the first castle before 1330 when he died fighting the Moors while accompanying Sir James Douglas to Palestine with Bruce's heart. Henry St Clair, Earl of Orkney added a large keep in the late 14th   century. His successor of 1417, Sir William Sinclair, built the south east wall, drawbridge, offices, chapel and hall before living here in regal splendour with his princess Elizabeth Douglas. Suffering a fire in 1452 after a servant tried to find one of Lady Douglas's greyhounds with a candle, it was quickly repaired for it was used as a prison for William Hamilton after his failure with William Douglas, to topple King James II in 1455. Though severely damaged by the Earl of Hertford in 1544 during the Rough Wooing of the young Queen Mary by Henry VIII, its reconstruction by 1580 included the 16th century mansion house on the east side with a richly decorated dinning room by William Sinclair, who in 1622 made more additions. It was again challenged, this time by Cromwell's forces under General Monck, who destroyed its north west side before plundering it. The last attack upon its walls was by a lawless mob in 1688, when much of the castle and nearby chapel were destroyed.

ROSYTH CASTLE
FIFE

Located on the north side of the Forth opposite South Queensferry. In 1435 the barony was granted by James I to Sir David Stewart, who became patron to Walter Bower the Abbot of Inchcolm, who wrote 'Scotichronicon' (a historical work from earliest times to the 15th century). Basically an L plan courtyard castle started by a relation of the former in the late 15th century. A panel above its porch was inscribed with the Crown above the letters M.R (Mary Regina) and the date 1561, which marked the arrival of Queen Mary at Leith on her return from France, as the family were distantly related. A courtyard with additional wings was added in 1635 or 1655 by John Stewart for his wife Margaret Napair, probably after it was damaged by Cromwell in 1651. Passing to the Hopetouns in the 19th century, it is now an interesting ruin.

ROTHESAY
ARGYLL & BUTE

Coastal town situated on the east side of the Isle of Bute. The name probably derives from the 'Rodericks Isle' which is itself from Rudri or Ruari, the progenitor of the Macdonalds, who was granted the island in the 13th century by King Haakon of Norway for his loyalty. Later belonging to the Stewarts, this was the site of a castle by the 11th century and figured during the invasions by Norsemen, who occupied it until it was retaken by the Scots after the battle of Largs in 1263. The town's popularity with Robert III moved him to erect it into a Dukedom, 1398, for his oldest son David Earl of Carrick, and before dying here in 1406 he made it a Royal Burgh with grants of land and privileges which in turn brought parliamentary representation in 1488. Apart from its occupation by Cromwell in 1650 and the Earl of Argyll during his failed rebellion in 1685, much of the towns' earlier history revolves around its castle. Its failure to match the growth of its neighbour Campbelltown was compensated for by the benefits accrued from the Stewardship of the Marquis of Bute, starting with the Customs House Station in 1765 for Irish colonial trade. While by no means an industrial town it did operate woollen mills in the 19th century but it was as a centre for the West Coast herring fishing that by 1855 the town became a prospering hub of activity for its 1600 fishermen and boys. Both of these groups benefited from government grants whose real objective was to obtain recruits for the navy. A new harbour followed by a tramway, precipitated the town's rise as an attractive summer retreat by 1885 when up to twenty passenger steamers berthed here daily, earning Bute the appellation 'The Madeira of Scotland'. Encouraged by its appeal, the authorities invested heavily in its infrastructure with roads, housing and public buildings throughout the 20th century, but with the advent of cheap air travel in the 1970s the trade's rapid decline helped it regain some of its former tranquillity. Nine miles to the west of the town is St Blane's Chapel, once the parochial church for the island; its Norman arch dates from 1100 but it was thought to have been preceded by a 6th century monastery nearby. To the south is Mount Stuart, the home of the Marquis of Bute. First built in 1718 but completely destroyed by a fire in 1876, it was rebuilt in the 1930s in a Gothic style with an Italian marble chapel, and opened to the public in 1995. See Castle

ROTHESAY CASTLE
ARGYLL & BUTE

Built in the town which bears its name on the Isle of Bute. From an early period this was the site of a castle built to repel attacks from Norsemen, who took it with 80 ships in the 13th century and held it until it was retaken by the Scots after the battle of Largs in 1263. Essentially a 14th century courtyard keep with surrounding walls flanked by round towers and a ditch. Its occupation by the English under John Balliol led to its submission to Bruce, who levelled it in 1311, but it was rebuilt either by Robert II or Robert III and seized by the English in 1334 before being retaken by the Scots. Visited by King Robert II in 1371, and the place where Robert III died broken hearted in 1406, it was taken by the Earl of Lennox, 1544, during the Rough Wooing of Queen Mary by Henry VIII. In the 17th century Cromwell's forces damaged its walls, 1650 and in 1685 when the Earl of Argyll wreaked revenge on the town it was reduced to ruin. Though partly rebuilt by the Marquis of Bute, it is now a substantial ruin.

ROWALLAN CASTLE
EAST AYRSHIRE

Located 3 miles NE of Kilmarnock town. After the battle of Largs, 1263, the land was granted by Alexander III to Gilchrist Moir who may have built the original house where Elizabeth Muir, wife of Robert II, was born. However, today's edifice is a 16th century courtyard mansion with towers flanking its doorway, above which is the name of the builder John Muir and the initials of his wife Margaret Cunningham with the date 1562. Known for his gardening skills, he planted an orchard here before his death in 1591. Further developed by his descendants, including William Muir and his wife Jane

Hamilton in 1639. As a member of Parliament he supported the Solemn League and Covenant in 1643, and consequently the house was the scene of Conventicle meetings which led to his persecution, something illustrated in one of his poems, ' The Cry of Blood and of Broken Covenants '. In the 19th century the castle was the property of the Earl of Loudoun.

ROXBURGH
SCOTTISH BORDERS

Town situated 3 miles SW of Kelso. The name is derived from the Old English 'Hrocs' meaning 'rook' (castle) therefore 'fortified burgh'. The original village, which stood closer to Kelso, was thought by some historians to be a place of some importance before the 12th century, when the present town and castle comes on record as the property of the Earl of Northumberland, later David Ist. Created a Royal Burgh on his accession in 1124, Roxburgh prospered through royal favour and in 1214 was the site of a Royal Mint. As a Border town it suffered the fluctuating fortunes of its castle, which, though now a fragmentary ruin above the River Teviot, was once a place of intrigue and pomp which was often held by the English and traded in cross border politics. In the 13th century Roxburgh became a member of The Four Courts of Burghs (arbitrary body for settling burgh disputes) and in 1241 had the distinction of being the birthplace of Alexander III. Burnt by Edward III in 1369 when the old timber village disappeared, plundered by the Earl of Douglas, 1398, for sympathising with the English, and while besieging its castle with heavy artillery James II was killed by bursting cannon, leaving the remaining pieces of ordinance to reduce it to a ruin that was captured in verse:

*Roxburgh ! how fallen, since first in Gothic
pride,*
Thy frowning battlements the war defied,
*Called the bold chief to grace thy blazoned
halls,*
And bade the rivers gird thy solid walls !

After the death of James II it was deprived
of burgh status until the grant made by
James IV of the ruined castle and town to
Walter Kerr of Cessford in 1499 helped restore the burgh's standing. In 1616 it was
raised to an Earldom for Robert Kerr, a
descendant, thus helping it to regain its
position as County Town and elevate it
to a Dukedom, 1707, for the 5th Earl. The
building in 1752 of the Parish Church on
the site of an earlier church from the
Middle Ages, which had been wholly
underground for safety, was a reflection
of the the country's return to peace and
stability and enabled Roxburgh to enjoy
the benefits of a rural Border town which
had eluded it during the centuries of
cross border strife.

ROYAL & ANCIENT GOLF CLUB OF ST ANDREWS
FIFE

The birth of golf which took place in the
Royal & Ancient Burgh of St Andrews
was to have a baptism of fire, for in 1457
the game was banned in Scotland by
James II who sought to advance the practice of archery to strengthen the nation's
defences. The first evidence of golf in St
Andrews appears in a charter of 1552
when the Archbishop of St Andrews confirmed the rights of the citizens to play
golf on the links. As one of the oldest golf
clubs in the world, the Royal & Ancient's
records go back to 1754 when the nobility and gentry of Fife formed the 'Society
of St Andrews Golfers' and wasted no
time in purchasing a Silver Club. For this
prize the players competed annually
with the winner, becoming 'Captain of

the Golf' for a year and marking the occasion by attaching a silver ball to the silver club. This tradition continued until
1824, after which by 1825 the post of
Captain was determined by the individual's personal qualities. The first known
written rules of golf were laid down by
the Gentlemen Golfers of Edinburgh in
1744 for a similar challenge and were
largely adopted by St Andrews in 1754.
Members played on the town links and
often gathered at Baillie Glass's and the
Black Bull Tavern before and after the
game, until 1835 when, members began
using the Union Club parlour on the site of
the later Grand Hotel. With King William
as patron it was around this time that the
Royal and Ancient began to establish its
status in the golfing world. In 1854 the
present clubhouse was built with funds
from the Union Club on land owned by
the R & A and in 1877 both clubs were
amalgamated. The first Open Championship in 1860 and the Amateur Championship, 1885, owe everything to the
Prestwick Golf Club and the Royal Liverpool Golf Club respectively who helped
initiate the involvement of other clubs
annually. The setting up in 1897 of the
Rules of Golf Committee formalised its
position as an authority on the rules of
golf which is now recognised by all the
countries of the world except the United
States, Mexico and Canada. Though the
club itself does not own a course, it plays
over six courses on St Andrews Links,
which are controlled by the St Andrews
Links Trust and run by The Links Management Committee. On the Old Course,
a round used to consist of 22 holes, 11 out
and the same 11 back. In 1764, the members of the Society of St Andrews Golfers
decided it would be an improvement if
the first four holes of the course were
combined into two. The first known map
of the Old Course was dated 1821. The
years subsequent to this saw the courses
continued development which included

the land reclamation of the 1840s and later the course was carefully tended by Tom Morris who was Keeper of the Green here between 1864 and 1913. On land bought by the Town Council in 1895 the R & A laid out a new course which was open to the public and later used it for the qualifying rounds for the Open Championships. Shortly after in 1897, the Jubilee Course named to mark Queen Victoria's Diamond Jubilee, opened with 12 holes, but was extended in 1904 to 15 and in 1905 to 18 holes. Since then it has been redeveloped in 1938 by H.S Colt and Willie Auchterlonie and completed in 1946. Latterly it underwent an extension and improvements that have left it a more daunting challenge to players. To cope with the game's growing popularity the Eden Course was opened in 1914, and gave rise to the Eden Tournament which became a central feature every August. The 9 hole Balgove Course was opened in 1972 for children and beginners. In 1948, requests were made for the Royal & Ancient to take over the boys' section and, in 1963, the youth championship, from private interest. The additional 18 hole Strathtyrum Course was opened in 1993. Among the club's objects of interest are the paintings which adorn its walls as reminders of its former captains, course designers and champions. These include Field Marshal Earl Haig, Captain in 1920; Prince of Wales, Captain in 1922; Tom Morris, course designer and Open Champion winner in 1861, 1862 and 1867; and Her Majesty the Queen, patron of the club who visited here in 1982. Included in the club's trophy cabinet are the Silver Club with balls attached, the Silver Putter donated by John Whyte Melville in 1833; the Silver Cross of Saint Andrew, presented by Major Murray of Belshies in 1883; as was The Calcutta Cup, presented by the Royal Calcutta Golf Club. Today the Royal & Ancient is limited to 1800 members, of whom 1,050

may be resident in the United Kingdom and 750 from abroad.

ROYAL BRACKLA DISTILLERY
HIGHLAND

One of the early examples of 19th century enterprise. It is situated close to Nairn but with a proximity to Inverness, the Capital of the Highlands, that undoubtedly reassured its founder, Captain William Fraser of Brackla House, when he built the distillery on the Cowder Estate near its water source at the Cawder burn in 1812. In ages past the area provided the setting for part of Shakespeare's 'Macbeth' in which the Thane of Cawder figured. A more personal tragedy, however, was that which befell the Captain when a law prohibited him from selling whisky within 120 miles due to the number of illicit stills. After being sucessfully contested in Parliament in 1821, the Captain developed markets in the south and became the first distiller to be granted a Royal Warrant of Appointment by William IV in 1835, which was followed by a second Royal Warrant by Queen Victoria in 1838. Renamed the Royal Brackla Distillery, its fortunes were boosted further by the opening of the Inverness-Nairn Railway in 1855, and its partnership from 1860 with Andrew Usher & Co, the whisky merchants and blenders of Edinburgh, its whisky being one of the earliest blended whiskies to be sold to the public. In 1890 the lease was granted by Lord Cawder to Andrew Usher Junior, who rebuilt the distillery and also left funds to build the Usher Hall in Edinburgh before his death in 1898. Owned by John Bisset & Co Ltd in 1925, and sold to Scottish Malt Distillers in 1943, it was closed and modernised in 1964, when its stills were doubled to four and their heating switched from coal firing by hand to a steam-fired boiler in 1969. Owned by United Distillers but later mothballed, Royal Brackla is again used for blending and is now available in bottles.

OWNERS
John Dewar & Sons Ltd ?

REGION
Highland

PRODUCT
Royal Brackla 15 year old single malt 43% vol

NOTES
A medium sweet nose with a smooth, slightly fruity character to its taste.

ROYAL LOCHNAGAR DISTILLERY
ABERDEENSHIRE

Taking its name from the nearby mountain which, through its foothills, has provided its clear water since 1845. The nearby town of Crathie was where Queen Victoria and Prince Albert attended church during their annual sojourns at Balmoral, moving its founder John Begg to invite the royal couple on a tour around the plant which quickly led to a Royal Warrant of Appointment and the right to use the royal prefix before the name. After John Begg's death in 1880 it was run by his son Henry, but was acquired by the Dewar family in 1916. Despite being comparatively small in size, its two copper pot stills produce a quality Highland Malt and a Royal Lochnagar selected preserve for a specialist market. The casks of the latter are chosen at a small ceremony each year on the anniversary of the Queen's visit. The distillery also provides the malt at the heart of the world's best selling deluxe blend Johnnie Walker Black Label and also Old Parr, a favoured deluxe blend in Japan.

OWNERS
Diageo plc ?

REGION
Highland

PRODUCTS
Royal Lochnagar 12 year old single malt & Royal Lochnagar select Reserve 43%

NOTES
A gentle, smoky aroma with a mellow, malty, sweet taste
A slightly peppery nose with a rich, full, smooth flavour.

ROYAL MUSSELBURGH GOLF CLUB, THE
EAST LOTHIAN

The club was formed in 1760 by the Rev Alexander Carlyle and other gentlemen of the town and wider area who sought an alternative to the long-established recreational activities of the town. Nicknamed 'Jupiter', he was the revered Minister of the Parish of Inveresk from 1748, and was winner of the club's first trophy, the Silver Cup, in 1775. In keeping with accepted practice, the winner then assumed Captaincy of the club for one year and attached the gold or silver medal to the cup before the competition. In 1784, from which year the club's first minutes date, members numbered 26 and frequently met in the local Inns and Taverns in the afternoon after playing foursomes for 6d a hole. In later years, the club's capricious pattern of development was indicative of the sport's fluctuating popularity on a local and national level, which sometimes left the club dormant, but in 1828, in response to a resurgence of interest, a committee of four were appointed to revise the rules and regulations. This was again revised in 1834, two years after the course had increased to 8 holes. With consistency still eluding its development between 1838 and 1870 it went through a period of relative inactivity that eventually gave way to frenzied organisation of official positions, subscriptions and entry fees along with the sporting calendar. This culminated in a proposal to build a clubhouse, thus providing a focal point for members, who numbered 87 in 1871. One of the more distinguished club Presidents was HRH Duke of Connaught, 1876-1942, while his son HRH Prince Arthur was Vice President between 1912 and 38. It was during this chapter that the club owes the prefix of Royal and the Connaught Cup. Its acquisition of more trophies reflected the clubs dynamism which kept it going through the First World War, 1914-18, when naval and army officers used the course, and was enriched further after the war when in 1926 the new 9 hole course by James Braid was opened. The event was marked by the eminent professional foursome Braid, Taylor, Vardon and Herd who played in a Scotland versus England match resulting in a decisive win for Scotland. In 1939 a new course of 6,200 yards was laid out by Mungo Park. With its course used for grazing and the clubhouse used by the RAF, during World War II, 1939-45, club functions were suspended until eventually revived after protracted post-war reconstruction work, and ambivalence by its members happily ended in the purchase of the course and clubhouse in 1957. Prominent among the club's other awards are the Powel Cup, presented in 1897, for winter meetings the Coronation Cup from 1953 and the Mixed Foursomes Cup, 1966.

ROYAL TROON GOLF CLUB
SOUTH AYRSHIRE

Owing to the long standing practice of golf in 19th century Ayrshire, many of the local burghers of Troon became followers of the game after playing on the various neighbouring courses. So in 1878 it was with this in mind that Dr John Highet, Medical Practitioner, convened a meeting of 24 guests at the Portland Arms Hotel with a view to establishing a club. Following its successful outcome and prior to the inaugural meeting, Cap-

tain James Dickie had secured some land between Craigend burn and Gyaws burn on the Fullerton Estate owned by the Duke of Portland. Under the guidance of Charles Hunter, Custodian of Prestwick Links, the land was cleared and the course of 5 holes laid out by 1879, but with additions made at different stages, the course had taken the form of 18 holes by 1888. Two years before, a new clubhouse replaced the old wooden hut. In the early days playing was encumbered by sand blowing in from the sea, by farmers with carts full of sea ware from the beach, and bullocks roaming free. Regretfully after these issues were settled, mainly due to the pragmatism of the Dukes factor, course congestion returned once more when local members claiming an ancient right to play on the course refused to desist. With this in mind and an increasing number of lady members, (who had formed a club in 1882) more land was leased from the Duke for the construction of the Portland Course, or Relief Course, which was opened in 1895. Subsequent to this was the ladies' course which was laid out in 1896 on the east side of Crosbie Road. In 1904 Miss Lottie Dod won the first ladies major championship to be held at Troon, while the club's first male professional was George Strath followed by Willie Fernie. The land was still leased before the Great War (1914-18) when it took the form of the course we see today after work by W. Fernie in 1909 including the famous postage stamp at the 8th hole. After the war moves were afoot to purchase the courses from the Duke, so in 1923 with the sale made, James Braid was recruited to make further changes that included bunkers on the left hand side of the green. Now firmly established as a premier golf course which by 1938 had hosted two major ladies championships, 1904, 1925; an Open Championship, 1923; and an Amateur Championship in 1938, Troon's development was consistent apart from the unsettled periods during both World Wars when activity was suspended. But through out the 1950s and 60s the course was the scene of two Open Championships won by Bobby Locke of South Africa, 1950 and Arnold Palmer of USA, 1962. One ladies' championship was won by Moira Paterson, 1952; and two amateur championships, 1956, were won by John Beharrel youngest winner of such and Michael Bonallack, 1968. The course was extended in 1962 to (7,045 yards) as was the clubhouse in 1971 with the new Ailsa lounge and to date both have witnessed seven Open Championships.

RULLION GREEN, BATTLE OF, 1666
CITY OF EDINBURGH

Fought outside Edinburgh during the Covenanting Wars between Colonel Wallace, who led his insurgents into the Pentland Hills to do battle with Charles II army, headed by Sir Thomas Dalyell of Binns. The subsequent victory of Dalyell gave momentum to his cause and eventully to the barbaric supression of the Covenanters in the west. See Pentland Rising

RUSCO CASTLE
DUMFRIES & GALLOWAY

On a sloping hillside 3 miles N of Gatehouse stands an oblong keep built by the Gordons by 1550. The land was originally called Glenskyreburn when owned by the Carsane family, and passed to Robert Gordon through his marriage to the daughter of Sir Robert Carsane. He later assumed the title, and that of Lochinver, after his brother's death at Flodden in 1513, when it became the seat of the Gordons of Lochinver. Used as a hunting lodge in the 19th century when Rusco House was built, the tower is now occupied.

RUTHERGLEN
CITY OF GLASGOW

Town situated 2 miles SE of Glasgow centre. Name derived from the Gaelic 'ruadh gleann' meaning 'red glen'. The likely site of a castle and settlement when the area was overrun by Caledonian tribes before the Roman Invasion. The village comes firmly on record when it became a Royal Burgh of David I around 1126, and by 1250 it was one of the chief towns on the lower Clyde with confirmatory charters from William I, 1189, who granted its church to Paisley Abbey. Rutherglen's involvement in the cause of the Stewarts was mainly due to its castle, which was occupied along with the town by Edward Bruce after a failed attempt by his brother Robert the Bruce. The castle remained intact until burnt by the Regent Moray after the battle of Langside, 1568, but continued to determine Rutherglen's importance, affording it a seat in parliament prior to 1478. Consequently the burghers were espousing the cause of electoral reform before 1671 prior to introducing their advanced social policy providing compulsory education for children between 6-12 years. The scene of celebrations marking the Restoration of Charles II, in 1679 the town was occupied by the Covenanters, who, after making the public Declaration of Rutherglen supporting Episcopacy at the Mercat Cross, were pursued by John Graham of Claverhouse, resulting in their defeat at Drumclog. In 1695 this was a quite rural community dwarfed by its larger neighbour Glasgow, but by the time Rutherglen bridge was built in 1776 the place was fast becoming a growing manufacturing suburb of the city, later producing chemicals, paper, pottery, rope and dyes, along with its more traditional cattle and horse fairs and the supply of cotton and coal. Despite its rejection of integration with Glasgow in 1912, the housing developments of the late 19th and early 20th centuries made its physical assimilation inevitable. This left Rutherglen's long-standing landmark, the Town Hall, built in 1861 and dominating the town centre with its Baronial clock tower, as a symbolic legacy of the civic pride of the burghers' forbearers.

RUTHVEN CASTLE/BARRACKS
HIGHLAND

Positioned on a hill in the Spey Valley 1 mile SE of Kingussie. For a long time the site of a castle which became a 13th-century stronghold of the Comyns and chief fortress of the 'Wolf of Badenoch'. The 16th century structure built by George, 6th Earl of Huntly, which was frequently besieged until it was destroyed by Claverhouse in 1689, was eventually rebuilt in 1718 as a bastion of the Government's authority in the unruly north during their pacification of the Highlands after the Jacobite Rebellion of 1715. As such, Ruthven played an important part in the 1745 Rebellion. The present ruins of the courtyard fort resulted from its burning by the Jacobites after the battle of Culloden, 1746.

RUTHVEN CASTLE
PERTH & KINROSS

Perched on a bank overlooking the River Almond 2 miles NE of Perth. The original keep was followed in 1488 by Lord Ruthven's second tower, both being linked by a moveable plank at the battlements, which was a 13th century mode of defence, as one tower served as a fall back position when under attack. This was called 'maiden's leap', after the Earl's daughter leapt over it after being found with her lover by her mother. Shadowy figures in the clandestine politics of the day, in 1566, Patrick, 3rd Lord Ruthven, played an active role in the Rizzio murder, his son William, made Earl of

Gowrie in 1581 when the towers were joined, was involved in the kidnapping of the boy King James VI, 1582, resulting in the King's recapture (Ruthven Raid) and the Earl's execution. In 1600 his sons John and Alexander threatened the life of King James VI in Perth (the Gowrie Conspiracy), which led to their forfeiture. Becoming the property of the Stewarts of Tullibardine, it was later acquired by the Murrays of Atholl, who held it until the 19th century.

RUTHWELL
DUMFRIES & GALLOWAY

Village situated 7 miles E of Annan. Name derived from the Old English 'Rod well' meaning 'rood' or 'cross well'. Other than its creation as a Burgh of Barony for Sir John Murray of Cockpool in 1507, with the right to hold markets and fairs, Ruthwell's early history is concerned with the Ruthwell Cross, which is housed in the Parish Church. Following the years of controversy it is thought to date from the Synod of Whitby (assembly of the English Church held to reconcile the differences between the Celtic and Roman Churches) in 664. Standing 18 ft high, the front and back depict finely carved vines, animals and biblical scenes including the Crucifixion and the Annunciation, and Latin inscriptions, while on its sides are carved vines, scroll work and runic verse. Regarded as the oldest example of English (Anglo Saxon) language and one of the most important monuments of its kind in Scotland, in 1842 it was proven by the Cambridge scholar John Kemble to be part of the very early religious Anglo- Saxon poem 'The dream of Rood'. Held in the church long before the Reformation, in 1642 it was cast down and broken into several pieces then left to decay in the churchyard until 1802 when it was restored and preserved in the manse by the then minister, Rev. Henry Duncan. The village also boasts the first savings bank founded in 1810 by the Rev. Henry Duncan, who developed it in the face of strong opposition from the ' Times' newspaper and eventually convinced Parliament to regulate it.

S

SADDEL ABBEY
ARGYLL & BUTE

Near the village of the same name on Kintyre NE of Campbeltown are the few remains of Saghadul or Saddel Abbey. Founded for Cistercian monks in the late 12th century by Ragnall or Reginald, the second son of Somerled, whom he succeeded, 1164 as the Lord of the Isles and Argyll, before dying in 1207. It enjoyed only a few centuries functioning as an abbey, partly owing to its marginal status, despite being united to the Bishopric of Argyll by James IV in 1507. Saddel was ruinous by the 16th century when its stone was used to build Saddel Castle. Of the church and the various other sections arranged around the cloister only part of the church's north transept and the refectory survive. See Castle

SADDEL CASTLE
ARGYLL & BUTE

Located at the head of Saddel Bay 8 miles NE of Campbelltown. Shortly after 1508, when the nearby Saddel Abbey and its lands were erected into a barony, David Hamilton, Bishop of the Isles, built this oblong keep, but in the 17th century it had become ruinous. Between 1640 and 1674 it was saved from further decline by William Ralston, a fugitive from the Covenanting Wars, and is now in a well preserved state owing to more recent restoration work.

SAINT ANDREWS
FIFE

A University Town and ancient burgh situated on the east coast of Fife. Bearing various names throughout its early history ranging from Mukross denoting 'boar-wood', Kilrymont meaning 'church of the royal hill', and Kilrule, indicating 'church of St Regulus'. According to leg-

end it became Saint Andrews either because St Regulus landed here in the 4th century with the saint's relics or the 8th century Pictish King Ungus, son of Urguis, invented the story to increase the importance of a Culdee Church which he had founded previosly. Its ecclesiastical history would seem to add weight to the latter. The land once formed part of the hunting ground of Pictish Kings, which along with the disciple gave the place its coat of arms, a wild boar tied to a tree below St Andrew crucified on a Saltire. Its first prelate, Bishop Cellach, attended King Constantine's Great Council meeting at Scone in 908 which resulted in Saint Andrews replacing Dunkeld as the seat of the Scottish Church. Often coming from the leading families in the kingdom, the Prelates of Saint Andrews, who were, distinguished by their talents and education, gave the place its most remarkable institutions that included the Augustinian Monastery (forerunner of Cathedral) founded in 1144 by Bishop Robert, for whom David I erected the town into a Royal Burgh 1140-44. This enriched its already privileged status as an ecclesiastical and administrative centre which was to revolve around its Cathedral, founded in 1160, and its castle, built in 1200. A charter of free trade conferred by Malcolm IV (1153-65) led to frequent disputes with its neighbours before being settled in favour of the Royal Burgh. Once compelled to travel to seats of learning abroad, the founding of St Mary's College by Bishop Wardlaw in 1411, later to become Scotland's first University, gave students access to degree course classes in theology, canon and civil law, medicine and the liberal arts which were authorised by Papal Bulls. These were eventually brought under one roof when the Bishop provided accommodation in the Pedagogy in South Street. Witnessing the fluctuating fortunes of its Cathedral and castle, in 1304 the town was occupied by Edward I who summoned the Scottish nobles here to swear fealty, a commitment that proved to be impracticable because it was occupied again in 1336 by Edward III during his subjugation of Scotland. Under the patronage of James II, its seat of learning continued to expand when Bishop Kennedy founded St Salvators College, which was confirmed in Papal Bulls from Pope Pius, 1458, and Pope Paul, 1468. This was followed by the College of St Leonards (forming United College with St Salvators, 1747), by Prior John Hepburn and Archbishop Stewart, 1512, and St Mary's Theological College founded in 1538 by Archbishop James Beaton. Formed along a small natural creek at the mouth of the Kinness burn, its harbour enjoyed great prosperity in the 15th and 16th centuries when its traders exchanged local produce with merchants from Holland, France, Flanders and other parts of Europe. During its annual fair, the Senzie, the coastline sometimes berthed as many as 300 vessels. In 1538 the town celebrated the marriage of James V and Mary of Guise when the royal couple returned here after the Queen's arrival at Crail. Rocked by the Reformation debates between 1525 and 1560, when the heretics Patrick Hamilton and George Wishart were burnt at the stake and its institutions declined, its problems were further added to by the plague in 1586 and 1604 and by a proposed plan to move the University to Perth owing to the general decay. Fortunately the plan proved short-lived and the burgh continued in the ruins of its former magnificence. During the 18th century the town was tainted by its Jacobite sympathies and leanings towards Episcopacy, bringing the University under an investigation by a Royal Commission which proved inconclusive and led to further expansion with the founding of Madras College in 1833 with a bequest

from Dr Bell, son of a local barbour. A prosperous but brief trade in calcined ironstone with the iron works on the Tyne brought slight relief before the advance of the railway reduced it to a Sub Port, sparing it the scars from commercial activity and preserving its tranquil residential ambience with the fresh air and sandy beaches that were to make it a Mecca for golfers. This presently contrasts well with its role as a centre for shopping and professional services. St Rules Romanesque Church, SE of the Cathedral, has a 112ft high tower and probably dates from the 12th century. In South Street are Blackfriars Chapel, once part of the Dominican Friary founded by Bishop Wishart in the 13th century, and damaged at the Reformation, it still retains some interesting work. Queen Mary's House is a 16th century merchant's house reputed to be where Charles II and Mary I stayed; the West Port Gate, a vestige of the fortified burgh, was built in 1589 but has some 19th century work, while the Church of the Holy Trinity has its 15th century tower. See Castle, Cathedral & Golf Club

SAINT ANDREWS CASTLE
FIFE

It stands on a rocky headland NE of the town facing the North Sea and was the site of a fortification from a very early period. The present castle was started by Bishop Roger as an Episcopal residence between 1188 and 1202. While growing along with the town, which was at the centre of the affairs of church and state, in 1332 it was taken and strengthened by the Scottish Barons led by Edward Balliol, then retaken by Sir Andrew Moray for David II and dismantled, but was reconstructed by Bishop Trail (1385-1401) who died here. The castle then started to develop into a built-up courtyard structure with enclosing walls, adjoining towers surrounded by a moat on its south front and west side to the sea. In 1452, James II recorded the birth of his first-born son in the chief mansion in the blessed City of St Andrews. During a dispute about the succeeding bishop, the Douglases, led by Bishop Gavin Douglas, seized it 1509-13 until they were driven out by Prior James Hepburn ending in the former being reconciled with Archbishop James Beaton (1522-39) and the Earl of Lennox. In the ensuing religious strife of the 16th century, additions were made by Archbishop David Beaton, (1543-46) who was murdered here by the Reformers in retaliation for the burning of George Wishart (martyr) outside the castle walls, but it was retaken and garrisoned by French troops, 1547 to prevent the arrival of an English force sent by Henry VIII. This resulted in the Reformer John Knox being sent to the galleys in France. Between 1550 and 1571 rebuilding work was carried out by Archbishop Hamilton, adding the south west section with gateway in an early Renaissance style which afforded refuge to James VI after the Ruthven Raid in 1583. Although owned by the Earl of Dunbar in 1606 and restored to the Archbishopric in 1612, after which some minor additions were made, its last function was as a prison after the battle of Philiphaugh in 1645, when Montrose's supporters James Spottiswood and Gordon of Haddo were interned here before being executed. In the same year the Town Council ordered that its 'sleatts and timmers' be used for the town pier.

SAINT ANDREWS CATHEDRAL
FIFE

At the east end of the town are the ruins of the Cathedral founded on the site of a Culdee Church by Bishop Arnold and Malcolm IV in 1160. Cruciform in design and built near to a 12th century priory, now gone. Today's remains include 12th 13th and 14th century work in a mainly Gothic style restarted by Bishop Wishart following severe storm damage, and completed in 1318 by Bishop Lamberton for its Augustinian Canons. The structure was of a considerable length and had a twelve bayed nave, twenty four support pillars, two lateral aisles, along with north and south transepts with three bays each and an eastern aisle with a Lady Chapel at its eastern extremity. From the south extended the domestic buildings which formed the quadrangle. Caught in the tempest of Scotland's history during the 14th century, it was pillaged for its stone and lead by Edward I, 1304, and witnessed the first Parliament, 1309 held by the Bruce and Bishop Lamberton in the presence of Scotland's clergy and nobility. This was the culmination of the Church's vital support and was followed by the jubilation of Bannockburn and its consecration by the Bishop and the King in 1318. Repairs necessitated by a fire and storm damage were carried out by Prior James Haldenston in the 15th century, precipitating its elevation to a Metropolitan See around 1472, and set the seal on its status as the ecclesiastical centre of the Scottish Church. The building suffered severely at the Reformation, 1559, after John Knox had preached here to the rascal multitudes, whose orgy of destruction reduced it to a shadow of its former grandeur. Its ruinous state was hastened on by the weather and now includes the west entrance, the east gable with twin towers and interlaced arches, the south wall of the nave and parts of the south transept with Chapter House. St Rule's Tower close by, a former Augustinian Priory Church retains a sanctuary, choir and western tower, all built between the 12th and 16th centuries.

ST ANDREW'S CATHEDRAL
ABERDEENSHIRE

An Episcopalian Cathedral in all but appearance, it stands in Aberdeen's King Street near the old castle site and was built in 1817 by Archibald Simpson. Perpendicular in plan, it includes an aisled nave with five bays and a chancel built by G.Street (R.A) in 1880. Having little history of its own, much of its richly decorated interior revolves around an event in 1784 in a nearby house when Dr Samual Seabury (1744-1816), the first Bishop of the United States was consecrated by Bishop Skinner. This event marked the beginning of the American Episcopalian Church and was commemorated with a stained glass window in the east wall. The building's plaster, marble and wood work contrast with its colourfully painted ceiling emblazoned with a fine array of local Jacobite family heraldry and American States. Plans for new building work were restricted by the Depression of the 1930s leaving today's Cathedral to symbolise the cradle of the American Episcopalian Church.

ST ANDREW'S CATHEDRAL
HIGHLAND

On the bank of the River Ness in the City of Inverness stands the Episcopal Cathedral for the United Diocese of Moray, Ross and Caithness. The first Cathedral built in Scotland since the Reformation, it was designed by Alexander Ross in an English Gothic style and opened in 1867 after its founding by the Archbishop of Canterbury. Smaller than the average cathedral, it measures 166 feet long, 72 ft wide while the ridge of its roof is 88 ft high. Its remoteness and relatively modern foundation, however, leaves one focusing on its architectural features, of which its clerestoried nave terminated by two massive towers is central. Among other interesting features are the choir

stalls, built in memory of Bishop Kelly and containing some of its finest woodwork, which is overshadowed by the granite pillars and vaulted roof and houses over 600 seats facing its altar and highly sculpted pulpit of stone and marble. Crowning this is its tower and peal of bells which, with its organ by Hill, create the perfect atmosphere.

ST BEAN'S CHURCH
PERTH & KINROSS

On the bank of the River Earn in a small churchyard 5 miles NE of Crieff stands a post-Reformation church. According to Skene, St Bean or Beanus dwelt here in the first half of the 10th century, while in a 16th century account the Knights of St John were thought to have a Commandery here, but in the 14th century the benefice appears as an independent parsonage. Probably built in the late 16th century, within a hundred years repairs were carried out at the behest of the Bishop and Synod of Dunblane, but following the absorption of Kinkell into the Parish Church of the Holy Trinity of Gask the building fell into ruin. Excavations carried out by the Duke of Hamilton in the 19th century showed this to be originally of Norman construction. The attractive little church we see today owes much to the restoration work carried out in 1927.

ST BLANE'S CHURCH
ARGYLL & BUTE

This interesting ruin stands in a valley at the south end of the Island of Bute. Although essentially a Norman structure the areas rich ecclesiastical history, in particular its ties with St Blane who was born on the island and played an important role in evangelising Scotland in the 6th century, suggests this was a site of some kind of a church before the 11th century. Consisting of an oblong nave and a chancel separated by a wall with an interesting Norman chancel arch, the building is in the middle of a graveyard with enclosing wall and in former times it was customary to bury the menfolk at the upper churchyard and the women-folk at the lower section.

ST BRIDGET'S CHURCH
SOUTH LANARKSHIRE

Located about 12 miles WSW of Lanark. The Church of St Bridget or St Bride has strong connections with the Douglas family who were responsible for the ear-lier 12th century foundation. At one time belonging to Kelso Abbey and in the 14th century becoming a Preband of Glasgow Cathedral, the then church played a prominent role in the Wars of Indepen-dence along with the Douglases. They in-cluded the Good Sir James Douglas, whose audacious attack on the English garrison from Douglas Castle, in prayer on Psalm Sunday, resulted in their death to a man. The Earl himself died in Spain in 1331 while attempting to take Bruce's heart to the Holy Land. The church was destroyed in the wars of that period and was rebuilt in the 14th century, for in 1448 William Earl of Douglas petitioned the Pope for its erection into a Collegiate Church which was followed by its re-building in 1450. During Cromwell's oc-cupation it was used as a stable when it suffered some damage, and continued to be used as the Douglas family vault. The area itself was a favoured meeting place for the Covenanters in the 17th century, and in the 18th century the Douglases ceased to be buried here. In the late 19th century it was saved from ruin by Lord Home and repaired. All that remains today is the choir and south side of the nave chancel and remains of south transept. Its memorials include an effigy of the Good Sir James and his wife Beat-rice Sinclair, daughter of the Earl of

Orkney, and a tomb of Archibald 5th Earl of Douglas (Bell the Cat).

ST CLEMENT'S CHURCH
WESTERN ISLES

One of the more interesting and best pre-served ecclesiastical structures in the ex-treme NW of Scotland is located in the south of the Island of Harris. The church is thought to have been founded by an emissary from Iona but fell into decay during the Norse occupation. Today's 16th century church includes part of its predecessor and was re-built by Alexan-der Macleod who died in 1527 and whose tomb housed within ranks as one of the more interesting features. Burnt and restored in the late 18th century, today's structure is cruciform in plan, with a square tower at the west end the same width as the nave, from which the choir is not distinguished. After falling into a dilapidated state it was repaired again in 1866 by Mr Alexander Ross. Apart from the tombs, the church displays some fine examples of Celtic decorations.

ST DUTHAC'S CHURCH
HIGHLAND

The original chapel of St Duthac adjoined the Parish Church to the N of the town of Tain overlooking the sea. A missionary from Ireland, St Duthac was said to have been the Bishop of Ross in the 11th cen-tury. It was here in 1306 that Isabella, wife of Robert I, and his daughter Marjo-ry with their retinue were abducted by the Earl of Ross and delivered to Edward I of England. After its destruction by fire in 1427 a second church was built and styled as a Collegiate Church of St Dut-hac of Tain in 1457, with a chaplainry en-dowed by James II. Although many of the early Scottish monarchs visited the Shrine of St Duthac, it was James IV who made numerous pilgrimages to do penance for his involvement in his father's death before his own death at Flodden in 1513. The tradition was later carried on by his son James V whose visit in 1527 involved the King walking barefoot along its causeway, which still bears the name the Kings Causeway.

ST GILES CATHEDRAL
CITY OF EDINBURGH

Located on the Royal Mile in the city's former administrative centre. This was probably the site of a 9th century church which was followed by a Norman structure erected by David I in the early 12th century, which was destroyed in 1385 during the invasion of Richard II. The new church, built shortly after in an early Gothic style and completed in 1391, forms the foundations of today's structure. Its limited history up to the early 16th century had everything to do with the gradual acceptance of Edinburgh's official status as Capital. It incorporates a southern aisle or Assembly Aisle, added in 1454 and where the General Assembly met after the Reformation. Following the enlargement of its choir in 1462 it was made a Collegiate Church by James III in 1466 and confirmed by Pope Paul II in 1467 when its interior took on a more heraldic appearance. Further developments included the St Anthony Aisle, and on the east side the Chapman Aisle after Walter Chapman, a Clerk at Holyrood Palace whose financial support for Scotland's first printing press, 1507, was to accelerate the religious strife in the 16th and 17th centuries. This was particularly apparent at the Reformation when St Giles was used as a platform by John Knox and divided into four churches. Its short-lived elevation to a Cathedral by Charles I, 1633-38, and his introduction of the Scottish Prayer Book provoked the alleged stool-throwing incident when a Jenny Geddes threw a stool at the Dean during its first reading. The event marked one of the many gestures of dissent that led to Episcopacy being abolished and Presbyterianism being restored. In 1648 its steeple was rebuilt by John Mylne, the King's Master Mason. Used as a Public Exchange, Police Station and a Prison for Covenanters taken at Rullion Green, 1666. After being developed by the various local commercial enterprises St Giles faded into relative obscurity until the restoration work of 1817, when it lost its cruciform shape and much of its Norman work, leaving a plain Gothic structure with some 14th-century work. In later decades its character was harmonised by a Mr William Burn while retaining its 15th century tower with its crown top from 1500. The interior work in the choir in 1872 revealed many of the beautiful features in the pillars, wall and roof and brought with it the installation of royal pews, stalls for the Lords of Session, civic dignitaries and open seats for the congregation. In 1911 Sir Robert Lorimer designed the Thistle Chapel in a Gothic style for the Knights of the Order of the Thistle. Presently St Giles is a skilful blend of a church, war memorial and hall of fame with many of its aisles named after noblemen. See Edinburgh City

ST MACHAR'S CATHEDRAL
CITY OF ABERDEEN

Standing in the Old Town overlooking the river is the well preserved granite structure. Possibly built on the site of a 6th century Columban Church after David I transferred the see from Mortlach, confirmed in a Papal Bull in 1157. Amongst its numerous bishops was Alexander Kininmoth (1356-80) who founded the present Cathedral of St Mary and St Machar but after its destruction by Edward III in 1336 it was carried on by his successors, notably bishops Dunbar and Leighton. By 1532 it included a five-bayed nave, an aisles choir, a transept, the Lady Chapel, and consistory, with two western octagonal steeples and a central tower in which hung fourteen bells. The destruction suffered by iconoclasm in the 16th century and during the Civil Wars of the 17th century, when it proudly stood with its west front and massive twin towers as the only granite Cathedral in the world reached a crescendo in 1688 when its central tower fell, demolishing its choir and transepts. Although it was later pillaged for its stone, its oak ceiling emblazoned with the arms of its benefactors, many of whom were from the noble houses of Europe, is a reminder of its 19th century restoration. See Aberdeen City

ST MAGNUS CATHEDRAL
ORKNEY

The first Cathedral which was moved from Birsay to Kirkwall by 1065, was subordinate to York but by 1137 Earl Rognvald founded St Magnus Cathedral in honour of his uncle the Earl of Orkney, who had been slain by his cousin Haakon, and both Earl and nephew are interred here. Cruciform in design, it was built of red sandstone in a Norman-Gothic style by masons brought from Durham, and rose like a colossus above the town, where its pre-eminence endured for more than 700 years. Added to by several bishops, it blends the work of five different periods between 1137 and 1500. The eastern section of its nave is thought to have been built by Bishop Edward Stewart in the 16th century, while its western section with its curious southern doorway was erected by the celebrated ecclesiastic and lawyer Bishop Robert Reid, who in 1548 helped arrange the marriage of Mary I to the Dauphin of France but died on the return journey. In the interim Bishop Maxwell ornamented its interior by building stalls and provided three church bells before receiving

James V here in 1536. The building's grandeur is best exemplified by the double row of 24 gigantic columns, supporting double tiers of arches and transepts with their three tiers of carved arched Norman windows ascending to the vaulted groined roof. The pyramid roof of the central tower replaced an earlier spire struck by lightning in 1671. Although escaping damage at the Reformation, the Cathedral was nearly destroyed by the Earl of Caithness during the rebellion of Patrick, Earl of Orkney (executed, 1615) and was later visited by Cromwell's forces in 1652, after which it suffered a long period of decline. During the period of reparation between 1805 and 1850 some of the bishops' tombs were desecrated and their remains removed. The nearby Earl's Palace (ruin), built in 1605 with slave labour by Patrick Earl of Orkney, displays a French Renaissance style as it rises three storeys high with protruding bay windows, but conforms to the Scottish courtyard plan. Seized by Royal troops during the Earl's rebellion, it was retaken by the Earl's son and inhabited by Bishop Mackenzie until 1688, but was roofless by 1745. See Kirkwall

ST MAGNUS CHURCH
ORKNEY

Situated on the highest point on the Isle of Egilsay NW of the mainland. Although now ruinous the church of St Magnus still retains as its best architectural feature its round tower, which served as a place of refuge during the Norse incursions and was modelled on the traditional Irish Round Tower, one of three left in Scotland. The building would seem to have reached its high point in the country's history when it was the scene of the murder of Magnus by his cousin Haakon around 1116, when the latter became Earl of Orkney. This church probably superceeded the earlier building, and its present ruins comprise the round tower with adjoining oblong nave and chancel.

ST MARY'S CATHEDRAL
ABERDEENSHIRE

One of the three cathedrals built during Aberdeen's 19th century expansion, and known as the Roman Catholic Cathedral of St Mary of the Assumption. It was erected in Huntly Street in 1860 and designed by Alexander Ellis in white granite in a second pointed style with seating for 1200. Its aisled nave, which is 156 feet by 73ft and 72ft high has life size statues of the twelve apostles and is terminated by the chancel and rood screen built in 1879 and adorned with a crucifix and the figures of the Virgin Mary and St John. Above the High Altar of 1881 is the large stained glass rose window, while at the west end is the baptistery with its granite font. The spire by R.G.Wilson was completed in 1877 and a peal of bells cast by John Foster was added in 1878. See Aberdeen City

ST MARY'S CATHEDRAL
CITY OF EDINBURGH

Located at Palmerston Place on the western fringes of the New Town near Princes Street. It was built on land bequeathed by a Mrs Walker of Coates. In 1874 work began to designs by George Gilbert Scott, after whose death it was completed by his son John and consecrated in 1879. A colossus of its day and the largest Cathedral in Scotland. In keeping with its Gothic style, its plan is cruciform, with a lofty central tower (275 feet) and spire which houses ten bells. The nave, transepts and choir are respectively seven, two and four bays in length while each of the four arms has aisles on both sides, and by the arrangement of the reredos the choir aisles are connected at the east end. Later additions included a Chapter

House built in 1891, spires added to the towers in 1917 which terminate the west end nave aisles (named after Mary and Barbra Coates), while the War Memorial side altar and hanging rood was by Sir Robert Lorimer and its organ was built by the renowned Father Willis. The Jacobean Laird's House in the grounds, formerly the Walkers' Manor House of the Easter Coates and Drumsheugh Estate, was opened as a Choir School in 1880 but now operates as a Music School..

ST MARY'S CHAPEL
ARGYLL & BUTE

The ruined chapel of St Mary stands on the Island of Bute 1 1/2 miles S of Rothesay town. Probably built in the 13th century, it was one of the cathedral churches of the isles and has associations with the Stewarts, who held Rothesay Castle from the 14th century. In 1692 the nave was removed to make way for the Parish Church which was in turn removed in 1795 to allow the present church to be built. Todays ruins include the walls of the choir, while the most interesting feature is the monument of a knight represented as a recumbent figure in a 14th century style of armour, along with two other tombs. According to some 19th century sources this was built on the site of an earlier Celtic church that was converted into a mortuary chapel by the Stewards of Scotland Lords of Bute around 1315.

ST MONANCE VILLAGE. SEE ST MONAN'S CHURCH.

ST MONAN'S CHURCH
FIFE

Giving its name to the fishing village in which it is situated 12 miles S of Saint Andrews. Although this quaint fishing village is one of long-standing, its history is surpassed by the antiquity of its church. The church was built on a rocky bank in the SW of the village and is dedicated to the 6th century missionary who converted the local Picts before suffering martyrdom at the hands of the Danes on the Isle of May. The earlier church was reputed to be erected in honour of the saint whose relics were brought from Ireland in the 9th century and was later rebuilt in a grander scale. The earlier church was founded by David II in 1370 and built by William Dishington, Master of Works. In the following century it was re-founded by James III who bestowed it on the Dominican Friars, and by a Papal Bull was given conventual status in 1477, by which time it had established a reputation for royal pilgrimages. However, this development receded and by 1519 the building was in ruins. Suffering greatly in 1544 during Hertford's invasion, from 1646 it was used as the Parish Church but by 1772 was again in a ruinous state and was again restored. However, the state of preservation we see today owes much to the restoration work of 1828. The church is essentially cruciform in plan with a chancel transepts and a spire over the crossing. Features of special interest are the sedila, a good pointed doorway and elaborate carvings on some of the windows.

ST NINIAN'S CHAPEL
DUMFRIES & GALLOWAY

Formerly situated on an island but now connected with the mainland, the ruined chapel stands about 3 miles SE of Whithorn. Its an area steeped in Scottish religious tradition and in particular the work of St Ninian who is regarded as Scotland's first missionary. Although it faded into the mists of obscurity there are some claims which assert that this was the original Candida Casa site of the 4th century saints, which in English means 'white house'. The saint's cave is located in the area by the coast. The tranquility of the place is certainly conducive to self-examination, which is how the early Christian hermits found solace from the savagery of the times. Today's ruins were probably built by the priors of Whithorn as a place of worship for the islanders, and probably for pilgrims on route to the saint's shrine. The ruins are of a structure that is unroofed but retains the walls and has been in a state of preservation.

SALTCOATS
NORTH AYRSHIRE

Town situated 7 miles NW of Irvine. Called Saltcotis in 1471, the name probably comes from the saltworkers' cottages or huts. Originally consisting of a small community living in clay-built cottages who eked out a living extracting coal and salt with the their pans and kettles. It was constantly overshadowed by the growing town and also by the Parish of Ardossan of which it was part. To safeguard the rights of Hugh, Earl of Eglinton, during the long-standing feud with the Cunninghams of Glencairn who burnt Ardrossan Castle, the family seat was erected into a Burgh of Barony in 1528 by James V but did not receive a charter until decades later. Despite this its decline was under way, resulting in it numbering four houses by 1660. It was, however the later endeavours of Sir Robert Cunningham, nearly a generation later, that arrested the decay and revived its fortunes, when he built several large saltpans and opened various coal pits with plans to develop its harbour as a Coal Port. Saltcoats then rapidly grew into a large village and henceforth a small town. Continued growth, along with its neighbours Ardrossan and Stevenston owed much to the landed gentry jostling for the industrial development of their respective estates. In 1802 it was the site of the first

Magnesia Works in Scotland. Saltcoats suffered in later decades from the repeal of the salt duty but was buffeted by the prosperity of its neighbours and the precarious though vigorous efforts in shipbuilding, followed by weaving and its coal trade with Ireland which was dominant by 1880. Its industrial status prevailed in later decades but in the 20th century it drew much benefit from the seaside retreat of Ardrossan of which it is now a virtual extension.

SALTCOATS CASTLE
EAST LOTHIAN

Situated 1 mile S of Gullane village are the fragmentary remains of the Livingstone's courtyard castle with round towers on its left side. Built in 1590 by Peter Livingstoun de Saltcoats, whose family arms, along with those of his wife, Margaret Fettis of Fawside, appeared on a panel. It was once surrounded by an extensive garden and orchard where the enclosing wall was built by a George Livingstone in 1695. Still inhabited in the 17th century, the main part of the castle was removed for the purposes of farming in the early 19th century.

SANQUHAR
DUMFRIES & GALLOWAY

Town situated 27 miles NW of Dumfries. Name derived from the Gaelic 'seann cathair' meaning 'old fort'. Once the site of an earthen defensive structure, the land was originally held by the Ross family but passed through marriage in the 14th century to William de Crichton for whose descendants, Sir Robert de Crichton, it was raised to a Burgh of Barony in 1484 and a Lordship in 1485. Along with the castle, the land and Lordship were purchased in 1639 by William Douglas, Viscount Drumlanrig whose descendant, the 3rd Duke of Queensberry, developed the town and its trade in

stockings with the Virginia market. This disappeared during the American War of Independence, 1776, and was later supplanted by carpet weaving and in later years a trade in coal and shovels. Scene of the Sanquhar Declaration in 1680 and 1685, when the Covenanters Richard Cameron and James Renwick declared their opposition to the King at the Mercat Cross. The site is now marked by a monument erected in 1860. Sanquhar's Old Tolbooth (now a museum), built by William Adam in 1735, predates Britain's oldest post office which was started here in 1763. See Castle

SANQUHAR CASTLE
DUMFRIES & GALLOWAY

It stands on a steep bank above the valley near the village of Sanquhar. The ruins of this outer and inner courtyard castle were started as a 14th century keep, built when William Crichton married the Ross heiress. In 1485 additional curtain walls were built when William Crichton was created Lord Crichton of Sanquhar after benefiting from the Douglases, fall in 1455. The scene of a royal reception in 1617, given in honour of James VI by William Crichton, who was created Earl of Dumfries in 1633. It was repurchased in 1639 by Sir William Douglas of Drumlanrig who, preferring the place to Drumlanrig, stayed here until his death in 1640. After this the family made some additions up until the death of the 2nd Duke in 1711, when it was pillaged for its stone by the local people.

SAUCHIE CASTLE
CLACKMANNAN

Erected 9 miles NE of Stirling by the River Deveron. With walls six foot thick, it stands two storeys high and is peppered with shot holes. The barony conferred by Robert the Bruce on Henry Annand in 1324 later passed through marriage to the

Shaws of Greenock, whose descendant James Shaw of Sauchie built the tower around 1430. The nearby mansion house, probably built as a replacement, bears the inscription above the main door.' I MEIN WEILL' above the date 1631, and the scroll inscribed 'BY PROMIS MADE RESTORED VE BE TO HAVE A BLESSED ETERNITY' while its southern pediment is the family motto which reads " JE ME CONTENTE " which paraphrased means 'IN WELL DOING I SATISFY MYSELF ' .

SAUCHIEBURN, BATTLE OF, 1488
STIRLING

To the south of Stirling. In response to a rebellion by Prince James, along with Archibald, Earl of Angus and other nobles resentful of the advancement of the King's low born favourites, King James III led an army estimated by some sources to be around 30,000 men to crush the insurgents. The benefits of the rebels' numerical superiority were furthered when their spearmen gained an advantage which was driven home, causing the royal army to flee and hastening their defeat. The King's murder in a nearby mill led to the crowning of Prince James and the elevation of the rebel Lords to the highest offices in the land.

SCALLOWAY CASTLE
SHETLAND

Above the village 5 miles SW of Lerwick are the ruins of an L plan castle built in 1600 by Patrick Stewart, the tyrannical Earl of Orkney. Built three storeys high with forced local labour on pain of losing their property, it was sometimes used as the local Law Courts and was occupied by Cromwell's forces in 1652, but fell into ruin after their departure.

SCHIVAS HOUSE
PERTH & KINROSS

Located 5 miles NW of Ellon. This old mansion house was built around 1640 by the Greys, who were practicing Roman Catholics and a branch of the Kinfauns family. Once containing the relics of its pre-Reformation Chapel, Schivas was used as a farmhouse in the 19th century but is now restored.

SCONE PALACE
PERTH & KINROSS

The palace stands near the River Tay 2 miles N of Perth. After the destruction of the old palace in 1559, a new edifice was built by William, Ist Earl of Gowrie, which was forfeited to the Crown on his execution in 1584. The Chevalier St George lived at Scone in splendour for three weeks in 1716 and his son Prince Charles Edward also visited the house in 1745. The succession of the Stormonts to the Mansfield title led in 1808 to the mansion being replaced by William Atkinson's palace built in a Gothic style fronting its magnificent halls and spacious apartments which house much of the original furniture and artefacts of the earlier house. The fine trees in its grounds include a sycamore planted by Mary I and an oak and sycamore planted by James VI. Visited by Queen Victoria and Prince Albert in 1842, today it still ranks as one of Scotland's premier palaces. The Moot Hill of Scone in the palace grounds was where the Old Scone village is reputed to have stood, and was the ancient site of the coronations of Pictish Kings, with the Stone of Destiny as its nucleus. According to one legend it was the stone which Jacob used as a pillow at Bethel and came via Spain and Ireland to Dunstaffnage, from where Kenneth Macalpine had it brought before uniting the Picts and the Scots under one kingdom. According to Fordun (historian) ' No king was ever wont to reign in Scotland unless he had sat upon this at Scone '. The last of these was John Balliol before it was carried off by Edward I in 1296 to London where it remained for 700 years until it was returned and housed in Edinburgh Castle.

SCONE ABBEY
PERTH & KINROSS

It occupies land by the River Tay 2 miles N of Perth. Stretching back into antiquity, Scone was the Capital of Pictavia when Scotland was divided into four Kingdoms and was the site of a castle and church (Mote Hill, Hill of Belief) where the Pictish King Nechtan embraced the church of Rome. Around 838 Kenneth Macalpine brought the Stone of Destiny (Stone of Scone) here from Dunstaffnage. The Abbey which occupied the site of the present palace and was founded by Alexander I for Augustinian monks was where Malcolm IV was crowned in 1153, and replaced the Culdee Church to eventually become the established place of coronations, which had been held at Dunadd. After 1296 when Edward I carried off the stone to London it served as a coronation stone for British monarchs for 700 years. In spite of its destruction during the Wars of Independence Scone witnessed the crowning of Robert the Bruce, 1306, with the full support of the Scottish Church. Between 1165 and 1488 it was the scene of the crowning of no fewer than eleven monarchs including William I, Alexander II, Alexander III, Robert I, David II, Robert II, Robert III, James I, James II, James III, and James IV. The Abbey and old palace was destroyed at the Reformation when the lands passed to the Earl of Gowrie but the remains of the former are now incorporated in the new palace. In 1624 David Murray, who was made Baron Scone in 1605 (after the Gowries' forfeiture) built a new church on Moot Hill where Charles II was crowned in 1651.

SCOTSCRAIG GOLF CLUB
FIFE

Situated SE of Newport on Tay. The club began life in 1817 after William Dalgleish galvanised enough support to build a course on his own land. From its inauspicious start as the 13th golf club in the world, in their uniformed red coats and green velvet collars, the members played for gold and silver medals up until the club went into abeyance for 50 years, when members resorted to playing on neighbouring courses. Following a meeting at the Templars Hall at Tayport (5 May 1887) interested parties led by Admiral Maitland Dougall, the then owner of the land, resolved to restart the club with its former name and gold and silver medals, which still figure amongst the club's trophies. In 1890 Scotscraig merged with Newport Golf Club taking the number of members to 100 and bringing the need for a clubhouse to the fore, as the present convenience at Tayport Hospital was proving unsuitable. The completion of the new clubhouse in 1896 and the opening of an extended course of 18 holes designed by James Braid in 1905 were significant milestones in the club's ongoing development. These marked the close of one century and the beginning of another, when a challenge match was arranged that included J Gordon Simpson, F H Scroggie, Andrew Kirkaldy and also Willie Auchterlonie, the Open Champion of 1893. After the purchase of the course in 1923, alterations and extensions were carried out by James Braid whose work is largely responsible for the course of today. This has often been used as the qualifying course for the Open Championship at Saint Andrews. One of the few traditional Scottish courses, its position so far from the seashore provides better conditions for one of its more unique features, its trees, particularly its firs, which with the rich turf and smooth greens provide a perfect setting and challenge to players today.

SCOTSTARVIT TOWER
FIFE

Positioned on high ground 3 miles N of Cupar. The land and tower of Tarvet was incorporated into the Barony of Scotstarvit when Sir John Scott purchased it from Alexander Inglis in 1612. A traditional battlemented L plan tower built by 1629, it once contained a panel dated 1627, with the Scott and Drummond family arms including the initials of the builder Sir John Scott, his wife Dame Ann Drummond of Hawthornden, and their son also John Scott.

SEAFIELD TOWER
FIFE

The ruins of an early 16th century L plan tower stand near the sea, 1 mile NE of Kinghorn. Built in 1542 by John Moutry of Seafield, whose family retained possession of it until 1631, the last of the family died in the Jacobite Rebellion of 1715.

SELKIRK
SCOTTISH BORDERS

Town situated 7 miles SW of Galashiels. The name is derived from the Old English 'sele' meaning 'a hall' or 'royal court' and the Scots 'Kirke' denoting 'a church' probably after the chapel used by the King while hunting in the nearby Ettrick Forest. With its strong royal links this was once the site of a Tironesian Abbey (removed to Kelso, 1128) founded in 1113 by the Earl David, later David I, and it was around the same period a castle was built which was frequently visited by William the Lion, Alexander II, and Alexander III before its decline in importance by 1306. Suffering the fluctuating

fortunes of a Border town, in 1328 it was created a Royal Burgh by Robert the Bruce who also granted Selkirk Forest to his lieutenant Lord James Douglas after Bannockburn. Represented in Parliament in 1469, the town was also the scene of the Justice Courts, held in the 15th and 16th centuries to curb the lawlessness, leading to James IV ordering the erection of Newark Tower. Following the burning of the town by the English after Flodden, 1513, when a Selkirk weaver had captured the English banner, James V granted the burghers 1000 acres of Ettrick Forest. The chapter is now commemorated on the towns armorial bearings and with the Common Riding Festival held in June. The former depicts the Virgin Mary and a child sitting on a sarcophagus to symbolise a widow and child, with the Scottish Lion below and a wood in the background. The latter is marked by a procession of mounted local tradesmen (The ancient Selkirk Merchant Company) led by a standard bearer who, after surveying the acres of the royal grant, lowers the colours in the Market Place in memory of Souter Fletcher, one of the few survivors of the battle whose return with the news is celebrated in the song:

Up wi' the sutors o' Selkirk,
And down with the Earl of Hume!
And up wi' a the braw lads
That sew the single-soled shoon!

Erected into an Earldom in 1646 for Lord William Douglas whose family held extensive tracts of land in this area for centuries. As already described, in addition to their bravery, the Souters of Selkirk had an established reputation for their single-soled shoes, making the town an attractive stopping place for armies from the north and south. In 1645 it gave a lukewarm reception to Montrose prior to his defeat by the Covenanters at Philiphaugh, and in 1745 its coolness towards the Stewart cause cost it dearly when the Prince ordered 3,000 pairs of shoes. During the threatened French invasion of 1804 the burgh committed its yeomanry and in 1811 it was the site of a camp for prisoners of the war. Among its literary associations are included Robert Burns, who wrote his Epistle to Willie Creech at the Forest Inn at the West Port (now marked by a plaque), 1787. It was Walter Scott who, while Sheriff Depute of Selkirkshire between 1799 and 1832, used the nearby Newark Tower as a setting for his 'Lay of the Last Minstrel' (pub. 1805), a period now marked by a statue of Scott in the Market Place. By the mid-19th century, shoe-making was being replaced by wool and tweed production owing to the abundant supply of running water and the nearby sheep farms which continue to supply the trade to this day. Standing in the Market Place outside the Municipal Offices is a statue of Mungo Park, the African explorer who was born at the nearby Foulshiels in 1771 but was murdered by natives on the River Boussa while travelling down the Niger. Although dating from the 17th century its Grammar School was replaced by the Selkirk High School in 1948 to accommodate the influx from the new housing developments, when the town's boundaries were extended. Today most of the town's history can be seen in the 18th century Halliwell House museum in the High Street.

SETON CHURCH
EAST LOTHIAN

In the grounds of Seton Castle 2 miles E of Prestonpans. The foundation of this church is uncertain but records seem to point to it functioning in the 13th century, when it is rated in the ancient Taxatio at 18 Merks. Strongly linked to the Sinclair family, in 1390 a reference to Kathrine Sinclair wife of William Ist Lord

Seton states she was buried in the "Biggit ane yle on the south side of the Buroche Kirk of Seytoun". In 1493 George 2nd Lord Seton made it collegiate for a Provost six prebendaries, a clerk and two singing boys, but the developments were not finished. Added to at various periods, ostensibly due to its position on the main invasion route from England, in particular 1544 when it is recorded that the Earl of Hertford's forces 'tuk away the bellis and organis and other tursable (movable) thingis and put thame in thair schippis, and brint the tymber wark within the said kirk'. The 2nd Lord's work was completed by George 3rd Lord Seton, but it was the Dowager Lady Seton who erected the transepts tower and part of the incomplete spire in the 16th century after her husband's death at Flodden. After the Reformation (1560) the church was an independent charge but was united with Tranent in 1580. The building was defaced by the Lothian Militia in response to Earl Winton's (formerly Lord Seton) Jacobite sympathies. Designed as a cross without aisles and central tower with spire over the intersection, the building owes its present state to the 19th century work of the Earl of Wemyss who, along with his Countess, is buried within.

SHERIFFMUIR, BATTLE OF, 1715
STIRLING

East of Dunblane. The first battle of the 1715 Jacobite Rising involved around 9,000 of the Earl of Mar's Jacobites who, after failing to secure Dunblane, halted and took up positions near the moor before the Earl of Argyll's 4,000 man force. On commencing battle the following morning, the haphazard attack by the Jacobites against the thoroughly disciplined government troops had little bearing on the outcome, which after attack and counter attack was inconclusive. Despite this, some weeks later the Old Pretender (Chevalier St George) landed at Peterhead and the 1715 Rising began in earnest. See Jacobite Rebellion

SHIRTS, BATTLE OF, 1544
HIGHLAND

At the E end of Loch Lochy S of Laggan. One of the many battles fought between feuding clans, namely Clan Ranald and the Frasers under Lord Lovat. It acquired its name owing to the combatants discarding their shirts in the summer heat. With the defeat of the Frasers came the death of 300 of the clan, along with their chief and his eldest son, which ushered in a long period of Frasers inheriting the title as teenagers, while Clan Ranald escaped the wrath of retribution.

SHOTTS
NORTH LANARKSHIRE

The town situated 15 miles SW of Livingstone once formed part of the land called Bertram-Shotts after an outlaw who terrorised the area in the 14th century but the name itself probably comes from the Old English 'sceat' meaning 'corner of land'. A church dedicated to St Catherine of Sienna which existed at a desert place called Bertram-shotts was mentioned in a Papal Bull in 1476 and the name was applied to the whole Parish until the first half was dropped in the 16th century. As part of the Lordship of Bothwell Moor the land was held by the Hamiltons from the 15th century and often figured in historical events owing to its position on the main highways between north and south and east and west. Scene of a religious revival in 1630, the town was visited by Cromwell's forces in 1650, who encamped here in 1651 and was later distinguished in the Covenanting struggles. The towns menfolk, fired with religious fervour during the many Conventicles held locally by

their leaders Alexander Pedan and Donald Cargill, fought in the Pentland Rising, Drumclog, and Bothwell Brig, 1666-1679. Apart from a visit from the Jacobites in 1745, most of its history is connected with commerce, which began when the railway made it part of the industrial corridor between Glasgow and Edinburgh, through which travelled most of its coal which fired its two iron works from 1787 and 1802. Since the closure of the hot blast furnaces in 1948 and the gradual rundown of its coal mines in the 1960s the town has fallen back on its oldest industry, farming, which benefited from its annual cattle and horse fairs and by the demands for the maximum yield required during both world wars.

SKELMORLIE CASTLE
NORTH AYRSHIRE

Situated 3 miles S of Wemyss Bay. The lands were held by the Cunninghams but later passed to the Montgomeries, for in 1461 Lord Montgomery bestowed it on his son George. Built in 1502, it was described in 1608 as being ' pleasantly seated, decorred with orchards and woodes'. In 1852 it was left to John Graham, a Glasgow merchant who incorporated it into a large mansion.

SKIPNESS CASTLE
ARGYLL & BUTE

Strategically positioned at a channel cross point 9 miles SE of Tarbert. Once surrounded by a ditch, the oldest part of this L plan keep with enclosing walls and projecting towers dates from the 13th century. Though originally a stronghold of the Macdougals, who built the 15th century priest's tower, it passed with most of Argyll to the Campbells long after the fall of the Macdougals Lords of Lorn in the 14th century. Acquired by the Montgomeries whose kinsman Alexander Montgomerie, author of 'Cherrie and the Slae' (allegorical poem concerning virtue and vice) stayed here in the 16th century. It later reverted to the Campbells who occupied it until the late 18th century. In 1880 the nearby house was built by a Mr Graham.

SKIRLING
SCOTTISH BORDERS

Village situated 2 miles NE of Biggar. Although the name's meaning is uncertain it either derives from the Gaelic 'sgrathlin' meaning 'turf land' or the Old Norse 'sker' and the Gaelic 'lin' meaning 'rock land'. The Barony of Scrawlin was granted by King Robert the Bruce to John Monfode by 1329 but was later held by the Cockburns whose castle was destroyed by the Regent Moray in 1568 due to Sir James Cockburn's support for the defeated Queen Mary. Despite being elevated to a Burgh of Barony for Cockburn of Skirling in 1592, by the late 17th century it was held by the Carmichaels, under whose stewardship it once enjoyed annual cattle and horse fairs which failed to generate the expansion some of the neighbouring towns enjoyed. As a result the Skirling of today consists of a small cluster of houses.

SMAILHOLM
SCOTTISH BORDERS

Village situated 6 miles NW of Kelso. Name derived from the Old English 'smoel ham' meaning 'small village'. From 1408 the lands were held by the Pringles who in the 16th century built Smailholm's L plan tower (now restored) with walls nine foot thick and three storeys high which overlook the River Tweed between Melrose and Kelso. The view from its battlements of Berwick, the Cheviots, triple Eildon and the Lammermuirs made it an important part of the Borders' defensive network. Acquired by the Scotts of Harden by 1725, the tower was frequently visited by the young Sir

Walter Scott (1771-1832), who stayed for five years at his grandfather's farm at nearby Sandyknow and later eulogised it in his 'Marmion' of 1808:

I deemed such nooks the sweetest shade
The sun in all his round surveyed;
And still I thought that shattered tower
The mightiest work of human power;
And marvelled as the aged hind
With sane strange tale bewitched the mind

The Parish Church, built in 1632 in a Norman style but added to periodically, includes a stained glass window gifted by the late Lord Binnning in memory of Scott.

SMAILHOLM TOWER. SEE VILLAGE

SOLWAY MOSS, BATTLE OF, 1542
DUMFRIES & GALLOWAY

To the W of the Solway Firth near Gretna. Fought during the reign of James V when after advancing into England, the Scots, led by General Oliver Sinclair, encountered a band of 400 English borderers under Thomas Dacre. Sinclair's indecision brought about the rout of the Scots in the direction of Solway Moss and his own capture, but on his subsequent release he promised to advance English interests in Scotland.

SORBIE CASTLE
DUMFRIES & GALLOWAY

About 1 mile E of the village are the ruins of an L plan structure. From the early 16th century to the late 17th century the land belonged to the Hannays' who some decades before their departure probably built the tower which stood four storeys high with pepper pot turrets and was surrounded by trees. A Patrick Hannay served Elizabeth the Winter Queen of Bohemia (Daughter of James VI of Scotland) in the Thirty Years War 1618-48.

SPEDLINS CASTLE
DUMFRIES & GALLOWAY

Located on the bank of the Annan 4 miles NNE of Lochmaben is a well preserved massive keep. The home of the Jardine family, who in the 15th century started the castle, of which two vaulted storeys remain that were added to in 1605 when the upper structure was rebuilt. Despite the horror stories that the castle was haunted by a miller who was accidentally starved to death in its pit, the family stayed here until 1814 when they moved to Jardines Hall.

SPEYBURN DISTILLERY
MORAY

It sits majestically in a corner of the Spey Valley SW of Rothes, near its water source of the Granty burn, one of the main tributaries of the River Spey. A traditional Victorian distillery founded by John Hopkins & Co Ltd, it produced its first batch of whisky mainly for blending on 15th Dec 1897 in a windowless unfinished still house in the middle of winter, when the men worked in overcoats to fill casks within the year which marked the diamond Jubilee of Queen Victoria. The only Highland distillery to use this particularly soft water, its original annual capacity was 100,000 gallons. It was built with the stones from the bed of the River Spey. With its familiar pagoda roof rising from the valley floor against a backdrop of pines as viewed from the Rothes and Elgin road, the distillery is also known as 'The Gibbet' because of its closeness to the ancient 'Cnock na Croiche' or 'Hillock of the Gibbet'. The first in Scotland to install a steam-driven mechanical malting system, Speyburn continued to be used for blending until 1992 when the then owners Inver House Distillers took the opportunity to bottle its ten year old malt.

OWNERS
Blairmhor Ltd ?

REGION
Speyside

PRODUCT
Speyburn 10 year old single malt 40% vol

NOTES
A honey bouquet with a balanced, malty taste and a warm, dry finish.

SPYNIE
MORAY

Town situated 3 miles N of Elgin. While its name derivation is a little obscure it may derive from the Latin 'spina' meaning 'a thorn'. Once the site of a Cathedral for the See of Moray founded by Malcolm Canmore in 1057, although its removal to Elgin in 1224 reduced its status, by the 15th century Spynie had become the site of the Bishop's Palace which with the church as its main landowner was at the heart of the town's development. The 13th century church of the Holy Trinity, which sometimes served as a Cathedral, was rebuilt in 1736 on the present site giving rise to the name New Spynie. In future years the area's essentially agrarian economy encouraged fluctuating population levels which continued despite land reclamation for re-forestry but with its marked increase in the 20th century came housing developments which virtually made the village a dormitory for its larger neighbour Elgin. See Castle.

SPYNIE CASTLE
MORAY

The ruins of this fortified palace stand on rising ground 2 miles NE of Elgin and once stood next to Loch Spynie, now no longer. Once the site of an early residence of the Bishops of Moray until their removal to Elgin in 1224. The gateway built by Bishop John Innes, who was consecrated in 1406, included a portcullis and a stairway leading to the battlements which probably surrounded the original keep. In response to a threat from the Chief of the Gordons, Bishop David Stewart built a tower (David's tower) between 1461 and 1476 which now forms part of the ruins. The first floor, which included the Great Hall, large bedrooms and vaulted closets, was where Queen Mary supped and slept on 17th September 1562. On the south side of the courtyard there was a tennis court running parallel to a chapel, while on the east side was the kitchen and offices surrounded by gardens and orchards. In 1590, James VI created it a Temporal Barony for Alexander Lindsay, Lord Spynie, but it was resold to the Crown in 1606. Fortified and garrisoned by the deposed Bishop Guthrie, who was forced to surrender in 1640 to General Munro, during the ensuing Covenanting Wars it was held for Montrose, becoming an Episcopal Residence again after the Restoration of Charles II in 1660. While held by the Crown it was allowed to fall into ruin, when much of the stone was used for building by local people.

STAIR CASTLE
SOUTH AYRSHIRE

It occupies ground by the River Ayr 8 miles NE of the town. The land once belonged to the Kennedys but passed to William Dalrymple on his marriage to Agnes Kennedy in 1450. Their descendant John Dalrymple (1648-1707), created 1st Earl of Stair in 1703, who also distinguished himself as a soldier and philosopher, was largely responsible for the Massacre of Glencoe, 1692, while Secretary of State. Given the style is of a 17th century house it is fair to assume he either built all of it or was responsible for its later development.

STANDARD, BATTLE OF, 1138

During the second invasion of the year, the Scots led by David I overran Durham before being opposed by an English force assembled by Thurston, Bishop of York, who defeated them at Northallerton with the might of the mail clad Norman Knights. The battle owes its name to the many consecrated banners of the saints carried by the English, and served as a milestone as it led to the northern counties coming permanently under English control (Treaty of York, 1237).

STEVENSTON
NORTH AYRSHIRE

Town situated 2 miles E of Ardrossan. The town derived its name from the one time owner of the land, a Stephen Lochart or Lochard whose father was granted the land in 1170 by Richard de Morville, Lord Cunningham and Constable of Scotland. After being acquired by a number of owners it was bought in 1656 by Charles II's physician, Robert Cunningham, whose nephew developed the town's trade in coal and salt mining and accessed the Dublin market after building Saltcoats harbour close by in 1700. The nearby village of Ardeer (now gone) which bore the curious name of Piper-Heugh owing to the long standing production of the Jews Harp gave the townsfolk a reputation as lovers of music, something which was frequently displayed at St Marnochs Fair that was held annually. The long standing rivalry with its neighbours Saltcoats and Ardrossan was spearheaded by the landed gentry of the respective towns, with the main focus concerned with the markets in Glasgow, where it traded its cotton and coal. Its mining greatly benefited from the Nobel Explosive Company which was founded near here in 1873 but was latterly replaced by the Imperial Chemical Industries factory as the main employer.

STIRLING
STIRLING

City situated 25 miles NE of Glasgow. Also known as Struelin, 1125: Strivling, 1455: and Sterling in 1470. The present name probably comes from the Gaelic 'Struth' and 'lann' meaning 'land by a stream'. The castle rock around which the town grew was probably the site of a primitive defensive structure and was followed in the 1st century by a Roman outpost due to its strategic importance, which continued throughout history. Though lost in the mists of obscurity between the 5th and the 10th centuries, owing to its importance this was undoubtedly an eventful period and by 993 Stirling comes back on record as it was the gathering point for the Scots before their defeat of the Danes at Luncarty. After the country's unification in the 11th century the town took on the appearance of a capital city with a Royal Burgh Charter granted between 1124 and 1127 and membership of the Four Courts of Burghs in the 13th century, when its inextricable links with the fate of its castle made it the scene of much activity relating to the affairs of state. Its Royal Burgh status was confirmed by Alexander II whose father had founded a Dominican Friary here in 1233. Playing a central part in the Wars of Independence, when Stirling Bridge to the north east of the town was the scene of Wallaces victory, 1297; in keeping with his scorched earth policy the burgh was burnt by the Scots, 1298, but was occupied by Edward I between 1298 and 1300. Attempts to restore the town's fortunes with the granting of customs and fishing rights by Robert II after its burning by Richard II in 1385 proved somewhat optimistic and it was not until the 15th century that it returned to something resembling its former state, by which time it had lost out to Edinburgh as the Capital City. Consequently the town retained its strategic importance through its castle and also developed some worthy religious houses like the Church of the Holy Rood, founded in 1457, where James VI was crowned, 1567, Greyfriars Monastery, established by James IV, 1494, the elevation of the Chapel Royal into a Collegiate Church, 1501, and the founding in 1530 of a hospital by Robert Spittal (former tailor to James IV). All of which gave Stirling the ecclesiastical importance which unleashed the destructive forces of the Reformation in 1560. Continuing to figure in the country's dynastic struggles, it was occupied by the Covenanters for Charles I, 1645, when the plague deterred the forces of Montrose en route to Kilsyth, was held by Argyll's forces in 1715 and by the Jacobites, followed by the Hanoverians in 1746. The outward expansion in the 19th century helped preserve the Old Town, where its Mercat Cross once provided a focus for its successive trades in tartan, cloth linen, tweeds and carpets from the 18th up to the 20th century, when the emphasis had switched to the more industrial products like rubber, wool, engineering, printing and upholstery. For a long time serving as the administrative centre for the area, the University development of 1967 was the culmination of an educational tradition which was started by the monks in the 12th century. Of its many historical buildings, the main places of interest are located in the north of the town and consist of: the Earl of Mar's Wark, an unfinished palace started in 1572, Argyll's lodging, a typical 17th century Town House where Charles II stayed in 1650 and the Duke of Cumberland in 1746, the Old Tolbooth, built in 1701 to designs by William Bruce, and the Mercat Cross. The Church of the Holy Rood was built in 1457 in a Gothic style and has long had royal associations while Cowan's Hospital or the Guildhall was erected in 1639 with a bequest from a local merchant, John Cowan, for 'the entertainment of decayed Gild Breither'. See Castle, Battle & Golf Club

STIRLING CASTLE
STIRLING

Rising from a rock above the town, this was the site of a fort stretching back into antiquity and was probably occupied by the Romans as the Roman road from Camelon northward passed through here. Stirling was the scene of much strife until its emergence from obscurity in the 12th century, when in 1124 it witnessed the death of Alexander I, and by 1127 was a Royal Burgh and one of Scotland's main strongholds. Garrisoned by the English after being pledged to Henry II as surety for the release of William the Lyon, 1175, but later restored to the Scots. Ironically it was the scene of King William's last Parliament and where he died in 1214, when it began to be favoured as a royal residence. It was here that Alexander II introduced the law of trial by jury and where in 1295 John Balliol held his convention which proposed a defensive league with France, precipitating the Wars of Independence when it was occupied by Edward I's forces until its recapture by William Wallace after the battle of Stirling Bridge, 1297. The siege by Edward I in 1304, which held down the English army for three months, resulted in its capture and destruction and rebuilding in stone to a Norman design. In Walter Scott's 'The Lord of the Isles' is described the preparations for a response by Edward II, to a later siege by Robert the Bruce:

England was roused on every side
Courier and post and herald hied,
To summon prince and peer,
At Berwick bounds to meet their leige,
Prepared to raise fair Stirling's siege,
With buckler, brand, and spear.

Surrendering to the Scots after their victory at Bannockburn, 1314, it was taken and retaken until Sir Robert Erskine Mar was made Hereditary Governor by David II, becoming a popular residence for the Stewarts, particularly Robert II and Robert III. It was here in 1452 that James II murdered the treacherous William, 8th Earl of Douglas, which led to the fall of the Douglases in 1455. The Royal Chapel built by James III was rebuilt by James VI for the baptism of Prince Henry, which took place amidst great pomp and rejoicing in 1594. King James III is also credited with building the Parliament Hall in a late Gothic style, along with the outer gateway, wall and towers. Preceded by a Lions den, though the palace was begun for James V (1513-42) by French masons and finished in its Renaissance style in the time of Queen Mary (1542-1567), its short-lived usefulness was to become apparent after it was the scene of the last Parliament of James VI, the last monarch to reside here before the Union of the Crowns in 1603 when the court had removed to London. Stirling was pillaged and damaged by Cromwell's forces under General Monck in 1651, but withstood an attempted seizure by the Jacobites in 1746. To the west of the chapel, which suffered a fire in 1855, the skeleton of the ill-fated Earl of Douglas was discovered in 1797. In the 19th century the castle was used as an infantry barracks by the Argyll and Sutherland Highlanders and now houses the regimental museum.

STIRLING BRIDGE, BATTLE OF, 1297
STIRLING

One of the most momentous battles during the Wars of Independence was fought just NW of Stirling Castle. After taking up their positions, the Scots, under William Wallace and numbering 40,000 foot and 180 horse, dealt a decisive blow to the invasion force of Edward I of around 50,000 men led by the Earl of Surrey. Wallace's rejection of the English terms as a precursor to attack saw half of Surrey's army cross the bridge and the Scots descend from Abbey Craig to exploit the situation. Looking on helplessly, the English army found themselves divided by the river and on the receiving end of a stratagem that resulted in mass slaughter and the full scale retreat of their forces. The victory stiffened the Scots' resolve and swelled the ranks of Wallace's supporters, who continued the struggle.

STIRLING GOLF CLUB
STIRLING

The ground on which the course is situated, within sight of the castle, has long been used as a place for recreation since the 12th century, when William I enclosed the area later known as Royal Park or King's Park. Thereafter the land and environs were used by other monarchs for hunting and fishing when it bore witness to some notable events. For in 1440 James II was ambushed and taken prisoner here while out hunting; his grandson James IV played golf here in 1505 during his stay at Stirling Castle; and in 1715 the forces of the Government led by the Duke of Argyll encamped here for ten weeks before the battle of Sheriffmuir. More recently in 1805 a racecourse was built which survived until 1854. The club was formed in 1869 in the Golden Lion Hotel at a meeting chaired by Provost John Murrie. Gradually acquiring all the physical manifestations of a club, in 1873 Tom Morris (Jnr) was made club Professional and over the years oversaw the Spring and Autumn meetings that helped engender a need for a standardised course of 9 holes, which Morris, being his usual proficient self, had planned for in 1892. As in many clubs at the turn of the century the

game's growing popularity provoked a desire for more security of tenure which resulted in the granting of a lease by the Crown Commissioners in 1904 and the adoption of Willie Fernie's plan for an 18 hole course in 1912. The years before World War II saw the preparations made by James Braid to lengthen the course and include the ladies' 9 hole course, but with the onset of war in 1939 work was suspended. During the years following the war the members reached another milestone and a new era beckoned as, following the passing of austerity and the lifting of rationing and the uncertainty that engendered, the club amalgamated with Stirling Victoria Golf Club in 1953, increasing the role of members further. The 1960s saw the opening of a new clubhouse, later followed by an extension to the course from 6000 to 6400 yards to plans presented by Henry Cotton a year before the clubs centenary in 1969. From this course can be seen the back of the Grampian Mountains and Stirling Castle. Latterly the Working Group appointed in 1988 oversees the club's long-term development and assures its future prospects in the decades ahead.

STOBHALL CASTLE
PERTH & KINROSS

Built on the bank of the Tay 8 miles N of Perth. Originally a mansion with extended courtyard and dower house of the Drummonds. The family's elevation came when the barony was bestowed by Robert the Bruce on Malcolm Drummond after Bannockburn, 1314, and continued when Annabella Drummond became the Queen of Robert III in 1367. Her position however, gradually diminished Stobhall's importance, and in 1488 the family built Drummond Castle which became the family seat. The chapel was built by David, 2nd Lord Drummond, who succeeded in 1520, and whose initials, along with those of his wife Lilias (daughter of Lord Ruthven) appear on the fireplace lintel above the chapel wall. Although the other member to leave his mark was John, 2nd Earl of Perth, who succeeded in 1612 and married Jane Kerr (daughter of the Earl of Roxburgh), both of whose initials and family arms appear above the door, it was the 4th Earl, created Duke of Perth in 1695, who completed the house in a blend of Gothic and Renaissance styles. In the 18th century the 3rd Duke, who was a Jacobite, built its boathouse before being wounded at Culloden, 1746, and died on a frigate en route for France. The building was later used as a caretaker's residence and now consists of a cluster of individual buildings built around a courtyard.

STONEHAVEN
ABERDEENSHIRE

Seaport town situated 18 miles SW of Aberdeen. Name derived from the Old Norse 'steinn hofu' meaning 'stony haven'. Comprising of Old and New Stonehaven (built 1759), the Old Town which stands on the bank of the Cowie, forms part of Dunnottar Parish, while the New Town situated between the River Carron and Cowie is part of Fetteresco Parish. Essentially a fishing village, its natural harbour probably made it an attractive site for a settlement during the Mesolithic period and in less remote times undoubtedly led to the granting in 1587 of a Burgh of Barony Charter for the Earl Keith Marischal who ruled from the family seat at Dunnottar Castle. By 1607, when the Sheriff Court was transferred here from Kincardine, its neighbour and rival, the town had surpassed its rival as a trading burgh with strong Continental trade links. This was undermined however by its involvement in the religious struggles and the fate of the Stewart Kings which brought about its burning

by Montrose in 1645, its occupation by Cromwell in 1652 while he was besieging Dunnottar Castle, and its pro-Jacobite stance in 1715 and 1745. The building of the New Town in 1759 by the Barclays of Urie ushered in an era of growth which became concentrated around its harbour built by an Act of Parliament, 1825 and designed by Robert Stevenson. Comprising a harbour with sea wall and additional jetties to protect vessels during storms, it extended over five acres and facilitated its greatly enlarged herring fishing fleet which numbered 100 boats in 1884, providing its chief export to mainly Baltic Ports, but today it caters mainly for pleasure craft. The westward expansion of the New Town from the low ground near the beach after 1850 brought about a period of house building by the new local Authorities after the First World War, resulting in an extension to the burgh boundaries in 1946. Sadly lacking in historical buildings, the main place of interest is the 16th century Old Tolbooth which now houses the museum exhibiting artefacts from Stonehaven's ancient and more recent past. See Golf Club & Dunnottar Castle

STONEHAVEN GOLF CLUB
ABERDEENSHIRE

Attractively situated on the Braes of Cowie just to the North of Stonehaven Town. The report in the 'Stonehaven Journal' and the 'Kincardineshire Advertiser' of 16th Feb 1888 described how an initiative of Postmaster J C Robertson resulted in a gathering in the Town Hall that unanimously agreed to the founding of a club on land next to the local cricket and football grounds. In April of that year an agreement had been secured with a Mr Captain Innes of Cowie for I shilling annually and was quickly followed by the framing of rules and the appointment of officials. Included among these were Mr Innes of Cowie, the club's first Captain, whose descendants carried on the practice of charging the same minimum rent. Flanked by the railway line and the sea, the course of 10 holes was described as being of an excellent standard and well adapted to test the skill of the most experienced players. Play began for the first time in July for the monthly handicap medal, with later competitions and developments appearing in the local press with an increasing regularity, such as the opening of the new clubhouse in 1889 overlooking the sea and the reduction of the course to 9 holes. One of the more prominent club officials to be connected with lasting fame was the Secretary Albert Wood who was nephew of Robert Thomson, inventor of the pneumatic tyre in 1845. During the closing years of the century the more farsighted members proposed the building of a new course and clubhouse; this started with the course in 1896 under the supervision of Archie Simpson Professional at the Royal Aberdeen Golf Club. Regretfully, after the opening of the new clubhouse in 1897 its limitations became all too apparent as with the admission of the first lady members in 1898 came the need for better accomodation that was eventually completed in 1900. In 1906 the club witnessed one of the more memorable competitions before the Great War of 1914-18 when the distinguished James Braid and Archie Simpson, played on the new 18 hole course that had been built in 1904 by Alex Mason of Cowie. Restrictions experienced during the war gave way to a more liberal climate and the restoration of the course at a time when the motor car was replacing the horse, thus providing greater mobility. In the 1920s and 30s the club's trophy collection was enlarged with the Scott Cup given in 1929 by the Liberal MP James Scott; the Barclay Harvey Cup, 1931 from Mr C M Barclay MP; and the Coronation Cup, 1937 bought by

the club. During the war of 1939-45 the course was altered to prevent the landing of enemy aircraft who in 1940, dropped an incendiary bomb, causing a 30 ft creator. Following the armistice of 1945, plans for repair work were set in motion which facilitated the first competition held in peacetime in 1946. In the 1950s and 60s the club benefited from the efforts of Archie Nicol, the County Architect who was also Captain 1961-64 and club champion seven times, leading to further improvements carried out in the 1970s with a car park to cope with the rising membership that had reached 406 men, 68 ladies and 144 juniors by 1975. The year was also marked by the death of Major Alexander Innes whose family's munificence over the years, particularly the low rent of the ground were consummated by the sale of the course and the Den of Logie for £24,000 . At the end of the 1990s with membership approaching 800, the committee appointed a manager to run the club which with its fresh air and good views is proving to be a popular tourist attraction in its own right.

STONEYPATH TOWER
EAST LOTHIAN

About 1 mile E of Garvald village are the ruins of a 15th century L plan tower built by the Lyle family. A John Lyle of Stonepath is mentioned in a charter from James II in 1446. Passing to Alexander Hamilton and then to Archibald Douglas in the 17th century, it later became part of the March estate and was eventually owned by the Seatons.

STORNOWAY
WESTERN ISLES

Town and Capital of the Hebrides situated on the NE Isle of Lewis. Name derived from the Old Norse 'stjorn vagr' meaning 'stearing bay'. Anciently inhabited by the Celts, from the 8th to the 13th century the Norsemen held sway here but were in turn followed by the Macleods of Lewis, the probable descendants of Leod, a Scandinavian sea rover. Coming firmly on record in 1607, when James VI erected it into a Burgh of Barony for Lord Balmerino, Stornoways remoteness encouraged Cromwell to build a fort here in 1652, which stood like a distant outpost of his Protectorate until the garrison was slain by the islanders. During the 1745 Rising the fugitive party of Prince Charles Edward was prevented from buying a boat here by two ministers, an event now marked by a statue of the Prince by the harbour. The area's sheer remoteness spared it the vicissitudes of Scotland's history, leaving its church and the Gaelic language to develop freely. Held by the Mackenzies of Seaforth in the 18th century (whose lodge stood on the site of Stornoway Castle), the island was bought by the tea merchant James Matheson in 1844 when large tracts of land were reclaimed, its farming further developed, and its fishing industry expanded. Stornoway was Head Port of the Outer Hebrides by 1885, with the lighthouse built on Arnish Point in 1833 guiding vessels in distress to the sanctuary of its natural harbour. The end of the war in 1918 saw the return of its menfolk from naval service and the purchase of the island by Viscount Leverhulm (soap magnate). His ambitious plans for the land's transformation instilled a sense of hope and optimism that was later dashed by bureaucratic wrangles, resulting in the land being broken up into small holdings. Although continuing to provide mariners for the Royal Navy during World War II, the gradual decline of its herring drifters from nine in 1946 to none by 1986 marked the passing of most of the town's traditional trade, which was later replaced by tweed. During the waulking or shrinking of the tweed the housewives beat the fabric on a wooden table to the accompaniment of traditional songs. About 16 miles to the west of the town are the Callanish monoliths. Thought to be a Cruciform sacrificial sun temple built by the Iberian Celts 3,000 years ago, the dimensions of the gnome are 16`5 ft high by 4 ft broad and 1 ft thick, placed in the centre of a circle 40 ft in diameter, formed of 12 stones averaging 10 to 13 ft high.

STRANRAER
DUMFRIES & GALLOWAY

Town situated at the head of Loch Ryan 50 miles SE of Ayr. Name derived from the Gaelic 'sron' and 'reamhar' meaning 'thick point' which is probably a reference to the nearby Rhinns of Galloway. A town of some antiquity, the community which sprang up around the 16th century Kennedy Castle with its natural harbour served as a ferry port with links to Ireland from ancient times but unusually it was not until 1596 that it received its first Burgh Charter, followed by Royal Burgh status in 1617. Stranraer continued to exercise superiority over its affairs until the 19th century when the jurisdiction of its Custom House was subsumed by Ayr. In the Covenanting Wars, the burgh was occupied by John Graham of Claverhouse (Bloody Claverse) who as Sheriff of Galloway persecuted the dissenters in the south west when the Rev. John Livingstone, a Covenanting Divine, was Minister here, 1638-48. Because of the absence of water power and the high price of fuel the town traded mainly in agricultural produce which during its heyday as a ferry rail port for the west of Wigtownshire was exchanged for imported goods brought by cargo ships attracted by its excellent harbour facilities and railway links. The decline in trade due to the opening of the Girvan-Portpatrick railway line in 1877 was offset by the Locomotive & Engineering Works and the Stranraer ferry service, which plied daily to Larne in Ireland, weekly to Glasgow, and fortnightly to Liverpool. So by the 20th century the town had assumed a new character with a strong Irish influence. This coupled with the influx of Allied Service Personnel to the nearby transit camp built in 1940, and followed by the stationing of RAF flying boats at Loch Ryan in 1942, prompted the building of military camps that greatly boosted the local economy. Apart from its Town Hall, which dates from 1776, its architecture is mainly 19th century, including the North West Castle Hotel built by the Arctic explorer Sir John Ross (1777-1856). See Castle

STRANRAER CASTLE
DUMFRIES & GALLOWAY

The castle is situated in the town. Though very little is known of its history its style is of the 16th century L plan. Built by Adair of Kinhilt, it passed to the Kennedys of Chapel, from whom it once took its name and was later occupied by the Dalrymples. The additions made in the 17th century, when it was occupied by John Graham of Claverhouse, who as Sheriff of Galloway used it as a prison, included its passive exterior which indicated a need to keep people in rather than repel attacks from outside. In the 19th century it was briefly used as a merchant's store before becoming derelict.

STRATHISLA DISTILLERY
MORAY

Located in Keith, a town long known for the production of alcohol on the site of a Brassina, or brewery. In 1545 a distillery stood here called Milton, named after the ruined Milton Castle which was home to the Ogilvies of Milton. Built by George Taylor on a rich tradition, Strathisla is now acknowledged as the oldest operat-

ing distillery in the Highlands dating from 1786. It draws its water from the Fons Bulliens, a revered spring that is steeped in local folklore and was once thought to be guarded by water spirits or Kelpies. In 1828 the distillery was purchased by William Longmore under whom it flourished, and on his death in 1882 was floated as William Longmore & Co Ltd. Beautifully situated, Strathisla has all the characteristics of a traditional malt distillery, the pagoda style roof of the 1890s and the Doig vents giving it listed building status. In contrast, its efficiency combines the old and the new to produce a spirit that is used in the Chivas Regal, a premier deluxe malt and namesake of the Chivas Brothers (now The Chivas & Glenlivit Group) who have restored and operated it since the 1950s.

OWNERS
Chivas Brothers Ltd ?

REGION
Speyside

PRODUCT
Strathisla 12 year old single malt 40% vol

NOTES
A complex array of hay-like aromas and dry oakiness with a mellow, smooth sweetness that creates a nutty finish.

STRATHAVEN
SOUTH LANARKSHIRE

Market town situated 16 miles SE of Glasgow. Name derived from the Gaelic 'srath' meaning 'valley' and the Avon River. Therefore 'valley of the River Avon'. Preceded by a castle built by Andrew Stewart grandson of the Duke of Albany, in 1456 the Barony of Avondale was obtained by the former who was made Lord Avondale. The reversal of the towns decline after the decay of its castle post 1717 and the great fire of 1844 when forty houses were destroyed was assisted by its traditional weaving industry and later by its cattle and horse fairs which were established during the First World War. But by the 1960s its weaving trade had been replaced by three factories producing textiles: wools and silk. Due to its growing popularity as a retreat during World War II, after 1945 a number of young families settled here, attracted by its healthy atmosphere and proximity to industrial centres. The area's private mansions include Dungavel, a former shooting lodge and one time home to the Dukes of Hamilton, and Lauder Ha', which for fifteen years was the home of the music hall performer Sir Harry Lauder. In the John Hastie Museum can be gleaned a broader picture of the town's history.

STRATHMIGLO
FIFE

Village situated on the River Eden 2 miles SW of Auchtermuchty. Name derived from the Gaelic 'srath' meaning 'open valley' and 'miglo' a small tributary, meaning 'bog or marsh'. Flanking the River Eden are the north and south sides of the village, with the latter including the area at the south of the main street called Templelands, once occupied by the Knights Templars. On the suppression of the order in 1312, the land was acquired by the Knights of St John of Jerusalem. Also situated on the main street were the Kirklands, while on the extended Skene Street were the Cash Feus used to house the tradesmen of the village. A Burgh of Barony for William Scott of Balwearie in 1509, it subsequently became the property of Balfour of Burleigh in 1600, until its forfeiture to the Crown in 1715, and was later acquired by Balfour of Birnie in 1754. The possession of the Town House and village green (bleachfield) by the burgh feuars is a reminder of the time when the area was broken up into small holdings. In 1734 the demolition of its castle provided a ready supply of stone for the building of its church which now fronts the Town House. Its once-thriving hand weaving industry was incorporated into two factories producing damasks and diapers for export to the United States and Canada, but by the 1950s suffered from a labour shortage owing to the decline of the village population.

STRATHPEFFER GOLF CLUB
HIGHLAND

Located to the SW of Dingwall on land which once formed part of the Cromartie Estate. At the clubs opening in 1888 the areas fashionable ladies and gentlemen ushered in a new era in recreation for the district with a Hungarian Band. The view from the original 9 hole course over the woods around Castle Leod down the Strath to the Cromarty Firth and over to the Black Isle has provided a welcome distraction for players over the years, of which, unlike many other golf clubs who admitted ladies later, the first was a lady: Miss Lawson of Leys Castle Inverness. With all the officials in place and an extended 18 hole course built by Tom Morris, by 1896 the clubs development was underway and by 1903 a new clubhouse, which replaced the old croft house, was opened by Mrs Mackenzie of Seaforth. In 1907 the Open Champion, Arnaud Massy, was beaten by Alex Herd after playing two exhibition matches that were the last recorded events over the original 18 hole course. In the following year the celebrated Tom Vardon introduced pot bunkers (now gone). The club's function as the heartbeat of the area enabled many of the members to excel in many of the fund raising activities which took the club from strength to strength. In 1922 the members played the newly formed Dingwall Club for the Sir George Hastings Cup. It is likely that the history of Strathpeffer Spa up to the 1920s was determined by economic cycles, fashionable trends and events of national importance, but due to a fire in the house of the Secretary, Mr Maclean in 1927 the minute books and correspondence of preceding years were lost. It's with some irony that the next milestone in the club's history was the installation of electricity in 1930 as a safer source of power. As already implied the ladies have had a strong presence since its beginnings and held their first ladies' championship in 1931. The Lady Paget Cup, granted in 1933, became a longstanding prize in succeeding matches. It is thought that the ladies became members of the Golfing Union in 1937 but again the fire has left the history somewhat jaded. Things did get on a sounder footing after World War II when a rapid increase in competitions and activity generally amongst the ladies marked a new era for the club with inter-club matches against Tain and Muir of Ord being held in 1952. The first Ladies' Open was held in 1976. Regarding the juniors, although demand for membership existed in the early days, it was not until 1976 that the first Junior Championship was held. The upgrading work to the clubhouse including better facilities which started in 1968 was concluded with an opening ceremony in 1974 performed by the Earl of Cromartie.

STROMNESS
ORKNEY

Town situated on the SW mainland west of Kirkwall. Name derived from the Old Norse 'straumr' meaning 'river' or 'current' and 'ness' meaning 'cape' or 'point of land'. Probably a cluster of dwellings during the Norse occupation. The village, with its natural harbour, emerged from obscurity in the late 18th century after it successfully contested the right of the Royal Burgh of Kirkwall to tax the revenue from its growing trade as a dis-

tribution centre for American rice ships. The ruling by the House of Lords in 1754 overturned an obscure Act of 1690 giving Freemen of Royal Burghs the sole right to import and export, thus enabling all Scottish villages to become independent of Royal Burghs by 1758. A Burgh of Barony from 1817, the village continued to derive most of its income from maritime trade, while also providing the amenities for the docking in 1779 and 1780 of Captain Cook's ships the Discovery and Resolution, the setting up of an agency for the Hudson Bay Co in 1885 and for a thriving trade in herring fishing. Most of today's town dates from around these periods. The discovery of the ancient Stone Age settlement at Skara brae in 1850 sparked a worldwide interest in the area's Nordic past and isolated setting, something that was again affected by the naval base at Scapa Flow between 1914 and 1945 and the oil exploration in the 1970s. Founded in 1858 by the Orkney Natural History Society, the Stromness Museum provides an interesting insight into the area's natural, maritime and military history.

SWEETHEART ABBEY
DUMFRIES & GALLOWAY

Situated about 8 miles S of Dumfries. The substantial ruins of this Cistercian House were founded around 1275 by Devorgilla, a great-granddaughter of David I and wife of John Balliol, whose heart along with his wife was buried here in 1289, hence the name Sweetheart Abbey. The title New Abbey was applied to distinguish it from the Cistercian Dundrennan Abbey. Built in a Norman and Early English style, the conventual buildings were pillaged for their stone, leaving its church as the chief ruin. In 1513 the monks placed themselves under the protection of Lord Maxwell and in 1544 feued the Barony of Loch Patrick to his

family. The two dates mark the battle of
Flodden and Hertford's invasion respectivly. During the Reformation the Abbey
records were destroyed or carried abroad
by the monks. Their last and most noted
abbot was Abbot Gilbert Brown who was
the prototype for Sir Walter Scotts 'The
Abbot', and was denounced as a Papist
and Jesuit and banished abroad before
dying in Paris in 1612. Vested in the Crown
by the Annexation Act of 1587, the property was granted to Robert Spottiswood in
1624 but decayed in the hands of subsequent owners until 1779, when the Parish
Minister raised £42 for work which facilitated its use as a Parish Church until 1877.
After years of stone pillaging the church is
left as its chief ruin with its choir without
aisles, a nave with an arcade of six arches,
the west wall with a rose window frame
and the north and south transepts below a
square tower over the crossing.

T

TAIN
HIGHLAND

Town situated 14 miles NE of Alness. Name derived from the Old Irish 'Tain' meaning 'water' but in Gaelic was called Baile Dhuthaich owing to its long standing ties with St Duthac whose remains were buried here in 1253 long after his death in Ireland. Tain was a burgh from the 11th century probably one of the oldest in Scotland and in 1439 was raised to a Royal Burgh. Long serving as a place of pilgrimage, St Duthacs Chapel was burnt by Macneil of Creich in 1427 but was rebuilt and made collegiate in 1487 and continued to be visited by Scottish monarchs in particular James IV visited here up to the month before his death at Flodden in 1513. Although situated on the traditional land of the McCullochs with the chief landlords being the Earls of Ross, part of the charter granted by Malcolm II which states that 'they have never paid and never shall they pay, on any account, any contribution to the Kings of Scotland or the Earls of Ross' clearly strengthens the towns claim to be Scotlands oldest burgh. Described in 1695 by Thomas Tucker as being 'a small town lying near the mouth of the river of that name'. Like most of the island towns its economy was mainly concerned with fishing and farming but was later complemented by the production of wool and whisky. Used as the Parish Church from the Reformation, the old chapel's replacement by a new church in 1815 to the east of the town led to its gradual decay until its restoration between 1857 and 1877. Largely built of local sandstone and regarded as one of the finest in Britain, its Court House was built in 1849 to replace an earlier one destroyed by fire, and now adjoins the Tolbooth with its central tower housing a bell cast in Holland in 1716. Next to this is the Tain Museum. The town's long tradition in education started by the Collegiate Church was advanced by its Grammar School, established by 1646, and later by Tain Academy, set up by Royal Charter in 1809 and opened in 1813. This was united with the parochial school in 1937. See Golf Club & St Duthac's Church

TAIN GOLF CLUB
HIGHLAND

Picturesquely situated on the outskirts of the Royal Burgh with a coastline view of the Kyle of Sutherland stretching to the Ord of Caithness. Tain was the inspiration of Alexander Macbean, a retired banker, whose passion for the game during his time in India brought about the founding of 'St Duthus Golf Club' in 1890 when the course was laid out by Tom Morris, the illustrious champion of the day. Originally comprising 15 holes, owing to its slow beginnings a grant was given by the Town Council and the course reduced to 12 holes and a new clubhouse built. The planning would seem to have been driven by the need for quality over expansion. One of the more macabre links with the past is the Gallows Hill where judgement was dispensed on the accused in times past. Its development began in earnest with the extension of the course to 18 holes in the late 19th century, bringing it into line with the standards of the day and more recognition from the press like the 'Golfing Annual' of 1895-96, which reported 'It consists of a full round of 18 holes of the most sporting character, no kind of hazard of a legitimate nature which might lend interest to the game being awanting'. In 1911 a new clubhouse was built and in 1912 further changes were made to the course. This, along with its rail links, brought Edinburgh and Glasgow only eight hours distant and a growing number of visitors among whom the Right Hon H H Asquith PM 1908-16 was the most distinguished. Falling into a state of disrepair during the First World War, in 1924 The Tain Open Tournament was held when a scratch cup was donated by the famous biscuit makers Mcvitie & Price, along with another presented by Sir John Stirling (Stirling Cup) for the handicap competitions. Both of these still rank among the club's more favourable awards. The granting of the first licence to the clubhouse in 1938 and the practice of playing golf on Sundays was in many ways hastened by the visits to nearby Invergordon of the Home Fleet, whose golf enthusiasts were only available on Sundays. This gave rise to the mutual hospitality and the annual competition for the Marineau Cup presented by Sir William Marineau of Kincraig in 1937. The Navy's associations with the town were indirectly given royal approval before World War One when King George VI, then Duke of York, played over the course while serving as a midshipman and, later, officer. Similarly the club has forged social and sporting ties with many of its inter-club matches with Royal Dornoch, Alness, Tarbert, Inverness and Fortrose, something that has become increasingly rare with the holding of many tournaments. When the clubhouse was refurbished in 1975 Tain saw a steady rise in membership owing to the oil rig manufacturing at Nigg but in 1990 it had fallen back to around 400. Since first applying for a seat on the committee in 1919 the ladies have come a long way with more recent winners like Lindsay Anderson, the 16 year old winner of the Golf Foundation Award and Margaret Vass who before 1990 won the Ladies' Championship eight times 1979-87. The oldest of the club's trophies are the Abdul Ghany and Baden-Powell along with the Jackson Cazenour. And among the men members

R W Graham ranks as the best club champion in modern times, winning nine times between 1950-67.

TALISKAR DISTILLERY
HIGHLAND

On the shore of Loch Harport near the Cullin Hills is the Isle of Sky's only distillery, built in the early 1830s by the brothers Hugh and Kenneth Macaskill. Dependent on supplies from small puffers before their return journey with whisky to a ready-made local market, Taliskar is a classic island malt and was made by the family up until 1863, when they were followed by a number of owners, including a consortium led by Dewar's & Johnnie Walker. Undergoing three distillations up until the early 1920s, today it is included in the famous Johnnie Walker, the world's best selling whisky. Acquired by Distilleries Co Ltd in 1925, the building had been constantly enlarged throughout the 19th century, but was mostly rebuilt in 1960 following a fire, and was latterly re-equipped and modernised in 1988. Today the building still retains the substantial whitewashed walls with grey slated roof crowned with pagoda-style vents.

OWNERS
Diageo plc ?

REGION
Highland

PRODUCT
Taliskar 10 year old single malt 45.8 % vol

NOTES
A rich seaweedy aroma with a sweet peaty flavour and a lingering peppery aftertaste.

TAMDHU DISTILLERY
MORAY

Located by the River Spey about 8 miles SW of Aberlour is another of Speyside's success stories. Its name in Gaelic means 'little dark hill'. The main factors that contributed to its growth were the uniqueness of the water from the Knockando burn, the coming of the railway, the growing popularity of blended whisky, and the investment from wine and spirit merchants in the 1890s. These moved William Grant, the director of Highland Distillers and agent for the Caledonian Bank in Elgin, to recruit the distinguished Charles Doig of Elgin to design Tamdhu in 1896. Described in 1898 by the authority on whisky, Alfred Bernard, as "one of the most modern distilleries", following good production levels its output peaked in 1903 at 135,000 bulk gallons, but was halved by the downturn in the industry between 1906-10. Closed in the run up to World War I, output recovered strongly in the early 1920s but gradually fell away with the depression of the 1930s and remained low until after World War II (1939-45). Latterly its fortunes were revived when in 1972 it was so prized by blenders that it doubled in size with two extra stills, increased to four in 1975, and in 1976 the Tamdhu single malt was launched.

OWNERS
Edrington Group Ltd, The ?

REGION
Speyside

PRODUCT
Tamdhu 10 year old single malt 40% vol

NOTES
A sweet, light smoky nose and a fine sweet smoky palate with a hint of malt.

TAMNAVULIN-GLENLIVET DISTILLERY
MORAY

It stands on the banks of the Allt a Choire, meaning 'stream of the corries' in Gaelic, which is a tributary of the River Livet 15 miles NW of Dufftown and takes its water from a subterranean spring at Easterton. One of Speyside's more modern distilleries, it was built by Invergordon Distillers in 1966 during a whisky boom. The name in Gaelic means 'mill on the hill' after the old carding mill nearby, which once served the local wool traders but was attractively restored and converted into a visitor centre. As one would expect of a modern distillery, the aesthetics are subordinate to an efficiency which has enabled its producers, in contrast with other distillers, to create a malt that is mild rather than brutish, sweet rather than bitter and with a subtle peaty taste that comes from its water source. Its winter isolation has necessitated a self-reliance that involves four large malt storage bins with a total capacity for 220 tonnes and on-site maturation where its two warehouses can house over 40,000 casks of its distilled whisky, which first appeared as a single malt in 1974.

OWNERS
Kyndal International Ltd ?

REGION
Speyside

PRODUCT
Tamnavulin 12 (40%) & 18 year old single malt 46% vol

NOTES
A slightly honey, nutty taste with a warm creamy aftertaste
A nutty, medium sweet nose with a smooth, oaky, velvety, nutty flavour

TANTALLON CASTLE
EAST LOTHIAN

Strategically positioned by the sea about 3 miles E of North Berwick are the ruins of a massive quadrangular courtyard structure comprising curtain walls, round corner towers, a drawbridge fronted by a ditch, and the sea on three sides. Although started by the Earls of Fife, the barony was acquired in 1370 by the Douglases when most of the castle was built. While the property of Archibald Douglas (The Grim), the Duchess of Albany (Countess of Fife) was imprisoned here in 1425, as was Alexander, Lord of the Isles in 1429, but following its forfeiture to the Crown, James II granted it to George Douglas Earl of Angus in 1452 before the whole family's forfeiture in 1455. It was besieged by James V with the cannon Mons Meg in 1528 and taken after the 6th Earl's flight to England, when some additions were made. After the King's death over a decade later, more work was done in 1542 when the Earl was reinstated while acting as an agent of Henry VIII. It continued to bear witness to dynastic struggles of the day (Rough Wooing) when it provided sanctuary for the English Ambassador Sir Ralph Sadler after their schemes were exposed. After a twelve-day siege in 1651 it was taken by Cromwell's 3,000 man force under General Monck. The castle's reputation as a bulwark on Scotland's east coast defensive network was immortalised in verses of Sir Walter Scott's 'Marmion' in 1808:

Many a rude tower and rampart there
Repelled the insult of the air,
which, when the tempest vexed the sky,
Half breeze half spray came whislting by ...
Above the booming ocean leant
The far projecting battlement ;
The billows burst, in ceaseless flow,
Upon the precipice below.
Where'er Tantallon faced the land,
Gate-works, and walls were strongly manned

The Royalist stance of the Earl of Douglas in 1639 brought about its capture and destruction by the Covenanters and its eventual dismantling by Hugh Dalrymple in the 18th century.

TARBERT
ARGYLL & BUTE

Coastal town situated 35 miles NE of Campbelltown. Name derived from the Gaelic 'tairbeart' meaning 'isthmus' after Magnus Barelegs ordered his Norsemen to drag their ships across Loch Fyne in the 11th century and so laid claim to Kintyre. Once the site of a Norse Fort followed by a 13th century castle around which the town grew. Tarbert greatly benefited from the ancient trade links with Ireland, begun when Kintyre formed the cradle of the Kingdom of Dalriada, and was developed further along with its castle, by Robert the Bruce in 1325, who sought to pacify the surrounding islands by making it an administrative centre for the region. This was contiguous to the King raising it to a Sheriffdom around 1327 which lasted up until the 17th century. Alas, early records of its Royal Burgh Charter have been lost. Though primarily concerned with horses but latterly second only to the herring fishing which reached its peak in the 20th century, was the annual Tarbert Fair which was an important event in the local calender. The event was later replaced by the cattle and market fair which benefited the long standing steamer service from Glasgow via Kyles of Bute and Gourrock. Similarly these have largely given way to pleasure craft drawn to its natural harbour and picturesque setting. See Castle

TARBERT CASTLE
ARGYLL & BUTE

In a favourable position above the town on the W side of Loch Fyne are the ruins of a courtyard keep with surrounding walls and drum towers. As a royal fortress it was held by John Balliol in 1292 but was strongly associated with Robert the Bruce, who repaired it and used it as a garrisoned stronghold to subdue the local clans, firmly establishing its strategic importance that continued down to the 18th century. During his suppression of the Western Isles in 1494, James IV dispatched his courier from here to the local lords, demanding their allegiance. The King was to visit Tarbert again when most of its development work was completed in 1497.

TARBOLTON
SOUTH AYRSHIRE

Village situated 8 miles NE of Ayr. Name derived from the Gaelic 'torr' meaning 'hill' or 'castle' and the Old Norse 'bol' meaning 'dwelling' or 'settlement'. Although originally a rural farming community, coal was mined here as early as 1497, later giving the village its main resources while sustaining its domestic weaving industry. A Burgh of Barony for Cunningham of Etterkine in 1671. Like many parts of the west coast, Tarbolton was affected by the Covenanting struggles and it was here around 1650 that the Covenanting Prophet Alexander Pedan was a school teacher. Nevertheless its main claim to fame is its associations with Robert Burns, who after becoming a member of the local Masonic Lodge started a debating society called The Bachelors Club in 1780 while living at the nearby farm at Lochlee (1777-84). It was from Tarbolton that he drew on some of the local characters for his poetry. The self taught sculptor James Thom (1799-1850) featured in 'Tam O' Shanter' and 'Souter Johnny', while the local schoolmaster and dispenser of medicine John Wilson figured in his 'Death and Mr Hornbrook' . Today the Bachelor's Club House is in a good state of preservation and houses a number of interesting objects from this period.

TARLAND
ABERDEENSHIRE

Town situated 5 miles NW of Aboyne. The name probably derives from the Old Gaelic 'tarbh-lann' meaning 'Bull-enclosure'. Of the ancient Parish of Tarland and Migivie the latter was once the site of St Moluag's Church which was granted to St Andrew's Priory in the 12th century by Morgund Earl of Mar whose seat was the Migivie Castle (now gone). The stone circle about half mile to the south of the church on Tomnaverie Hill, which is said to mean 'Hill of truth', was either a Druid temple or feudal Justice Court. As a Burgh of Barony for Irvine of Drum from 1683, Tarland subsisted on mainly agricultural produce from its relatively small rural economy, that revolved around its weekly market which provided the backdrop for most of its history, in which its churches were a central part. The building of Migvie Church in 1777 and the Gothic church of Tarland which was dedicated to St Moulag by the brother of Lord Aberdeen, 1870, led to the disjoining of the parishes in 1891. It was then that Tarland was much reduced in size. Still retaining the relics of its ancient past, in Migvies Church grounds are the remains of a 9th century Pictish Cross slab, while the old Parish Church at the east end of the village square had its walls and belfry preserved as an ancient monument. Among the area's other old and ancient buildings are Cromar House, one time home of Lord Aberdeen, but developed in 1947 as a home for RAF officers from many countries. This contrasts strikingly with the ancient Pictish house at nearby Calsh which though once looked after by a Margaret Anderson, a local worthy, is now preserved by the local authorities.

TARVES
ABERDEENSHIRE

Village situated 6 miles W of Ellon. Name derived from the Gaelic 'tarbh-ais' meaning 'place of the bull'. The land that formed part of the Regality which was bestowed on the Abbot of Arbroath by Robert I in the 14th century passed to Gordon of Haddo at the Reformation and became a Burgh of Barony for a descendant in 1673. Despite the modest prosperity derived from its farming the village remained relatively underdeveloped and consequently its farm workers houses are ironically included with Haddo House and Tolquhon Castle among the area's more interesting buildings. The castle built in the 16th century by William Forbes along with a hospital and Gothic tombstone in the churchyard was once considered the great glory of Tarves.

TAYMOUTH CASTLE. SEE BALLOCH CASTLE

TEANINICH DISTILLERY
HIGHLAND

Beautifully situated by the sea just outside Alness. Although the first attempt at distilling by Captain Hugh Munro on his own land in 1817 was stifled by illicit distilling, by 1830 lower taxes and a more regulated market had increased its output by 30 to 40 times. Under its second owner, Lieutenant General John Munro, it was leased in 1850 during his absence in India and was eventually taken over in 1895 by John Munro, a spirit merchant and Robert Innes Cameron, a formidable figure in the industry and friend of the Prime Minister Ramsay Macdonald. Redesigned with a capacity for producing 4000 gallons (18,000 litres) of malt at a time, by 1904 Innes Cameron had become sole proprietor and ran the distillery until his death in 1932. Acquired by Scottish Malt Distillers Ltd in 1933,

Teannich closed between 1939-46 and underwent big changes in 1962 with electricity replacing its steam engine and its water wheel. Owing to increased demand, a new distillation system and six new additional stills were added in 1970. Mothballed between 1985-91, today it continues in its former function amidst the many species of wildlife and a nature conservation area by the sea shore.

OWNERS
Diageo plc ?

REGION
Highland

PRODUCT
Teaniaich 10 year old single malt 43% vol

NOTES
Light, smooth and rounded, with a slightly spicy finish.

TERPERSIE CASTLE
ABERDEENSHIRE

In a secluded glen near Alford 28 miles NW of Aberdeen stands a ruined Z plan castle with diagonally opposite round towers, built by William Gordon of Lesmoir in 1561, who fought in the local clan battles at Corrichie in 1562 and Tillyangus in 1571. The castle was once surrounded by a moat. The last of the family suffered a cruel death at the hands of the Hanoverians after Culloden, 1746, when he hid in the surrounding land, and the property was subsequently acquired by the York Building Company.

TERRINGZEAN CASTLE
SOUTH AYRSHIRE

Positioned on a steep bank by the River Lugar NW of Cumnock. Although the site of an earlier castle, the ruins of today are of a 15th century courtyard castle built by the Crawford family. Of little historical note, it passed in 1467 to Thomas Boyd, Earl of Arran, and husband of Mary the sister of James III, but was forfeited to the

Crown in 1469 and was held by numerous owners until it was purchased by the Marquis of Bute in the 19th century.

THORNHILL
DUMFRIES & GALLOWAY

Village situated 15 miles NW of Dumfries. The name is probably from the Old English meaning 'hill of Hawthorn trees'. Built in Morton Parish by the Duke of Queensberry around 1714, the village was greatly improved by the 5th Duke of Buccleuch in 1833 when it was noted as "a clean healthy and populous village with a main street by which the high road from Dumfries passes to Edinburgh". Boasting a brewery, three banks, two hotels, a telegraph office, Parish Church and a subscription library (started 1814), by 1885, the column in the town centre crowned with the Queensberry Arms, 1714, is a reminder of its intended purpose as a Market Town. The village has associations with Robert Burns, who lived at Elliesland Farm with Jean Armour, 1788-90, and the African explorer Joseph Thomson (1858-95) who was born here. In the face of fluctuating population levels determined by commercial investment, the strides taken in later decades through improved amenities and rural projects reversed its fortunes to make it a centre for the whole of Nithsdale by the mid-20th century.

THIRLESTANE CASTLE
SCOTTISH BORDERS

Situated 17 miles SW of Selkirk are the ruins of a 16th century border pele tower. Built by Sir Robert Scott and his wife Mary Cranston between 1590 and 1620 as part of the Borders defensive network. It was abandoned in the 17th century when another house was built.

THIRLESTANE CASTLE
SCOTTISH BORDERS

Located just outside Lauder village on the banks of the river is a castellated mansion house, possibly erected on the site of Lauder Fort, built by Edward I in 1296 on land belonging to the Maitlands. It was developed by Chancellor Maitland into an oblong block by 1595 after he had been created Lord Maitland of Thirlestane in 1590; it now consists of a T shape edifice with four large round towers incorporating an older building. After John, 2nd Earl (1616-82), was created Duke of Lauderdale in 1672, he recruited the celebrated architect William Bruce (1630-1710) who added its new front and wings, giving it the distinctive T shape. This was eventually developed through the extensive alterations and embellishments of succeeding dukes into what we see today. By the 19th century it was held by Major Henry Maitland but now accommodates passing tourists.

THOMASTON CASTLE
SOUTH AYRSHIRE

Erected just SE of Culzean Castle 1 mile from Kirkoswald. Once a castle of some size and importance, thought to have been started in the 14th century by a nephew of Robert the Bruce. The present L plan structure was probably built by Thomas Carry after receiving a charter from James IV in 1507. The estate passed to the Mcilvanes of Grimmet around 1650 but by the early 18th century the building was unoccupied.

THREAVE CASTLE
DUMFRIES & GALLOWAY

The ruined stronghold of the Douglases stands on an island on the River Dee 3 miles W from Castle Douglas. Originally an oblong keep, once defended by a drawbridge and was probably built by Archibald Douglas in 1389 after he had succeeded to the Earldom. He was nicknamed Archibald the Grim owing to his savage brutality, and died here in 1400. Forfeited to the the Crown after being taken by James II in 1455, it was held by Keepers in 1545, when it was besieged by the Regent Arran. In the civil strife of the 17th century Threave was held by Lord Nithsdale for Charles I, 1649, and a war council under the Covenanting Laird of Balmaghie ordered its demolition. During the Napoleonic Wars it was used as a prison for French soldiers.

THURSO
HIGHLAND

Seaport town situated 20 miles SW of John O Groats. At one time thought to mean Thors River the name is probably derived from the Old Norse 'thjorsa' meaning 'Bulls River'. An important site for Norsemen from an early date and a great centre for trade between Scotland and Scandinavia. Apart from attempts to adopt its weights and measures system as the standard for the whole of the kingdom in the 12th century, its limited involvement in the country's historical milestones resulted in Thurso's somewhat short-lived resurgence being confined to the 19th century. From 1633 this was a Burgh of Barony and during the 200 years it served as the County Town of Caithness the spacious New Town was built by Sir John Sinclair before the rebuilding of Thurso Castle in the 1870s. The visit made by the Princess of Wales in 1876 to open an art exhibition in the Town Hall (built, 1870) marked a high point in the towns 19th century industrial development when the main High Street was renamed Princess Street. Sited to the east of the castle is Harold's Tower built by Sir John Sinclair on the grave of the Norsemen Harold, grandson of Rognvald, who was ruler of Orkney Shetland and Caithness in the 12th century. Close by is the Sinclair burial ground. To the north, at what was once Scrabster Bay, was the seat of the Bishops of Caithness and is now the site of a 12th century church to St Peter which comprises an apside cell with its nave and transepts dating from the 16th century. In 1828 the town's official standing was undermined when the Burgh of Wick raised an action over Thurso's legal jurisdiction, and so began the gradual removal of the Sheriff Courts to the former, leaving Thurso unable to muster a weekly debtors court by 1842. Its harbour, described as a creek of Wick in 1885 was the departure point for its main exports grain, flagstone and fish, while making it an integral part of the ferry supply line to the Orkney Islands. The oldest Municipal records of the town date from the 19th century when it became a Police Burgh. In the redevelopment plans of 1936 under Sir Frank Mears, the main focus was on the long term overall plan not on single entities, and proved to be as important for the New Town as the plan, for the Old Town by Sir John Sinclair was in the 19th century. During the 1950s Thurso served as a base for the construction workers of the UK Atomic Energy Authority's fast breeder nuclear reactor at nearby Dounreay.

TILLYCAIRN CASTLE
ABERDEENSHIRE

Situated 5 miles SW of Alford. Essentially a four-storey L plan with walls of varying thickness. Above its fireplace is a lug (ear), above which is a concealed staircase connected to the hall from which a trap stair led to the dungeon below. This is a simple but good example of a 16th century house designed to accommodate the intrigue of the pre-Reformation period.

TILLICOULTRY
CLACKMANNAN

Town situated 3´ miles NE of Alloa. Name derived from the Gaelic 'Tulach cul tire' meaning 'hill at the back of the land'. Once the site of a Pictish Hillfort on Castle Craig, the ruined House of Tillicoultry was probably where the ancient Culdee Cell stood that St Serf visited in the sixth century. The odd stones in the old churchyard must have belonged to an ecclesiastical building nearby. In 1263 the land was granted by Alexander III to the ancestor of the Earl of Mar but became the property of the Colvilles of Culross in 1483 until purchased by the poet Alexander Menstrie (later Earl of Stirling), for whom it became a Burgh of Barony in 1634. Famed for its woollen blankets from the 16th century, the industry's gradual expansion took Tillicoultry from a village in 1780 to a thriving town by 1880, when production had increased in the area's numerous factories to include the weaving of tartan tweeds and silks. From a one industry town its business diversified in the 20th century.

TILQUHILLY CASTLE
ABERDEENSHIRE

On ground 3 miles S of Crathes stands a 16th century house on the plan of a central keep with two diagonally opposite angle towers. The land belonged to a Walter Ogston in 1479 and later passed through marriage to David Douglas, son of Lord Dalkeith, whose grandson started the house in the late 16th century, but its exterior was completed in the 17th century.

TIMPENDEAN TOWER
SCOTTISH BORDERS

On rising ground 3 miles NW of Jedburgh are the ruins of a 15th century oblong tower built by the Douglases, who held the territory once known as Bonjedworth from 1479 until the 19th century.

TINNIES CASTLE
SCOTTISH BORDERS

Occupying land about 12 miles SW of Peebles. The site of a defensive structure since ancient times as it overlooks Merlin's Grave and had associations with the ancient bard Ossian. The present limited remains are of a quadrangular structure with 13th century curtain walls and round towers at each angle, built later as part of the Borders early warning network. Once held by the Tweedies, the cause of its destruction is inconclusive, but it was vacated by the family in the 16th century for Drumelzier Castle.

TIPPERMUIR, BATTLE OF, 1644
PERTH & KINROSS

This was the first victory of Montrose during his brutal campaign to crush the Covenanters. With an army of 6,000 foot and 600 horse, the Earl of Wemyss confronted the Marquis of Montrose's 1700 Highlanders who inflicted a heavy defeat, costing 2,000 slain and 200 captured. The battle marked the beginning of a series of defeats for the Covenanters, whose fortunes eventually turned at the battle of Philiphaugh.

TOBERMORY
ARGYLL & BUTE

Seaport town situated on the Isle of Mull 28 miles NW of Oban. Name derived from the Gaelic 'tobar Moire' meaning 'well of Mary' after a fountain dedicated to the Virgin Mary which was popular before the Reformation. Once the site of a primitive settlement, its proximity to Iona and its likely associations with the early Celtic missionaries are at odds with the present town's history, which is comparatively modern. In 1481 the nearby 'bloody bay' was the scene of a battle when John, the last Lord of the Isles, had his position challenged by his upstart son Angus Og. It was here in 1588 that the Florida, a galleon from the Spanish Armada, thought to be carrying gold, sheltered before it sank to the bottom. Since then rumours have abounded as to its cargo, with some sources mentioning large quantities of gold ducats, but as yet attempts to recover it have been unsuccessful. Shortly before his execution in Edinburgh, Archibald the 9th Earl of Argyll, 1685, landed here with Monmouth's small invasion force en route to Campbelltown. The town was rebuilt in 1788 by the British Fisheries Co as an assembly point for herring vessels but it was not until 1876 that the place acquired burgh status with a Provost, two Baillies and six Councillors. With the main street built in the form of a crescent fronted by a landlocked harbour, for a short time the town possessed a certain provincial importance which was further enriched by the coming of the railway, which marked the decline of its marine-based economy. This resulted in the building of the upper town with holiday villas on the outskirts and pleasure sailing from its harbour. Thus its tourism-based economy was established, with visitors increasingly more numerous than the local population, whose numbers have latterly been steadily dwindling. See Distillery

TOBERMORY DISTILLERY
ARGYLL & BUTE

Located in the town and once known as Ledaig. The distillery owes its existence to the late 18th century prosperity of the town, its natural harbour making it the ideal site for a fishing station in 1788. When a local merchant named John Sinclair applied for a licence in 1797 he was refused owing to the other stills operating in the area, and he in turn rejected the offer to build a brewery instead. With a ready supply of water available from the nearby private loch, a licence was eventually granted in 1823 which made To-

bermory the only legal distillery on the island, and it remained under Sinclair's control until it was closed in 1837. The long period of inactivity was to be the norm rather than the exception, for after being revived in 1878 it was to be run by a number of owners including DCL, while enduring the instability and uncertainties of the early decades of the 20th century. In 1930 the distillery was closed for a long period and did not open again until 1972, when its new owner's attempts to revive it failed and it was bought in 1975 by the Yorkshire property firm, Kirkleavington Properties. Fortunately this saga ended in some success when in 1993 it was bought by Burn Stewart Distillers, one of the largest independent Scotch Whisky companies, whose substantial investment brought the distillery into the late 20th century, producing a million litres of alcohol every year.

OWNERS
Burn Stewart Distillers plc ?

REGION
Highland

PRODUCT
Tobermory no age statement 40% vol
Ledaig no age statement 40% vol

NOTES
A fresh, slightly peaty, smoky nose, with a medium dry, smooth fruity taste and a well-rounded finish
A peaty, slightly floral nose with a rich, quite dry, spicy & peaty taste.

TOLQUHOUN CASTLE
ABERDEENSHIRE

On a hill near the village of Udney are the ruins of a quadrangular courtyard keep, built in 1584 by William Forbes whose descendants had acquired the estate in 1420 through marriage from the Prestons who had built the first tower. The most distinctive features are the arched gateway with flanking round towers and the large western tower. It was purchased in 1716 by Lieutenant Colonel. Farquhar, but was later sold to the Earl of Abercorn.

TOMATIN DISTILLERY
HIGHLAND

Latterly becoming Scotland's largest and most modern distillery, it is located by the River Findhorn about 16 miles SE of Inverness, taking its name from the Gaelic meaning 'the hill of the bushes'. Tomatin's position 1028 feet above sea level once made it the highest and most isolated distillery in Scotland, with the old distillery looking more like a cluster of warehouses around a main building with chimney stack. Tomatin was born of the whisky boom in 1897, but was probably the site of a much earlier, cruder still; while its water source the 'Alt-na-Frith' means 'free burn' in Gaelic. This was often frequented by drovers who filled their rams' horns at the still nearby the 17th century Laird's House en route to the cattle pens at Tomatin. The outline of the cattle pens are still visible by the Free-burn Hotel near the distillery entrance. Following the time honoured process of malting, mashing, fermentation and distillation, Tomatin made steady progress up to World War II. It was, however, the resumption of production during the post-war period that sparked its golden age; with a 20 year improvement plan started in 1951 and completed in 1974; enabling its 12 wash stills and an extra 11 spirit stills to produce 5 million proof gallons (12975 million litres), of alcohol. Acquired by Japans biggest alcoholic drinks producer, Takar Shuzo, and trading company Okura & Co in 1986, Tomatin is now widely used in blends at home and abroad.

OWNERS
The Tomatin Distillery Co Ltd ?

REGION
Highland

PRODUCT
Tomatin (Big T) 10 year old single malt 40% vol

NOTES
A malty, slightly sweet, fruity aroma and sweetish perfume toffeish taste.

TOMINTOUL DISTILLERY
MORAY

Once abounding in illicit stills, Tomintoul takes its name from the nearby village, one of the highest in Scotland and located 14 miles SE of Grantown on Spey. A latecomer to the whisky industry, it grew out of the whisky boom of the 1960s and first started production in 1965, seven years before it first appeared in a bottle. The building's modern appearance is in stark contrast with its natural setting on the edge of a forest near the Rivers Avon and Livet and the Cromdale and Ladder Hills which foreshadow the Cairngorm mountains. All of these combine to provide the essential ingredient, its Ballantruan Spring water, to make a malt that is one of the lightest in the district, though with a little more body than its neighbours. In 1974 its stills doubled from two to four. Bought by Scottish Universal Investment Trust (part of Lonroho) in 1973 and managed by Whyte & Mackay, by 1990 it was owned by American Brands Inc. but has again changed hands.

OWNERS
Angus Dundee Distillers plc ?

REGION
Speyside

PRODUCT
Tomintoul 10 & 16 year old single malt 40% vol

NOTES
A sweet fruity nose with a nutty vanilla taste

A sweet peaty nutty nose with a rich sweet palate that is slightly peaty.

TONGLAND ABBEY
DUMFRIES & GALLOWAY

Above the River Dee 2 miles N of Kirkcudbright is the foundation of Fergus, Lord of Galloway from 1220. Built for Premonstratensian monks from Lanarkshire, in 1325 the Gallowegian rebels slew the Abbot in the church because they were foreigners and had sworn allegiance to Edward I of England. This was consistent with the Parliament held in Brigham, 1290, when it helped settle the succession to the Scottish Crown. Enriched by grants from successive Stewart Kings including James IV, who in 1503 appointed as its last and one of its more notable abbots an Italian named Damiane. A known alchemist, his botched attempt at flying to France from Stirling Castle ended in a rapid decline and crash into a midden.

TORFNESS, BATTLE OF, 1040
MORAY

Near Burghhead is thought to be where one of the battles aimed at reasserting the claim of the Scottish King Duncan to land in Caithness and Sutherland was fought. With his nephew Modan leading one army, the King sought to sandwich Earl Thorfin with his own force, but was eventually engaged and defeated by the Earl. The battle was a milestone in the attempts by the Scottish Crown to erode the power of the Celtic Mormears and the Norwegian Earls of Orkney that eventually came to pass in the 15th century.

TORMORE DISTILLERY
MORAY

In the shadow of the Cromdale Hills, overlooking the River Spey, 12 miles SW of Dufftown, is the region's first 20th century distillery. Built in 1958 by the architect Sir Albert Richardson, once President of the Royal Academy, Tormore skilfully combines modern techniques with traditional aesthetics which blend with its natural setting and its distinctive clocktower which stands like a milestone in distillery design. Meaning 'great hill' in Gaelic; Tormore takes its water from the Achvochkie burn after it has flowed over peaty moors and through granite hills, providing the essence which, with the barley and ten-year maturation, has produced a quality Highland Malt since its inception in 1959 and opening in 1960. Its popularity by the 1970s prompted the increase of stills from four to eight in 1972. Sold to Whitbread & Co Ltd in 1975, Tormore became part of Allied Distillers in 1990.

OWNERS
Allied Distillers Ltd ?

REGION
Speyside

PRODUCT
Tormore 10 year old single malt

NOTES
A honey sweet nose with a smooth, soft, balanced, malty flavour which creates a smooth, well-rounded finish.

TORTHORWALD
DUMFRIES & GALLOWAY

Village situated 4 miles NE of Dumfries. The name probably derives from the Gaelic 'Torr' meaning 'mound' or 'hill tower' and Thorald therefore 'hill of Thorald'. This was once the site of two Caledonian Camps, with the nearby Nithsdale Wood providing the area's inhabitants with the vital timber for their many defensive structures down through the ages. To the south of the village stands a 14th century tower. The land held by a Sir James of Torthorwald who fell at Bannockburn in support of Edward II, 1314, later passed to the Kilpatricks followed by the Carlyles, and was later created a Lordship for a John Carlyle, 1473. However, it eventually passed to the Douglases, including a nephew of the Regent Morton, Sir James Douglas, who was Lord Torthorwald in 1590. The most famous person linked to the village is William Paterson (1658-1719), founder of the Bank of England, who was born at Skipmyre. The Torthorwald of today was largely developed around 1800, when the main trade here was weaving which was sustained by the mill owners of Carlisle. See Castle

TORTHORWALD CASTLE
DUMFRIES & GALLOWAY

Overlooking Lochar Moss 4 miles E of Dumfries is the ruinous shell of a 14th-century courtyard keep. In 1320 the barony was conferred by King Robert the Bruce on the Kirkpatricks, but had passed through marriage to the Carlyles by 1443. Built by either Thomas or William Carlyle, a John Carlyle was created Lord Carlyle of Torthorwald in 1474. Held by Sir James Douglas by 1500, who had married the Torthorwald heiress, it remained in the family and in 1622 was held by their descendants, who later became the Earls and Dukes of Queensberry.

TORWOODHEAD CASTLE
FALKIRK

It occupies land 2 miles NW of Larbert which was once part of the Caledonian Forest . Essentially a ruined 17th century Scottish L plan mansion, it was built by the Baillies of Castlecary when a James Baillie received a charter from the Forresters before he married a daughter of the family and became Lord Forrester.

TOUCH CASTLE
STIRLING

Erected 3 miles W of Stirling. Developing from a 15th century keep, additions were made in the 17th century and it was incorporated into a mansion house by the Seatons in the 19th century.

TOWARD CASTLE
ARGYLL & BUTE

On a ridge inland from the sea opposite Rothesay is a 15th century courtyard keep built by the Lamonts. In 1646 it was besieged and taken by the Campbells, and in the savagery which followed, 36 of the Lamonts were hanged and 200 wounded. Afterwards it fell into a long period of disuse but has since been restored along with its richly embellished gateway.

TOWIE CASTLE
ABERDEENSHIRE

Positioned by the River Don 10 miles SSW of Rhynie. The original structure was built in 1136 by Alexander Barclay of Tolly. Completed by 1550 on the site of the 12th century structure with a chapel included, which was probably used for mass during the Reformation. As supporters of Queen Mary the Forbses were persecuted after her fall. In 1715 a force under Captain Ker ordered its surrender to the Crown but after a hostile response from Lady Forbes, in which the Captain was wounded, it was burnt, causing the deaths of the Lady, her children and the servants. Following the removal of two storeys in 1792 it fell into ruin but was reroofed in 1874 and later restored and was used as a dwelling house.

TRANENT
EAST LOTHIAN

Village situated 9 miles E of Edinburgh. Name derived from the Brythonic 'tref' and 'nant' meaning 'homestead by a brook' or 'village by a river'. The Parish land of Tranent, incorporating Preston-pans, Gladsmuir and Pencaitland (until 1595) was held in the 12th century by the monks of Holyrood Abbey, who mined for coal here, but by the 14th century was owned by the Seton family, who as feudal overlords further developed its coal-mining with the monks of Newbattle. The near surface coal-seams, of the limestone coal group, encouraged the development of an export market to England and Holland in the 16th and 17th centuries, while also serving as a place of refuge for the local people during the battle of Pinkie in 1547. After the forfeiture of George 5th Earl of Winton for his part in the Jacobite Rising, 1716, the land was acquired by the York Building Co, 1719, which developed its many lower coal seams at a time when most of the large family landowners were being replaced by smaller holdings. In 1722 the railway line to Port Seton, the first rail link in Scotland, was extended to Cockenzie Port. The rioting witnessed here in 1797 after the introduction of the Militia Act, when seven people died, was indicative of the egalitarian values of the mining communities throughout Southern Scotland during the 19th and 20th centuries. Among which Tranent played a significant part, with large scale mining developments that have all but disappeared.

TRAQUAIR HOUSE
SCOTTISH BORDERS

Situated 1´ miles S of Innerleithen. The land's original use as a Royal hunting seat gave the first structure strong royal connections as Kings David I, Alexander II , and Alexander III all dated charters from here. Granted by Robert the Bruce to Sir James Douglas, after a number of owners it was purchased in 1478 by Sir James Stuart, Earl of Buchan, whose son

developed it as a border tower before he died at Flodden in 1513. The family's continued ties with the Royal Stewarts brought about a visit from Queen Mary and Lord Darnley, who stayed here in 1566, months before Darnley's murder in 1567, and much later assisted in Sir John Stuart's elevation in 1628 to Lord Stuart and Earl of Traquair in 1633. At one time Lord High Treasurer and Lord High Commissioner of the Church of Scotland, he presided over the Assembly when it ratified the Scottish National Covenant which rejected Episcopacy. An additional SE wing was added in 1642 projecting from the first block with angle turrets and ground floor entrance, prior to a visit by the Marquis of Montrose, who stayed here before his defeat by General Leslie at the battle of Philiphaugh in 1645. Further additions in 1695 included lower wings, the enclosure, the terraces, pavilions and gateway. Traquair's last welcome to the ill-fated Stewarts was to Prince Charles Edward in 1746 during his retreat from Derby, and at the end of the century the house was closed by the Earl after the death of his Countess. On the death of Lady Louisa Stuart of Traquair, it passed to the Maxwells, Earls of Nithsdale, who assumed the name Stuart, and for their descendants, the Maxwell Stuarts of Traquair, it is still a family home.

TROON
SOUTH AYRSHIRE

Seaport town situated 7 miles N of Ayr. Name derived from the Brythonic 'trwyn' meaning 'nose' or 'cape'. In the 17th century these natural advantages, including its harbour, almost led to Troon pre-empting Port Glasgow as the main harbour for the Glasgow merchants. Their failure, however, left the site undeveloped until 1805, when the 3rd Duke of Portland purchased the then Fullarton

Estate and built a pier followed by a wet dock, two graving docks, a lighthouse and warehouses that gave rise to a town where only salt pans and a smugglers Inn once stood. Reinforced with a breakwater after the storms of 1839, its harbour, which once ranked as a creek of Irvine, became a thriving coal port with frequent shipments to Ireland, Galloway and elsewhere, hastening further developments through an Act of Parliament in 1837, resulting in Head Port status in 1863. The founding of its main industry, shipbuilding, through the opening of a yard in 1860, later followed in 1886 by the Ailsa Yard where steam yachts, cargo ships and paddle steamers were built, contrasted with residential Troon, then being built by the Duke of Portland for a growing merchant class; something that no doubt influenced the granting of a Burgh Charter in 1896. Thereafter the town slowly developed its leisure trade with putting greens, bathing facilities and a reputation for golf which it still enjoys today. In 1919, its most famous son, Charles Kerr Marr, bequeathed a large sum of money from profits accrued from his business ventures for an educational institute, which became Troon's best architectural feature, the Marr College, which opened in 1935 and quickly established a reputation for academic excellence. Witnessing the decline of its harbour from 1918, its total ruin was averted by the onset of World War II in 1939, when yachts and trawlers were converted into minesweepers for the Admiralty. In addition the more profitable ship breaking contracts after 1945 spawned a thriving trade in scrap metal. See Royal Troon Golf Club

TULLIBARDINE DISTILLERY
PERTH & KINROSS

About 21 miles SW of Perth near Blackford is one of the Highlands' most southerly distilleries. Preceded by an earlier distillery established in 1798, the present building was designed by Delme Evans (designer of Jura) and built in 1949. Two years later production started on the site of an ancient brewery which once produced ale for the court of James IV in 1488. It is famed for its water which comes from the Dany burn in the Ochil Hills. The neighbouring Highland spring and Gleneagles mineral waters are from the Blackford River, which according to legend was so named after the drowning of a royal personage in a nearby ford on the Allan Water. The distillery was purchased in 1971 by Invergordon Distillers who built and enlarged it in 1974, when its stills doubled to four. Although mothballed in 1995 it has since reopened.

OWNERS
Tullibardine Ltd ?

REGION
Highland

PRODUCT
Tullibardine 10 year old single malt 40% vol

NOTES
A soft, malty, sweetish nose with a grassy, malty sweetness.

TULLIBODY
CLACKMANNAN

Village situated 2 miles NW of Alloa. Name derived from the Gaelic 'Tulachboth' meaning 'hill house'. Although a settlement was here as long ago as the 9th century the place firmly comes on record in 1149 when David I built a church which was subordinated to Cambuskenneth Abbey. In 1559 a retreating French force under Doysel, being pursued by Kirkaldy of Grange, an opponent of Queen Mary I, used the slabs of the old church to repair the Tullibody Bridge and in 1649 the place was again involved in military manoeuvres when

Montrose's army encamped in Tullibody Wood. The main landowner and benefactor of the town was Sir Ralph Abercromby (1734-1801) who resided at Tullibody House and developed the kirk as the burial vault of his family, who held the land up until 1924, when it was sold off to sitting tenants. Chiefly involved in coal mining and the tanning of leather, followed by glass making, these, like most of the old intimate village have been replaced since the community's enlargement .

TULLIBOLE CASTLE
PERTH & KINROSS

About 6 miles W of Kinross stands a fine example of a 17th century Laird's House which was the site of a castle from the 13th century and held by William Oliphant (Knight). The lands were bought from the Herron family in 1590 by John Halliday (Advocate) and passed to his son John who was married to Helen Oliphant before building the house in 1608. Also an advocate, he was knighted before his death in 1620. The epigraph on its walls reads 'THE LORD IS/MY ONLY DEFENCE/2 APRIL 1608; PEACE BE/ WITHIN THY WALLS AND PROSPERI-TIE/WITHIN THY HOUSE'. Prior to 1800 the castle was unroofed but shortly after it was modernised internally and a new wing was added.

TURNBERRY CASTLE
SOUTH AYRSHIRE

On a rock 6 miles W of Girvan are the fragmentary ruins of a courtyard tower. Once the site of a stronghold of the Celtic Lords of Galloway, it passed to Robert de Bruce (grandfather of King Robert the Bruce and competitor for the Crown) in 1271 and it served as a rallying point for the Scottish Barons who pledged their support. Occupied by the English until retaken by Robert I (grandson) in 1307,

when the present castle was built. Although a structure of some size it was empty by 1400 and eventually surrendered to the forces of the elements. In 1874 a lighthouse was built here.

TURRIFF
ABERDEENSHIRE

Town situated 35 miles NW of Aberdeen. Name probably derived from the Gaelic 'turach' meaning 'place of the tower' or 'hill'. A church is supposed to have been built here by Malcolm Canmore which was probably preceded by a much earlier church dedicated to St Comgan but by the 12th century it had given way to a monastery. This was bestowed on Arbroath Abbey by Marjory, Countess of Buchan. In 1272 a hospital was added by Alexander Comyn, Earl of Buchan for thirteen poor people, which by 1412 had become a prebend of Aberdeen Cathedral. Probably the site of a settlement of the Knights Templars until the order's dissolution in 1312, by a charter of 1511, the Kirklands village and Glebe (church holding) were created a Burgh of Barony for Thomas Dickson. In 1639, during the Covenanting Wars the Marquis of Huntly assembled his forces here prior to occupying Aberdeen, and it was here months later in what came to be known as the Trott of Turry that the Royalist Earl of Huntly's Gordons dispersed a force of Montrose's Covenanters. After failed attempts at the manufacture of carpets, linen and thread in the 1760s, the burghers fell back on farming which with new drainage methods and the introduction of the reaping machine, 1860, helped establish its yearly fairs on the local farming calender. Through constant growth this culminated in the Turiff Annual Show being attended by 30,000 people in 1948. Though the wider area is dotted with castles, Turriff's oldest building is the ruined church which, standing on top of an earlier foundation, retains its choir and belfry with a bell dated 1557.

TYNINGHAM
EAST LOTHIAN

Village situated 2 miles NE of Prestonkirk. Name derived from the Old English 'tyn' 'ing' 'ham' meaning 'river' 'descendants of' and 'farm' therefore 'home of the dwellers on the Tyne' . The church founded here by St Baldred of the Bass in the 8th century was burnt along with the village by the Danes around 941 but was rebuilt in a Norman style and subordinated to the church of Durham by David I in the 12th century. With the patronage of the church, the Manor of Tyningham anciently belonged to the Bishops of St Andrews as part of their Regality on the south side of the Forth, but by 1628 it was held by the Earl of Haddington and later became a family seat. One of the first projects of Thomas the 6th Earl, an early pioneer of afforestation was the 300 acre Binning Wood planted on Tyningham Moor at the behest of his Countess. Later becoming well known for its holly hedges, it provided timber for the 1939-45 war effort. Annexed to Whitekirk Parish in 1751, Tyningham has the scant remains of its Norman Church, while in the former is a fine example of 15th century Gothic architecture which was restored by Robert Lorimer after a fire in 1914. Nearby is the site of a holy well that attracted large numbers of pilgrims up until the Reformation. Still used as the family home, Tyningham House, built by successive earls, was greatly enlarged in 1829 by a Mr Burn in a Scottish Baronial and semi-Elizabethan style .

U

UDDINGSTON
SOUTH LANARKSHIRE

Village situated 4 miles NW of Hamilton. Possibly occupied by the Norsemen as the original name of Odingstone in 1475 is thought to derive from Odin. The village developed in the 18th century as a community of weavers and agriculturists but is chiefly remembered for its manufacture of agricultural implements. Significant among these was John Wilkie's Iron Plough (100% iron from 1800), which revolutionised farming. Between 1800-45 over 10,000 were made around here and sold worldwide, thus inspiring John Grey in 1850 to found the Uddingston Iron Works which was the forerunner of the Uddingston Engineering Works.

UDNEY CASTLE
ABERDEENSHIRE

It stands on rising ground 20 miles NE of Aberdeen. The land belonged to the Udney family, who built this three-storied oblong tower between 1500 and 1600 and bankrupted three successive lairds in the process. As with many other castles in the north its position denied it an important part in events of national importance so it is presently in a well preserved state.

URQUHART CASTLE
HIGHLAND

This massive ruin is positioned on a rock on the W side of Loch Ness at Urquhart bay. Although the site of a defensive structure for a very long time, the oldest part of this tower with enceinte wall is its 13th century wall. It was held by the Durwards and the Cumins for William I in the 13th century, it was besieged and captured by Edward I in 1297 and 1304, but was Crown property in the reign of Bruce, whose grandson David, Earl of Strathearn, acquired it in 1371. Repaired in 1429, it belonged to the Earl of Ross in 1450, but reverted to the Crown in 1476. Developments by James IV in 1509 in favour of John Grant of Freuchie, whose service against the Lord of the Isles had engendered political stability in the area, saw the rebuilding of its tower, ramparts, hall, chamber and kitchen. Attacked in 1545 by the Macdonalds and Camerons who raided its artillery. In 1700 its roof and woodwork were destroyed which hastened its decline.

URR
DUMFRIES & GALLOWAY

Village situated on the River Urr 10 miles SW of Dumfries. The name may derive from the Celtic 'ur' meaning 'water' or from the Old Norse 'orr' meaning 'swift'. With traces of a Roman presence, the Motte of Urr, the chief antiquity (once an island) was one of the largest earthen mounds in Scotland and thought by Skene (historian) to mark the site of the Carbantorigum, a town of the Caledonian Selgovae tribe mentioned by the geographer Ptolemy. The village which grew up around it was mentioned as a barony in 1262 when the Motte (as revealed by excavations in 1951) was a baronial fortalice crowned by a Norman-style fort. Despite figuring in the Covenanting conflict, Urr's failure to expand has consigned its importance to an early period of the country's history.

V

VAYNE CASTLE
ANGUS

About 6 miles W of Buchan are the ruins of a 17th century Z plan castle with its square and its round towers. In the early 15th century the barony was held by the Lindsays who started the castle which was eventually bought by the Earl of Southesk around 1658, when some additions were made. The carved initials of the Earl and his family motto are still visible.

VIKING INVASIONS,
8-11TH CENTURY

In the face of the relentless advance of the Roman Empire to the north west, the peoples of Europe became used to instability and singularly developed forms of organised and disciplined defence. So it was in the wake of the empire's fall that some of the resettled peoples tried to reassert themselves. For Norsemen, who included the Danes, the next step was Scotland and England. Naturally predisposed to plunder and rapine, Norway was the perfect base for the pursuit they lived by, with its countless harbours of refuge in its majestic fiords flanked by mountains; in many ways the country was more suited for protection than production. The success of their ventures owed everything to the skill of their ships' carpenters who made their ships light, narrow and fast with a reversible helm giving them a speedy element of surprise and escape when they descended on coastal communities. The orgy of destruction wrought by them on the Island of Lindisfarne in 793 was to mark the beginning of their many onslaughts, which for centuries severely affected Scotland's trade, particularly with Ireland, for in the 8th century Olaf the White had established a powerful base on the island. When Harold Harfagr seized power in Norway in 872, many of his enemies took refuge in the Orkneys and the Hebrides. Not to be slighted, in 875 with his two sons Hausaklyfur the skull splitter and Eric the bloody axe, he captured the islands and shortly after conferred the Jarldom of Orkney on Sigurd, who was to conquer a large portion of Caithness and Sutherland along with Ross and Moray before establishing a base in Thurso. It was from this expansion that a link was forged with the Scottish mainland. This created much conflict between successive earls and the Celtic Mormaers, notably Finleiker or Finlay, the father of Macbeth who later allied himself with the Jarl after killing Duncan in 1040. Between 798-802, the Island of Iona was plundered three times. Latterly, in 806, the monastic buildings were burnt and the monks slain, forcing them to remove from the Western Isles to Ireland for a time with the remains of St Columba's relics. But in 878 the monks were murdered here for refusing to reveal the rich copious shrine of the saint. Ironically, the monasteries which they pillaged and destroyed were instrumental in converting many of the settled Vikings to Christianity. Raids continued on a more sporadic scale until 1093 when Magnus Barelegs, the King of Norway, seized the Western Isles from Malcolm I and was succeeded by Olav as ruler of the Isles. While attempting to throw off the Norwegian yoke, Alexander II of Scotland failed to regain control of the Hebrides from King Haakon which eventually came in 1266 (Treaty of Perth), after the battle of Largs when Haakon ceded the Isles to Alexander III. The final step in this process came in 1470 when the Orkneys and Shetlands were annexed to the Scottish Crown by James III.

W

WEDDERLIE HOUSE
SCOTTISH BORDERS

It stands at the base of the Lammermuir Hills 6 miles NW of Greenlaw. A 17th-century mansion house which incorporates an earlier keep, both of which were built by the Edgars, who held the land from the 14th to the 18th century, when it was sold to Lord Blantyre. Wedderlie played an important role in local politics in the late 17th century when John Edgar sat in Parliament for Berwickshire and Alexander Edgar represented Haddington. The mansion was decayed in the 19th century but was later restored.

WESTHALL CASTLE
ABERDEENSHIRE

A 16th century mansion house, it is situated 2 miles W of Oyne. The land belonged to the Diocese of Aberdeen from the 13th century but passed at the Reformation to the Horn family, and was later held by the Dalrymple-Horn-Elphinstone family who built the house. In the 19th century it was the property of Lady Leith, who added a modern house.

WEST CALDER. SEE MID CALDER

WEST LINTON GOLF CLUB
SCOTTISH BORDERS

The town owes the existence of a club here to its founding father Robert Miller, who first played golf while a student at St Andrews. After taking up a teaching post at the local school, he eventually won over the more distinguished villagers to the idea at a time when they were increasingly being made aware of the benefits from the local railway links that were making the area popular with commuters from Edinburgh, drawn by its fresh air, scenic walks, and cycle runs.

With the committee made up of the local doctor, minister, banker, and merchants, ground was made available by the tenant farmer Mr Kerr who sub-let the land on Slipperfield Moor which was once used by the Highland Drovers for resting and grazing their cattle. Around 1830, it was also used for grouse shooting by the exiled Charles X of France. In 1890 the course was laid out to 2100 yards with an inaugural competition over the 9 holes for the Lewis Medal. With Miller's fund raising skills and influence with prominent local figures of the day, the club enjoyed a period of stability and by 1907 male and female members enjoyed their own facilities. Meanwhile on the course the club motto 'Cherish The Good Turf' was very much in evidence. Before the founder's death in 1909, attempts to acquire a licence for the club were hampered by the local Temperance Movement, and it wouldnt be until 1963 that ale was sold in the club bar. During the First World War, 1914-18, the club's finances became strained and although attempts to extend the course were thwarted by the Kerrs they finally got underway in 1927, under the celebrated champion and course designer James Braid. This was a decade which also saw the emergence of member Andrew Jamieson, the Scottish Internationalist 17 times. War was to continue to hamper the course's development, for in 1939 Braid's work was suspended and the club witnessed the usual reduction in manpower and numbers until normality returned. So by 1957 electricity had been installed and the club members enjoyed more catering facilities. A new clubhouse with lounge and bar was built in 1964, along with men's and ladie's facilities but it was to be another ten years before the full 18 hole course was opened. The event was marked by a match between some of Scotland's more distinguished golfers, like Bernard Gallacher who went on to represent Scotland in five World

Cups and appeared in eight Ryder Cups. The club continued to play an active role in the town and wider area, and in 1980 was able to purchase the land from Col Sutherland for £55,000, which was followed by the creation of new holes, extensions, tree planting and many minor improvements. The year also marked the fifth win for H J Bruce ladies' club champion and the start of S. Obrien junior champion's reign.

WHITEKIRK
EAST LOTHIAN

On the coast 4´ miles SE of North Berwick is St Mary's Whitekirk which is one of the few rural Medieval Parish Churches still in use. The lands were held by the Canons of Holyrood Abbey in the 12th century while the Kirk developed from a chapel founded by Black Agnes, Countess of Dunbar after recovering from injury following drinking the water from Whitekirk Well. In the century it was built Aeneus Sylvius Piccolomini later Pope Pius II walked barefoot to the church after landing nearby, which led to him being carried back to the town in a litter and to him contracting rheumatism which remained with him for life. On record as being a place for pilgrims where numerous miracles were said to have taken place. Records state that in 1413 over 15,000 pilgrims of many nations visited the site. Today's church dates from the 15th century and like many of the period is cruciform in shape with an unaisled nave, north and south transepts and chancel with a massive square tower with a pyramid timber spire. Behind the church is the age old barn which the monks used to store their grain.

WHITHORN
DUMFRIES & GALLOWAY

Town situated 33 miles SE of Stranraer.

Anciently called 'Candida Casa' which in Old English means the same as Whithorn 'white house'. In the 2nd century AD this was the site of the Caledonian Novantae settlement. Strongly linked with St Ninian, who, fired with religious fervour travelled to Rome and was consecrated Bishop of the Britons before returning here to found Scotland's first stone built church (built on site of Roman Camp), and dedicated it to St Martin of Tours around 400 AD. After converting the southern Picts, St Ninian died and was buried here. It later became a seminary for religious instruction known throughout the Celtic world, its 8th century bishopric being re-established by Fergus Lord of Galloway who also founded its Premonstration Priory about 1177. The Priory Church later became the Cathedral and St Ninian's shrine. Erected into a Free Burgh by Robert I, 1325, a Burgh of Barony for the Prior of Whithorn, 1451, its church became a suffragen of St Andrews in 1472 and of the Glasgow Archbishopric in 1492. For centuries this was a place of pilgrimage for peasants, nobles, royals, all. The royal visits made yearly throughout the reign of James IV, who raised it to a Royal Burgh in 1511, increased its popularity as a place for spiritual and religious benediction so much that its allure continued until long after the Reformation, until an Act of 1581 made it illegal. The subsequent neglect means that the chief vestiges of its former magnificence are a Norman doorway and the remains of the vaults leading to the priory. All that remains above ground are the walls of the roofless nave with its richly ornamented doorway to the south west while to the south east is an emblazoned 15th century doorway. In the 17th century, restoration work was done to its nave which became the Cathedral of the Protestant Bishops of Galloway and in 1822 the Parish Church was built on part of the site. Uniting with Wigtown, New Galloway and Stranraer in sending a member to parliament before 1885, its harbour built by the monks and where it operated its fishing fleet and cattle trade with Liverpool was later run by the Isle of Whithorn Harbour Co. Old accounts stating that animals roamed freely in the streets were in stark contrast to 19th century Whithorn when its Town Hall was opened, 1885, along with its banks and hotels which brought the more structured surroundings that we see today. With its castle to the north, the main thoroughfare is George St which was probably at the centre of the ancient burgh. Its coastline, which was once dotted with defensive structures to repel attacks from the Vikings based on the Isle of Man, have along with the Roman Camp south west of the town, been places of interest for archaeologists since the 19th and early 20th centuries. St Ninian's cave to the west of the town has revealed 8th and 9th century Celtic crosses and headstones with Runic inscriptions which are now housed in the museum with many other artefacts. See St Ninians Church

WHITTINGHAME CASTLE
EAST LOTHIAN

Near the edge of a steep bank 2 miles SE of East Linton is a 16th century battlemented L plan tower of the Douglases. In 1372 the family acquired the land when Sir James Douglas of Dalkeith married Agnes, the sister of the Earl of March. His descendant James Douglas, 4th Earl of Morton, held a meeting here with the Earl of Bothwell and Secretary Lethington in 1567, when the plan to murder Lord Darnley was hatched. It was forfeited to the Crown in 1581 and passed in 1660 to the Setons, who probably made the additions that included its richly panelled wood and plaster work ceiling. Later held by the Hays of Yester, in 1817 it passed to James Balfour, who built the nearby house.

WICK
HIGHLAND

Coastal town situated 17 miles SE of John O Groats. Name derived from the Old Norse 'vik' meaning 'little bay'. Its original Celtic settlers were followed by the Scandinavian pirates who found its harbour a suitable haven and so encouraged many to settle here. Visited by Rognvald Earl of Orkney in 1160 whose descendant Harold the wicked used the town as a winter retreat. By 1330 when the power of the Orcadian Earls was waning Wick Castle had become a stronghold of the de Cheyne family and passed through marriage to the Earl of Sutherland. The nearby Tannach Moor was the scene of a victory in 1464 for the Keith Clan over their rivals the Gunn family. Although constituted a Royal Burgh in 1589, owing to the naivety of the townsfolk it continued to function as a barony under a feudal superior until the Municipal Reform Act of 1833 when the boundaries were extended to include Louisburgh, and by 1900 it was joined with its arch rival and suburb Pultneytown. The suburb was started by the British Fisheries Society in 1808 prior to the building of its harbour by Thomas Telford, 1810, which replaced the old trading point at the river mouth. When enlarged in 1844 to accommodate an expanding herring fishing fleet, Wick was considered a model fishing town with weekly steam boat links to Lerwick, Aberdeen, Kirkwall and Granton in addition to being a net exporter of fish, cattle, grain and agricultural produce. Following their service in the convoys during World War II, 1939-45, its fishermens' receipts of government subsidies failed to reverse the industry's (remembered in its heritage centre) decline which was somewhat softened by the rise in Wick's regional status with good road, rail, sea and air links.

WIGTOWN
DUMFRIES & GALLOWAY

Coastel town situated 7 miles SE of Newton Stewart. The name either derived from the Old English 'wic' and 'ton' meaning 'village by a hill' or from 'wic' and 'ton' meaning 'a bay by a town', both of which are supported by the town's location. In the Old Churchyard is St Machute's Church (ruin) which retains some original 12th century work and was founded by Edward Bruce and given to the monks of Whithorn, later becoming a free rectory with royal patronage. Rebuilt in 1730, repaired 1770 and re-roofed, 1831, this served as the Parish Church until 1850 when the present church was built. The early fort which became the castle (now gone) to the south of the town was held by a Walter de Currie for Edward I in 1291, who later granted it to his vassal John Balliol, King of Scots (1292-1296): and was used as a royal residence until taken by William Wallace in 1297. The town's swift rise in importance owed much to its ties with the Crown and Church that began with the founding of a Dominican Priory in 1290 by Devorgilla daughter of Alan Lord of Galloway, its elevation to a Royal Burgh, 1292 which became an Earldom for Malcolm Fleming in 1341, but passed to the Douglases who were forfeited in 1455, and finally its seat in Parliament in 1469. During his frequent visits to St Ninian's shrine at Whithorn between 1488 and 1513 James IV often lodged in its priory. As a Sheriffdom for John Graham of Claverhouse, 1681, Wigtown became synonymous with the persecution of Covenanters and witnessed the burning at the stake of two women field Conventiclers in 1685 (Wigtown Martyrs). The site is now marked by a stone. Other memorials marking this bloody period stand in the churchyard and on Windyhill. A ruin by 1684, its priory only survives in names such as Monkhill, Friarland, and Friars well. As County Town with a market its population increased after the building of its harbour, which attracted many Irish migrants during the potato famines of 1845 and 1846 but quickly became derelict after the opening in 1875 of the Wigtownshire Railway line. Its old and new Mercat Crosses in the square include a fine example of an 18th century pillar cross dated 1738 and another erected in 1816 to commemorate the battle of Waterloo. Today Wigtown has reverted to something resembling a provincial town. At Torhousie, 3 miles to the north, are the conjectured druidical remains of a monument to the Scottish King Caldus who defeated the Romans here.

WINTON CASTLE
EAST LOTHIAN

Suitably situated by the River Tyne just NW of Pencaitland. The original tower built by George, 4th Lord Seaton, was burnt by the English. In 1620, George the 10th Lord Seton, 3rd Earl of Winton commissioned William Wallace, the King's Master Mason, to build this semi-octagonal tower with orchard and gardens. A blend of the Renaissance style with some Jacobean additions, the interconnected apartments on the first floor are elaborately decorated in a florid 17th century manner while a wall is inscribed with the Seton dragon and the Earl's coronet along with his initials G .S. and those of his wife A.H. Ann Hay. The King Charles Room in the east chamber, so named after he stayed here for a night while en route to Edinburgh, and for a week on his return journey to London, includes a Renaissance fireplace and is handsomely decorated with a plaster frieze and ceiling. Sold to the York Building Co after the 5th Earl was forfeited for supporting the Jacobites in 1715. The additions made in 1805 were destroyed in the fire of 1861 but since the restoration work it has stood as a good example of its period.

Y

YETHOLM
SCOTTISH BORDERS

Comprising Kirk Yetholm (KY) and Town Yetholm (TY) it is situated on either side of the Bowmont Water SE of Kelso. Called Jetham, 1233 and Yethan, 1224 the name is thought to derive from the Old English 'geat' and 'ham' meaning 'a pass' and 'a village'. The area was once occupied by Caledonian tribes whose forts stood on Castlelaw hill and Camphill, while Yetholm Law is reputed to be the site of a Roman Fort. Beginning as Kirk Yetholm, its church was a favoured burial place for border chiefs. Often figuring in border conflicts, Edward I spent two days here in 1304; its Kirk (rebuilt in 1837) was the rendezvous point for the Scots before the battle of Otterburn, 1388 and was where many Scottish nobles were buried after Flodden in 1513. A writ issued by James V in 1540 in favour of 'oure louit Johnne Faw, Lord and erle of litill Egipt' established Yetholm as an assembly point for gypsies. By 1861 a ragged school had been founded by Rev Baird for children whose parents were prepared to leave them here during their travels. Erected into a Burgh of Barony for Wauchope of Niddrie in 1665. An Esther Faa Blythe, Queen of the Gypsies, who died here in 1883, once described Yetholm as "sea mingle mangle that ane micht think it was either built on a dark nicht or sawn on a windy ane the inhabitants maistly Irish and nane o her seed breed and generation". The town's associations with the Jacobites who marched through here in 1745 mainly centred around Jean Gordon, who was ducked to death in the River Eden for her Jacobite sympathies, later becoming the prototype for Sir Walter Scott's Meg Merilees. For a long time a haunt of smugglers, up until 1835 the smuggling of whisky into England once involved a fifth of the villagers, bringing in a considerable annual revenue.